# The Golden Lotus

## JIN PING MEI

## 金 瓶 梅

## Volume I

Lanling Xiaoxiaosheng (Pseudonym)

*A translation from the Chinese by* Clement Egerton,
*with the assistance of* Shu Qingchun (Lao She)
*With a new introduction by* Robert Hegel

**TUTTLE** Publishing

Tokyo | Rutland, Vermont | Singapore

Published by Tuttle Publishing, an imprint of Periplus Editions (HK) Ltd.

**www.tuttlepublishing.com**

Copyright © 2011 by Periplus Editions (HK) Ltd.

Based on the edition first published in 1939 by Routledge & Kegan Paul Ltd.
Pinyinized and corrected for this first Tuttle edition.

**Library of Congress Cataloging-in-Publication Data**

Xiaoxiaosheng.
  [Jin ping mei ci hua. English]
 The golden lotus = Jin ping mei / Lanling Xiaoxiaosheng (pseudonym) ;
a translation from the Chinese by Clement Egerton, with the assistance
of Shu Qingchun (Lao She); introduction by Robert Hegel —1st Tuttle ed.
    p. cm.
 ISBN 978-0-8048-4170-2 (v. 1 : pbk.) -- ISBN 978-0-8048-4171-9 (v. 2 : pbk.)
1. China—Social life and customs—960–1644—Fiction. 2. Domestic
fiction. I. Egerton, F. Clement C. (Frederick Clement Christie) II.
Lao, She, 1899–1966. III. Title. IV. Title: Jin ping mei.
 PL2698.H73C513 2011
 895.1'346—dc22         2010049040

ISBN 978-0-8048-4170-2

**Distributed by**

**North America, Latin America & Europe**
Tuttle Publishing
364 Innovation Drive
North Clarendon, VT 05759-9436 U.S.A.
Tel: 1 (802) 773-8930; Fax: 1 (802) 773-6993
info@tuttlepublishing.com
www.tuttlepublishing.com

**Asia Pacific**
Berkeley Books Pte. Ltd.
61 Tai Seng Avenue #02-12, Singapore 534167
Tel: (65) 6280-1330; Fax: (65) 6280-6290
inquiries@periplus.com.sg
www.periplus.com

First Tuttle edition
15 14 13 12 11        6 5 4 3 2 1       0611TP

Printed in Singapore

# Contents

# General Introduction
*by Robert Hegel*

For centuries now, the novel in your hands has been denigrated as a "dirty book" (*yinshu*), one that describes, and might encourage the reader's own, illicit behavior. Consequently it has frequently been proscribed, and many editions are expurgated. Yet even before it was completed, perhaps around 1590, leading Chinese writers of the time shared the manuscript among themselves, avidly poring over it, marveling at its rich and nuanced representations of daily life and individual social interactions. They also commented on its intricate structure and its biting indictment of the immorality and cruelty of its age, especially on the part of the leaders of the state. *Golden Lotus* was without precedent in China and was not to be equaled in sophistication in any of these areas for another two centuries.

In contrast to more "sprawling" sagas in other languages and all previous Chinese-language novels, *Golden Lotus* is tightly focused on one household, and for much of its length on two individuals. One is the prominent merchant Ximen Qing, a handsome, well-placed, and fortunate young man; his connections in the imperial government lead to his appointment in the local judicial administration. But unlike the other Chinese novels of the time that narrate great military campaigns and the far-ranging adventures of outlaws, this text focuses on Ximen's private life: his parents are dead, leaving him with a substantial inheritance and no one to rein in his excessive self-indulgence. Much of the novel takes place within his extensive household, at the center of which is his beautiful fifth wife, Pan Jinlian (literally, "Golden Lotus"). Initially, she had been the helpless plaything of older men. But after her seduction by Ximen Qing she becomes insatiable in her desire to exert control over her husband and, through him, the entire household. Jinlian's primary weapon in this struggle is simply sex: she employs any and all activities to monopolize his desire. *Golden Lotus* reveals the inner politics of this wealthy family, particularly the machinations of Jinlian and others as she claws her way to a position of dominance. The intertwined lives of these two central characters bring out their brutality in their incessant concern for momentary pleasure; both are heedlessly self-destructive, and that tendency brings about the ultimate collapse of the entire household. Throughout this process, parallels between events within the Ximen household and the attitudes and activities of the emperors of the time suggest a scathing condemnation of petty self-indulgence on the part of Ming imperial house.

## Approaches to the Novel

*Jin Ping Mei cihua*, its original title, combines elements from the names of three female protagonists: Pan *Jin*lian ("Golden Lotus"), Li *Ping*'er ("Vase"), and Hua Chun*mei* ("Spring Plum"), to read "The Plum in the Golden Vase, a ballad tale." The title provides rich clues to its meaning. Although its final element celebrates the inclusion of large numbers of poems and songs, the novel is primarily about characters, not just these three but dozens of others as well, and about their complex interactions as each makes his or her way through life always on the lookout for personal advantage. From the perspective of the seventeenth-century critic Zhang Zhupo (1670–1698), placing beautiful "flowers" (women) in elegant surroundings allows them to be appreciated properly by the refined reader. Yet the title would seem to refer to an anonymous earlier poem suggesting that when these most beautiful flowers are placed in an elegant vase, the aesthetic elements clash with each other, and the combined effect cheapens both the blossoms and their receptacle. From its very title, the novel suggests ambiguity and calls for the reader's engagement in interpreting its various meanings, ranging from the elegant to the decidedly vulgar.[*] Thus from the outset the perceptive reader is warned to be aware of multiple levels of signification.

The novel is justly famous for two very conspicuous elements: its detailed characterization and its frequent narrations of sexual encounters. The denizens of the Ximen house and his contacts outside are realized primarily through extensive dialogue; the novelist creates a multiplicity of voices, dialects, and social registers to suggest the texture of contemporary society. Pan Jinlian seems to mimic the language of popular romantic songs, even though their plaintive lyrics contrast sharply with her often cold-blooded plots against her rivals. Ximen Qing adopts the language of official documents when communicating with his prospective patrons.[†] Efforts to identify the native place of the author through these voices and that of the narrator have been unconvincing; the novelist was simply a master of many voices.[‡]

Chinese editions regularly delete portions of the novel's numerous scenes of sexual activity, considering these frank descriptions a liability appropriately

---

[*] Roy, *Plum*, Vol. 1, p. xvii. The conventional epithet for the tiny bound foot, *sancun jinlian*, "three inch golden lotus," makes Jinlian's name itself into an erotic image; "vase," too, appears in erotic descriptions.

[†] Shang, "*Jin Ping Mei* and Late Ming Print Culture," pp. 201–02.

[‡] Roy, *Plum*, Vol. 1, pp. xxiii, 451n30.

kept away from the delicate eyes of a susceptible reading audience. Few editions preserve the entire text as it was first printed in 1618. The present translation, its first complete rendition in English, deletes much of the original poetry and yet it retains all of these problematic scenes. However, they were put under wraps. Even though many are comprised of flowery phrases in the original, the translator initially (1939) rendered selected terms and phrases into Latin. A subsequent edition (1972) translated the Latin passages into an English that is often more anatomically correct than the original, as they appear in this version. Yet when one counts up the passages Egerton found offensive, or those deleted from even the most heavily bowdlerized Chinese editions, we find the novel to have been only slightly diminished: for all its notoriety, only a very small portion of this complex narrative—some fraction of one percent of the total text—is devoted to describing sex. Instead, the bulk records the speech and recounts the more mundane daily activities of its many characters. This does not make the narrative any less troubling to read, however; its view of humanity is generally far from positive.

As early readers clearly perceived, the text is structured with mathematical precision. The novel is a hundred chapters in length, with a pivotal scene in Chapter 49. Up until that point, and apparently slightly thereafter, Ximen Qing's fortunes are on the rise: he grows in wealth, prominence, and power. The novel's second half narrates his decline: he is overextended financially and socially and physically depleted. The first twenty chapters introduce the novel's main characters; they are mirrored by Chapters 80 to 100 in which they scatter after Ximen Qing's death in Chapter 79. Scenes set in cold places are balanced by those set in hot locales; frigid comments occur in hot places, and heated encounters happen where it is cool. In terms of their narrative flow, chapters occur in groups of ten throughout the work: decades generally reach an emotional peak in the fifth chapter with a narrative twist in the seventh, while a dramatic climax is reached in the ninth. This is a major reason the novel was so celebrated: close reading reveals that it was meticulously constructed by a highly self-conscious—and remarkably innovative—author.[§]

*The Golden Lotus* is considered the first single-authored novel in the Chinese tradition. To a great extent, this is true. However, a substantial portion of the early chapters was borrowed from an earlier novel, a short story and other prose texts; likewise, hundreds of popular songs, common sayings, and current jokes have been adapted here. Yet each earlier text is woven into the fabric of the novel so skillfully that they do not necessarily stand out to later readers. Recognizing popular stories and songs that would have delighted

§ See Roy, *Plum*, vol. 1, pp. xxxiii, xxxv; Plaks, *Four Masterworks*, pp. 72-82.

the novel's original readers is a pleasure now lost to us; only a few of these adapted texts are visible in this translation. Critics from the seventeenth century onward have complained that readers tend to overlook what was an ongoing and very complicated literary game successfully crafted to impress and enthrall the author's highly educated contemporaries—with whom the critics identify. The novelist's endless sampling of texts from contemporary culture does contribute a degree of choppiness in his style, as translators and some critics have noted. Even so, generations of readers have found the novel gripping, its characters mesmerizing in their tragic vulnerability even as they treat others with callous lack of concern or even cruelty.

At the most obvious level, the novelist demands that his readers understand his essential message: the inevitable consequences of self-indulgence, particularly in the four vices of drunkenness, lust, greed, and anger, are suffering and ultimate destruction. In this he offers the "counsel" that Walter Benjamin saw in all stories.* The novel offers glimmers of hope of release through Buddhist salvation, but even these are compromised by contradictory versions of the role of Ximen's posthumous son in his father's ultimate salvation, for example. Some critics consider such indeterminate interpretations to be evidence of sloppy editing on the part of the novelist;† I see them as his means of throwing into question any quick and easy escape from the consequences of one's actions or the pervasive venality of his age.

The historical setting of the novel is itself ominous. As the first chapter tells us, the fictitious Ximen Qing lived during the reign of the Emperor Huizong (r. 1101–1126) of the Song Empire (968–1279). This monarch was an accomplished painter and calligrapher; his work can be found in major museum collections around the world. But he was a far better artist than he was administrator; during his reign bandits pillaged widely, in numbers far beyond the ability of his imperial armies to control. Moreover, growing tensions along the northern frontier erupted into a full-scale invasion by the Jurchens, a nomadic people who had established a sedentary empire of their own in 1114, the Jin. Song imperial guards were no match for their disciplined and dedicated forces. Huizong and his successor, the Song emperor Qinzong, were taken captive in 1127 and eventually died of exposure and disease after long periods of detention in the north by the Jin. As a consequence of that military disaster, the Song Empire hastily moved its capital south to the modern city of Hangzhou; there the Southern Song persisted until the Mongol conquest brought the dynasty to an end in 1279.

---

*   Walter Benjamin, "The Storyteller," in *Illuminations,* ed. Hannah Arendt, Harry Zohn trans (New York: Schocken Books, 1969), p. 86.
†   See Hsia, *Classic Chinese Novel,* pp. 164–202, esp. 170–73.

The novel regularly refers to six major villains at the imperial court; these are historical ministers who garnered great wealth and power for themselves at the expense of their talented but ineffective liege. Ximen Qing wins his position in the local judiciary by currying favor with their ringleader, Cai Jing (1046–1126): he uses major portions of the wealth brought by his marriage to sixth wife, Li Ping'er, to secure lavish birthday presents for Cai—who was later impeached by the censor Yuwen Xuzhong, (1079–1146). By setting the novel at this particular juncture, the novelist casts a pall over the heedless merriment of Ximen and his fellows, rendering all his activities even more frivolous in the face of the looming cataclysm. Not surprisingly, the novel was produced at a time (ca. 1590) when central power in the Ming Empire (1368–1644) was at the mercy of similar strongmen in the position of central ministers; late Ming rulers were among the least competent in Chinese history. The novel was first printed during the decades when the throne was in thrall of the ruthless eunuch Wei Zhongxian (1568–1627) and the gang of bureaucrats at his bidding. Its unmistakable resonances between the fall of the Northern Song and contemporary events imbue the novel with an air of prophecy—about the potential in the author's own time for another disaster similar to what befell the Song. That did come to pass before long, of course. Banditry rose and spread during the last decades of the Ming, to become so powerful that one of the major rebels captured Beijing in 1644, driving the last Ming emperor to kill his wife and daughters and then to hang himself on the hill just north of the Forbidden City, the present Imperial Palace Museum. This act provided the necessary rationalization for the Manchus—who saw themselves as successors of the Jin—to invade and overrun the Ming in order to restore social order. They rapidly succeeded; their empire, the Qing ("Pure"), lasted until 1911.[‡]

## The Literary Context for the Novel

*The Golden Lotus* appeared toward the end of the century that witnessed the birth of both the novel and the short story in vernacular Chinese. Before then, and indeed until the twentieth century, Chinese narratives had generally been written in the classical literary style. Ultimately derived from a written version of the language spoken during the time of the great philosophers Confucius (Kong Zhongni, 551–479 BCE) and Mencius (Meng Ke, 371–289? BCE), the succinct ancient style was the vehicle for philosophy, history, and especially poetry—the major form in the Chinese literary tradition.

---

[‡] For a succinct history of the period during which the novel was produced and initially circulated, see Mote, *Imperial China*. David Roy discusses these historical references very persuasively in his introduction to *Plum,* vol. 1, pp. xxix–xxxvi. For biographical sketches of the Jiajing and Wanli Emperors of the Ming, see *Dictionary of Ming Biography*, pp. 315, 325.

Despite its generally didactic function, narrative was often considered more utilitarian than artistic, and could be written with less formality as a consequence—in contrast to refined classical prose essays that often incorporated the arts of the poet. Writing in the vernacular, especially when it imitated the verbal art of the professional storyteller, seemingly took this educational function seriously as it focused on the mistakes and crimes committed by people at all levels of society. However, the vernacular literature of late imperial China demonstrates the authors' uses of these new forms to develop the art of writing.

The earliest novel in Chinese was *Sanguo zhi tongsu yanyi*, "A Popular Elaboration on *The Chronicles of the Three Kingdoms*," commonly referred to in English as *The Romance of the Three Kingdoms*. Its first imprint was dated 1522, although one preface bears the date 1494, suggesting that it was completed two decades earlier. By tradition it has been attributed to a fourteenth-century playwright named Luo Guanzhong, but there is no evidence to suggest that the text is anywhere that old. Starting around 1550 there appeared a virtually unbroken series of fictionalized histories of the individual empires that occupied portions of the Chinese landmass of today; most of these texts were dreary adaptations and rewordings of historical chronicles demonstrating little sense of how to develop a good story. By contrast, a second novel, the *Shuihu zhuan* (known in English as *The Water Margin* or, more recently, *Outlaws of the Marsh*) relates the adventures of 108 bandits whose individual exploits and misadventures draw them together as an ever-growing rebel band in a Shandong mountain fastness called Liangshan. The product of many hands, this novel circulated in versions of dissimilar lengths; it was "finalized" to a degree by the seventeenth-century editor Jin Shengtan (1608–1661) whose annotated seventy-chapter version has been the standard ever since. Late in the sixteenth century two other major novels appeared, *The Golden Lotus* and *Xiyou ji* (*Journey to the West*). *Journey* relates the adventures of a timid cleric based on the historical monk Xuanzang (600–661) who traveled from Chang'an, the capital of the Tang Empire, through various Central Asian kingdoms to India to obtain Buddhist scriptures. On this fictional pilgrimage he rides a horse that is really a transformed dragon and is guarded by a pig monster, a man-eating ogre known as Sand, and the Monkey King. For his wit and mischief, along with his physical and mental prowess, the Monkey becomes the novel's central character. Together these works have been termed the "Four Masterworks," *si da qishu*, in the Ming novel form. All are now available in fine English translations.

Due to their heavy debts to earlier texts, the other three novels should be considered compilations and adaptations, rather than the creative writing of single authors. *Three Kingdoms* makes this clear from its title: it refers to the earliest survey of the turbulent third century compiled by historian Chen Shou around the year 280. Its proximate source was one of the proto-novels known as *pinghua* ("plain tales") printed in the 1320s. By contrast, *Outlaws of the Marsh* drew upon a fertile tradition of oral and theatrical narratives about this heroic bandit troupe who ultimately come together to struggle against the evil ministers at court who are misleading their ruler—Emperor Huizong of the Song. They nominally retain their loyalty to the throne nonetheless. *Journey to the West* rewrites a broad range of plays, shorter vernacular tales, and historical accounts about the great Tang pilgrim to create a original composition that ultimately imitates the narrative structure of an esoteric Buddhist scripture. All three are essentially collective works that have been edited by one or more writers into their present forms. Although its multifaceted reliance on earlier texts is unmistakable, *Golden Lotus* represents a major step in the direction of originality.[*]

The best known textual source for *Golden Lotus* is, of course, *Outlaws of the Marsh*. There Wu Song is a stalwart hero, known, as are many of the others, for righting wrongs on behalf of the powerless. One is his misshapen brother, a dwarf whose attractive wife Pan Jinlian falls for the rake Ximen Qing and kills her husband to get him out of their way. Virtually all Chinese readers would have been familiar with the earlier novel and this episode in particular because of its long and detailed seduction scene—and for the equally detailed scene in which Wu Song kills a tiger with his bare hands. By building on that tale, *Golden Lotus* draws attention to the stark contrast between Ximen Qing's urban world of sex and commerce and the marginal realm of "rivers and lakes" (*jianghu*) inhabited by Wu Song and the other heroic outlaws; the adapted material merely sets the stage for a new location and far more developed characterization in *Golden Lotus*. Wu Song's revenge for his brother's murder comes swiftly in the parent novel; by contrast, in *Golden Lotus* he is exiled for most of the text, returning only at the end to wreak bloody vengeance on Jinlian after Ximen's death.[†]

While the other early vernacular novels regularly narrate the violence of individual combat but avoid all explicit descriptions of sexual activity, *Golden Lotus* draws on a then-current fashion for erotic novellas in the classical language for many of its scenes. Of the fewer than twenty of these

---

[*]   For brief surveys of the history of the Chinese novel, see Hegel, "Chinese Novel," and Idema and Haft, *Guide to Chinese Literature*, pp. 198–211, 219–30. An extensive study of these four major novels as a group is Plaks, *Four Masterworks*.

[†]   See Hanan, "Sources of the *Chin P'ing Mei*." For a translation of *Shuihu zhuan*, see Sidney Shapiro, trans., *Outlaws of the Marsh* (Beijing: Foreign Languages Press, 1981), where the Wu Song-Pan Jinlian episode takes up chapters 23–27.

medium-length compositions still extant, all deal with the sexual exploits of one young scholar and many, many women. One has thirty wives by the end of the tale; others have fewer formal wives but more wide-ranging conquests among the other women their tireless heroes meet. Most detail sexual activity in the flowery language found in this novel as well.[*] By adapting this tradition of mindless titillation into serious vernacular fiction, the novelist has in effect harshly parodied a fashionable trend in reading of his day.

*Golden Lotus* appeared just as the vernacular short story in Chinese was developing. Around 1550 the eminent Hangzhou publisher Hong Pian edited a collection of sixty of these tales. They circulated in six collections of ten stories each; only twenty-seven of the total survive today, having been driven off the market by the success in the 1620s of more refined stories edited by Feng Menglong, a scholar who produced three collections of forty stories each before finally becoming a local administrator. Some of these were his original adaptations of earlier tales; many reflect older turns of phrase and thematic concerns. A number dating from around the middle of the Ming narrate the misadventures of merchants. Patrick Hanan has aptly described this theme as "folly and consequences." Here, again, our anonymous novelist developed this fairly commonplace idea from the short story form into the central motif of his novel.[†] In essence, *Golden Lotus* narrates the terrible consequences of excessive desire in its multiple forms.

Adaptation in *Golden Lotus* involves the use of earlier narrative material in new and original ways. Instead of simply copying both the text and the thematic content of pre-existing fiction, songs, jokes, and the like, our unidentified novelist carefully fitted each piece into his own overarching theme, adapting every one to suit his larger narrative project. He signaled this practice by following the conventions of presentation in the printed versions of these materials.[‡] It is tempting to imagine that the novelist simply wrote out of his own personal collection of popular literature. Although large private libraries were not uncommon among the learned who could afford them, to have a large collection of these ephemera was only possible because of the rapid development of printing during the Ming period: a broad range of printed texts would have been available at that time for a relatively modest investment.[§]

---

[*]   The first detailed study of this genre in English is R. G. Wang's *Genre, Consumption, and Religiosity.*
[†]   See Hanan, *Chinese Short Story*, pp. 133–51; see also his *Chinese Vernacular Story*, pp. 54–74.
[‡]   See Shang, "*Jin Ping Mei* and Late Ming Print Culture."
[§]   A number of important studies of the developing print culture in late imperial China have appeared in recent years; for a review, see Brokaw, "On the History of the Book."

## About the Edition Translated Here

*Golden Lotus* apparently was written during the early years of the Wanli era (1573–1620) of the Ming Empire, late in the sixteenth century. Several prominent scholars of the day commented on it as it circulated in manuscript around 1605;[¶] its earliest extant printed edition, entitled *Jin Ping Mei cihua* ("Ballad Tale of ..."), is dated 1618. A second version, impoverished in style by some critical estimates, was produced somewhat later, during the Chongzhen reign period (1628–1644); it deletes a number of the poems from the older edition and other wording throughout to shorten the text somewhat. The Chongzhen edition was the only one available for centuries; this is the version translated here.[**] The earlier *cihua* edition was considered lost until 1932, when a copy was discovered in Shanxi and was purchased by the Beijing National Library. The Chongzhen edition also formed the basis for the most heavily annotated version, produced early in the Qing period by Zhang Zhupo (1670–1698); Zhang also wrote extensive prefatory notes pointing out the novel's artistic features. His preface is dated 1695.[††] Until David Roy began his monumental five-volume complete translation of *Jin Ping Mei cihua*, there were only Japanese and French renditions of the older and fuller version. The versions also vary in what comes first: the Chongzhen edition begins with Ximen Qing's oaths of brotherhood with his party-loving cronies, laying the emphasis from its first page on the protagonist's excessive indulgence. The older *cihua* edition first traces Wu Song's rise to prominence by killing a tiger with his bare hands; this episode leads, elliptically, to an introduction of his stunted brother, the latter's wife Pan Jinlian, her affair with Ximen Qing, and then to life in the merchant house. Chapters 53–57 in both versions seem to have been written by yet another author, perhaps because that portion of the manuscript had been lost while being circulated among the small circle of its initial readers before it was completed.[‡‡]

---

[¶] They include poet and critic Yuan Hongdao (1568–1610) and his brother Yuan Zhongdao (1570–1624), dramatist Tang Xianzu (1550–1617), and painter Dong Qichang (1555–1636). Tang has been identified as one possible author for *Golden Lotus*; see Roy, *Plum*, vol. 1, pp. xliii.

[**] Egerton omitted most of the remaining poems, translating the few remaining into a generally very wordy style of English. The Chongzhen and later versions omit *cihua* from the title; presumably that term referred to the large number of popular songs incorporated into the original text but deleted subsequently.

[††] See Roy, *Plum in the Golden Vase*, Vol. 1, pp. xvii–xlviii, esp. pp. xx–xxi. The first major study of these questions in English is Hanan, "Text of the *Chin P'ing Mei*." For a translation of Zhang's lengthy critical introduction to his edition, see Chang, "How to Read," pp. 196–243.

[‡‡] Hanan, "Text of the *Chin P'ing Mei*." Given the time required to copy a lengthy text by hand, there were generally only one or two manuscript copies of an unprinted or unfinished novel available at any given time, making the loss of pages or even whole chapters not uncommon.

## About the Author

As with the three other "masterworks" of the Ming novel, *Golden Lotus* was produced anonymously, using an untraceable pseudonym. In fact, the idea of individual authorship of vernacular fiction in Chinese only developed during the seventeenth century. Before then (and afterward as well) writers freely adapted and improved on earlier texts with no apparent concern for either originality or proprietary control over what they had written—even of the loose sort writers held for their poetry and essays. That is, writing lines parallel to, alluding to, or even quoting from earlier texts was not only acceptable, it was a common practice. By doing so a poet demonstrated his ability to appreciate an earlier writer by locating himself emotionally and intellectually in the same place as his predecessor; this practice was intended to expand the scope and significance of his own composition by generalizing, even universalizing, an individual's personal experience and insights.

Earlier novels, even the "masterworks," recast older material from the oral, theatrical, or print traditions, quoting or paraphrasing while writing new portions to create a unique compilation. Most authors did not derive income from publishing their novels directly, as far as can be known; most texts circulated in manuscript among limited circles of the elite, often the novelist's friends and acquaintances. In addition to the segment adapted from *Shuihu zhuan* which every reader would immediately recognize, this novelist incorporated dozens of songs, jokes, stories, and anecdotes then in circulation, and innumerable passing references to other narratives. Shang Wei has argued successfully that the novel could only have been written by a man who had access to hundreds of written texts, perhaps a collector of ephemera as suggested above.* But all *Golden Lotus* sources were substantially modified to fit one overriding vision of the decline and fall of virtually all of his characters.†

For that reason, *Golden Lotus* is the first substantially single-authored novel in Chinese, despite its reliance on other sources: the artistic vision is clear, consistent, individual, and unprecedented in its focus. Whoever he was, this novelist possessed keen insights into human weaknesses, had a broad knowledge of society, and felt considerable political outrage. He is usually identified with the prefacer of the first edition, "Lanling Xiaoxiao sheng," the "Scoffing Scholar of Lanling." Lanling is the old name for a place in Shandong province, as is the supposed setting for the novel, Qinghe County. And yet attempts to find Shandong dialectal expressions in the novel have not been particularly successful. American scholar David Roy uses these facts to bolster

---

* Shang, "*Jin Ping Mei* and Late Ming Print Culture."
† See Hanan, "Sources of *Chin P'ing Mei*."

his argument that the novelist based his social critique on the teachings of the pessimistic Confucian philosopher Xun Qing (312?–240? BCE)—who held office in a place called Lanling and was later buried there. Roy argues that the philosopher's argument about human nature—that it is basically selfish and needs the discipline provided by proper ritual behavior in order to reform it—is amply exemplified in *Golden Lotus*.[‡] Moreover, Master Xun's contention that leaders must serve as strong moral exemplars lies behind the novel's castigation of Ximen Qing, of the Song Emperor Huizong, and, by implication, the Ming Jiajing and Wanli emperors as well. Chinese scholar Wu Xiaoling also demonstrates that the nominal setting for the novel, the city called Qinghe ("Clear River," in practice an epithet of praise for the emperor's sagacity), has many features unique to the Ming imperial capital, Beijing.[§] Here again as with so many elements in the novel, the Shandong location is an ironic reference to the novelist's here and now, by implication the capital of a realm doomed by moral weaknesses to suffer a disastrous end.

## About the Translator

Frederick Clement Christie Egerton was born around 1890, the son of an English country pastor. In 1910 he published a book of church music and the following year was consecrated as a bishop of the Anglican Church, an *episcopus vagans* of the Matthew Succession, a highly controversial move at that time. This heresy led a church scholar to remark that Egerton subsequently was "reconciled with the Holy See, became a soldier and performed no ministerial functions."[¶]

During the Great War Egerton served in the British Army, where he rose to the rank of Lieutenant Colonel. After a divorce from his first wife—with whom he had run away when she was quite young and with whom he had four children—in 1923 he married Katherine Aspinwall Hodge (b. 1896) from New York; later she would work as a secretary at the American Consulate in London.[**] The couple had no children. During the 1920s he visited Japan and later commented on the beauty of Mount Fuji. Apparently he began his study of Chinese soon after returning from East Asia.

---

‡  See Roy, *Plum*, vol. 1, pp. xxiii–vii, xxix–xxxii, for his argument about the novel's moralistic perspective.

§  Wu Xiaoling, "*Jing Ping Mei cihua* li de Qinghe ji yi Jiajing shiqi de Beijing wei moxing chutan," *Zhongwai wenxue* 18.2 (1989), 107–22; cited in Roy, *Plum*, vol. 1," pp. xxxvi, 453n64.

¶  Henry R. T. Brandreth, *Episcopi Vagantes and the Anglican Church* (London: Society for Promoting Christian Knowledge, 1947), pp. 16, 22n8.

**  Class of 1879 Hartford Public High School (http://www.ctgenweb.org/county/cohartford/files/misc/hphs.txt), accessed July 10, 2010.

After the war Egerton's profession was listed as "editor." He was a skilled and prolific writer of broad experience and interests. From his early dedication to religion, Egerton turned to education, and then two decades later he published his translation of *Golden Lotus*. About the same time his highly detailed travelogue appeared, *African Majesty: A Record of Refuge at the Court of the King of Bangangté in the French Cameroons* (1938). This was followed by a short political treatise, *Reaction, Revolution, or Re-birth,* and in the 1940s by his biography of the right-wing Catholic prime minister of Portugal, António de Oliveira Salazar. He published two more books on Angola in the 1950s, presumably in favor of Salazar's policies toward Portugal's African colonies; Egerton had been highly favorable of the French colonial administration of the Cameroons in the 1930s.

In *African Majesty* Egerton described himself in his forties as "a fattish, bespectacled, middle-aged, would-be slightly cynical publisher" (p. xvii) who was largely bald (p. 189) and who resided on Lime Street in London, presumably near the Leadenhall Market. He had taken part in seminars offered at the London University School of Economics by the widely influential pioneer in that field, the Polish anthropologist Bronislaw Malinowski (1884–1942) (p. 4). He was also "very fond" of reading travel books, and yet he had little patience for "travelers" who seldom left their comfortable carriages to engage with the people they purported to be describing. His travel diaries demonstrate far more contact with local people.

Egerton's anthropological interests in learning more about the differences among human cultures is what drew him to West Africa (xvii) and to other subsequent adventures. It may also have informed his tackling *Golden Lotus* as a novel of social behavior. Although he was a prolific photographer who took innumerable still photos and even motion pictures while on his journeys, he admitted that he lacked the technical skills to keep his cameras functioning (p. 260). Egerton likewise acknowledged about his first African expedition,

> I was very eager to find out, so far as I could, the attitude of the Bangangté people to what we call the problem of sex. We, ourselves, seem to have gone more wrong on sex than on anything else, and that is saying a great deal. It absorbs our energies out of all measure. It permeates every department of our lives. It arouses the bitterest controversies. It is the most popular form of amusement. It saturates our art and literature. It fills our gaols; it lurks in the background of most of our murders and suicides. Even the advertisers who try to sell us motor-cars or cigarettes endeavor to do so by appealing to our sex interest. When all other topics of conversation fail, there is always sex to fall back upon. And, most amazingly,

we conventionally behave like ostriches and keep up a polite pretence that sex is not really important or, if it is important, it is too disgusting to be mentioned in decent society. With all this atmosphere behind me, I cannot pretend to be uninterested, or even purely scientifically interested, in the matter of sex. (p. 296)

From this perspective, a consuming interest in *Golden Lous* would seem perfectly natural for Clement Egerton.*

Egerton's work on the novel began soon after his second marriage. Short on cash and dependent on his new wife's meager income, Egerton suggested sharing an apartment with a friend he had made at London University, the man he referred to as C. C. Shu (Shu Qingchun, 1899–1966)—who was soon to become famous among Chinese readers as the Beijing novelist Lao She. At that time Shu was a lecturer in Chinese at the School of Oriental Studies, where he taught from 1924 to 1929; they agreed that he should pay the rent while Egerton and his wife provided food for the three of them. He and Egerton also exchanged language lessons for their mutual benefit.

Although in his 1936 essay "My Several Landlords" ("Wode jige fang-dong") Lao She says that they lived together for three years, 1924 to 1926, he never mentioned their collaborative work on *Golden Lotus,* although he did admit that he read fiction avidly as a means to develop his own English reading skills. Undoubtedly he encouraged Egerton to do the same for Chinese.† Shu was extremely productive himself, however; in addition to his teaching duties, during those years he completed two Dickensian novels in Chinese, *Old Zhang's Philosophy* (*Lao Zhang de zhexue,* 1926), and *Master Zhao Says* (*Zhao zi yue,* published 1928), and then his humorous and sensitive study of cultural differences, *Ma and Son* (*Er Ma,* also published 1928).

Many decades later and without citing his sources, martial arts film maker King Hu (Hu Jinquan) commented that the *Golden Lotus* translation was the product of close collaboration between the two men, and surely it must have been.‡ Egerton had begun to study Chinese in London not long

---

* For a photograph of Egerton in the mid 1930s, see his *African Majesty,* Plate 121, "Saying Good-bye" to King N'jiké (facing p. 329); Egerton is wearing a pith helmet along with tie, white shirt, sweater, jacket, and glasses; his face is in profile.

† Lao She, "Wode jige fangdong," http://www.eduzhai.net/wenxue/xdmj/laoshe/zw14/048. htm. For a photograph of Lao She during those years, perhaps taken in the apartment shared with the Egertons, see: http://baike.baidu.com/image/718e25c7a0f8959dd0006023 (both sites accessed August 16, 2010). For Shu's references to reading English fiction as language learning material, see Zhang Guixing, ed., *Lao She nianpu* (Shanghai: Shanghai Wenyi, 1997), vol. 1, p. 43.

‡ Hu Jinquan, *Lao She he ta de zuopin* (Hong Kong: Wenhua Shenghuo, 1977), pp. 32–36, translated as "Lao She in England," pp. 46–47. In his 1939 preface to *The Golden Lotus,*

before he and Lao She met. Lao She notes that Egerton finally landed a job just as he was moving out in 1926; whether Egerton continued his study of Chinese thereafter is not clear. Given the complexity of the various voices and the innumerable contemporary references in *Jin Ping Mei*, it is highly unlikely that a foreigner could translate the text after only a few years of language study, even for a gifted language learner (Egerton reportedly was able to read Latin, Greek, German, and French). It seems much more likely that as his Chinese tutor Shu might have provided a rough translation, which Egerton then spent years polishing into its present form. Ironically, Egerton complains that the novel's style was "telegraphese," more likely a characteristic of Lao She's imperfect English than an attribute of the Ming novelist writing in his own language.* But Egerton had a fine sense of English style, which is clearly visible in the resultant translation. For his part, even though he praised *Jin Ping Mei* as "one of the greatest Chinese works of fiction" and considered its author "very serious" in his intent, Lao She never acknowledged his role in this translation project. Perhaps he was embarrassed—not by its morally objectionable content as many have claimed, but by the linguistic mistakes he may have inadvertently introduced there.† Lao She need not have worried; generations of readers have found very few problems in this *Golden Lotus* translation. His efforts have surely contributed to a far more widespread appreciation of the Chinese novel of the late imperial period.

Egerton's translation of *Jin Ping Mei* has undergone 25 editions since its first appearance in 1939. The first major alteration came in 1972 when Routledge published an edition in which Egerton's Latin passages (inadvertently except one) had been rendered into English (that overlooked line has been translated from the Chinese for this edition); recently an abridgement has appeared (Rockville, MD: Silk Pagoda Press, 2008). *Golden Lotus* has been published in London, New York, Singapore, Tokyo, and, in 2008, by Renmin wenxue (People's Literature Press) in Beijing. The online

---

Egerton notes that he had begun the translation fifteen years before and that he had spent many years polishing it with advice from various scholars, apparently after Lao She was no longer working on the project. I am grateful to Dr. Rüdiger Breuer for his unstinting assistance in locating sources of information about Lao She's activities in England.

* This supposition seems to be confirmed by a comment made by Lionel Giles in his 1940 review of *Golden Lotus*. There he finds Egerton mistranslating *zhuli* as "bamboo fans" when instead it means literally "bamboo fence" (introductory poem to Chapter 79). The characters for "fans" (*shan*) and "fence" (*li*) look nothing alike, but a Chinese learner of English might well pronounce the two similarly.

† See Hu, "Lao She in England." For Lao She's comments on the novel: *Zhongguo xiandai wenxue yanjiu congkan* 1986, no. 3, quoted in Li Zhenjie, *Lao She zai Lundun* (Beijing: Guoji wenhua, 1992), p. 13.

bibliographical source *WorldCat* lists 366 separate printings to be found in participating libraries around the globe. It is my hope that this updated edition extends its life to reach yet another generation or two of readers.

## About This Edition

Until around 1980, the dominant scheme for representing the standard pronunciation of Chinese was the Wade-Giles Romanization system, named after a missionary and a scholar, both British, of the late nineteenth century. But with the death of Mao and China's reemergence on the world stage, the Romanization system authorized by the People's Republic government and adopted by the United Nations has become the standard for Chinese language textbooks and, increasingly, for scholarly writings in Western languages. This edition has been reset in this international system, designated Hanyu pinyin, to make it easier for new generations of readers to equate the names given here with what they have read in other sources. Most of the secondary works in the bibliography that follows still use the Wade-Giles system, rendering the novel's original title as *Chin P'ing Mei tz'u-hua*.

Through the nineteenth and the first half of the twentieth century, English translators of Chinese fiction regularly Romanized the names of male characters while translating the names of all women and girls, ostensibly to make identification easier for readers unfamiliar with Chinese transliterations. Egerton followed this practice in his 1939 edition. But literal translations often produced odd or confusing renditions; two different names in Chinese could well turn out looking very similar in English. To avoid such confusion (and to avoid the sexist overtones of treating male names differently from women's names), this edition renders all names in the modern standard *pinyin* and provides a character finding list, as did Egerton's original, in the hope that this facilitates following each of them through the various chapters in which they appear. The work of Romanizing all names was ably carried out by Dr. Rumyana Cholakova. I am extremely grateful for her care and thoroughness in editing; through this process she also discovered and corrected occasional misidentifications of minor characters in Egerton's translation. I have corrected several other small errors here, including those pointed out by Lionel Giles in his 1940 review of the first edition.

## Useful Sources in English

Brokaw, Cynthia. "On the History of the Book in China." In *Printing and Book Culture in Late Imperial China*, ed. Cynthia J. Brokaw and Kai-wing Chow (Berkeley: University of California Press, 2005), pp. 3–54.

Carlitz, Katherine. *The Rhetoric of Chin P'ing Mei*. Bloomington: Indiana University Press, 1986.

Chang Chu-p'o [Zhang Zhupo]. "How to Read the *Chin P'ing Mei*." Trans. David T. Roy, in David L. Rolston, ed., *How to Read the Chinese Novel* (Princeton, NJ: Princeton University Press, 1990), Chapter 4, pp. 196–243.

*Dictionary of Ming Biography*. Ed. L. Carrington Goodrich and Chaoying Fang. 2 vols. New York: Columbia University Press, 1976.

Egerton, Clement C. *African Majesty: A Record of Refuge at the court of the King of Bangangté in the French Cameroons*. London: G. Routledge & Sons, 1938.

Egerton, Clement C., trans. *The Golden Lotus: A Translation, from the Chinese Original, of the Novel, Chin P'ing Mei*. 4 vols. London: G. Routledge, 1939.

Giles, Lionel. Review of: *Golden Lotus*. In *Journal of the Royal Asiatic Society of Great Britain and Ireland* 3 (1940), 368–71.

Hanan, Patrick D. *The Chinese Short Story: Studies in Dating, Authorship, and Composition*. Cambridge, Mass.: Harvard University Press, 1974.

_____. *The Chinese Vernacular Story*. Cambridge, Mass.: Harvard University Press, 1981.

_____. "Sources of the *Chin P'ing Mei*." *Asia Major*, n. s. 10.1 (1963), 23–67.

_____. "The Text of the *Chin P'ing Mei*." *Asia Major*, n. s. 9.1 (1962), 1–57.

Hegel, Robert E. "The Chinese Novel: Beginnings to Twentieth Century." In *Encyclopedia of the Novel*, ed. Paul Schellinger (Chicago: Fitzroy Dearborn, 1998), Vol. 1, pp. 205–11.

Hsia, C. T. *The Classic Chinese Novel: A Critical Introduction*. New York: Columbia University Press, 1968. Esp. Chapter 5, pp. 165–202.

Hu, Jinquan [King Hu]. "Lao She in England." Trans. Cecilia Y.L. Tsim, *Renditions* 10 (1978), 46–51.

Idema, Wilt L., and Lloyd Haft. *A Guide to Chinese Literature*. Ann Arbor: University of Michigan Center for Chinese Studies, 1997.

Martinson, Paul V. "The *Chin P'ing Mei* as Wisdom Literature: A Methodological Essay." *Ming Studies* 5 (1977), 44–56.

Mote, F. W. *Imperial China 900–1800.* Cambridge and London: Harvard University Press, 1999. Esp. Chapter 29, "The Lively Society of the Late Ming," pp. 743–75.

Plaks, Andrew H. *The Four Masterworks of the Ming Novel: Ssu ta ch'i-shu.* Princeton: Princeton University Press, 1987. Esp. Chapter 2, pp. 55–180.

Roy, David Tod, trans. *The Plum in the Golden Vase or, Chin P'ing Mei.* 5 vols. Princeton: Princeton University Press, 1993–.

Shang Wei. "*Jin Ping Mei* and Late Ming Print Culture." In *Writing and Materiality in China: Essays in Honor of Patrick Hanan,* ed. Judith T. Zeitlin and Lydia H. Liu (Cambridge, Mass.: Harvard University Asia Center, 2003), pp. 187–219.

Shapiro, Sidney, trans. *Outlaws of the Marsh.* 2 vols. Beijing: Foreign Languages Press, 1981.

Wang, Richard G. *Genre, Consumption, and Religiosity: The Ming Erotic Novel in Cultural Practice.* Hong Kong: Chinese University Press, 2011.

# Translator's Introduction

It is now fifteen years since I set to work on this translation of the *Jin Ping Mei,* and nearly ten since it was, as I imagined, almost ready for press. I did not flatter myself that it was a perfect translation—it would have needed the research of many years to clear up a number of difficult points —but I thought a few months' work would make possible a fairly adequate rendering of what I had come to regard as a very great novel. Now, looking at the proofs, I wish I had another ten years to spend on it. I have made no attempt to produce a "scholarly" translation, but it is not easy, from the staccato brevity of the original, to make a smooth English version and, at the same time, to preserve the spirit of the Chinese. It would, doubtless, have been possible to escape some of the difficulties by omitting the passages in which they occur, but I could not bring myself to do this or even to cut down occasional passages that seem to me a little dull. I made the best I could of them. The position was not quite the same with the poems. Nobody would, I think, claim that they are masterpieces of Chinese poetry, and some of them, turned into English, seemed very much like gibberish. I have allowed myself much more liberty with them and have omitted a great many. After all, they are merely conventional trimmings to the story, and I have no qualms of conscience about them. But for the rest, I confess that I have not even read the proofs. My long-suffering publishers knew that I was so anxious to go on polishing the translation that they thought the book would be indefinitely delayed if I was allowed to handle the proofs. They have been corrected by Mr. A. S. B. Glover.

There was one other problem that I must mention. I have already said that I could see no excuse for tampering with the author's text. He set out, coldly and objectively, to relate the rise to fortune and the later ruin of a typical household at a time when Chinese officialdom was exceedingly corrupt. He omitted no detail of this corruption, whether in public or in private life. Such detail he obviously considered essential to his story. If he had been an English writer, he would have avoided some subjects completely, skated over thin ice, and wrapped up certain episodes in a mist of words. This he does not do. He allows himself no reticences. Whatever he has to say, he says in the plainest of language. This, of course, frequently is acutely embarrassing for the translator. Again I felt that, if the book was to be produced at all, it must be produced in its entirety. But it could not all go into English, and the reader will therefore be exasperated to find occasional long passages in Latin. I am sorry about these, but there was nothing else to do.[*]

Perhaps I may be allowed to say how I came to translate the book. Some time after the Great War I became interested in the social applications of a certain modern school of psychology. I thought I should like to study these applications in the case of a developed civilization other than our own. So I began to learn Chinese and to search about for documentary material. The novel was the obvious field to be investigated.

The Chinese have never regarded novel writing as anything more than a rather doubtful diversion for a literary man. Literature, to them, was almost a sacred art, hedged about by conventions. It had a language of its own, and this language must not be profaned. For this reason, though there is a mass of novel "Literature" in Chinese, it has never been accepted as such, and novels were written in the colloquial language of the period and not in the literary language. It is only within the present generation that scholars like Hu Shi have come to appreciate the value and the interest of the Chinese novel.

This depreciatory attitude to the novel of the learned class in China is, perhaps, responsible for the absence of any true development of style. The *Jin Ping Mei* is written in a sort of telegraphese. There are no flowers of language. And when the author goes beyond plain narrative, his descriptions are bare and devoid of any very picturesque quality. But the narrative is so detailed and so ruthless in its searching delineation of character that there is little need for any attempt to convey atmosphere by deliberate means. It is this power of conveying the essential with the utmost economy in the use of literary devices that seems to me to make the *Jin Ping Mei* a great novel. It has something, surely, of the quality of a Greek tragedy in its very ruthlessness. It proceeds slowly and, apparently, unsuspectingly to its climax: and so suddenly, but inevitably, to its end.

In view of its limitations, the characterization of the book is very striking. There is a multitude of characters—Ximen Qing's wives, the women of the household, the singing girls with whom he associates, his disreputable *sponging friends,* the officials with whom he comes into contact—but there is no confusion among them. Each is a living character, clearly drawn and perfectly distinct. This distinctness comes, not from any deliberately drawn picture of each individual, but from his words and actions. I know no other book in any language in which such an effect has been produced

---

[*] The passages formerly cloaked in Latin appear in English in thie edition. EDS.

by such means. It is partly for this reason—though my main reason was a very strong belief that a translator has no right to mutilate any author's book—that I felt it necessary not to cut out any of the details of behavior given by the author. I am convinced that such details were included in the original not for the purpose of titillating the reader's palate for the salacious, but because they, too, indicate shades of character that, given the author's stylistic limitations, could not be indicated by any other means.

It was more or less accident that made me choose the *Jin Ping Mei* as a suitable novel for my original purpose. I first came across it in Cordier's *Bibliotheca Sinica.* He says of it there, "In it there is set before us a whole company of men and women in all the different relationships that arise in social life, and we see them pass successively through all the situations through which civilized human beings can pass. The translation of such a book would render superfluous any other book upon the manners of the Chinese."

Grube, in his *Geschichte der chinesischen Literatur,* says that "the author of this book ... displays a power of observation and description so far above the average that all the remaining novel literature of China put together has nothing to compare with it."

Finally, Laufer in his *Skizze der manjurischen Literatur* declares that "As an artistic production, this work belongs . . . among the highest of its class. . . . That the novel is unmoral must be flatly denied: it is as little unmoral as any work of Zola or Ibsen, and like them a work of art from the hand of a master, who well understands his fellow men; who depicts them with their passions, as they are and not as . . . they ought to be."

In view of such opinions as these, it was clear that the *Jin Ping Mei* must be a mine of psychological and cultural material. I began its translation. And it is such a mine and it is unique. But, as the work of translation progressed, I found that I was becoming more and more absorbed by the book as a work of art, and, I am afraid, its value as a psychological document soon faded into the background. I have no doubt that a deliberately strictly literal translation, with an elaborate apparatus of notes and explanations, would be extremely valuable, but my interest in the book as a masterpiece of novel writing has made me try to render it in such a form that the reader may gain the same impression from it that I did myself. He will need patience occasionally, but his patience will be rewarded.

There is not much that I can say about the history of the book. Since novels were not "Literature," its authorship and history were not recorded with the care and solemnity that Chinese bibliographical study gives to canonized works. It deals with life in the Song Dynasty, in the reign of Huizong (1101–26 CE), but it was written towards the end of the Ming Dynasty. The identity of its author is not absolutely certain, but most writers attribute it to Wang Shizhen, who died in 1593. A popular tradition says that he poisoned the pages of his manuscript and then offered it to his enemy, the Prime Minister, Yan Shifan, in the hope that he would become engrossed in the reading of it and absorb the poison as he turned over the pages. The book existed in manuscript only for many years and, when it was first printed nearly a hundred years after its assumed author's death, the fifty-third and fifty-seventh chapters had been lost and were supplied by another unknown hand. The first edition was promptly placed on the list of prohibited books by the famous Emperor Kangxi, though his own brother made a translation of it into Manchu, which is one of the few literary masterpieces in that language.

## Translator's Note

Without the untiring and generously given help of Mr. C. C. Shu, who, when I made the first draft of this translation, was Lecturer in Chinese at the School of Oriental Studies, I should never have dared to undertake such a task. I shall always be grateful to him.

I have to thank also Dr. Walter Simon, formerly Professor of Chinese in Berlin University, and now Reader at the School of Oriental Studies, for most valuable assistance in clearing up certain doubtful points that I have submitted to him. He has always taken the greatest interest in this translation.

Further, my thanks are due to Mr. A. S. B. Glover, who has had the objectionable and difficult task of going through the proofs, and to Mr. L. M. Chefdeville, who checked the Chinese names throughout.

Finally, Mr. Cecil Franklin deserves special thanks for the trouble he has taken in coordinating the labors of such a miscellaneous host of proofreaders and correctors. His was a most exasperating occupation, fulfilled with his accustomed imperturbable serenity.

# List of Principal Characters

LI GUIJIE (Cassia) or GUIJIE, a singing girl, niece of Ximen's Second Lady, sister of Li Guiqing

LI JIAO'ER (picture of Grace), Ximen's Second Lady; later wife of Zhang the Second

LI MING, a young musician, brother of Li Guijie

LI PING'ER (Lady of the Vase), wife of Hua Zixu, later Sixth Lady of Ximen

LIN, LADY, a lady of quality, mother of Wang the Third, and mistress of Ximen

LIU, "Old Woman," a procuress

MENG YULOU (Tower of Jade) or YULOU, Third Lady of Ximen; later, wife of Li Gongbi

PING'AN, boy of Ximen

PAN JINLIAN (Golden Lotus) or JINLIAN, originally a singing girl, later wife of Wu Da, and afterwards Fifth Lady of Ximen

PAN, "Old Woman," mother of Jinlian

PANG CHUNMEI (Plum Blosson) or CHUNMEI, maid to Wu Yueniang and later to Pan Jinlian; afterwards wife of Major Zhou

QITONG, boy of Ximen

QINTONG, boy of Meng Yulou; later lover of Pan Jinlian

QIUJU (Chrysanthemum), kitchen maid of Pan Jinlian

RUYI'ER (Heart's Delight), or Zhang the Fourth, nurse of Guan'ge

SHUTONG, Zhang Song, secretary to Ximen.

SONG HUILIAN (Wistaria), wife of Laiwang and mistress of Ximen

SUN GUAZUI or SUN TIANHUA, or Crooked-headed Sun, associate of Ximen and member of his brotherhood

SUN XUE'E (Beauty of the Snow) or XUE'E, originally a maid in Ximen's household; afterwards Ximen's fourth wife; also known as the Kitchen Lady

WANG, a Buddhist nun

WANG, "Old Woman," a procuress

WANG CAI (Wang the Third), a young nobleman; son of Lady Lin

WANG JING, brother of Wang Liu'er, later servant of Ximen

WANG LIU'ER (Porphyry), wife of Han Daoguo and mistress of Ximen

WEN BIGU, a dissolute scholar, secretary of Ximen

WEN, "Old Woman," a procuress

WU "The Immortal," a fortune-teller

WU, "Uncle," or Wu the Elder, brother of Wu Yueniang

WU DA, brother of Wu Song and first husband of Jinlian

WU DIAN'EN, friend of Ximen and member of his brotherhood

WU SONG, brother of Wu Da, and avenger of his murder

WU YIN'ER (Silver Maid), mistress of Hua Zixu, adopted as ward by Li Ping'er

WU YUENIANG (Moon Lady), or the Great Lady, Ximen's principal wife

WU ZONGJIA, abbot of the Temple of the Jade Emperor

XIA YANLING, a magistrate, friend of Ximen

XIAOGE, posthumous son of Ximen by Wu Yueniang

XIAOYU (Tiny Jade), maid of Wu Yueniang; later, wife of Daian

XIE XIDA, friend of Ximen and member of his brotherhood

XIMEN QING, the central figure of this book, originally the owner of a considerable estate at Qinghe, later a magistrate

XIMEN DAJIE (Orchid), daughter of Ximen and wife of Chen Jingji

XIUCHUN (Hibiscus), maid to Li Ping'er and later to the Second Lady

XUE, a eunuch of the Imperial Household, friend of Ximen

XUE, "Old Woman," a procuress

YANG GUANGYAN, also Yang the Elder or Iron Fingernails, manager of one of Ximen's shops

YING BAO, eldest son of Ying Bojue

YING BOJUE, friend of Ximen and member of his brotherhood; known as Beggar Ying

YINGCHUN (Welcome Spring), maid of the Sixth Lady, later of Wu Yueniang

YING'ER (Jasmine), daughter of Wu Da by his first wife and stepdaughter of Pan Jinlian

YUN LISHOU, friend of Ximen and member of his brotherhood

YUXIAO (Autumn), maid of Wu Yueniang.

ZHANGJIE, Qiao Zhangjie, infant daughter of Madam Qiao, betrothed to Guan'ge

ZHANG SHENG, servant of Major Zhou

ZHENG AIXIANG (Perfume) or AIXIANG, a singing girl, sister of Zheng Feng and Zheng Aiyue

ZHENG AIYUE (Moonbeam) or AIYUE, a singing girl

ZHENG FENG, a young actor

ZHONGQIU, maid of Wu Yueniang

ZHOU, Major, later General Zhou, neighbor of Ximen

ZHU SHINIAN, friend of Ximen and member of his brotherhood; called Pockmarked Zhu

# The Golden Lotus

# The Golden Lotus

When wealth has taken wing, the streets seem desolate.
The strains of flute and stringed zither are heard no more.
The brave long sword has lost its terror; its splendor is tarnished.
The precious lute is broken, faded its golden star.

The marble stairs are deserted; only the autumn dew visits them now.
The moon shines lonely where once were dancing feet and merry songs.
The dancers are departed: the singers have gone elsewhere.
They return no more.
Today they are but ashes in the Western Tombs.

Beautiful is this maiden; her tender form gives promise of sweet
    womanhood,
But a two-edged sword lurks between her thighs, whereby destruction
    comes to foolish men.
No head falls to that sword: its work is done in secret,
Yet it drains the very marrow from men's bones.

This poem was written by one Lū Yan [Lū Dongbin], an immortal whose name in religion was Master Chunyang. He lived in the dynasty of Tang and spent his days in the pursuit of virtue and the mortification of the flesh. So he attained to paradise, leaving this mortal world, and there was given to him a seat in the Purple Palace. The gift of immortality was bestowed upon him, and he was made the Governor of the Eight Caverns that are above, whence he brings succor to them in trouble and adversity.

It seems, unfortunately, too true that they who live in this world can never wholly free themselves from their bondage to the Seven Feelings and the Six Desires. There is no escape from the fatal circle of Wine and Women, Wealth and Rage. Sooner or later the end comes to every man, and he must give up his hold upon all of these, for, after death, they will avail him nothing. Experience would seem to show that of these four evils, women and wealth most surely bring disaster. Let us for a moment consider the case of one who falls upon evil times, so that he finds himself in sore need, suffering misfortunes whereof he never dreamed. At night he searches dili-gently for a grain of rice, and finds the morrow must be foodless. In the morning he rises and looks around the kitchen, but cannot discover even the makings of a fire. His family is hungry and cold; his wife and children are starving, and he knows not where to turn for food. Where shall he find the money to buy wine? Worse even than this, his relatives and friends turn aside their eyes, and show him nothing but coldness and contempt. There may have been a time when the poor wretch had ambitions; now they must perish, for he is in no position to enter into rivalry with others.

Then there is the man who squanders his wealth to purchase the delights of love. It matters not how great that wealth may be, in one adventure he may cast away ten thousand golden pieces. Should he crave for wine, he will find it precious indeed, precious as molten jade, for to the outpour-ing of amber cups there is no end. Should it be rank he seeks, his wealth may conjure up spirits; a gesture may bring servants running to serve him, and a nod may summon his attendants. Men will flock to his presence and press forward to curry favor with him. They will hasten to abase themselves before his majesty, even to lick his sores and set their tongues where tongue should not be set. Only so long as he maintains his power will this con-tinue: when once his influence is gone, they will shrug their shoulders and wait on him no more. No trial is more hard to bear than this change from hot to cold. Are not both the upstart and they who fawn upon him sufferers from the plague of wealth?

Then there is the danger that is to be had from women. Look around the world, I pray you. Liuxia Hui, though a fair lady seated herself upon his knee, remained unmoved. Where in these days shall we find conduct such as his? And he of Lu, who when a maid would have come to him, made fast his door and would not let her enter; where shall we find one like him? Or to Guan Yunchang who, with a lighted candle, kept chaste watch until the dawn? How many such heroes can history make known to us? What shall we say of those who, though they have four wives already, daily go forth to spend their substance on unlawful loves, unceasingly craving amorous delights? For the moment we will leave them, for there is that kind of lustful beast who cannot see a woman of even ordinary comeliness, without devis-ing a hundred or a thousand plots to seduce her. He ensnares the woman, craving the pleasure of a moment, and for this neglects the affection of his friends, and takes no heed for the governance of his own household. To attain this paltry end, he pours forth countless wealth and casts immea-surable treasure to the dogs. His wantonness exceeds all bounds, and then come disputes, bloodshed, and all manner of evil. He is doomed. His wife and children are forever ruined and his business brought to the dust.

Such a man was Shi Jilun who, for love of his mistress Lu Zhu, died wretchedly in prison, though, at one time, the masses of his wealth were high enough to touch the skies. Another was Bawang [Xiang Yu] of Chu, whose heroism might have uprooted mountains. Because of his madness for Yu Ji [Concubine Yu], his head hung in Gaixia. The gate of Love may be the gate of Life, but just as surely is it the gate of Death. Time and time again our common sense reminds us of this fact; and yet our hearts still carry us away. So do men fall victims to the plague of love.

It is easy to talk thus of women and of wealth, yet there is none who is forever free of these plagues. If, in all the world, there be one who appreciates the truth, he will tell us that all our piles of gold and silver, all the jade we treasure, can never follow us beyond the grave. They are but refuse, no more worth than dust and slime. Our wealth may be so great that nothing can contain it, our rice so plentiful that it may rot because we cannot consume it: to our dead bodies it will be of no avail; all will become corruption and decay. Our lofty palaces and spacious halls will bring no joy to us when we are in the grave. Our silken gowns and our embroidered skirts, our robes of fur and wraps of sable, what are they but worthless rags, for all the pride our bones will take in them?

Those charming dainty maidens who serve our lusts so well, whose skill in self-adornment is so exquisite: when once the veil is torn aside, what shall we find in them but falseness? Are they not like a general who, when the signal is given for battle, can only manifest his valor by the noise he makes?

Those scarlet lips, those white and glistening teeth, that flashing of eyes and dallying with the sleeve: if true understanding were vouchsafed us, we should know them for the loathsome grimaces of the powers of Hell within the palace of the Prince of Hades.

The silken hose, the tiny feet are like the pick and shovel that dig our graves. Soft dalliance upon the pillow, the sport of love upon the bed, are but the forerunners of an eternity wherein, within the Fifth Abode of Hades, we shall be boiled in boiling oil.

Well does the *Diamond Sutra* speak of this foolish life "as dream and as illusion; as lightning and as dew." For though at the end of life all things are vain, during life men cannot bear the loss even of a trifle. We may be so strong that, unaided, we can lift a cauldron or tow a ship, but, when the end draws near, our bones will lose their strength and our sinews their power. Though our wealth may give us mountains of bronze and valleys of gold, they will melt like snow when the last moment comes. Though our beauty outshine the moon, and the flowers dare not raise their heads to look on us, the day will come when we shall be nothing but corruption, and men will hold their noses as they pass us by. Though we have the cunning of

Lu Jia and Sui He, it will avail us nothing when our lips are cold, and no word may issue from our mouths.

Let us then purify our senses, and put upon us the garment of repentance, that so, contemplating the emptiness and illusion of this world, we may free ourselves from the gate of birth and death, and, falling not into the straits of adversity, advance towards perfection. Thus only may we enjoy leisure and good living and still escape the fires of Hell.

I am brought to these reflections upon the true significance of wine and women, wealth and rage, remembering a family that, once flourishing, sank at length into a state of deepest misery. Then neither worldly wisdom nor ingenuity could save it, and not a single relative or friend would put forth a hand to help. For a few brief years the master of this household enjoyed his wealth, and then he died, leaving behind a reputation that none would envy. There were many in that household who always sought to flatter, to do well for themselves, to join in amorous pleasures, to stir up strife, and to turn their influence to their own profit. At first it seemed that all was well with them, yet it was not long before their corpses lay in the shadow, and their blood stained the deserted chamber.

# CHAPTER I

# The Brotherhood of Rascals

IN the mighty dynasty of Song, when Huizong was Emperor, and in the Zhenghe period of his reign [1111–1119], there lived at Qinghe, a city of the prefecture of Dongping in Shandong, a dissolute young man whose name was Ximen Qing. He was about twenty-seven years old, and the master of a fine estate. A gay, good-looking fellow, he was, unfortunately, flighty and unstable. His father, Ximen Da, had once traveled through Sichuan and Guangdong dealing in raw medicines, and later he opened a shop near the Town Hall of Qinghe. He lived in a splendid house that had a frontage of five rooms upon the street, and wings that went back even farther. He had a host of servants, and a very considerable number of horses and mules. Though, perhaps, he was not quite a millionaire, he was certainly one of the richest men in the whole district.

Ximen Da and his wife showered affection upon their only child, and allowed him to do exactly as he pleased. While he was still comparatively young, they died. The boy paid scant attention to his studies, idled about, and finally gave himself up entirely to dissipation. Indeed, after his parents' death, he was seldom to be found at home, but spent all his time in the pursuit of forbidden pleasures. He learned to box, to wield the quarterstaff, and to play a good game of chess. He gambled a great deal, and became so skilled in the game of *pai* that he could distinguish the different pieces by simply touching them. In fact, so far as such accomplishments were concerned, there was very little he did not know.

His friends and acquaintances were wastrels and spongers who spent all their lives in amusing themselves at other people's expense. The chief among them was Ying Bojue, the son of a silk merchant. He had squandered the wealth his father had left him, and had sunk so low that he spent all his time waiting about the Town Hall, ready to go with anyone to the bawdy house, or to dine with the first-comer who would pay for a meal. People nicknamed him Beggar Ying. He was an expert at kickball, backgammon, chess and all sorts of other games.

Then there was Xie Xida. This man's grandfather had been a minor official at Qinghe, and his parents had died while he was still a youth. He wasted his time, and paid no attention to his duties, so he lost his position, and now led a life of leisure. He played the lute.

These two and Ximen Qing were as thick as thieves, and there were several more, of varying degrees of disreputability. One was Zhu Shinian; another Sun Tianhua, also known as Greedy Chops. Then there was Wu Dian'en, who had once been Master of the Yin Yang for the district. He had been dismissed, and now was always to be found hanging about the Town Hall in the hope of finding a job as witness for the officials in their money-lending transactions. In this way he made the acquaintance of Ximen Qing.

Other friends were Yun Lishou, a younger brother of Colonel Yun; Chang Zhijie; Bu Zhidao; and Bai Laiguang, who was also known as Guangtang. When people remarked that this was a strange name, he would become very indignant and enter upon a long explanation, which, by reference to the *Book of History*, was supposed to show that his tutor, when he had conferred that name upon him, had made an admirable choice. "If there had been anything objectionable about it," he used to say, "I should have changed it long ago, but, obviously, it has important historical associations, and I shall most certainly retain it."

There were, perhaps, ten of them in all, and, when they discovered that Ximen Qing was not only a very rich man, but ready to throw his money about, they led him on to gamble, drink and run after women.

The House of Ximen had fallen upon evil days. It had given to the world an unworthy son, who chose his friends from among those destitute of every virtue. It was inevitably doomed to impoverishment.

Ximen Qing was reckless, but when he took it into his head to bestir himself, he was capable of showing that he was no fool. He lent money to the officials and even had dealings with the four corrupt ministers, Gao, Yang, Tong and Cai. So he came to be mixed up in all kinds of official matters, acting as intervener for people at law, arbitrating in cases of dispute, and, sometimes, acting as stakeholder. The people of Qinghe stood in awe of him and spoke of him as "His Lordship Ximen." His first wife, a Miss Chen, died young, leaving him with a little daughter, and this daughter was now betrothed to Chen Jingji, a relative of Marshal Yang, the Commander of the Imperial Guard at the Eastern Capital.

After the death of his wife, Ximen found himself without a housekeeper, and married the daughter of a certain Captain Wu. This lady was about twenty-five years old. As she was born on the fifteenth day of the eighth month, her parents called her Yueniang ["Moon Lady"], and she was still known by that name after her marriage to Ximen Qing. She was gentle and quiet, a good wife, and faultlessly obedient to her husband. She had three or four maids and serving women to wait upon her, and Ximen Qing had taken his pleasure with all of them.

As a second wife, he married a girl from the bawdy house, called Li Jiao'er, and as his third, a young woman from South Street, who had been his mistress. She was not very strong, and suffered from so many different illnesses that Ximen Qing again went off to "fly with the wind and sport with the moon!"

One day, when Ximen Qing was at home with nothing to do, he said to his wife:

"It is the twenty-fifth day of the ninth month, and on the third of next month, I am supposed to be meeting my friends. I think I will entertain them here, and engage a couple of singing girls, so that we can have our amusement at home without needing to go elsewhere. Will you make the necessary arrangements?"

"I wish you wouldn't mention those horrible creatures to me," Wu Yue-niang said. "There isn't a decent fellow among them. Day after day, they come here, like messengers of Hell, putting ideas into your silly mind and making an absolute fool of you. Never, since you've known them, have you spent a whole day in your own house. The Third Lady is anything but well, and I think you might give up these drinking parties, for a while at least."

"Generally," Ximen Qing said, "I find your conversation delightful, but today your remarks are a little wearying. To hear you talk, all my friends might be beyond the pale. I don't mind so much what you say about the others, but surely Brother Ying is an honest, entertaining fellow. If we ask him to do anything for us, he never raises any objection, and what he does, he does well. Then Xie Xida is clever as well as conscientious. But there is this much to be said. So long as our meetings are irregular and uncertain, we can never develop our friendship on the proper lines. The next time we all come together, the best thing we can do will be to form a brotherhood, and ever afterwards we shall be able to count upon receiving assistance, if we need any."

"I have nothing against this brotherhood idea," Yueniang said, "though I have no doubt whatever that the others will get more assistance out of you than you are ever likely to get out of them. They will be as much use to you as dancing dolls, and not half so lively."

Ximen Qing laughed. "If I find, by experience, that they are to be trusted, why shouldn't I trust them? As a matter of fact, I'm expecting Brother Ying any moment. When he comes, I'll see what he thinks of the idea."

At that moment an intelligent-looking boy with delicate eyebrows and charming eyes came in. This was Daian, Ximen Qing's body servant. "Uncle Ying and Uncle Xie are outside," he said. "They would like to speak to you."

"I was just talking about them," Ximen said. He hastened to the hall. Ying Bojue was dressed in a new black hat and a shabby blue silk gown.

He was sitting in the place of honor with Xie Xida opposite. When Ximen Qing came in, they both jumped up and saluted him with great deference. "We are glad to find you at home, Brother," they said. "We have not seen you for some time." Ximen asked them to sit down, and called for tea.

"You are a nice pair," he told them. "I have had a very anxious time lately. I could not leave the house, but I haven't seen even so much as your shadows."

"What did I say?" Bojue cried. "I knew our brother would be annoyed!" Then he turned to Ximen Qing. "I am not surprised that you are angry with us, but, really, I have been so busy that I haven't known what to do. It is all very well for you to give your orders, but it is not so easy for me to carry them out."

"Where have you been, these last few days?" Ximen asked them.

"Yesterday, I went to the Li's to see a young lady called Li Guijie. She is Li Guiqing's younger sister, a niece of your Second Lady. I hadn't seen her for some time, and I must say she has become a very pretty girl. There's no telling what she will be like in the future. Her mother urged me to find a handsome young man to make a woman of her. Really, you yourself would not find her too bad."

"If she is so attractive," Ximen said, "I must go and have a look at her."

"Brother," said Xie Xida, "if you don't trust him, you can at least take my word for it."

"Well," said Ximen, "that accounts for yesterday, but what about the day before?"

"A little time ago, our friend Bu Zhidao died, and I have had to spend several days at his house in connection with the funeral arrangements. His wife asked me to tell you how grateful she is for the incense and things you sent her. Her place is so small and the only entertainment she can offer so unworthy, that she did not venture to invite you to the funeral."

"Alas!" Ximen Qing said, "it seems only a few days since I first heard he was ill. I never thought he would die so soon. He once made me a present of a gilded fan, and I was thinking of giving him something in return. Then I heard of his death."

Xie Xida sighed. "Once there were ten of us, now one has gone. By the way, the third of next month is the day for our meeting. We shall be troubling His Lordship to spend some small sum on the day's amusement."

"I have just been telling my wife," Ximen said, "that these meetings, at which we do nothing but eat and drink, do not represent the essential element in our friendship. We ought to decide upon some temple, have an appropriate document drawn up, and band ourselves into a definite brotherhood. Then we shall be pledged to help one another ever afterwards.

When the day comes, I will buy the three offerings needed for the sacrifice. I presume you will all be ready to give something towards the expenses, each according to his means. I do not insist on this, but it seems to me that, since we are forming a brotherhood, it will be much more satisfactory if every brother makes some little contribution."

"Certainly, Brother," Ying Bojue said hastily. "A man who never says his own prayers cannot expect to get credit for the incense his wife burns. We must all do something to show that we are in earnest, but I'm afraid we're rather like the warts on a rat's tail, there is not much to be got out of us."

"Oh, you funny dog," Ximen said, laughing. "Nobody expects you to give very much."

"If the brotherhood is to be complete," Xie Xida said, "there should be ten of us. Brother Bu Zhidao is dead. Whom can we find to take his place?"

Ximen Qing thought for a while. Then he said: "My neighbor, Brother Hua, the nephew of Eunuch Hua, is the very man. He spends his money without stint, and goes regularly to the bawdy house. He lives next door, and we are very good friends. I will send a boy to invite him to join us."

Bojue clapped his hands. "Do you mean Hua Zixu, who keeps a girl called Wu Yin'er?"

"That is the man," Ximen Qing said.

"Ask him by all means," Bojue said. "If I can only make friends with him, it will mean another house of call for me."

"You silly rascal," Ximen said, laughing. "To hear you talk about eating, one would imagine you were always on the point of starvation."

They all laughed. After a while, Ximen called Daian, and sent him to Hua's house. "Tell him that we are going to form a brotherhood on the third of next month, and that I shall be honored if he will join us. When you have heard what he says, come back and tell me."

"Shall we come here, or go to a temple?" Bojue asked.

"There are only two temples to go to," Xie Xida said. "One is the Buddhist temple of Eternal Felicity, and the other, the Daoist temple of the Jade Emperor. Either of them would do."

"Not at all," Ximen said. "This forming of a brotherhood is not a Buddhist practice, and, in any case, I don't know the priests of that temple very well. We must go to the Temple of the Jade Emperor. The abbot, Wu, is a good friend of mine; it is quiet there and we shall have room enough."

"You are right, Brother," Bojue said. "He only suggested the temple of Eternal Felicity because the monks there are on such good terms with his wife."

"You old villain," Xie Xida said, laughing. "Here we are, discussing a most serious matter, and you think it a suitable occasion to fart."

They were laughing and talking when Daian came back. "Master Hua was not at home," he said, "but I gave the message to his lady. She was very pleased. 'If Uncle Ximen is so kind as to invite my husband,' she said, 'I am sure he will not fail to come. He shall have the message as soon as he comes in, and when the day for the meeting comes, I will remind him.' She gave me two cakes for myself, and told me to give you her respects."

"Brother Hua's wife," Ximen said, "is not only a very pretty woman, but she has intelligence."

They drank another cup of tea, and the two men rose to go. "We will tell the other brothers," they said, "and collect their share of the expenses. Will you make the arrangements with Abbot Wu?"

"Yes," Ximen Qing said, "I'll see to that. Don't let me keep you any longer." He took them to the gate. Before they had gone very far, Ying Bojue turned. "Don't you think it would be fun if we had some singing girls?"

"Yes, indeed," Ximen said, "it will be more amusing if the brothers have someone to laugh and joke with." Bojue made a reverence and went away with Xie Xida.

It was soon the first day of the tenth month. Ximen Qing rose early and was sitting in Yueniang's room when there came a serving boy whose hair had been dressed in grown-up style. He brought with him a gilded and polished card case. First he made a reverence to Ximen Qing; then he came forward and said: "My master, Hua Zixu, sends his compliments. Some time ago you sent your servant with an invitation, but he was out on business and did not personally receive the message. He was told that you are arranging a party on the third of the month, and has sent this small gift, which he trusts you will use as you think fit. Afterwards he hopes you will tell him what his proper share of the expenses amounts to, and he will make up what is lacking."

Ximen Qing took the packet, examined the label upon it, and wrote a receipt for one tael of silver. "This is more than enough," he said; "your master must certainly not send any more. Remind him to keep the day free. He will have to get up very early so as to be ready to go to the temple with the rest of us."

When the boy was going away, Yueniang asked him to wait a moment. She told Yuxiao, the elder of her two maids, to give him two pieces of fruit-cake. "This is instead of tea," she said to him. "When you get home, give my kind regards to your mistress, and tell her that one of these days I am going to ask her to come and have a talk with me." The boy took the cakes, made another reverence, and went out.

A few moments later, Ying Bao, Ying Bojue's boy, came. He, too, was carrying a visiting case. Daian introduced him. "My father has collected these presents from the others," he said, "and hopes you will accept them." Ximen Qing looked at the packets, saw that there were eight in all, and handed them to his wife without opening them. "Use them," he said to her, "to buy something for our visit to the temple." He dismissed Ying Bao.

Soon afterwards he got up and went to see his third wife, who was ill, but he had only just reached her room and sat down when Yuxiao came to tell him that her mistress would like to speak to him again. "Why didn't she say all she had to say before?" Ximen Qing said. He got up and went back to her, finding her with all the packets opened and spread out before her.

"Look here!" she said, laughing. "Ying sends a *qian* and two *fen* of bad silver, and the rest, three or five *fen* apiece. Judging by the color, some red, some yellow, it might be gold. Certainly, I've never seen anything like it in this house before. If you accept it, our reputation will be gone forever. You must send it back at once."

"What a fuss about nothing!" Ximen said. "This is all right. Don't let me hear any more about it." He went out.

The next day, he weighed four taels of silver and told his servant Laixing to buy a pig, a sheep, five or six jars of Jinhua wine, some chickens and ducks, candles and paper offerings. He put five *qian* in an envelope and told his man Laibao to take it and the other things, and go with Daian and Laixing to the temple of the Jade Emperor. They were to say to the abbot: "Tomorrow, our master proposes to form a solemn brotherhood, and he takes the liberty of asking you to compose an address suitable to the occasion. He would like to take dinner at your temple in the evening, and would be very grateful if you would make the necessary preparations. He will arrive in the morning."

Daian soon returned. He said that he had given the message, and that the abbot agreed.

The day soon passed. The next morning, Ximen Qing washed and dressed, and told Daian to go and ask Hua Zixu to come for breakfast before they joined the others on the expedition to the temple. Soon afterwards, Ying Bojue and the others arrived. They came in, and forming a circle, made reverence together.

"It is time to start," Bojue cried.

"No, breakfast first," Ximen Qing said. He called for tea and refreshments. Afterwards, he changed his clothes for brighter and more handsome attire, and they all set out together for the temple of the Jade Emperor.

Before they had gone very far, they could see the temple gateway. It was lofty and imposing, but the sanctuary, with walls reaching almost to the skies, was more commanding still. It was approached by a gate in the shape of the character *ba*, covered with a red wash. Within the precincts were three paths, like the character *chuan*. The buildings were of marble with wave-like markings. The sanctuary, its lofty eaves glittering in green and gold, was in the center. Images of the Three Pure Holy Ones stood in due order in the middle, and at the far end was Laozi, the Old Lord of the Most High, riding upon his black ox.

They entered the second sanctuary, went around, and passing through a side door, came to the abbot's quarters. On either hand grew grasses as green as jasper and flowers as red as coral. There were pine trees and bamboos. On either side of the door hung scrolls. One bore the inscription: "In Paradise, unending are the months, the years," and the other, "In the Vessel of Heaven there lies another world." On the north was a hall the size of three rooms, where the abbot officiated every day at morning and evening prayer.

The temple had been specially decorated for the occasion. In the middle of the north wall hung a picture of the Jade Emperor in the Golden Palace of Paradise, and on both sides were the nobles of the Purple Palace. The four generals, Ma, Zhao, Wen and Guan were there too.

Abbot Wu was standing outside the Hall of the Sacred Scriptures. He welcomed them with a priestly reverence, and Ximen Qing and his friends went in. After taking tea, they all got up and began to look at the pictures. Bai Laiguang took Chang Zhijie by the hand, and they examined the portrait of General Ma. He looked very brave and fierce, but he had three eyes. "I don't understand this," Bai Laiguang said. "We mortals find that with only two eyes it is well to keep one closed. Can he need an extra eye to keep a watch on us and on our misdeeds?"

Ying Bojue overheard him and went over to them. "You silly fellow," he said. "It is on your account alone that he needs an eye more than anybody else."

Everybody laughed, and Chang Zhijie pointed to the picture of General Wen. "Now here," he said, "there really is something out of the ordinary. He is blue from top to toe. I suppose he must be one of Lu Qi's ancestors."

Bojue burst out laughing. "Come over here, Father Abbot," he cried, "and I'll tell you a story.

"Once upon a time, a priest died and came before the Prince of Hades. The Prince bade him give an account of himself. 'I am a priest,' he said quite simply. Then the Prince ordered one of his officers to search the records and find out what was known of the man. They discovered that he was indeed a priest and a man of excellent character. So the Prince of Hades reprieved him and sent him back to earth.

"When he was once more in the land of the living, he met a man he knew, who worked at a dye works. 'However did you succeed in getting back, Father?' this man said to him. 'I only said I was a priest and they sent me back again,' his friend answered. The man remembered this, and when his time came to go before the Prince of Hades, he too declared that he was a priest. The Prince told his officials to examine the man's body. When they came to his hands, they found them both bright blue. 'What does this mean?' he was asked. 'That comes from the work I have done on General Wen's thing.' "

They laughed. Then they went to the other side to look at the pictures of red-faced Guan and Zhao. Zhao was a black-faced warrior, with a great tiger standing beside him. Bai Laiguang pointed to the tiger, and cried: "Look at that tiger! He must be one of the kind that don't eat meat, or he wouldn't be going about with a man so amiably."

"What!" said Ying Bojue. "Don't you know the tiger is his most trusted servant?"

Xie Xida, who had been listening, said, "If I had a servant like that, a quarter of an hour of his company would be quite enough. I should always be afraid he might take it into his head to eat me."

Bojue laughed: "That's a nice thing to say," he said to Ximen Qing.

"What's that?" said Ximen.

"Well," Bojue said, "Xie here says he would be afraid a trusted comrade might eat him. You certainly ought to go in fear of your life, for there are seven or eight of us, all trusted comrades, and all ready to feed at your expense at any time."

At that moment the abbot came back to the hall. "Do I hear you speaking of tigers, Gentlemen?" he said. "In this very district of Qinghe, one has recently caused very serious trouble. Scores of travelers, and more than a dozen hunters, have found that to their cost."

"Really?" Ximen Qing cried.

"Yes," said the priest. "I am surprised you gentlemen have not heard about it. I should not have known myself, but a little while ago, one of my young novices went to ask alms at Master Cai's house in Cangzhou, and he had to stay there several days before it was safe to return. Between Qinghe and Cangzhou there is a ridge called Jingyang, and it seems that a dragon-eyed, white-headed tiger has recently been making raids from there in search of human prey. Travelers have been afraid to pass the hill, and have had to form parties when they went that way. The local authorities are now offering a reward of fifty taels to anyone who kills the tiger, but so far, though several attempts have been made, they have all come to nothing. Indeed the hunters have been most unfortunate: they have had nothing but maulings for their pains."

Bai Laiguang jumped up. "We are too busy today, since we have this brotherhood to form, but tomorrow we will go and catch the tiger. It will be one way of putting a little money in our pockets."

"Evidently you don't value your life very highly," Ximen Qing said. The other laughed. "Let me get hold of something to spend, and I don't care what happens."

"That reminds me of another funny story," Ying Bojue said. "Once a man fell into a tiger's clutches, and his son, who wished to rescue him, took a knife and went to kill the beast. But the man, though the tiger had him actually in his jaws, cried out anxiously: 'Son, mind where you stick that knife. For goodness' sake, don't spoil the tiger's skin.' "

Abbot Wu was now preparing the offerings for sacrifice. When everything was ready, he came forward and said: "Gentlemen, it is time to burn the sacred papers." Then he produced a document. "I have already written the address," he said, "but I should be glad if you would tell me which of you is the elder brother and in what order I am to put the others. If you will kindly arrange yourselves in your due rank, I shall find it easier to write down your honorable names."

At this there was a chorus: "His Lordship comes first, of course," but Ximen Qing held back. "We should rank according to our age," he said. "Brother Ying is older than I am, and it is for him to take the first place." This was not at all what Ying Bojue wished. "Oh, no, Father!" he cried, I should be ruined. In these days, a man is judged by his wealth or by his position, and since there is no getting away from that, there is no point in taking age into consideration. Besides, there are others older than myself. And there are many other reasons why I should not be made elder brother. Both in dignity and moral standing, I do not rank so high as his Lordship. He is a paragon to the whole world. Then again, I have always been called Ying the Second, and if I were made elder brother I should have to be called Ying the Elder. If I met two acquaintances, and one addressed me as Ying the Elder and the other as Ying the Second, I shouldn't know which of them I ought to answer."

Ximen Qing laughed. "You talk such nonsense, anybody might die of laughing," he said. Xie Xida urged him not to decline, but Ximen continued modestly to prefer the others. Finally, after further pressure from Hua, Ying and the rest, he could hold out no longer and took the place of honor. He was followed by Ying Bojue and Xie Xida, and Hua, out of respect for his wealth, was allotted the fourth place. The others arranged themselves in the lower positions. The abbot then filled up the document, lighted candles, and, with all the men standing shoulder to shoulder in their due order, the address was solemnly unfolded and read aloud.

## IN THE EMPIRE OF THE GREAT SONG, THE PROVINCE OF SHANDONG, PREFECTURE OF DONGPING AND DISTRICT OF QINGHE

The faithful, Ximen Qing, Ying Bojue, Xie Xida, Hua Zixu, Sun Tianhua, Zhu Shinian, Yun Lishou, Wu Dian'en, Chang Zhijie and Bai Laiguang, here assembled, do wash their hands and burn incense to ask a blessing.

The oath of fidelity sworn within the Peach Orchard is the model of all loyalty; with humble hearts we seek to take it as our example, and strive to emulate the spirit that inspired it.

The love of Bao and Guan was as the depth of the ocean, and animated by the same spirit, we hope to imitate their solemn purpose.

The peoples of the four oceans may yet be as brethren and they of different names as of the same blood.

*Therefore*

In this period of Zhenghe—Year—Month—Day, devoutly offering meat offerings of pig and sheep before the phoenix chariot, we humbly bow before this holy altar and make our supplications.

We make our obeisance unto the Highest Heaven, where in a golden palace dwell the Jade Emperor, the Guardian Angels of the Five Directions, the Tutelaries of City and Village, and all the spirits who come and go.

We beseech them to accept the incense of our sincerity. May they deign to protect us in all our doings.

We, Qing, etc. . . . , though born each at a different hour, pray that death may find us united. May the bond between us remain ever unbroken. Our pleasures will we take together, and in time of need will we succor one another. The memory of our friendship shall be ever green, and in our wealth will we remember the unfortunate. Thus, at the last, shall our confidence be confirmed: thus, coming with the sun and going with the moon, shall our fellowship be established as high as the heavens and as firm as the earth.

Henceforth, from this our solemn act of friendship, may our love be eternal and our peace unending. May each of us enjoy length of days, and his household unceasing felicity.

In Heaven alone do we place our trust, until our lives' end.

In token whereof, we diligently set this down.

REIGN PERIOD OF ZHENGHE.

YEAR.

MONTH.

DAY.

When the abbot had finished the reading of this declaration, the men worshipped, bowing together eight times before the shrine. One last time they bowed, and when the paper money had been consumed, the sacred utensils were removed. The abbot told his acolytes to remove the sacrificial animals and cut them up. Chicken, fish and fruits of every kind were set out in profusion upon two tables. Ximen Qing took the seat of honor, and the rest seated themselves in accordance with their rank. The abbot presided over the feast. Soon the wine had been passed around several times, and the men began to amuse themselves telling riddles and guessing fingers, making the hall ring with noisy laughter.

> They saw the sun rise in the distant east
> They watched it set behind the mountains.
> Deep have they drunk, and now unsteadily go forth
> While o'er the trees there hangs the tiny crescent moon.

In the midst of their enjoyment, Daian suddenly came in. He whispered to Ximen Qing, "Mother has sent me to take you home. She says the Third Lady has had a fainting fit, and you must not be late." Ximen rose at once.

"I don't wish to disturb the party, or to be the cause of its breaking up," he said, "but my third wife is ill, and I am afraid I must leave you."

"I go the same way as Brother Ximen," said Hua Zixu. "We will go together."

"If you two rich men both go away," Ying Bojue cried, "how can we stay? Brother Hua, you really must not go."

"There is no man in his house," Ximen said. "We must go back together and set his wife's mind at rest."

"Just as I was coming away," Daian said, "Mistress Hua was telling Tian Fu to saddle a horse and come here."

At that moment the boy arrived. He went to Hua and said, "Your horse is here, and Mother would like you to return."

Before leaving, they thanked Abbot Wu for his kindness, and saluted Ying Bojue and the others. "We are compelled to go now," they said, "but you must stay and have a good time." They went out, jumped on their horses, and rode away. Those who remained were indeed so ravenous that they would have devoured Taishan without leaving a particle of earth. They lingered in the temple and drank deep, and there we may leave them.

When Ximen Qing reached home, he said good-bye to Hua Zixu, and went at once to ask Yueniang how his third wife was.

"I only said she was ill," said Yueniang, "to get you away from those fellows. That is why I made Daian tell you that story. But in truth she has been steadily getting worse, and you ought to stay at home and devote a little of your time to her."

Ximen went to the other side of the house to visit his third wife, and for a few days continued to pay her some attention. On the tenth day of the tenth month, when Ximen Qing had just dispatched a boy to summon the doctor, he was still in the hall when Ying Bojue came in, smiling. Ximen greeted him, and asked him to sit down.

"How is my sister-in-law?" Bojue asked.

"I'm afraid she will never get any better," Ximen said, "it is very doubtful indeed whether anything can be done for her. What time did the party break up the other day?"

"Abbot Wu kept urging us to stay, and it was nearly the second watch before we left. I was very drunk. It was a good thing for you that you came home so early."

"Have you had dinner yet?" Ximen Qing said.

Ying Bojue could not make up his mind whether to say "Yes" or "No," so he asked Ximen to guess.

"I should say you have."

Ying politely put his hand before his mouth, laughed, and said, "You silly man, you've guessed wrong."

"Well, if you haven't, why didn't you say so, you greedy beast?" Ximen said, laughing. "I can't imagine what makes you such a donkey." He told a servant to prepare a meal for Bojue and himself.

"I should have dined," Bojue said, "but I have just heard a most extraordinary piece of news, and I had to come and tell you all about it. We can go and see for ourselves."

"What is this marvelous piece of news?" said Ximen.

"You remember the abbot telling us about the tiger of Jingyang Ridge?" Bojue said. "Well, yesterday a man killed that tiger with his bare fists."

"Don't talk such nonsense," Ximen said. "I don't believe a word of it."

"You say you don't believe me, but wait till I've told you all about it," Bojue went on, waving his arms and stamping his feet in his excitement. "The hero is a certain Wu Song, who some time ago got into trouble at Master Chai's house, and had to run away. He fell ill, and, when he recovered, thought he would like to come and see his brother again. On the way here, he had to pass Jingyang Ridge. There he came upon the tiger and killed it with no weapons but his hands and feet." Ying Bojue told this story in such minute detail that he might himself have been an eyewitness. Ximen Qing shook his head.

"In that case," he said, "as soon as we have finished dinner, I'll go with you and see what the tiger looks like."

"Don't let's wait for dinner, or we may be too late," said Bojue. "Let's go to the High Street, and spend an hour or two in the tavern there."

Laixing was setting the table, but his master told him not to trouble about the meal, and to ask Yueniang to have some clothes set out for him to wear. In a few moments he had changed, and set off arm in arm with Bojue. In the street they ran into Xie Xida. "Hullo, Brothers," he said, laughing, "are you coming to see the man who killed the tiger?"

"We are," said Ximen.

Xie Xida told them that the crowd was so great as to make the roadway almost impassable, and they went to a tavern overlooking the street. They had not long been there when they heard the sound of drums and gongs. The people were all craning their necks to see. Hunters, marching two by two, carrying their tasseled spears, went before the tiger's body. It was so huge that four men could hardly carry it, and it looked like a great embroidered sack. Then, riding upon a splendid white charger, came the bold fellow who had killed it. Ximen Qing gazed at him, bit his nails, and said, "Just look at that man. He must have the strength of a hippopotamus, or he could never have vanquished that great beast." They drank their wine and discussed the heroic deed.

> Full seven feet tall is this majestic figure
> A hero striking terror into all beholders
> With stern and rugged face, and sparkling eyes that blaze like glittering stars
> Clenched fists like sledgehammers.
> If he but raise his foot, the tigers in their mountain lair feel their courage wane
> One blow with that fist, and the great bear trembles in his lonely valley.
> He wears a magic cap with silver flowers
> And his long-sleeved gown is soaked with his victim's blood.

This was the man of whom Ying Bojue had spoken. His home was in the district of Yanggu, and it was only because he had taken a sudden fancy to pay a visit to his elder brother that the opportunity of killing the tiger had come to him.

The magistrate had summoned the hero to his presence, and a host of people were waiting to see him arrive at the Town Hall. As Wu Song dismounted, the magistrate took his place in the Hall of Audience, and the people carried the great beast to the front of the Hall. His Honor was greatly impressed by the hero's bearing, and reflected that a man must be strong indeed to kill such a tiger. He called Wu Song forward.

The hero paid his respects, and then told the story of his prowess so vividly that the officials were half paralyzed by fright. Then, in the Hall of Audience, the magistrate solemnly offered him three cups of wine, and from the public treasure that was stored there took fifty taels of silver.

"By your Honor's leave," said Wu Song, "I owe my victory over the tiger more to good fortune than to ability. I have no right to this reward. The hunters here have incurred your Honor's displeasure on account of this same brute, and I shall be grateful if you will give them the silver rather than myself."

"I will do so if you wish it," said the magistrate, and the money was distributed among the hunters. Seeing that Wu Song was generous-hearted and honest as well as a hero, he thought it would be a good idea to offer him a position. "You are a native of Yanggu," he said; "but that is not a great distance from here. I should like to offer you the appointment of captain of my police, and entrust to you the task of sweeping out the brigands that infest the neighborhood. What do you say?"

Wu Song knelt down. "I shall be eternally grateful to your Honor." The magistrate called his secretary, told him to prepare the necessary papers, and they were sent forward the same day. The notabilities of the district all came to offer their congratulations, and there was feasting for several days.

So Wu Song, who had only thought of his desire to see his elder brother, secured the appointment of police captain in Qinghe. He was delighted with the way things had turned out, and in all the prefecture of Dongping there was none who did not know the name of Wu Song.

> A hero this! A mighty hunter
> Who climbed the Jingyang Ridge with eager tread.
> With strong wine firing his veins he slew the terror of the mountain
> And now his fame is spread to every corner of the earth.

One day, as Wu Song was strolling along the street, he heard a voice behind him, crying: "Brother, Brother! Are you too proud to know me, now that you have become captain of the police?" He turned, and to his surprise, recognized the speaker. It was his brother Wu Da, the very man he had been hoping so long to meet. During a period of severe famine the brothers had been compelled to separate. Wu Da had moved to Qinghe and taken a house in Amethyst Street. He was a simple-minded man, not impressive in appearance. In fact people called him sometimes Tom Thumb and sometimes Old Scraggy Bark. (This was because his body was deformed and his face pinched.) The poor man was neither very strong nor very intelligent, so he became a constant butt for the wits of the neighborhood.

Wu Da had no established business, but scraped together a living by hawking baskets of cakes. His wife had died, leaving him with a little daughter, Ying'er, who was now about twelve years old. They lived alone together for some months, and then Wu Da fell into low water and removed to the house of a rich man named Zhang who lived in the High Street. Here he obtained a lodging of a single room. Zhang's people found him a very honest fellow, and they did their best for him, and started him off selling cakes. When they had time to spare, they used to go to his little place, and he was very attentive to them. They all liked him and spoke well of him to their master, and he, in consequence, did not worry Wu Da for his rent.

This rich man Zhang was more than sixty years old. He was wealthy and prosperous, but he had no children. His wife, a daughter of Master Yu, managed his household with a rod of iron, and he had no pretty maids to amuse him. He was always beating his breast, sighing and lamenting: "Here I am, aged and childless, and though perhaps I am not exactly poor, what use is all my wealth to me?"

"If you feel like that about it," his wife said one day, "I will tell the go-between to buy a couple of girls for you. They can study, morning and night, and learn how to play and sing for your entertainment, and then perhaps you will feel better."

At this, the rich man was delighted, and thanked his wife again and again. Before long, she redeemed her promise, sent for the go-between, and the two girls were bought. One, surnamed Pan, was called Jinlian, and the other, whose surname was Bai, was called Yulian. Yulian was about sixteen years old, and had been born in a bawdy house. She was fair, clear-skinned, dainty, and intelligent. Jinlian was the daughter of a certain Pan Cai who lived outside the South Gate. She was his sixth child, and had been given her name because she was very beautiful even as a child. Her tightly bound feet were particularly charming. When her father died, her mother had been entirely without resources, and when she was only nine years old, she was sold to General Wang. In his house, she learned to play and sing, and, in her spare time, to read and write also. She was clever and industrious, and before she was twelve years old acquired a host of accomplishments. She learned, for example, how to darken her eyes, powder her face, and rouge her lips, and she could play more than one musical instrument. Her needlework had not been neglected and she could read the characters in books. With her hair dressed in a braid, and wearing a simple gown, she made a very pretty picture.

When Jinlian was fifteen years old, General Wang died, and her mother sold her to Master Zhang for thirty taels of silver. She and Yulian were both given music lessons, but since she had had some previous experience, she did not find them very difficult. It was decided that she should play the lute and Yulian the zither. They shared the same room.

When the two girls first came to the house, their mistress was very kind and gave them gold and silver ornaments to make them look pretty. Then Yulian died, and Jinlian was left alone. By this time she was eighteen years old and as beautiful as a peach flower. Her eyebrows were arched like the crescent moon. Many times Master Zhang hungered for a closer acquaintance, but, under the austere eye of his wife, no opportunity was forthcoming. One day, however, when the mistress of the house had gone to take wine with one of her neighbors, the rich man secretly summoned her to his room, and had his way with her.

Unhappily, after he had thus disported himself with Jinlian, all sorts of troubles came upon him. His nose ran, tears streamed from his eyes, and he could not hear. He had severe pains in the loins, and difficulty in making water. He had not long suffered from these complaints before his lady got to know his secret. She upbraided him for several days, and devised all manner of punishment for Jinlian. Master Zhang, though he knew he was doing something he ought not, secretly provided the girl with a trousseau, and looked about for a suitable man to whom to marry her. Everybody said, "Wu Da is a widower and a very honest fellow," and it occurred to him that no one could be more desirable, for Wu Da lived in the same house, and there would be no need for him to lose sight of the young lady. So he married the girl to Wu Da without asking for anything in return. The marriage once celebrated, Zhang heaped kindnesses upon the bridegroom. If he needed money for the ingredients with which to make his buns, the rich man provided it, and when Wu Da went out with his baskets, the rich man, after making sure that there was no one about, would go to console Jinlian in her loneliness.

Wu Da could not help seeing that Zhang treated his wife as though she belonged to him, but he was not in a position to object. Master Zhang came in the morning and stayed until evening, until one day he was overcome by exhaustion and died on the spot. His wife had not been blind to all that was going on, and now, in a rage, she told her servants to turn Wu Da and his wife into the street. The poor man went to Amethyst Street, and there rented a couple of rooms in a nobleman's house, and continued to sell his cakes.

It did not take Jinlian very long to discover that her husband was not much of a man. He was by no means a model of manly vigor, and she came to hate him with an intense hatred. Never a day passed but she found some quarrel to pick with him, and she even cursed Master Zhang. "There is no lack of men in the world," said she. "Why should he have married me to a thing like this? It is always the same. Drive him as hard as I will, he never does a stroke of work, and if I try to push him forward, he only goes backward. No matter how busy the day, he malingers and will not touch his tools. I must have been a great sinner in my last existence to have been doomed to marry such a creature as this. My life is wretched indeed." And when she was quite alone, she sang this song :

> This was an ill-made match.
> A man I thought him; now I know that he is no true man.
> I would not boast, but it is plain
> The crow can ne'er be mated with the phoenix.
> I am as gold deep buried in the ground
> And he a lump of common brass
> Who may not hope to stand beside my golden glory.
> He is nothing but stupid clay.
> Shall my jade body, lying in his arms, thrill him with ecstasy
> As from a dunghill the dainty sesame springs?
> How can I pass my days with him forever?
> How can I suffer him so long as life shall last?
> I, that am purest gold, can never rest upon a bed so vile.

Women, my dear readers, are all very much the same. If a girl is pretty and intelligent, all goes well so long as she marries a fine specimen of a man. But if her husband turns out a simple-minded sort of fellow like Wu Da, it does not matter how virtuous she may be, some degree of hatred will sooner or later affect her attitude to him. And we must remember that seldom do beautiful maidens succeed in finding handsome husbands. The man who has gold to sell never seems to meet the man who wishes to buy.

Every day, Wu Da took his baskets and went out to sell his cakes, returning only at sunset, and when the woman had rid herself of him, she used to sit beneath the blind, chewing melon seeds and pushing forward her tiny feet in the hope of attracting the attention of some young ne'er-do-well. And, indeed, there was a constant stream of courtiers before the gate, who spoke in riddles and called out such remarks as:

"What a pity that such a tasty piece of lamb should fall into a dog's mouth!" They poured out smooth words like oil, till Wu Da came to the conclusion that Amethyst Street was no place to live, and decided to remove elsewhere. But when he talked to his wife about the matter, she cried, "You low creature, you are nothing but a fool. You take a wretched little place like this, and of course dishonorable fellows come and say whatever they think fit. The best thing you can do is to scrape together a few taels, find a decent house, and take a couple of rooms in it. Then perhaps we can live more respectably, and people will cease to treat us like dirt."

"Where am I to get the money from to take a house?" Wu Da said.

"You are not a baby, you lump of mud! Why can't you? Are you going to allow your wife to be continually insulted in this way? If you have no money, take my hair ornaments and sell them, then buy a house with the proceeds. We can buy them back again sometime if we wish to."

Wu Da succeeded in getting together ten taels of silver, and took a place not very far from the Town Hall. It had four rooms on two floors, and there were two small courtyards. The whole place was very clean. When they had taken up their abode in West Street, he still continued to make a living by selling cakes.

Now, unexpectedly, he had come across his younger brother, and their hearts overflowed with joy. Wu Da at once invited his brother to go home with him, and took him upstairs to sit down. Then he called Jinlian to come and see Wu Song. "You remember," he said, "the man who killed the tiger on Jingyang hill. He is none other than your brother, the son of the same mother as myself. He has just been appointed captain of police."

Jinlian made a reverence to her brother-in-law, and Wu Song knelt down to return her greeting. She would not allow this, and made him stand up, saying that such condescension on his part would embarrass her beyond measure. Wu Song, however, persisted, and for some time they carried on a polite dispute, until at last they both knelt and kowtowed down to one another. Soon afterwards, the little Ying'er brought tea for the two men. Wu Song, realizing the seductive charm of his sister-in-law, modestly refrained from looking at her. Wu Da, who was anxious to offer his brother some entertainment, went downstairs to buy some wine and refreshments, and left his wife alone with Wu Song in the upper room.

Jinlian admired his manly qualities and the nobility of his bearing, remembering how he had killed the tiger, and thinking what immeasurable vigor he must have. She said to herself: "These two men are both the sons of one mother; why should my husband's body be so ill-shapen that he seems more like a ghost than a man? In which of my former lives did I so misbehave that I should be doomed to marry an object like him? Wu Song is strong and lusty. Why should I not invite him to make his home with us? He seems the very man for me." She smiled sweetly, and said, "Where are you living, Uncle? Who looks after you?"

"I have just been appointed captain of the police," Wu Song said, "and, as I have to be ready for duty at all times, I live near the Town Hall. Two soldiers wait upon me and cook for me."

"Why not come and live here?" the woman said. "It would be much pleasanter for you than living near the Town Hall with only those nasty dirty soldiers to look after you. If you come and live with us, you will find it much more convenient and, any time you want any little thing to eat or drink, I shall be only too glad to prepare it for you myself and it will be perfectly clean."

"It is very good of you to suggest it," said Wu Song.

"Perhaps your wife is living somewhere in the neighborhood," Jinlian said delicately. "I hope you will ask me to call on her."

"I have never married," said Wu Song.

Then Jinlian inquired politely how old he was, and when he told her he was twenty-eight, she remarked that he was three years older than herself. Finally, she asked where he had been living.

"I have been at Cangzhou for more than a year. I didn't know my brother had moved here, but thought he still lived at the old place."

"Ah," Jinlian said, "that is a long story. We had to come here because, ever since I married your brother, people have taken advantage of his excessive meekness and never ceased to insult us. If only he were as strong as you, Uncle, no one would dare to answer him back."

"My brother has always been a good steady fellow," said Wu Song, "not a good-for-nothing like me."

"Don't be so absurd," the woman said, smiling. "There is an old saying that a man who has no spunk cannot long maintain his independence. I have some spirit myself, and I don't care for the sort of man who lets you hit him without turning a hair, and spins round and round like a top the more you strike him."

"If my brother does not make trouble," Wu Song said, "it is because he wishes to spare you unhappiness."

They were still talking in the upper room when Wu Da came back with a host of things to eat, and set them down in the kitchen. He came to the foot of the stairs and called, "Wife, Wife, come down!"

"Where are your manners?" Jinlian cried. "Why do you call me down? There is no one except myself to entertain your brother."

"Please do not trouble about me," Wu Song said.

"Why don't you go next door," the woman said, "and ask old woman Wang to come and get the dinner ready? That's what you ought to do."

Wu Da went off and asked the old woman to come. She busied herself, and when all was ready, took the food upstairs and set it on the table—fish, meat, fruit and cakes. The wine was heated, and Wu Da, having asked his wife to take the host's place, himself sat at the side and put his brother in the seat of honor. When they were all in their places, the wine was poured out.

Wu Da himself heated it and served the other two. "Uncle," Jinlian said, as she took her cup, "please excuse our having made no special preparations for you. I am afraid this is very inferior wine."

"Please don't say that," said Wu Song. "It is most kind of you to trouble about me at all."

While Wu Da busied himself with the heating of the wine, Jinlian, all smiles, and with the word "Uncle" continually upon her lips, kept saying, "Will you not have something tasty?" and, taking the choicest parts from different dishes, herself offered them to her brother-in-law.

Wu Song was a simple-hearted fellow and treated her like a sister, not knowing the sort of woman she was. Cleverly enough, she assumed a modest air, and it never occurred to him that she was deliberately trying to seduce him. They sat together and drank several cups of wine, but she could not keep her eyes away from him, and this finally embarrassed him so much that he turned his head away. By this time, he had drunk much wine and, as he began to feel a little tipsy, he decided it was time to go and stood up to take his leave.

"What is your hurry?" Wu Da cried. "Stay and have a little more to drink. You have nothing to do now."

"Thank you," said Wu Song politely, "but I shall see you both some other time."

They went downstairs with him, and as he was going out of the door, Jinlian cried, "Don't forget to make arrangements to come here to live. If you don't, the neighbors will have a very poor opinion of our hospitality. Brothers are not strangers, and your company will be a pleasure to us."

"It is very kind of you," Wu Song said. "I will bring my things here this very evening."

"We shall be waiting for you," the woman said.

# CHAPTER 2

# Pan Jinlian

Wu Song went to the inn near the Town Hall, packed his baggage and his bedclothes, and told a soldier to carry them to his brother's house. When Pan Jinlian saw him coming, she was as delighted as if she had discovered a hidden treasure. She bustled about preparing a room for her brother-in-law and setting everything to rights. Wu Song sent back the orderly, and stayed the night at his brother's home. The next day, he rose very early, and Jinlian hastened to heat water for him. He washed, combed and tied his hair, and then made ready to go to the office to sign the roll.

"Uncle," Jinlian said, "when you have signed the roll, be sure to come home for lunch. You mustn't think of taking your meals anywhere but here."

After signing the roll, Wu Song waited all the morning in attendance at the office, and finally went home. Jinlian had taken the greatest pains over the cooking, and the three sat down together to lunch. Taking a cup of tea in both hands, the woman offered it to Wu Song.

"You take so much trouble on my account," he said, "that it makes me quite embarrassed. Tomorrow I will arrange for a soldier to come and wait on us."

"Please do no such thing," Jinlian cried anxiously. "We are the same flesh and blood, and this house is home to us all. I am not waiting upon a stranger. Certainly this little Ying'er is not much use, and I can't rely upon her. She always seems to do the wrong thing. But if we get a soldier to help about the house, I shall find him in the way in the kitchen, and it will fidget me to watch him."

"In that case," Wu Song said, "I can only accept your kindness gratefully."

Not long after Wu Song had taken up his abode in his brother's house, he gave Wu Da some money and asked him to make arrangements to give a party for the neighbors. They came with presents to pay their respects to Wu Song, and a little later Wu Da gave another party in return. Wu Song presented his sister with a length of colored silk to make dresses.

"Oh, Uncle," she cried delightedly, "I can't possibly accept such a magnificent present," but she hastened to add: "Since you have already bought it, I suppose I must not refuse." She made a reverence, and took the silk.

From that time, Wu Song was definitely established as a member of his brother's household. Wu Da, as before, went to the street every day to sell his cakes, and Wu Song went to the Town Hall to perform his official duties. Whether he returned early or late, Jinlian always had something ready for him, and seemed delighted to wait upon him. He noticed this, but thought no more about it. Nonetheless, the woman was forever trying to lead him on by pretty speeches, though she found it no easy task, for he was really incorruptible. If he had anything of importance to say, he would stay long enough to say it, but if not, he went straight about his business.

A month soon passed. It was the eleventh month, and they began to experience seasonable weather. The north wind blew violently for several days and black clouds gathered on every hand. Then the snow began to fall, and soon it filled the skies.

> For miles and miles the skies were filled with thick dark clouds.
> Snowflakes, dancing past the window ledge, in midair formed a screen
>     like tiny flowers of jade.
> Zi Yu's boat, on the Yan River, was held and forced to tarry.
> Soon was a mantle laid on the high palaces
> River and mountain bound with a chain of silver
> The skies filled with winged salt and driving, powdery dust.
> That day, Lū Meng, in his little hut, sighed
> For all his wretchedness.

The snow continued without ceasing until the first night watch; the world was silver everywhere, and it seemed as though the earth had arrayed itself in a glorious garment of jade. Next morning, Wu Song went to the office and stayed till noon. Jinlian bade her husband go and sell his cakes and she went to ask her neighbor, old woman Wang, to go and buy some food and wine for her. Then she went to Wu Song's room, and made up the fire, thinking: "Today I will make sure of him. Beyond a doubt I can do something to wake him up." Afterwards, feeling quiet and lonely, she went and stood beneath the lattice and waited till she saw Wu Song trampling down the glistening snow as he hastened home.

She quickly raised the lattice for him and smiled. "You look frozen, Uncle." He answered her politely and came in, taking off his hat. Jinlian offered to take it, but he brushed the snow away himself and hung it on the wall. Then he unloosed his girdle, took off his outer gown of parrot green, and went into the living room.

"I have been expecting you all the morning," Jinlian said. "Why didn't you come back to lunch?"

"One of my friends asked me to lunch," Wu Song replied, "and just now I had another invitation, but I decided not to accept it, and came home instead."

"Is that so?" said the woman. "Won't you come a little nearer the fire?"

Wu Song thanked her and, taking off his oiled boots, changed his socks and put on a pair of slippers. Then he brought a bench and sat down by the fire. Jinlian told Ying'er to bolt the gate and shut the back door. She herself went to fetch some of the dishes she had cooked, and set them on the table before Wu Song.

"Where is my brother?" he said.

"He has not come back from business yet," the woman answered. "Let us drink a few cups of wine together."

"It is not late," Wu Song said. "We had better wait for him."

"Oh, why should we bother about him?" Jinlian cried.

At that moment Ying'er came in with the wine already warmed. Wu Song again apologized politely for causing so much trouble. Jinlian said nothing, but brought a bench to the fire and sat down. There were several dishes on the table, but she only took a cup of wine, looked at Wu Song, and invited him to drink it. This he did in one breath. She poured a second cup and handed that to him, saying, "It is so cold, you must drink this to keep the other company." This, too, Wu Song drank straight off. Then he filled a cup for her. She took the wine and sipped it delicately, then poured out still another cup and offered it to him. Her milk-white breast was partially uncovered, and her disordered hair was like a beautiful cloud. Desire had given color to her cheeks.

"People tell me you keep a singing girl over there by the Town Hall," she said slyly. "Is that true?"

"People always talk nonsense like that, but you shouldn't believe them, Sister," Wu Song said. "I never was that kind of man."

"I don't believe you," said Jinlian. "Your heart speaks one language and your tongue another."

"Ask my brother, if you don't believe me."

"What on earth is the use of bringing him into it?" Jinlian said. "His life is one long dream. Judging by the way he goes about, you might think he was always half tipsy. He would not have to spend all his days selling cakes if he had a particle of intelligence. But have another cup of wine."

She filled three or four cups one after the other, and Wu Song drank them all. She drank a few cups too, till the spur of desire pressed her more acutely and the passion within her blazed so that she lost all control of herself and could hardly speak. By this time, an inkling of the true state of affairs was beginning to dawn upon Wu Song, and he looked away from her.

After a while she rose and went to heat some more wine. Wu Song, left alone in the room, took up the poker and began to poke the fire. Jinlian was soon back again with a jar of wine that she had warmed. In one hand she held the jar and with the other she gently pressed his shoulder. "Uncle," she said, "you must be cold with so few clothes." Wu Song was now beginning to feel thoroughly uncomfortable, and made no answer. Seeing him thus silent, she snatched the poker from his hand and cried, "You don't know how to poke. Let me do it for you. I want it as hot as a bowl of fire."

Wu Song felt even more uneasy, but he still said nothing. Jinlian was not in any way put out. She set down the poker and poured out another cup of wine. She drank a mouthful, looked meaningly at Wu Song, and said, "If you feel like it, drink what I have left."

This was too much. He snatched the cup from her hand and dashed the wine upon the floor, crying, "Don't be so shameless," and at the same time pushed her so violently that she almost fell. Then he gazed haughtily upon her.

"My feet are steadfast upon the earth and I aspire to reach the heavens. I am a man with teeth in my mouth and hair upon my head. I am a man, I say, not a swine or a cur, that I should pay no heed to the sacred laws of honor or flout the precepts of common decency. You must not behave in this shameless way. If I hear any whisper of your ever doing such a thing again, my eyes may tell me that you are my sister, but my fist will not recognize you."

This made Jinlian so confused and angry that her face became crimson. She called Ying'er to clear away the dishes, and muttered, "I was only joking. How could you think I was in earnest? You are not an honorable man." When the dishes had been removed, she went down to the kitchen.

So Jinlian came to realize that her blandishments were without effect, except that Wu Song had treated her roughly, while he, now sitting alone, grew angrier and angrier and thought very seriously about the matter.

It was still early, about the hour of the Monkey, when Wu Da came back, carrying his baskets over the snow. He opened the door, put down his burden, and going into the house at once saw that his wife's eyes were red with weeping. "With whom have you been quarreling now?" he said.

"If you were not such a mean-spirited creature," his wife cried, "things like this would not happen. But you never care whether outsiders insult me or not."

"Who has been insulting you?" Wu Da said.

"If you really wish to know, it was that scoundrel, your brother. When the snow was very heavy, I saw him coming back, and I was kindly getting something ready for him, when he saw there was nobody about, and tried to seduce me. It is perfectly true: Ying'er saw him."

"My brother is not that kind of man," her husband said. "He has always been high-principled and straightforward. Don't make so much noise, or the neighbors will hear you and laugh." He went to see Wu Song.

"You haven't eaten your cakes, Brother," he said. "I'll come and have some with you." But Wu Song did not answer him and, after brooding there a while, started to leave the house.

"Where are you going?" cried Wu Da, but his brother went off without replying. Wu Da went back to the room and said to his wife, "I called him, but he would not answer, and now he has gone down the road to the Town Hall. I'm sure I don't understand what all the bother is about."

"You thievish, stupid worm," Jinlian cried. "There is nothing to understand. The wretch is ashamed and dare not face you. That's why he has gone out. Probably he has not the audacity to inflict himself upon us any longer, and has gone to tell somebody to come and take his things away. I can't imagine why you bother about him."

"If he goes away," Wu Da said, "people will certainly laugh at us."

"You silly creature," Jinlian cried. "He is a shameless, immoral fellow, and he tried to seduce me. Is that a laughing matter? If you want him so much, go and live with him. I won't put up with it. Give me divorce papers if you like, and then the pair of you can live together."

After this, Wu Da did not dare to open his mouth again, and he had to suffer his wife's ill-temper for a long time. They were indeed still quarreling when Wu Song, with a soldier carrying a long pole, came back, packed up his luggage, and went off. Wu Da went after him, crying, "Why are you going away, Brother?"

"Ask no questions," Wu Song answered. "If I tell the truth, your good name will be ruined. Let me go."

Wu Da did not dare to question him any further, and was obliged to let him go with his luggage. Meanwhile his wife was scolding in her room: "That's better. Relations always prove a nuisance in the long run. People don't know the truth. Just because here is a young brother with a position at the Town Hall, they must needs conclude that he keeps his brother and sister. They never think that he is really eating us out of house and home. He is like a yellow quince, good to look at and rotten inside. I shall thank my lucky star if he takes himself off for good and all. Indeed there is nothing I hope more than that I may never set eyes on that piece of ill-fortune again."

Wu Da could not avoid hearing all his wife said, but still he could not make out what had really happened, and his heart was troubled. Now that his brother had gone back to live at the inn near the Town Hall, he still sold buns and cakes upon the street. He longed for an opportunity to go to the Town Hall and have a talk, but his wife gave him strict instructions that he must not dare to do anything of the sort, and he did not venture to disobey her. After Wu Song's departure, the snow suddenly stopped. Ten days passed.

The magistrate of Qinghe had been stationed there for more than two years and had amassed much gold and silver. Now he wanted a man of courage to take his treasure to the Eastern Capital, so that his relatives might take charge of it. In three years his term of office would expire, and knowing that he would then have to make his report to the Emperor, he thought it would be well to have this gold and silver in hand when he came to deal with officials more exalted than himself. But he felt the need of a stout fellow for the job, as thieves often beset the way. Then he thought of Wu Song. He was just the man. That very day he sent for Wu Song and said to him:

"I am thinking of sending an important present to one of my relatives at the Eastern Capital. I mean Zhu Mian, one of the Grand Marshal's officers. There may be some danger about the journey, but if you undertake it, I am sure all will be well. If you will do this for me, I will reward you handsomely when you get back."

"You have shown me so much kindness, Sir, that I should never think of refusing," Wu Song replied. "I will set off as soon as you give me your orders."

The magistrate was now perfectly satisfied. He gave Wu Song three cups of wine, and handed him ten taels of silver as journey money. After receiving his instructions, Wu Song went to the inn and, after getting his orderly to buy some food and a jar of wine at a shop in the street, went to his brother's house. When Wu Da returned, he found his brother waiting on the doorstep. He had told his servant to take the wine and food into the kitchen.

Jinlian had not abandoned all hope, and when she saw Wu Song coming with wine and other delicacies she said to herself: "He must still be thinking about me, or he would not have come back. I may get him yet." So she went upstairs to powder her face and arrange her hair, and when she had changed into a prettier dress, she came down to welcome him.

"I can't imagine what can have displeased you, Uncle," she said, as she made a reverence. "For several days you haven't been near us, and I have often wondered why. It is delightful to see you home again, but why did you trouble to bring wine and food?"

"I have something to say to my brother," Wu Song said. "That is why I have come."

Jinlian invited him to go upstairs, and they all three went to the upper room. Wu Da and his wife sat in the places of honor, and Wu Song sat down on a long bench. The orderly brought up the food and Wu Song invited his brother and sister to take some. From time to time, Jinlian glanced meaningly at her brother-in-law, but he paid no attention to anything but the wine he was drinking. When they had all drunk several cups, Wu Song asked Ying'er to bring a loving cup and, when the orderly had heated the wine, he took this cup in his hands and said to Wu Da:

"Honorable elder brother: today the magistrate has ordered me to go to the Eastern Capital for him. I am starting tomorrow, and it may easily be two or three months before I get back, though I hope it will be less. What I have come to say to you is this: you have always been a long-suffering kind of man, and I don't intend you to be imposed upon in my absence. Now, listen to me. You have been in the habit of selling ten trays of cakes, but in future you must only make five. Then you will be able to go out later and come home earlier. Don't let anyone persuade you to drink; pull down the shutters and bolt the door as soon as you get home. If you do this, you will be saved a great deal of unpleasantness, but if anything disagreeable should happen, don't let yourself be drawn into a quarrel. Wait till I come back, and I'll soon settle the matter. Now, my dear brother, if you agree, drink this cup of wine."

Wu Da took the cup and drained it. "I will do whatever you think fit," he said.

Wu Song filled up the cup again and spoke to Jinlian. "Sister, you are no fool, and I don't think I need say any more. My brother is so simple-hearted that the real management of the household is in your hands. You will remember the old saying that a proud appearance is not always the mirror of an honest heart. If you attend to your household duties as you should, my brother will have nothing to worry about. As our fathers used to say: 'When the fence is safe, dogs cannot get in.'"

Jinlian listened, and the crimson color spread across her face. She shook her finger at Wu Da, and addressed Wu Song through him. "You fool! What do you think you will gain by insulting me like this? I have to wear a woman's clothes, it is true, but I am as good as any man. I am always steady and reliable. A man might stand upon my fist or a horse ride over my arm. I am not a turtle to be wounded without bloodshed. Never, since I married Wu Da, has even an ant dared to sneak into my room. How dare you talk about dogs getting in if the fence is not safe? Tell the truth, not a pack of lies. I don't care in the slightest what you say."

Wu Song laughed. "Don't lose your temper, Sister. So long as your heart keeps company with your mouth, all will be well. But I shall remember what you have said. And now, won't you drink this cup?"

Jinlian dashed the cup aside and ran downstairs. Before she reached the bottom, she turned and cried, "You think you're very wise and clever, but how is it you don't seem to know that a brother's wife should be respected as a mother? When I first married Wu Da, nobody ever mentioned his having a brother. Where have you come from? Are you really a relative or are you not? One would think you were the master of the house. Oh, it makes me wild to have to put up with such nonsense." She went down the rest of the stairs, sobbing.

The brothers drank several more cups of wine together till they could stay no longer, while Jinlian affected many airs and graces. At last they both went downstairs, and took their leave of one another with tears streaming down their cheeks. "Brother," Wu Da said, "you must go, I suppose, but come back as soon as you can and let my eyes rejoice in you once more."

Wu Song said, "Wouldn't it be better if you stayed away from business altogether, and let me arrange with somebody to supply you with funds?" Finally, he cried, "Remember what I say, Brother, and keep a watch on your door." Wu Da promised.

So Wu Song parted from his brother. He went back to the inn, packed his luggage, and saw to his weapons. The next morning he took charge of the magistrate's presents, secured a horse, and set off for the Eastern Capital.

After his brother's departure Wu Da had to endure his wife's scoldings for several days, but he held himself in check, swallowed his wrath, and let her scold him. He did what his brother had told him, and made only half the number of cakes he had made before. Every day he returned before sunset and, setting down his baskets, pulled down the shutters and closed the outer gate before he came to sit down in the room. His wife saw this, and grew more and more resentful every day. "You horrible creature," she said at length, "one would think you couldn't tell the time. Even jailers don't bar the prison gate while the sun is still in the heavens. Our neighbors must be in fits of laughter and think we are afraid of ghosts. You are just like a new-born babe who has to do what his brother tells him. Aren't you ashamed to have everybody laughing at you?"

"Let them laugh," Wu Da said. "What my brother said is true enough, and may save us much trouble yet."

"Pah, you vile creature!" his wife shouted, and spat in his face. "You, a grown-up man, have no will of your own, but have to do whatever anybody tells you."

"Say what you like," Wu Da said with a gesture of weariness. "To me my brother's words are as gold and precious stones." He continued to go out late and return early, and he still shut the door as soon as he got home. This so infuriated his wife that she almost had a fit; she quarreled with him so incessantly that trouble seemed to have become a habit. About the time for his return, she would pull down the shutter and bolt the door, thinking that so she would annoy him, but instead of making him angry, this gave him considerable secret satisfaction and he thought: "If she takes things like this, so much the better for all concerned."

The sun's bright horses galloped past the window, and the sun and moon raced like a weaver's shuttles. It seemed but a moment since the winter solstice passed and it was the season when the plum trees blossom, yet now the weather was giving warning of spring's return. One day, in the third month, the sun shone so pleasantly that Jinlian decided to dress herself in her best clothes. Wu Da was out, and she was standing by the door beneath the lattice. Thinking it was nearly time for his return, she prepared to pull down the shutter and go back to the room to wait for him. But now the fates intervened. A man passed beneath the lattice.

In affairs of the heart we always find that Fate brings the lovers together, and a story would not be worth the telling if accidents never happened. Jinlian was holding the pole and preparing to pull down the shutter, when a gust of wind suddenly blew it out of her hand. She could not catch it, and it fell upon the man's head. She smiled her apologies, and stole a look at him. Upon his head he wore a tasseled hat, and golden filigree hairpins, with one of the signs of the zodiac edged with jade. Over slender hips he wore a green silk gown and on his feet a pair of fine but heavily soled shoes, with socks as white as the purest water. He was fanning himself with a gilt fan. He was indeed as handsome as Master Zhang, and worthy of comparison with Pan An.

Jinlian peeped at him from under the lattice. When first the pole struck him, he stopped and seemed on the point of an angry outburst, but, as he turned, he suddenly beheld an incredibly pretty woman.

Her hair was black as a raven's plumage; her eyebrows mobile as the kingfisher and as curved as the new moon. Her almond eyes were clear and cool, and her cherry lips most inviting. Her nose was noble and exquisitely modeled, and her dainty cheeks beautifully powdered. Her face had the delicate roundness of a silver bowl. As for her body, it was as light as a flower, and her fingers as slender as the tender shoots of a young onion. Her waist was as narrow as the willow, and her white belly yielding and plump. Her feet were small and tapering; her breasts soft and luscious. One other thing there was, black-fringed, grasping, dainty, and fresh, but the name of that I may not tell. Words fail to describe the charm of so beauteous a vision.

Her luxuriant coal-black hair was as thick as the clouds. On each side she wore small pins and, at the back, a pair of combs with a cleverly fashioned flower. Two peach flowers adorned her willow-leaf eyebrows. The jade pendants she wore were remarkable, but the glory of her uncovered bosom was that of jade beyond all price. She wore a blue gown bound with a long silk-embroidered sash, and in her cuff a tiny satchel of perfumes. Beneath her delicate throat, a many-buttoned corsage concealed her breast.

Her feet were graced by tiny shoes made like the mountain crow, with tips embroidered to look like the claws. Their high heels were of white silk, so that she seemed always to walk upon a fragrant dust. Her scarlet silken trousers were decorated with birds and flowers and, as she sat or when she rose, the wind would puff out her skirts and flowing undergarments. From her mouth there came a perfume as delicious as that of orchides and musk, while her cherry lips and beautiful cheeks had the glory of a flower. One glimpse of this vision, and the souls of men would flutter away and die. Many handsome young men might perish at the sight.

No sooner had the man set eyes upon all this beauty than he became almost beside himself with desire. His anger sped to Java and his face was quickly wreathed in smiles. Jinlian knew that she was to blame for the disaster, so she made a graceful reverence and said, "The wind suddenly blew the pole out of my hand, and I had the misfortune to strike you. Please do not be angry with me."

The man set his hat straight with one hand, and made a reverence so low that he almost swept the ground. "Lady," he said, "it was not of the slightest consequence. You may do with me what you will."

It so happened that the neighbor, old woman Wang, the tea seller, had seen everything that happened. She was greatly entertained. "Who may you be, Sir," she cried, "who pass by this house to be welcomed with blows upon the head?"

The man laughed. "It was all my fault. I should have been more careful. Please don't be vexed with me, Lady."

"Don't beat me," said the old woman Wang, still enjoying the joke. The man laughed again, and bowed most profoundly to express his regret. His roguish eyes, experienced in amorous adventure and well versed in the value of a woman's charms, could not look away from Jinlian. At last he went off, strutting and waving his fan, though not without turning around seven or eight times.

Jinlian had no sooner set eyes upon the man with his engaging manner and lively ways, no sooner heard him speak so winningly and brightly, than she fell head over heels in love with him. She had no idea who he was or where he lived, but she rightly concluded that he would not have turned his head so often unless he reciprocated her feelings in some measure. She stayed beneath the lattice until he was out of sight and then, pulling down the shutter, closed the door and went back to her room.

You may have guessed who this man was. None other than that chief of those who sought the pleasures of the couch, that captain of those who gather precious treasure and pursue unlawful fragrance, his Lor Ximen. His third wife had just died and been given a solemn burial and, being distressed in mind, he was taking a stroll along the street intending to call upon Ying Bojue and thus secure a little distraction from his gloom. As he passed by Wu Da's house, he received, as we have seen, an unexpected blow on the head. But now that he had seen Jinlian under the lattice, Master Ximen went home again. "That was a splendid woman," he thought. "I wonder how I can get hold of her." He suddenly remembered old woman Wang, the neighbor who kept a tea shop. "She seems a clever old body," he said to himself, "and, if she can bring this affair to the conclusion I desire, she shall have a few taels of silver." He did not stay to eat anything, but hurried off to the street and dashed to old woman Wang's tea shop. He went in and took a seat, looking out beneath the awning.

"That was a very fine bow you made, Sir," said old woman Wang, laughing.

"Please come here, Stepmother," Ximen said. "That young neighbor of yours—er—that young woman—ahem— whose wife is she?"

"Oh," the old woman replied, "she is the sister of the King of Hell, the daughter of General Wu Dao. What makes you ask?"

"Don't treat the matter as a joke," Ximen said. "I am speaking seriously."

"Surely you know, Sir," said old woman Wang. "Her husband sells cakes outside the Town Hall."

"What! Xu the Third?" Ximen said.

The old woman shook her head. "No, if it were he, they would be something like a pair. Guess again, Sir."

"Perhaps it is Li the Third, then: he sells cakes."

The old woman shook her head again. "No, if he were the man, I should think they were perfectly matched."

"Well, then," Ximen cried, "it must be Liu Xiao. You know: the man they call Tattooed Arms."

Still the old woman laughed. "No," she said, "even if it were he, I should say they were a well-mated couple. Guess once more, Sir."

"I can't guess, Stepmother," Ximen said almost in despair, while the old woman roared with laughter.

"Well, I'll tell you. Her husband is that fellow Wu Da, who hawks his cakes about the streets."

When Ximen Qing heard this, he nearly jumped out of his chair. "You can't mean that Wu Da whom people call Tom Thumb or Old Scraggy Bark."

"That is the man," replied the old woman.

"Good Heavens," Ximen cried. "What a tasty piece of lamb to fall into a dog's mouth. However can it have happened?"

"It is always the same," old woman Wang replied. "You always find a beautiful horse ridden by some fool of a man, and a pretty girl sleeping with a husband who is not fit to be seen. The old Man in the Moon works things that way."

"How much do I owe you?" Ximen said.

"Nothing worth mentioning," the old woman replied. "We will leave it till another time."

"With whom is your son Wang Chao working now?" Ximen asked.

"He is away with a merchant, a native of Huai, but really he has been away so long that I don't know whether he's alive or dead."

"Why not let him come to me? He seems to be a smart lad."

"I am glad he meets with your approval."

"Very well," Ximen said, "when he comes back we must talk about the matter again." He thanked the old woman and went away. But in less than no time he was back again, sitting once more near the door that looked upon Wu Da's house.

"May I offer you some damson broth, Sir?" said old woman Wang, when she came out.

"I should like some very much," Ximen said, "but let it be a little sour, if you don't mind." The old woman made the broth, and offered it to him with both hands. When he had finished it, he put down the cup. "You make excellent damson broth, Stepmother," he said. "Have you got many damsons in your room there?"

"I have dealt in damsons all my life," the old woman said, "but I never keep them in my room."

"I was talking about damsons, not damsels," said Ximen. "You are getting a little mixed up."

"It was damsels you were thinking about, nonetheless," the old lady retorted.

"Well," said Ximen, "you admit you sell damsels. What about finding one for me? If you can let me have a nice tasty one, you won't lose by it."

"You are only teasing me," the old woman said. "If your wife heard about it, my old face would have a rough time."

"Not at all," Ximen said. "My wife is a most amiable woman, and I have several girls already, but none of them is exactly what I want. If you have a really good girl on your books, you must introduce her to me. I don't care whether she is somebody else's leavings or not, but she must be a woman who will satisfy me."

"Ah," the old woman said, "a few days ago I did hear of an excellent girl, but I'm afraid she wouldn't do for you."

"If she is the right stuff, just go ahead, and you shall be well paid for your pains."

"She is more than usually good-looking," said the old lady, "but rather old, perhaps."

"Well," said Ximen, "people have always said that a middle-aged woman has a charm all her own. It will not put me off if she happens to be a year or two older than I am. But how old is she?"

"She was born under the planet Mercury and her animal is the Pig, so as my reckoning goes, she will be ninety-three years old next New Year."

"You crazy old woman," Ximen cried. "Why do you screw up your silly old face and make fun all the time?" It was getting late and he decided to go away. The old woman had lighted her lamp and was going to fasten the gate, when Ximen Qing once again appeared. He sat down under the awning and gazed with longing eyes at Wu Da's house.

"Would you like a little allspice soup?" old woman Wang said.

"Yes, please," said Ximen, "but let it be sweet." The old woman hastily brought some soup, and he ate it all. He sat there till it was very late. At last he stood up. "Please make out my bill, old lady, and I will pay you next time I come."

"Don't worry about it," the old woman said; "we shall certainly have another opportunity of settling it." Ximen Qing laughed and went away.

At home, he could take no pleasure either eating or sleeping; his heart was consumed with desire for Jinlian. Wu Yueniang saw him in this sad state, but thought it was because of his third wife's death, and did not trouble him. Next morning, as soon as it was light and old woman Wang came out to unbolt her gate, Ximen Qing was already striding down the street.

"Ah," she thought, "new brooms sweep clean, and this one seems to be doing all its sweeping in this direction. I must keep the young man on tenterhooks for a while. In his dealings with the people here, he always manages to come off best, but if I get him into my clutches, I shall be surprised if I can't squeeze a little bawdy money out of him."

Old woman Wang's past history was none too creditable. She had been an efficient and busy go-between all her life, and occasionally dealt in children. She had also practiced midwifery, applying the requisite pressure to the mother and receiving the little ones on their arrival. In short, she was a thoroughly accomplished rogue.

The old woman had just opened her door to throw out the tea leaves when she saw Ximen Qing pacing up and down. Finally he came towards the tea shop and stood underneath the awning facing Wu Da's door. He was looking up at the lattice as though he could not take his eyes from it. The old woman pretended not to see him, and went on making a fire in her tea shop, until Ximen Qing, finding that she did not come out to offer him any tea, called to her to bring two cups.

"Ah," the old woman said, "is that you, my lord? Why have you allowed so long a time to pass without coming to see me? Please take a seat." In a few moments, she had made two cups of very strong tea and set them on the table.

"You'll take a cup with me, Stepmother, won't you?" Ximen said.

"I am not your shadow," the old woman said, laughing. "Why should I always drink tea with you?"

Ximen Qing laughed. "What do these neighbors of yours sell?"

"Roasted love darts; dried cuckoo's nests with parsley all around them; good fresh mincemeat; rolls all ready to be stuffed; oyster dumplings, and warm-heart pastries."

"You mad old woman," Ximen said, laughing. "I do wish you would talk sense."

"I am not mad by any means," said the old woman. "If you would rather go and ask the master of the house, you will find him at home."

"I am quite serious," Ximen said. "If they have good buns there, I should like to buy forty or fifty and take them home with me."

"There is no need to go to the house to buy them. The man will be going to the street in a minute or two, and you can get as many as you like."

"That is true," said Ximen. He drank his tea, lingered for a while, and at last went away. Old woman Wang watched him with her stony eyes, and saw him pacing to and fro, looking first to the right and then to the left. This he did seven or eight times. At last he came back to the tea shop.

"How do you do, Sir?" the old lady said. "I had almost forgotten what you look like."

Ximen Qing took a tael of silver from his sleeve and handed it to her. "This is for my tea," he said.

The old woman smiled. "Why do you give me so much?"

"I should take it if I were you," said Ximen, "and not trouble how much it is."

"Now," thought the old woman, "my chance has come. It is time this broom lost some of its bristles. I will take this today, and it will doubtless come in for my lodging tomorrow." She said aloud, "I see there is something you have set your heart upon."

"What makes you think that?" Ximen said.

"It is not very hard to see. There is an old saying, 'When a man enters your door, don't trouble to ask whether he is in luck or not. Look at his face.' I can assure you I've guessed things far more difficult than that."

"If you can guess what I am thinking about," said Ximen, "you shall have five taels of silver."

Old woman Wang laughed. "One guess will be enough. Let me whisper in your Lordship's ear. You have been haunting this neighborhood for two or three days, and it is quite clear that you have your eye on the lady next door. Am I right?"

Ximen Qing smiled. "Your intelligence, Stepmother, is worthy of Sui He, and you are even sharper than Lu Jia. I shall not attempt to hoodwink you. I don't know how it is, but ever since I saw her face under the lattice I seem to have lost both my heart and my head. Day and night I can think of nothing else. When I am at home, I can neither eat nor drink, and work is out of the question. I wonder if you can think of some way to help me."

"I shall not try to hoodwink you either," the old woman said. "People imagine that I keep a tea shop here, but to tell you the truth, a ghost playing the night watchman would fill the part as honestly as I do mine. One day, I certainly did sell some tea. It was three years ago, to be precise, when snow fell in the sixth month; but I've sold none since. No, sir, I make my living in quite another way."

"And what may that be?" Ximen asked.

"When I was thirty-six years old, my husband died. He left me with a young boy and not a penny to live on. So I took up the business of a go-between, and also made a little money by making clothes, acting the midwife, and introducing people to one another. Sometimes I let blood for people who are ill."

I had no idea your accomplishments were so many," Ximen said. "If you can arrange this matter to my satisfaction, I will give you ten taels of silver for your coffin. All you have to do is to get that woman to meet me."

"I was only joking," the old woman said. "Why did you take me seriously?"

# CHAPTER 3
# The Old Procuress

Ximen Qing was desperately anxious to possess Pan Jinlian. He gave the old woman no peace.

"Stepmother," he said, "if you bring this business to a happy end, I will give you ten taels of silver."

"Sir," said the old woman, "you may have heard, perhaps, of setting a love snare. The expression implies much that is difficult and is, indeed, what is more commonly known as wife stealing. Before a man can set about this wife-stealing business with any prospect of success, five things are essential. He must be as handsome as Pan An. His member must be at least as large as a donkey's. He must be as rich as Deng Tong, and reasonably young. Finally, he must have plenty of time on his hands, and almost endless patience. If you are possessed of all these qualifications, you may think of going in for this sort of entertainment."

"I think I may say I do possess them all," Ximen Qing said. "I would not venture to compare my handsome figure with that of Pan An, but it will serve. Ever since I was a boy, I have played in the lowest and most unsavory haunts, and I must say I have succeeded in keeping a very fat turtle well content. I may not have as much money as Deng Tong, but have a good deal put away, certainly sufficient to live upon. As for my patience, I should never think of retaliating though I received four hundred blows. Finally, if I had not plenty of time to waste, you would not be seeing me here so often. Stepmother, do this for me, and you shall not be disappointed with your reward."

"There is one thing more, Sir," the old woman said. "You tell me that you possess the five essential qualifications, but I fear this too is indispensable."

"What do you mean?" Ximen Qing cried.

"Forgive my speaking plainly," the old woman said, "but when a man would run off with somebody else's wife, there are very considerable difficulties in the way. A man may spend almost his last penny, and still fail. He must go to the absolute limit. I happen to know that you particularly dislike parting with your money, and that is the difficulty."

"It shall be no difficulty in this case," Ximen said, "for I will do anything you suggest."

"Very well," the old woman said, "if you are really prepared to spend a few taels, I have a plan that should enable you to secure the lady."

Ximen would have liked to hear it, but the old woman said, with a laugh, "It is too late today, and time you went home. Come back in six months, or perhaps three, and we will see what we can do."

"Stepmother," said Ximen, "don't joke about it. Only do this for me and you shall have a really handsome present." But the old woman laughed all the more.

"You certainly seem to be very keen," she said. "Nobody ever comes to say his prayers to me at the temple of Wu Cheng Wang, but my plan is as good and better than any that fellow Sun Wuzi could have made. He was able to turn girls into soldiers, but I could have captured eight out of ten of them. Let me tell you all I know about this woman. She comes of a poor family, but she is as clever as can be. She knows how to play and sing, her embroidery is excellent, and she is expert at many games. In fact, there is nothing she doesn't know. Her surname is Pan, and her personal name, Jin-lian. Her father was Pan Cai, who used to live by the South Gate. Originally, she was sold to Master Zhang, and at his house she learned to sing and play. When Zhang was very old, he made a present of her to Wu Da. She does not go out very often and, when I am not busy, I go over to her place and get anything she happens to want. She always calls me Stepmother.

"These last few days, Wu Da has been going out early. If you wish to clinch the matter, you must buy some silk, one roll of blue, another of white, another of the finest white silk, and ten taels of good raw silk. Give them to me. I will go to her house to borrow a calendar, and ask her to tell me a day of good omen so that I can engage a dressmaker to come and make me some clothes. It may be that she will find a day for me, but not offer to come herself to make the clothes. In that case, there is nothing to be done. If she is very pleasant and says, 'Don't get a dressmaker. I will come and make the clothes for you,' that will be one to us. If I can persuade her to come here to sew, that will be another one to us. If she comes at noon, I will set out refreshments and invite her to have some. She may say, 'I am very sorry but I can't,' and go off home and, in that case, we shall have to give up. On the other hand, she may say nothing, but sit down and eat my lunch, and then we score again.

"You must not come tomorrow, but the day after. Put on your smartest clothes. Give a cough of warning, and then come to the door and call, 'How do you do, Stepmother? May I come in and have a cup of tea?' I will come out and ask you in. It is possible that, as soon as she sees you, she may want to go home, and, if she does, I cannot stop her. That will be the end. But if she stays where she is, we shall be four points to the good.

"When you sit down, I shall say to her, 'This is the gentleman who gave me the clothes. I can't tell you how grateful I am to him,' and I shall say all sorts of pretty things about your generosity. Then you will compliment her on her sewing. If she does not answer, we are done. If she does answer, and enters into conversation with you, our fifth point is gained.

"Then I shall say, 'Isn't this good lady kind to make my clothes for me?' and praise you both—you for giving me the money and her for making the clothes. I shall say, 'This lady is indeed good-hearted. I was lucky to be able to persuade her to come. Perhaps you would like to offer her some refreshment.' You will take some silver out of your pocket and ask me to go and buy something. If at that moment she decides to go, I can't hold her, and all is over. But, if she doesn't move, we shall have gained our sixth point.

"I shall take your silver and, as I go out, I shall say, 'I wonder if you would mind keeping this gentleman company?' She may jump up at that and, if she does so, I can't very well put my arms around her and hold her, but, if she doesn't, we shall have gained another point.

"When I come back with the things, I shall put them on the table and say, 'Lady, put the clothes aside for a while and let us drink a little wine. This gentleman has been good enough to spend his money on us.' If she will not join us, but takes her leave, the matter is ended. But if she says, 'Oh, really I can't stay,' but does not make any effort to go, the eighth point is ours.

"If she drinks her wine contentedly and begins to talk to you, I shall say, 'There is not enough wine,' and you will ask me to buy some more, and some fruits too, and give me silver for the purpose. Then I shall shut the door upon you both. If she is shy and tries to run away, we can do no more. But if she lets me fasten the door and does not get angry, we are within an ace of our goal. The last stage is the critical one. You, Sir, will stay in the room with the woman and talk prettily to her, but you must not be too rough when you begin to take liberties. If you touch her, and spoil the whole game, it will not be my fault. But it is possible that you might knock down a pair of chopsticks with your sleeve, and touch her foot when you pretend to pick them up. If this makes her angry, I shall come in and make peace between you, but all our chances will be gone and we can never hope to retrieve the position. If she says nothing, we gain our tenth point, and the game is ours. If I lead you to victory, what reward may I expect?"

Ximen Qing listened to all this, and was perfectly delighted. "Your plan may not come from the Ling Yan temple," he said, "but it is absolutely flawless."

"Don't forget those ten taels of silver," old woman Wang said.

"If I get but a single piece of orange peel," Ximen said, "I shall never forget the Dongting lake. But when do you propose to put this scheme into operation, Stepmother?"

"Come back this evening," the old woman said, "and you shall know. By this time Wu Da has gone out, and I will go over about the calendar and say my part. You send somebody with the silk as quickly as possible. Don't waste any time."

"I'll see to it at once," Ximen Qing cried. "You may count upon me absolutely." He went to the street to buy the three rolls of silk and the ten taels of raw silk, and told Daian to wrap them up and take them to the old woman. She received them with great satisfaction and sent the boy away.

When the silk had come, the old woman opened her back door and went across to Wu Da's house. Jinlian took her upstairs, and they sat down.

"Why have you not been to take tea in my poor house lately?" asked the old woman.

"I haven't been well these last few days," Jinlian replied, "and somehow I have not felt inclined to move."

"Have you a calendar in the house?" the old woman said. "I should like to see one. I wish to find a day favorable for making clothes."

"What clothes are you thinking of having made?"

"I am always suffering from something or another," the old woman said. "One of these days I shall find myself as high as the mountains and as deep as the ocean. And my son is not at home."

"Where has he been all this time?" Jinlian said.

"He went away with a stranger, and I have never had a word from him since. I worry about him all day long."

Jinlian asked how old the boy was, and when the old woman told her he was seventeen, she said, "Why don't you find him a wife? You would save yourself a great deal of work."

"You may well say that," the old woman said. "There never was a place so lonely as mine. I potter about, as best I can, and sometimes I do think I'll find a wife for him. When he comes home, I really must see about it. Day and night I have trouble with my breathing, and I cough till my body shakes as though it were being torn in pieces. And I can't sleep. I've come to the conclusion that it's time I was getting my funeral clothes together. Fortunately for me, there is a rich gentleman who often comes to have tea at my shop. When there is anybody ill at his place, he sends for me; I buy maids for him and see about marriages. He knows I am to be trusted; that I never neglect any little point, however unimportant it may seem to others. He has given me the material for a full set of funeral clothes, and all the trimmings too. I have had this stuff put away for more than a year and have done nothing with it. But this year I have not felt at all well, and as there is an extra month in it, and I am not very busy, I have taken my chance and I am going to have it made up at last. Unfortunately, all the dressmakers say they are too busy to come and make my clothes. You've no idea how ill all this anxiety makes me."

Jinlian listened to this long story, and smiled. "I'm afraid I can't make the clothes as well as they should be made, but I have nothing particular to do, and, if you like, I'll see what I can do for you."

The old lady smiled delightedly. "With your precious hands to make the things, even if I die, my poor old body will rejoice. I have always heard what a good needlewoman you are, but I have never dared to come and trouble you."

"Why should I not make them?" Jinlian said. "Anyhow, I've promised now, and I must do them for you. Take the calendar, and get someone to find an auspicious day. Then I'll begin."

"Do you think I don't know that you can read all the characters in the poems and the hundred dramas? Why should I take the calendar to anybody else?"

"I have never had any education," Jinlian said, with a smile.

"Oh, thank you, thank you," the old woman cried, handing her the calendar. Jinlian examined it, then she said, "Tomorrow is no good, and the day after that is no good either. We shall have to wait."

The old woman took the calendar and hung it on the wall. "If you are willing to do the work you yourself are my lucky star. I need not bother whether the day is lucky or not. Others have looked at the calendar and told me that tomorrow is not a good day for the purpose, but that doesn't trouble me."

"Well," Jinlian said, "it may be that a day unlucky for other purposes is most suitable for the making of funeral clothes."

"If you don't mind, then come to my poor house tomorrow."

"Why not bring the material here?" said Jinlian.

"Because I should like to watch you sewing, and there is nobody to look after my house."

"Very well," Jinlian promised, "I will come to your house tomorrow after lunch."

"God bless you! God bless you!" the old lady cried. She went downstairs and away. That evening she told Ximen Qing the result of her efforts, and asked him to come two days later. The next morning the old woman swept out her room, prepared needles and thread, made some tea, and waited for Jinlian.

When Wu Da had eaten his breakfast, he went out with his baskets. His wife pulled up the lattice and ordered Ying'er to look after the house.

Then she went by the back door to old woman Wang's house. The old lady, who was as pleased as could be, welcomed her and made her sit down. Then she made a cup of very strong tea, with walnuts and beechnuts, and gave it to Jinlian. After wiping the table, she brought out the three rolls of silk. Jinlian measured them and cut all the garments out. Then she began to sew. The old woman watched her and poured forth a stream of compliments.

"What marvelous skill! I have lived nearly seventy years and never have I seen so swift a needle or such cunning fingers."

Jinlian sewed till noon. Then old woman Wang prepared lunch, and asked her to have some. Afterwards, Jinlian sewed till it was nearly dark; then she packed up the silk and went home. When Wu Da came in with his baskets, she closed the door and pulled down the blind. Wu Da saw that his wife's face was red, and asked her where she had been.

"I have been with our neighbor, Stepmother Wang," Jinlian said. "She asked me to make some funeral clothes for her and at lunchtime she set out some wine and cakes and insisted that I should have some."

"You ought not to eat her food," Wu Da said. "It is our place to invite her. She asked you to make these clothes, it is true, but you should take your meals at home and not trouble her. If you go tomorrow, take some money with you and buy some food and wine in your turn. The proverb says: 'Better a neighbor at hand than a relative far away.' Don't let us spoil the friendship between us. If she will not allow you to return her hospitality, you must bring the clothes here and make them."

Jinlian listened, but said nothing. The next day, after breakfast, Wu Da took his baskets and went out. Old woman Wang came over to invite Jinlian to go to her house, and soon they had brought the clothes out and were at work upon them again. Old woman Wang made a cup of tea for Jinlian, but at lunchtime Jinlian took three *fen* from her sleeve and gave them to the old woman.

"Stepmother," she said, "it is my turn to buy a cup of wine."

"Oh dear!" the old woman cried, "what can you be thinking about? It was I who asked you to come and make these clothes, and I can't possibly allow you to spend your money as well. Why, if I did, your wine and food would poison me."

"You must blame my foolish husband," Jinlian said, "but he said, if you did not take it kindly, I was to go home."

"If your husband feels like that about it," the old woman said, "I suppose I must keep it." She was very much afraid of doing anything that might interfere with her plans, so she put some of her own money to it and went out to buy better food and wine. Then she invited the woman to join her.

It would seem that in all the world there is not a single woman, no matter how intelligent she may be, who cannot be led astray by some trivial act of kindness. Nine women out of every ten are caught this way.

The old woman prepared some refreshments and enjoyed them with Jinlian. Afterwards they went on sewing and, when evening began to fall, the old woman thanked her very heartily, and she went home once more.

After breakfast on the third day, the old woman waited till Wu Da had gone out, then she went to the back door and called out: "Lady, may I make so bold . . ." Jinlian said she would come in a moment, and soon they were again in the old woman's room, sitting down to work upon the clothes. The old woman made tea as usual. About midday, Ximen Qing arrived.

He had waited anxiously for this day, and now he dressed himself very elegantly, put three or four taels of silver in his sleeve, and sauntered off to Amethyst Street, with a golden fan in his hand. When he came to the old woman's house, he coughed. Then he called, "Where are you, Stepmother Wang? I haven't seen you for ever so long."

"Who is that calling me?" the old woman cried.

"Ximen Qing."

"I could not imagine who it might be," the old woman said, hurrying to the door, "and here you are! You have just come at the right moment. Come in and see what I have to show you." She took him by the sleeve and led him to her room. "This is the very gentleman who gave me the silk," she said to Jinlian.

Ximen Qing opened his eyes wide and gazed at the woman. The masses of her piled-up hair seemed like clouds of the darkest hue. Her rosy cheeks had all the freshness of spring. She was wearing a white linen coat, a dark red skirt, and a blue stomacher. When Ximen came in, she was sewing, but she rose at once and made a reverence to him. He came forward and bowed profoundly. Then she put down the clothes and made a more profound reverence.

"I owe this gentleman a great deal," old woman Wang said. "It was he who gave me this material. I had it in the house a year before I could get anyone to make it up." Then she added, "I am greatly indebted to this lady too, for making the clothes for me. Her sewing is as fine as fine can be. Anything so good and fine is seldom seen in these days. Come and look at it, Sir."

Ximen Qing took up the clothes and examined them. "Indeed," he said, "the lady sews so exquisitely that only an angel could rival her."

Jinlian shyly looked at the ground, but she smiled. "Do not make fun of my poor efforts," she said.

"Stepmother,' Ximen Qing said, "I hardly dare to ask you, but who is this lady?"

"Guess," said the old woman.

"How can I guess?"

"Sit down then, and I will tell you. Do you remember passing by one day and getting a knock on the head?"

"Yes," Ximen said, "I know it is she who struck me that day, but I still don't know who she is."

Jinlian bowed her head more deeply and said with a smile, "It was very careless of your slave to strike you. Please don't be angry with me, my lord."

"How could I possibly be?" Ximen said hastily.

"This lady is the wife of my neighbor, Wu Da," the old woman said.

"Is that so?" Ximen said. "I am afraid I was forgetful of my good manners."

The old woman turned to Jinlian and asked if she knew the gentleman.

"I do not," the woman replied.

"He is one of the wealthiest men in our district and a very good friend of the magistrate. It is Master Ximen. He has thousands and thousands of strings of cash, and keeps a medicine shop near the Town Hall. The money in his house is piled so high that it touches the North Star and even his spoiled rice is enough to fill many barns. His gold is yellow and his silver white. His pearls are round and his precious stones brilliant. He has rhinoceros horns and elephants' tusks. It was I who arranged his first marriage. His wife is the daughter of Captain Wu, a very intelligent woman indeed." Then she turned to Ximen. "Why have you not been to have tea with me lately?"

"I have been very busy attending to my daughter's betrothal," Ximen said, "and that has left me very little leisure."

"Whom is your daughter going to marry?" the old woman said, "and why didn't you get me to arrange the marriage?"

"She is going to marry Chen Jingji, the son of that Chen who is related to General Yang, who commands the Imperial Guard. The young man is seventeen years old and still at his studies. I should have asked you to arrange this marriage, but a woman named Wen came from his family to ask for the betrothal papers, and Xue, the flower seller, acted for us. They arranged everything between them. But, Stepmother, we shall be giving a party very soon, and, if you care to come, I shall be delighted to have you join us."

"I was only joking," the old woman said. "The go-betweens in this city are all bitches. When they arranged the marriage, I had no finger in the pie, and, now that the dinner is cooked, they certainly won't wish me to have a bite. There is an old saying that there is never any love lost between those who follow the same profession. No, I will wait until the wedding is over and then I will come with a few humble presents, and I may pick up some of the leavings. That will be the best thing I can do. I can't allow myself to be left completely out of it." They chattered away in this strain, the old woman flattering him, and he muttering any nonsense in return. Meanwhile, Jinlian kept her head modestly bowed and went on with her needlework.

Ximen Qing glanced at her from time to time, and could see the passion within her growing stronger. This delighted him beyond measure, and he was more eager than ever to bring the matter to its consummation. The old woman made two cups of tea. She gave one to Ximen Qing and the other to Jinlian, and said: "Lady, won't you take a cup of tea with this gentleman?" She looked at Ximen, and stroked her cheek gently; it was a sign that five of their ten points were already gained. The power of tea to exhilarate, and the power of wine to bring people together, have always been acknowledged as the go-betweens of love.

"If you had not come here," old woman Wang said, "I should never have had the courage to go to your house and invite you. Good fortune brought you here, and good fortune, again, decided the moment of your coming. But there is an old saying: 'One guest never troubles two hosts.' You have given me money, and this kind lady has been good enough to work for me, and I don't know how I can express my gratitude to either of you. If the fates had not been kind, I should have found it hard to bring you two together. I suggest, Sir, that you take my place as host, and give me something to buy a little wine for the lady."

"I don't know whether I have any money with me," Ximen Qing said, feeling in his sleeve. He brought out a tael of silver, gave it to the old woman, and asked her to buy something with it.

"Not for me, please," Jinlian said, but she made no attempt to move. The old woman took the silver and, as she prepared to go out, said, "Lady, I wonder if you will be good enough to keep the gentleman company till I come back. I shall only be a few minutes."

"Stepmother, please don't trouble," Jinlian said, but still she remained in her place. The old woman went out, and left Ximen Qing and Pan Jinlian alone together.

Ximen's eyes seemed to devour the woman. She looked up at him coyly, then bowed her head again and went on with her sewing. Before long, the old woman was back again with cooked goose and roasted duck, meats of various kinds, and some luscious-looking fruits. She put them on dishes and set them on the table. Then she said to Jinlian: "Won't you put the clothes aside for a while, and take a cup of wine?"

"You drink with his Lordship," the woman said. "It is not for me to take such a liberty."

"You mustn't say that," the old woman cried, "it has all been arranged in your honor." She placed the dishes before them and, when they had taken their places, poured the wine.

"Stepmother," Ximen Qing said, "will you ask the lady to take wine with me?"

Jinlian thanked him. She dared not drink, she said, because a very little wine went to her head.

"Oh, you can hold a good deal," the old woman said, "I know that. Don't make a fuss about a cup or two." Jinlian took the wine and raised her glass to the others. Ximen Qing took up his chopsticks. "Stepmother," he said, "ask the lady to take something to eat." The old lady picked out some tidbits and passed them to the woman. The wine went around three times, and old woman Wang went out to warm some more.

"May I ask your age?" Ximen said.

"I am twenty-five," Jinlian said, bowing her head again.

"Then you and my wife are the same age. Her animal is the Dragon, and she was born on the fifteenth day of the eighth month."

"You are putting Earth and Heaven on the same plane," Jinlian said. "You pay me too great a compliment."

"This lady," old woman Wang said, "is as clever as can be, besides being such a good needlewoman. She knows all the philosophies of all the philosophers, not to speak of backgammon and chess. She can write very nicely too."

"Ah," Ximen said, with a sigh, "but where shall we find another like her?"

"I wouldn't say anything impertinent for the world," old woman Wang said, "but though you have many ladies in your house, I doubt whether there is one among them equal to this lady."

"That is true, I fear," Ximen said. "It is a long story. The fates have been unkind to me and I must own that none of them is really any use."

"Your first wife was good enough," the old woman said.

"Don't talk about her," Ximen cried. "If she had lived, things would have been very different, but now there is no real mistress in the house and the whole place is going to rack and ruin. There are three, five, nay seven people—all ready enough to eat my food, but not so ready to attend to their household duties."

"How long is it since your first wife died? I have forgotten."

"I hate to talk about it," Ximen said. "My first wife Chen came from a very poor family, but she was a clever woman and did all I needed. Unhappily, she died more than three years ago. I have married again, but my present wife is always ailing and the business of the household is too much for her. My domestic affairs are in complete disarray. Perhaps that is why I spend so much of my time away from home. If I didn't there would be trouble."

"You must excuse me, Sir," said the old woman, "but your late wife and your present wife together were not so skilled in needlework as this lady, or so attractive in appearance."

"My other wives also," said Ximen, "cannot compare with her."

"But what about the establishment in East Street?" the old woman said, laughing. "Why do you never ask me to tea there?"

"You are thinking of Zhang Xichun, the singing girl?" Ximen said. "I found she was a flighty creature and I have given her up."

"That may be," the old woman continued, "but what about Li Jiao'er, who used to be in the bawdy house? You have been on very good terms with her for a long time."

"Oh, I took her into my household some time ago and, if she proves satisfactory, I shall marry her."

"Then there was Miss Zhuo," the old woman suggested.

"Do not mention her name," Ximen said. "I made her my third wife, but a short time ago she fell ill and died."

"Dear me! Dear me!" cried the old woman. "Suppose I found a lady like this, one whom you really liked, and came to your house to talk over the matter? Don't you think it would cause a disturbance?"

"My parents are both dead, and I am my own master. Who would dare say a word to me?"

"However, I may try. Where can I find a lady so much to your liking as this one?"

"Oh, there may be one for all we know," Ximen said. "But I loathe the Fates who control my matrimonial affairs. If they had been more indulgent, I might have found such a woman."

They chatted in this way for some time. At last old woman Wang said, "Just when we are ready for a little more wine, it all seems to have gone. I am sorry to trouble you, Sir, but may I buy another jar?" Ximen Qing put his hand in his sleeve. There were still three or four taels there. He gave them all to the old lady, "Here you are," he said. "Any time we are short of wine, you need only go and get it."

The old woman thanked him, and got up. She glanced at Jinlian, who, after drinking three cups of wine, was already consumed with passion. The words that passed between them seemed only to add fuel to the fires that burned within. She bowed her head, but still she did not move.

# CHAPTER 4
# Ximen Qing Attains His End

The sun streams through the painted doorway into the bedchamber.
There stands a maiden whom no gold can buy.
She leans against the door
Her lovely eyes, like beams of sunshine, seek to pursue her lover
But he has gone so far, her tender feet may never hope to follow.

Old woman Wang took the money and started for the door. Smiling, she said to Jinlian, "I must go to the street to buy a jar of wine; you will keep his Lordship company, won't you? If there is a drop left in the jar, warm two cups and drink them with him. The best wine is to be had in East Street. I shall have to go there for it, so I may be away some little time."

"Really I can't drink any more," Pan Jinlian cried. "Please don't go on my account."

"You and his Lordship are no longer strangers," said the old woman, "and you have nothing else to do. Drink a cup of wine with him. Why should you be afraid?"

With her lips Jinlian said she did not wish to drink, but her body told another story. The old woman shut the door and fastened it on the outside with a chain, imprisoning the two young people in her room. Then outside in the roadway, she sat down and began to roll some thread. Jinlian saw the old woman go, and pulled her chair to one side. As she settled down again, she glanced swiftly at Ximen Qing. He was sitting on the other side of the table, his eyes wide open, staring at her. At last he managed to speak.

"I forgot to ask your honorable name."

The woman bowed, and answered, smiling, "My unworthy name is Wu."

Ximen Qing pretended that he had not heard properly. "Did you say Du?" he said. Jinlian looked up, and said in a very soft voice, "I did not think you were deaf, Sir."

"I am sorry," Ximen said, "it was my mistake. You said 'Wu.' There are not many people called Wu in Qinghe. There is indeed one fellow who sells cakes outside the Town Hall, but he is no bigger than my thumb. His name is Wu, Master Wu Da. Is he a relative of yours by any chance?"

Jinlian flushed. "He is my husband," she said, hanging her head.

Ximen Qing was silent for a long time, and seemed to be thinking very seriously. "How sad! How wrong!" he murmured at last. Jinlian smiled, and glanced at him.

"You have no reason to complain. Why should you say, 'How sad!'?"

"I was thinking how sad it must be for you," he said. He muttered many things, almost unintelligibly. Jinlian still looked down. She played with her skirt, nibbled at her sleeves, and bit her lips, sometimes talking, sometimes glancing slyly at him. Ximen pretended to find the heat trying, and took off his green silk coat.

"Would you mind putting my coat on the old lady's bed?" he said. Jinlian did not offer to take the coat. Keeping her head still turned away, she played with her sleeves and smiled. "Is there anything wrong with your own hands?" she said. "Why do you ask me to do things for you?" Ximen Qing laughed.

"So you won't do a little thing like that for me? Well, I suppose I must do it myself." He leaned over the table and put his coat on the bed. As he did so, he brushed the table with his sleeve and knocked down a chopstick. Luck favored him; the chopstick came to rest beneath the woman's skirt. Ximen, who had already drunk more wine than was good for him, invited her to join him. Then he wanted his chopsticks to help her to some of the dishes. He looked about. One of them was missing. Jinlian looked down, pushed the chopstick with her toe, and said, laughing, "Isn't this it?" Ximen Qing went to her, and bent down. "Ah, here it is!" he cried, but instead of picking up the chopstick, he took hold of her embroidered shoe.

Jinlian laughed. "I shall shout, if you are so naughty."

"Be kind to me, Lady," Ximen said, going down on his knees. As he spoke, he gently stroked her silken garments.

"It is horrid of you to pester me so," Jinlian cried. "I shall box your ears."

"Lady," he said, "if your blows should cause my death, it would be a happy end."

Without giving her time to object, he carried her to old woman Wang's bed, took off his clothes and, after unloosing her girdle, lay down with her. Their happiness reached its culmination.

In the days when Jinlian had performed the act of darkness with Zhang, that miserable old man had never been able to offer any substantial contribution to the proceedings, and not once had she been satisfied. Then she married Wu Da. You may imagine the prowess that might be expected from Master Tom Thumb. It could hardly be described as heroic. Now she met Ximen Qing, whose capacity in such matters was unlimited and whose skill was exceptionally refined and cunning.

The mandarin ducks, with necks entwined, sport upon the water.
The phoenix and his mate, their heads close pressed together, fly
    among the blossoms.
Joyful and tireless, the tree puts forth twin branches
The girdle, tied in a lovers' knot, is full of sweetness.
He, the red-lipped one, thirsts for a close embrace
She, of the powdered cheeks, awaits it eagerly.
The silken hose are raised on high
And two new moons appear above his shoulders.
The golden hairpins fall
And on the pillow rests a bank of lowering clouds.
They swear eternal oaths by ocean and by mountain
Seeking a thousand new delights.
The clouds are bashful and the rain is shy
They play ten thousand naughty tricks.
"Qia Qia," the oriole cries.
Each sucks the nectar from the other's lips.
The cherry lips breathe lightly, lightly.
In those willowy hips the passion beats
The mocking eyes are bright like stars
Tiny drops of sweat are like a hundred fragrant pearls
The sweet full breasts tremble
The dew, like a gentle stream, reaches the heart of the peony
They taste the joys of love in perfect harmony
For stolen joys, in truth, are ever the most sweet.

Just when they had done and were putting on their clothes again, old
woman Wang pushed open the door and came in, clapping her hands as
though she had never been more surprised in her life.

"A fine state of affairs," she said. Ximen Qing and Jinlian were extremely
embarrassed.

"Oh, splendid, splendid!" the old woman said to Jinlian. "I asked you to
come here to make clothes, not to make love with someone else's husband.
If your Wu Da found this out, he would blame me. I shall have to go and
explain the matter to him at once." She turned, and started out. Jinlian
caught her quickly by the skirt. She hid her blushing face and could only
get out a single sentence: "Spare me, Stepmother."

"You must make me a promise, then," the old woman said. "From this
day forward, you must deceive Wu Da and give his Lordship here whatever he desires. If I call you early, you must come early. If I call you late,

you must come late. Then I will say no more about it. But, if there should be a day when you do not come, I shall tell Wu Da."

Jinlian was so abashed that she could find nothing to say. "Well," said the old woman, "what are you going to do about it? I must have an answer now." "I will come," the woman whispered. Old woman Wang turned to Ximen Qing. "I need say no more to you, Sir. This is a fine piece of work, and you owe it all to me. You must not forget your promise. You must keep your word. If you try to wriggle out of it, I shall be compelled to speak to Wu Da."

"Don't worry, Stepmother," Ximen said, "I shall not go back on my word."

"I haven't too much confidence in either of you," old woman Wang said. "Give me a pledge of some sort and then I'll believe you."

Ximen Qing took a golden pin from his head and set it in Jinlian's hair. She took it out again and put it in her sleeve, for she was afraid that if she went home wearing it, Wu Da would wish to know where it had come from. She hesitated to produce any pledge herself, but the old woman caught her by the sleeve and, finding a white silk handkerchief, handed it to Ximen Qing. Then they all drank several cups of wine. By this time it was getting dark and, saying that it was time for her to go home, Jinlian said good-bye to old woman Wang and Ximen Qing and went to her house by the back way. She pulled down the blind and, soon afterwards, Wu Da came in.

Old woman Wang looked at Ximen Qing.

"Did I play my cards well?" she said.

"No one could have done better," said Ximen.

"Were you satisfied?"

"Perfectly."

"She comes of singing girl stock," the old woman said, "and she must have had plenty of experience. I am very proud that I have been able to bring you two together, especially since I did it all by my own cleverness. Mind you give me what you promised."

"I will send you the silver as soon as I reach home."

"My eyes have seen the banner of victory and my ears have heard a sweet message," the old woman said, "but don't wait until my coffin is being carried out for burial, and then send money for the choirboys."

Ximen Qing laughed. He saw that the street was deserted, put on his eyeshades, and went home.

The next day he came again to the old woman's house. The old lady made tea for him and asked him to sit down. He took ten taels of silver from his sleeve and gave it to her. Money seems to produce an extraordinary effect upon people everywhere. As soon as the old woman's black eyes beheld this snow-white silver, she was as happy as could be. She took it, and twice made reverence to him. "I thank you, Sir," she said, "with all my heart."

"Wu Da is still at home," she continued, "but I will go over to his house and pretend I wish to borrow a gourd." She went by the back way to her neighbor's house. Jinlian was giving her husband his breakfast when she heard the knocking at the door, and told Ying'er to see who was there. It is Grandmother Wang," the girl said, "she has come to borrow a water gourd."

"I will lend you a water jug, Stepmother," Jinlian said, "but won't you come in and sit down a while?"

"There is nobody to look after my house," the old woman said, beckoning with her finger to Jinlian, thus giving her to understand that Ximen Qing had come. She took the gourd and went away, and Jinlian hustled her husband over his breakfast and packed him off with his baskets. She went upstairs and redressed herself, putting on beautiful new clothes, and told Ying'er to watch the house. "I am going to your Grandmother Wang's, but I shall be back in a moment. If your father comes home, let me know at once or it will be the worse for your little bottom." She went to the tea shop.

Jinlian came, and to Ximen Qing it seemed that she had come straight down from Heaven. Side by side, close pressed together, they sat. Old woman Wang gave them tea. "Did Wu Da ask you any questions when you got home yesterday?" she said.

"He asked me if I had finished your clothes, and I told him that the funeral shoes and socks had still to be made."

The old woman hastily set wine before them, and they drank together, very happily. Ximen Qing delighted in every detail of the woman's form. She seemed to him even more beautiful than when he had first seen her. The little wine she had taken brought roses to her pale face and, with her cloudlike hair, she might have been a fairy, more beautiful than Chang E.

Ximen Qing could not find words to express his admiration. He gathered her in his arms, and lifted her skirts that he might see her dainty feet. She was wearing shoes of raven-black silk, no broader than his two fingers. His heart was overflowing with delight. Mouth to mouth they drank together, and smiled. Jinlian asked how old he was. "I am twenty-seven. I was born on the twenty-eighth day of the seventh month." Then she said, "How many ladies are there in your household?" and he said, "Besides the mistress of my house, there are three or four, but with none of them am I really satisfied." Again she asked, "How many sons have you?" and he answered, "I have no sons, only one little girl who is shortly to be married." Then it was his turn to ask her questions.

He took from his sleeve a box, gilded on the outside and silver within. There were fragrant tea leaves in it and some small sweetmeats. Placing some of them on his tongue, he passed them to her mouth. They embraced and hugged one another; their cries and kissings made noise enough, but old woman Wang went in and out, carrying dishes and warming the wine, and paid not the slightest attention to them. They played their amorous games without any interference from her. Soon they had drunk as much as they desired, and a fit of passion swept over them. Ximen Qing's desire could no longer be restrained; he disclosed the treasure that sprang from his loins, and made the woman touch it with her delicate fingers. From his youth upwards he had constantly played with the maidens who live in places of ill-fame, and he was already wearing the silver clasp that had been washed with magic herbs. Upstanding, it was, and flushed with pride, the black hair strong and bristling. A mighty warrior in very truth.

> A warrior of stature not to be despised
> At times a hero and at times a coward.
> Who, when for battle disinclined,
> As though in drink sprawls to the east and west.
> But, when for combat he is ready,
> Like a mad monk he plunges back and forth
> And to the place from which he came returns.
> Such is his duty.
> His home is in the loins, beneath the navel.
> Heaven has given him two sons
> To go wherever he goes
> And, when he meets an enemy worthy of his steel,
> He will attack, and then attack again.

Then Jinlian took off her clothes. Ximen Qing fondled the fragrant blossom. No down concealed it; it had all the fragrance and tenderness of fresh-made pastry, the softness and the appearance of a new-made pie. It was a thing so exquisite that all the world would have desired it.

> Tender and clinging, with lips like lotus petals
> Yielding and gentle, worthy to be loved.
> When it is happy, it puts forth its tongue
> And welcomes with a smile.
> When it is weary, it is content
> To stay where Nature put it
> At home in Trouser Village
> Among the scanty herbage.
> But, when it meets a handsome gallant
> It strives with him and says no word.

After that day, Jinlian came regularly to the old woman's house to sport with Ximen Qing. Love bound them together as it were with glue; their minds and hearts were united as if with gum.

There is an old saying: "Good news never leaves the house, but ill news spreads a thousand miles." It was not long before all the neighbors knew what was going on. Only Wu Da remained ignorant.

In Qinghe there lived a boy called Qiao; he was about fifteen years old. As he had been born in Yunzhou, where his father was on military service, he was called Yun'ge. His father was now grown old, and they lived together alone. The boy was by no means without craft. He kept himself by selling fresh fruits in the different wineshops, and Ximen Qing often gave him small sums of money. One day he had filled his basket with snow-white pears and was carrying them about the streets, on the lookout for his patron. Somebody he chanced to meet said to him, "Yun'ge, I can tell you where to find him."

"Where can I find him, Uncle?" the boy said. "Tell me if you please."

"Ximen," the man said, "is carrying on with the wife of Wu Da, the cake seller. Every day he goes to old woman Wang's house in Amethyst Street. Most likely you will find him there now. There is nothing to prevent you going straight into the room."

Yun'ge thanked the man, and went along Amethyst Street with his basket till he came to old woman Wang's tea shop. The old woman was sitting on a small chair by the door, making thread. The boy put down his basket, looked at her, and said, "Greetings to you, Stepmother."

"What do you want, Yun'ge?" the old woman said.

"I have come to see his Lordship in the hope of getting thirty or fifty cash to help support my father," the boy told her.

"What 'Lordship' are you talking about?" asked the old woman.

"You know him."

"Well, I suppose every gentleman has some sort of a name," the old woman said.

"This gentleman's name has two characters in it."

"What two characters?"

"You are trying to fool me," Yun'ge said. "It is his Lordship Ximen to whom I am going to speak." He started to go into the house. The old woman caught him. "Where are you going, little monkey? Don't you know the difference between the inside and the outside of people's houses?"

"I shall find him in the room," the boy said.

The old woman cursed him. "What makes you think you will find his Lordship in my house, you little rascal?"

"Stepmother, don't try to keep all the pickings for yourself. Leave a little gravy for me. I know all about it."

"What do you know?" the old woman cried. "You are a young scoundrel."

"And you are one of those people who would scrape a bowl clean with a knife. You don't mean to lose even a single drop of gravy. If I began to talk about this business, I shouldn't be surprised if my brother, the cake seller, had something to say about it."

This made the old woman furious. She was touched to the quick. "You little monkey," she screamed, "how dare you come to my house to let off your farts."

"Little monkey I may be," said Yun'ge, "but you're an old whoremonger, you old lump of dog meat."

The old woman caught him and boxed his ears twice.

"Why are you hitting me?" cried the boy.

"You son of a thief, you little monkey, make a noise like that and I'll thrash you out of the place."

"You knavish old scorpion," Yun'ge cried, "you have no right to beat me."

The old woman struck him again, and drove him out into the street, tossing his basket after him. The pears rolled all over the street, four here and five there. There was nothing the little monkey could do. He grumbled and cried as he picked them up. He shook his fist in the direction of the tea shop, and shouted, "Wait, you old worm! When I've told about this, you will be ruined, and then there will be nothing at all for you."

The young monkey picked up his basket and went off to the street to see if he could find Wu Da.

# CHAPTER 5
# The Murder of Wu Da

When deep in mystic contemplation
Sounding the shallows of this world's emptiness,
Even the marriage most blessed by Fate seems full of evil.
Men in their folly crave for love,
Yet, when in calm collectedness they study it,
Hateful it seems.

Leave the wild grasses
Gather not the idle flowers
So, thy truest self, the vigor of thy manhood,
Will know the peace of Nature.
A simple wife, young children, and plain fare
With these need no man suffer the pangs of love
Or lose his fortune.

Yun'ge could not contain his anger at the way old woman Wang had treated him. He took his basket and went to find Wu Da. He had gone through two streets before he met the man for whom he was looking. Wu Da, carrying his buns, was coming towards him. The boy stopped. "It is some time since I saw you last," he said, looking hard at the man. "How fat you have grown."

"Fat?" said Wu Da. "What do you mean? I am just the same as I always was."

"A few days ago," Yun'ge said, "I wanted some chicken food. I went for miles, but couldn't get any. Yet everybody tells me you have lots of it at your house."

"I keep neither geese nor ducks," Wu Da said. "Why should I have chicken food?"

"So you say," Yun'ge retorted, "but what makes you so much like a capon? Why! If you were held topsy-turvy, you would never turn a hair; you'd keep quite cool if you were being boiled in a cauldron."

"This is an insult, you young scoundrel," Wu Da cried. "My wife has not run off with anybody's husband. What makes you call me a capon?"

"Indeed?" the boy said. "So your wife has not run off with anybody's husband, hasn't she? Perhaps I should have said she has run off with *somebody's* husband."

"Who is the man?" Wu Da cried. "Tell me."

"You make me laugh. You can do what you like with me easily enough, but you won't find your wife's new friend so easy to dispose of."

"Good little brother, tell me who he is and I will give you ten cakes."

"Cakes won't do. I'd rather you were my host and gave me some wine. Three cups, and I'll tell you the whole story."

"If it's wine you want, come along," Wu Da said. He led the way to a little wineshop. Calling for a jar of wine and some meat, he took cakes from his basket and invited Yun'ge to join him. "Good little brother," he said, "you really must tell me."

"There is no hurry. Wait till I have finished my food. Then I'll tell you. You mustn't be impatient. I'll help you to catch them."

Wu Da waited till the young monkey had finished, and again asked him to explain himself.

"If you would like to know," the boy said, "put your hand on my head and feel the bumps."

"How did you get them?"

"I'll tell you. Today I have been carrying my pears about looking for his Lordship, Ximen. I walked and walked, but couldn't find him anywhere. Then somebody in the street told me he was at old woman Wang's tea shop, amusing himself with Mistress Wu; that he went there every day. I thought I might see him there, and get thirty or fifty cash from him, but the old sow Wang wouldn't let me in. She drove me away, and then I thought I'd come and see you. I was rather rude, but, if I hadn't made you wild, you wouldn't have asked me any questions."

"Is this the truth?"

"Don't you believe me?" the boy cried. "Didn't I say you were a white-livered fellow? Those two are making merry at this very moment. They wait till you have gone out, and then they go and meet at the old woman's house. You say, 'Is this the truth?' What reason have I for deceiving you?"

"Little brother, it is true. My wife goes every day to this old woman's house to make clothes and shoes, and when she comes back she has a red face. My first wife left me with a little daughter. This woman beats her every morning and scolds her every night. She gives her hardly anything to eat. Lately she certainly has been looking as if something was on her mind. She looked balefully at me, and I wondered whether anything was wrong. You have told the truth. I will put my baskets down and go and catch these evil-doers in the act."

"You may be old as years go," Yun'ge said, "but for the little you know of the world, you might be a child. That old bitch Wang is not afraid of anybody. She would throw you out of the house. Besides, your wife and Ximen have a secret signal. If they knew you were coming, Ximen Qing would hide your wife. He is a very strong man and could dispose of twenty like you. You will never be able to touch him; much more likely you'll find his fist in your mouth. He is so rich and powerful that he would bring an accusation against you, and have you hauled to the courts. You have nobody to help you, and you'd come to an unhappy end."

"You are right, little brother, but what can I do to revenge myself?"

"I want revenge too," Yun'ge said, "for the old woman beat me. Listen to me. Go home today, show no sign of being angry, and don't say one word about the matter. Just behave as usual. Tomorrow, don't make more than a few cakes. Go out with them. I shall be waiting at the entrance to the lane. If Ximen Qing comes, I will give you a call, and you can take your baskets and wait for me somewhere near by. I will go first and plague the old bitch. She will certainly come out to hit me. I will throw my basket far into the street, and then you can run in. I will hold the old woman, and you can rush into the room, and tell them what you think about them. Don't you think that's a good plan?"

"I am greatly indebted to you," Wu Da said; "here are two strings of cash. Come early tomorrow and wait at the entrance to Amethyst Street."

Yun'ge took the money and some of the cakes, and went off. Wu Da paid the reckoning, picked up his baskets, and went back to the street to sell his cakes. A little later he went home.

His wife had never ceased to grumble at him and had found a hundred ways of making life unpleasant to him, but of late her conscience had smitten her and she showed signs of relenting. This evening, when Wu Da came home with his baskets and said nothing, as was usual, she asked him to have some wine. He refused, saying he had already taken wine with some merchants. She laid out his supper, but still he did not offer to speak, and next morning, after breakfast, he made only two or three trays of cakes, and put them in his baskets. Jinlian was so taken up with her thoughts of Ximen Qing that she did not notice how many cakes he made. She waited impatiently until he had gone out and then went to the tea shop to wait for her lover.

Wu Da took his baskets to the entrance to Amethyst Street. Yun'ge, also with a basket, was looking around.

"Well?" Wu Da said.

"It is too soon yet. Go and sell your cakes till he comes. Wait at the corner, and don't go far away."

Wu Da hurried away, but was soon back again. "The moment you see me throw down my basket," the boy said, "dash into the room." Wu Da put down his own basket and waited.

Yun'ge went to the tea shop. "You old pig," he said, in the most irritating tone he could command. "What did you mean by hitting me yesterday?"

Old woman Wang jumped up at once. "I have not done anything to you, you little monkey. Why have you come to insult me again?"

"For a very good reason, you old bitch, you old strumpet mistress. My ramrod to you!"

This made the old woman furious. She dashed at Yun'ge and tried to hit him. "Would you beat me?" he cried, and threw his basket as far as he could into the street. The old woman tried to hold him, but the little monkey cried, "Hit me if you can," put down his head, and butted her in the belly. She would have fallen if there had not been a wall behind her. The young monkey pushed as hard as he could and pinned her against the wall, while Wu Da pulled up his skirts and strode into the tea shop. The old woman saw him, and would have stopped him if she could, but the boy kept her close against the wall and she could not free herself.

"Wu Da is here," she cried.

Jinlian and Ximen Qing did not know what to do. Jinlian threw herself against the door, and Ximen Qing crawled under the bed. Wu Da tried to force open the door but failed. "This is a fine game you're playing," he cried. Jinlian was filled with confusion, but she succeeded in holding the door against him.

"You talk about the strength of your fists," she said to Ximen Qing, "and you are always boasting about your skill with the staff; why don't you come out and do something? Why, even a paper tiger is enough to frighten you." This she said to shame him into coming out, so that he might strike down Wu Da and make his escape. Ximen, in his hiding place under the bed, did grow bolder when he heard what she said. He crawled out nervously.

"I wasn't afraid," he said, "only a little taken by surprise." He threw open the door, and cried, "Stand back there!" Wu Da tried to close, but Ximen kicked out at him and, as the man was very small, the foot caught him in the ribs, and he fell backwards. Ximen Qing went out, and Yun'ge, seeing that matters had not turned out as he had hoped, released the old woman and ran away.

The neighbors knew Ximen Qing's power, and none of them dared to come and interfere. Old woman Wang lifted up Wu Da. His face was as yellow as a tallow candle, and he was spitting blood. She told Jinlian to bring a cup of water to revive him and then, each holding him by one arm, they took him home by the back way and put him to bed.

Next day Ximen did not hear any bad news, so he went as usual to the old woman's house to make merry with Jinlian. He hoped that Wu Da would die, and indeed for five days the poor man was very ill, and unable to leave his bed. He longed for food and could obtain none; he sighed for a drink and none was given him. Day after day he appealed to Jinlian, but she never answered. She went out, dressed in her best clothes, and came back with a flushed face. His daughter Ying'er had been forbidden to do anything for him. "If you dare to do anything for him and don't tell me," the woman had said, "you shall pay for it." After this the child did not venture to give her father a spoonful of soup or even a drop of water. Several times Wu Da fainted in his anger, but nobody paid the least attention to him. One day he cried to his wife, "You have done this because I found you out. You told that wicked man to kick me over the heart. And now I can neither die nor live. And the pair of you are as happy as can be. If I die, it is a small matter; you have nothing to fear from me. But don't forget Wu Song. Sooner or later he will come back, and he will have something to say about all this. Show me a little kindness and help me to get well as quickly as possible and I won't tell him anything. But if you still refuse to do anything for me, I shall have my reckoning with you on his return."

Jinlian listened, but made no answer. She went next door and told old woman Wang and Ximen Qing everything Wu Da had said. Ximen shivered as though a bucket of cold water had been poured over him. "This is most awkward," he said. "This brother is the Captain Wu who killed a tiger on Jingyang Hill. And now I have learned to love you. We get on together so perfectly. It is not conceivable that we should separate, but it means thinking out some way of dealing with the problem. Really, it is most unfortunate."

Old woman Wang laughed. "I've never seen such a man. You are at the helm and I am only at the oar, yet, while I see no difficulty, you seem to have no notion what to do."

"I am ashamed," Ximen said, "but I must admit I don't know what to do. Have you any plan for getting us out of the difficulty?"

"If you really wish for my help, I have a plan," the old woman said. "First, I must know whether you wish your relations to be permanent or temporary."

"What do you mean, Stepmother?"

"If you will be satisfied with a temporary arrangement, you must separate today. When Wu Da is well, you must ask his forgiveness. Then nobody will say anything to Wu Song about this affair. You will have to wait till some business takes him away again, and then you can meet once more. That is what I mean by 'temporary arrangement.' If you wish for something more permanent, I have an excellent idea, but it is one that I hesitate to tell you."

"Stepmother," Ximen said, "please do anything you can to keep us always together."

"There is one thing I need for this plan. It is not to be had everywhere, but I have no doubt you have some of it."

"If you want my eye, you shall have it," Ximen cried. "What is it you mean?"

"Wu Da is dangerously ill. Let us take the chance while we have it. Go to your shop, get some arsenic and give it to this lady. Then she can buy some medicine for Wu Da's sore chest and put the arsenic into it. So we shall rid ourselves of that little man. When he is dead, we will burn his body till not a trace remains. When Wu Song comes back, he can do nothing about it. A young man, when he takes a wife, marries to please his parents, but when he marries again he makes his own choice. What can a younger brother do? Six months or a year later, when the lady is out of mourning, there is nothing to prevent you marrying her. If you live together happily all your lives, won't that be permanent enough for you?"

"It is an admirable plan, Stepmother. As the proverb says: 'The treasure of a happy life can only be secured by desperate deeds.' Yes, one evil deed deserves another."

"So you think my scheme a good one!" the old woman said. "Well, there is nothing like pulling up the roots when we cut the grass. It never grows again. Go home, Sir, and bring the stuff to me. I'll show the lady what to do with it. But, when all is over, I shall expect a present worth having."

"Of course," Ximen said, "that goes without saying."

He went at once to his shop and soon returned with a packet of arsenic, which he gave to old woman Wang. She looked at Jinlian.

"Now, Lady, I am going to tell you how to use this. Wu Da has begged you to save him, and that gives you an opening. You must make a great show of affection. When he asks you for something to make him better, put this arsenic into some medicine to soothe his chest. When he complains of pain, pour it down his throat. As soon as the poison has got to work, his bowels will burst and he will cry out. So put the bedclothes over him, and press down the coverlet, and make sure that no one hears him. One thing you must do is to heat some water, and put a napkin into it. When the poison has taken effect, blood will stream from the seven openings of his body, and there will be marks on his lips. As soon as he is really dead, you must take off the bedclothes, and wipe away the blood. All that remains is to put him into a coffin and get him out of the way."

"I see," Jinlian said, "but my arms are weak. I shall not have strength enough."

"That doesn't matter. Knock on the wall, and I will come and help you."

"You must both be very careful," Ximen Qing said. "I will come tomorrow at the fifth watch to hear what news you have."

Old woman Wang powdered the arsenic and gave it to Jinlian, who went home. Wu Da was breathing so feebly that it seemed as though his soul had already left him. She sat on his bed, and pretended to cry.

"Why are you crying?" Wu Da said.

Jinlian dried her tears. "Because I allowed myself to be led astray by that Ximen Qing and, for a time, yielded to temptation. But I never meant him to kick you in the chest. Now, I have heard of some very good medicine, and I would go and buy some to make you well, if I were not afraid you would be suspicious. As it is, I don't dare go."

"If you will only save my life," Wu Da said, "I'll forgive you everything, and never hold this business against you. And I won't tell Wu Song anything about it, when he comes home. Go and buy the medicine, and save my life."

The woman took a few coins, and went to old woman Wang's, to make it appear as though she had asked her neighbor to go and buy it. When she came back, she showed the medicine to her husband. "This will soon cure you," she told him. "The doctor says you must drink it during the night, and cover yourself with one or two blankets to make you sweat. Then go to sleep, and tomorrow you will be able to get up."

"Splendid," Wu Da said. "I am very grateful to you. Don't go to sleep, but make up the medicine for me in the middle of the night."

"Go to sleep again," the woman said. "I will bring it to you without fail."

It was beginning to grow dark. Jinlian lighted the lamp. Then she went downstairs, put a great cauldron of water on the fire, and dipped a cloth into it. The watchman sounded the third night watch. She put the arsenic into a cup, filled it up with water, and took it upstairs.

"Brother, where is the medicine?"

"Here, underneath the mattress. Please make it for me at once."

Jinlian lifted the mattress, and took the medicine. She put it into a cup, then filled up the cup with the liquid she had brought, stirring it with a silver pin she took from her hair. With her left arm she supported her husband. Then she poured the medicine down his throat. Wu Da drank a mouthful.

"Sister," he said, "this medicine is very nasty."

"We are only trying to make you well. Don't be put off by the bitter taste."

Wu Da drank again, and the woman emptied the cup down his throat. She lowered him on to the bed again, herself got down from it. Wu Da groaned.

"Sister, I have taken the medicine, but the pain in my belly feels worse, worse. Oh, I can't bear it."

Jinlian took two coverlets from behind his head, and pulled them entirely over his head.

"I can't breathe," Wu Da cried.

"It is what the doctor told me to do. It will make you sweat, and you'll be better much sooner."

Wu Da again tried to speak, and Jinlian was afraid he might struggle. She leaped upon the bed and, riding astride his body, pressed down the bedclothes so that he could not move at all.

His lungs were fried in boiling oil, his liver and bowels burned with fire,
His heart was pierced as by a butcher's knife, his belly stirred as by a
    sword's sharp edge.
Then froze his body to an icy cold, the seven openings all streamed
    with blood.
Through clenched teeth his three spirits sped to the city of ghosts.
From his parched throat his seven souls fled to the watchtower of Hell.
Thus to the ghosts of all the poisoned deep in Hades
Was joined another,
And in the world of living none was left
To hinder wantonness.

Wu Da groaned twice, and gasped for breath. Then his bowels burst, and he died.

Jinlian pulled down the bedclothes. Wu Da's teeth were tight clenched, and blood streamed from the seven openings. She was frightened and, getting down from the bed, knocked on the wall. When old woman Wang heard the knocking, she came to the back door and coughed. Jinlian went downstairs and opened the door.

"Is it all over?" the old woman asked.

"Over? Yes, it is over. My hands and feet fail me, and I can do no more."

"What is the matter with you?" the old woman said. "I'll help you." She rolled up her sleeves, took a tub of boiling water and put a napkin in it. Then she took them upstairs and gathered up all the bedclothes. She wiped Wu Da's lips, and cleaned away the blood from the seven openings. Then she piled the clothes on his body and, step by step, the pair of them carried him downstairs. There, they took an old door, and lifted the corpse onto it. They combed his hair and put a hat on his head, dressed him, and put shoes and socks upon his feet. They covered his face with a piece of white silk, and set clean bedclothes over him. Then they went upstairs again, and straightened the place. Old woman Wang went home, and Jinlian pretended to mourn for Wu Da, crying, "Husband! Husband!"

Readers, though there are many women in the world, they have but three ways of lamenting. Sometimes they weep and sob at the same time; sometimes they sob and do not weep; and sometimes they weep and do not sob. Jinlian sobbed for half the night, but not a tear accompanied her sobbing.

Next morning, just before dawn, Ximen Qing came to hear how the thing had gone. Old woman Wang told him all about it. He gave her some silver to pay for the coffin and the funeral expenses, and they called Jinlian to discuss the arrangements. When she came, she said to Ximen Qing:

"Wu Da is dead, and you are all I have in the world. All I have done, I have done for you. You must not, some day, cast me aside like a woman's hairnet that is no more needed."

"There is no fear of that."

"But what if ever you change your mind?"

"If I do, may I have the place that now is Wu Da's."

The old woman interrupted them. "There is one thing that must be attended to at once. We must have him put in his coffin without any delay. The coroner's officers might see that there is something wrong, especially He the Ninth, who is a smart man. He might even refuse to put Wu Da in his coffin."

"There will be no trouble from that quarter," Ximen said. "I will speak to He the Ninth. He will do anything I wish,"

"In that case," the old woman said, "you had better go and speak to him at once. Don't waste a moment." So Ximen Qing set out to find He the Ninth.

The sun, the moon, the stars, all cast their shadows
We cannot reach them.
The multitude of happenings, which have no roots save in themselves,
Comes into being.

The herons are behind the clouds
We see them only when they fly.
The parrot is hidden in the willow tree.
We hear him only when he speaks.

# CHAPTER 6
# The Funeral

When Ximen Qing left the old woman's house, it was broad daylight. Old woman Wang went out and bought a coffin, some paper offerings, incense, candles and paper money. When she came back, she lighted a lamp, and set it before Wu Da's body. The neighbors came to offer their condolences, and Pan Jinlian covered her lovely face and pretended to sob.

"How did the gentleman die?" the neighbors asked.

"There was something amiss with his heart, and, although we never expected anything like this, he got worse and worse and at last we saw that he could not get better. Last night, about the third watch, he died." Jinlian pretended to sob.

The neighbors thought that there was something mysterious about the manner of this man's death, but they did not venture to ask any more questions. They consoled Jinlian. "The dead are dead," they said, "but the living must live in peace. Do not grieve so much, Lady. It is too hot."

Jinlian thanked them, and they went away. Old woman Wang had the coffin brought, and went to see He the Ninth, the undertaker. She made all the arrangements, not only for the funeral, but for the household generally. She went to the Temple of Eternal Felicity and asked for two choirs of monks to come that night and sing a dirge for the departed.

He the Ninth sent some of his assistants in advance to set everything in order, and it was some time before he sauntered along himself. At the entrance to Amethyst Street, he met Ximen Qing.

"Where are you going, old Ninth?" Ximen said.

"I am just going to perform the last offices for Wu Da, the cake seller," said He the Ninth.

"Wait a moment, I want to speak to you." He the Ninth went with Ximen Qing till they came to a small wineshop at the corner of the street, and there they went into a small room.

"Take the upper seat, old Ninth," Ximen said.

"Who am I," said Ho, "that I should take the liberty of being seated in your presence?"

"Don't stand on ceremony, old Ninth; please sit down." They argued politely for a while, and then took their places. Ximen Qing ordered the waiter to bring a bottle of good wine. Refreshments were set out, and the wine warmed. He the Ninth wondered what was to come. "Ximen Qing has never taken wine with me before," he said to himself. "I wonder what he wants." They drank together for a long time. At last Ximen took from his sleeve a piece of pure silver, and put it down on the table before his companion.

"Old Ninth," he said, "do not think this too poor a present. I will express my thanks more worthily tomorrow."

"I have done nothing for you, Sir," He the Ninth said, making a reverence. "How can I take your silver? Any matter that you may care to entrust to me will naturally receive my most careful attention."

"Old Ninth," Ximen said, "don't behave as though you were a stranger. Please take it."

"Tell me what I can do for you," He the Ninth said.

"Only this. You are going to see about the disposal of Wu Da's body and, of course, his people will pay you for what you do there. But if in the course of your duties you should happen to notice anything, pay no attention, but cover him up with the bedclothes. That is all."

"I expected you to ask something really important," He the Ninth said, "and it is nothing more than this. It will be no trouble, and I couldn't think of taking your money."

"If you won't accept my money, I take it that you refuse to do this for me."

He the Ninth was aware of Ximen Qing's influence in official circles, and hesitated to offend him. He could not refuse to accept the money. They drank several more cups of wine, then Ximen Qing said to the waiter: "Put this down to my account, and come to my shop tomorrow for the money." They went downstairs and left the inn. As they took leave of one another, Ximen Qing said:

"Old Ninth, don't forget what I have told you, but not a word must be said about this. Later on, I will show my appreciation more tangibly." He walked away.

He the Ninth pocketed the silver. "I don't know what all this means, but it is evidently something to be kept quiet. Anyhow, here is the silver and if, as I expect, Wu Song has a few questions to ask when he comes back, I can produce it as evidence." A little later, he said to himself, "I need some money very badly just now, so I had better use this. When Wu Song comes back, I must think of something else." He came to Wu Da's house, where his men were all waiting for him at the door. Old woman Wang was also waiting anxiously.

"What did Wu Da die of?" He the Ninth said to his men.

"His wife says he suffered from pains at the heart, and died," his men said.

He the Ninth pulled up the lattice and went in.

"We have been waiting a very long time for you," old woman Wang said, "and the Master of the Yin Yang has been here half a day. Why are you so late, old Ninth?"

"I had some business to attend to. That made me late."

Jinlian, wearing plain clothes, with a white covering on her head, sobbed as though her heart were breaking. "Do not grieve so, Lady," He the Ninth said. "Your husband is already on his way to Heaven."

"My sorrow is greater than I can bear," Jinlian said, drying her eyes. "My husband suffered from his heart and, after only a few days' illness, he died and left me inconsolable."

He the Ninth looked the woman up and down. "I have often heard people speak of Wu Da's wife," he said to himself, "but this is the first time I have seen her. So this is the lady Wu Da married. Ximen Qing is getting good value for his ten taels of silver."

He went to the bed and examined the body. By this time the Master of the Yin Yang had finished his ritual, so He the Ninth pulled aside the mortuary emblems and removed the white silk. He stared. Wu Da's fingers were green and his lips purple; his face was yellow, and his eyeballs protruded. The undertaker saw at once that a crime had been committed.

"Why is his face purple?" the two assistants asked. "What is the cause of these teeth marks and the blood on his lips?"

"Don't be silly," He the Ninth said. "It is very hot. How can you expect a corpse not to alter?" The men put the body into the coffin and nailed it up with two longevity nails. Old woman Wang asked He the Ninth to give his men a thousand cash between them.

"When is the funeral to be?" the undertaker asked. "The lady says," old woman Wang told him, "that we will take the body outside the city wall to be burned, three days hence." He the Ninth went away. That night, Jinlian prepared wine for the funeral supper, and the next day four monks came and read the funeral service. On the third day at the fifth watch the bearers came to carry the coffin, and some of the neighbors followed behind. Jinlian, dressed in mourning clothes, seated herself in a sedan chair and, all the way along the street, pretended to bemoan her husband. At last they came to an open place outside the city. Here the funeral pyre was, and word was given for the fires to be lighted and the coffin burned. Soon everything was consumed and the ashes thrown into a pond. All the fees at the temple were paid by Ximen Qing.

The woman returned home, and, in the upper room, set up a tablet with the words "In Memory of Wu Da, my beloved husband." Before it she placed a lamp, golden flags, paper money, and ingots of imitation gold and silver. That day, she sat with Ximen Qing and bade the old lady go home. So these two enjoyed each other's company without hindrance, not as before at the house of old woman Wang, where their pleasure had been as uncertain as that of a chicken thief. Now Wu Da was dead they were alone in the house. They were able to spend the whole night together without thought of consequences. At first, Ximen Qing was afraid the neighbors might discover what was going on, and he used to go to old woman Wang's house, wait there for a little while, and then go to Jinlian's back door. But afterwards they seemed to find it almost impossible to separate, and for three or five nights at a time he would not go home. His household was at sixes and sevens, and everybody was unhappy.

The days passed quickly, the sun and moon crossed and recrossed like a weaver's shuttles. It was now two months and more since Ximen Qing had first possessed the woman. It was the Dragon Boat Festival.

Ximen Qing was on his way back from the Temple of Yue and, calling at the old woman Wang's tea shop, he sat down there. The old woman quickly made him a cup of tea.

"Where have you been, Sir? Why haven't you been to see your lady?"

"I have just been to the Temple," said Ximen, "and as it is the Summer Festival, I thought of her and came to see her."

"Her mother, old woman Pan, has been here today," the old woman said. "I fancy she is still here, but I'll go and find out for you." She went to the back door and found Jinlian drinking wine with her mother. They asked her to sit down.

"Drink a welcoming cup," Jinlian said, smiling, "and have a lovely baby."

"But I have no husband," laughed the old woman. "Where shall I get a baby? You are still young. You're the one to have babies."

"The young tree bears no fruit; but the old tree bears well," Jinlian said, quoting an old saying.

"Do you hear your daughter making fun of me?" the old woman said, turning to Madam Pan. "She calls me old beggar, but she'll be glad enough of her 'old beggar' one of these days."

"She has always had a sharp tongue, Stepmother," old woman Pan said, "but you must not pay too much attention to it."

"Yes, indeed, your daughter is as clever as they make 'em. She is a good woman. Some lucky man will snap her up one of these days."

"You are a go-between, Stepmother," old woman Pan said, "and it rests with you." She set out a cup and chopsticks, and Jinlian poured out some wine. The old woman drank several glasses, and her face grew red. She was afraid that Ximen Qing would grow tired of waiting, so she gave a sly wink to Jinlian, said good-bye to them, and went back to her own place.

Jinlian understood that Ximen Qing had come and hurriedly sent her mother away. She tidied the room, burned some fine incense, took away what was left of her mother's food, and prepared some special dishes for Ximen Qing. Then she went down to the back door to meet him.

She took him into the room, made a reverence to him, and sat down. She had given up wearing mourning very soon after Wu Da's death, and had put his tablet aside with a sheet of white paper over it. She never dreamed of putting offerings of soup or food before it. Every day she painted her face, put on colored dresses, and looked very charming indeed. Ximen Qing had not been to see her for some days, and she scolded him.

"What a fickle rascal you are! Why have you run away from me? Have you another sweetheart hidden somewhere that you leave me in the cold?"

"I have been very busy these last few days," Ximen said, "but today I have been to the temple to buy you some ornaments, and some pearls and clothes."

This pleased her. Ximen called Daian and, unfastening the package, showed the things one by one to Jinlian. She thanked him and put them away. She no longer troubled to keep the matter secret from Ying'er, who was afraid of being punished, and told her to bring tea for Ximen Qing. She herself laid the table, and then sat down with him.

"You should not take so much trouble for me," he said. "I have given Stepmother some, money to go and buy a few things. Now that the Summer Festival is here, the only thing I want is to sit here with you."

"It was for my mother originally," said Jinlian, "but this is quite fresh. If we wait for Stepmother to come back with her purchases, we shall have to wait a long time. Let's eat some of this." She pressed her cheek close against his, entwined her legs with his, and, side by side, they drank their wine.

The old woman had taken a basket and gone to the street to buy wine and meat. It was the beginning of the Fifth Month, and the rain was incessant. At one moment the sun was bright in the sky, the next it was hidden by black clouds, and there came down a torrent like the emptying of a washbasin.

Lowering clouds gather from the four corners of the sky
A chain of mist binds the far distances.
*Xi-la-la.* The air is filled with flying drops that veil the sun.
*Pit-pit.* They beat upon the plantain tree.
The winds blow, and the old juniper tree is uplifted,
Uplifted and overthrown.
Once its topmost branches threatened the sky.
The crashing thunderclaps grow louder,
The mountains of Tai and Song are shaken as by an earthquake,

Yet now the sultry heat is washed away, its heaviness is banished.
The fields of young corn are fresh again
New water races down the four rivers.
The green bamboo and scarlet pomegranate
Are made clean once more.

The old woman had just bought a jar of wine and a basketful of green stuff and fruits, and was walking along the street when the downpour came. She ran under the balcony of a house and tied her kerchief over her head, but her clothes were wet through. She waited a while till the rain began to slacken, then rushed home like a flying cloud and set down her wine and meat in the kitchen. Ximen Qing and Jinlian were drinking wine.

"Yes, my Lord and Lady," cried she, laughingly, "you are drinking, but look at me! My clothes are drenched. I shall have to have a new dress."

"Oh, you old woman," Ximen said, "you are one of those spirits who always find somebody to throw the blame on."

"I am not a spirit at all," the old woman said, "but you will have to make me a present of a roll of the deepest indigo silk."

"Drink a cup of hot wine, Stepmother," Jinlian said.

The old lady drank three cups of wine with them and then said she must go to the kitchen to dry her clothes. When she had dried them, she made ready chicken, goose, and rice, carving and chopping till all was to her liking, set the other things on plates and dishes, and then took them into the room and warmed the wine. Ximen Qing and Jinlian again poured the wine and, close pressed together, drank from the same glass.

While Ximen was drinking, he saw a lute hanging on the wall. "A long time ago, I was told how well you play. You must play me a tune, and I shall enjoy my wine all the more."

"When I was a small child," Jinlian said, "I learned one or two bits of tunes, but none too well. Please do not make fun of me." Ximen took down the lute and made the woman sit on his knee. She placed the lute in her lap and, gently stretching her delicate fingers, slowly plucked the strings and sang in a low sweet voice:

I set no headdress on my brow; my idle hands refused to serve me.
Round and round I furled the silken tresses, black as night, the curls
    like clouds in shadow.
Golden pins, thrust crosswise, restrained the lowering masses.
"Oh, maiden, open wide the chests," I cried
And dressed in robes of whitest silk
I came forth from my tiring room, glorious as Xi Shi.

"Oh, maiden dear, throw back the lattice for me, come and burn a
    stick of evening incense."

This song sent Ximen Qing almost into ecstasy. He drew his loved one
to him and put his arms about her white neck.

"I never realized how clever you were," he said. "I have often wandered
through the haunts of singing girls, but never were their songs or music so
exquisite as yours."

"It is kind of you to praise me, my Lord. I am ready to do whatever you
wish. All I pray is that the time may never come when you forget me."

"How can I forget you?" Ximen cried, as he stroked her soft cheeks.
Then, lazily, they played the game of rain and clouds, joking with one
another and making merry. Ximen took off one of her embroidered shoes,
poured a cup of wine into it, and drank.

"My feet are small enough," cried Jinlian. "Why should you make fun
of them?"

Soon they had taken their fill of wine and, shutting the door of the
room, they undressed and got onto the bed. Old woman Wang closed the
gate, and sat down in the kitchen with Ying'er. Jinlian and her lover turned
over and over, like the cock pheasant and his mate, and played as merrily
as the fishes in the water. Her skill in the arts of love was a hundred times
greater than that of any strumpet, and Ximen Qing himself was no mean
performer. They were at the age when a woman's beauty is at its loveliest
and a man's vigor at its highest. Youth was theirs.

Ximen Qing spent the whole day at his lover's house, and gave her several taels of silver for household expenses. At last she could not persuade
him to stay longer; he put on his eyeshades, and went home. Jinlian pulled
down the lattice and fastened the gate, then she and old woman Wang
drank wine together, and went their ways.

# CHAPTER 7
# Ximen Qing Meets Meng Yulou

One day there came to Ximen Qing's house an old woman called Xue. She was a seller of flowers made of kingfisher feathers, and was carrying a box of them. She could not find Ximen, but seeing Daian, asked him where his master was.

"My father," said the boy, "is in the shop, going through the accounts with Uncle Fu."

The old woman went straight to the shop door, pulled aside the lattice, and looked in. Ximen Qing was going through the books with his manager. With a movement of the head she signaled to him to come out. He left the shop at once, and they sought a quiet place in which to talk.

"What is your business with me?" Ximen Qing asked her.

"It is just an idea about a marriage that has come into my head," the old woman said. "The marriage I am thinking of should be satisfactory to you in every sense of the word, and it would fill the gap left in your household by the death of your Third Lady."

"Who is the lady?" Ximen asked.

"You probably know her. Her family name is Meng, and she is the widow of a cloth merchant, named Yang, who used to keep a shop outside the South Gate. She is by no means poor. She has a couple of Nanjing beds, and four or five chests so full of clothes for every season of the year that there isn't room to put a finger inside them. Her jewelry is beyond counting. She has about a thousand taels of ready money, and two or three hundred rolls of cloth woven with three shuttles. It is a year or more now since she became a widow, and she has no children of her own, only a younger brother of her husband, who is about ten years old. She is quite young, with no one to love, and her aunt thinks it is time she married again. She is about twenty-four years old this year, and very tall and beautiful. When she is dressed, she looks like a figure on a painted lantern. She is lively and charming, and just as intelligent as can be. She can govern a household, do needlework, and play backgammon and all kinds of games. There is nothing to hide. The lady's name is Meng, and she is the third of her family. She lives in Stinking Water Lane. I forgot to mention that she can play the moon guitar too. You will certainly fall in love with her the moment you see her."

Ximen was delighted when he heard that the girl could play the moon guitar. "When can I see her?" he cried.

"I don't anticipate any difficulty," the old woman said, "but one thing you must bear in mind. There is only one member of her family who counts for anything, and that is her aunt. There is indeed another relative, Zhang the Fourth, but he is like a mountain walnut, all shell. Many years ago this aunt married Crooked-Headed Sun, and they used to live in Master Xu's house on the north side of the High Street. But Sun has been dead these forty years. She has no children, and is entirely dependent upon her nephew and niece.

"She is the only person we have to consider. She cares about nothing but money, and she knows quite well that her nephew's widow has property. It is nothing to her whom her niece marries, so long as she gets a few taels of silver for herself. You have plenty of excellent silk. I suggest you take a roll of it, buy some presents, and call upon this old aunt. You might give her a little silver at the same time. If you do that, you will have disposed of her once and for all. Later, if anybody should venture to raise objections, the old lady will have her way and the objector will find himself powerless."

All this pleased Ximen Qing immensely. His face beamed with delight. They decided that the next day would suit their purpose, and that he should buy some presents and take them to the house of the young lady's aunt. Xue took up her box and went off, and Ximen Qing went back into the shop and continued to go through the books with Fu.

The next morning, Ximen rose early, and dressed himself in his finest clothes. He took a roll of silk and, buying four large dishes of beautiful fruits, had them put into carrying baskets and told a man to carry them. Then, on horseback, with Daian in attendance and old woman Xue leading the way, he set out to Aunt Yang's house. Xue went in to give the old lady warning.

"One of our neighbors," she said, "a very rich man, would like to have a word with you about your niece's marriage. I told him that you are the only person of any account in the family, and that he must come and see you before he goes to see the lady. I have brought him here today, and at this moment he is at the gate waiting your pleasure."

"Oh dear!" said the old lady. "Why didn't you tell me before?" She told a maid to prepare some fine tea, and gave orders that Ximen Qing should be asked to come in. Xue suggested that the presents should be sent in first, so that the empty baskets might be brought out again, and that then he should go and see the old lady.

He was wearing a large hat of woven palm and a pair of white-soled boots. When he came into the old lady's presence he made four reverences. Leaning on her stick, she hastily prepared to return them, but he would not allow this. "Please, Aunt," he said, "be so kind as to accept my greeting."

They disputed amicably for some time, and the matter ended with half the required reverences. Then they sat down, hostess and guest in their proper places, and old woman Xue sat down beside them.

"May I know your honorable name, Sir?" said the old lady.

"This gentleman," answered Xue for him, "is the richest or the second richest man in Qinghe. He is Master Ximen, who keeps a medicine shop by the Town Hall. The money in his house reaches higher than the North Star, and his barns are filled with more spoiled rice than is to be found in the Imperial Storehouses. Now his household is without a mistress and, since he has heard that our lady is ready to marry, he has come expressly to talk to you about the marriage."

"Sir," the old lady said, "if you wanted my niece, you had only to come and tell me. Why have you spent your money upon a present for me? It has put me in the position that if I refuse it, I shall be impolite, and if I accept it, I shall feel ashamed."

"Most worthy Aunt," Ximen said, "this is not fit to be called a present." The old lady made two reverences as a sign of thanks and accepted the present. Tea was brought in and, as they were drinking it, the old lady said:

"You will think me lacking in intelligence if I fail to make myself quite clear. My nephew, when he was alive, was very rich, but unfortunately he is dead, and all his wealth has come into my niece's hands, probably no less than a thousand taels of silver. I am not in the least concerned whether you want her for the mistress of your household or as a second wife, but I should like to have a requiem sung for my nephew's soul—I am his own aunt—and a little money for my coffin. Of course, all this will cost you nothing. I would do anything to get the better of that old dog Zhang the Fourth, and I will see that this marriage is arranged. Perhaps, when you are married, you will allow her to come occasionally to see her poor old aunt, on my birthday and perhaps at the Summer Festival. I don't imagine you will find my poverty infectious."

Ximen Qing laughed. "Please make your mind quite at rest," he said. "I understand perfectly. If you arrange this matter for me, you may have a dozen coffins if you like."

He told Daian to bring his visiting box. From it he took six bars of the purest white official silver, worth thirty taels, and set them before her. "This is only a trifle, Lady, but I hope you will use it to buy a cup of tea. After the marriage, I will give you another seventy taels and two rolls of silk. That may suffice for your funeral. And at the four seasons and the eight festivals, I will certainly allow her to visit you."

When the cunning old woman set her black eyes on the thirty taels of shining white silver, her face became all smiles. "Honorable Sir," she said, "don't think that I am grasping, but it has always been considered the wisest plan to be quite definite at the very beginning. It avoids disputes later on."

"You are a very intelligent woman," old woman Xue said, "and, really, you need not have any fears. His Lordship is perfectly reliable. If he had not been, he would not have brought his box with him when he came to discuss the matter. Perhaps you are unaware that he is on friendly terms with the local officials. They know how open-handed he is. You need not be afraid of exhausting his resources."

The old lady was more and more delighted, and gave vent to her feelings in more ways than one. They drank two more cups of tea, and Ximen stood up to take his leave, though the old lady urged him to stay longer.

"Now that we have seen you," old woman Xue said, "we will go tomorrow to pay our respects to the young lady."

"His Lordship need not trouble to go and see my niece," the old lady said. "You go and tell her that I say if she won't marry a gentleman like this, I should like to know whom she will marry."

Ximen Qing prepared to leave.

"A poor old woman like me," the old lady said, "could never have dreamed that you, Sir, would condescend to come and see me, so I was taken unprepared. Please forgive my allowing you to go away empty-handed."

She took her stick and hobbled a few steps with him, till he begged her to return. As he was mounting his horse, Xue said, "Wasn't that a good idea? Go home now, I have a little more to say to the old lady. I will call for you early tomorrow morning."

Ximen Qing gave her a tael of silver to pay for the hire of a donkey, mounted his horse, and rode home. Xue went back again to the old lady, and they talked and drank together till the sun was setting. Then she went home.

The next morning Ximen Qing dressed himself exquisitely, put his purse in his sleeve, and rode on a white horse. His two boys, Daian and Ping'an, were in attendance, and old woman Xue rode on a donkey. They set off for the South Gate and soon reached the young lady's house.

The gatehouse was as large as an ordinary room and had a black-and-white screen. Xue asked Ximen Qing to dismount, and they went in together. They came to the inner door with another screen and a low fence of bamboo. There were flower pots with pomegranates in the courtyard and, on the steps, a row of blue jars and two long benches for beating cloth. The old woman pushed open the scarlet double doors and they went into a parlor, with seats arranged as for host and guests. The tables and chairs were new and brightly polished, and the curtains and blinds in excellent taste.

Old woman Xue told Ximen Qing to sit down, and she went to the courtyard. Very soon she returned and whispered, "The lady has not finished dressing yet. Do you mind waiting?" A boy brought in some Fujian tea and, while Ximen Qing was drinking it, the old woman with much gesticulation gave him what information she thought fit.

"Apart from the aunt, this young lady is the only person of consequence in the family. Her husband had a brother, but he is still very young and ignorant. When Master Yang was alive, they used to sell enough to fill two large baskets with coins, not to speak of silver, every day. He charged three *fen* a foot for the black cloth used for making shoes and twenty or thirty men were employed in the dye shop. This lady managed everything. She has two maids and a boy. The elder maid is fifteen, and has already had her hair dressed as a woman. That is Lanxiang. The little maid, Xiaoluan, is twelve. When she marries, they will go with her. If I bring off this marriage, I only ask one thing. I should like to be able to take a couple of rooms to live in."

"There will be no difficulty about that," Ximen said.

"But last year," the old woman said, "when you bought Chunmei, you promised me several rolls of silk. I have never had them. Perhaps you will remember that when you reward me on this occasion." A maid came to call her, and in a little while Ximen Qing heard the tinkling of ornaments and there came to him the fragrance of exquisite perfume. The old woman pulled up the lattice and Mistress Meng came in.

Ximen Qing was delighted with her the moment he saw her. She came into the room, modestly made a reverence, and sat down opposite him. He stared at her so fixedly that she bowed her head. "Lady," he said at last, "it is now a long time since my wife died, and I should like to take you to wife to govern my household. May I know your honorable wishes in this matter?"

The lady looked at him. He seemed a pleasant-looking fellow and she was well enough satisfied. She said to old woman Xue, "How old is this gentleman and how long is it since his lady died?"

"I have misspent twenty-eight years," Ximen Qing said, "and my wife unfortunately died more than a year ago. May I know how many fruitful springs you have seen?"

"I am thirty years old," the lady said.

"Then you are two years older than I am."

"When the wife is two years older than the husband," the old go-between said, "the yellow gold increases day by day; and when the wife is three years older, the yellow gold is piled up mountains high."

The little maid brought three cups of tea and some preserved golden oranges. Mistress Meng stood up, took one of the cups, and with her slender finger wiped the water from its rim, then offered it to Ximen Qing, at the same time making a reverence. Old woman Xue found an opportunity to lift the lady's skirt slightly, displaying her exquisite feet, three inches long and no wider than a thumb, very pointed and with high insteps. They were clad in a pair of scarlet shoes, embroidered in gold with a cloud design, with white silk high heels. Ximen Qing observed them with great satisfaction.

Mistress Meng gave a cup of tea to Xue, then took one herself and sat down. Ximen Qing told Daian to bring in the box of presents. In it were two silk handkerchiefs, a pair of jeweled pins, and six gold rings. Ximen took them out of the box and, putting them on a tray, presented them to the lady. The old woman prompted her to thank him. "When do you wish the ceremony to be performed?" she asked. "I shall have preparations to make."

"I take this as a pledge of your kind intention," Ximen Qing said. "On the twenty-fourth day of this month I will send my small gift, and I would suggest the second of next month for the wedding day."

"I must speak to my aunt about the matter," Mistress Meng said.

"His Lordship called upon your aunt yesterday, and discussed the matter," old woman Xue said.

"What did she say?" Mistress Meng asked.

"She was very pleased. Indeed, she said that if this gentleman was not good enough for you, she didn't know who would be. She will be very satisfied with you when she learns that you have agreed to marry his Lordship."

"If she really said that, all will be well."

"Ah, Lady," the old woman said, "you have to thank me for this good fortune."

Ximen Qing rose and said good-bye. Old woman Xue went with him as far as the entrance to the lane.

"Well," she said, "you have seen the lady. What do you think of her?"

"Sister," Ximen Qing said, "I thank you."

The old woman asked him to go home without her. She said that she had still something to say to Mistress Meng. Ximen mounted his horse and returned to the city, and the old woman went back to the room.

"You must feel satisfied, now that you have arranged to marry this gentleman," she said.

"But he may have a wife already for all I know," said Mistress Meng, "and I have no idea what his business is."

"My good lady," the old woman said, "supposing he is married, I can assure you that none of his ladies has any intelligence to speak of. When you marry him, you will find that I am telling the truth. As for his reputation, everybody knows that he is the famous medicine merchant, money lender to the officials, and the first or second richest man in the district. The magistrates, both of the prefecture and of the district, are on very intimate terms with him, and only recently he became a relation by marriage of Marshal Yang of the Eastern Capital. With a relative like that, who dare interfere with him?"

Mistress Meng prepared some refreshments. While they were eating, a boy came from Aunt Yang's house. He brought a box in which were four pieces of cake made of yellow rice and dates, two pieces of sweetmeat, and several dozen little pastries.

"My mistress would like to know whether you have accepted the man's proposal," the boy said. "She says if you don't accept him, she can't imagine whom you will have."

"Thank your mistress for her kind message," Mistress Meng said, "and tell her that I have accepted him."

"Now you have a proof that I was not lying to you," the old woman said. "Your aunt did know all about it."

Mistress Meng took the cakes out of the box, and gave it back filled with buns and cured meats. She gave the boy a handful of coins, and said, "Thank your mistress for me. Tell her that he is going to send his present on the twenty-fourth, and the wedding is to be on the second of next month." Then the boy went home.

"What did your aunt send you?" the old woman asked. "May I have some to take home to my children?" Mistress Meng gave her a piece of sweetmeat and a dozen pastries, and she went away.

Now, the lady's uncle, Zhang the Fourth, was very anxious to secure the guardianship of his nephew Yang Zongbao in order that he might get the woman's property into his own hands. He hoped that she would become the second wife of a certain Scholar Shang, who was the son of a local magistrate. Had it been any less important person, a few words would have settled the matter, but he knew that Ximen Qing was on good terms with the officials, and dared not oppose him openly. After thinking over every possible way of dealing with the situation, he decided that the best plan was to introduce some element of discord between them. So he came to see his niece.

"You mustn't think of accepting Ximen Qing's proposal," he said. "Shang is the man for you. He is a poet of distinction, owns several farms, and enjoys a very comfortable existence. He would be a much better match than that fellow Ximen, who has had too many dealings with the officials and is a truculent upstart and a ne'er-do-well. Ximen has one wife already. She was a Miss Wu. If you marry him, you won't be the mistress of his house; you'll be nothing but an underling. He has three or four other wives, and several young maids. No, if you marry him, with so many people already in the household, I'm afraid you'll have to put up with a great deal of unpleasantness."

Meng realized that Zhang the Fourth wished her to break off her engagement, and she decided to tease him. "There is an old saying," she said, "that though there are many ships upon the water, the traffic still goes on. I see no reason why we should not all get along very well. If he has a wife already, I will gladly revere her as an elder sister. If he has other wives, I will place absolute confidence in him. If I afford my husband pleasure, I don't mind how many wives he has; if not, even if I should be his only wife, life would be utterly miserable. In every rich family there are four or five ladies. My dear old uncle, don't trouble yourself any more about the matter. When I get there, I shall know how to look after myself. I don't anticipate any trouble on that score."

"But that is not all," Zhang the Fourth continued. "He is continually beating his women and ill using his wives. He makes a business of buying and selling young people, and if anyone in his establishment gives him the slightest cause for annoyance, he sends for the go-between and gets rid of her. Are you ready to put up with that sort of treatment?"

"No, Uncle, you are mistaken," his niece said. "Even a bad-tempered husband cannot punish a wife who does her duty and keeps her wits about her. If I marry him and perform my household duties properly, and if I know when to keep my mouth and other people's mouths shut, he will find no excuse for treating me badly."

"I am told," Zhang the Fourth persisted, "yes, I am told that he has a young unmarried daughter about fourteen years old, and I can't help thinking, if you marry him, that the girl will take every possible opportunity of annoying you."

"Why do you think that, Uncle? If I marry him, old is old and young is young. I treat children very kindly. I don't believe either that my husband will be dissatisfied with me, or that my daughter will be undutiful. If he had ten daughters, it wouldn't worry me."

"One more point," said Zhang the Fourth, "and perhaps this is the most serious of all. The fellow's behavior is atrocious. Strumpets and bawdy houses are the only interest he has in life. Moreover, he is a man of straw and frightfully in debt. What I fear most of all is that he will involve you in his downfall."

"Uncle, you are mistaken again. The man is young and occasionally he may philander away from home. There is nothing extraordinary about that, and there is no way in which wives can prevent their husbands from so amusing themselves. As for his financial position, you should remember the old saying: 'Money has no roots.' We have no means of telling whether a person will always be rich or always be poor. No, Uncle, marriages are made in Heaven, please don't distress yourself so much about this one."

Zhang the Fourth was forced to realize that there was nothing he could say to change his niece's purpose. She paid no heed to anything he advised. So he made a wry face, drank two cups of plain tea, stood up, and went home extremely crestfallen.

He talked over the matter with his wife, and they decided to wait until the wedding day, and then to use their nephew Yang Zongbao as an excuse for laying hands on Mistress Meng's belongings.

On the twenty-fourth Ximen Qing sent his marriage pledge. On the twenty-sixth twelve monks came to chant a dirge for the repose of the soul of the late Master Yang, and burn his tablet. Aunt Yang was definitely on Ximen's side, but, on the eve of the wedding, Zhang the Fourth asked a number of neighbors to accompany him and went to make a last attempt to dissuade his niece. Old woman Xue, with Ximen's servants and ten or twenty soldiers of the garrison, came to bring away the lady's bed, her curtains, and all her boxes. Zhang met them and stopped them. "Madam Go-between," he said, "please do not remove these things. I have a few words to say about the matter." Then he and all the neighbors went in to see Mistress Meng. They sat down and Zhang the Fourth addressed the company.

"Honorable neighbors all, please listen to what I have to say." Then he turned to his niece. "You are the mistress here, and I have nothing against that. But your husband Yang Zongxi and his younger brother Yang Zong-bao were both nephews of mine. The elder of these two nephews is now dead and what he possessed has been inherited by others. That is right and fitting. But my second nephew Yang Zongbao is still a child, and the burden of this matter falls upon me. He was born of the same mother as your late husband, and has naturally a right to some share in the property. I call upon these honorable neighbors to witness. We will open all the boxes and everybody shall see what there is. Then we shall know whether there is much or nothing."

"Honorable neighbors," Mistress Meng said, beginning to cry, "now hear what I have to say." She turned to Zhang the Fourth. 'You are mistaken, old gentleman. I did not wickedly murder my husband, so that I might marry again to my dishonor. It is no secret that he had money. He laid by many taels of silver, and spent them on the building of this house. I am not taking this house away. I leave it for my young brother-in-law. I am not even taking away a single article of furniture. Three or four hundred taels of silver were due to me, but I handed over to you the contracts and documents, you collected the money, and I have used it to live upon. What else could I do?"

"Doubtless you have no money," Zhang said. "I am quite ready to agree. But in the presence of these good people, let the boxes be opened so that everyone can see for himself. Even if they turn out to be full of silver, you can take it away. I don't want it."

"Perhaps you would like to see my shoes too," Mistress Meng cried.

They were in the midst of this dispute when Aunt Yang came in, leaning on her stick. "Here comes the aunt," all the neighbors cried. They saluted her respectfully. She returned their greeting and sat down. Then she began.

"Honorable neighbors here present. I am her aunt, and it is natural that I should have something to say about all this. He who is dead was my nephew, and he who lives is just as much my nephew. If any one of our fingers is bitten, it is no less painful than any other. It has been stated that her husband was rich. Well, even if he had a hundred thousand taels, you should still treat her fairly. She has no children and she is young. What right have you to prevent her marrying again?"

"Quite right, quite right," said all the neighbors.

"Do you claim the things that came to her from her own family?" the old lady continued, addressing Zhang the Fourth. "She has had no secret understanding with me. All I want is justice." She turned again to the bystanders. "If my niece had not always been so good-hearted and sweet-natured, honorable neighbors, I should not be bothering my old bones about her. I hate to see her leave this place."

Zhang the Fourth glared at the old lady. "Oh," said he, "I know how full of fine ideas your mind is. I also know that the phoenix does not lay his head where there is no treasure."

This remark infuriated the old lady. Her face became purple. She shook her finger at Zhang the Fourth. "Don't talk such rubbish, Zhang the Fourth. I may not be the rightful representative of the Yang family, but as for you, old slippery tongue, what have you to do with the Yangs?"

"Even if I am not a Yang, these two nephews are my sister's sons. You biting old reptile, a woman ought to consider her husband's family. What is the use of lighting a fire with one hand and pouring water on it with the other?"

"You good-for-nothing old dog bone," the old lady cried. "She is a young and helpless woman. You wish to keep her in this house, but what is it you are really after? Either you have nasty lustful designs upon her yourself, or you are devising some scheme to grow fat upon her money."

"I don't want her money," Zhang the Fourth retorted, "but there will be nothing for Yang Zongbao when he grows up. I am not your sort, ripe for the slaughter, one who takes up with the rich and deceives the humble. You are like a yellow cat with a black tail."

"Zhang the Fourth, you offshoot of generations of beggars, you miserable old slave, you old mealy mouth, how dare you be such a humbug and talk like this? What utter nonsense! There will be no cords to tie your coffin when you die."

"You garrulous old whore, you want the money yourself to put a little warmth under your tail. No wonder you never had any children!"

The old lady became more and more wild.

"Zhang the Fourth, you son of a bawd. Pig! Dog! So I have no children, eh? Well, that's better than having an old woman who goes to the temple to sleep with the monks and carry on with the priests. You don't know what you're talking about."

By this time the pair were on the point of coming to blows. Fortunately, the neighbors stopped them. "Uncle, let the lady have her say," they said to Zhang the Fourth.

Old woman Xue, while the dispute was at its height, told Ximen's servants and the soldiers to hurry in. They carried out all the chests and beds, some on their shoulders and others on poles. It was like a whirlwind. Zhang the Fourth was furious, but he could only look on, speechless. The neighbors could not understand what the trouble was all about. They tried to make peace, and finally they went away.

On the second day of the sixth month Ximen Qing sent a large sedan chair, with four pairs of lanterns, for Mistress Meng. Yang Zongbao, his hair dressed in a knot, wearing green clothes, rode on a horse and acted as his sister-in-law's escort. Ximen Qing gave him a roll of silk and a piece of jade. Lanxiang and Xiaoluan, the two maids, went with her to be her chambermaids. Qintong, her boy, was now fifteen years old, and he too went to serve her. On the third day after the marriage Aunt Yang and Mistress Meng's sisters-in-law called to offer their congratulations. Ximen Qing gave Aunt Yang seventy taels of silver and two rolls of silk, and from that day forward their friendship was never broken. He prepared three rooms in the western wing for Mistress Meng, and established her there as his third wife, calling her "Yulou" [Tower of Jade] and giving orders to his household that she must be spoken of as the Third Lady. For two nights he slept in her room. The golden hangings seemed to indicate the coming of a new bride, but the story told by the scarlet silk coverlets was not new.

# CHAPTER 8
# The Magic Diagrams

Higher and yet higher the red dawn
Creeps slowly up the casement.
She wakes and throws her silken wrapper
Carelessly across one breast.
Is it not strange
This rising while the sun is not yet high?

Blown by the gentle breeze
The hastening flowers wander through the tower of jade.
She could not sleep
The image of her loved one lingered always with her.

Now that Ximen Qing had married Meng Yulou, their love was so deep that they could not bear to be away from one another even for a moment. One day old woman Wen came on behalf of the Chen family to propose that the marriage arranged between their son and Ximen's daughter should be celebrated on the twelfth day of the sixth month. Ximen Qing, in a great state of excitement, took one of his new wife's gilded Nanjing beds for his daughter. For more than a month he was so busy preparing for the ceremony that he could not find time to go and see Pan Jinlian. Day after day she leaned upon the door, and looked out for him till her eyes could see no longer. At last she asked old woman Wang to go to his house. The old woman went, but the servants knew whence she had come and paid no attention to her. Jinlian waited and waited, but still Ximen did not come and, after old woman Wang's fruitless visit, she told Ying'er to go to the street and see if she could see him. The girl did not venture to enter the great house, or even the courtyard, but stood in the gateway and peeped inside. But she too could see no sign of Ximen Qing and had to go back again. When she got home, Jinlian spat in her face, cursed and beat her, because, she said, she was no use. She made the child kneel down until midday, and would give her nothing to eat. Then, finding the hot weather very trying, she told Ying'er to heat some water that she might take a bath, and to cook some little meat pasties for Ximen Qing to eat if he should come.

Jinlian was wearing a thin gossamer shift, and she sat on her little bed. When her lover did not come, she cursed him for a fickle rogue. This made her only the more sad. With her slender fingers she took off her red embroidered shoes, and began to use them for working out the magic diagrams of love. There was no one she could talk to, and she used coins to try and find out what her absent lover was thinking of.

Jinlian played at the love diagrams for a long time. Then she tired of them and lay down to sleep. An hour later she awoke in a very bad temper. "Mother," Ying'er said, "the water is hot now; will you take your bath?"

"Are the pasties cooked?" Jinlian asked. "Bring them here and let me see." Ying'er hastily brought them, and Jinlian counted them with her dainty fingers. She had made a tray of thirty but, though she counted again and again, she could not find more than twenty-nine.

"Where is the other one?" she cried.

"I haven't seen it," Ying'er said; "you must have counted wrong."

"I have counted them twice. I want thirty for your father to eat. How dare you steal one? You are an impudent, whorish little slave. I suppose you were dying of starvation, and couldn't do without one of these particular pasties! A bowl of rice, whether large or small, is not good enough for you. Do you imagine I made them for you?"

Without giving the girl a chance to say a word, she stripped off her clothes and beat her twenty or thirty times with a whip, till she squealed like a pig being killed. "If I have to ask you again, and you still lie to me, I will most certainly beat you a hundred times."

The girl could bear no more. "Mother, don't beat me," she cried, "I was so hungry I had to take one."

"Why did you say I'd counted them wrongly, when you knew you'd stolen one? I knew it was you, you little whore, you thief. When that turtle was alive, you knew one or two things, and told him a great deal more than you really knew. Now he is not here. You play your tricks right in front of my eyes. I will break every bone in your whorish little body."

She beat the girl for some time longer, then made her put on her drawers, and told her to stand beside her and fan her. When the girl had fanned her for a long time, Jinlian cried, "Turn your face to me, you little strumpet, and I'll pinch it." Ying'er turned and the woman, with her long sharp nails, pinched it till the blood came. Then she let go. After a while, she went to the dressing table to dress again before going to stand at the door.

At last the Heavens relented. Daian on horseback, carrying a parcel, passed her door.

"Where are you going?" she cried.

The boy was by no means lacking in intelligence, and he had often come with his master to this house. Jinlian was in the habit of giving him little presents. He knew her quite well. He dismounted and said, "I have been with a present to one of the officers and now I'm going home."

"What is happening at your Father's?" Jinlian said. "Why hasn't he been here? It looks as though he had another sweetheart."

"He has no new sweetheart. But for the last few days everybody in the house has been very busy, and he couldn't get away."

"If he has been so busy, why didn't he send me word? I have been worried about him for ever so long. Tell me, what is he really doing?"

The boy smiled. He did not answer, and this made Jinlian think there must be something behind it all. Once again she asked him eagerly, "What has been happening?"

"Well, if there was anything," Daian said, smiling, "why should you want to know all about it?"

"If you don't tell me, little oily mouth, I will hate you all your life."

"If I tell you," the boy said, "you mustn't let my master know I did so."

Jinlian promised, and Daian told her how his master had married Meng Yulou. The woman could not prevent the tears from falling over her beautiful face. Daian was very much embarrassed. "Oh, Aunt," he said, "how easily upset you are. That is just why I didn't want to tell you." Jinlian leaned upon the door and sighed deeply.

"You don't understand," she said, "you don't know how fond of one another we used to be. And now he has cast me aside." Her tears fell faster and faster.

"You shouldn't let yourself be so distressed," Daian said. "Even our Great Lady can't keep him in order."

"Listen to me, Daian," said Jinlian. She sang a song to him about the fickleness of men.

Then she began to cry again. "Please don't cry," Daian said, "I'm sure he will come and see you very soon. Write him a short note and let me take it to him. He will certainly come when he gets it."

"I will, indeed," Jinlian said, "and, if you will be so kind, you shall have a fine pair of shoes for your pains. I should like him to come in time for me to congratulate him on his birthday, but whether he comes or not will depend absolutely on your little oily tongue."

She told Ying'er to put some of the pasties onto a dish, and asked Daian to have some tea. Meanwhile she went into her room, took a sheet of flowered paper, and wrote with a sheep's-hair brush in a jade holder. In a few minutes she had written this poem:

The words upon this flowered paper come from my heart.

I remember that our hair once mingled on the pillow.

How often I have leaned upon the door, under the lattice, filled with
    countless fears.

Now, if you are false to me, if you will not come

Give back to me my dainty handkerchief.

When she had written this, she folded the paper in a lover's knot and gave it to Daian. "Tell him he must come on his birthday. I shall be waiting most anxiously for him."

When the boy had eaten the cakes and the pasties, Jinlian gave him a handful of coins. As he was about to mount his horse, she said, "When you get home and see your Father, tell him that I am very angry with him. Tell him that if he does not come here, I shall get a sedan chair and come to him."

"Lady," the boy said, "you mustn't do anything of the sort. You would be like a dumpling seller trying to do business with a fortune-teller. You would never get a fair deal." He rode away.

Day after day, early and late, Jinlian waited for Ximen Qing, but he did not come. It was the end of the seventh month and his birthday was approaching. To Jinlian every day seemed like three autumns and every night like half a summer. Still no word came from him. She clenched her pearly teeth and rivers of tears flowed from her eyes. One evening she prepared a meal, and asked old woman Wang to come and see her. She took a silver pin from her hair and gave it to the old woman, entreating her to go to Ximen's house and ask him to come.

"This is no time to go," the old woman said, "he will certainly not be able to come now. I will go and see him tomorrow morning."

"You must not forget, Stepmother."

"I am not unused to such business," the old woman said. "I'm not likely to lose any time in a matter of this sort."

Old woman Wang never did anything without being paid. This time the pin was her reward. She drank till her face was very red, and then went home.

Jinlian burned incense to perfume the bedclothes, and lighted the silver lamp. Long and softly she sighed to express the inmost feelings of her heart. All through the long night she played the lute, till the silence and loneliness of the empty house made her feel that she could play no longer. And as she played, she sang.

She tossed about all night, unable to sleep. As soon as it was light, she sent Ying'er to see whether old woman Wang had gone to see Ximen Qing. The little girl came back and told her that the old woman had gone.

It was still early when old woman Wang reached Ximen's gate. She asked the servants about him, but they all said they knew nothing. She waited a long time, standing by the wall opposite the gate, till Clerk Fu came out and opened the shop. She went over and greeted him respectfully. "Excuse me," she said politely, "but is his Lordship at home?"

"What do you want with him?" Fu said. "Yesterday his Lordship entertained a number of guests to celebrate his birthday and, after drinking all day here, they went to the bawdy house last night. He has not come back yet, and you will probably find him still there."

The old woman thanked him and set off down East Street to the lane in which the bawdy house was. There she met Ximen, on horseback, coming from the opposite direction, and two boys attending him. He was half drunk, nodding to and fro upon his horse, and his bleary eyes could hardly see. "You ought not to get as drunk as this, Sir," old woman Wang shouted. She took hold of his bridle.

"Hello, Stepmother Wang, is that you?" Ximen Qing drunkenly mumbled. "I suppose Sister Wu has sent you to look for me?"

The old woman whispered something. "My boy said something about it some time ago," Ximen said. "I hear she is very angry with me. I'll go and see her now." He chatted with the old woman as they went along. When they came to the door, old woman Wang went in first.

"Now you ought to be happy, Lady," she said. "In less than half an hour I've brought his Lordship to you."

Jinlian was so delighted that he seemed like a visitor from Heaven. She ran downstairs to meet him. Ximen Qing waved his fan airily and went in, still neither drunk nor sober. He gave the woman a nod, and in return she made a profound reverence.

"You are indeed a nobleman, my Lord, and not the sort of man who is to be gazed upon any day. Where have you been all this time? I suppose you have been so taken up with your new wife that you haven't had time for me?"

"My new wife!" Ximen said. "What do you mean? Surely you don't believe all the tittle-tattle you hear. I have not had time to come and see you. I have been busy making arrangements for my daughter's wedding."

"Still trying to deceive me, are you?" Jinlian cried. "Well, if this is not a case of off with the old love and on with the new, you must take oath upon your body."

"If I have forgotten you," Ximen Qing said, "may my body become the size of a bowl of rice and may I suffer for three years or more from yellow sickness. May a caterpillar as large as a carrying pole bite a hole in my pocket."

"You fickle rascal, what harm will it do you if a caterpillar as large as that does bite a hole in your pocket?" She went up to him and, snatching off his hat, threw it on the floor. Old woman Wang hastily picked it up and put it on the table.

"Lady," she cried, "you were angry with me because I didn't make his Worship come, and, when he does come, you treat him like this."

Jinlian pulled a pin from his hair, held it up, and looked at it. It was of gold, with two rows of characters engraved upon it.

The horse, with golden bridle, neighs on the sweet turf.
In the season of apricot blossoms, they who dwell in the jade tower
    drink till they are merry.

This pin belonged to Yulou, but Jinlian thought some singing girl had given it to him. She thrust it into her sleeve. "Now will you say you haven't changed? Where is the pin I gave you?"

"The other day," Ximen said, "I was rather tipsy and fell off my horse. My hat blew away and my hair was all in a mess. I looked everywhere for the pin, but could not find it."

Jinlian snapped her fingers in his face. "Brother, you are so drunk you don't know what you're saying. A child of three would see through a story like that."

"Don't be so hard on his Lordship," old woman Wang said. "He is one of those men who can see a bee piddling forty miles away, but not an elephant outside their very own doors."

"When she is nearly done," Ximen Qing said, "you begin."

Jinlian saw a scarlet-trimmed finely gilded fan. She snatched it from him and took it to the light to look at. She was well skilled in the arts of love, and she was sure that certain marks upon it had been caused by teeth. She came to the conclusion that some girl must have given him the fan, and without a word tore it into pieces. Before Ximen Qing could stop her it was in shreds.

"My friend Bu Zhidao gave me that fan," he said, "and I've kept it put away for a long time. I've only been using it for two or three days, and now you've gone and spoiled it."

Jinlian plagued him a little longer, and then Ying'er brought in tea. The woman told her to put down the tray and kowtow to Ximen Qing.

"You two have been quarreling quite long enough," old woman Wang said. "Don't forget that you have more important business to attend to. I'll go into the kitchen and get something ready for you."

Jinlian told Ying'er to bring wine and refreshments in honor of Ximen's birthday. The girl obeyed and soon a meal was set upon the table. Jinlian brought out her own present and, setting it on a tray, offered it to him.

Besides a pair of black silk shoes, there was a pair of breeches made of purple silk, double sewn and embroidered with a design of pine, bamboo, and plum blossom, the three cold-weather friends. They were lined with green silk, scented with fragrant herbs, and the braces were again of purple. The stomacher was embroidered with roses. There was also a pin like the petals of the double lotus, on which was engraved a verse of four sentences, each sentence consisting of four characters:

> A double lotus, I,
> To dress your hair.
> Do not forget me
> Like a neglected ornament.

Ximen Qing was delighted with these presents. He caught Jinlian to him and kissed her. "I never knew you were so clever," he said.

Jinlian told Ying'er to bring the wine jar that she might offer Ximen a cup of wine. As she bowed four times in reverence before him, she seemed as graceful as a branch laden with blossoms, and each time she stood up as straight as a candle. Ximen Qing quickly lifted her up, and they sat together side by side. Old woman Wang drank several cups of wine with them and then went home, her face very red. Then they abandoned all restraint, and drank for a long time till darkness fell.

> Dark clouds have gathered over the mountains
> A chain of deepest mist stretches far into the distance.
> Stars come out to challenge the brightness of the moon
> And the green waters of the lake mirror the sky.
> The monks return to their ancient temples
> While, in the depths of the forest, the crows fly, crying
> Caw, caw, caw.
> People hasten back to the distant villages
> And in the tiny hamlets the dogs bark
> Bow, wow, wow.

Ximen Qing decided to stay the night with Jinlian, and ordered the boys to take his horse home. That night they spent their whole strength in the enjoyment of one another, and their passionate delight knew no bounds. Yet, as the proverb says, "When joy is at its height, there comes sad news." The time flew by.

*          *          *

We must now return for a while to Wu Song. He had taken the magistrate's treasure to the palace of the Grand Marshal in the Eastern Capital. When he had safely handed over the letters and the chests, he stayed some time waiting for the return letter, and then ordered his men to start back to Shandong. When he had started, it was the third or fourth month; now it was already autumn. Rain fell incessantly, and they had to halt for a few days. He had already been away about three months, and somehow, on this journey homewards, he seemed unable to rid himself of a feeling of great uneasiness. At last he made up his mind to send one of the soldiers before him to carry a report to the magistrate and a letter to his brother, Wu Da. In this he said he would be home some time during the eighth month.

The soldier arrived and, after giving the letter to the magistrate, went off to find Wu Da. It so happened that old woman Wang was standing outside her door when the soldier was just about to knock at Wu Da's house. She went across and said to him, "What is it you want?"

"I have orders from Captain Wu," the soldier said, "to give this letter to his brother."

"Master Wu Da is not at home," the old woman said. "He has gone to visit his family tombs. Give me the letter and he shall have it as soon as he comes back. That is the best thing you can do."

The soldier saluted, took out the letter, and gave it to the old woman. Then he jumped on his horse and rode away. Old woman Wang immediately brought the letter to Jinlian's back door. She and Ximen Qing were not yet up; they had spent half the night in amorous combat.

"Get up, Master and Mistress," the old woman cried, "here is news for you. Wu Song has sent a soldier with a letter for his brother to say he is coming back shortly. I took the letter and sent the soldier about his business, but you will have to do something about it, and not waste any time."

Ximen Qing was feeling perfectly contented with life, but, when he heard this news, it seemed to him that the eight pieces of his skull had fallen apart and somebody was pouring a great jar of ice and snow through the opening. He and Jinlian quickly leapt out of bed, threw their clothes on, and asked the old woman to come in. She gave the letter to Ximen Qing to read. It only said that Wu Song would be back not later than the Autumn Day, but this was enough to make the lovers beside themselves with anxiety.

"What shall we do, Stepmother?" they cried. "If you can only think of some way out for us, we shall be so grateful that we shall find a splendid reward for you. We are so fond of one another that we cannot bear to be apart. But, if Wu Song comes back, we shall be obliged to separate, and life won't be worth living."

"Sir," said the old woman, "why all this to-do? I told you once before that first marriages were arranged for people by their parents, but that second marriages are the concern of no one but the parties themselves. Nobody has ever suggested that a man and his brother's wife belong to the same family. Wu Da has been dead a hundred days or so. Lady, you must ask a few monks to come and burn his tablet before Wu Song comes back. Then you, Sir, must send a sedan chair and take her into your establishment. When Wu Song does come back, I will have a word with him, and what is there he can do? You will be able to spend all your lives together. Isn't that good enough for you?"

"You are right, Stepmother," Ximen Qing said. He and Jinlian breakfasted together, and it was decided that on the sixth day of the eighth month there should be a final requiem for Wu Da, when they would send for monks and have the tablet burned. Two days later Ximen Qing would take Jinlian into his own household. When all these arrangements had been made, Daian came with a horse and Ximen went home.

Time sped like an arrow in flight. The sun and moon crossed and recrossed like a weaver's shuttles. It was the sixth day of the eighth month. Ximen Qing brought several taels of silver to Wu Da's house, and told old woman Wang to go to the Temple of Eternal Felicity and ask six monks to come and sing a dirge for Wu Da and to burn his tablet the same evening. Before it was fully light the temple attendants came with their sacred books and instruments. They set up a lectern and hung their pictures all around, and old woman Wang in the kitchen helped the cooks to prepare vegetarian food. Ximen Qing spent the whole day there. Soon the monks arrived, tinkling their bells and beating their drums. They read their sacred books and intoned their exorcisms.

Jinlian would perform none of the due purifications. She slept with Ximen Qing till the sun was high in the heavens, and she would not have risen then, had not the monks come to invite her to burn incense, sign the documents, and make her reverence to Buddha. Finally she dressed herself in white and went to worship Buddha.

As soon as the monks saw her, their Buddhist hearts were troubled and their Buddhist natures stimulated to a furious degree, so that their passions ran away with them, and they were in such a state that they did not know what they were doing.

> The precentor lost his wits and, as he read the sacred books
> Knew not if they were upside down.
> The holy priests went mad and read their prayers
> By no means sure what line they read.

The thurifer upset the vases, and the acolyte seized the incense boat
Thinking it was his candle.
The lector should have read "The Mighty Empire of Song"
But called it "Tang" instead.
The exorcist, who should have chanted "Master Wu" cried "Mistress
    Wu."
The old monk's heart so wildly beat
He missed the drum and struck the young monk's hand.
The young monk's mind was so distraught
He used the drumstick on the old monk's head.
Long patient years of novicehood were all undone
And had ten thousand saints come down to earth
It would have been no better.

Jinlian burned incense before the image of Buddha, signed the papers, and made a reverence. Then she went back to her room and began again to play with Ximen Qing. She never even dreamed of abstaining from wine or any kind of food.

"If there should be anything that requires attention," Ximen said to old woman Wang, "you attend to it, and don't let anybody come to disturb the lady."

"You young people enjoy yourselves," the old woman said, laughing. "If there is anything to be done for these shaven-headed fellows, I'll do it."

Now that the monks had seen how beautiful Wu Da's widow was, they could not put her out of their minds. When they came back again from their temple after the evening meal, Jinlian was still drinking and making merry with Ximen Qing. There was only a wooden partition between her room and the temporary chapel. One of the monks had come back before the others and was washing his hands in a basin outside the window of her room when he heard soft whisperings and gentle murmurings that left him in little doubt about what was going on. He stopped washing his hands and stood still to listen. He heard Jinlian say, "Sweetheart, how long will you continue? The monks will be back soon and they may hear us. Do let me go. We must finish."

"Don't be in a hurry," Ximen's voice said. "I should like to 'set the cover on fire' just once more." It never occurred to them that there was a monk listening to every word they said.

Then all the monks came back, and they began to make music and intone their orisons. One told another, till there was none who did not know that Wu Da's widow was entertaining her lover in the house. They waved their arms and feet wildly without the slightest idea of what they were doing. Thus were the Buddhist services performed, and thus, this night, they sped Wu Da's spirit on its lonely journey.

Jinlian took off her mourning robes, dressed herself beautifully, and came to stand with Ximen Qing behind the lattice. They watched the monks preparing to burn the tablet and old woman Wang carrying water and fire. At last the tablet and the Buddhist pictures were completely consumed.

Thievish shaven-heads peered with cold eyes through the lattice. A man and a woman standing shoulder to shoulder could vaguely be seen. This brought to their minds the remembrance of what had happened before, and they struck their instruments discordantly. An old monk's hat was blown off by the wind and his bluish bald pate appeared. He did not pick up his hat, but went on thumping his instrument and roaring with laughter. Old woman Wang called, "Reverend Fathers, you have finished your service. Why do you beat your instruments any longer?"

"We haven't set fire to the cover of a paper stove yet," one of the monks cried. Ximen Qing heard this, and told the old woman to give them their fee and send them packing, but the old monk insisted that they must see the lady first and thank her.

"Please tell them that is quite unnecessary," Jinlian said, but the monks answered with one voice, "Do let us go." Then, roaring with laughter, they all went off.

# Chapter 9
# Wu Song Seeks to Avenge His Brother

So Ximen Qing and Pan Jinlian burned Wu Da's tablet. The next day they invited old woman Wang to a farewell party, and gave Ying'er into her charge.

"When Wu Song comes back," Ximen Qing said, "how am I to prevent his learning that I have married this lady?"

"I shall be here," the old woman said, smiling, "and no matter how inquisitive Wu Song may be, I shall have an answer ready for him. Don't worry about that."

Ximen Qing was only too glad to receive such a comforting reply, and gave the old woman three taels of silver. The same evening he took all Jinlian's belongings to his own house; the furniture and clothes were given to old woman Wang. The next day he sent a sedan chair with four lanterns, and Jinlian in her best clothes seated herself in it. Old woman Wang went with her as though she represented the bride's family, and Daian acted as escort. So Jinlian went to her new home. Everybody in the neighborhood knew what was happening, but people feared the rich and powerful Ximen Qing, and nobody dared to interfere. But someone composed a little poem in honor of the occasion.

Ximen Qing received his new bride, and had an apartment of three rooms set aside for her in the garden. There was a small gate in one of the corners of the courtyard, easily overlooked for it was hidden by flowers and flowerpots. Few people came that way. It was very secluded. One of the three rooms was furnished as a sitting room, and one as a bedroom. Ximen paid sixteen taels of silver for a bed of black lacquer and gilt with a crimson silk net. The chairs and tables were beautifully carved, and everything was arranged with excellent taste.

Wu Yueniang had two maids, Chunmei and Yuxiao. Ximen Qing directed that Chunmei should act as maid to his new wife, and paid five taels for a little girl called Xiaoyu to take her place with the Great Lady. For another six taels he bought a maid called Qiuju and gave her to Jinlian as a kitchen maid.

Ximen Qing's first wife, Chen, had brought with her a servant called Sun Xue'e. She was now about twenty years old, fairly tall and not bad-looking. Ximen had allowed her to assume the position of his fourth wife, so that Jinlian ranked as the fifth of his ladies.

Now that Jinlian was actually established in his own house, Ximen spent every night with her. They played together as merrily as fishes in water, and nothing could have surpassed their pleasure in each other. On the day after her arrival Jinlian put on her finest clothes and, when Chunmei had served her with tea, went to Wu Yueniang's room to make the acquaintance of the other members of the household. She took with her as a present a pair of shoes. Yueniang sat in her place as mistress of the house, and looked closely at the new bride. She was about twenty-five years old, and very beautiful.

Yueniang looked at her from her head to her feet; every inch of that exquisite body seemed endowed with the power of fascination. She looked at her from her feet to her head; this extraordinary charm seemed to issue from her as water from a fountain. She was like a translucent pearl lying on a crystal dish, like the early morning moon shining above the topmost branches of a pink apricot tree. Yueniang gazed at her without speaking, and she said to herself, "When the boys came home, they used to say, 'How strange that Wu Da should have so beautiful a wife.' I have never seen anyone so beautiful. No wonder that brave husband of mine fell in love with her."

Jinlian kowtowed to Yueniang, and offered her a present. When the Great Lady had acknowledged her reverence, she turned to Li Jiao'er, Meng Yulou, and Sun Xue'e, and greeted them as sisters. Then she stood till Yueniang bade a maid give her a chair and speak to her as the Fifth Lady.

Jinlian sat down and secretly considered her new sisters. Yueniang was about twenty-seven years old; her face was as beautiful as a bowl of silver and her eyes were like the kernel of an apricot. Her manner was gentle and her speech careful. Li Jiao'er, who had been a singing girl at the bawdy house, was inclined to be corpulent and not so attractive. Though she had been a famous strumpet, her skill in the arts of love was not to be compared with that of Jinlian. Yulou was about thirty years old. Her face was like the pear blossom, and her waist as slender as the willow. She was tall, and her oval face was marked by a few slight scars. But she was very beautiful, and it would have been difficult to say whether the tiny feet that peeped from beneath her skirt were larger or smaller than those of Jinlian herself. Xue'e had been a maid; she was not very tall and her manner was sharp. But there was no kind of soup she could not make and her skill with dishes and plates was almost miraculous.

In a very short time Jinlian had made herself acquainted with the characteristic features of her companions.

When the first three days were over, she rose early every morning and, as soon as she was dressed, went to Yueniang's room to sew and make shoes.

She pretended to be very eager to do anything she could, moving things that did not need to be moved, calling Yueniang Great Lady, as all the maids did, and giving her little presents. This delighted Yueniang. She called Jinlian Sister, and gave her some clothes and ornaments of her own that she valued highly. They always took their meals together.

Li Jiao'er and the others became very jealous of the attentions that Yueniang paid Jinlian, and in secret had much to say about it. "We are wives of old standing," they said, "but the Great Lady cares not a whit about us. This woman has been here only a few days, and she is shown all these favors. Our eldest sister is not discreet."

Ximen Qing was now married to Jinlian, living in a splendid house and wearing the finest of clothes. So close was the attachment between this fascinating woman and her dissolute bridegroom that nothing could have separated them. Everything was as merry as could be, and Ximen Qing took advantage of the situation without ceasing.

It was the beginning of the eighth month when Wu Song reached Qinghe. First, he went to the Town Hall to give the magistrate the letters he had brought from the Eastern Capital. The magistrate was glad to know that his presents had been duly delivered. He gave Wu Song ten taels of silver and entertained him. After this, Wu Song went back to his own place, changed his clothes, put on a new hat, locked the door, and went straight to Amethyst Street. The neighbors saw that he was back and were tremendously excited, breaking into a perfect sweat. "Now the trouble will begin," they said. "This prince of the haughty spirit will not let this matter pass lightly."

Wu Song went to his brother's door and pulled up the shutter. Ying'er was sitting outside the room, making thread. He called, "Brother," but there was no reply. Then he cried, "Sister," but still there was no answer. He thought, "I must be getting deaf if I can't hear one or other of them." He spoke to Ying'er, but she was so terrified she could not utter a word.

"Where are your father and mother?" Wu Song said. Ying'er burst into tears.

Meanwhile old woman Wang had heard that he was back, and she was afraid that all would be discovered. She hurried over. When Wu Song saw her coming, he saluted.

"Where is my brother, and how is it my sister-in-law is not here?"

"Sit down, please," the old woman said, "and I will tell you. Some time during the fourth month, shortly after you had gone away, your brother was taken very ill, and died."

"When did he die? What did he die of? Who attended him?" Wu Song cried.

"About the twentieth of the fourth month your brother suddenly began to suffer from pains at the heart. After a week or so we went to make supplication to Heaven. We called in soothsayers, and got every medicine we could think of, but it was all no use. He died."

"My brother never suffered from anything of the sort before," Wu Song said. "It is a very curious thing that he should die of heart trouble so unexpectedly."

"Captain," the old woman said, "you should not say things like that. Heaven sends its storms upon us without warning, and, though we may take off our shoes and socks tonight, who can tell whether tomorrow morning we shall put them on again? Nobody can be certain that some sudden calamity will not befall him."

"When was my brother buried?" Wu Song asked.

"When your brother gave up the ghost," the old woman said, "he had not a halfpenny in the world. His wife was no better off than a crab without feet. She could never have bought a grave for him. Fortunately, one of our more wealthy neighbors, who happened to be a friend of your brother, provided a coffin, and, when Master Wu had been dead three days, we had the funeral ceremonies and cremated him."

"Where is my sister-in-law now?" Wu Song asked.

"She was a young and tender woman, with nothing to live on, so she wore her mourning for a hundred days, and then her mother persuaded her to marry some stranger who lives a long way from here. She left this troublesome little girl in my care, and said I was to give her to you when you came back. When I have done that, I shall have done all I was called upon to do."

Wu Song listened to this story, and pondered it for a while. Then he left old woman Wang. He went to his own rooms near the Town Hall and changed into white clothes. Then he told his servant to buy a hempen cord, a pair of cotton socks, and a mourning hat. He bought fruits, cakes, candles, and paper money. Returning to Wu Da's house, he prepared a new tablet, made ready soup and food, lighted the candles, set out the wine and food, and hung up all the paper offerings. By the time he had done this, it was already the first night watch.

Then Wu Song burned incense, and knelt down and said: "Brother, may your spirit draw near. When you were on earth, you were weak and feeble. Now you are dead, and I do not know the cause of your death. If you met your death at the hands of others, and your brooding spirit can find none to avenge it, send me a dream, and I will avenge you." He poured wine upon the ground, and burned all the paper money. Then he sobbed aloud. The neighbors heard him and were sorry for him, for they knew that Wu Song was brother to Wu Da.

When all was done, he gave the wine, food, and dishes to the soldiers. Then he brought two pallets, and told the soldiers to sleep in the outer room. Ying'er was asleep in the inner room, and he himself took a pallet and lay down before Wu Da's tablet. It was now midnight. He tossed over and over, unable to sleep. He could only sigh. The soldiers were sleeping as soundly as the dead. He rose, and it seemed that the lamp on the table was flickering, half light, half dark. He sat up on his pallet and said to himself, "My brother was very weak, and there is something very mysterious about his death. . . ." He had not finished this sentence when, over the table that supported his brother's tablet, there came an ice-cold wind.

> Formless and shadowless, neither mist nor smoke
> Round and round it moved,
> Like a spirit wind striking cold to the marrow,
> Gloomy and dark,
> Like the icy mist over a war-stricken land
> Chilling the flesh.
> The lamp before the tablet lost its brightness
> Sad and uncanny.
> The paper money hanging on the wall
> Whirled round and round.
> It seemed as if, within this mist, the souls of all the poisoned marched,
> Their ghostly standards fluttering in the wind.

The cold wind made Wu Song's hair stand on end. He stared at the tablet and it seemed to him that there slowly emerged the form of a man who cried, "Oh, younger brother, I died in agony." Wu Song could not distinguish the figure very clearly and would have gone forward to question it, but, as he waited, the cold mist faded away and the figure vanished.

Wu Song sank down upon the pallet. "This is truly a strange thing," he thought, "a dream yet not a dream. My brother seemed to wish to tell me something, but the vigor of my body was too much for his frail spirit. Nevertheless, I am sure there is a mystery about his death." Then he heard the watchman striking the third watch. He went to look at the soldiers, but found them fast asleep. His soul was troubled. He watched till daybreak, when the cocks began to crow and the dawn broke in the eastern sky. Then the soldiers got up and heated some water for him, and he washed his face and cleansed his mouth. Calling Ying'er, he told her to look after the house, and went off with the soldiers.

As he passed down the street, he asked all the neighbors to tell him how his brother had died, and whom his sister-in-law had married. They knew all there was to be known, of course, but they were afraid of Ximen Qing and did not wish to get mixed up in the matter. "Captain," they said, "it is no use asking us. Old woman Wang is the nearest neighbor, go and ask her. Then you will learn the truth." One of the more talkative added: "Yun'ge, the pear seller, and He the Ninth know all about it, too."

Wu Song went down the street to find Yun'ge. At last he found that young monkey carrying a basket, coming back from buying some rice. He hailed him. When the boy saw that it was Wu Song who called him, he said, "Captain Wu, you have come back too late. You will not find it easy to get to the bottom of the matter and, if you take it to the courts, there will be no one to look after my poor old father."

"Come with me," Wu Song said. He took the boy to an eating house, and ordered two bowls of rice. "Brother," he said, "you are not very old, but I see that you pay proper respect to your father. That is as it should be." He took five taels of silver from his sleeve. "Take this for the present," he said, "and when I have attended to this matter, I will give you another ten taels to set you up in business. Now, I want you to tell me who it was who quarreled with my brother, who is responsible for his death, and who has married my sister-in-law. Tell me the whole story and don't hide anything."

Yun'ge took the silver. He decided that it would be enough to supply his father's needs for three or four months, and that he need no longer be anxious about going to the law courts. "Brother," he said, "listen, but do not be impatient." Then he told the whole story from beginning to end. Wu Song listened attentively. "Is this absolutely true?" he said. "Who took my sister-in-law away?"

"Ximen Qing took your sister to his place," the boy said. "She has given herself to him absolutely. Why do you ask whether I am telling the truth?"

"It is essential that you shall not tell any lies," Wu Song said.

"What I have told you is what I shall say at the law courts," the boy replied. Wu Song called for food and, when they had finished it, he paid the reckoning and they left the shop.

"Go home and give the silver to your father," Wu Song said, "and tomorrow morning come to the Town Hall to give your evidence. Tell me, where does He the Ninth live?"

"You won't find him," the boy said, "he disappeared three days ago, as soon as he heard you had come back."

Wu Song left Yun'ge and went to his own place. The next morning, he asked Master Chen to write an accusation for him, and went to the Town Hall. Yun'ge was already waiting for him. He went into the Hall of Audience, knelt down, and presented his accusation. The magistrate recognized Wu Song at once and asked what was the accusation he wished to make.

"My brother Wu Da has been murdered by that villain Ximen Qing, who was carrying on an intrigue with my sister-in-law. First, my brother was kicked in the chest; then old woman Wang devised a plan for murdering him. After his death the undertaker He the Ninth allowed his body to be cremated without properly examining it, and now Ximen Qing has carried off my sister-in-law to be one of his concubines. This boy, Yun'ge, is here to give evidence as to the facts, and I pray your Lordship to see that justice is done."

"Why is the undertaker He the Ninth not here?" the magistrate said.

"When he knew that the secret was out he ran away," Wu Song said. "Nobody knows where he is."

The magistrate examined Yun'ge and wrote down his evidence. Then he withdrew and called together his officials. The magistrate himself, his deputy, and all the other officers were very intimate with Ximen Qing, and the case was one they did not care to decide. The magistrate came back to Wu Song and said, "You are a captain in my district, and I am surprised to find that you don't seem to know the law. In cases of alleged adultery, it has always been customary to require that the guilty pair should be caught in the act; and, in cases of murder, to insist upon direct evidence. Your brother's body has been burned, and you did not, in fact, lay hold of the adulterers. It would not be right for me to give judgment in the case simply upon the evidence of this little fellow. Think over the matter for yourself, calmly."

"Sir," Wu Song replied, "what I have told you is the simple truth, not some fantastic tale of my own imagining. I beg you to order the arrest of Ximen Qing, the woman Pan, and old woman Wang. Let the law take its ordinary course with them, and the truth will come out. If I lie, I am ready to suffer the consequences."

"Well," the magistrate said, "I must think this over. If I decide that they ought to be arrested, I will arrest them." Wu Song rose and went out, leaving Yun'ge in the court.

By this time Ximen Qing had heard what was going on. He was greatly alarmed, and at once gave large sums of money to his trusted servants, Laibao and Laiwang, and sent them to bribe the officials. The next morning, when Wu Song went to the court in the hope of persuading the magistrate to have the criminals arrested, he found that all the officials had accepted Ximen's bribes and refused to have anything to do with his accusation.

"Wu Song," one said, "don't believe busybodies who simply wish to make trouble between you and Ximen Qing. There is really no evidence in this case, and it would be impossible to give a fair judgment upon it. A wise man says: 'Things I see with my own eyes, I can hardly credit; how shall I believe what others tell me?' You must not be so impetuous."

"You work in this office," another said, "and of course you understand the law. You know all that is to be known about murders and murderers. Now, before the case can be opened, five things are essential: the corpse, the wounds, the disease, the instruments by which the crime was committed, and the traces of the crime itself. Your brother's body has already disappeared. How can we decide this case?"

"If that is how you look at it," Wu Song cried, "my brother's murder will never be avenged. It is clear that the magistrate does not intend to deal with the matter, and I must do things my own way." He took away his accusation and went back to his place, sending Yun'ge home. Then he gazed towards the heavens and sighed deeply, gnashed his teeth, and cursed his sister-in-law's wantonness. Wu Song at that moment was ferocity itself! His anger was beyond control. He set off at once for Ximen Qing's shop, with his mind made up to engage Ximen in single combat. But only Fu the manager was there.

"Is your master at home?" Wu Song said.

Fu recognized Wu Song. "No," he said, "he is not at home. Is there anything I can tell him for you, Captain?"

"I must trouble you to come here," was the only reply. Fu did not dare refuse, and went with Wu Song to a secluded place. Suddenly, Wu Song turned and caught him by the throat, glaring wildly at him.

"Do you wish to live or to die?"

"Captain," Fu cried, "I have never done you any harm. Why are you so angry?"

"If you wish to die, say nothing. If you wish to live, tell me the truth. Now, where is that fellow Ximen? When did he marry my sister-in-law? Tell me everything, and I will let you go."

Fu was a poor-spirited creature, and Wu Song's rage made him panic-stricken. "Pleas don't be so angry, Captain," he stammered; "I work in his shop and he pays me two taels a month. My business is to look after the shop, nothing else, and I have no notion how he spends his time. Truly, my master is not at home now. He and his friends have gone to a wineshop in Lion Street. I would not dare to tell you a lie."

Wu Song released Fu, and rushed off to Lion Street as though possessed of wings. Fu was so terrified that he could not move for a long time. While Wu Song was striding towards the wineshop, Ximen Qing was drinking there with a man called Li the Merchant of Secrets. This man was one of the court runners and had a finger in the pie in all the matters that came up at the District Office. He used to find out everything that was to be found out and use the knowledge to his own advantage. If any dispute arose, he would suggest courses of action to both parties, and, if they thought of bribing the magistrate, he smoothed over any little difficulties. So he came to be called Merchant of Secrets. Today, after the magistrate had rejected Wu Song's accusation, he was reporting the matter to Ximen Qing. Ximen invited him to take wine and made him a present of five taels of silver.

They were contentedly drinking their wine when Ximen Qing happened to glance around to see what was going on in the street, and saw Wu Song, like an angry god, coming over the bridge towards the inn. He knew that Wu Song could have no peaceful intent, and was frightened out of his wits. He would have escaped, but could not get down the stairs in time, so he pretended he wished to change his clothes and hid himself somewhere at the back of the inn.

Wu Song came to the door and asked the waiter where Ximen was. "Master Ximen is taking wine with one of his friends upstairs." Wu Song pulled up his skirts and dashed upstairs. Ximen Qing had vanished. There was only a man sitting before a table, and a couple of singing girls on either side. Wu Song recognized the runner Li and knew that he must have been telling Ximen Qing what had happened. In a fury, he went forward and shook his fist at Li.

"You villain," he cried, "what have you done with Ximen Qing? Tell me at once or I'll give you a drubbing."

The very sight of Wu Song had terrified the runner, and, when he was spoken to so roughly, he could not get out a word in reply. Wu Song, finding that he received no answer, grew angrier and angrier, and kicked down the table. The cups and dishes were smashed. The two singing girls were so frightened that they swooned away. The runner realized that Wu Song meant him no good, and, though he did not find it easy, managed to pull himself to his feet and tried to shuffle downstairs. Wu Song pulled him back.

"I have asked you a question and you don't answer. Where do you think you're going? Be so kind as to eat one of my fists. I'll see whether you'll answer me or not." He struck Li a terrific blow in the face.

"Oh dear!" the man cried, finding his tongue at last, and agonized by the pain. "Ximen Qing has gone to the back to change his clothes. Please let me go, it has nothing to do with me."

Wu Song with both hands lifted the runner and hurled him out of the window. "If you wish to get out, there you are," he cried, and flung the merchant of secrets into the street.

Wu Song went to the back of the house to find Ximen Qing. Ximen had heard the disturbance and was in a terrible state of fright. Without giving a thought to the danger, he jumped out of the window, ran along the balcony, and found his way to somebody's courtyard. Wu Song could not find him and, thinking that Li had lied to him, he ran downstairs to where the runner was stretched out on the ground, half dead, though his eyes still moved. Wu Song kicked him twice in the guts, and he died.

"This is runner Li," the bystanders said. "What has he done to annoy you, Captain, that you should kill him like this?"

"It was Ximen Qing I was really after," Wu Song said, "and this ill-starred fellow happened to be with him. So he met his death at my hands."

The policeman saw that a man had been killed, but did not venture to take Wu Song by force. He went slowly towards him and tried to detain him by persuasion. A bond was put on the waiter and the two singing girls, and they were all taken together to the Town Hall. The news soon spread through the street and everybody was talking about it. They did not know that Ximen Qing had escaped, but thought Wu Song had killed him.

# CHAPTER 10

# The Exiling of Wu Song

Wu Song was taken by the watch to the city jail. Meanwhile Ximen Qing, who had jumped out of the wineshop window, found himself in a courtyard that belonged to old Doctor Hu. One of the maids had just gone to the privy and had lifted her skirts. Suddenly she saw a man crouching at the foot of the wall. As she could not run away, she called, "Thief! thief!" as loudly as she could, and Doctor Hu ran out to see what was the matter. He recognized Ximen Qing, and said:

"My Lord, I must congratulate you on your escape from Wu Song. He has killed a man, and they have taken him to the lockup. But you may go home now, Sir, I don't think there is likely to be any more trouble."

Ximen thanked the doctor, and went home with all the assurance in the world. He told Pan Jinlian what had happened, and they clapped their hands with delight to think that all their troubles were now over. Jinlian advised Ximen to send bribes to all the officials, so that they might make sure that Wu Song would be sentenced to death, for they by no means desired to set eyes on him again. Ximen Qing called his servant Laiwang, and told him to take the magistrate a set of gold and silver drinking cups, with fifty taels of silver, and sums of money for all the other officials, both great and small, and to ask that Wu Song should be punished with all the rigor of the law. The magistrate accepted the bribe and, the next morning, as soon as he entered the Hall of Audience, had Wu Song brought before him, with the waiter and the two singing girls. His manner had now completely changed.

"Wu Song," he said, "you are a desperate fellow and have brought accusations against perfectly innocent people. I have overlooked this more than once. Now you yourself have killed a man, without the slightest cause. Why don't you obey the laws?"

"My quarrel was really with Ximen Qing," Wu Song said, "but, as ill luck would have it, I met this man. He refused to tell me where Ximen Qing was, and I lost my temper and killed him. My Lord, I implore you to give me justice, and bring Ximen Qing to answer to the law for my brother's death. As for myself, I am ready to give my life for this dead man's."

"You are talking nonsense," the magistrate cried. "Do you mean to say you did not know he was an officer of this court? You must certainly have had some other reason for killing him. Why do you try to drag Ximen Qing into the matter? I can see that I shall never get the truth out of you without a beating."

He ordered his attendants to punish Wu Song. Three or four of them pulled him down and gave him twenty strokes of the rod, like drops of rain falling. Wu Song continued to insist that he was being unjustly dealt with. "I have done much for you," he cried, "and you should deal with me accordingly and not have me beaten so severely."

This only made the magistrate more angry. "You killed a man with your fist," he cried. "Now your boldness seems to have gone into your mouth." He ordered the thumbscrews to be put on, and Wu Song's fingers were pressed and his hands beaten fifty times, after which a cangue was put about his neck and he was returned to prison.

Some of the officers had been Wu Song's friends and knew that he was a man who had taken upon himself to avenge another's quarrel. They would have liked to clear him, but, as they had accepted Ximen Qing's bribes, their mouths were sealed and they were unable to do anything. As Wu Song persisted in demanding justice, the magistrate waited a few days and then drew up a dossier without hearing any evidence. All he did was to appoint an officer to go to Lion Street to examine Li's body and fill in the necessary particulars. Then the crime sheet was drawn up as follows:

> The accused Wu Song called to see Li, and there was a dispute with regard to the division of certain moneys. The parties became drunk and began to fight. The deceased was kicked and beaten and thrown from a high place. Green and red marks were found on his left side, his face, ribs, and groin.

After completing their examination, the officials went back to the office, and a document was drawn up to be sent with Wu Song to the Prefect of Dongping, where the matter would have to be further investigated and the final judgment made.

The Prefect of Dongping, His Excellency Chen Wenzhao, was a native of Henan and an official of exceptional probity. As soon as the documents were brought to him, he began the hearing of the case.

Chen Wenzhao went to his court and ordered everyone to be brought before him. He read through all the documents that had come from Qinghe and examined the depositions. The indictment said:

## PREFECTURE OF DONGPING DISTRICT OF QINGHE
### An Indictment

The accused Wu Song is twenty-eight years of age, formerly domiciled in the District of Yanggu. On account of his splendid physique he was appointed Captain of the Police in this District.

After returning to this District from a tour of duty, the accused visited his brother's tomb. He ascertained that his sister-in-law had not observed the required period of mourning, but had remarried. The same day he inquired from people in the streets concerning the matter, and ultimately proceeded to a wineshop in Lion Street, where he met Li Waichuan. Being drunk, he endeavored to recover the sum of three hundred cash that he alleged Li had previously borrowed from him, but Li refused to pay the money and the two men fought. Li was struck and kicked, and so severely injured that he died shortly afterwards.

In proof whereof the singing girls Niu and Bao are witnesses.

The watch arrested Wu Song, and officers deputed for that purpose proceeded to the place where Li's body lay and made a careful examination. We then heard Wu Song and prepared the accompanying depositions. We trust that upon further investigation you will find the particulars to be correct.

It is our submission that Wu Song fought with and killed the man, and that he should be executed in accordance with the law for the capital offense, not for fighting or the dispute over money. The waiter Wang, and the two girls Niu and Bao, appear to be guiltless in the matter, and we only await your permission to release them.

Dated this eighth day of the eighth month of the third year of Zhenghe:

>Li Dadian, *Magistrate*
>Luo He'an, *Deputy Magistrate*
>Hua Helu, *Keeper of the Archives*
>Xia Gongji, *Prosecutor*
>Qian Lao, *Chief Jailer*

When the Prefect had read this document, he asked Wu Song how he had come to kill Li Waichuan. Wu Song kowtowed.

"My Lord of the Blue Heavens," he said, "I trust that, in your court, justice may be done. If you will allow me to speak, I will tell the truth about the matter."

"Say on," the Prefect ordered.

Wu Song told him the whole story, not omitting a single detail, from Ximen Qing's seduction of Jinlian to the rejection of his accusation at the

Qinghe court. He ended by saying: "I wished only to avenge my brother, and it was Ximen Qing of whom I was in search. Unhappily, I did kill this man, but the fault is not mine alone. Ximen Qing is very rich, and the officers did not dare to arrest him. I am not afraid of death. My sole desire is to avenge my murdered brother, whose remains lie in the tomb awaiting vengeance."

"I understand the case," the Prefect said. "That will do for the present." He called forward Qian Lao and ordered him to be given twenty strokes. "Your magistrate does not seem to know how to perform his duties. He should not allow himself to be moved by personal interest and sell justice in this way."

Again he questioned Wu Song, and amended the indictment that had come from Qinghe. Finally he said to his officers: "This fellow was anxious to avenge his brother and killed this man more or less accidentally. He seems a good man and he ought not to be treated like a common criminal." He gave orders that the cangue should be removed from Wu Song's neck and a lighter one put in its place, and that he should be detained in the prison. The rest of the party were sent back to Qinghe with instructions to the magistrate that Ximen Qing, Jinlian, old woman Wang, Yun'ge, and He the Ninth should be sent to the Prefect to be examined. When all this had been done, the Prefect said, he would send forward the documents to the Imperial Court.

Wu Song was still in prison, but the officials soon found what a good fellow he was, and sent him wine and food without taking anything in return. The news reached Qinghe and, when Ximen Qing heard it, he was greatly alarmed. He knew that Chen Wenzhao was incorruptible, and did not dare to try to bribe him, but he decided to send word to his relative Chen and ask for help. He told Laiwang to go to the Eastern Capital in all haste with a letter to Marshal Yang, the Provincial Commander-in-Chief, begging him to use all his influence with the Imperial Tutor Cai. When Cai heard of the matter he was afraid that the magistrate Li would suffer, so he secretly wrote to the Prefect of Dongping asking him not to proceed with the examination of Ximen Qing and Jinlian. Now Chen Wenzhao had been the chief magistrate of Dalisi before he had been appointed to the Prefecture of Dongping. He had been befriended by Cai, and knew that Marshal Yang was in high favor at court. He finally decided that the best thing he could do was to settle the matter without injury to either side.

He reprieved Wu Song, but ordered him to be given forty strokes, branded, and banished two thousand li. In Wu Da's case, it was declared that, as the body had been burned, the matter must be considered closed. The others were ordered to be sent home. This was all duly written down, and the documents sent, first to the Provincial Office, then to the Court. They were returned by the higher authorities with orders that the Prefect's proposals should be put into execution. Chen Wenzhao took Wu Song from the jail, read over the papers in the case, gave him forty strokes, and set a cangue upon him. Two columns of characters were branded on his face, and he was ordered to leave for Mengzhou in the charge of two officials, who took the document with them. Then the other parties in the case were dismissed.

That day Wu Song, in the charge of two officers of the court, left the prefecture of Dongping for Qinghe. There, he sold all his furniture and gave the money to the officers, and asked one of his neighbors, named Yao, to look after Ying'er. "If His Majesty pardons me," he said, "I will pay you back. I can never forget your kindness."

Wu Song's neighbors knew well that he was a good man in misfortune, and they gave him, some silver, some a little wine; others offered food, money, and rice. He went once again to his own rooms and got a soldier to bring his personal belongings, and the next day they set off from Qinghe along the high road for Mengzhou.

When Ximen Qing heard that Wu Song had really started for Mengzhou, he felt secure at last. The canker that had ravaged his heart so long was now removed, and he felt completely at ease. He gave orders to Laiwang, Lai Po, and Laixing to make preparations in the garden. They set up folding screens and arranged embroidered hangings in the Hibiscus Arbor; a banquet was prepared, and a band of musicians engaged to sing and dance. Yueniang and the other ladies enjoyed the repast, and menservants, serving women, and maids waited upon them.

> Incense was burned in precious censers, and flowers set out in golden
>     vases
> Treasures from Xiangzhou in all their glory.
> When the lattice was raised, the shining pearls from He Pu gleamed.
> Flame-like dates and pears from Jiao heaped on crystal dishes
> Cups of green jade filled with a precious juice, a liquid jade.
> Of roasted dragon's liver, of fried phoenix giblets, one chopstick's load
>     was worth ten thousand pence.
> The palms of black bears, the hooves of purple camels
> Mingled their sweet savor with the wine's, filling the air.
> Then were ground the phoenix balls of tea,
> And a small clear wave rose in the white jade cups.
> As the precious liquid was outpoured, there came fragrance from the
>     golden jar.
> The lord Meng Chang was now outdone
> The wealth of Shi Chong rivaled.

Ximen Qing and Yueniang sat in the place of honor, and the other ladies arranged themselves according to their position in the household. As they passed the cups from one to the other, they seemed as full of grace as the flowers of a posy or the pattern upon a piece of brocade.

They were drinking when Daian brought in a boy and a young maid of great beauty, whose hair was dressed in a fringe upon her brows. She was carrying two boxes.

"Our neighbors the Huas," Daian said, "have sent some flowers for the ladies."

The maid came before Ximen and Yueniang, kowtowed to them, and said, "My mistress has sent me with this box of cakes and these flowers for you." Yueniang opened the boxes. One contained pastries, some of which were stuffed with fruit, and others with peppers. They were like those made in the Imperial palaces. The other box contained freshly picked lilies. She was greatly pleased, and told the little girl to thank her mistress. After giving them something to eat, she presented the girl with a handkerchief and the boy with a hundred coins.

"Tell your Mistress," she said, "that I am most grateful to her." She asked the little girl her name.

"I am called Yingchun, and this boy is Tian Fu." Then they both withdrew.

"Mistress Hua is really very kind," Yueniang said to Ximen Qing. "She is always sending her servants with something or other for us, and I have never made her any return."

"Brother Hua married the lady two years ago," Ximen said. "He himself told me what a sweet disposition she has, but that is clearly to be seen from the excellence of her maid."

"I saw her once," Yueniang said, "at her father-in-law's funeral. She is moderately tall and has a round face. She has two delicately arched eyebrows and a very clear skin. She certainly seems very gentle, and still quite young, not more than twenty-four or twenty-five, I should think."

"You may not know," Ximen said, "that before she married Hua, she was one of the second ladies of Minister Liang. She brought Hua a very good fortune."

"Well, she has sent us these two boxes," Yueniang said, "and we must not be less courteous than she is. I will send her something in return tomorrow."

The family name of Hua Zixu's wife was Li. She was born on the fifteenth day of the first month, and on that day somebody had sent the family a pair of fish-shaped vases. She was given the name of Li Ping'er. She had once been the concubine of Minister Liang of the Prefecture of Daming, a son-in-law of the Imperial Tutor Cai. His wife was a very jealous woman, and had made an end of several maids and concubines, and buried their bodies in the garden. So Li Ping'er had to live hidden away in his study, with an old woman to wait on her.

On the fifteenth of the first month in the third year of Zhenghe, Minister Liang and his wife were in the Green Jade Pavilion, when the whole family except Li Ping'er and her servant were murdered by Li Kui. They succeeded in escaping, Li Ping'er taking with her a hundred large pearls and a pair of jewels as black as a raven's wings. They went to the Eastern Capital in the hope of finding some relatives there. At that time Eunuch Hua, one of the Imperial Chamberlains, had just been appointed to the Governorship of Guangnan. His nephew Hua Zixu was unmarried, so the eunuch secured the services of a go-between and arranged a marriage between his nephew and the woman. The eunuch went to Guangnan and they with him, but they had not been there very long before old Hua fell ill, had to resign his appointment, and go home again. His home was in the district of Qinghe. Then he died, and all his property came to his nephew. Every day this gentleman and his friends frequented the bawdy houses, and he had become a member of the brotherhood that Ximen Qing had founded.

With Ying Bojue, Xie Xida, and the rest, he amused himself with singing girls, and they were all most intimate. It was well known that he was a nephew of one of the Imperial Chamberlains and very free with his money, and his friends were always dragging him away to the bawdy house. Often he did not return for three or four nights at a time.

Ximen Qing and his ladies made merry in the Hibiscus Arbor. They drank till it was late, and then went to their own apartments. Ximen Qing went to Jinlian's room. He was already half drunk, and soon wished to enjoy the delights of love with his new lady. Jinlian hastily burned incense, and they took off their clothes and went to bed. But Ximen Qing would not allow her to go too fast. He knew that she played the flute exquisitely. He sat down behind the curtains of the bed, and set her before him. Then Jinlian daintily pushed back the golden bracelets from her wrists and stimulated his penis with her lips, while he leaned forward to enjoy the delight of her movements. She continued for a long time, and all the while his delight grew greater. He called Chunmei to bring in some tea. Jinlian was afraid that her maid would see her, and hastily pulled down the bed curtains.

"What are you afraid of?" Ximen said. "Our neighbor Hua has two excellent maids. One of them, the younger, brought us those flowers today, but there is another about as old as Chunmei. Brother Hua has already taken her virginity. Indeed wherever her mistress is, she is too. She is really very pretty, and of course no one can tell what a man like Brother Hua may do in the privacy of his own home."

Jinlian looked at him.

"You are a strange creature, but I will not scold you," she said. "If you wish to have this girl, have her and be done with it. Why go beating about the bush, pointing at a mountain when you really are thinking about something quite different. I know you would like to have somebody else to compare with me, but I am not jealous. She is not actually my maid. Tomorrow, I will go to the garden to rest for a while, and that will give you a chance. You can call her into this room and do what you like with her. Will that satisfy you?"

Ximen Qing was delighted. "You understand me so well!" he said. "How can I help loving you?" So these two agreed, and their delight in each other and in their love could not have been greater. After she had played the flute, they kissed each other, and went to sleep.

The next day Jinlian went to the apartments of Yulou, and Ximen Qing called Chunmei to his room, and had his pleasure of her.

From that day, Jinlian showered favors on this girl. She would not allow her to go and wait at the kitchen, but kept her to attend to her bedroom, and serve her with tea. She chose beautiful clothes and ornaments for her, and bound her feet very tightly.

Chunmei was a very different kind of girl from Qiuju. She was extremely intelligent and full of fun, and she had a pretty skill with her tongue, besides being very beautiful. Ximen Qing found her irresistible. Qiuju, on the other hand, was both simple and stupid: Jinlian was always punishing her.

# Chapter II
# Li Guijie, the Singing Girl

Pan Jinlian, now settled in her new home and confident of Ximen's favor, grew more and more arrogant, and made so much trouble that the whole place was in a turmoil. She was suspicious too, and spent much time listening at doors and peeping through windows.

Chunmei was not a model of patience. One day she had been doing some trifling thing for her mistress, and Jinlian found fault with her about it. She could not vent her bad temper upon her own mistress, so she went to the kitchen and there began to thump the table and knock the chairs about. Sun Xue'e did not appreciate such behavior, so she said:

"You strange creature, if you are so anxious to find a husband, kindly try some other place. Why come here to display your nasty temper?"

Chunmei was already very angry, and this made her even more furious. "Who is the wretch who accuses me of wanting a man?" she cried.

It was quite clear that she was in a very bad temper, and Xue'e pretended not to hear her. Chunmei, however, continued in the same strain, and finally went to the front court where, with a few additions of her own, she related the story to Jinlian, to annoy her. "She says you asked his Lordship to have me so that we could try to keep him all to ourselves."

Jinlian was herself in the worst of moods. She had been obliged to get up very early to help Yueniang to dress for a funeral. She was tired, and decided to lie down for a while. When she awoke, she went to the arbor and there met Meng Yulou, who looked as charming as ever.

"Why are you looking so miserable, Sister?" Yulou said.

"Don't ask me," Jinlian said, "I had to get up very early, and I am tired. Where have you been?"

"I have just come from the kitchen."

"And what did you hear there?"

"I didn't hear anything."

Jinlian hated Xue'e, but she said nothing to Yulou. They sewed for a while in the arbor. Chunmei brought them tea and, after it, they wearied of their work and set out a chess table. Then Qintong came and told them that Ximen Qing had returned. Before they had time to clear their game away, he came through the garden gate.

The two women were wearing white silk hairnets, and their hair peeped out beneath. They had black jeweled earrings, and, in their white silk dresses, red bodices, embroidered skirts, and little red shoes, so tiny, arched, and tapering, they looked like figures carved in jade. Ximen Qing smiled at them.

"You are like a pair of singing girls," he said. "You must be worth a few hundred taels of silver."

"We are not singing girls," Jinlian said, "but if you want one you will find one in the back court."

Yulou was going to leave them, but Ximen Qing pulled her back. "Where are you going?" he said. "The moment I come in, you try to run away. Tell me, what do you do when I'm not here?"

"We were both feeling very miserable," Jinlian said, "so we came here to have a game. We don't play tricks behind your back, but we didn't expect you so early." She took his cloak. "The funeral was soon over," she said.

"There were many court officials at the temple, and it was so hot I couldn't stand it any longer. That is why I am home so early."

Yulou asked if Yueniang had come back, and Ximen said that he had come away before her, and had sent two boys to meet her. "I see you are playing chess," he said, sitting down. "What is the stake?"

"We are playing for love," Jinlian said. "Why should we have a stake?"

"I will play you both in turn," said Ximen, "and the loser shall spend a tael of silver, and treat us."

"We have no money," Jinlian said.

"Well, if you have no money, take one of your hairpins and pawn it with me. That will do."

The chessmen were set up, and Ximen Qing played against Jinlian. She was beaten, but, as soon as Ximen began to count the pieces, she jumbled them all together and ran away to a rock garden where there were many flowers, and pretended to be gathering them.

"Here, little oily mouth," Ximen Qing cried, and ran after her, "you lose, and then you run away." Jinlian laughed at him.

"You wonderful creature," she cried, "it was Yulou you beat, go and bother her instead of coming and plaguing me."

She had some flowers in her hand and, pulling them to pieces, she threw them at him. Ximen Qing went up to her and, taking her in his arms, set her down upon the rock garden, and gave her some sweets from his own mouth. They were amusing themselves in this way when Yulou came up. She told them that Yueniang had returned, and asked Jinlian to go with her to the back court that they might greet her. Jinlian left Ximen Qing, and, as she went, she called out, "Young man, I shall have something to tell you when I come back." She and Yulou then went to make their reverence before the mistress of the house.

"What are you laughing about?" Yueniang said.

"The Fifth Lady has been having a game of chess with Father," Yulou said. "She lost a tael of silver to him. Tomorrow, she is going to give a party. Of course, you must come."

Yueniang smiled. Jinlian stayed only a few moments, and then went back to the front court to Ximen Qing. She told Chunmei to burn incense in her room and to prepare the bath, that they might enjoy the pleasures of fishes in the water that evening.

Yueniang was the first wife, but she was always ill, and could not take her proper place in the management of all the household affairs. Engagements with friends and relatives and all the financial business of the household were attended to by Li Jiao'er. Xue'e acted as housekeeper and attended to the preparation of meals in the kitchen for the whole family. Wherever Ximen Qing happened to be spending the night, if he wished for anything, Xue'e would get it ready, and the maid of the lady with whom he was staying would go to the kitchen for it.

That night Ximen Qing slept in Jinlian's room. They drank wine, took a bath, and went to bed. The next morning it soon became apparent that trouble was brewing. Ximen Qing had promised Jinlian that he would go to the temple and buy a jeweled ornament for her hair. He got up very early and asked for some lotus cakes and soup. He told Chunmei to go to the kitchen for them, but Chunmei did not move.

"Just as well not tell her to go," Jinlian said. "Someone has said that I allow her liberties so that she and I may keep you all for ourselves. They called us all the nasty names they could think of. It will be much better not to send her."

"Who said such a thing? Tell me," Ximen Qing said.

"I shall not tell you," Jinlian said. "The basins and jars in this house have a way of hearing things. Just don't send her, that's all. Tell Qiuju to go."

Ximen Qing told Qiuju to go to the kitchen and tell Xue'e what he wanted. A very long time passed. Jinlian set the table, but there was no sign of food, and Ximen Qing grew more and more angry. Jinlian told Chunmei to go and find her fellow maid. "Go and see what that slave is doing. She doesn't seem to be coming; she must have taken root there." Chunmei went angrily to the kitchen and found Qiuju still waiting for the food.

"You thievish slave," she cried, "mother is going to take your trousers down. Why have you been all this time? Father is all ready to go to the temple, and he wants his cakes. He is in a terrible temper, and has sent me to fetch you."

Xue'e was greatly annoyed. "You marvelous little whore," she cried, "you behave like a Mohammedan Ma keeping a feast day. You think that if you want anything, you have only to run over here for it. I assure you the pans are made of iron, and things take time to cook. I made some gruel, and he won't eat it. Now he must have something new, cakes and soups and so on. I should like to know who is the worm at work in his belly."

This was too much for Chunmei. "Don't you begin any of your indecencies," she cried. "If Father hadn't sent me, I shouldn't be here. Are you going to get it ready or are you not? We will go and see what the master of the house has to say about it." She took Qiuju by the ear, and set off with her to the front court.

"Mistress and slave are far too insolent," Xue'e shouted after her, "but my time will come."

"Time or no time," Chunmei said, "we shall see what happens." She rushed off in a terrible temper.

Jinlian saw her pulling Qiuju along, and noticed that her face was very pale. She asked what was the matter.

"Ask her," Chunmei said. "When I got to the kitchen, she was acting the lady in there, waiting while they slowly stirred the flour. I just said a single sentence: 'Father is waiting, and Mother wants to know why you have not returned.' The one who lives in that little place cursed me in every way she could think of, as if I were a slave. She said Father is like some Mohammedan Ma, who thinks everyone's as devout as he is. She supposed Father had to ask permission from somebody or other before he could have anything to eat. She said they had made gruel for him, and then he has to have soup and cakes. She cursed everybody in the kitchen and would not do a thing."

"I told you so," Jinlian cried. "I told you not to make her go there, or somebody would make trouble with her, and say that we are always monopolizing you, and overwhelm us with insults."

Ximen Qing flew into a rage. He went to the kitchen and, without waiting to hear any explanation, kicked Xue'e several times.

"You crooked, thievish bone," he cried, "I told that maid to come here and ask for some cakes. What right had you to curse her? You called her a slave; but if you want to see a slave you'd better piddle and look at your own image in the pool you make."

Xue'e had to suffer Ximen's ill-usage. She was very angry, but dared not offer any excuses. When he had left the kitchen, she said to the Beanpole, Laizhao's wife:

"You see what bad luck I'm having today. You heard all that went on this morning. I didn't say anything very terrible, but in she came like a roaring demon and created all that disturbance. Then she dragged off the other maid, and went and told his Lordship, making a mountain out of a molehill, and he came here and made all this trouble. There's no rhyme or reason in it. But I will keep my eyes open and be on the watch for them.

The mistress and the slave are both of them haughty, but one of these days they will take a false step."

Unfortunately for Xue'e, Ximen Qing heard everything she said. He went back, and struck her several blows with his fist. "You thievish slave, you strumpet," he cried, "you can't say now that you didn't insult her, for I have just heard you saying things about her." He continued to chastise the poor woman, causing her considerable pain. Then he went back to the front court. Xue'e shed many tears and sobbed loudly. Yueniang had just risen and was dressing herself. She said to Xiaoyu, "What is all that noise in the kitchen?"

"Father is going to the temple and he wished for some cakes before he left," Xiaoyu said, "but the Kitchen Lady was rude to Chunmei. Father heard about it. He kicked the Kitchen Lady several times and made her cry."

"I never heard of such a thing," Yueniang cried. "If he wants anything to eat, it is her business to make it for him as soon as she can, and be done with it. There is no reason for her to be rude to the maid."

She told Xiaoyu to go to the kitchen, stir up Xue'e and the maids, and order them to make some soup at once. They did so, and sent it to Ximen Qing. Then he set off to the temple.

Xue'e could not settle down. She went to Yueniang and told her all that had happened. While she was talking, Jinlian happened to come that way and stood outside the window to listen. She heard Xue'e say: "Why should she try to get our husband all for herself and make him do everything she wishes? It seems to me, Mother, you don't realize that this strumpet is more lustful than a woman who has half a dozen husbands. She can't bear to sleep alone even for a single night. Nobody else would ever have dreamed of making such a plot. She poisoned her husband, and now she wants to bury us alive. She has made our husband like a black-eyed chicken. He looks at us, but never gives us a thought."

"In my opinion, it is you who are in the wrong," Yueniang said. "He told the maid to come to you for some cakes, and, if you had given them to her, there would have been no trouble. There was no need for you to insult her."

"Well, I only brought more trouble upon myself," Xue'e said. "There was a time when that maid served in your part of the house. She was disobedient even in those days, and once I had to use the back of a knife upon her. You never said anything then, Mother. Why should she have become so high and mighty now that she belongs to the Fifth Lady?"

Then Xiaoyu came in and said, "The Fifth Lady is here," and a moment later Jinlian entered the room.

"Let us suppose I did murder my husband," she said, looking straight at Xue'e. "Why didn't you do something to prevent your husband from marrying me? There would have been no question then of my getting him all for myself and your nest being empty. Chunmei is not my maid. If you have anything against her, kindly tell the Great Lady, and let her return to her service. Then there will be no further trouble between you, and I shall be well out of the matter. As for the present state of affairs, there need be no difficulty about that. When he comes back, let him give me papers of divorce, and I will go away. Then, perhaps, you'll be satisfied."

"These squabbles are beyond me," Yueniang said, "you'd better both be quiet."

"Mother," Xue'e cried, "you must realize that her mouth is as the Huai River. There is not a person living who could get on with her. It is perfectly clear that she deceives our husband, but, even if she winks, she denies it the next moment. If you had your way," she added, turning to Jinlian, "you would have us all kicked out, except, perhaps, our mistress, so that you could be in sole possession."

Yueniang sat and said nothing, letting them bandy insults as they wished. Soon they began to curse each other. "You called me a slave," Xue'e cried, "but you are the genuine article and no doubt about it." At this, there was nearly a fight, but Yueniang would not allow things to go so far, and told Xiaoyu to take Xue'e to her room. Jinlian went to her own apartments, took off her beautiful dress, washed the powder from her cheeks, and pulled her dark hair about till she was hardly fit to be seen. She cried till her eyes had the color of peaches, and then lay down on the bed.

The sun was going down in the west when Ximen Qing came back from the temple with four taels of pearls. He went to Jinlian's room and asked what was the matter, but she sobbed louder than ever and demanded papers of divorce.

"From the very beginning," she cried, "I have cared nothing about your wealth. You were all I wanted. And in return you let everybody trample on me. They said I murdered my husband. If I had had no maid, there would have been no trouble. Why did you give me somebody else's maid, and then allow other people to insult her?"

Ximen Qing flew into a terrible rage. He rushed like a whirlwind to the back of the house, caught Xue'e by the hair, and thrashed her as hard as he could with a short stick until, fortunately, Yueniang came and stopped him.

"You should behave yourselves, all of you," she said. "Why do you make your master so angry?"

"You thievish, crooked bone," Ximen cried to Xue'e, "I heard you in the kitchen cursing them, yet you still try to blame other people. I don't care if I break every bone in your body."

If Jinlian had not carefully plotted the whole scheme beforehand, Ximen Qing would never have struck Xue'e that day. It was all her doing.

When he had done with Xue'e, Ximen Qing went back to Jinlian's room and gave her the pearls he had brought from the temple. Now that her husband had taken her side and vented her spite for her, there was no reason why she should remain upset, so for one loving overture on his part she repaid him tenfold. Their delight in each other grew unceasingly.

One day, it was Hua Zixu's turn to give a party in his house, next door to Ximen Qing's. There was a great feast, and all the brothers were present. Ximen Qing had another engagement, and did not arrive until the afternoon. They would not take their wine without him, and waited. When at last he came, they made reverences to one another and took their seats, with Ximen in the place of honor. Two singing girls played the lute, the cithern, and the flute.

Soon the wine had been passed three times, and the musicians had played twice. The singing girls put down their instruments, and came towards the guests. They had all the delicacy of a branch of flowers. When they had kowtowed, Ximen Qing told his servant to take two envelopes from his purse, each of which contained a small sum, and give it to them. They thanked him, and went back to their places. Then Ximen Qing said to his host, "These girls sing extraordinarily well. Who are they?" Hua said nothing, but Ying Bojue replied:

"My Lord, you have a very poor memory. Don't you remember them? The one who plays the cithern is Brother Hua's sweetheart, young Wu Yin'er. She lives in one of the back streets in the bawdy district. The one who plays the lute is the girl I told you about some time ago. Her name is Li Guijie, and she is the younger sister of Li Guiqing. One of your ladies is her aunt. It's no use pretending you don't know her."

Ximen Qing smiled. "Oh, that's who she is! I haven't seen her for about six years. I never thought of her as being grown up."

A little later the girls came to pour wine for them. Guijie pressed Ximen to drink a great deal, and murmured loving words in his ear.

"What are your mother and sister doing now?" Ximen said. "Why do they never come to see your aunt?"

"Since last year," Guijie said, "my mother has not been at all well. Even now she can hardly get about, and she has to have someone to lean upon if she wishes to walk. My sister Guiqing has taken up with a merchant from Anhui, and for some months she has been staying at the inn with him. He will not allow her to come home even for a few days, so there is no one at home but me. I have to support the household by going out day after day to sing at parties, and I'm very tired of it all. We are always thinking about coming to see Aunt, but really we never get an opportunity. Why have you not been to see us for so long, Father? It would be kind of you to send my aunt to see her sister one of these days."

Ximen Qing thought the girl very pleasant, and she talked intelligently. He soon found himself falling in love with her. "I think I shall invite one or two friends to help me take you home tonight," he said. "What do you say?"

"Don't make fun of me, Father," the girl said. "How can such noble feet as yours tread our unworthy ground?"

"I am not making fun of you," Ximen said. He took a handkerchief, a toothpick, arid a box of tea leaves from his sleeve, and gave them to her.

"When will you come?" Guijie asked. "I must tell the servant to go home, and give them a chance to get ready."

"We shall start as soon as the party is over."

Soon the wine was finished and it grew dark. Ximen Qing invited Ying Bojue and Xie Xida, and, without going home first, they went off together to Guijie's house in the bawdy district.

> A dark, deep pit is this for man's ensnarement
> Built like a prison pen, a cavern for the enticement of souls
> Like a butcher's yard, with corpses piled and laid in order.
> Here love brings death, and only money lives.
> The sign is written in great characters:
> "Here, golden brothers, would you purchase love, pray do not offer
>     silk for hairdresses.
> Before she yields her blossoms to you, Madam must have cash.
> In this house, sisters are to be had only for ready money."

Ximen Qing followed Guijie's sedan chair to her door. Guiqing opened it, and took them into the hall, and, after greeting them with due politeness, went to ask her mother to come and receive them. Soon the old procuress came, supporting herself on a stick, for she was almost paralyzed. As soon as she saw Ximen Qing, she cried, "Heavens, Sir, what wind has blown you here?"

Ximen Qing smiled. "Please forgive me, but I have been so busy, I couldn't come."

The old woman turned to Ying Bojue and Xie Xida. "Why haven't you two been here?"

"I have been busy too," Bojue said. "We have been to a party at Hua's house today, and we met Guijie there. Master Ximen and we have brought her home. But give us some wine as quickly as you like, and let us drink a cup or two and have some fun."

The old woman made the three sit down in the place of honor, and offered them tea. Meanwhile the table was laid, and wine and refreshments set out. Candles and lamps were lighted, and a plentiful repast was set before them. Guijie changed her clothes and came to sit beside them.

The two sisters, their jade wrists keeping time together, filled the golden cups. They passed the wine and sang songs.

"I have been told," Ximen said to Guiqing, "that your sister can sing songs of the South. Here are these two gentlemen. Won't you ask her to sing a song in their honor?"

"Oh, I really could not trouble her," Bojue said. "I am only basking in your reflected glory, Sir, but I shall of course clean my ears the more respectfully to hear the exquisite melody."

Guijie sat and smiled, but did not get up. Ximen Qing really wished to make a woman of her, and that was why he asked her to sing. Her old mother was experienced in such matters and saw what was in the wind.

"My sister," Guiqing said, "has always been very independent. She won't let anybody hear her sing unless she thinks fit."

Ximen Qing told Daian to take five taels of silver from his purse, and set it on the table. "This is a mere trifle," he said, "but it may suffice to buy you some powder and rouge. I will send you some pretty clothes one of these days."

Guijie jumped up and thanked him, and, telling the maid to take the present away, she prepared to sing. Now, though she was very young, she was much more seductive and clever than many another. There was no flurry or haste about her. She gently touched her silken sleeves, and swung her dainty skirts. A handkerchief, tasseled and embroidered with a design of flowers and water, hung from her sleeve.

When she had ended her song, Ximen Qing was delighted beyond all measure. He told Daian to take the horse home, and spent the night with Guijie. He had been ready enough to make a woman of this girl, and, when Ying Bojue and Xie Xida urged him to do so, he yielded to their suggestions without raising any difficulties. The next day he sent a boy home for fifty taels of silver and four sets of clothes. These were to be the present customary on such occasions. When Li Jiao'er heard the news, she was delighted, for Guijie was her niece. She gave Daian a piece of silver, and he brought the clothes to the bawdy house. There a banquet was prepared, and there was singing, dancing, and wine for three days. They were all as merry as could be. Ying Bojue and Xie Xida brought along Sun Guazui, Zhu Shinian, and Chang Zhijie, and they all offered a few coins in token of congratulation. Ximen Qing provided the silken bedclothes, and every day there was wine and food without stint. They enjoyed themselves immensely.

# Chapter 12

# Pan Jinlian Narrowly Escapes Disaster

The tree is pitiful that stands alone
Its branches fragile and its roots uncertain.
The dew may give it moisture, but the wind
Blows it to one side and the other.
There is none to raise the silken coverlet
I must sit and keep my watch from night to morning.
Sorrow has made me thin
No loving wish of yours has given me
This slender waist.

Ximen Qing was so delighted with Guijie's beauty that he stayed at the bawdy house for several days. Many times Wu Yueniang sent servants with horses to bring him back, but Guijie's family hid his hat and clothes, and would not let him go. The ladies of his own household were for once at a loss for something to do. Most of them were quite content, but Pan Jinlian was still not thirty years old, and her passions were by no means under control. Day after day, she made herself look as pretty as a jade carving, and stood at the main gate with gleaming teeth and scarlet lips, leaning upon the door and waiting for her husband to return. Not until evening did she go to her room, and there the pillow seemed deserted, and the curtains forlorn, and there was none to share the joys of her dressing table. Sleep would not come to her, and she went to the garden, walking delicately upon the flowers and moss and, when she saw the moon reflected in the water, she thought of the uncertainty of Ximen's nature, and as she watched the tortoiseshell cats enjoying each other's company, it brought only disturbance to her own sweet heart.

Qintong, the boy who had accompanied Meng Yulou when she married Ximen Qing, was now sixteen years old, and for the first time took his place in the household as a full-grown youth. He had finely arched eyebrows and eyes full of intelligence, and was indeed both clever and attractive. Ximen Qing had entrusted him with the care of the garden, and he slept every night in a small room there. Jinlian and Yulou sometimes sewed or played chess in an arbor in the garden, and at such times Qintong waited upon them attentively, and, whenever Ximen Qing was about, would come and give them warning. Jinlian liked him and often summoned him to her room and gave him wine. So morning after morning, and evening after evening, they exchanged understanding glances, and were not entirely indifferent to one another.

It was now about the seventh month and Ximen's birthday was drawing near. Yueniang was well aware of her husband's doings, and once again told Daian to take a horse and go for him. Jinlian privately wrote a note, and told the boy to give it to Ximen Qing in secret. "Tell him," she said, "that I hope it will not be long before he comes back." Daian rode off to the bawdy house, and there found all Ximen's boon companions keeping company with him, kissing the girls, and being very merry.

"What has brought you here?" Ximen Qing said, when he saw Daian. "Is there anything wrong at home?" "No," said Daian. "Well, tell your uncle Fu to collect the money that is owing, and, when I come back, I'll settle up with him."

"He has been collecting some during the last few days," the boy said, "and he is only waiting for you to come home to go through the accounts."

"Did you bring the clothes for your Aunt Guijie?"

"Yes," the boy replied, "here they are." He took a red vest and a blue skirt from a parcel, and gave them to the girl. She made a reverence to him, and called for food and wine to be given him. When he had finished, he came over to Ximen and whispered in his ear: "The Fifth Lady has given me a note for you, asking you to go home soon."

Ximen Qing was just about to take the note when Guijie saw it. She thought it was a love letter from some other girl, and made a dash for it. When she opened it, she found a sheet of patterned paper, with several columns written in black ink, and handed it to Zhu Shinian, asking him to read it for her.

> I think of him as evening falls; I think of him when the sky is bright.
> I think about my lover till my thoughts overwhelm me, and I faint
> Yet still he does not come.
> For him I am wounded; for him my spirit faints.
> Oh, it is sad.
> I lie alone under the figured coverlets; the flickering lamp is nearly out.
> The world is sleeping, and the moonbeams creep across the window.
> That heart is unrelenting, like a wolf's
> How can I bear this agony another night?

Guijie listened to this, then left them and went to her room, where she threw herself face downwards on the bed. Ximen Qing saw that she was upset, tore the note to pieces, and kicked Daian. Twice he implored Guijie to come back, but she paid no heed. Finally, getting more and more excited, he went to her room and carried her out.

"Get on your horse and go home," he said to Daian. "As for the strumpet who told you to come, when I get home, I'll beat her till she comes to a disgusting end." Daian went home with tears in his eyes. "Please don't be so angry," Ximen said, "it is only from my fifth wife. She wants me to go home to talk about something or other. There is nothing else."

Zhu Shinian teased them. "Don't believe him, Guijie. He is deceiving you. Jinlian is his latest flame, a very pretty girl too. Don't let him go."

Ximen Qing slapped him. "You ruffian! You'll be the death of somebody with these silly jokes of yours. She is angry enough without your talking rubbish."

"Brother," Guiqing said, "you are not fair. If you were a good husband, you would not run about teaching singing girls the arts of love, you should stay at home. Then all would be well. Why, you've only been here a few hours, and now you're getting ready to go away again."

"That's quite true," Bojue said. "You had better take my advice, both of you. Your Lordship must stay here, and you, Guijie, must not lose your temper. The first person to leave will have to spend a couple of taels and treat the rest of us."

Ximen Qing took Guijie on his knee, and they drank together happily. Soon afterwards seven cups of the most delicious tea were brought and handed around.

"Now we'll have a song from everyone who can sing," Xie Xida said. "He who can't sing must tell a funny story, and we'll persuade Guijie to take a little more wine with us. I'll begin."

"Once, a bricklayer was doing some paving in a house, and the lady of the house treated him shabbily. So he quietly took a brick or two and stopped up the drain. Not very long afterwards it began to rain and, of course, the water flooded the whole place. The woman didn't know what on earth to do, and ran to find the bricklayer. This time she gave him a meal, and offered him some money, and got him to make the water flow again. When he had eaten his fill, he went to the gutter, took the bricks out, and the water flowed away at once. "What was the matter with it?" the lady of the house asked him. "Just what is the matter with you," the bricklayer replied. "If there is any money about, the water gate will open; but, if not, there will be no admission."

Guijie thought that this story was aimed at her, and she lost no time before retaliating.

"I should like to tell you a story," she said. "Once upon a time, Sun, the Immortal, thought he would give a banquet to his friends, and sent his tiger around to invite them. As ill luck would have it, the tiger gobbled them all up on the way. The Immortal waited until it was dark, but nobody came. At last the tiger came back. 'Where are my guests?' the Immortal said. 'Master,' said the tiger, 'I fear I am not a success at inviting people. Somehow I seem much better at eating them up.' "

This did not please the brothers at all. "Oh, indeed," Ying Bojue said, "so we are always sponging, are we?" He took a small silver pin from his hair. Xie Xida found in his hat a pair of gilt rings of no great value. Zhu Shinian took from his sleeve a tattered old handkerchief worth a pittance. Sun Guazui took a white apron from around his waist. Chang Zhijie had nothing, so he borrowed a small piece of silver from Ximen Qing. They handed all these things to Guiqing, and asked her to provide a feast in honor of Ximen Qing and Guijie. She turned them over to a servant to buy some pork and a chicken, but all the rest she had to pay for herself. Soon everything was brought in, and they sat down. The order was given: "Chopsticks into action." Our description must take time, but there was nothing slow about the movements we describe.

Then every mouth was opened wide and every head was bent.
No sun or sky was to be seen; it was like a cloud of locusts.
They blinked their eyes, their shoulders heaved.
Starvelings they might have been, from some dark dungeon.
One quickly snatched a piece of leg, as though no food
Had passed his lips for years.
One waved his chopsticks thrice, it was as though for years and years
He had not seen a meal.
Sweat trickled down the cheeks of one, he carved a chicken bone
As though inspired by hatred.
Gravy adorned his comrade's lips. With copious drafts of spittle
He gobbled down the pork, with hair and skin.
They ate, and in a flash, the cups and plates were clean
It might have been a den of wolves.
They ate, and in a flash again, the flying chopsticks
Crossed and recrossed the table.
This is the marshal of the King of Gluttons
This, the general of the Lickers-up.
Though it has long been empty, from the wine jar
They try to fill their cups.
Though all the food has gone long since,

They search and search again.
The luscious meal, with all its hundred flavors
Has vanished in a moment.
To worship has it gone,
To worship in the temple of the belly.

They cleared up everything till the plates and dishes looked like the head of a shining bald-pated Buddha. Ximen Qing and Guijie could get nothing but a cup of wine each. They did indeed pick out a few pieces of food, but the others snatched them away. Two of the chairs were broken. The boys, who were looking after the horses, could not get in to share in the repast, and contented themselves by pulling down the statue of the divinity of the place and piddling upon it. When the time came for them to go away, Sun Guazui took a gilded image of Buddha, which was venerated in an inner room, and slipped it inside his trousers. Ying Bojue pretended to kiss Guijie, and stole a gold pin from her hair. Xie Xida went off with Ximen's fan. Zhu Shinian went secretly to Guiqing's room and stole her mirror. As for Chang Zhijie, he did not hand over the money he had borrowed from Ximen Qing, but had the sum put down to his account. They were all in the highest spirits.

When Daian reached home, he found Yueniang, Yulou, and Jinlian sitting together. They asked him if his master was coming. "Father kicked me and cursed me," the boy said, his eyes still red. "He says that anyone who tries to get him away will find herself in trouble."

"What an outrageous fellow he is," Yueniang cried. "It is quite bad enough that he refuses to come, without ill-treating this poor boy."

"It was bad enough for him to kick the boy, but why should he threaten us?" Yulou said.

"The affection of a dozen of these strumpets wouldn't amount to anything," Jinlian said. "There is an old saying that a shipload of gold and silver would never satisfy people of their sort."

Li Jiao'er had seen Daian return, and, as Jinlian was speaking, she came to the window and listened. They could not see her. She heard Jinlian speak of her family as a host of strumpets. After that, she hated Jinlian from the bottom of her heart, and there was always enmity between them.

Jinlian, while Ximen was away, found that the days passed very slowly. When she realized that he did not mean to return, she waited till her two maids had gone to bed and then, making believe to go and walk in the garden, called Qintong to her room and made him drunk. Then she shut her door, undressed, and the pair made love together.

After this, she called the boy to her room every night and kept him there until daybreak. She gave him two or three of her golden pins, and put them in his hair. On another occasion she gave him a perfume box that she wore on her skirt. Unfortunately, the boy was not very discreet and, as he frequently went drinking and gambling with his fellow servants, it was not long before the affair became known. As the proverb says: "If you would have none to know your secret, you must do no evil." One day the rumor came to the ears of Xue'e and Li Jiao'er.

"That thievish strumpet has been high and mighty for a long time," they said, "but now we have her." They went and told Yueniang. She would not believe a word they said.

"You only wish to make things unpleasant for her," she said, "but you will annoy the Third Lady, and she will say you are slandering her boy." They said no more, and went away.

That evening Jinlian and the boy were amusing themselves. The woman had forgotten to shut the kitchen door. The maid Qiuju chanced to use that door on her way to the privy, and saw everything that was going on. The next morning, she told Xiaoyu, and Xiaoyu told Sun Xue'e.

Once again Xue'e and Li Jiao'er went to tell Yueniang. They gave her all the details, and added: "Her own maid told us about it; it is not something we have invented to get her into trouble. If you will not do anything in the matter, we will tell Father ourselves. If he can forgive a whore like this, he can forgive a scorpion."

It was the twenty-seventh day of the seventh month when Ximen Qing came back from the bawdy house to celebrate his birthday.

"He has just come back," Yueniang said to the two women, "and this should be a happy day for him. If you will not listen to me, and are still determined to tell him, I will not be responsible for the consequences."

They paid no attention to her, and, as soon as Ximen came in, they both ran up and told him that Jinlian was carrying on with one of the boys. Ximen Qing had been in an amiable mood, but at this he flew into a towering rage. He went to the front court, and called, "Qintong! Qintong!" over and over again. Jinlian had heard what was happening, and, with trembling hands and feet, she told Chunmei to call the boy to her room. She begged him not to say a word to his master, and took the pins out of his hair, but she was so excited that she forgot the perfume box.

Ximen Qing ordered the boy to the hall, and made him kneel down. Then he told some of the other servants to get a large bamboo and make it ready for use.

"You rascally slave," he cried, "do you confess your guilt?" Qintong made no reply.

"Take out his pins and let me see them," Ximen said to the boys. They looked, but could not find any.

"What have you done with the silver pin with a golden head?"

"I have no silver pin," Qintong said.

"Ah, you slave, you think you will deceive me, do you?" Ximen said, and ordered the boys to take down his trousers. Three or four of them stripped Qintong. On the jade-colored short trousers he was wearing the perfume box hung. As soon as Ximen caught sight of it, he made the boys show it to him, and recognized at once that it was the same one that used to hang on Jinlian's skirt.

"Where did you get this?" he cried in a fury. "Tell me the truth. Who gave it to you?"

The boy was so terrified that it was a long time before he could speak, but at last he said, "I was tidying the garden one day, and picked it up. Nobody gave it to me."

This reply made Ximen still more angry. He bit his lips, and told his servants to beat the boy with all their strength. Qintong was bound and given thirty terrible stripes till his flesh was torn and the blood ran down his legs. Then Ximen told Laibao to cut the boy's hair at the temples and turn him out, and on no account to allow him to return. Qintong kowtowed, wept, and went away.

Jinlian soon heard all that had happened and felt as though a stream of icy water had been poured over her. It was not long before Ximen Qing arrived. She was so frightened that she trembled, and the blood in her veins seemed to freeze. She went forward to take his clothes, but Ximen Qing boxed her ears so hard that he knocked her down. Then he told Chunmei to shut all the doors and keep everybody out. He took a small chair, went out, and sat in the courtyard in a shady place. Then he took a horse whip, and made the woman take off her clothes and kneel before him. She bowed her white face, but did not dare to make a sound.

"You rascally whore," Ximen cried, "don't pretend you are dreaming. I have questioned that slave and he has confessed everything. You had better tell me the truth. When I was away, how many times did you play your games with that boy?"

"Oh, Heavens! Heavens!" Jinlian said, sobbing, "somebody has been telling lies about me, and I shall die if you believe them. All these days you've been away, I have spent my whole time sewing with Yulou. As soon as it was dark, I locked my door and went to bed. Unless there was something very urgent, I never even ventured to go beyond the corner door. If you don't believe me, ask Chunmei. There was nothing I could do without her seeing." She called to Chunmei: "Sister, come here and tell your Father all about it."

"You rascally whore," Ximen said again, "I know you gave the boy two or three gold pins. Why don't you admit it?"

"These suspicions will be the death of me," Jinlian cried. "Some nasty-minded strumpet who will come to a foul end has been telling you lies. I suppose she was, jealous because she saw you always coming to sleep in my room. You know how many pins there were, there is not one missing. Count them yourself, and see. How can you suspect me of being so base as to carry on with a slave? If he were a full-grown slave, they would prob-ably tell the same story, but this short-haired lad is hardly out of his cradle. There is not a word of truth in the story. They have made up the whole chapter of scandal."

"We will leave the pins out of it," Ximen said, taking the perfume box from his sleeve. "This, I think, belongs to you. How do I come to find it on that boy's person? Now perhaps you will not have so much to say." And, with these words, Crash! fell the whip on her delicate white body. The pain was so great that she burst into tears.

"Oh, dear good Father," she cried, "you mustn't treat me like this. If you will only give me a chance, I can explain everything. If you won't give me the chance, but beat me to death, you'll make a very nasty mess here. As for that perfume box, one day when you were away Yulou and I were doing some needlework in the garden. It wasn't firmly attached, and it must have fallen down as I was going through the flower arbor. I looked everywhere for it, but the boy must have picked it up. I am sure I did not give it to him."

This certainly seemed to agree with what Qintong had said. Ximen looked again at the woman. Her flower-like body, unclothed, was kneel-ing as she uttered these softening words and wept so touchingly. His anger flew to Java, and he began to cool down. He called Chunmei and kissed her.

"Did she play heads and tails with that boy? If you tell me I ought to forgive the little strumpet, I will do so."

Chunmei sat on his knee, and made herself most charming and affec-tionate. "Father," she said, "you are making a fool of yourself. Mother and I never left one another the whole time. How can you possibly imagine that she would have anything to do with that slave? No, the whole thing is a plot made up by somebody, who is jealous. You must deal with the matter your-self, Father. If the story gets about, and you make yourself a laughingstock, that won't be very pleasant."

Ximen Qing could say no more. He told Jinlian to stand up and dress, and bade Qiuju prepare a meal. Jinlian poured out a full cup of wine and, offering it to him with both hands, knelt to wait for its return.

"This time I forgive you," Ximen said. "Whenever I am away, you must keep your mind pure and your ways clean. Shut your door early, and be on your guard against thoughts of evil. If I ever hear of anything of this sort again, there will be no more forgiveness."

"Your word is my law," Jinlian said meekly. She kowtowed four times, and sat down to drink with him.

So Jinlian, despite the high favor in which she was held by her husband, brought shame upon herself.

Ximen Qing was drinking wine in Jinlian's room when a boy knocked at the door and told him that Yueniang's two brothers, Fu, the manager of his shop, Ximen's daughter Ximen Dajie and her husband, and several other relatives had called to congratulate him on his birthday. He left Jinlian and went to receive his guests. Ying Bojue, Xie Xida, and the other brothers had also brought presents. Even Guijie had sent a servant with a gift. Ximen Qing was soon very busy receiving all his presents and sending out letters of invitation in return.

Meanwhile Meng Yulou, who had heard all about Jinlian's trouble, seized the opportunity while Ximen was not there, and went to see her without the others knowing anything about it. When she came, Jinlian was lying on the bed.

"Do tell me what it is all about, Sister," she said.

Jinlian cried bitterly. "That little strumpet has been telling tales about me. She made our husband so angry that he thrashed me. I hate those two whores with a hate as deep as the ocean."

"If you had to play tricks with the boy," Yulou said, "you might at least have made sure that I shouldn't lose him. But don't be unhappy. Our husband is bound to look at things from our point of view. If he comes to see me tomorrow, I shall tell him what I think about him."

"It is good of you to trouble about me," Jinlian said. She called Chunmei, and told her to serve tea. They chatted for a while, and Yulou went back to her own rooms. That night, Mistress Wu was staying with Yueniang and Ximen Qing went to sleep with Yulou.

"It was very wrong of you to distress Jinlian so unreasonably," Yulou said. "She did not do anything. This trouble has all come from her quarrel with Xue'e and Li Jiao'er. Without taking the trouble to make any inquiries, you had my boy beaten. You have certainly been most unjust, and it makes things very awkward for the poor woman. Do you imagine our mistress would not have told you, if there had been any truth in the story?"

"I did ask Chunmei," Ximen Qing said, "and she said exactly what you say."

"The Fifth Lady is very much upset," Yulou said. "Why don't you go and see her?"

"I will go and see her tomorrow," Ximen promised.

The next day was Ximen's birthday, and many visitors came to take wine with him, Major Zhou, the magistrate Xia, Captain Zhang, and Uncle Wu, Yueniang's brother. Ximen Qing sent a sedan chair for Guijie, and engaged two singing girls, who performed throughout the day.

As soon as her niece arrived, Li Jiao'er took her to visit Yueniang and the others, and she drank tea with them. They asked Jinlian to come and see her, and twice a maid went to her room to invite her, but she said she was not very well and refused to come. Later in the evening, when Guijie was about to go home, Yueniang gave her a silk handkerchief and some artificial flowers, and went with Li Jiao'er to see her off. Guijie was anxious to go to the garden and pay her respects to Jinlian, but as soon as Jinlian heard she was coming, she told Chunmei to bolt and bar the corner door. When Guijie got there, Chunmei said, "My Mistress's orders. I dare not open the door." Guijie had to go away, greatly abashed.

That evening Ximen Qing went to see Jinlian. Her beautiful tresses were all in disorder, and she seemed very weary and faded. But when he came, she took her clothes, served him with tea, and hot water to wash his feet, and showed him a hundred signs of affection. That night, as they played together, she did for him whatever he asked of her.

"Brother," she said, "who in all this household really cares about you? They are all just stale married women, nothing more. I am the only one who understands you, and you understand me. The others see that you show me favor and spend most of your time here; it makes them jealous, and they try to vent their spite on me. How could you be caught by such talk, and treat me so unkindly? There is an old saying: 'When a farmyard chicken is beaten, it turns round and round; a wild one flies away.' You may beat me to death, but I shall never run away. The other day, when you were at the bawdy house and kicked Daian, I never complained. The Great Lady and Yulou know that quite well. I said I was afraid the girls there would do you no good. I said singing girls in places like that care for nothing but money. What is true love to them? Is there a single one of them who really loves you? That is all I said. Somebody came slyly up and secretly listened, and then they plotted together to get me in disgrace. Fortunately, while people may injure others, they cannot kill them; it is only those whom Heaven wishes to destroy who die. In the future you will realize that I am speaking the truth, and you will know what to do if such a thing happens again."

Ximen Qing was completely won over, and his delight in her was greater than ever.

Some days afterwards he mounted his horse and went off to the bawdy house, attended by Daian and Ping'an. Guijie had other visitors, but as soon as she heard he was coming, she went to her room, washed off her powder, removed her rings and ornaments, lay down on the bed, and pulled the bedclothes over her. Ximen Qing came in. He waited for a long time before the old woman appeared and made a reverence to him.

"Why is it so long since you were here?" the old lady said. She asked him to take a seat.

"I was very busy on my birthday," Ximen Qing said, "and there is no one at home who seems able to attend to things."

"I am afraid my daughter must have been a trouble to you," the old lady said.

Ximen asked why Guiqing did not come to see him on his birthday. The old woman told him that she had been away; a traveler had taken her to stay with him at the inn, and she was still there. They talked for a while, and the old woman offered him tea.

"Where is Guijie?" Ximen said at length. "Don't you know, Sir!" the old woman said. "Ever since the child came back from your house, she has been terribly overwrought. She is not at all well. I can't tell you what is the matter with her, but she has stayed in bed all the time and refused to leave her room. You must have a heart like a wolf's not to have been to see her before."

"This is the first I have heard of it," Ximen said. "Where is she? I will go and see her."

"She is lying down in her bedroom," the old lady said. She told a maid to go and raise the lattice. Ximen Qing went into the room. Guijie, covered with the bedclothes, was sitting on the bed, her face turned to the wall; her hair was in disorder and she seemed in a sad way. She did not move when Ximen came in.

"Why have you been ill since you were at my place?" Ximen said. The girl did not reply.

"What has made you so angry? Tell me." He questioned her for a long time, and at last she said:

"It is all your Fifth Lady's doing. Since you have someone in your own home who is as good as any strumpet, I can't imagine why you come here and make love to a wicked girl like me. I may have been brought up in this house, but I don't believe I'm any worse than some in other houses I could mention. I did not go as a singing girl that day; I came to give you a present. Your great lady was very kind and gave me flowers and clothes, and when I heard you had a fifth lady, I asked to be allowed to pay my respects to her. If I hadn't done so, she would have said that the girls from the bawdy house are very ill-mannered, but I *did* ask, and she refused to see me. When I was leaving your house, I asked once more, and she ordered her maid to shut the door in my face. Really she is lacking in the very elements of politeness."

"You mustn't blame her too much," Ximen Qing said. "She wasn't very well that day. If she had been, I'm sure she wouldn't have refused to come and see you. But I've often felt like giving that little strumpet a beating. She's always hurting somebody with that sharp tongue of hers."

Guijie slapped him lightly on the face. "Why haven't you beaten her, then, you shameless fellow?"

"You don't know how severe I can be," Ximen Qing said. "I have punished most unmercifully all the women and maids in my house, except, of course, my first wife. Sometimes I use a whip upon them twenty or thirty times or even more, and sometimes I cut their hair off."

"Oh," said Guijie, "I've met men before who talk about cutting the hair off their womenfolk, but never one who did more than brag about it. You may have bowed three times and made reverence twice to them for all anybody could prove. If you mean what you say, go home and cut off a single tress, bring it here, and show it to me. If you do that, I'll believe you are the greatest hero there is in this part of the world."

"Your hand upon it," Ximen cried.

"A hundred times, if it pleases you."

Ximen Qing spent the night with Guijie, and the next day, as he was mounting his horse to go home, she called after him: "If you don't bring it to me, don't dare to show your face here again."

This made Ximen very excited, especially as he was already half drunk. As soon as he got home, he went straight to Jinlian's room. She saw that he had had some wine, and was most careful in her attentions. She offered him something to eat, but he would have none of it. He told Chunmei to make the bed, then sent her away and shut the door. He sat on the bed and ordered the woman to take off his shoes. She took them off. Then he got on to the bed, but he would not go to sleep, and sat on a pillow. He bade Jinlian undress and kneel down. She was so terrified that the sweat rolled down her body. She had not the faintest notion what was amiss, and could only kneel down sobbing quietly.

"Father," she said, "tell me what is wrong, even if it kills me. I have been so careful all day, and still I don't seem to satisfy you. You are just sawing me asunder with a blunt knife. How can I bear it?"

"You rascally little whore," Ximen cried, "if you don't take your clothes off, I will show you no mercy." He called to Chunmei: "Bring me the whip that is hanging behind the door."

Chunmei would not go into the room, and he had to call for a long time before she slowly pushed the door open and went in. Jinlian was on her knees, and the lamp had fallen down beside the table. In spite of Ximen's orders, the maid did not obey him.

"Chunmei, Sister, please help me," Jinlian cried, "he is going to beat me again."

"Don't worry about her, little oily mouth," Ximen said. "Give me the whip. I am going to beat the strumpet."

"How can you be so shameless, Father?" Chunmei cried. "What has Mother done wrong? You seem to listen to anything any bad woman likes to tell you, making a storm in a teacup all the time. Mother is one heart and mind with you. What makes you so changeable? I shall not do what you say." She shut the door and went out. Ximen Qing could only burst out laughing.

"I won't beat you this time," he said to Jinlian. "Come here. I want you to give me something. Will you give it me or not?"

"My precious darling," Jinlian said, "I belong to you, heart and soul. Whatever you ask, it is yours. What do you want?"

"I want some of your hair," Ximen said.

"Heavens!" Jinlian cried, "if you had asked me to set myself on fire, I would have done it. But to cut off my hair . . . that is too much. You must wish to frighten me to death. From the day of my birth, twenty-six years until this very day, I have never done such a thing. And lately my hair has been falling out of its own accord. Do, please, spare me that indignity."

"You are always complaining about my bad tempers," Ximen Qing said, "yet you won't do a single thing I ask you."

"If I don't obey you, I don't obey anybody. But tell me, why do you want my hair?"

"I am thinking of having a hairnet made," Ximen said.

"If you want a net, I will make one for you, but you must not take my hair to that strumpet to lay a spell on me."

"I won't give it to anybody," Ximen said, "but I must have your hair to make the foundation for a net."

"Very well," Jinlian said, "in that case I will let you cut some off." She parted her hair. Ximen took a pair of scissors and cut a large tress from the crown of her head. He wrapped it in paper, and put it in his sleeve. Jinlian pressed close to him and wept quietly.

"I will do anything you wish," she said. "The only thing I ask is that you love me always. You may play with others as much as you please, but you must not forget me."

That night their joy in each other seemed more glorious than ever. The next morning, when Ximen Qing got up, she served him with tea; then he mounted his horse and rode to the bawdy house.

"Where is the hair you were going to cut off?" Guijie cried.

"Here you are," said Ximen. He took the hair from his sleeve, and handed it to her. She opened the packet. It contained a tress of beautiful hair, as black as the blackest coal. She put it into her sleeve.

"You have seen it now," Ximen said. "Give it back to me. She was terribly upset because I insisted on cutting off that hair, and, until I changed countenance and frightened her, she wouldn't hear of my cutting it off. I told her I wanted it to make a net. You see, I have brought it to you. Perhaps now you will believe that I always do what I say."

"I don't see why you should be so alarmed," Guijie said. "There is nothing so very extraordinary about it. I'll let you have it before you go. You shouldn't have taken it, if you are so frightened of her."

"What makes you think I'm afraid of her?" Ximen Qing said, laughing. "If I were, I shouldn't tell anybody."

Guijie asked her sister to take wine with Ximen Qing, and, going to a quiet place, put some of the hair into her shoe, that she might tread it underfoot every day. She kept Ximen a prisoner for several days and would not allow him to go home.

Jinlian was very unhappy for several days after her hair had been cut. She refused to leave her room and seemed too languid to take food or tea. Yueniang sent one of the boys to bring old woman Liu, an old favorite of hers, to see what was the matter.

"The lady is suffering from some secret grief," the old woman said, "and because the trouble is insistent and she can't free herself from it, she has headaches and gnawing pains at the heart, and does not feel inclined to take her food."

She opened her medicine box, and, taking out two black pills, told Jinlian to take them in the evening with some ginger water. "I will bring my husband tomorrow," she said. "He will tell your fortune for the coming year and see whether there is any bad luck in store."

"Can your husband really see what is in one's life?" Jinlian asked.

"He is blind," the old woman said, "but there are three things he can do. He can tell fortunes and read the Yin-Yang, and so save people from misadventure. He can bleed the sick, cauterize, and cure wens. The third thing is only to be mentioned with discretion, but, as a matter of fact, he can make philters to change people's hearts."

"What are these philters for?" Jinlian said.

"Well," old woman Liu said, "suppose father and son do not agree as well as they might, or there is a slight misunderstanding between brothers, or a quarrel between wives, if my husband is told the true state of affairs, he will make a spell and write a charm. This is put in water, and the people concerned are given it to drink. Three days after drinking this water, father and son will love one another again, brothers will reach a perfect understanding, and wives will live in harmony together.

"Again, when a man is unsuccessful in business, or his lands and family are not doing very well, my husband can produce the necessary money and increase profits. And when it comes to curing illnesses and making people immune, praying to the stars and invoking the planets, my husband is absolutely a master. People call him Liu the Master of the Stars. I remember the case of a household where there was a new wife who came from a family that was none too well off. She was inclined to be light-fingered, and was always stealing things from her mother-in-law to give to her own people. When her husband found her out, he beat her. My husband exercised his art on her behalf, made a charm, and when it had been burned to ashes, the ashes were put into the cistern. The whole family drank the water from this cistern, and afterwards, even if they actually saw her stealing, they didn't seem to realize what she was about. He also put another charm under her pillow, and when her husband had once slept on that pillow, his hands might have been tied, for he could not beat her any more."

Jinlian listened to this and stored it away in her mind. She told the maid to give the old woman some tea and cakes, and, when she was about to take her departure, she gave her not only three *qian* of silver for her fee, but five more to buy the materials needed for making a charm. She told her to bring the blind man early the next day so that he could burn the charm. The old woman went home, and next morning very early she brought the blind old rascal to the gate, and was about to go to the inner court. Ximen Qing was standing in the courtyard, and the gatekeeper asked the blind man what his business was.

"We have come to burn some papers for the Fifth Lady," the old woman said.

"Very well, in you go," the boy said, "but mind the dog doesn't bite you."

The old woman led her husband to Jinlian's apartments, and they waited some time for her. When she came, the blind man made a reverence to her; then they sat down, and Jinlian told him the eight characters of her destiny. The blind rascal reckoned for a while on his fingers, and said; "Lady, I will now interpret the eight characters of your destiny. They are *Gengchen* for the year, *Gengyin* for the month, *Yihai* for the day, and *Jichou* for the hour of your birth. The eighth of the month is the Spring Day, we must reckon your fate as from the first month. According to the admirable doctrine of Zi Ping, though your eight characters are indeed both clear and remarkable, you will never have the husband star in a favorable conjunction. The question of children, too, does not seem to be decided in your favor. The *Yi* tree grows in the first month and, though this would seem to show that you will enjoy good health, you must be careful lest you overdo things. *Geng* gold appears twice, and the *Yangren* star is unduly prominent, while the husband star is very troublesome. I should say that you will only reach contentment when you have outlived two husbands."

"I have already outlived one," Jinlian said.

"I beg you to excuse me, Lady," the blind rascal went on, "but though your life appears to be of the type known as *Shayin,* you are handicapped by the fact that there is the water of *Gui* in the *Hai* as well as in the *Chou.* This is decidedly a superabundance of water, and it rushes out of a single *Ji* earth. The stars *Guan* and *Sha* are confused. In the case of a man, if the influence of the *Sha* star is predominant, he will attain to dignity and prominence, but, in the case of a woman, such a state of affairs indicates that she will be dangerous to her husbands. The fact that you belong to this class shows that you know very well what you're about and that you attract men.

"With regard to your fortune for the present year, this year is *Jiachen* in the cycle, and this is a sign of coming calamity. The two stars *Xiaohao* and *Goujiao* are influencing you, and, though this does not indicate any real catastrophe, you will have trouble from friends and relations, and backbiters will prove a nuisance."

"It is kind of you to have gone so carefully into all this for me," Jinlian said, "and now I should like you to make a spell for me. Here is a tael of silver to spend on a cup of tea. All I want is that backbiters shall leave me in peace, and that my husband shall have a high esteem for me." She went to her room, found a couple of hair ornaments, and gave them to the blind man. He put them in his sleeve.

"If you would like me to make a spell," he said, "I shall take a piece of willow wood and fashion it into two figures, one male and the other female. On one I shall write your husband's eight characters and on the other your own. Then I shall bind them together with forty-nine red threads. I shall cover the man's eyes with a piece of red cloth and stuff him with the leaves of artemisia. I shall put a needle through his hands and stick the feet with gum. You must put the figures under his pillow, secretly. I shall also write a charm in red ink, and the ashes of this you must put into his tea. Then providing he sleeps on this pillow, you will see the result in three days at the utmost."

"What is the meaning of all this?" Jinlian said.

"I will explain," the old rogue replied. "The covering of the eyes with cloth will make you appear to him as beautiful as Xi Shi. Stuffing the figure with artemisia will make him love you. If I put a needle through the hands, that will ensure that, whatever your faults, he will not be able to raise his hand against you. Finally, the sticking of the feet with gum will prevent his wandering away from you."

Jinlian found this extremely satisfactory, and she wasted no time in getting candles and paper to burn the charms. The next day old woman Liu brought them, with water and the spell figures. Jinlian did with them as she had been told. She burned the charm to ashes, and prepared some of the best tea. When Ximen Qing came back, she told Chunmei to give him some of the tea. That night they slept on the same pillow. Two or three days passed, and their happiness was as great as that of fishes sporting in the water.

Readers, every household, no matter whether it be great or small, should make a rule that nuns, priests, nurses, and procuresses like these should always be kept at a distance.

# CHAPTER 13
# Li Ping'er

One day, when Ximen Qing went to Wu Yueniang's room, his wife told him that Master Hua had sent a boy to invite him to take wine that day. Ximen looked at the message. It said: "Come and talk with me this afternoon at Wu Yin'er's house. Call for me, and we will go together. I greet you heartily."

He dressed quickly and, summoning two boys to attend him, set off upon a fine horse to call on Master Hua. He was surprised to find that Hua was not at home, but Li Ping'er was standing on the steps that led to the inner part of the house. She wore a silken hairnet, with golden earrings set with amethysts, a coat with white trimmings, and an embroidered skirt, beneath which peeped forth a pair of dainty little feet. Ximen had entered hurriedly, and they bumped into one another.

Although he had seen her once before, in the country, he had not paid any particular attention to her, but she had made some impression upon him. Now they met face to face. She was pale and clear-skinned, rather short, with a face as oval as a melon seed, long, with two finely arched eyebrows. He was enraptured. Quickly he went forward and made a reverence to her, and she as quickly returned his greeting. Then she turned and went to the inner court. She sent to him a maid whose name was Xiuchun, a girl who had just grown out of childhood, and told her to ask Ximen to take a seat in the hall. She herself stood at the door of the courtyard, so that only half her charming face was visible.

"Pray sit down for a while, my lord," she said. "My husband has gone out, but he will be back in a few moments."

The maid brought Ximen a cup of tea.

"My husband has asked you to take wine with him today," Mistress Hua said, "but please, for my sake, persuade him to come home early. The two boys will be with him, and there will be nobody here but the two maids and myself."

"You have every right to speak as you do," Ximen Qing said. "The claims of a man's household should have his first attention. Since you wish it, we will not only go together, but come back together."

At that moment Hua Zixu returned, and his wife retired to her own room. The two men exchanged greetings.

"It was very good of you to come," Hua said. "I had to go out for a moment on business, and I hope you will forgive me for not being here to welcome you."

They sat down in the places appointed for host and guest, and Hua ordered a servant to bring tea. When they had drunk it, he said to the boy: "Ask your mistress to prepare some refreshments for us. I should like to drink some wine with Master Ximen before we go." He turned to Ximen and said, "It is Wu Yin'er's birthday today. That is why I asked you to come and have a little amusement."

"Why didn't you tell me earlier?" Ximen said. He told Daian to go home at once and bring five *qian* of silver. The servants were setting the table, but he said, "Don't let us stay any longer. We might as well take our wine at the bawdy house."

"I will keep you a very short time," Hua Zixu said, "but stay for a minute or two."

In a few moments refreshments were brought, and they drank a few cups of wine together. The cups were of silver with long stems like a sunflower. They ate some little buns, and gave what were left to the servant. When Daian had brought the silver, they went out and, mounting their horses, rode to Wu Yin'er's house to celebrate her birthday. There was singing, dancing, and music, and they were as happy as the flowers in a posy, drinking wine together till the first night watch. Ximen Qing deliberately made Hua very drunk, and then took him home, as Li Ping'er had asked him. The boys called for the gate to be opened, and they helped Master Hua to a chair in the hall. Li Ping'er and one of the maids brought a lamp, and took him to the inner part of the house.

Ximen Qing told her all that had happened, and was going away when she thanked him again.

"My foolish husband," she said, "has very little sense. He is too fond of wine, and I am afraid you must have found him a nuisance. It was out of kindness to me that you brought him back. Please, my lord, do not be too scornful of him."

"Not at all," Ximen said, bowing politely, "it was your desire. How could I do other than set your words in my heart and engrave them on my bones? If I had not brought him back, not only would you have been uneasy, but I should have shown myself no gentleman. My brother went to the bawdy house and they tried to keep him there, but I made him come home. When we were passing the Hall of the Joyful Star, he saw one of the girls standing outside. She was a very pretty girl and he would have liked to go in, but I would not let him. I told him that you were waiting anxiously for his return, and we came on together. If he had stayed there, he would not have come back tonight. Sister-in-law, it is not for me to say that my brother is a fool, but you are so young, and this is such a large house to be in. He ought not to leave you here alone at night. It is not right."

"No, indeed," Li Ping'er said. "He is always roaming about and making a fool of himself. I have reproached him till I have made myself quite ill. I do beg of you, my lord, if you meet him at the bawdy house, do, for my sake, persuade him to come home early. I shall always be grateful to you."

There never was a man more clever in the ways of women than Ximen Qing. He had spent many years pursuing them, and there was very little about such matters he did not know. It was perfectly clear to him that the woman was making overtures, and he appreciated the situation admirably. He smiled.

"Sister-in-law," he said, "there is really no need for you to say this. What are friends for? I cannot help feeling that my brother is very much to blame, but do not worry about it a moment longer."

Li Ping'er made a reverence to him, and told a maid to bring tea and fruits. Ximen drank the tea. "I must go home now," he said. "I hope you will see that all the doors are shut safely after me." Then he said good-night and went home.

From that day Ximen Qing racked his brains for a plan whereby he might make this woman his own. Several times he got Ying Bojue, Xie Xida, and the others to take Hua to the bawdy house to drink and pass the night, but he himself escaped from them and went home. He used to stand outside his own gate, and Li Ping'er, with her two maids, would stand outside hers. When he saw her, he would cough affectedly and walk up and down, or he would stand outside his gate and look towards her. When she saw him, Li Ping'er used to hide inside her gate, and put the door between them, but, as soon as he went away, she would put her head out to look after him. They longed for each other in their hearts, but showed their feelings only with their eyes.

One day Ximen Qing was standing outside the gate when Xiuchun brought him an invitation.

"Why does your lady invite me?" he said, pretending not to know. "Is your master at home?"

"Master is not at home," the maid said, "but my mistress would like to have a chat with you."

Ximen Qing did not wait for more, but set out at once. He went into the hall and sat down. After some time Li Ping'er came to him, made a reverence, and said: "I am extremely grateful for your kindness the other day. Indeed

I have engraved it on my heart, for my gratitude is beyond expression. My husband has now been away two days. Perhaps you have seen him?"

"He was at the Zhengs' house yesterday, drinking with a few friends," said Ximen, "but I had some business to attend to and came away. Today I haven't been there, so I don't know whether he is still there or not. If I had been there, I should have considered myself in honor bound to persuade him to come home and not to make you so unhappy."

"He will not do a single thing I ask, and it is almost more than I can bear," Li Ping'er said. "He spends all his time playing with women of that sort and cares nothing at all about his home."

"If it were not for that one failing," Ximen said, "my brother's character would be beyond reproach."

The maid brought tea, but Ximen was afraid that Hua Zixu might return, and did not venture to stay very long. Li Ping'er said to him, "Whenever you do see my husband, please beg him to come home, and I shall be eternally grateful to you."

"We are such good friends," Ximen said, "that I should do so without your asking." He went home.

Next day Hua Zixu came back from the bawdy house. "All you care about," his wife said, "is strong wine and strange women. It is a good thing our neighbor, Master Ximen, has more than once taken some interest in our establishment. If you wish to keep his friendship, I should advise you to buy him a present to show your gratitude."

Hua wasted no time, but bought four boxes of presents and a jar of wine, and sent a servant with them to Ximen Qing. When he had accepted them and given the boy a present, Yueniang asked: "Why has Hua sent you these things?"

"Some time ago," Ximen said, "Brother Hua asked me to go with him to celebrate the Wu Yin'er's birthday. He got drunk, and I brought him home. Indeed, more than once I have urged him not to stay so late at the bawdy house, but to go home early. His lady seemed very grateful, and I imagine she must have told him to send me this present."

Yueniang folded her hands in an attitude of devotion. "I think you might begin by practicing a little self-control yourself. To me this seems a, case of a Buddha made of clay preaching to a Buddha made of mud. Why, there isn't a day when you don't go off to play with some woman or other, and here you are giving pious exhortations to other people's husbands. We can't accept this present without making some return. Whose name is written on the card? If it is Mistress Hua's, I must write and ask her to call. I'm sure she would like to come. If it is his name, you can invite him or not as you please. It is no concern of mine."

"It is Brother Hua's name," Ximen said; "I will ask him to come tomorrow." He sent an invitation to Hua Zixu to come and take wine with him.

"We must not be lacking in politeness," Mistress Hua said, when her husband returned. "We sent him a few small presents and in return he has asked you to take wine with him. Next time, you must get some wine and ask him."

The days passed quickly. It was the Feast of the Ancestral Tombs. Hua Zixu engaged two singing girls and sent to ask Ximen Qing to come and admire the chrysanthemums. He also sent invitations to Ying Bojue, Xie Xida, Zhu Shinian, and Sun Tianhua to come and play at passing the flower while the drums beat. So, in the best of good spirits, they drank their wine.

They drank till the lamps were brought. Then Ximen Qing left the table and went out to wash his hands. Li Ping'er was standing behind a screen peeping in at them. Ximen did not see her until he had almost run into her. She went to a door in the corner and told her maid Xiuchun to go over in the shadow to Ximen Qing and whisper, "My mistress asks you not to drink much wine, but to go home early. She has something to tell you tonight."

No message could have been more welcome to Ximen Qing, and though, after washing his hands, he went back to the table, he would not drink. The singing girls pressed wine upon him, but he pretended to be drunk and would have no more. It was about the first night watch. Li Ping'er paced up and down on the other side of the screen. She could see Ximen Qing lolling in his chair pretending to be half asleep. Ying Bojue and Xie Xida showed not the slightest intention of leaving, and sat there as if they were nailed to their chairs. Even when Zhu Shinian and Sun Guazui took their leave, the others still did not move, much to Mistress Hua's annoyance. Once Ximen Qing started to leave, but Hua Zixu stopped him. "It must be that I have not yet offered you becoming entertainment," he said.

"Really, I'm quite drunk already," Ximen said, "I can't possibly drink any more. He rolled about till Hua sent him home with two boys to assist him.

"I can't think what's wrong with him today," Ying Bojue said. "He won't drink. He has taken very little, yet he's drunk. You have been very kind, and so have these two good little sisters. May I have a large cup? We must drink ever so much more before we think of parting."

At this Li Ping'er, who was on the other side of the screen, secretly cursed them as a set of unprincipled ruffians, and told Tian Xi, one of the boys, to ask her husband to come out and speak to her.

"If you must drink with rascals like these," she said, "get off to the bawdy house at once. Don't stay here making yourselves a nuisance. It is midnight, and you have wasted fire and oil enough. This sort of behavior I will not have."

"You encourage me to go to the bawdy house as late as this?" said Hua Zixu. "Very well. If I can't get back, you mustn't blame me afterwards."

"Run along. I won't blame you."

Hua Zixu was only too pleased to receive such instructions. He went back to the others and said, "Now we will go to the bawdy house."

"Really?" cried Ying Bojue. "Don't try to be funny. You must see what your lady has to say about it first."

"I have spoken to her," Hua said, "and she says I may stay until tomorrow."

"Of course," put in Xie Xida, "Beggar Ying is too clever. Master Hua knows what he is about. Let us go without more ado." With the two singing girls they set off to the bawdy house. The two boys Tian Fu and Tian Xi went with them. It was about the second night watch.

Ximen Qing had gone home, pretending to be drunk. He went to Jinlian's room, but, as soon as he had changed his clothes, he went and sat down in the garden. There he waited for a summons from Li Ping'er. Some time passed; he heard the dog being driven out and the gate fastened next door. Then the maid Yingchun climbed up on the wall in a dark place, pretending to call the cat. Seeing Ximen Qing sitting in the arbor, she made a sign to him. He took a bench, mounted it, and got down a ladder that had been placed for him on the other side of the wall.

When Li Ping'er had made sure that her husband had gone, she took off her headdress and allowed the clouds of black hair to fall about her. Dressed simply, but still charming, she stood in an arbor. When Ximen came, she was delighted and quickly took him indoors. She had already prepared a table with wine, refreshments of various sorts, and fruit. The lamp was burning brightly. The wine jar was filled with a most fragrant wine, and, taking a jade cup in her hands, she offered it to Ximen Qing and made a most profound reverence.

"I have been anxious to show my gratitude to you for a long time," she said, "but you have given us present after present and put yourself out so much that I feel unbearably embarrassed. Today I have made ready this poor cup of wine and asked you to come so that I may at least give some expression to my feelings. Unfortunately those two shameless rogues stayed on and on, till I grew angry and packed them out of the house."

"I suppose Brother Hua will be coming back," Ximen said.

"He will not come back," the woman replied. "I told him to spend the night somewhere else. Both the boys have gone with him. There are only my two maids here, and old woman Feng who acts as doorkeeper. She is my old nurse and absolutely devoted to me. All the doors have been bolted."

This was all very pleasing to Ximen Qing. They sat as closely together as they could and drank each from the other's cup. Yingchun served the wine, and Xiuchun came in and out to take away the dishes. Under the silken net incense perfumed a coral bridal bed. When they had drunk together long enough, the two maids took away the jar and the dessert, and shut the door. The lovers went to bed to enjoy what pleasure they might.

The houses of wealthy families usually have double windows, the outer of which is called the window proper and the inner the casement. When Li Ping'er sent the maids away, she shut the casement so that, though there were lights in the room, they could not be overlooked from outside. But Yingchun was seventeen years old and not without experience. Realizing that her mistress and Ximen Qing were enjoying their unlawful loves, she quietly went between the windows and made a hole in the paper with a pin, so that she could see all that happened. The lovers accomplished their destiny, and all they did was seen by Yingchun as she stood outside the window.

"May I ask your age?" Ximen said.

"I am twenty-three," Li Ping'er said. "What is your lady's honorable age?"

"She is twenty-six."

"Three years older than I am. I should like to buy a present and call upon her, but perhaps she does not care to make friends."

"She is extremely good-natured."

"Does she know you come here?" Li Ping'er said. "What will you say if she asks you questions?"

"She lives well within the house," Ximen said. "My fifth wife, Jinlian, lives in the garden where she has a little house all to herself. But she dare not interfere."

"What is the honorable age of your Fifth Lady?" Li Ping'er said.

"She is the same age as my first wife."

"Good! Unless she considers my poor self too unworthy, I shall be happy to call her Sister. Tomorrow I will ask the size in shoes of your two ladies and make two pairs as a sign of affection." Then she took two golden pins and put them on Ximen's head. "Don't let Hua Zixu see them, if you go to the bawdy house."

Ximen Qing promised. Then they renewed their pleasures together as though they would never part. It was the fifth night watch. Outside the window a cock crew, and the light flooded the eastern sky. Ximen Qing was afraid lest Hua Zixu should take it into his head to come back, so he dressed and climbed back over the wall. Before he went they agreed upon a secret signal. When Hua Zixu was not at home, one of the maids should come to the wall and cough, or throw over a piece of brick, and, if there were nobody about on Ximen's side of the wall, she should climb up and he should get a ladder and come over. So this naughty couple made love over the wall, stealing hours of happiness together. Since they never went around by the gate, the neighbors could not possibly know what was going on.

> The moonbeams shine upon the flowers
> The water clock seems very slow.
> They meet. It seems like Gao Tang's dream.
> She takes the silver lamp to light them
> In the deep night.
> Fearful lest, through the crevices, the light should pass.

When Ximen Qing had climbed over the wall, he went to Jinlian's room. She was in bed.

"Where have you been?" she asked. "You have been away all night and you never told me where you were going."

"Brother Hua sent a boy," Ximen said, "and asked me to go with him to the bawdy house. We drank till the small hours of the morning, and then I was able to get away."

Jinlian suspected him, but she pretended to be satisfied. One day, however, when she and Yulou were sewing in the arbor after dinner, a piece of brick suddenly seemed to drop from the skies quite close to them. Yulou was bending down to fasten her shoe and did not see it, but Jinlian looked everywhere till at last she saw a pale face at the wall. She could not be certain whose it was. The face appeared once and vanished. Jinlian pulled Yulou by the sleeve.

"Look there! There's the elder of Hua's two maids. She must have been admiring our flowers, and jumped down as soon as she saw that we were here." They thought no more about it.

That evening when Ximen Qing came home from a party, he went to Jinlian's room. She took his clothes and asked if he would like anything to eat, but he said no. She offered him tea, but he would not drink it. He paced to and fro in the garden, and Jinlian watched him quietly. Soon the maid's face appeared again over the top of the wall. Ximen Qing took a ladder and climbed over to join Li Ping'er, who was waiting for him on the other side. Jinlian went to her room and tossed about on her bed. She did not sleep the whole night through. At daybreak Ximen Qing came back. He opened the door, but Jinlian pretended to be asleep and did not speak. Ximen, somewhat embarrassed, went and sat on her bed. Jinlian jumped up and caught him by the ear.

"You fickle scamp!" she cried. "Where have you been? All night long I have been worried about you, but now things are so clear that I don't need to ask you for an explanation. The best thing you can do is to tell me the truth at once. What have you been doing with that strumpet who lives next door, and how many times did you do it? Tell me every little thing and I'll forgive you, but miss out a single word and tomorrow you shall march in front, and I'll march behind and I'll tell the whole world what you've been up to. You disgraceful rogue, I'll make you so dead you won't need to be buried. You have got a lot of fellows to keep her husband in the bawdy house, while you go and visit her. Very well, but I'll show you what's what. No wonder yesterday when Yulou and I were sewing, we saw that maid bobbing up and down over the wall, and in full daylight too. She is playing the part of the devil who runs after lost souls, and enticing you away to that whore. You don't think you can deceive me any longer. Only the day before yesterday that turtle of a fellow fetched you away in the middle of the night to go to the bawdy house. Why! his own house would have done as well."

This was extremely disturbing to Ximen Qing. He knelt down as though to make himself small.

"You funny little oily mouth," he said, smiling. "Don't speak so loud. I won't tell you any lies. She asked me how old you are, and one of these days she is going to find out your size in shoes and make you a pair. She would love to consider you her elder sister."

"I don't want a strumpet like her to consider me a sister, or a brother either for that matter. First she seduces another woman's husband, and then tries to offer some insignificant courtesy in return. I will not have dust thrown in my eyes. Why should I let people play such tricks on me?"

She pulled down Ximen's trousers and perceived that the warrior seemed anything but ready for the strife, though he still wore his silver armor.

"Tell me the truth," she cried, "how many times has this fellow returned to the attack?"

"That is an easy question to answer," Ximen said. "Once was enough for him."

"Will you swear that it was only once?" Jinlian said. "Why should he be so dejected, then? He seems half paralyzed. If he showed the slightest sign of courage, I might credit his master with some manly qualities at least." She stripped the warrior of his armor, and cursed him.

"You abandoned scoundrel. There cannot be another like you in all the world. You take this thing with you on the sly when you go to play with that wicked creature."

"You funny little strumpet," Ximen cried, "you are enough to drive a man crazy. She asked me several times to tell you that she is coming to kowtow to you, and she is going to make you a pair of shoes. Yesterday she sent a maid to find out what size Yueniang takes, and today she has given me this pair of pins, with the character *Shou* engraved upon them, for you." He removed his hat, took the pins from his hair, and gave them to Jinlian. She examined them. The lucky character was designed in gold upon an emerald ground. They were of very fine workmanship, for they had been made in a royal palace. She was delighted with them.

"Ah well," she said, "if that is how the land lies, I'll say no more about it. Indeed, when you go to call on her, I'll keep a lookout for you on this side, and the pair of you can enjoy yourselves in peace. Now what do you say?"

Ximen Qing was delighted. He took Jinlian in his arms. "You are a darling," he said. "The sort of baby I like is one who knows how to deal with a situation when it arises, as you do, not a miraculous creature who brings forth gold and silver when he performs his natural functions in the privy. Tomorrow I will show what I think about you by buying you a suit of fine embroidered clothes."

"I don't believe that honeyed tongue and that sugary mouth of yours," Jinlian said; "if you want me to help the pair of you, you must promise three things."

"I promise," said Ximen; "ask what you will."

"To begin with, I forbid you the bawdy house. Secondly, when I ask you to do anything, you must do it. And thirdly, every time you go to visit your sweetheart, I must know all that happens; you must not keep a single thing back."

"That will be easy," Ximen said. "I agree to all your conditions."

The next time Ximen Qing went to spend the night with Li Ping'er, he told Jinlian how white and flawless was the body of his lady love, as yielding as the softest down; how amorous her temperament; and how she loved wine. "We took a basket of fruits into the net with us," he said, "and played dominoes and drank wine, before we went to sleep." He took something from his sleeve and handed it to Jinlian.

"Her father-in-law brought this from the palace and, when we had lighted the lamp, we used it as a model of deportment."

Jinlian unfastened the roll of pictures and looked at it from end to end. Twenty-four subjects were painted upon it, and it was most exciting. She decided to keep it. She handed it to Chunmei and said, "Put this away in my chest. No doubt I shall find much to learn from it."

"You may have it for a few days," Ximen Qing said, "but I must have it back again. She thinks a great deal of it, and I only borrowed it to look at. I must return it to her."

"You shouldn't have given it to me, then," Jinlian said. "I didn't steal it from her. You will find it loves me so much it won't leave me."

"Little slave," Ximen cried, "don't be such a tease." He tried to take back the roll.

"If you try to snatch it," Jinlian said, "we will have a snatching match. I'll tear it into shreds and then it will be lost to all of us forever."

Ximen Qing laughed. "Have it your own way. I can't help myself, but I beg you to give it back to her when you've done with it. She has something else that is very interesting and, if you let her have this back, I'll ask her to let me show you the other."

"I wonder who trained you in artfulness, young man," Jinlian said. "You shall have this back when you bring me the other."

They talked for a long time, and that night Ximen stayed with Jinlian. She perfumed the bed and lighted the silver lamp. She dressed herself with all the skill at her command, performing her most intimate toilet, and they looked at the roll so that they might emulate the lovers who were painted upon it.

Readers, the wonders of witchcraft have been known to us since the most remote periods of antiquity. Very soon after the blind Liu had made a spell for Jinlian, her shame was turned to happiness and Ximen's displeasure to favor. He dared refuse her nothing. Though he had all the cunning of a ghost, he was compelled to drink the water in which she washed her feet.

## Chapter 14
# The Cuckold

One day, Wu Yueniang was not feeling well, and her brother's wife came to see her. Yueniang pressed her to stay a few days, and they were sitting together in her room when Ping'an came to announce his master's return. Mistress Wu went to Li Jiao'er's room.

Ximen Qing came in, took off his cloak, and sat down. Xiaoyu brought tea, but he did not drink it, and his wife noticed that he was very pale.

"Why have you come back so early?" she said.

"It was Brother Chang's turn today," he replied, "but his house is not very large, and he asked us to go to the Temple of Eternal Felicity outside the city. Brother Hua and Brother Ying—there were four or five of us in all—went to the Zhengs' bawdy house for some wine. We were enjoying ourselves when several constables appeared. Without a word they seized Hua and took him off with them. This scared us all. I went to Guijie's house, and hid there for a long time. I was so worried that I sent a man to find out what had happened. It seems that Hua's brothers have some grievance about the disposal of the family property. They made complaint at the Eastern Capital, and the courts have sent an order for Hua's arrest. When I had heard this, I didn't worry so much, and the rest of us came back."

"The best thing you could do," Yueniang said. "You have been going with those scamps day after day, gadding about and neglecting your home. Now, you see, there has been trouble. After this, I trust you will break with them completely. If you don't, you will find yourself involved in squabbles and disasters, and you will end by being beaten till you look like a rotten sheep's head. You will never believe what I tell you and stop this unbecoming manner of life, but the whores in the bawdy house can tell you any old story and you'll listen to them with your donkey's ears. You are the kind of man who lets the advice of his own people go in at one ear and out at the other, and treats everything outsiders tell him as if it were written in the golden characters of a sacred book."

"Who do you imagine would have courage enough to strike me?" Ximen said, laughing.

"Oh, you are a splendid braggart by your own fireside," Yueniang said.

Daian came in. "Our neighbor, Mistress Hua, has sent her boy to ask Father to go and talk to her."

Ximen Qing tried to escape as quietly as he could.

"Aren't you afraid people will talk about you?" Yueniang said.

"We are only neighbors. There's nothing in it. I must go and see what she has to say." He went to Hua's house.

Li Ping'er had given instructions that he was to be taken at once to the inner part of the house, and there Ximen Qing found her, wearing a silken gown. She looked disheveled and weary, and her face was as pale as wax. She came and knelt down before him.

"My lord," she said, "the priest may be nothing to you, but I pray you consider the glory of Buddha. There is an old maxim that when disaster over-takes a household, neighbors should do what they can to help. My husband has never paid any attention to me; he has never troubled in the least about domestic affairs, but has always gone elsewhere and played the fool. Now he has got into serious trouble and is in a difficulty, he sends one of the servants to say that I must get him out of it. I am a woman, and no more use than a crab without feet. How am I to find anybody who will take the trouble to do anything for him? When I realize how he has always refused to listen to me, I can't help thinking that it serves him right even if he is sent to the Eastern Capital and beaten till he rots. But my father-in-law's memory must be con-sidered, and this would bring disgrace upon him. I feel bound to ask you to help me to persuade the officials not to send him there. Think of my poor face, and plead for him. I should not like him to suffer hardship."

Ximen Qing saw her kneeling before him and asked her to get up. "It can't be anything very serious," he said, "but so far I don't know what the trouble is."

"It will take some explanation," Li Ping'er said.

"My late father-in-law had four nephews. Ziyu was the eldest, Ziguang the third, and Zihua the fourth. My husband was the second. They are all blood relations. My father-in-law was very wealthy, but he knew that my husband was a fool and, when he came back from Guangnan, gave every-thing into my charge. The other three had all annoyed him in some way, and never dared to visit the old man. Last year, my father-in-law died. The other brothers divided between them a good deal of the furniture and some of the beds and curtains, but they got none of the money. I told my hus-band several times that he should give them something, but he would do nothing at all in the matter. Now, he has got himself into a hopeless situa-tion, and the others have the whip hand." She burst into tears.

"Sister," Ximen Qing said, "don't distress yourself about it any more. I was under the impression that the matter was really serious, but it is only a family squabble. You have told me what you wish, and I will give my brother's business as much attention as if it were my own. Tell me what you wish me to do and I will do it."

"My lord," Li Ping'er said, "if you are really willing to undertake this, I could wish for nothing better. Tell me how much you will need for presents, and I will get it ready for you at once."

"Not very much," Ximen said. "I believe the Governor of Kaifengfu is a ward of the Imperial Tutor Cai. Both Cai and my relative, Marshal Yang, have a certain influence with his Majesty. If we send two presents and get those gentlemen to speak to Governor Yang, I don't think he will refuse anything they ask, no matter how serious the case may be. We must send a present to the Imperial Tutor, but, as Marshal Yang is a relative of mine, he can hardly accept a present from me."

Li Ping'er went to her room and took from a chest sixty large bars of silver each worth fifty taels. She gave them to Ximen Qing. The total value was three thousand taels of silver.

"Half of this will be enough," Ximen said. "Why do you give me so much?"

"Keep anything that is left for me," Li Ping'er said. "There are four chests behind my bed, full of the finest embroidered ceremonial clothes, jade girdles, and so on, without mentioning cap buttons, jewelry, and things of that sort. They are worth a great deal of money. Will you look after them for me and keep them in your house, so that when I want anything I can ask you for it? I feel very unsafe with all this stuff here. If anybody should come and take it away from me, I should be in a desperate fix."

"But what will you say when Brother Hua comes back and asks questions?" Ximen said.

"My father-in-law gave me all these things secretly," Li Ping'er said. "My husband knows nothing about them. You can take them without hesitation."

"I must go and see what my wife says," Ximen Qing said. "When I get home, I will send somebody for them." He went home to discuss the matter with Yueniang.

"We can tell the boys to take food boxes for the silver," she said, "but the chests and big things we must bring over the wall when it is dark. Then we shall be sure that the matter is kept secret; for, if we bring the stuff around by the gate, everybody in the neighborhood will know what is happening."

Ximen Qing thought this an excellent plan. He told Daian, Laiwang, Laixing and Ping'an to take two food boxes and bring the three thousand taels of silver. That evening, when the moon had risen, Li Ping'er and her two maids, Yingchun and Xiuchun, brought benches to the wall and lifted up the chests. On Ximen's side, Yueniang, Jinlian, and Chunmei set up a ladder and put a blanket on the top of the wall to receive the various articles one by one. Everything was taken to Yueniang's room.

In this manner Ximen Qing got into possession of many fine and delicate things, both gold and silver, while his neighbors had not the faintest inkling of what was afoot. He quickly prepared several loads of presents, and, after getting someone to write a letter to go with them, sent Laibao to the Eastern Capital. He was to ask Marshal Yang to send the presents to the Imperial Tutor, asking him to communicate with Governor Yang of Kaifengfu.

The Governor's name was Yang Shi, and he was also known as Guishan. Born at Hongnong in Shaanxi, he had obtained the third literary degree in the period of Guiwei. He had formerly been an official at Dalisi, and had been promoted to his present position at the Eastern Capital. He was an honest and fair-dealing official, but the Imperial Tutor had been his guardian, and Marshal Yang was in high favor at the palace, so he could not but fall in with their wishes.

When the presents arrived, the Governor went into his hall and, bringing Hua Zixu and the others from prison, questioned them about their property. Hua Zixu had received a message from Ximen Qing, so he knew how matters stood.

"When my worthy ancestor departed this life," he said to the Governor, "I spent what money there was upon his funeral expenses and the reading of the Buddhist sutras. There was nothing else beyond a parcel of land and a couple of houses. The furniture has already been distributed among the members of the family."

"It is never possible," the Governor said, "to be quite certain about the amount of a chamberlain's wealth. It comes easily, but it goes easily too. If you have spent all you had, I will send instructions to the magistrate at Qinghe to put up for sale your two houses and the parcel of land, and to share the proceeds between Ziyu and the others."

Hua Ziyu pleaded that his brother should be made to hand over to them all his property, but the request irritated the Governor. "You seem to be asking for trouble," he said. "When the chamberlain died, you made no complaint. Why are you trying to rake up matters that are over and done with?"

Hua Zixu escaped without the chastisement he had anticipated. The Governor sent a document to Qinghe, ordering the officials there to make a valuation of the houses and land, and dispose of them.

As soon as Laibao had heard the decision, he traveled posthaste to give the news to Ximen Qing, who was delighted to hear that Hua Zixu was free and on his way back. Li Ping'er sent for him to talk over the situation, and suggested that he should take some of her money and buy the house.

"I shall be yours entirely then," she said. Ximen again went home to discuss the matter with Yueniang.

"I don't see how her husband can fail to have his suspicions," Yueniang said, "if he finds that you intend to buy his house. How do you propose to manage it?"

Ximen Qing considered what she said, but he did not answer.

In a few days Hua Zixu returned, and the magistrate of Qinghe appointed his deputy to make an inventory of the old chamberlain's estate. One house in the Street of Peace and Good Fortune was sold to the princely family of Wang for seven hundred taels, and the land by the South Gate to Major Zhou for six hundred and fifty-five taels. The house in which Hua Zixu had been living was valued at five hundred and forty taels, but nobody made an offer for it, because it was so near to Ximen Qing's house. More than once, Hua Zixu sent a messenger to ask Ximen to buy it, but he always said he had no money and didn't care to pass the transaction through his accounts. Meanwhile, seeing that the local authorities seemed anxious to get the matter over and done with, Li Ping'er grew more and more anxious, and secretly sent old woman Feng to Ximen to beg him to take five hundred and forty taels from the money that she had left in his care. Finally Ximen consented, and paid the money to the officials. Hua Zixu hurriedly signed all the documents, and his three brothers divided the eighteen hundred and ninety-five taels between them.

Hua Zixu was at last clear of the law, but he had not a penny to bless himself with, and both houses and land had been taken from him. The large bars of silver, amounting to three thousand taels, which he had had in his two chests, seemed to have completely vanished, a circumstance that he found exceedingly annoying and disturbing. He wished Li Ping'er to ask Ximen how much had been spent on his behalf and what was left, so that he could buy a house with the remainder, but the only reply he got from his wife was ill humor for several days.

"You idiot," she cried, "you have never paid the slightest attention to your own affairs; you have spent all your time chasing after women, and as a result you found yourself in a hole and were thrown into jail. You then condescended to ask me to find somebody to help you. I am not a woman given to gadding about. What do I know about matters of this sort? Whom do I know and where should I have found anybody to do anything for you? I am a creature of such insignificance that, if my body were made of iron, very few nails could be made out of me. All I could do was to go around like a baby, appealing for help, and, fortunately for you, Master Ximen remembered that you had once been his friend, and when things looked cold and bleak for you, sent his servant to the Eastern Capital to get everything settled for you. It was exceedingly kind and thoughtful of him. Now you are out of the mess and your feet are once more on dry land, you begin to think about money, though your life has only just been given back to you. As soon as your troubles are over, you forget all you have gone through, come back to rake up a business that has already been done with, and want to know whether there is any money left.

"Here is a letter from you, written in your own hand. Without this authority I should never have dared to spend your money on getting assistance for you. I am not so bold that I would steal your money and give it away."

"Although I said so in my letter," Hua Zixu said, "I did hope to keep a little something, sufficient, at least, to buy a house to live in."

"Pah, you dirty fool!" Li Ping'er cried, "you ought to have thought about that before. When you had money, you never gave it a thought; but it seems a very different matter now. You keep on saying that I have spent too much money. What was three thousand taels? Do you imagine that the Imperial Tutor Cai and Marshal Yang are so moderate in their desires? If I hadn't sent them a handsome present, do you think they would have attended to the matter so effectively that you never even felt the weight of a straw on your turtle's body, but got off scot-free? And you are proud of the fact! You have no influence with them. You are no relative of theirs that they should trouble to be kind to you. Unless it was for something worthwhile, why should they go tearing about to save your skin? Yet you come home, and instead of preparing a banquet and showing your gratitude by entertaining Ximen Qing, you brush everybody on one side and only think about reopening the whole business."

This was like a blow in the face to Hua Zixu. He said no more. Next day Ximen Qing sent Daian with a present to console him in his distress. In return he prepared wine, and invited Ximen Qing, hoping that he might get an opportunity to ask him about the money. As a matter of fact, Ximen would gladly have sent him a few hundred taels to buy a house with, but Li Ping'er would not hear of it. She sent old woman Feng to tell him not to come, and to send her husband a falsified account, making it appear that all the money had been spent.

Hua Zixu had not brains enough to see through the trick. He sent repeated invitations to Ximen Qing. But Ximen went off to the bawdy house, and told his servants to say that he was not at home whenever a message came for him. This so upset Hua Zixu that he almost fainted, yet he could do nothing but stamp his feet with impatience.

Readers, if a woman once ceases to love her husband and becomes unfaithful to him, he will never be able to find out her secrets, though he have strength enough to bite through iron. It is traditionally a man's duty to attend to matters outside the household and a woman's to govern within it, but over and over again a man's good repute has been brought to nothing by his wife. Why is this? It is because he has not treated his wife as the Sacred Principle requires. The relations between husband and wife should be based upon a generosity of spirit that gives rise to mutual understanding and brings their feelings into complete accord. When this is the case, the husband sets the tune and the wife follows; there is no reason to anticipate trouble. Hua Zixu lost his head and was blown hither and thither by every wind; he had no ideas at all about the management of a household. This being so, it could hardly be expected that he would exercise any control over his wife's doings.

Soon after this Hua Zixu succeeded in borrowing two hundred and fifty taels of silver and bought a house in Lion Street. But he was still smarting beneath a load of anger, and had not long been in his new house before he fell ill of a fever. At the beginning of the eleventh month he took to his bed, and never rose from it again. Early in his illness he was attended by a doctor, but he objected to the expense and allowed the illness to run its course till, on the twentieth, he breathed his last. He was only twenty-four. While he was ill, Tian Xi, one of his boys, stole five taels of silver and made off.

Hua Zixu was no sooner dead than his wife sent old woman Feng to ask Ximen Qing to come and talk to her. A coffin was bought, Hua was put into it, monks were engaged, and the coffin was sent to the tomb. The brothers Hua with their wives all came in deep mourning to assist at the funeral. Ximen Qing asked Yueniang to prepare a funeral offering of wine and food. Li Ping'er went to the funeral and returned in a sedan chair. She set up a tablet in her room, but, though it was a time when she should have respected her husband's memory, she could think of nobody but Ximen Qing.

While Hua Zixu was still alive, Ximen Qing had taken over the two maids, but after his death the two households were practically united. One day Li Ping'er heard that it was Pan Jinlian's birthday, and, though it was not five weeks after her husband's death, she bought some presents and went in a sedan chair to offer her congratulations. She wore a white silk gown and a blue skirt with gold embroidery, and upon her head was a white covering adorned with pearls. Old woman Feng attended her, and Tian Fu walked behind the sedan chair.

Li Ping'er kowtowed four times to Yueniang. "I am sorry," she said, "that at the graveside I had nothing better to offer you. It was kind of you to send such a handsome offering." After her reverence to Yueniang, she asked to see Li Jiao'er and Meng Yulou. Jinlian came in.

"Is this the Fifth Lady?" Li Ping'er said, preparing to kowtow to her. She repeatedly called her Elder Sister, and begged her to accept her reverence. But Jinlian would not do so, and, after disputing amicably for a long time, they ended by making equal reverences. Jinlian thanked her for her birth-day present. After greeting Mistress Wu and Madam Pan, Li Ping'er asked after Ximen Qing.

"He has gone to make his devotions at the Temple of the Jade Emperor," Yueniang said. She asked Li Ping'er to sit down, and offered her tea. A little later Sun Xue'e came in. Li Ping'er saw that her attire was not so rich as that of the others, but she stood up. "Who is this lady?" she said, "I should have asked to be presented, had I known there was anyone else."

"She is one of my husband's ladies," Yueniang said. Li Ping'er would have made a reverence to Xue'e, but Yueniang would not allow her to do so. "Lady," she said, "you should make the reverence of an equal." So they greeted each other. Yueniang took Li Ping'er to her own room to change her clothes, and ordered the maids to set a table in the middle room. Char-coal was put into the brazier, and wine and food were brought. Mistress Wu, Madam Pan, and Li Ping'er sat in the place of honor; Yueniang and Li Jiao'er in the hostess's place, and Yulou and Jinlian sat at the side. Xue'e went to the kitchen to see to the serving of the meal, and it was some time before she took her own place.

Yueniang saw that Li Ping'er never refused any cup of wine that was offered. She herself poured wine for everyone, and told Li Jiao'er and the others that they must do so in their turn.

"Mistress Hua," she said, "since you have gone so far away, we do not see so much of one another, but I often think about you. It has been cruel of you not to come to see us."

"You would not have come today," Yulou said, "if it had not been the Fifth Lady's birthday."

"Good ladies," Li Ping'er said, "it is very good of you to say such kind words. I should have been only too glad to come, but I am still in deep mourning and there is nobody to leave at home. Even now it is only about five weeks since my husband died, and if I had not been afraid of incurring the Fifth Lady's displeasure, I should not have come today." She turned to Yueniang, and asked the date of her birthday.

"It is still a long way off," Yueniang said, but Jinlian contradicted her.

"Our Great Lady's birthday is the fifteenth day of the eighth month. You must come and see us that day." Li Ping'er promised to come. Yulou suggested that she should spend the night with them.

I should enjoy the pleasure of your company very much indeed," Li Ping'er said, "but, as you know, I have only just removed to this new place and, since my husband died, there is not a soul in the house. The back of my house adjoins the garden of the princely family Qiao; it is very lonely and desolate. There are many nights when foxes come and throw bricks and tiles into my house, and it makes me very nervous. I used to have two serving boys, but the older of them has run away, and there is only young Tian Fu to attend to the front door and no one at all to keep watch at the back. Very fortunately for me, old woman Feng, an old friend, comes in frequently to do my washing."

"How old is Madam Feng?" Yueniang said. "She seems a very decent quiet old body."

"She is fifty-six this year," Li Ping'er replied. "She has no children, but lives upon her earnings as a go-between and what she makes by washing clothes for me. When my husband died, I asked her to come and live with me, and now she and the maid sleep in the same bed."

"Since there is old woman Feng to look after your house," Jinlian said, "there can be no possible reason why you should not spend the night here. In any case, Master Hua is dead, and you are not answerable to anybody but yourself."

"Do what I tell you," Yulou said, "and tell old woman Feng to send the sedan chair away. You don't go back today."

Li Ping'er laughed but said nothing.

The wine had now gone around several times. Old woman Pan was the first to rise, and she went to the front court with her daughter. Li Ping'er repeatedly declined to drink any more, but Li Jiao'er said, "Mistress Hua, you drank everything the other ladies offered you, yet you refuse me. That isn't fair." She took a large cup and filled it to the brim.

"My dear lady," Mistress Hua said, "I can't drink any more. I am not pretending."

"Just one cup more," Yueniang said, "and then we will let you off."

Li Ping'er took the cup, and put it down on the table. She went on talking to the ladies. Suddenly Yulou noticed Chunmei standing beside her.

"What is your mistress doing in the front court?" she said. "Go and tell her and old lady Pan to come back at once. The Great Lady wishes them to help to entertain Mistress Hua."

Chunmei went away, but was soon back again. "The old lady is not very well and has gone to bed," she said. "My mistress will be back in a moment. She is powdering her face."

"I never saw such a hostess," Yueniang said, "running away and leaving her guest like this. She is a good soul, but she behaves like a child at times."

When Jinlian came back, Yulou saw that she had dressed herself in her most beautiful clothes. She certainly looked very charming.

"Fifth Maid," Yulou said, jokingly, "my good woman, this is the feast of your donkey and horse, yet you ran away to your own room and left your guest behind. Do you call yourself a human being?"

Jinlian laughed, and slapped her playfully.

"You hussy of a fifth maid," Yulou cried, "come and pour out the wine."

"The Third Lady has given me too much wine already," Li Ping'er said, "I have had as much as I can take."

"What she gave you is her affair," Jinlian said, "but you must take a cup from me." She poured out a large cup for her guest. Li Ping'er took it, but did not drink it. Yueniang noticed that Jinlian was wearing in her hair a pin with the lucky character in gold. "Where did you buy your lucky character pins?" she said to Li Ping'er. "They are exactly like those the Fifth Lady is wearing. I must get a pair with the same design."

"If you would like some," Li Ping'er said, "I have several more pairs, and tomorrow I shall be delighted to offer a pair to each of you. They are some that my late father-in-law brought from the palace, and it is impossible to buy them outside the Court."

"You mustn't take me seriously," Yueniang said, there are too many of us. You can't possibly give us so many pins."

The ladies laughed and drank till the sun went down in the west. Old woman Feng had been drinking in the kitchen with Xue'e, and her face was very red. At last she went into the room and said to Li Ping'er, "Are you ready to go now? I must arrange about the chair."

"Don't go, Mistress Hua," Yueniang said. "Tell Madam Feng to send the chair away."

"There is no one at home," Li Ping'er persisted. "I will come and see you again some other day."

"You are very obstinate, Mistress Hua," Yulou said. "It looks as though you don't care in the least what we should like, since you won't send the chair away. If Father had been here, he would soon have persuaded you."

They finally persuaded her to give her key to old woman Feng. "These ladies have all urged me to stay," she said to the old woman, "and if I don't, it will be discourteous on my part. Send the sedan chair away and tell the men to call for me tomorrow. You take the boy home, and see that all the doors are shut." She added in a whisper: "Tell Yingchun to unlock the small box in my room. There is a little gilt case in it, and I want her to take four pairs of gold lucky-character pins out of it. Bring them to me tomorrow morning. I wish to make a present of them to these four ladies."

Old woman Feng made a reverence to Yueniang and went home. A little later, seeing that Li Ping'er would not drink any more, Yueniang asked her to go to the upper room and take tea with Mistress Wu.

Shortly afterwards Daian brought in the wrapper, and Ximen Qing came in. He pulled up the lattice and, as he entered the room, said, "Surely this is Mistress Hua!" Li Ping'er rose and made a reverence to him. Yueniang told Yuxiao to take his clothes.

"I have been outside the city to worship at the Temple of the Jade Emperor," Ximen Qing said. "I have to preside this year, and the Abbot and I had to go through the accounts in great detail. That is why I am so late. Are you staying the night, Mistress Hua?"

"Mistress Hua has made several attempts to get away," Yulou said, "but we succeeded in persuading her to stay."

"My only reason for wishing to go was that there is no one to look after my house," Li Ping'er said.

"That is nonsense," Ximen Qing said. "The constables have been very active lately, and there is nothing to be afraid of. If you should feel the least bit anxious, I would send my card to Major Zhou. He will do anything I ask him. But why do you sit there like a mouse, Lady Hua? Have you had any wine?"

"We have tried to persuade her to drink some, but she would not," Yulou said.

"You are none of you any good," Ximen cried. "Let me see what I can do. She can really drink quite a lot more."

Li Ping'er kept declaring that she could not drink another drop, but her objections were only half-hearted, and the maids once more set the table. Some dishes and dessert had been kept for Ximen Qing, and these were now brought out. Mistress Wu declined to drink any more, and went to Li Jiao'er's room. Li Ping'er now sat in the seat of honor, with Ximen Qing opposite to her, and Yueniang sat on the bed and warmed her feet at a small brazier. Yulou and Jinlian sat at the side. The wine was poured again, and they pledged each other in large cups. They drank so long that Mistress Hua's eyebrows grew heavy and her eyes could hardly see.

When Yueniang saw that both her husband and Li Ping'er had drunk more than was good for them, and were chattering nonsense to each other, she waited no longer but went to join her sister. The others stayed drinking till the third night watch, and then Li Ping'er could neither see straight nor stand upright. Jinlian helped her to the back court to wash her hands, and Ximen Qing, who was rolling in all directions, went to Yueniang's room.

"Where is she going to sleep?" he asked.

"In her hostess's room, I imagine," said his wife.

"Where shall I sleep, then?" Ximen said.

"Anywhere you like, though I expect you will go after her," Yueniang said.

"Nonsense," Ximen Qing said, laughing, "I'll stay here." He called Xiaoyu to help him undress.

'Don't be dirty," Yueniang said. "Where is my sister-in-law going to sleep if you stay here? Don't provoke me or I shall tell you what I think about you."

"All right! all right!" Ximen cried. "I'll go and sleep with Yulou." He went off to her room.

When Jinlian had shown her guest where to wash her hands, she took her to the front court and they slept with old woman Pan. Next morning Li Ping'er got up and dressed with the aid of Chunmei. She knew that the girl had passed through Ximen Qing's hands. She gave her a set of golden hair ornaments. Chunmei immediately went to tell Jinlian, and the Fifth Lady thanked her guest most effusively.

"I feel as though we were imposing on you, Mistress Hua," she said

"Not at all, Fifth Lady, you are fortunate to have so admirable a maid."

When they were dressed, Jinlian took her and old woman Pan into the garden, sending Chunmei to open the gate. Li Ping'er saw that a new gate had been made in the wall, and asked when Ximen was going to rebuild the house.

"The Master of the Yin Yang has been here," Jinlian said, "and he suggests our starting on the foundations in the middle of the second month. His Lordship proposes to make your old house and ours into one. In the front he is going to build an artificial mound, a pergola, and a large garden. At the back he will build a garden house of three rooms like mine."

Li Ping'er listened attentively. Then Yueniang sent Xiaoyu to invite them to take tea in the back court, and the three women went to her room. Yueniang, Li Jiao'er, Yulou, and Mistress Wu were waiting for them.

While they were having breakfast old woman Feng came in. She took an old handkerchief from her sleeve, in which were wrapped four pairs of gold pins, and gave the pins to her mistress. Li Ping'er gave them in turn to Yueniang, Li Jiao'er, Yulou, and Xue'e.

"I feel that I ought not to accept them," Yueniang said. "It is really too kind of you."

Li Ping'er smiled. "There is nothing very wonderful about them," she said, "I only offer them as playthings." Yueniang and the others thanked her, and put them in their hair.

"I believe the Feast of Lanterns is to be held near your house," Yueniang said. "It will be very lovely, and, when I go to see it, I will pay you a call. That is, unless you tell me you won't have me."

"I shall be only too glad to invite you all," Li Ping'er said.

"Perhaps you do not know, Sister," Jinlian said to Yueniang, "that it will be Mistress Hua's birthday on the fifteenth."

"In that case," Yueniang said, "we will make a definite arrangement now to come and offer our congratulations that day."

"My little room is no better than a snail's," Li Ping'er said, smiling, "but if you will condescend to come, I shall be only too happy."

They finished their breakfast, and wine was brought. It was now late in the morning, and the sedan chair came for Li Ping'er. She said good-bye to them all and, though they urged her to stay still longer, she prepared to go. As she was about to start, she asked for Ximen Qing, but Yueniang told her that he had gone early to say farewell to one of his friends who was going away. Li Ping'er got into her sedan chair and went home.

# CHAPTER 15

# The Feast of Lanterns

The days passed quickly. It was the birthday of Li Ping'er on the fifteenth of the eleventh month. The day before it Ximen Qing told Daian to get ready four courses of food, a large jar of wine, birthday cakes, and pastries. He himself added a suit of quilted silken clothes embroidered in gold. He wrote Wu Yueniang's name on a card, and sent everything as a birthday present from Yueniang to Li Ping'er.

Mistress Hua was dressing when Daian brought the present. She ordered the boy to be brought to her.

"It is only a few days," she said to him, "since your lady last troubled herself on my account. Now she has placed me in her debt again by sending this magnificent present."

"I was told to say that this is only a trifle, which you may well pass on to your maids."

Li Ping'er told Xiuchun to give Daian some cakes. As he was about to go, she gave him two *qian* and a colored handkerchief. "Tell your ladies," she said, "that I am going to send old woman Feng to ask them all to brighten my poor house by their presence."

Daian kowtowed and went away. Li Ping'er paid the porters, and sent old woman Feng with five cards of invitation to ask the ladies to come the following evening. Secretly she was to ask Ximen Qing to come later and take wine with her.

The next day Yueniang left Sun Xue'e to look after the house. She and the other ladies, all most charmingly dressed, got into their sedan chairs to go to Lion Street, where the Feast of Lanterns was being held. Laixing, Laian, Daian, and Huatong escorted them.

The house in which Li Ping'er now lived had three rooms at the front, and went back for the same distance. On the street it was two stores high, and, as one entered the gate, there were rooms on either side. Three formed a hall and one served as a passage to the third court, where there were three bedrooms and a kitchen. At the back of the house a wall separated the property of Li Ping'er from the garden belonging to the princely family of Qiao.

Yueniang and the others were coming specially to see the lanterns, and Li Ping'er set out screens, tables, and cushions, and hung up floral lanterns in the rooms that overlooked the street. When her guests arrived, she welcomed them and took them to the inner court for tea. They sat down, and two singing girls, Dong Jiao'er and Han Jinchuan, sang for them and served the wine. Afterwards refreshments were set out in the upper rooms, and she invited her guests to go upstairs and look at the lanterns. The windows had been decorated with bamboo shades, lanterns, and silken streamers.

Yueniang was dressed in a red-quilted cloak with an emerald green skirt, and she wore a mantle of leopard skin. Li Jiao'er, Meng Yulou, and Pan Jinlian were wearing white silk gowns and blue skirts. Li Jiao'er had a brown wrap embroidered in gold, Yulou a green one, and Jinlian a red one. They all wore masses of pearls and jade on their heads, and phoenix pins peeped out from their hair. They looked out of the window at the fair.

There were hosts of people at the fair, and it was a wonderful sight. Dozens of arches, with lanterns hanging all around them, had been set up in the street. There were all kinds of booths, surrounded by crowds of men and women admiring the lanterns, some red as roses, and some green as willows. Horses and carriages made a noise like thunder.

> Dragons flit through mountain peaks and sport in couples in the water.
> Lonely storks gaze at the skies, shining as the clouds themselves.
> Lanterns of the golden lotus; lanterns like towers of jade, glimmering like a mass of jewels.
> Lanterns of mimosa, lotus lanterns, shedding a thousand radiant hues.
> Lanterns of gossamer, light and dainty; sunflower lanterns, bobbing in the wind
> Student lanterns, bowing back and forth, attentive to the bidding of Confucius and Mencius.
> Wife lanterns, tender and obedient, picturing the virtues of Meng Jiang.
> Monkish lanterns, with Yue Ming and Liu Cui standing side by side.
> Lanterns of the Scribe of Hell, Zhong Kui and his sisters, sitting down together.
> Lanterns like witches with fluttering fans, conjuring up evil spirits.
> Lanterns of Liu Hai, with a golden frog, devouring precious treasure.
> Camel lanterns and green lion lanterns bearing gifts beyond price.
> Monkey lanterns and white elephant lanterns, with treasure worth the ransom of many cities.
> Crabs sporting with the incoming breakers, on their backs, all hands and feet.
> Bull-headed fishes, with monstrous mouths and long beards, swallowing the river plants.

Silver moths, vying in beauty; snow-white willows, each more glori-
    ous than the last.
Fishes and dragons playing on the sands.
The seven immortals and the five ancients with their sacred books
The nine barbarians and the eight uncivilized coming to offer pre-
    cious gifts.

The drums at the fair beat sharply twice.
A hundred toys, each more cunning than its neighbor
The lanterns move round and round
The hanging lanterns bob up and down
There are glass vases painted with delicate maidens and exquisite
    flowers
There are screens of tortoiseshell, with Ying Zhou and Lang Yuan
    painted on them.

The young men gather at the rails where the ball is kicked as high as
    the eyes.
Hand in hand the maidens go to the upper floors that the beauty of
    their charms may be seen.
The booths of the palmists are like the clouds, and the tents of the
    readers of faces like the stars
They tell the fortunes of the coming year and read in the lives of men
    the joy and sadness that are to come.
They who sing the song of Yang Gong stand on the slopes.
Elsewhere, the wandering priests strike their cymbals and tell the
    story of San Cang.
There are sellers of Yuan Xiao, their pastries stuffed with fruits
And sellers of plum blossom with the dried branches cut away.
Hair ornaments sporting with the winds of spring; cold weather orna-
    ments brightening the hair, their golden glory gleaming in the sun.
Round screens, painted with the gorgeous net of Shi Chong.
Lattices of mother of pearl, adorned with plum blossom and crescent
    moon, charming to the eyes.
We may not see all the beauties of Ao Shan
But before us is a year of happiness and joyful living.

Yueniang looked out upon the lanterns until the noise became too great
for her. Then she and Li Jiao'er went back to their places to drink for a
while. Jinlian, Yulou, and the two singing girls, stayed and still looked out
of the window at the fair.

Jinlian flaunted her silken sleeves and pointed with her fine fingers, show-ing off the gold rings on them. She leaned half out of the window, biting melon seeds and throwing the skins at the passersby. She and Yulou laughed all the time. She pointed to something in the street, and cried, "Great Sister, come and look at the two hydrangea-lanterns over at that house. They look so pretty, as the wind blows them to and fro." Then: "Second Sister, come and look at the great fish lanterns hanging over that door, and all the little fishes, crabs, and lobsters below. They are ever so funny." And again: "Third Sister, come and look at the old-man-and-woman lanterns."

Suddenly a gust of wind made a large hole in the lower part of the old-woman-lantern, and Jinlian laughed merrily. People standing below the window stared up at her, crowding till they almost trampled on each other. There were several dissolute young fellows among them. They pointed at the woman, and began to discuss her.

"She must have come from the palace of some duke or earl," one said.

"She is a concubine of one of the princely households, come to see the lanterns," another said. "She must be, or she would not be dressed in such splendid style."

"She is one of the little girls from the bawdy house, and some nobleman has engaged her to come here and sing," said a third.

Then another young man spoke. "You will never guess who they are. But I know. Those two women indeed belong to a distinguished family: they are the wives of the King of Hades, concubines of the General of the Five Directions. In other words, they belong to Master Ximen who keeps a medicine shop near the Town Hall and lends money to the officials. He is not at all the sort of man to fall out with. Probably they have come with the mistress of their household to see the lanterns. I don't know the one wearing the green wrapper, but the other, in red with the artificial flowers, looks like the wife of Wu Da the cake seller. Wu Da caught them misbehaving in old woman Wang's tea shop. His Lordship kicked Wu Da to death, and then took the woman to be one of his ladies. Her brother-in-law, Wu Song, went to the courts to bring an accusation, but, in mistake, killed the runner Li, and his Lordship had him punished. It is a year or two since I saw her last. She has certainly become very beautiful."

Yueniang saw that a crowd was collecting in the street, and told Jinlian and Yulou to come and sit down. They drank wine and the two singing girls sang the Lantern Song to them.

Yueniang was anxious to go home. "I have had as much wine as I can drink," she said, "and I and the Second Lady must leave you. But the others may stay and entertain you, Mistress Hua. My husband is not at home today, and there are only a few maids to look after things. I can't help being anxious."

Li Ping'er tried to persuade her to stay. "Good lady," she said, "if you go, it must be because I have entertained you so poorly. Today is a great holiday, and the lamps are not yet lighted or the food prepared. You mustn't think of going home. Even if Master Ximen is out, you have a number of maids. Why should you be uneasy? As soon as the moon rises, I will see you all home."

"Mistress Hua," Yueniang said, "I am afraid that is impossible. I never drink much wine. But I will leave the others here to take my place."

"Great Lady and Second Lady," Li Ping'er said. "Neither of you will drink with me. It is not fair. When I was at your house, your ladies would not let me off though I drank one cup after another. Today you have come to this poor place of mine, and though I can offer nothing worthy of you, I should like to do something to show my feelings."

She took a great silver cup, and asked Li Jiao'er to drink. Then she turned to Yueniang. "I dare not offer you so large a cup," she said, "but here is a small one." She poured out a cup of wine and offered it.

Yueniang gave each of the singing girls two *qian* of silver and, when Li Jiao'er had finished her wine, they prepared to leave. "We will go first," Yueniang said to Yulou and Jinlian, "and I will send the boys with lanterns to bring you home. You must not be too late, for there are not many of us at home." Li Ping'er took Yueniang and Li Jiao'er to the door, and saw them off in their sedan chairs. Then she came back to drink wine with Yulou and Jinlian. It was getting dark, and the lamps in the room were lighted. As they drank, they listened to the playing and singing of the two girls.

Ximen Qing dined at home with Ying Bojue and Xie Xida, and afterwards they set out to the Lantern Fair. When they reached the end of Lion Street, Ximen was afraid his companions might see the ladies drinking wine at Mistress Hua's house, so he turned aside into another street to look at the large lanterns. They went as far as one of the great booths and then came back. They met Sun Guazui and Zhu Shinian.

"It is a very long time since we saw you last," the newcomers said. "Our hearts were thirsting for the sight of you." They turned to Ying Bojue and Xie Xida. "You are a fine pair of rascals! You have been enjoying yourselves with our brother and never said a word to us about it."

"You are unfair to them," Ximen said. "I only met them in the street a moment ago."

"Well," Zhu Shinian said, "now that we've had enough of the lanterns, where shall we go?"

"Let us go to the wineshop and drink," Ximen Qing said. "I will not ask you to my place, because all my women have gone to a party."

"Why a wineshop?" Zhu Shinian said. "Why not call on Li Guijie? This is a great occasion. We will go and wish her a Happy New Year and enjoy ourselves at the same time. A few days ago we were at her place, and the very thought of you brought tears to her eyes. She told us she had been ill ever since the twelfth month, but not even your shadow had crossed her threshold. Brother, you have nothing else to do, and we shall be very glad to go with you."

Ximen Qing remembered that he had to go and see Li Ping'er that evening. He declined. "I have certain matters to attend to today," he said, "I'll go with you tomorrow." But they hustled him and dragged him till he found himself at the bawdy house in spite of himself.

When Ximen Qing and his companions reached the house, Guiqing, dressed very daintily, was standing outside the door. She brought them into the hall and made a reverence to each in turn.

"Come here at once, Mother," Zhu Shinian cried at the top of his voice. "We have been lucky enough to persuade his Lordship to come." The old procuress came, hobbling along with the help of her stick. She greeted Ximen Qing.

"I am a poor old body who has never done you any wrong," she said. "Why have you kept away from your sisters so long? Perhaps you have another girl somewhere."

"A good guess," Zhu Shinian said. "His Lordship has made the acquaintance of a very pretty girl, and he goes to see her every day. Now you know why he never bothers about Guijie any more. If we hadn't run into him at the Feast of Lanterns and dragged him along, he would not be here now. If you don't believe me, ask Sun." He pointed to Ying Bojue and Xie Xida. "Those unholy rascals belong to the same family of immortals as Master Ximen himself."

The old woman found this very amusing. "Good brother Ying," she said, "I have always treated you well. Why couldn't you speak for us to his Lordship? He is a busy man, and, of course, as the proverb says, a young man is never faithful to one girl. All the coins in the world are made with the same sort of hole. I don't mean to boast, but my daughter is a good-looking girl. Your own eyes, Sir, will tell you that much."

"Let me explain," Sun Guazui said. "His new girl does not live in any bawdy house. She is independent."

Ximen Qing ran after Sun Guazui and slapped him. "Don't believe this old oily mouth and all his crazy stories. His proper place is the slaughter-house."

Sun and the others roared with laughter. Ximen took three taels of silver from his sleeve and offered it to Guiqing, saying that he would like to give his friends a treat on this festival day. Guiqing would have nothing to do with it; she passed it on to the old procuress.

"What does this mean?" the old woman cried. "Do you think that on a festival day like this I cannot myself entertain your friends? If you offer me this silver, it is quite clear you believe we never think of anything but money."

Ying Bojue went to her. "Take my advice and accept the money," he said, "and get us some wine at once."

"It is not right," the old woman mumbled, still pretending to refuse the money, though she put it into her sleeve. Finally she thanked Ximen Qing, and made a profound reverence to him.

"Wait a moment, Mother," Bojue cried. "I have a funny story to tell you. There was once a young man who kept a girl at the bawdy house, and one day, when he called to see her, he pretended to have been ruined. The old woman saw how shabby his clothes were and would have nothing to say to him. He sat for a long time, and she never even offered him a cup of tea. 'May I have some rice, Mother?' the young man said at last. 'I am very hungry.' 'My rice bin is empty,' the old woman replied. 'Where shall I find rice for you?' 'If you have no rice,' said the young man, 'perhaps you will give me a little water to wash my face?' But the old woman said, 'I can't afford to buy any water; we have had none for days.' But then the young man produced a piece of silver, about ten taels in weight, and put it on the table. Again he asked for rice and water. The old woman became quite excited. 'Eat your face and wash your rice, Brother,' she cried, 'and when you have washed your rice, eat your face.'"

They laughed. "You are trying to make fun of me," the old woman said. "I have heard stories like that before, but I don't believe a word of them."

"Listen," Bojue said, "I'll tell you something. This girl his Lordship has been courting is Brother Hua's girl, Wu Yin'er, who lives in the back lane. He doesn't care for Guijie any more."

"I don't believe you," the old woman said, laughing. "I don't wish to boast, but my daughter is certainly as good-looking as Wu Yin'er. Brother is so wrapped up in us that not even the sharpest of knives could cut him away from us. And he is not a fool either. He can tell real gold when he sees it." With this, she went to see about the preparation of the feast.

In a short time Guijie came in. Her hair was dressed in the Hangzhou style, with pins inlaid with gold, and green plum ornaments. She wore a pearl headdress, a pair of golden earrings, a crimson silk skirt and a white silk coat. She looked as beautiful as a carving in jade. When she had greeted them all, she sat down by the side of her sister, and a little later tea was brought in. Guijie handed the tea and kept a cup for herself. Then a maid came to clear away the tea things and set the table.

Suddenly several men, whose dress showed that they were of low degree, appeared before the lattice, and looked in on them. Then they came in and knelt down. They brought three or four measures of melon seeds.

"We bring you this present," their spokesman said, "in honor of the festival."

"Who are you?" Ximen asked. He only recognized the leader, Yu Chun.

"Nie Yue is outside," said Yu Chun. "He belongs to our party."

Nie Yue came in. When he saw Ying Bojue, he said, "So you are here, Master Ying." He kowtowed.

Ximen Qing took the melon seeds and threw a tael of silver to Yu Chun. Then the fellows thanked him politely and went away.

When Ximen Qing had got rid of them, he settled down to his wine. Guijie filled the golden cups, making great play with her crimson sleeves. The food was of the rarest and the dessert of seasonable fruits. The men reveled in the fragrance of the two girls, and the wine they drank only seemed to add to the charm. The cups were filled twice, then Guijie and her sister sang "The Sweetness of the Glorious Day," one playing the cithern and the other the lute. While they were singing, three members of the Ball Club came in, wearing dark clothes and bringing two roast geese and a couple of jars of wine. They made a profound reverence to Ximen Qing, and offered their gifts. Ximen knew them all. There were Bai Tuzi, little Zhang Xian, and Mohammedan Luo.

"Wait for us outside," he said, "and, as soon as we have finished our wine, we will come and have a game with you." He gave them four dishes of food, a large jar of wine, and some cakes. They got their ball ready and waited. When Ximen had drunk a little more wine, he went out to the courtyard to watch the ball game and asked Guijie to play with two of them, one to pitch and one to strike. She jumped about, kicked, elbowed, and struck the ball to the great admiration of those looking on. If sometimes she could not catch it, they hastily caught it for her. When the game was over, they went to Ximen Qing for money.

"Guijie's form has very greatly improved," one said. "When she elbows the ball, it takes us all our time to hold it. In a year or two, she may well be the finest ball player in all the bawdy houses. She is infinitely better than the Dong girls who live in the second lane."

By the time Guijie had played two games, dust covered her eyebrows and her cheeks were damp with sweat. Her limbs ached and she panted for breath. She took the fan from her sleeve and fanned herself, then held Ximen Qing's hand, while they watched Guiqing, Xie Xida, and Zhang Xian play a game. The others stood at the sides to pick the ball up for them.

Ximen Qing drank wine as he watched them. Then Daian came with a horse. "My mistress and the other ladies have now been gone some time," he whispered. "Mistress Hua hopes that you will come as soon as you can." Ximen told the boy to take the horse to the back and wait for him there. He refused to drink any more, but took Guijie to her room for a while, and then pretended to go out to wash his hands. Leaving her room, he opened the back door, mounted his horse, and was off like a flash. Ying Bojue saw him go and told a servant to detain him, but Ximen would not wait; he declared that he had business at home to attend to. He left Daian to give a tael and five *qian* to the ballplayers.

Thinking that Ximen had gone to Wu Yin'er's house, they sent a servant to follow him there. Bojue and the others drank till the second night watch, and then the party broke up.

# CHAPTER 16
# Li Ping'er Is Betrothed

Ximen Qing left the bawdy house. With Daian following, he went to see Li Ping'er at her house in Lion Street. When they found the gate closed, they knew that the guests had got into their sedan chairs and departed. Daian called to old woman Feng to open the door. She let Ximen Qing in. Li Ping'er, holding a candle, was waiting for him in the hall. She looked very charming in her pretty headdress and soft white clothes. She had been leaning on the framework of the lattice longing for him to come; and when he came, she ran downstairs to meet him, her lotus-like feet moving swiftly, her silken skirt fluttering.

"If you had been a little earlier," she said, smiling, "you would have found two of your ladies still here. They have only just gone. The Great Lady went away early, because she said you were not at home. If that is so, where have you been?"

"Brother Ying and Brother Xie asked me to go and see the lanterns with them," Ximen Qing said, "and we were passing your door when we met two other friends. They carried me off to the bawdy house, and I could not get away before this late hour. I thought you would be waiting for me, and, as soon as the boy came, I said I was going to wash my hands. I slipped away through the back door. If I hadn't done so, they would have kept me and I should never have been able to get away."

"Thank you very much for the splendid present you sent me," Li Ping'er said. "I could not prevail upon your ladies to stay. They said there was no one at home, but nonetheless I felt ashamed."

She heated some excellent wine and served food to him. The lanterns were lighted in the hall and the curtains drawn. Charcoal was put into the golden brazier and precious incense into the incense burner. She kowtowed before him and offered him a cup of wine.

"My foolish husband is dead now," she said, "and I have no other relatives. Today, my lord, I offer you this cup of wine and implore you to take me under your protection. Do not despise my lack of comeliness, for I wish nothing more than to be your slave and a sister to all your ladies. I have told you my wishes, but what you may think about it I do not know." As she said this, she shed tears.

Ximen took the wine and raised her up. "Do not kneel," he said, "I am grateful for your love. When your period of mourning is over, I shall know what course to take. You need worry no longer. This is your lucky day, and we can enjoy our wine without a care." He drank his own wine and poured a cup for Li Ping'er. Then they sat down and, in a little while, old woman Feng, who was in charge of the kitchen, brought them some dumplings.

"Who were the singing girls today?" Ximen Qing said.

"Dong Jiao'er and Han Jinchuan," Li Ping'er said. "They went after your ladies to get some flowers from them."

They sat on the bed and drank wine, exchanging cups. Xiuchun and Yingchun waited upon them. Daian came and kowtowed to Li Ping'er to congratulate her upon her birthday. She rose quickly and returned his greeting. She asked Yingchun to tell old woman Feng to give him some birthday dumplings, cakes, and a jar of wine in the kitchen.

"You may go home as soon as you have finished," Ximen told him.

"And when you get home," Li Ping'er said, "if any of the ladies ask where your master is, don't tell them he is here."

"I understand," the boy said. "I will tell them that Father is spending the night somewhere else. Tomorrow morning I will come back for him." Ximen nodded approval and Li Ping'er was very pleased. "What an intelligent boy he is," she cried. "You can see it in his eyes." She told Yingchun to give him two *qian* of silver with which to buy melon seeds. "Let me know what size you take," she said to him, "and I will make you a pair of shoes."

Daian kowtowed again, thanked her, and went away when he had had a meal in the kitchen. Old woman Feng bolted the gate. Ximen Qing and Li Ping'er guessed fingers, and then, taking a set of thirty-two ivory tablets, set a cloth upon the table and played dominoes as they drank their wine. Then they told Yingchun to light them with a candle to the bedroom. Now that Hua Zixu was dead, both Yingchun and Xiuchun had yielded to Ximen's desire. The lovers did as they pleased in the presence of these maids, and were quite at their ease. They called for the bed to be prepared and for fruit and wine to be placed within the purple silk net. Li Ping'er unveiled her white body and Ximen Qing sat beside her. They went on with their game of dominoes, and drank great cups of wine together.

"When are you going to begin the rebuilding of the house?" Li Ping'er asked suddenly.

"I shall get the work in hand at the middle of the second month," Ximen said. "I propose to make the two properties into one and let the gardens run together. At the front I am having an artificial mound and a shelter made, and at the back a garden pavilion of three rooms where we can go to enjoy the flowers."

"In some tea chests behind that bed," Li Ping'er said, "there are thirty or forty pounds of aloes, two hundred pounds of white wax, two jars of quicksilver, and eighty pounds of pepper. Take them all away and sell them; you can use the money to help pay the building expenses. If I find favor in your sight, when you get home tell the Great Lady that I hope to take a sister's place among your ladies. Give me any place you choose, but I cannot live without you." She began to sob again.

Ximen Qing took out his handkerchief and wiped away her tears. "I understand perfectly," he said, "but you must wait till the building is finished and your mourning is over. Until then there will be no place where you can live."

"If you really intend to marry me, you will build a little pavilion for me near that of your Fifth Lady. She is so nice, and I am very fond of her. The Third Lady too is very kind to me. One would never take them to be anything but sisters. The Great Lady is not quite so agreeable. Somehow those eyebrows of hers seem supercilious."

"My foolish wife is really one of the kindest of souls," Ximen Qing said, "or she would never have managed to keep such a large household in order. I will build a three-roomed pavilion with two little doors for you, as fine as the place in which you live now. What do you think of that?"

"Oh, Brother, what more could I wish for?" Li Ping'er said.

They played together unrestrainedly, as the male phoenix plays with his mate, and their delight was so great that it was the fourth night watch before they went to sleep. Then, close pressed in each other's arms, they slept until morning. Breakfast time came, but they did not rise, and Yingchun brought them some rice porridge. They ate a little of it, and then called for wine. Li Ping'er liked to play at being a horse. She made Ximen Qing take up his position on a pillow, and she placed herself in the manner of a flower inverted. They were enjoying themselves like this when Daian, who had brought Ximen Qing's horse, came and knocked at the door. Ximen called him to the window and asked what he wanted.

"Three merchants from Sichuan and Guangdong have come to see you," the boy said. "They are waiting with a host of fine things. They have shown them to Uncle Fu. All they ask for them is a hundred taels of silver on the signing of the contract, and the rest in the eighth month. My mistress told me to ask you to come and see them."

"You didn't tell her I was here, did you?" Ximen Qing said.

"No," said the boy, "I told them you were spending the night at Guijie's house."

"They have no sense," Ximen said. "Your uncle Fu could have managed this perfectly well. Why send and bother me?"

"Uncle Fu has talked to them," Daian said, "but the strangers will not settle with him. They will not sign the contract unless you go yourself."

"Your family has sent the boy for you," Li Ping'er said. "Business must come first. You must go, or the Great Lady will be angry."

"You don't know these thievish barbarians," Ximen said. "They miss the proper season, can't get rid of their goods, and then come to me. If I show myself at all eager to accept their terms, they will very soon ask for more. In the whole of this district mine is the only wholesale house, and they must come to me, whatever I choose to offer."

"In business matters," Li Ping'er said, "you should take care not to turn friends into enemies. Please do as I tell you. Go home, and get rid of them. There are still as many days before us as there are leaves upon a willow tree."

Ximen agreed to do as she wished. He got out of bed in a leisurely manner, combed his hair, washed his face, and put on his hairnet and clothes. Li Ping'er served him with food. When he had eaten it, he put on his eyeshades and rode home.

Four or five merchants were waiting in the shop for him to check the goods and give them the money. When this had been done, they signed the contract and went away. Ximen Qing went to Jinlian's room.

"Where did you spend last night?" Jinlian cried. "Tell me the truth, or I will stir the dust with my complainings."

"You were all drinking wine with Mistress Hua," Ximen said, "so I went to the Lantern Fair with my friends. Afterwards we went to the bawdy house and spent the night there. This morning Daian came to bring me back, and here I am."

"I know the boy went to fetch you, but pray, in which of the bawdy houses does your particular ghost live? You fickle rogue, you are trying to deceive me. Last night that strumpet turned us out and invoked the aid of gods and devils alike to get you to go to her. When you have had enough, you come home. That thievish lump of knavery, Daian, is cunning enough to tell one story to his mistress, but it is quite another one he tells me. Last night when he came back, the Great Lady said, 'Why hasn't your Father come back? Where is he drinking?' and he said you and Uncle Fu had gone to see the lanterns, and that you had gone to Guijie's house to drink, and he was going to bring you back this morning. But afterwards, when I questioned him, he laughed and kept his mouth shut. When I pressed him, he admitted that you were spending the night with Mistress Hua in Lion Street. You villain, how does he know that I always let you do as you please? I suppose you told him."

"Indeed I did nothing of the sort," Ximen Qing said. He told her how Li Ping'er had asked him to take wine with her, how sorry she was that

Jinlian had returned so early, how she cried and told him that she had no one to help her and was always terrified at night because her house was so lonely. "She begged me to marry her, and asked when I was going to rebuild the house. She has some incense and candles and all kinds of valuable stuff there, and she asked me to take it and use the money to pay the builder. She is very anxious that I should get the house finished quickly, so that she can come here and live with you as a sister. But it looks as though that won't suit you."

"One shadow more or less will not worry me," Jinlian said. "I shall be glad to have her, for, as things are, I'm very lonely, and, if she comes, she will keep me company. The fact that there are many ships on a river does not necessarily mean a block, and a road is not stopped because there are many carts upon it. There is no more reason why I should refuse to welcome her than others might have found when I came here myself. But I'm very much afraid you will not find everybody so amiably disposed as I am. You still have to see what our mistress thinks about it."

"Although I am talking about this matter now," Ximen said, "of course she is still in mourning."

Jinlian took Ximen's silken gown. Something dropped out of the sleeve, and fell tinkling to the ground. She picked it up and weighed it in her hand. It was like a little ball, but very heavy. She looked at it for a long time, but could not imagine what it was for. Jinlian stared at it.

"What is it?" she said, "and why does it seem so heavy?"

"Don't you know?" Ximen said, laughing. "They call it the Bell of Fecundity, and it comes from Burma, a country somewhere in the south. A good one is worth four or five taels of silver."

"Where do you put the thing?" the woman asked.

"First, you put it inside, then get on with what has to be done. The results are quite indescribable."

"Did you use it with Mistress Hua?" Jinlian asked.

Ximen Qing told her all that had passed during the night, and this so stirred up Jinlian's ardent mind that, though it was still day, these two disrobed themselves and behaved in a manner better befitting the night.

Ximen Qing went to see the valuers, taking with him the candles and wax and other things that belonged to Li Ping'er. They were all weighed up and sold for about three hundred and eighty taels of silver. Out of this Li Ping'er would take only one hundred and eighty taels, making Ximen Qing spend the rest on the house. He consulted the Master of the Yin Yang, and work was begun on the eighth day of the second month. He gave five hundred taels to his servant Laizhao and his manager Ben the Fourth, to buy bricks, tiles, timber, and stone, and gave them instructions to superintend the work and keep account of the expenditure. Ben the Fourth was a dissipated young fellow, something of a windbag, but efficient and cunning. He began life as servant to a eunuch, but was sent away because of some irregularity. Then he lent himself to practices of doubtful morality and, still later, took employment as domestic in a family of position. But he seduced the nurse and ran off with her. For a while he acted as a tailor's tout. He could play the lute, the flute, and the double flute. Ximen Qing, who appreciated such accomplishments, gave Ben the Fourth help from time to time, and finally found a place for him in his shop, so that he could earn commission. In this way Ben the Fourth came to have a finger in the pie of all Ximen's enterprises.

Ben the Fourth and Laizhao supervised the workers during the building of the house. To begin with, the old rooms of Hua's house were demolished, then the walls were pulled down and new foundations laid. They constructed the shelter, the artificial mound, and all the arbors and apartments. This took a considerable time.

The days passed quickly. The sun and moon crossed and recrossed like the shuttles of a weaver. A little more than a month after Ximen's setting to work upon the gardens, it was a hundred days since Hua Zixu died. Li Ping'er asked Ximen to go and see her, to talk over the future. "I will have Hua's tablet burned," she said, "and you must decide whether you wish to have this house sold or not. You need only to give your orders, but you must marry me as soon as you can. Give me any position you like in your household. So long as I can be your chambermaid, I shall be quite happy." Her tears fell like rain.

"Don't cry," Ximen said. "I have told the Fifth Lady that, as soon as the house is finished and your mourning is over, I am going to marry you."

"If you really want me," Li Ping'er cried, "get my apartment finished first, and take me there. If I spend a single day in it and then die, I shall die content. Anything would be better than staying here, where each day seems like a year."

"I know," said Ximen.

"Why should I not go to live with the Fifth Lady for a few days, as soon as the tablet has been burned, and move into the new apartment as soon as it is finished? Go home and see what the Fifth Lady thinks of that, and I will wait. The hundredth day is the tenth of the third month, and I will arrange to have the dirge sung and the tablet burned."

Ximen Qing agreed, and spent the night with Li Ping'er. The next day he went home and told Jinlian all she had proposed.

"Very well," Jinlian said, "I am quite ready to clear a couple of rooms for her, but you must go and ask the Great Lady first. As for me, I am like the water in the river, there is no reason why I should not do my part in washing the boats."

Ximen Qing went at once to see Yueniang. She was dressing her hair, and Ximen told her the whole story.

"It is not at all a suitable arrangement," Yueniang said. "To begin with, she is still in mourning. Secondly, you were a very intimate friend of her husband. Thirdly, you have already had dealings with her, purchased her house, and stored many of her goods. The proverb says, If the loom is not speedy, the shuttle is. I understand that one member of her family, Hua the Elder, is a rogue. If he gets wind of this, I very much fear we shall find many fleas about our heads. What I have said is plain common sense. By Zhao, Qian, Sun and Li, think the matter over and see if you don't agree with me."

Ximen could think of no answer to make. He went and sat on a chair in the hall, and pondered the matter. He was by no means decided how he should answer Li Ping'er, but he could not make up his mind to give her up. The problem troubled him for a long time, and finally he went back to Jinlian's room.

"What did the Great Lady say?" Jinlian said. Ximen told her all that had passed.

"She is right," Jinlian said. "You did buy her house and you do wish to marry the widow of one of your most intimate friends. And, for that reason, you must forgo what otherwise you might have had. If you do not, your influential friends will look upon you with grave suspicion."

"That doesn't trouble me in the least," Ximen said, "but I am anxious about that fellow Hua the Elder. I don't want him to start interfering. If he hears what is going on, he will bring pressure to bear upon her before she is out of mourning. What can I do then? But I really don't know what to say to her."

"I see no difficulty at all," Jinlian said. "All you need do is to go and say to her, 'I have mentioned the matter to the Fifth Lady, but it appears that there is a great stock of merchandise stored on the upper floor of her apartments, and there is no room for your things. You must wait a few days more. My place is nearly finished, and I will hurry on the workmen and get the painting and decorating done as soon as possible. By that time your mourning will be over and I will marry you. That seems much the best plan, far better than your staying with the Fifth Lady, packed like herrings in a barrel, neither one thing nor another.' That ought to satisfy her."

Ximen Qing was delighted with this counsel, and went at once to see Li Ping'er. "The Fifth Lady says: Wait till the painting and decoration of your apartment are finished, and go straight there. At present there is a whole heap of things in her place, and there would be no room for your belongings.

There is one thing more I must remind you of. May not your brother-in-law say that your period of mourning has not been duly fulfilled? What can we do about it?"

"He has no authority over me," Li Ping'er said. "We have already come to an arrangement about the property and we have signed a document in the courts to say that our relationship is at an end. We women certainly have our first marriages arranged for us, but for the rest we can surely please ourselves. There is a proverb that says: Brothers and sisters-in-law have no right to interfere in each other's affairs. My brother-in-law has not the slightest power to say a word in any matter that concerns myself alone. If I could not support myself, he would never raise a finger to help me. No, if that fellow dares to fart about, I shall tell him to die in his chair, and after that, he will not venture to die in his bed. Please don't let him worry you, my lord. He can do me no harm. When will the apartment be finished?"

"I have given orders for it to be painted and decorated before anything else. At the beginning of the fifth month it will certainly be ready."

"I will gladly wait till then, but you must do your best to hurry it on."

The maids brought wine, and they spent the night most pleasantly together. Thenceforth Ximen Qing went every few days to visit Li Ping'er.

It was not long before Ximen Qing had finished some of the side rooms and the three-roomed apartment. Only the arbor still remained to be done. It was the Summer Day, the fifth day of the fifth month.

Li Ping'er made preparations, and invited Ximen Qing to unfold the three-cornered dumplings, and also to talk over the arrangements for the wedding. She had decided to send for the monks to sing a dirge on the fifteenth day of the month, and then she proposed that Ximen should take her to his house.

"Are you going to invite the Hua brothers to the ceremony?" Ximen Qing said.

"I shall send each of them a card, and they may come or not as they please," Li Ping'er said. So the matter was settled.

On the fifteenth day of the fifth month, she asked twelve monks from the Temple of Eternal Felicity to sing a dirge at her house. The same day Ximen Qing took three *qian* of silver as a birthday present for Ying Bojue, and gave Daian five taels to spend in celebration of Li Ping'er's coming out of mourning. Just before noon Ximen mounted his horse and went to Ying Bojue's house. Ping'an and Shutong rode behind him. At Ying's house the ten brothers were already gathered, with Ben the Fourth, the latest accession to the band. Bojue had engaged two young actors to play and sing and serve them with wine. When everybody was seated, Ximen Qing called the actors to him. One of them, Wu Yin'er's brother, he knew already, but not the other, who knelt down and introduced himself as Zheng Feng, the brother of Zheng Aixiang.

Ximen Qing, who was sitting in the place of honor, gave each of the boys two *qian* of silver. They drank till it grew dark, and Daian appeared to escort his master home. The boy went to Ximen Qing and whispered, "Mistress Hua hopes you will not stay very late."

Ximen Qing winked at him and made to leave the table. Bojue cried, "You thievish bone of a dog! Come here and tell me what it is all about, or I will pull your little ears till they are both on the same side of your head. How many birthdays a year do you think I have? The sun is still high in the heavens, and you come here with a horse. Who told you to come? The ladies of your family, or someone else we know? If you don't tell me, I will never ask your father to find a wife for you, even if you live to be a hundred years old, you little bald-pated dog."

"Really," said Daian, "nobody told me. I thought it was going to be a rough night and that it would be better for Father to go home early, so I brought the horse and came to wait for him."

Ying Bojue questioned the boy for a long time, but Daian did not tell him the true story.

"So you won't tell me?" Ying Bojue cried. "Well, tomorrow I shall hear all about it, and then I'll settle with you, little oily mouth."

He gave Daian a cup of wine and half a dish of cakes, and told him to go away and eat them. Soon afterwards Ximen Qing came down to change his clothes. He called Daian to a quiet place.

"Who has been at the Huas' house today?" he asked.

"Hua the Third has gone to the country, and Hua the Fourth has something the matter with his eyes. Only Hua the Elder and his wife were at the funeral banquet. Master Hua went away first, and, before his wife followed him, Mistress Hua took her into her room and gave her ten taels of silver and two dresses. She kowtowed to Mistress Hua."

"Didn't she say anything?"

"Not a word, except that, when Mistress Hua was married, she would come to pay her respects on the third day."

"Did she really say that?" Ximen cried.

"I would not dare to lie to you," Daian said.

This was extremely satisfactory. Ximen asked if the service was over.

"The tablet has been burned and the monks have gone," said Daian. "Mistress Hua says she hopes you will go as soon as you possibly can."

"Very well," said Ximen, "go and get the horse ready."

Daian was about to do so, when Ying Bojue, who had been listening in the passage, suddenly shouted and frightened him. "You thievish little dog bone," he cried, "you wouldn't tell me, but now I've heard everything. This is a nice little plot you and your father are hatching together."

"Don't make so much noise, you funny dog," Ximen Qing said.

"Talk nicely to me and I won't," Bojue answered.

They went back to the party, and Bojue told them all that had happened. Seizing Ximen Qing's hands, he cried, "Do you really call yourself a man, Brother? You have something like this on hand, and not a word of it do you mention to any of us. Why, if Hua the Elder had tried to say anything, all you had to do was to tell us, and we would have gone and dealt with him. One word from him, and we would have raised a fine big bump on him. There would have been no difficulty in getting his assent. We had no idea that this marriage was decided. Tell us all about it, or what use is there in calling ourselves a brotherhood? If we can serve you in any way, we will gladly go through fire and water. That is how we feel about you. Yet you keep your secrets from us."

"If you won't tell us," Xie Xida said, "we will tell Guijie and Wu Yin'er tomorrow. Then there will be trouble."

"Give me a chance to tell you," Ximen said, laughing. "The marriage has been definitely arranged."

"When is our new sister-in-law going to your house?" Xie Xida asked. "We must come and pay our respects, and you must engage four singing girls to serve us with wine. So we will celebrate your wedding."

"Of course," said Ximen, "I shall do myself the honor of sending you invitations."

"Far better drink the wedding cup now," Zhu Shinian said. Ying Bojue took the cup, Xie Xida the wine jar, Zhu Shinian held the dish, and the others knelt down. The two young actors also knelt and sang the thirteen melodies known as "Happy Is This Joyful Day." Ximen Qing swallowed three or four cups one after the other.

"If you invite us to take wine with you on the wedding day," Zhu Shinian said, "you must have these two boys at the house." Turning to the young actors, he said, "You must make a point of going that day." Zheng Feng replied, "We will most certainly attend the banquet."

After a while the wine was finished, and they all sat down to dinner. By this time it was dark, and Ximen Qing would stay no longer. He seized the first opportunity, and got up. Ying Bojue would have stopped him, but Xie Xida said, "Let him go, Brother Ying. Don't make him late when he has such important business to attend to. Our sister-in-law will be angry." So Ximen managed to escape, and went to Lion Street.

Li Ping'er had taken off her mourning clothes and changed into a dress of bright colors. The fire and lamps were burning brightly in the hall.

She had prepared the finest of dishes and wine, and had set a single chair in the place of honor. She asked Ximen Qing to take it. One of the maids held the wine jar, and Li Ping'er poured out a cup of wine and kowtowed four times.

"This day the tablet has been burned," she said. "I am most grateful for the favor which will allow me to assist you at your dressing. The joys of marriage with you will be joys indeed." She rose, and Ximen Qing rose in his turn to offer her a cup of wine. Then they both sat down.

"Did Hua the Elder and his wife have anything to say?" Ximen said.

"I took them to my room after the banquet," said Li Ping'er, "and told them about our marriage. Hua said that, three days after it, he would tell his wife to come and see me. I gave them ten taels of silver and two dresses. They both seemed quite satisfied. In fact, they thanked me again and again."

"If they talk in that strain," Ximen said, "I shall have no objection to their coming. We have nothing to be ashamed of. But if they begin to talk any nonsense, I will never forgive them."

"If they dare to make a sound, I will never forgive them either," Li Ping'er said.

Xiuchun poured the wine into inlaid silver cups and handed them to her mistress. They drank many cups together. Though love may diminish with age, wine improves more and more. It is a question of circumstances. Li Ping'er rejoiced because her wedding day was drawing near, and was even more lively than usual.

"You were drinking at Ying's house," she said, smiling, "when Daian went to ask you to come and see me. Do they know anything about this matter?"

"Ying Bojue guessed," Ximen Qing said. "He tried to get the boy to tell them, and they teased me for a long time. The Brothers insisted on congratulating me. They asked me to give a dinner party and send for singing girls. They tossed the wine down their throats, cup after cup. When I thought I had a chance, I tried to get away, but they held me back. I gave them pleasant words and unpleasant words, and at last they were compelled to let me go."

"They know a thing or two, all the same," Li Ping'er said. "They let you come away."

Ximen Qing saw that she was burning with desire, and he was by no means cold himself. He could refrain no longer. They passed fragrant sweetmeats from one to the other, and pressed their cheeks together. Li Ping'er kissed him.

"If you love me truly," she said, "you will make me your wife soon. I feel like a prisoner here. Do not leave me here alone by day or night." They turned again to the delights of love.

# CHAPTER 17

# The Amorous Doctor

The twentieth day of the fifth month was Major Zhou's birthday. Ximen Qing wrapped up five taels of silver and a pair of handkerchiefs, dressed himself in his best clothes, and, with four boys in waiting, set off to pay his respects, riding on a great white horse. Magistrate Xia, Captain Zhang, and other military gentlemen were there, and music and drama were performed for their entertainment. Daian took Ximen's cloak and went home with the horse. In the afternoon he came back to escort his master home. On his way through West Street, he met old woman Feng and asked where she was going.

"Silversmith Gu," the old woman said, "has finished my lady's headdress. He brought it today and she has sent me to ask your master to go and have a look at it. She wishes to have a talk with him."

"He is at a party at Major Zhou's house," the boy said, "and I am on my way to bring him back. Go home. I'll tell him what you say as soon as I see him."

"Tell him that my lady is expecting him."

Daian went on to Major Zhou's house. The gentlemen were still drinking together. He went to Ximen and said, "As I was bringing the horse for you, I met old woman Feng. She says the silversmith has finished Mistress Hua's headdress, and that her lady would like you to go and see it." This made Ximen anxious to get away, but Major Zhou urged him to stay and pressed him to drink another great cup of wine.

"I am most grateful for all your kindness," Ximen said, "but really I mustn't drink so much. I have a number of things to attend to, and I'm sorry I can't permit myself the pleasure I should wish."

He drank the wine, said farewell to Major Zhou, mounted his horse, and rode off to see Li Ping'er. She welcomed him, and Daian was told to take the horse away and come back the next morning. Li Ping'er bade her maid take the headdress from its box, and show it to Ximen Qing. It was indeed very bright and handsome. They put it away again. Then they arranged that the wedding gifts should be sent on the twenty-fourth day of that month, and the bride should leave for her new home on the fourth of the following month.

Li Ping'er was now perfectly content. She brought wine and drank it with her lover in great delight. She told the maids to prepare the summer bed. The lovers took off their clothes and sat side by side within the silken net on coverlets of the rarest silk, perfumed with orchids and musk. They laughed and played together till the flush of desire mounted to their brows and the passion in their hearts made them tremble. Then they performed the mystery of clouds and rain, and did whatever the wine inspired. Ximen sat on the bed and made Li Ping'er place herself upon the cushions and play the flute for him.

> Not from bamboo or stone, not played on strings,
> This is the song of an instrument that lives,
> That makes the emerald tassels quiver.
> Who shall say whether the mode is *Gong* or *Shang*
> Or *Jiao* or *Zheng*?
> The red lips open wide; the slender fingers
> Play their part daintily.
> Deep in, deep out. Their hearts are wild with passion.
> There are no words to tell the ecstasy that thrills their souls.

Ximen Qing was more than half drunk. "Did Hua Zixu enjoy himself with you like this?" he said.

"His life was one long dream," Li Ping'er said, "and he was still dreaming when he died. I had never any desire to act with him in this way. Day after day he went out and played the fool, and when he returned I would never allow him to come near me. In my father-in-law's lifetime I never shared my husband's room, and I cursed him till the dog's blood went to his head. I was always telling my father-in-law about him and getting him into trouble. No, I should have died of shame if anything of this sort had passed between us. But who could satisfy the cravings of my heart as you do? You act upon me just like a drug. I can think of nothing else by day or night."

They played some time longer, and once again performed the mystery. Yingchun brought in a small square box with all sorts of dainties, and a small golden jar of precious wine. From early evening till the first night watch they drank and sported together. Then, suddenly, they heard a loud knocking at the gate, and sent old woman Feng to see who was there. It was Daian.

"I told you to come for me tomorrow," Ximen Qing said. "Why have you come back tonight?" He told the boy to come in.

Daian, in a great flurry, ran first to the door of the room, but, when he found that his master and Li Ping'er were in bed, he did not venture to go in. Standing outside the lattice, he said, "Sister and Brother-in-law have just come home, and brought all their luggage with them. The Great Lady has sent me to ask you to come home at once."

Ximen wondered what could have brought them at this late hour, and decided to go home. He jumped out of bed, and Li Ping'er helped him to dress. She gave him a cup of hot wine. He mounted his horse, and rode away.

In the hall the lamps and candles were lighted. His daughter Ximen Dajie and her husband were there with trunks, hangings, and furniture, all piled up. This alarmed him. He asked why they had come. His son-in-law, Chen Jingji, kowtowed and said, weeping, "A few days ago, the Censor brought an accusation against our kinsman, Marshal Yang, and his Majesty has given orders that he shall be put in the Southern Prison to await his trial. All his relatives and dependents have been put in the cangue, and banished. Yesterday Yang's people brought word to my father, traveling day and night without resting. My father was much upset and bade my wife and myself bring these things here for you to keep, for the time being. He has gone to the Eastern Capital to try to find out from my aunt what has really happened. When the danger has passed, he will make you a handsome present, and he will remember your kindness so long as he lives."

"Did your father send me any letter?" Ximen asked.

"Here it is," Chen Jingji said. He took a letter from his sleeve and handed it to Ximen, who opened it.

Your kinsman Chen Hong [he read] kowtows and offers this to the most worthy Ximen. The matter of which I have to speak is most urgent. Some time ago the border garrison sent word of a surprise attack, as a result of which the enemy have already invaded Xiongzhou. Wang, the Minister of War, did not send the necessary troops, and the military situation has become disastrous. In consequence of this our kinsman Yang has been accused by the Censor in the most direct terms. His Majesty is extremely angry and has ordered Yang's arrest and his incarceration in the Southern Prison. He is to be tried by three justices. Orders have been given that all those under him and his relatives shall be banished to the frontier.

When this news reached us, we were all much distressed, for we have no possibility of escape. I am sending my son and your honorable daughter, with their belongings, to stay with you for a while. I myself am just about to leave for the Eastern Capital, to visit my brother-in-law, Zhang Shilian, to see if I can hear any news. We hope to return when the matter has been settled.

I shall be eternally grateful to you for your kindness. Even in your district there may be some little difficulty, so I am giving my son five hundred taels, which perhaps you will be good enough to expend on his account.

I kowtow to express my gratitude, and so long as I have a tooth in my mouth I will remember your kindness.

Under the lamp, in haste, and without a proper expression of my affection.

Midsummer, the twentieth.

Your most obsequious kinsman Hong.

After reading this letter Ximen Qing was so perturbed that he did not know what to do with himself. He told Yueniang to give his daughter and her husband something to eat, and instructed the maids to make ready three rooms at one side of the hall for them to live in. The trunks and valuables were taken to Yueniang's room. Chen Jingji handed the five hundred taels to his father-in-law. Then Ximen gave one of his servants five taels, and sent him posthaste to the Town Hall to make a copy of the *Imperial Gazette* from the Eastern Capital. This is what it said:

### THE PROCURATOR FOR MILITARY AFFAIRS, YUWEN XUZHONG
#### A Memorial

This is respectfully to implore Your Sacred Justice to punish the traitors in high places, that the morale of the army may be reconstituted and the disturbance at the frontier quelled.

I am not unaware that during every Dynasty there have been frontier attacks. In the Zhou dynasty this happened at Taiyuan; in the Han dynasty at Yinshan; and in the Tang dynasty at Hedong. During the period of the Five Kingdoms these attacks went on unceasingly. Since the great dynasty of Song has been established, our four frontiers have more than once been threatened. It is common knowledge that signs of decay without are an indication of the depredations of worms within. There is an old saying that when the bell booms in the hall, it is a sign of frost; and when the foundations are flooded, we may know that there has been rain. Good fortune and ill fortune alike have their proper causes. This is apparent in every case of sickness. When the heart and stomach suffer from disease, that disease has long been acquiring strength, and the patient's physique has been gradually sapped from within. Then, one day a cold wind blows, and the chill affects every part of his body. Even the physicians Lu and Bian can do nothing for that man and his days are numbered.

The condition of this Empire is precisely that of such an invalid, thin and wasted to a most precarious degree. Your Majesty is the head; the Ministers are the stomach and heart; and the lesser officers the limbs. Your Majesty sits in sublime state above the Nine Degrees, and, if the officers whose duty it is to carry on the business of the Empire are loyal and dutiful in their less exalted stations, then the natural vigor of the Empire will be sound indeed; the armies will afford protection against attack from without; and the menace of these barbarians can remain unheeded.

Now, of those who are chiefly to be held responsible for the trouble between our soldiers and the barbarians, there is none more infamous than Cai Jing, the Minister of the Palace of Chong Zheng. His courses of action have been both dangerous and unpolitic, and he is, moreover, improvident and without shame. Since he but flatters your Majesty, he is unable to assist you and your ministers to maintain the Sacred Authority and to improve the condition of the people. He is unable to foster virtue and concord among the lower orders, thus promoting peace among the people. He maintains himself by selling profit and position, seeking only for favor and to make his own position secure. He has set up a faction of his own, and harbors evil designs. All this he has done in secret, deceiving your Sacred Majesty. He has done injury to all the well-affected, and faithful men have been alienated. There is in his household none who has not robed himself in red and purple garments of office. Lately, when there broke out disorder in He Huang, he suggested a declaration of war in the east, and lost three districts. The rebellion of Guo Yaoshi was the cause of the Jin country's denouncing its treaty with us; and we lost its friendship.

These are his greatest misdeeds, and they are due entirely to his disloyalty. Wang Fu is greedy for money and misconducts himself, behaving like an actor, but Cai Jing recommended him for appointment. Only a short time after securing this appointment, he led the army to disaster, and then, in the hope of saving his own skin, made a patched-up peace, without having any notion of further consequences. Now that Zhang Da has been defeated at Taiyuan, Wang Fu is terrified and all soldiers in a panic, so that by this time the invaders have already reached the interior, while he has escaped with his wife and children to the South. The guilt of such treasonable conduct deserves a punishment worse than death.

Yang Jian is nothing but a wealthy and ignorant young man, who relies upon the reputation of his ancestors and the favor of those in high official positions. He obtained a command but has succeeded very indifferently in this very vital position on the frontier. Though in reality he is a man of evil character, he poses as a devoted subject. His lack of determination is unrivaled.

These three officers have been in very intimate relations and, both within and without the Court, have been guilty of deceitful conduct. They are, as it were, the disease that has affected your Majesty's heart and stomach. For many years they have been the cause of troubles, and have brought upon us calamities that are sapping away the natural vigor of the body politic and undermining the State. Taxes have increased and the people have migrated in consequence. Bandits and thieves have shown unexampled boldness, and even bear arms against their lawful sovereign. The Imperial Treasury is exhausted and the laws of the Kingdom made of no effect. The crimes that these men have committed outnumber the hairs on their heads.

I accept responsibility for what I have said, but it is my duty to point out that which is in need of amendment, and if, when I perceive traitors meddling in the affairs of State, I fail to convey the fact to Your Majesty, I should be untrue to myself and unworthy the favor of a Lord and Father. I pray therefore that Your Exalted Justice will summon Jing and the others before the officers of the law that due chastisement may be awarded.

The penalties suggested are

> The Extreme Penalty
> The Cangue
> Banishment to a Far Country

Thus may the evil course be stayed and the favor of Heaven restored, while the desires of the common people will be satisfied. If the laws of this Empire are duly enforced, all disorders and troubles will come to an end of themselves. This would be indeed fortunate for our Empire, and for both officials and people.

Here follows the sentence of the Imperial Sage.

Cai Jing shall remain in office for the time being. Wang Fu and Yang Jian shall be sent before the Justices. Let them be tried with due care and the report sent to us.

### TAKE HEED, TAKE HEED, AND OBEY.
### The Findings of the Court

The traitors Wang Fu and Yang Jian are found guilty of negligence of duty as military commanders. They have permitted the soldiers of other nations to invade the interior, and many have lost their lives in consequence. Our armies have been defeated, many officers killed, and the territory of this Empire lost.

The Law decrees their execution.

Their households, secretaries, and underlings, Dong Sheng, Lu Hu, Yang Sheng, Bang Xuan, Han Zongren, Chen Hong, Huang Yu, Liu Sheng and Zhao Hongdao are all accessories in their crime, and, after wearing the cangue for one month, shall be banished to the frontiers as private soldiers.

When Ximen Qing had read this, his good humor vanished. He fell into a terrible state of agitation. At once he began to get ready gold, silver, and jewels, packed them with the greatest care, and, calling his two servants Laibao and Laiwang to his room, gave them secret instructions. They were to hire several beasts of burden, go to the Eastern Capital, traveling both night and day, and get all the information they could about the matter.

"It will be better for you not to go to Chen's house," Ximen said. "If the news you hear is bad, do what you can with these things, and come back and report to me." He gave them twenty taels of silver. Next morning, before it was light, they rose, hired drivers, and started for the Eastern Capital.

All that night Ximen Qing never closed his eyes. The next morning he ordered Laizhao and Ben the Fourth to cease work upon the garden and send all the workmen away. Every day he had the gate most carefully secured, and no one in his household was allowed to go out except on business of the utmost urgency. Ximen himself paced up and down his room like a centipede on hot earth, brooding over his sorrows and anticipating all manner of trouble. As for his marriage with Li Ping'er, all thoughts of that were banished to regions beyond the clouds. Yueniang saw how greatly his anxieties weighed upon her husband—his appearance showed that clearly— and tried to console him.

"You need not be so distressed over this misfortune of our kinsman Chen," she said. "Hatred and debt always pursue their proper object."

"Oh, woman! what do you know about it?" Ximen cried. "Chen is my kinsman, and so long as my daughter and her husband live with us, they will be a millstone about our necks. Nearly all our neighbors detest us, and as the old proverb says: Though the loom be slow, the shuttle is speedy, and Beat the sheep, and the young donkeys will stir up trouble. If there are any small-minded men among them who take it into their heads to uproot the tree to see what the roots are like, neither you nor I will be safe from them, to say nothing of the rest of the family. Even if we lie low here and keep our door shut, trouble will find its way through the roof."

Ximen Qing remained sadly at home.

Li Ping'er waited for him, one day, two days, but he did not come. She ordered old woman Feng to go to his house. The old woman went twice, but the gate was shut as closely as the iron cover of a well, and, though she waited a very long time, not a sign of life was to be seen and she could not find out what was amiss. The twenty-fourth day was drawing near, and again Li Ping'er told old woman Feng to take the headdresses to Ximen and ask him to come and talk to her. The old woman knocked at the door, but no answer was vouchsafed, so she took her stand beneath the eaves of a house opposite and waited. After a while Daian came out to water the horses, and saw her standing there.

"What are you doing here?" he asked.

"My mistress told me to bring these headdresses and find out why she has had no message from your master. She would like to see him."

"My master has been too busy to go out these last few days," Daian said. "Take the things back, old lady, and as soon as I have finished watering the horses I will tell him what you say."

"Take them in, good little brother," the old woman said, "and tell him that my lady is not at all pleased. I will wait here."

Daian tethered his horses, and went in. Some time later he came out again. "I have told my master, and he has taken the headdresses. He says you must ask your lady to wait a few days longer, and then he will come and see her."

The old woman went home and told her mistress all that had happened. For several days more she waited for him, till the fifth month had nearly come to an end. Morning and evening she longed for him to come, but there was not a word from him. Her dreams were dashed to the ground, her good fortune seemed to have come to an end.

Ximen Qing's absence made Li Ping'er lose her appetite. She became very languid. Night after night she slept alone, tossing about on her bed, the same ideas constantly re-echoing in her mind. Suddenly, she heard a knocking at the door. Ximen Qing had come at last. She opened the door for him and smiled, taking him by the hand to lead him within. She asked why he had so long delayed their marriage, and they spoke to each other the deepest thoughts of their hearts. They spent the whole night in the enjoyment of their love. When day broke and the cock crew, he rose and went away. It was a dream. The woman woke with a start, gave a great cry, and fainted away. Old woman Feng heard and quickly ran in.

"Master Ximen has just gone," Li Ping'er said. "Have you bolted the door?"

"Where is his Lordship?" the old woman said. "Your mind is wandering. Not even his shadow has been here."

From this time onward Li Ping'er dreamed many unseemly things and, night after night, foxes came, taking upon themselves human form, and sucked away her very life. By degrees her face grew pale and thin. She could neither eat nor drink, but lay all day upon her bed, unable to get up. With her permission, old woman Feng asked Doctor Jiang Zhushan of the High Street to come and see her. This Jiang was not more than thirty years of age, not very tall, and a very pleasant fellow. When he came in, Li Ping'er was lying on the bed with the bedclothes over her, her hair about her like a mist of cloud. The doctor could see that she was anything but well. After he had taken tea, a maid gave him a cushion, and he went to the bedside to feel his patient's pulse. This gave him an opportunity to find out how pretty she was.

"Lady," he said, "I think I know what is the matter with you. There is considerable irregularity in the pulse of the liver, which, above the wrist, appears to be too strong. As for that pulse which is peculiar to ladies, it is so weak above the wrist that it cannot be felt, but appears to have betaken itself to the hollow beneath the thumb. This is clearly due to the fact that the masculine and feminine principles are at war within you, thus interfering with the six passions and the seven emotions. So you sometimes feel hot and sometimes cold. Evidently you are suffering from repression of some sort. This produces a state of affairs rather like a fever, though it is not a fever, and makes you feel cold, though you are not cold. During the day it makes you weary, low-spirited, and anxious to lie down all the time; and at night you feel as though your spirit were on the point of departure, and dream that ghosts come and misconduct themselves with you. Unless something is done about it at once, the trouble will take a still more serious turn and you may even die. Oh, it is very serious, very."

"Doctor," Li Ping'er said, "please let me have some of your very best medicine, and when I am better you shall have a handsome fee."

"I will take the utmost care, Madam," Zhushan said, "and, when you take my medicine, you will soon be quite well again." He went away.

Old woman Feng took five taels of silver and went to the doctor's house for the medicine. The same evening Li Ping'er took it, and enjoyed an undisturbed night's rest. Gradually her appetite returned; she was able to get up and dress; and, in a very short time, was completely recovered.

One day she spent three taels, and sent old woman Feng to invite the doctor to dinner. As soon as Jiang Zhushan received the invitation, he dressed and went to the lady's house, for indeed, ever since he had first attended her, he had desired to possess her. Dressed in her most beautiful clothes, Li Ping'er received him in the hall. She made a reverence to him and offered him tea. Then she asked him to go into the inner room, where wine and dishes were set out and there was a delightful fragrance of orchids. Xiuchun came, holding a gilded tray upon which were three taels of white gold. Li Ping'er raised a jade cup high before her, and again made a reverence to the doctor.

"I was very ill," she said, "and I find it hard to express my gratitude to you for giving me such excellent medicine and curing me. Today, doctor, I have hastily prepared a poor cup of wine in token of my thankfulness, and now I beg you to accept it."

"It was no more than the business of a poor scholar like myself," Zhushan said. "It was my duty to come and attend you, and there was no occasion for you to give the matter a second thought." Then he saw the white gold. "I cannot possibly accept this," he said.

"It only represents a fraction of my gratitude," Li Ping'er said, "and is in no way what you deserve. But I hope, doctor, that you will condescend to accept it."

After much show of hesitation Zhushan finally accepted the present. Li Ping'er poured wine for him, and they sat down and drank together. Zhushan looked at her and realized how charming and attractive she was. He began to wonder what words he should choose to make an impression upon her.

"May I ask how old you are?" he said at last.

"I have lived twenty-four ill-spent years," she said.

"But that is a delightful age," Zhushan cried, "yet you live in such seclusion. You seem to be quite comfortably off and everything should be well with you. Why should you suffer so from depression?"

Li Ping'er smiled. "I will tell you, doctor," she said. "Since I lost my husband, things have been very lonely here. I live alone and worry. Does it surprise you that I should be ill?"

"When did your husband die?" the doctor said.

"It was the eleventh month of last year when he died of a fever. About eight months ago now."

"Ah," Zhushan exclaimed, "and whose medicine did he take?"

"Doctor Hu, who lives in the High Street, attended him."

"What? That foxy-mouthed Hu, who used to live in East Street in Eunuch Liu's house? He is not a member of the Royal Society of Medicine. He knows nothing about the pulse. What can have induced you to call him in?"

"The neighbors recommended him, and really I don't think it was his fault that my husband died so young."

"Have you any children?" Zhushan asked.

"None," said Li Ping'er.

"It is most unfortunate that you should have become a widow so young," Zhushan said, "especially since you have no children. Why do you not consider the desirability of another mode of life, something better than living by yourself like this and bringing sickness upon yourself?"

"As a matter of fact," Li Ping'er said, "I became engaged only a little while ago, and we are going to be married almost immediately."

"May I venture to ask to whom you are betrothed?"

"To Master Ximen, who keeps a medicine shop over by the Town Hall."

"Dear, dear!" Zhushan said. "Surely you haven't become engaged to him! I know him quite well. I often go to attend the members of his household when they are ill. He is the man who arranges things behind the scenes at the Town Hall and is mixed up in shady money-lending transactions. He makes quite a business of dealing in women. Apart from his maids, he must have at least half a dozen wives. He is always thrashing them. If one of his women upsets him in the slightest, he sends at once for the go-between and gets rid of her. In fact, he is a captain among wife beaters and a shining light among those who lead women astray.

"I am glad you have told me this, Lady, for otherwise you would have gone blindly to him, like a moth rushing headlong into a flame. If you do this, you will be in a hopeless position and it will be too late to repent. Moreover, only recently, one of his relatives has got into trouble. Ximen has had to hide away in his house and dares not go outside his own door. His new house is only half built, but all the work upon it has been stopped. An order has come from the Eastern Capital that he is to be arrested and his property confiscated to the State. How can you think of marrying him?"

Li Ping'er could think of no answer to make to this. She reflected that all her wealth was stored in Ximen's house, and her foot tapped nervously upon the floor. "Now I know why he has not been to see me though I have invited him more than once," she said to herself. "There is evidently something seriously wrong. Zhushan seems very agreeable and pleasant. If I married a man like him, I should not do so badly, but he may have a wife already for all I know."

"I am most grateful for your advice," she said aloud. "Thank you with all my heart. If you can think of anyone more suitable and will be kind enough to recommend him, I will take your advice."

Zhushan did not let this opportunity slip. "I have no idea what kind of man you would like," he said, "but I may be able to arrange matters for you, if you will speak quite frankly."

"Whether his family is of high or low degree is of no consequence to me," Li Ping'er said, "I should be quite satisfied with a man like you."

At this the doctor was so overjoyed he could hardly contain himself. He threw himself on his knees before her. "I have been long without a mistress in my house," he said, "and I am childless. Lady, if you will take compassion on me and link your destiny with mine, I can wish for nothing better. Even if you give me the work of a menial to do, I shall be eternally grateful."

Li Ping'er laughed and helped him to rise. "Please do not kneel," she said. "How long have you been a widower and under what star were you born? If you really wish to marry me, the Rites insist that you should send a go-between."

Zhushan kneeled down again. "I am now twenty-nine years old, and was born at the hour of the Hare on the twenty-seventh day of the first month. I grieve to say that my wife died last year. I am very poor, and, if you give me your promise, why should we trouble about a go-between?"

"If you cannot afford it," Li Ping'er said, smiling, "I have an old lady named Feng living with me, and we will make her our go-between. As for a betrothal present, don't worry about that. We will select an auspicious day, and you shall marry me and come and live here."

Zhushan bowed. "You are both father and mother to me, and have given me a new lease of life. Obviously our marriage was ordained several generations ago, and it is the greatest piece of luck I have had in any of my three lives."

They drank each other's health, and so this marriage was decided. Zhushan remained till nightfall. When he had gone away, Li Ping'er discussed the matter with old woman Feng.

"Ximen Qing," she said, "is now in a bad way. It is impossible to say whether his luck will ever turn. There is no one to bother about me, and I have been so ill I nearly died. The best thing I can do is to marry this doctor. There doesn't seem to be any reason why I should not."

The next day she sent old woman Feng with a letter to the doctor, saying that the eighteenth day of the sixth month appeared to be an auspicious day. He was to come then and live with her. Three days afterwards she gave Zhushan three hundred taels of silver, so that he could open a couple of rooms and decorate his surgery tastefully. Before this he had always gone on foot to visit his patients. Now he bought a donkey and rode up and down the street.

# CHAPTER 18

# Ximen Qing Bribes Officers of the Court

Laibao and Laiwang set out to the Eastern Capital to try to put matters right there. They traveled at early dawn when the rising sun threw a purple haze over their path; they traveled in the evening when its setting cast a rosy light upon the dust. At last they came to their destination and entered the city through the Gate of Eternal Life. They found an inn and rested there. The next day they set out to pick up what news they could in the street. They heard people saying that Wang, the Minister for War, had been tried the previous day, and that the Emperor had ordered his execution in the coming autumn. Of Marshal Yang it was said that his case was not yet done with, for his household and his staff had not all been arrested.

Laibao and Laiwang took the treasures they had brought and went in haste to the palace of the Imperial Tutor. They had been there before and knew the way well, but, when they came to the Arch of Dragon Virtue, they waited for a time to see if they could learn anything more of interest. After a while a man wearing black robes came hurriedly from the palace and went eastwards. Laibao recognized him as one of the household of Marshal Yang. He would have liked to go and ask a few questions, but his master had told him to keep in the background, and he let the man pass. At last they went up to the palace gate, politely greeted the keeper of the gate, and asked if his Eminence was at home.

"His Eminence is still detained at the Court," the keeper of the gate said. "What is your business?"

"We should like to see Master Zhai the Comptroller of the Household," Laibao said. "Will you be good enough to ask him to see us?"

"His Lordship is not at home," the keeper of the gate said.

Laibao realized that the officer was not telling the truth and that something was expected of him. He took a tael of silver from his sleeve and gave it to the gatekeeper.

"Whom did you say you wished to see?" the man said. "His Eminence or his Excellency the Vice Chancellor? Zhai Qian is the great Comptroller of the Household and matters affecting the Imperial Tutor are referred to him. The lesser Comptroller Gao An deals with the Vice Chancellor's affairs.

Their duties are quite distinct. The Imperial Tutor himself is not at home, but the Vice Chancellor is. What is the real nature of your business? Shall I ask Master Gao to come and see you? He will serve your purpose just as well."

"We are from Marshal Yang's palace," said Laibao, "and shall be very glad to see anyone."

The officer of the gate hastened into the palace, and, after a short delay, Gao An appeared. Laibao went forward and made a reverence, at the same time offering ten taels of silver. "I was to have come," he said, "with one of Marshal Yang's household. We hoped to see the Imperial Tutor to find out what is happening. But I had to stay for food, and so was late and missed the officer."

"Marshal Yang's courier has just gone," said Gao An, accepting the present, "but if you will wait a moment or two I will take you to see the Vice Chancellor." He took Laibao through the entrance hall, and passing through a side door they came to three large rooms on the north. Here was a green screen, with a scroll upon which the Emperor had written in his own hand 'The Music Chamber of the Vice Chancellor.' Cai Yu, the son of Cai Jing, was, like his father, a favorite at court. He was an Imperial Delegate at the Temple of the Great Monad and held high office at the Xiang He Palace and in the Board of Rites.

Laibao waited till Gao An, who had gone to announce him, came to summon him. Then he went in and knelt down. Cai Yu was dressed in his ordinary attire with a soft hat. He asked Laibao where he had come from.

"I am a servant of Chen Hong's household," said Laibao. "He is a kinsman of Marshal Yang. I was to have come with the Marshal's courier in the hope of seeing his Eminence and obtaining some information. Unfortunately, the courier got here before me." He took a paper from his sleeve and offered it to the minister. Cai Yu read on it the words "Five hundred measures of purest rice," and called Laibao nearer.

"His Eminence," he said, "has avoided becoming mixed up in this matter in view of the fact that his own name was mentioned to the Emperor in the Censor's report. Li, the Minister of the Right, dealt with the case yesterday. But so far as Marshal Yang is concerned, we heard from the Court that his Majesty is inclined to be merciful and will not deal severely with him, though his underlings, no doubt, will still have to be tried and sentenced. You must go and see Li."

Laibao kowtowed. "I am quite unknown at Li's palace," he said. "Pray have pity on me for Marshal Yang's sake."

"Go as far as the Bridge of the Heavenly River," said Cai Yu. "North of it you will see a very high building, and there you must ask for Li Bangyan,

Minister of the Right. Everybody knows him. But I will send someone with you."

He called for official paper, set his seal upon it, and instructed Gao An to go with Laibao and introduce him. The two men left the hall together. They called to Laiwang to bring the presents, went down the Street of Dragon Virtue, and, passing the Bridge of the Heavenly River, came to the palace of Li Bangyan.

The minister, who had just returned from the Presence, was still wearing his robes of crimson silk and a girdle around his waist, fastened by a jade clasp. After bidding farewell to some man of rank, he had gone to his hall when the gatekeeper informed him that Vice Chancellor Cai had sent his Comptroller, Gao An, with a message. Gao An was then summoned, and, after he had exchanged a few words with the minister, Laibao and Laiwang were called forward. They went into the hall and knelt down. Gao An stood beside them and handed Cai Yu's note and the list of presents they had brought to the minister. Bangyan looked at it.

"You are connected with Marshal Yang," he said, "and Cai has been good enough to send you to me. How can I possibly accept presents from you? Besides, his Majesty is now quite well disposed to Marshal Yang: he will not be troubled further. But I fear the Censor has been so severe upon some of the Marshal's subordinates that they can hardly escape punishment." He called for the memorial that the Censor had laid before the Emperor the previous day.

"Wang Fu's archivist, Dong Sheng; his chamberlain, Wang Lian; Captain Huang Yu; Yang Jian's servant, the scrivener Lu Hu; Yang Sheng, his administrator; Fu Quan, his comptroller; Han Zongren; Zhao Hongdao; Captain Liu Sheng; Chen Hong; Ximen Qing; and Hu the Fourth. These are all men of utter unworthiness, scoundrelly fellows who, like foxes, invest themselves with the dignity of a tiger. We pray that justice may be done upon them. Some should be banished to the frontier that there may be an end to their deceits. Some should be put to death that the majesty of the law may be vindicated."

When Laibao heard this document read, he was greatly excited. Again and again he prostrated himself before the minister. "In truth, your Excellency," he cried, "I am Ximen Qing's servant. I implore you to be generous and spare my master's life." Gao An knelt down and added his prayers to those of Laibao. The minister allowed his glance to fall upon the gold and silver. There were, in all, five hundred taels, and it seemed to him that such a present might suffice to purchase the name of a single man. Why should he hesitate? He called for writing materials, took up a brush, and changed the name of Ximen Qing to Jia Lian. Then he accepted the presents and dismissed the men, sending a polite message to the Vice Chancellor Cai Yu. To each of the three domestics he gave five taels of silver. Laibao and Laiwang took their leave of Gao An, returned to their inn, packed their luggage, paid their reckoning, and made haste back to Qinghe.

As soon as they reached home, they hurried to Ximen and told him all that had happened in the Eastern Capital. When he realized how narrowly he had escaped, he shivered as though he had been plunged into a bath of ice-cold water.

"If I had not bestirred myself at the right moment," he said to Yueniang, "I dare not think what would have happened. It would have been too late to do anything now."

A stone comfortably at rest upon the ground could not have felt more solidly established than Ximen Qing now. The gate was opened again; the work upon the garden restarted, and, in a little while, Ximen resumed his saunterings through the streets.

One day, Daian, riding down Lion Street, passed the house of Li Ping'er. He noticed that a large drug shop had been opened there, with a small red counter and a lacquer sign. It seemed to be prospering. When he reached home, he told Ximen Qing, but, as he knew nothing of the marriage between Li Ping'er and Jiang Zhushan, he said she had engaged a manager and opened a medicine shop. Ximen Qing did not pay much heed.

About the middle of the seventh month the autumn winds blew and the dew was cold and chill. Ximen Qing mounted his horse and set out for the main street. There he was hailed by Ying Bojue and Xie Xida, and got off his horse to greet them.

"Where have you been all this time, Brother?" they said. "We have been to your house several times, but the gate was fast shut and we did not venture to call. We could not imagine what was wrong. What have you been doing, keeping within doors like that? Have you married the lady? You never sent for us to take wine with you."

"It is not a very agreeable story," Ximen said, "but a near kinsman of mine, Chen, has been in trouble, and I have had to devote all my energies to getting him out of his difficulties. I had to put off my marriage."

"We knew nothing of any troubles," Bojue said. "Anyhow, now that we have run into you today, we shall not let you go. Come with us to see Wu Yin'er and drink some wine to drown your sorrows." They would take no refusal and rushed Ximen Qing to Wu Yin'er's house.

They drank all day, and not till night was falling and Ximen Qing was half drunk, would they let him go. On his way down East Street he saw old woman Feng hurrying along. "Where are you going?" he called, reining in his horse.

"My lady has sent me to the temple outside the city to burn paper offerings for my late master."

"How is your mistress?" Ximen said tipsily. "I'm going to come and have a chat with her one of these days."

"What is the use of asking after my mistress now?" the old woman said. "The rice was cooked, but you let someone else walk off with the pan."

Ximen was greatly agitated when he heard this. "You don't mean to say she's gone and married someone else?" he cried.

"My lady sent me to show you her wedding headdress, and I called at your house several times, but the gate was closed and I could not see you. I spoke to your boy and told him to ask you not to delay, but you paid no heed. It's no use complaining now if you find your place occupied by someone else."

"Who is the man?" Ximen cried.

Old woman Feng told him the whole story. She explained how Li Ping'er came to send for Jiang Zhushan, and finally married him, and how she gave him three hundred taels to set him up in a medicine shop.

"Terrible! Terrible!" Ximen cried. He flew into a furious rage and stamped his feet. "I wouldn't have minded so much if it had been anybody else, but that miserable little turtle! What use does she think he'll be to her?" He whipped up his horse and galloped home.

When he passed through the inner door, Wu Yueniang, Meng Yulou, Pan Jinlian, and Ximen Dajie were skipping in the courtyard. When Ximen came, they withdrew to the inner court. But Jinlian leaned against a pillar and began to tie her shoelaces.

"You little strumpet," Ximen cried, "have you nothing better to do than fool about like this?"

He kicked her twice and then went to the inner court, but, instead of going to change in Yueniang's room, he went to his own study in the wing and demanded bedclothes so that he could pass the night there. With unrelenting fury he beat the maids and cursed the boys, till all the women gathered together in terror, wondering what could be amiss. Yueniang blamed Jinlian. She said, "If you had got out of his way when you saw him in such a rage, all would have been well. Instead, you stayed there in front of him, laughing and playing with your shoelaces, and he cursed us like a host of grasshoppers, yes, and caterpillars too."

"It would not have mattered so much," Yulou said, "if he had only cursed us, but to abuse the Great Lady and call her a strumpet! Really, he is a most unmannerly fellow!"

"It was me he picked on," Jinlian cried. "You were all there, but I was the one to suffer. Why should I be selected to receive his special favors?"

This made Yueniang angry. "Why didn't you ask him to kick me?" she said. "You were treated neither worse nor better than anybody else. You don't know your place."

Jinlian saw that Yueniang was angry and she changed her tune. "Oh, Sister," she said, "I didn't mean that. He doesn't know what is the matter with him and he thought he would vent his spite on me. He set up a tremendous outcry and swore he would bring me to a doleful end."

"Nobody told you to make fun of him," Yueniang said. "He would have been all right if you had not given him cause to beat you."

"Great Sister," Yulou said, "let us send for the boy and find out where he was drinking this afternoon. He was in a perfectly good temper when he went out this morning. What has made him come back like this?"

Daian was summoned.

"You wicked young scoundrel," Yueniang said to him, "if you don't tell me the truth you shall have a thrashing. Ping'an too. You shall both have ten strokes of the rod."

"You need not beat me," Daian cried, "I will tell all there is to tell. Father spent the day drinking with Uncle Ying at Wu Yin'er's house. Afterwards, as he was going down East Street, he met old woman Feng and she told him that Mistress Hua had not waited, but had married the Doctor Jiang who used to live in the High Street. Father was fearfully angry, even in the street."

"So, just because that shameless hussy chooses another man, he must come home and take it out on us!" Yueniang said.

"That was not all," Daian said. "Mistress Hua has taken him to live with her and set him up in a fine medicine shop. I told Father so once before, but he wouldn't listen to me."

"It is only a few months ago since her husband died," Yulou said, "and she was not out of mourning. It is most unseemly."

"In these days," said Yueniang, "nobody stops to think whether things are unseemly or not. If she took a man before she was out of mourning, she was not the first one. Strumpets like her will drink or sleep with any man. How can one expect them to consider the virtuous estate of widowhood?"

This was a blow at Yulou and Jinlian. Both had married before their widowhood was over. Yueniang's remark made them feel so uncomfortable that they went to their own rooms and did not wait to hear what she would say next.

Ximen Qing spent the night in his study. The next day he sent his son-in-law, Chen Jingji, to the garden to superintend the work there and keep the accounts with Ben the Fourth. Laizhao, whose place he took, was given charge of the gate. Ximen's daughter, Ximen Dajie, took her meals in the inner court with Yueniang and the others, and only went to the front court to sleep. From morning till night Jingji labored in the garden. He never went into the other parts of the house unless he was invited, and, as all his meals were taken to him by the boys, the ladies of Ximen's household never set eyes on him.

One day, when Ximen Qing was at a farewell party for Captain He, Yueniang remembered that Jingji had to work very hard and that his services were poorly requited.

"If I do anything about it," she said to Yulou and Li Jiao'er, "his Lordship will say I meddle in things that don't concern me, but really I can't allow this sort of thing to go on. The boy is one of ourselves. He rises early and goes to bed late every single day, and all on our account. Nobody lifts a finger to make things more comfortable for him."

"Lady," Yulou said, "you are the mistress of the house, and if you do nothing, nobody else can."

Yueniang told a boy to lay a table for Jingji and ask him to join them. The young man at once handed over his work to Ben the Fourth and hurried to pay his respects to Yueniang. He made reverence to her and sat down. Xiaoyu brought tea and the table with refreshments was carried in.

"You work terribly hard," Yueniang said. "I should have asked you before to come and spend a few moments' leisure with us, but there has never been an opportunity. However, your father is away today and I am free. This is a poor sign of our appreciation of all you do for us."

"Mother," Jingji said, "you are too good to me. I have done nothing to deserve this."

They drank together, and Yueniang told a maid to invite his wife to come and join them. The maid told them that she was washing her hands and would be with them in a moment. Then they heard the clatter of dominoes in the next room, and Jingji asked who was playing there.

"It is your wife," Yueniang said, "playing with Yuxiao."

"She is most ill-mannered, not to come the moment you invite her."

Soon, however, she came, sat down, and drank with them. Yueniang asked her whether Jingji knew how to play. "He knows the difference between 'pleasant scent' and 'evil odor,'" Ximen Dajie said.

Yueniang believed that Jingji was all that could be desired as a son-in-law. She did not know that never was a rascal so well versed in poetry, backgammon, songs, and every other form of low amusement. "If you know how to play," she said, "why should we not go and take a hand?"

"Mother," Jingji said, "pray go and play with your daughter. It would be presumption on my part."

"Not at all," Yueniang said, "you are a close kinsman. Why shouldn't you join us?"

In the next room Yulou was playing, sitting on the bed on which a crimson coverlet had been laid. She rose when they came in and would have retired. "Our brother is no stranger," Yueniang said. "You must treat him as one of ourselves. This is the Third Lady," she said to Jingji.

The young man bowed, and Yulou returned his greeting. Then the three ladies began to play while Jingji stood and looked on. When Ximen Dajie was beaten, her husband took her place.

Jinlian came in. She was wearing a flower in her hair. "I wondered who was here," she said, laughing. "I see it is Brother Chen."

Chen Jingji turned quickly. When he saw Jinlian, his breath seemed to stop. It was as though, after five hundred years of separation, he met his loved one again.

"This is the Fifth Lady," Yueniang said, "you need only exchange simple greetings."

Chen Jingji rose to his feet and bowed low. Jinlian returned his greeting. Then Yueniang invited her to come and see how an old crow could be beaten by a greenhorn. Jinlian, with one hand resting on the bed and the other fluttering her fan, advised Yueniang how to set out her pieces, and they were all playing with great excitement when Daian came and told them that Ximen Qing had returned. Yueniang told Xiaoyu to take Jingji away by the corner door.

When Ximen had dismounted, he went to the outer court to see how the work in the garden was progressing. Then he went to Jinlian's room. She welcomed him and took his clothes. "You are back very early today," she said.

"Yes," said Ximen, "Captain He has just been promoted, and all the officials went out beyond the city gates to say good-bye to him. I was asked to join them, and I couldn't very well refuse."

Jinlian asked if he would like to drink, and told the maid to bring wine. Soon the table was laid. They sat together and enjoyed their food.

"We shall finish the work in the garden tomorrow," Ximen said; "I suppose some of our friends will be coming with presents and scrolls. We shall have to hire some extra cooks and have a banquet."

They talked for a while; then it began to grow dark. Chunmei went to her own room, and Ximen Qing and Jinlian went to bed. He had been up early and was very tired. A few cups of wine made him very sleepy. He was soon fast asleep and snoring like thunder.

It was the twentieth day of the seventh month, and the weather was very sultry. Jinlian could not sleep, the noisy buzzing of mosquitoes in the net annoyed her. Without putting on any clothes, she got up and with a candle in her hand searched all around the bed curtains for mosquitoes, burning each one in the flame as she caught them. Then she looked around. Ximen

Qing was fast asleep. She shook him, but he would not wake. His weapon, with the clasp still upon it, seemed limp and heavy. The sight of it set her naughty mind in a whirl. She put down the candlestick and fondled it with her exquisite hands. After doing this for a short time, she bent her head and kissed it. Ximen woke and stormed at her. "You funny little strumpet. Your darling is sleepy, and you are a terrible nuisance." But he got up. Sitting on the bed, he told her to go on with what she was doing. He watched her, and found the sight particularly attractive. Here is a poem about the mosquito:

> I love that dainty body, its wondrous lightness,
> The beauty and softness of that tender waist.
> Music and song go where it goes.
> When evening comes, before the crimson doors are shut
> It steals within and seeks the silken net,
> Settles so lovingly on the fragrant flesh
> And lightly falls upon the jade-like form.
> Where those lips touch, there stays a rosy flush.
> It sings a hundred songs in people's ears
> Allowing none to sleep though it be midnight.

Jinlian continued for a long time, then Ximen Qing thought of a new plan. He called Chunmei to heat some wine and come and stand beside the bed to hold the wine jar. He set the candlestick beside the bed and told Jinlian to go down on all fours before him. When he saw her like this, he was quickly excited again, and gave himself once more to the delights of love, drinking wine as he did so.

"What a naughty fellow you are," Jinlian cried. "Where did you learn to carry on like this? A fine thing, to let the maid stand by and watch us in such unseemly circumstances."

"Li Ping'er and I used to do it," Ximen said. "She always told Yingchun to stand beside us and hold the wine jar. I think it is most amusing."

"I can't tell you what I think of you," Jinlian said. "And what do I care for that woman? Why do you bring her into it? I had to wait for what I wanted, but she couldn't wait; she had to go and find another man. I haven't forgotten how, when the three of us were skipping in the courtyard, you came home drunk. You vented your spite on me, kicked me, and got me into trouble with the others. I must be one of those who are fated to be ill-used."

"With whom did you have trouble?" Ximen asked.

"When you had gone into the house, she who lives in the upper room made a fine to-do. She accused me of deliberately raising my voice against hers and swore I did not know my place. She doesn't want anyone to like me."

"That day," Ximen said, "Brother Ying dragged me to the Wu Yin'er's house to drink. On the way back I met old woman Feng, and she told me what had happened. It was that which made me so furious. If she had married anybody else, I should not have cared, but Doctor Jiang, the wretched little turtle! What could she be thinking about to marry a man like that, take him to live with her, and give him the money to open a medicine shop right in front of me? And the business seems to be doing well!"

"It's all very well talking like that now," Jinlian said, "but what did I tell you? The one who is the first to cook the rice is always the first to eat it. You wouldn't listen to me; you went and asked what the Great Lady thought about it. I tell you: those who must always take the opinion of somebody else will never get what they want. You went the wrong way about things, and nobody is to blame but yourself."

Ximen Qing flew into a temper. "Let her say what she likes, the strumpet! I will never speak to her again."

Thenceforth Yueniang and Ximen Qing would have no dealings with each other. When they met, they would not speak. Yueniang paid no heed to Ximen's goings and comings, and never asked any questions. If he went to her rooms for anything, she told her maid to attend to him, but would do nothing for him herself. Their hearts were cold to one another.

After this quarrel Jinlian knew that she could do what she liked with her husband and she became more arrogant than ever. She flaunted herself about and made herself as pretty as she could, all to secure Ximen's favor and attentions for herself. When she met Chen Jingji, she was so impressed by that young man's smartness and liveliness that the idea of seducing him came into her head, but she was too afraid of Ximen Qing to attempt it. But when Ximen was out, she sent a maid to invite the young man to take tea in her room and they played chess together.

At last the work in the garden was completed, and relatives and friends came to present red scrolls of congratulation, some bringing boxes of fruits also. Ximen gave all the workmen food and money, and received his guests in the hall, where the celebrations were kept up until noon, when the party broke up. Ximen had been up so early that he decided to go to the inner court for a rest, and Jingji went to see Jinlian and ask her for a cup of tea. He found her sitting on her bed, playing the lute.

"In the outer court," she said, "they have been house warming and drinking wine. How is it that you have had nothing, but must come to me for tea?"

"To tell you the simple truth," Jingji said, "I was up before dawn and have been busy ever since. I never had a moment for food."

"Where is your father?" Jinlian said. Jingji told her that Ximen was resting in the inner court. "Well," she said, "since I see you have had nothing to eat, Chunmei must pick out some of my own pastries for you."

The young man sat on her bed, and a small table with four plates of light refreshments was brought in for him. As he began to eat them, he saw that Jinlian had been playing the lute, and asked her whether she would not sing for him. She laughed. "My dear good Brother," she said, "I don't belong to you. Why should I sing for you? When Father gets up, I shall tell him what you have asked."

Jingji smiled. He knelt before her and said, "Please, Mother, forgive your son. I will never offend again." Jinlian laughed at him.

Ever afterwards they were on terms of intimacy, taking tea and meals together almost every day. Jingji used to go to her room to joke with her, and they sat close together without the slightest scruple. All this time Yueniang treated the young man as though he had been her own son, never dreaming how utterly faithless he was.

# CHAPTER 19
# Ximen Qing's Vengeance

After many months of labor the work in Ximen Qing's garden was com-pleted. The place seemed quite new. So many people came to offer congratulations that the feasting lasted for several days. One day, about the beginning of the eighth month, Xia, the magistrate of the military court, celebrated his birthday in his new house. He engaged four singing girls, a band of musicians, and a troop of actors. Ximen Qing was invited, and set off early in the morning. At home Wu Yueniang prepared a feast for the ladies of the household, and they all went to the garden to admire its arrangement. There were flowers and trees, and buildings specially placed so that they afforded a beautiful view, and everything was delightful.

There was a gatehouse, fifteen feet high and broad around, with a belvedere in each of the four directions. There was an artificial mound and a lake beside it. Bamboos, with their light green foliage, stood out against the darker green of the pines. Summerhouses, high and flat-roofed, contrasted with buildings that, though imposing, were not so high. There was provision for each of the seasons. In the spring could be seen the swallows flitting through the halls, and peach blossoms striving to outdo the apricots in beauty. In summer, from the arbors, you could look down upon the running rivulets, and delight in the gay colors of the artemisia. In autumn, from the Hall of the Humming Bird, one might gaze upon masses of golden chrysanthemums. In winter there was the Tower of Hidden Spring, where the white plum blossom held out its dainty petals.

The narrow paths were carpeted with lovely flowers, and sweet-smelling trees drooped their branches over the carven doors. There were willow trees sporting in the wind, touching, as it were, their eyebrows; and cherries, like raindrops, peeping shyly out.

Before the hall, where the swallows played, the lantern flowers were breaking into blossom; behind the Tower of Hidden Spring white apricots were just coming out. The marigold was opening beside the mound, and the bamboo shoots were springing up beside the balustrade.

The purple swallows flew daintily between the hangings; the twittering orioles flashed amid the green shadows.

There were windows shaped like the moon, and caverns of snow; halls of the wind, and halls of the waters. There were arbors of white roses and ramblers intertwined, and the thousand-leaved peach stood face to face with the willow of the Three Springs. The pine trees formed a wall, and the bamboos a passage. There were winding streams and square ponds. Palms stood gloriously upon the steps, with sunflowers making the round after the sun. Fishes swimming among the reeds suddenly jumped, and the powdered butterflies danced in couples among the flowers.

The white peony blossomed like the face of Buddha, and lichee covered the branches like the head of the King of the Demons.

Yueniang led the others into the garden. They held each other's hands, walked on the beautiful paths, and sat on the soft fragrant moss. One leaned against an arbor and admired the view, then tossed a red cherry at the goldfish. Another rested on the balustrade and laughingly frightened the butterflies with her silken kerchief. Yueniang herself went to the highest point, called the Hall above the Clouds, and there played chess with Li Jiao'er and Meng Yulou. The others stood at the flower summerhouse and looked down upon the white roses, the peonies, the ramblers, and the other flowers. They looked at the bamboos that bore the cold like supermen, and the proud pine trees boldly contemptuous of the snow. Throughout the four seasons the flowers never faded, and at the eight festivals it always seemed like spring. There was too much to appreciate in a single visit: it needed to be enjoyed slowly.

Wine was brought. Yueniang took the place of honor, Li Jiao'er sat opposite and the other ladies on either side. "I forgot to invite our brother," Yueniang said, and sent Xiaoyu to the outer court to invite Chen Jingji to join them. He came, dressed in a light blue hat, a long purple gown, and black boots with white soles. When he had greeted them, he sat beside his wife. After the wine had been passed around, Yueniang again played chess with her stepdaughter and Li Jiao'er. Sun Xue'e and Meng Yulou went up to admire the view, and Pan Jinlian, alone with her white silk fan, played with the butterflies near the lake by the mound. Jingji crept up behind her quietly.

"Fifth Mother," he said suddenly, "you don't know how to catch butterflies. Let me catch one for you. They go up and down. They are not quite sure what they want, and wander this way and that."

Jinlian turned and looked at him. "You must wish to die before your time, you rogue," she said. "It is clear your life means nothing to you." Jingji laughed, went closer to her, then took her in his arms and kissed her. She pushed him away and the young man stumbled. At that moment, Yueniang saw them from the steps. "Fifth Sister," she called, "I have something to tell you. Come here!" Jinlian left Jingji and went up the steps.

When Jinlian had left him, Jingji went sadly to his own room, and wrote a poem to express his melancholy.

> I saw her with a flower in her hair
> With lips uncarmined though they seemed so red.
> Once before, I met her, then today again
> And thought she loved me, though I could not see the love.
> She may give herself to me, but it is not likely
> She may reject me, but I do not think she will.
> When can we meet? When is the time for meeting?
> I think of her although I cannot see her
> And when I've seen her, think of her again.

Ximen Qing, after Magistrate Xia's party, passed through South Lane. He went so often about the streets and lanes, that he knew all the ne'er-do-wells who haunted them. To two of them he often gave money—Lu Hua, otherwise known as Viper in the Grass, and Zhang Sheng, who was nicknamed Rat Scurry down the Street. They were both scoundrels who spent all their time in chicken stealing and mean thieveries of every kind. Today, they were gambling as Ximen Qing passed. Reining in his horse, he called to them. They ran to him at once, made a reverence, and asked where he had been.

"It is Magistrate Xia's birthday," Ximen said, "and he invited me to take wine with him. There is a little matter I should like you to attend to for me. Do you mind?"

"Your Lordship," they said, "you need not ask. We have received too many kindnesses at your hands. If there is anything we can do for you, even if it means going through fire and water, we will do it."

"'Very well," Ximen said, "come and see me tomorrow and I will tell you what it is."

"Why wait till tomorrow?" they said; "please tell us now."

Ximen Qing lowered his voice and told them the story of Jiang Zhushan and Li Ping'er. "I want you to avenge my dishonor," he said, and pulling up his clothes, took about five taels of silver from his purse. "This will buy you some wine. If you do the business to my satisfaction, there shall be more for you."

Lu Hua would not take the money. "You have been so good to us," he said. "When you mentioned our doing something for you, I imagined you wished us to go to the Eastern Sea and take the horns from the Green Dragon, or to the Western Mountains, to draw the Magic Tiger's teeth— something really difficult. But there is nothing at all in this. We cannot accept your money for a job like this."

"If you will not take my money," Ximen said, "I shall not ask you to do it for me." He handed the money to Daian, and made ready to ride away.

Zhang Sheng stopped him. "Lu Hua," he said to his companion, "you don't understand his Lordship. If we refuse to take his money it will look as though we decline to do anything for him." They took the silver and made a profound reverence. "Your Lordship," they said, "wait for us. In less than a couple of days, we promise we'll bring a smile to your face." Zhang Sheng added that he hoped Ximen Qing would recommend them to Xia, and this he promised to do, a promise that he later redeemed.

When Ximen Qing reached home, the sun had set. Yueniang and the others went to the inner court, but Jinlian stayed in the summerhouse and watched the servants clear away the remains of the feast. Ximen went straight to the garden, and found her there.

"What have you been doing while I've been away?" he said.

Jinlian laughed. "The Great Lady brought us to see the garden," she said. "We did not expect you back so early."

Ximen Qing explained. "Xia was good enough to engage four singing girls, though there were only five guests. I remembered what a long way I had to come, and came back early."

Jinlian took his long gown. "If you have had no wine," she said, "I will order some for you." Ximen Qing told Chunmei to clear everything away, except some dessert, and a jar of grape wine.

He sat down on a chair, and gazed at Jinlian admiringly. She was wearing an incense-colored silken gown that opened down the middle, with varicolored ribbons at the sleeves. Below was a shimmering embroidered skirt, and beneath the skirt, red shoes with white high heels. On her head she wore a net of silvery silk, a gold inlaid comb, a plum-blossom pin, and many pretty ornaments. Her lips seemed redder, and her face whiter than ever before. Ximen was seized with sudden desire for her, took her hands, pulled her to him, and embraced her. When Chunmei brought the wine, they drank it together, and kissed more passionately still. Then Jinlian pulled up her skirts, and sat upon his knee. She passed wine from her own mouth to his, and picking a fresh lotus seed with her dainty fingers, offered it to him. But Ximen refused it; he said it was too bitter.

"My son," Jinlian said, laughing, "if you refuse anything your mother offers you, you are tempting the fates." But instead of the lotus seed, she gave him a walnut. Then Ximen wished to play with her bosom, and opening her silken gown, she uncovered her exquisite, flawless, fragrant breasts. He fondled them and kissed them, delighting in their firmness. So they sat together, and enjoyed each other's company. Ximen Qing was very happy.

"I have something to tell you that will make you laugh," he said. "You remember that Doctor Jiang set up a medicine shop. When I've done with him, he'll be setting up a vegetable shop on his face." Jinlian asked him what he meant, and he told her of the arrangement he had made with Lu and Zhang.

"If you do that," said Jinlian, "you will arouse a good deal of ill feeling. Is it the Doctor Jiang who sometimes comes to see us when we are ill? I have always thought him a most modest man. He always looks at the ground when he examines us. You ought to sympathize with him, instead of treating him like this."

"You don't understand his tricks," Ximen said. "You say he looks down, but, don't you see, he looks down so that he can look at your feet?"

"What a nasty-minded fellow you are!" Jinlian said. "I don't believe he ever thinks of women's feet. He is an educated man, and wouldn't dream of such a thing."

"If you judge him by appearance, you make a mistake. He pretends to be decorous, but he's a very dangerous fellow at heart."

They chattered and joked for a long time. Then the wine was finished, and the table cleared, and they went to bed.

It was now two months since Li Ping'er had married the doctor. In the early days of their marriage, he was very anxious to satisfy his wife. He prepared love potions, bought some interesting pictures and other devices for stimulating love, and did, in fact, everything he could to make the lady happy. But Ximen Qing had been a more strenuous lover, and Jiang failed to come up to her expectations. She came more and more to hate the sight of him. She took the instruments of love and smashed them with a stone. "There is no strength in your loins," she cried. "You are no better than an eel. What is the use of buying things like these? You have deceived me. I thought you a piece of good meat, but I find you are only good to look at, not to eat. You are like a waxen spearhead, a dead turtle."

Several times she sent him away in the middle of the night, and he had to go to the shop to sleep. She could only think of Ximen Qing, and would not allow the doctor to enter her room. Every day she went most carefully through his accounts.

It was on one such day as this, when Doctor Jiang had gone to sit down in his shop, that two men appeared. They were both tipsy, swaying from side to side, and their eyes stared wildly. They found chairs, and sat down. "Have you any dog-yellow in your shop?" they said.

Zhushan laughed, and asked them not to make fun of him. "I have ox-yellow, but no dog-yellow," he said.

"Well, if you have no dog-yellow, show me some ice ashes."

"The drug shops," said the doctor, "sell ice pieces that come from Persia over the Northern Sea, but no ice ashes."

"Don't ask him for such things," the other man said. "The shop has only been open for a few days, how can you expect him to have such things? We have more important business to talk about."

"Brother Jiang," he continued, "do not pretend not to know what you're about. Three years ago, when your wife died, you borrowed thirty taels of silver from Brother Lu. That and the interest now make quite a lot of money. We have come to call for it. It might have seemed discourteous if we had asked you for it as soon as we came into the shop, and you might have thought we had no consideration for you, seeing that you have just married and opened this shop. So we had our little joke. We suppose you will admit your indebtedness. But if you don't, you will have to pay just the same."

The doctor was startled. "I've never borrowed any money from you," he said.

"If you had not, we shouldn't be asking you to pay. Don't forget the old saying: If there is no crack in the egg, the flies can't get in. It's no use saying that."

"But I do not even know your honorable names," the doctor said, "and I have certainly never had the honor of your acquaintance. Why do you ask me for this money?"

"Brother Jiang, you are taking up the wrong attitude. Remember the old saying that those in authority are never poor, and men who don't pay their debts are never rich. Just think how poor you used to be. You used to go around ringing a bell and selling your plasters, when, fortunately for you, you met brother Lu, and he befriended you. You would not be where you are today, if it had not been for him."

"I am Lu Hua," the other man said. "In such and such a year you borrowed thirty taels from me and spent the money on your wife's funeral. Now you owe me forty-eight taels, counting the interest, and I want the money."

"I never had the money," cried the doctor excitedly. "If you say I did, let me see the contract."

"I was the witness," Zhang Sheng said. He took a document from his sleeve and handed it to the doctor.

Zhushan's face became the color of wax. "You meat fit for the gallows! You low hounds!" he cried. "Whence have you sprung to cheat me?"

Lu Hua's fist flew over the counter into the doctor's face and the doctor's nose was twisted to one side. They pulled all the medicines from the shelves and threw them into the street.

"Robbers," Zhushan wailed, "how dare you steal my things?" He called his boy to help him, but Lu Hua cuffed the boy away, and he dared not come again.

Zhang Sheng pulled the doctor over the counter, and rescued him from Lu Hua. "Brother Lu," he said, "he has been very slow to repay this debt, but we might give him a few more days. What do you say, Brother Jiang?" he added, turning to the doctor.

"I never borrowed his money," Zhushan cried, "and if I did, why can't he talk about the matter quietly? Why does he behave like a savage?"

"Brother Jiang," Zhang Sheng said, "you talk as if you had been eating something bitter, and still had the taste in your mouth. If you had behaved reasonably, I would have asked Brother Lu to forgive you some of the interest, and you might have paid him in two or three installments. That would have been the proper method of procedure. Why did you refuse to admit the debt, and so rudely too? Did you really think that he would not ask for his money?"

"My temper got the better of me," Zhushan said. "I will go with him before the judge, and then we shall find out who had his money."

"Dear, dear!" said Zhang Sheng, "you must be drunk again."

Lu Hua suddenly let fly his fist; the doctor stretched his length on the ground and indeed nearly fell into the gutter. His hair was disarranged and his hat covered with dirt. "Oh, blue skies and glorious sun!" he cried. At that moment, the policeman arrived, and took them all into custody.

Li Ping'er, hearing the noise, went to the lattice and, peeping through, saw the policeman taking her husband away. This alarmed her, and she told old woman Feng to take down the shop signs. Meanwhile all the things in the street had been stolen. She hastily bolted the door and sat down in her own room.

Ximen Qing very soon learned what had happened. Early the next day he sent a man to the court with a message to his friend Xia, the magistrate. Xia took his place in the hall, and ordered the doctor and the accusers to be brought before him. After reading the accusation he questioned Zhushan. "You are Jiang," he said; "why did you not pay Lu Hua the money you owed, instead of striking him? A most improper proceeding!"

"I do not even know him," Zhushan said. "Certainly I never borrowed any money from him. I tried to explain, but he would not listen. He beat me and kicked me and stole my belongings."

The magistrate called Lu Hua. "What have you to say about it?" he asked.

"Indeed he did." Lu Hua said. "He spent this money on his wife's funeral. For three years he has kept putting me off. I heard he had married again and had a fine shop, so I went and asked for my money. He insulted me for all he was worth, and now he says I stole his things. Here is the contract, and Zhang Sheng is the witness. I beg your Worship to investigate the matter thoroughly." He brought out the document and handed it to the magistrate.

"Jiang Wenhui, doctor of this town, writes this [it said]. His wife has died, and he has no money to pay for the funeral, therefore he engages, with Zhang Sheng as surety, to borrow thirty taels of pure silver from Lu Hua. The interest shall be three *fen* monthly. He will spend this money, and repay the thirty taels next year with the interest without any deduction. In witness whereof, this document is drawn up."

When the magistrate had read the paper, he banged his fist upon the table angrily. "Here," he cried, "are both the document and the surety. Do you think you can hoodwink me? I see you are a smooth-spoken rascal, but obviously you won't pay your debts." He told the attendants to pick out a strong bamboo and beat Jiang Zhushan with all their might. Three or four of them threw him to the ground and beat him severely thirty times, till his skin was torn and the blood flowed. Then the magistrate told two constables to take a white warrant board, and escort Zhushan to his house, there to collect the thirty taels for Lu Hua. If the money was not forthcoming, he was to be taken to prison.

The doctor, dragging his aching limbs, reached home, weeping. He begged Li Ping'er to give him the money for Lu Hua. She spat in his face and cursed him. "You shameless turtle," she cried, "have you ever given me any money that I should give some to you? I've known for a long time, you turtle, that you're nothing but a braggart and a sponger. Why, I must have been blind to marry a turtle like you, good to look at and useless for anything else."

The constables, who were standing outside, heard this squabbling and became more urgent. "If Jiang has no money," they said, "there is no use wasting time. We must get back to the court at once and let his Worship know." Zhushan went out to appease them and returned again to plead with Li Ping'er.

"Treat this matter in the spirit of charity," he begged, kneeling on the ground before her, "and let it be as an offering of thirty taels to the Holy Ones of the Four Mountains and the Five Shrines. If you will not, I must go back to the court, and how can I bear more punishment on my poor torn legs? It would mean my death."

Li Ping'er could hold out no longer, and gave him the thirty taels. He gave the money to Lu Hua in the presence of the constables. The contract was torn up and the matter ended.

After Lu Hua and Zhang Sheng had got the money they went straight to Ximen Qing. He offered them wine and food in the arbor, and they told him the whole story. He was delighted. "You have avenged me; that is all I want," he said, and when Lu Hua offered him the thirty taels, he refused them. "Keep the money to buy a jar of wine," he said, "and what I gave you too. One of these days I may want something more of you." They thanked him and went away to gamble.

After Jiang Zhushan had paid the money he returned, but Li Ping'er would have no more of him.

"I regard those thirty taels as money paid to rid me of a plague. Now you must go somewhere else, for if you stay here any longer, all I have in the house will not suffice to pay your debts."

The doctor wept bitterly. His legs pained him and he had nowhere to go, but he was obliged to find other quarters. Everything that Li Ping'er had given him he had to leave behind, and he hired a cart to take away his old medicine box and his mortar.

When he had gone, Li Ping'er told old woman Feng to throw a basin of water after him. "I am so glad that this plague is out of my sight," she said. She longed for Ximen Qing all the time, and when she heard that his difficulties were over, she was sorrier than ever. She languished so that she did not trouble about her tea or her food and left her eyebrows unpainted. She leaned upon the door and gazed till her eyes seemed to start out of her head, but nobody came.

One day Daian, riding past the house, saw that the gate was shut and the medicine shop closed. Everything seemed quiet. He went home and told Ximen Qing.

"I imagine," Ximen said, "that the little turtle has had such a good drubbing that he has to keep to his room. He won't be able to go out and attend to his business for a long time." He forgot all about the matter.

The fifteenth day of the eighth month was Yueniang's birthday, and many ladies came and were entertained in the great hall. Ximen Qing, who was still not on speaking terms with his wife, went to the house where Li Guijie lived, telling Daian to take back his horse and come again in the evening. He invited Ying Bojue and Xie Xida to play backgammon with him. Li Guiqing was there, and the two sisters together served the wine. After a while they all went to the courtyard to play Arrows through the Jar. In the afternoon Daian came back with Ximen Qing's horse, and found his master washing his hands in the back court. Ximen asked the lad what had happened at home during his absence. "Nothing particular," Daian said. "Most of the ladies have gone, and the Great Lady is in the inner court with Aunt Wu. Mistress Hua sent old woman Feng with a birthday present.

There were four plates of fruits, two long-life noodles, a roll of silk, and a pair of shoes. Mother gave old woman Feng a *qian*. She said you were not at home, and did not send an invitation to Mistress Hua."

Ximen Qing saw that the boy's face was flushed. "Where have you been drinking?" he asked.

"Mistress Hua," said the boy, "told old woman Feng to ask me to go and see her. It was she who gave me the wine. I told her that I never drink, but she pressed me to drink a cup or two. That's what has made my face red. She is very sorry now for what has happened, and cried for a long time. I told you before, but you wouldn't believe me. After Doctor Jiang was at the court, the lady would have no more to do with him. She is very, very sorry and still wishes to marry you. She is much thinner than she was. She told me I must ask you to go and see her, and if you can, please tell me, because she is waiting to hear what you say."

"The rascally whore!" Ximen cried. "She has a man already. Why can't she leave me alone? If you are telling the truth, say I'm too busy to go. Say she need not send presents, just let her choose an auspicious day and I'll take the strumpet home."

Daian said that, as Li Ping'er was waiting for an answer, he would leave Ping'an and Huatong to go home with his master. "Go along, then," said Ximen, "it is all perfectly simple."

Daian went to the house in Lion Street, and told Li Ping'er what his master had said. She was delighted. "My good brother," she said, "I am grateful to you for what you have done for me." She went herself to the kitchen to cook something for the boy. "I have not enough boys here," she said, "and you must come one of these days to help me to get my things removed."

The next day she hired five or six porters to carry her belongings, and they were busy for four or five days. Ximen Qing said nothing to Yueniang, but simply gave orders that the things were to be put in the new house. On the twentieth day of the eighth month, he sent a large sedan chair for Li Ping'er, with a roll of silk, and four pairs of red lanterns. Daian, Ping'an, Huatong, and Laixing were sent to escort the sedan chair. It was afternoon when they arrived. Li Ping'er sent her two maids in charge of old woman Feng, and when the old woman returned, she got into the sedan chair, leaving her house in the care of the old woman and Tian Fu.

That day Ximen Qing stayed at home and sat in the new summerhouse, wearing his everyday clothes and hat, waiting for Li Ping'er. The sedan chair reached the gate, but, for a long time, no one came out to receive it. Yulou went to Yueniang's room. "Sister," she said, "you are the mistress here. The woman has come, and, if you do not go out to welcome her, his Lordship will be angry. He is in the garden, and the sedan chair is at the gate. How can she come in if nobody goes out to receive her?"

Yueniang at last decided to go, fearing that if she did not, her husband would fly into a temper. So, after hesitating a while, she went to the gate to receive Li Ping'er. With a precious vase in her hands, the new wife went to the room which the maids had prepared for her, and there waited for Ximen Qing. He was still angry with her and would not go that night. The next day she was taken to Yueniang's room, and there was formally given her rank and place as the Sixth Lady in the household. For three days there were celebrations. Ximen Qing invited his relatives and friends, but still did not go to visit her. The first night he went to Jinlian's room.

"She is the last of us," Jinlian said, "and this is her first night. You should not let her room be empty."

"You don't realize that strumpet's eagerness," Ximen said. "I will leave her to herself for a day or two. Then I will go."

But even on the third day, when all the guests had left, instead of going to her, Ximen Qing went to Yulou's room.

Seeing that for three nights her husband kept away from her, Li Ping'er told her two maids to go to sleep, and, after sobbing for a long while, she stood upon her bed, and fastening her shoelaces to the beam, tried to hang herself.

The two maids woke. They saw that the lamp in their mistress's room was very low and got out of bed to turn it up. Then they saw the woman hanging there. They were frightened and ran at once to tell Chunmei. Jinlian got up and went to see Li Ping'er. She was hanging very stiff and straight above the bed, wearing a red dress. Jinlian and Chunmei quickly cut her down and laid her on the bed. After a while some saliva dribbled from her mouth and she began to come around.

Jinlian told Chunmei to go to the back court and ask Ximen Qing to come. He was drinking wine with Yulou and had not gone to bed. Yulou had been remonstrating with him. "You have married her," she said, "yet for three nights you do not go near her. She will be miserable and think that this is all our doing."

"You don't understand," Ximen said. "She is the sort of woman who, not content with the rice, must have the pan too. How do you expect me to be anything but annoyed? We were on the most intimate terms even before her husband's death, and I know all there is to know about her. Then she went and married that Doctor Jiang. Evidently I wasn't good enough for her. Now she wants me again."

"Oh, I understand how you feel," Yulou said, "but the other fellow deceived her."

While they were talking a knock came at the door. Yulou told her maid Lanxiang to see who was there. The maid came back and said that Chunmei had come to ask for her master because the Sixth Lady had hanged herself in her room.

"I told you so," Yulou said excitedly, urging Ximen Qing to go at once. "I told you to go to her, and you wouldn't listen to me. Now the trouble has begun." They took a lantern and went to the Sixth Lady's room.

Yueniang and Li Jiao'er also heard the news, and went to see the woman. When they arrived, Jinlian was holding her up. They asked whether she had been given any ginger broth. Jinlian told them that she had given her some as soon as she had been cut down. Li Ping'er made a gurgling noise and then began to show signs of coming around. Yueniang and the others were much relieved. They spoke consolingly to her and made her lie down. Then they went back to their own places.

The next day about noon Li Ping'er was persuaded to eat some gruel. "Don't give her a thought," Ximen Qing said to Li Jiao'er and the others. "She is playing this game in the hope of frightening me, but I will see she does not get away with it. Tonight I shall go to her room and see that she hangs herself again. If she refuses, she shall taste my whip. That's the only way to show her the kind of man I am."

When the ladies heard this, they were so afraid for Li Ping'er that the sweat rose upon their brows.

That night Ximen Qing took a whip and went to her room. Yulou and Jinlian told Chunmei to shut the door and allow no one to come in. They both stood outside and quietly listened to all that went on. Ximen went into the room where Li Ping'er was lying upon the bed, sobbing. She did not get up when he came in, and this annoyed him all the more. He ordered the two maids out of the room and sat down on a chair.

"Now, you strumpet," he shouted, pointing his finger at the woman, "you have already caused me trouble once. What do you mean by coming and hanging yourself in my house? You should have gone on living with your little turtle. Nobody asked you to come here. I have done you no harm. Why should you come here with your piddling tricks? Well, I've never yet seen a woman hang herself, and I'll begin by watching you." He threw a cord to her.

Li Ping'er remembered that Jiang Zhushan had told her of Ximen's prowess as a wife beater, and wondered what misdeed in a former existence had brought her to such a pass that day. She sobbed more loudly.

Ximen Qing, in a terrible rage, ordered her to get down from the bed, strip, and kneel before him. When she hesitated, he threw her to the ground and beat her several times. Then she took off her clothes and knelt down trembling. Ximen still sat still and related all her misdeeds. "I told you," he said, "that you must wait a while for me because I was busy. You paid no attention but married that fellow Jiang. If it had been anybody else, I would not have cared, but to marry a miserable creature like him . . . You took him to live in your own house and gave him money to set up a shop beneath my very eyes. I suppose you thought you would try to start a rival shop to mine."

"It is too late for me to be sorry now," the woman said. "But I did wait for you, and thought about you day and night till I became crazy. The garden of the noble family of Qiao is at the back of my house, and there were many foxes there, which came in the middle of the night in human form and sucked the marrow from my bones. When morning came, they disappeared. If you don't believe me, ask old woman Feng and my two maids. I nearly died, and they sent for Doctor Jiang to cure me. I was quite helpless and he deceived me. He told me you had gone to the Eastern Capital, and there was nothing for me to do but marry him. I didn't realize what a good-for-nothing braggart he was. Then someone came and set upon him at the door, there was trouble at the court, and it was all very troublesome for me. I lost my money and drove him away."

"You told him," Ximen said, "to accuse me of having detained your property. Why do you come back to me now?"

"Wherever did you hear that nonsense?" Li Ping'er cried. "I would have been torn in pieces first."

"It would not have mattered to me if you had," Ximen said. "You may have money enough to get a new husband when you want a change, but you shall not behave like that here. Let me tell you this. It was I who got the men to set upon Doctor Jiang. It was no trouble to me, but it was quite enough to set that fellow spinning round and round looking for a hole to crawl into. If I had taken the matter more seriously, you would have been taken to the court too, and made to give up everything you have."

"I knew it was your doing," Li Ping'er said, 'but forgive me, I beg you. If you treated me as you say, there would be nothing for me to do but die."

Ximen's ill temper was gradually dying away. "Tell me, you strumpet, which is the better man, Jiang or I?"

"How can he compare with you?" the woman said. "You are like the heavens, and he is nothing but a piece of clay. It was such a man as you who set the tiles upon the palace of the Jade Emperor in the thirty-third heaven, and he is fit only to dig coal for the King of Hell in the ninety-ninth abode beneath the earth. Don't mention yourself in the same breath with him. Why, such food as you have upon your table every day, he has never seen and never will see, though he live to be hundreds of years old. How can I compare him with you? Not only he, but Hua, my first husband too. Had he been the least like you, I should never have desired you. But you are just what I need. Ever since I came into your hands I have never ceased to think about you day and night."

With such words she made Ximen remember his old affection for her, and his heart was happy again. He threw the whip aside, lifted the woman up, made her put on her clothes again, and took her in his arms. "Daughter," he said, "you say but the truth. Indeed he has never seen a sky as large as a plate." He told Chunmei to set out a table and bring wine and food.

# Chapter 20
# The Reconciliation

They walk along the flowery glades
Where screening trees leave but a little space,
Hiding themselves from curious eyes
Always afraid lest others should see them.
The thorns upon the bushes cut and tear
They seek escape among the climbing roses.
They brush aside the rustling branches
Seeking to return again
And look for some forsaken corner.
The swallow, from his nest beneath the eaves,
Guides them to the silken curtains.

Li Ping'er, with her sweet ways and persuasive words, dispelled Ximen Qing's anger. He raised her up and made her dress again. They embraced and were perfectly happy. Ximen told Chunmei to set a table and go to the inner court for wine.

After Ximen Qing had gone in, Pan Jinlian and Meng Yulou stood outside the door to see what they could hear. As the other door was closed, there was no one but Chunmei about, and the two women peeped through the crack in the door. They could see the light but could not hear a word of what was said.

"Chunmei, the young rascal, is better off than we are," Jinlian said, "she can hear."

The maid stood outside the window for a while and then went over to them.

"What are they doing?" Jinlian whispered.

"Father made her take off her clothes and kneel down," Chunmei said. "At first she would not, and Father was angry and took the whip to her."

"Did she take her clothes off then?"

"Yes, when she saw that Father was really angry, she undressed and knelt down. Father asked her a lot of questions."

Yulou was afraid that Ximen would hear them, and, taking Jinlian by the hand, she drew her away to the other door.

It was about the twentieth day of the eighth month and the moon was late in rising. Jinlian and Yulou stood together in the dark, waiting for Chunmei.

"Sister," Jinlian said, "she thought she would get something good here. That's why she was so anxious to come. And now, at the very start, she has had a good thrashing. She seems to be one of those people who do not care for authority. If she does what she is told, all will be well, but if she behaves deceitfully, she will have to pay for it. Indeed, she will have to pay in any case. I remember how that young woman told stories to me and about me, and, although I was as careful as could be, I had to weep before him or I should not have been forgiven. You have been here for a long time. Do you understand him?"

The door opened. Chunmei came out and went to the back court. Jinlian, from the shadows, called to ask where she was going, but Chunmei only laughed and went on. Then Jinlian called her again, and this time she stayed. "She wept and told Father a long story," the maid said. "Now he is quite content. He has raised her up and made her put on her clothes again. He has told me to lay the table and bring them some wine."

"What a shameless creature!" Jinlian said to Yulou. "All that thunder, and so little rain to follow! It all ends in smoke. Nothing will come of it. She will just offer him wine. And you, you scamp," she said to Chunmei, "she has maids of her own, why should you fetch wine for her? When you get to the kitchen, that Xue'e woman will make a fuss, and I simply won't put up with it."

"I can't help it," Chunmei said, "I'm only doing what Father told me." She laughed and went away.

"The young rascal," Jinlian cried. "Ask her to do something that is her business and she is as lazy as a corpse. But when it's something she is not supposed to do, she rushes around and takes all the care in the world. That woman has two maids of her own. Why should Chunmei take this upon herself? She is a meddlesome young hussy."

"Oh, it is often so," Yulou said. "There is my maid Lanxiang. If I ask her to do anything for me, she takes no pains at all, but if *he* has any trick for her to play, she bustles about and doesn't mind what trouble she takes."

Yuxiao came to them. "Third Mother," she said to Yulou, "I have come to take you to your room."

"You frightened me, you little wretch," Yulou said. "Does your mistress know you're here?"

"I have just helped her to bed," the maid said, "and now I've come to see what is happening. I saw Chunmei going to the inner court. What is Father doing?"

Jinlian pointed to the door. "Go there," she said, "and you'll hear a strange story." Yuxiao wished to hear more, and Jinlian told her.

"Did Father really make her take off her clothes, and beat her?" the maid asked.

"He beat her," Yulou said, "because she would not take them off."

"Well," the maid said, laughing, "it is better to be beaten with them on than with them off. The bare skin is not too fond of punishment."

Chunmei brought the wine. Xiaoyu, with a square food box, came with her. They both went into the room.

"Look at those young rascals," Jinlian cried. "Why are they doing this? They are like rats flying in the skies. Take it in quickly," she said to Chunmei, "and let her own maids serve them. You must not occupy yourself there. I have something else for you to do."

Chunmei laughed and went in with Xiaoyu. After setting the things on the table they came out again, and her own maids served Li Ping'er and Ximen Qing. Yulou and Jinlian had many questions to ask Chunmei. Then Yuxiao said: "Third Mother, it is time for us to go," and they went away together. Jinlian told Chunmei to shut the door, and went to sleep by herself.

Ximen Qing and Li Ping'er drank together and talked till midnight, rejoicing in their love. Then they spread the coverlets and arranged the bed. In the bright candlelight they might have been the phoenix and his mate singing in harmony before a mirror. Fragrant incense was in the burner, and they were like a pair of butterflies dancing among the flowers. That night they took the silver lamp and gazed upon each other, fearful lest their coming together might be but fantasy.

Next day they slept till breakfast time. Then Li Ping'er got up and dressed her hair before the mirror. Yingchun brought in the breakfast. Li Ping'er rinsed her mouth and ate with Ximen, but very little. She told her maid to heat what remained of the wine, and drank it with her husband. After a little while she went on with her dressing. Then she opened her boxes and showed all her fine headdresses and clothes to Ximen Qing. There were a hundred pearls from the Western Ocean that had once belonged to Grand Secretary Liang, and a cap button of dark green that, she said, had been her father-in-law's. She weighed this and asked Ximen to take it to the silversmith's and have a pair of earrings made from it. Then she brought out a hairnet of gold thread that weighed about nine taels and asked him if the Great Lady or any of the others had a net like it. When she heard that they had silver nets but nothing to compare with hers, she said it would be unbecoming for her to wear it. "It will be better for you to take it to the silversmith's and get him to make a nine-phoenix pin, with pearls between the teeth. And with what is left he can make a comb like the Great Lady's, a Guanyin of gold and jade."

When Ximen Qing had taken the things and was about to go out, Li Ping'er said: "There is now nobody in my house. It would be well to send a man there to take care of it, and let Tian Fu come here to wait on me. Old woman Feng is too old to walk, and herself causes me more than a little anxiety."

Ximen Qing agreed and went out. On his way he came upon Jinlian, with her hair in disorder, standing by the gate.

"You are up very late, Brother," she called to him. "Where are you going?"

"I am going out on business," Ximen said.

"What is your hurry, you funny creature? Come here. I have something to say to you."

When Ximen saw that she was serious, he turned back and went with her into her room. She sat on a chair, and held his two hands.

"It is hard to find words bad enough for you," she said. "Are you afraid someone is going to put you in a pan and boil you, that you are in such a hurry to get away? Stay here. I want to tell you something."

"Oh, you little strumpet," Ximen said, "what is it you want? I have something to attend to, and you must wait till I come back."

He started out, but Jinlian caught him by the sleeve. It seemed very heavy. "What have you got there?" she asked. "Take it out and let me see."

"It is my purse," Ximen said.

Jinlian would not believe him. She put her hand into his sleeve and took out the golden hairnet. "This is her net," she said. "What are you going to do with it?"

"Well," Ximen said, "when I told her that none of you had one like it, she didn't care to wear it herself, and so she asked me to take it to the silver-smith's and change it for something else."

Jinlian asked how much it weighed, and what Li Ping'er wished to have made instead of it. Ximen told her.

"For such a pin," Jinlian said, "three taels and five or six *qian* of gold will be quite enough. The Great Lady's comb has only one tael and six *qian* in it. You must have one made for me with what is to spare."

"But she wants a solid stem," Ximen said.

"Even if she does, it will only take three taels, and there will be enough left to make a pin for me."

"You little strumpet," Ximen said, laughing, "you are never satisfied unless you are getting something out of somebody. You're always on the make."

"My son," Jinlian said, "don't forget what your mother tells you. If I don't get my pin there will be trouble."

Ximen Qing put the net into his sleeve again and laughed. As he passed through the door, Jinlian called to him: "You have come out of this business rather easily. He asked her what she meant. "Well," she said, "yesterday there was a great deal of thunder but very little rain. You told her to hang herself, and here you are with her hairnet. She has twisted you around her little finger, and she isn't afraid of you in the least."

Ximen laughed. "You're talking nonsense," he said, and went out.

Yueniang, Yulou and Li Jiao'er were sitting together in Yueniang's room when there was some excitement among the boys. They were looking for Laiwang. Ping'an pushed aside the lattice and was going in. Yueniang said: "Why do you want him?" Ping'an told her that Ximen Qing wanted him at once. After some time Yueniang told the boy that she had sent Laiwang on an errand. She had told him to go with a present of oil and rice to the nuns.

"I will tell Father that you have sent Laiwang on some business," Ping'an said.

"Tell him what you like, you young scamp," Yueniang said. The boy went away.

"If I open my mouth," Yueniang said to Yulou and the others, "he says I take too much upon myself. If I do not, I feel I am not doing my duty. Now that woman has come here, of course her house ought to be sold. There is a tremendous fuss, ringing of bells and beating of drums, and somebody must be sent to take charge of the place. Old woman Feng is there, and an unmarried boy was chosen to keep her company. That was all that was necessary. The house won't run away. Now he must have Laiwang and his wife to go there. There is always something wrong with Laiwang's wife, and who's going to wait upon her if she has to stay in bed?"

"Lady," Yulou said, "it is not for me to say anything, but, after all, you are the mistress of this house and you ought not to refuse to speak to him. It has made us all very unhappy, and the boys don't know to whom they must go. He is all muddled these days, and you really must take our advice and speak to him again."

"Third Sister," Yueniang said, "you don't know what you're talking about. I did not begin this quarrel. He flew into a temper without any excuse at all. I am not afraid of him, and no matter what he does, I shall not look at him with a friendly eye. He has said insulting things about me behind my back and called me a whore. What right has he to say things like that? He has seven or eight women here and he says I am not a lady. But it has always been the same. Fall in with other people's wishes and they will say nice things about you: tell the truth and everybody will hate you. I reproved him perfectly justly. I told him he had accepted things from her, bought her house, and that if he married her, all the gentlemen at the office would scorn him. Her mourning was not over, and I said it was not the right time to marry. I never dreamed that they were making plans the whole time. They used to meet regularly and I never knew a thing about it. It was like putting me inside a big jar. One day he would tell me he was at the bawdy house; the next night, he said, he was at another bawdy house. And all the time he was staying with her.

"Yes, he goes to the bawdy houses, where all the people are like beautiful foxes and behave like dragons and tigers. They swindle him and cheat him, and he thinks everything they do is perfect. I have done my duty by him and spoken to him fairly, and now he has not a word for me. But I want nothing from him. Let him give me three meals a day and I can do without a husband. Let him allow me to go my own way and he can go his."

Yulou and the others could think of no reply to make to this. After a while Li Ping'er came in, beautifully dressed. She wore a gown of red silk embroidered with gold and a skirt with an embroidered pattern of green leaves. Yingchun came with her, carrying a silver pot, and Xiuchun, with a box of tea leaves. They came to offer tea to Yueniang and the others. Yueniang told Xiaoyu to offer the Sixth Lady a chair. Then Sun Xue'e came and all the ladies had tea.

"Sister," Jinlian said to Li Ping'er, "you owe apologies to our Great Sister. Let me tell you that for a long time she and Father have not spoken to one another, and it is all on your account. We have done our best to smooth matters over. You must give a party and try to get the old couple to talk to one another again."

Li Ping'er agreed. She kowtowed four times before Yueniang. "Sister," Yueniang said, "she is teasing you. You must not urge me any more," she said to Jinlian. "I have taken an oath that I will not speak to him even if I live to be a hundred years old." There was nothing more to be said.

Jinlian took a brush and began to brush Li Ping'er's hair. She noticed that the new wife was wearing a set of golden hair ornaments with designs representing different insects, and a comb with an inlaid pattern showing the Three Friends of Winter, the bamboo, the plum and the pine.

"Sister," said Jinlian, "you should not wear these pins. They catch your hair. A golden Guanyin with a solid stem, such as the Great Lady wears, is much more suitable."

"I have thought of having one made like Great Sister's," Li Ping'er said.

Xiaoyu and Yuxiao, when they came in to wait upon the ladies, did not show due respect to Li Ping'er. Yuxiao said to her: "Sixth Mother, what office did your father-in-law hold at court?"

"He was in the Department of Forestry," said Li Ping'er.

"Ah," Yuxiao said, laughing, "so your acquaintance with the rod did not begin yesterday."

Then Xiaoyu began. "Last year," said she, "some old men, the elders of the village, were seeking you, to get you to go to the Eastern Capital."

Li Ping'er did not understand this remark. "Why were they seeking me?" she asked.

"Because you are so clever at dealing with floods," Xiaoyu said.

Then Yuxiao began again. "Where you come from, Mother, the ladies all worship the Thousand Buddhas. That, I suppose, is why you kowtowed so often yesterday."

And Xiaoyu said: "Yesterday, four officers were sent from the court to ask you to visit the Mongols in Tartary. Isn't that so?"

"I don't know what you mean," said Li Ping'er.

Xiaoyu laughed. "They said you knew how to speak the language."

Jinlian and Yulou were greatly amused at all this, but Yueniang upbraided her maids and told them to go and attend to their business. As for Li Ping'er, she flushed and paled in turns, and did not know whether she should stay or go away. After a little while she went back to her own room.

When Ximen Qing returned, he told her that he had given her ornaments to the silversmith. Then he said that on the twenty-fifth, he proposed to give a banquet and invite her late husband's eldest brother.

"There is no need to invite him again," Li Ping'er said, "I settled that with his wife, but, if you like to do so, by all means do.

"Old woman Feng can look after my house alone," she added; "all you need do is get someone to take turns with Tian Fu. There is no necessity to send Laiwang there. I hear his wife is not very strong and really not fit to go there."

"I did not know that," Ximen said. He called Ping'an and told him to go to the house on Lion Street every other day to relieve Tian Fu.

On the twenty-fifth Ximen Qing gave a banquet for all his relatives and friends. A band of players and four singing girls were engaged, Li Guijie, Wu Yin'er, Dong Yuxian and Han Jinchuan. They came about noon. The guests took tea under the awning, and, when they had all assembled, went to the great hall. The guests, who included the band of brothers as well as Ximen's relatives, sat at six tables. Ximen Qing himself sat in the host's place, with his son-in-law, Ben the Fourth, and Fu, the manager of his shop, at his table. The musicians played several melodies, and two youths, Li Ming and Wu Hui, sang a song. There was more music and then the four singing girls came to serve the wine.

"Today," said Ying Bojue, "is a very happy day in our brother's life. I say so with great diffidence, but I should very much like to pay my respects to our new sister-in-law and assure her of our affectionate regard. I do not wish to cause any inconvenience, but here are two venerable uncles, and I should like to know what they have come for if not to see her."

"My wife is not at all beautiful," Ximen said. "It will be better to dispense with this visit."

"Brother," Xie Xida said, "do not say that. We have told you what we wish. Why should we have come if we did not desire to see our sister-in-law? Then here is your honorable relative Hua the Elder. Once he was only a friend; now he is a relative. You cannot treat us as strangers. Please ask the lady to come and see us. There is nothing to be afraid of."

Ximen Qing laughed but did not move.

"Brother," Bojue said, "don't laugh. We have all brought our presents. We don't ask the lady to come out for nothing."

"Oh, you're talking nonsense," Ximen said. However, they pressed him again and again, and at last he told Daian to go to the inner court and ask Li Ping'er to come to them. There was a long delay. Then Daian came back and said that the Sixth Lady thought there was no need for such a ceremony.

"It is you, you little dog bone," Ying Bojue said. "You're playing tricks. You haven't been to the inner court at all. You have just come back and made up this story."

"I should not dare to do such a thing, Uncle," the boy said. "If you don't believe me, go yourself and ask her."

"You think I dare not go," Bojue said. "I know my way about your garden well enough. I will go and drag the lady out, whether you will or not."

"We have a strong dog and a fierce one," Daian said. "He will bite your legs."

Bojue left his seat and kicked Daian. "You young scamp," he said, laughing, "you have had your joke. Now be quick and ask the lady to come. If you don't succeed, I will give you twenty strokes with one of these palings."

The singing girls laughed. Daian went back a little way and looked to his master for instructions. Ximen Qing could not help himself. He told the boy to ask the Sixth Lady to dress and come to them. Daian went and after a while came back for Ximen Qing. All the menservants were dismissed and the second door was closed. Yulou and Jinlian urged Li Ping'er to go out, and arranged the flowers on her head. The servants spread beautiful rugs on the ground, and the four singing girls went to the inner court. They played their instruments and walked in front of Li Ping'er. The incense was delightfully fragrant and the music exquisite.

Li Ping'er wore a long gown of red silk embroidered in five colors. Her skirt was green and bore the design of the Hundred Flowers, with golden stems and leaves of many colors. She wore a girdle with a green jade clasp.

On her wrists were golden bangles. There were pearls upon her breast and jade tinkled at the hem of her skirt. Pearls and flowers were piled high upon her hair, and two jewels were upon her brow. Pendants came down over her white cheeks. Tiny shoes, with embroidered love birds on them, peeped out from beneath her skirt. The four singing girls played their instruments about her. She looked like the stem of a blossom bending in the wind; her embroidered girdle flowed behind her. She greeted them all with a low reverence, and they quickly left their chairs to return her greeting.

Yulou, Jinlian and Li Jiao'er stood behind the screen with Yueniang to watch the proceedings. They heard the song of congratulation to one who has reached exalted rank, the song that declares that Heaven has joined these two together and compares them to the phoenix and his mate living together in wedded bliss for generation after generation.

"Sister," said Jinlian, "do you hear that? That is not a fitting song for this occasion, for if they are to live together for generation after generation, what about you?"

Yueniang, in spite of her equable temperament, could not help feeling annoyed. Ying Bojue, Xie Xida and the others paid compliments to Li Ping'er as though they hated themselves because they had only one mouth to sing her praises. "Is this Sister-in-law?" they said. "Why! in all the world, we have never seen anyone so beautiful. We need not speak of the sweetness of her nature and her virtue. And how exquisitely she carries herself. There is no other like her in all the world. Brother, we envy you. Now that we have seen this lady once, we shall be happy if we die tomorrow."

"Take the lady back to her room at once," they said to Daian. "We must not let her tire herself."

Yueniang heard this and cursed them for a pack of rogues.

Li Ping'er retired. The four singing girls, seeing that she was rich, flattered her in their turn, calling her Mother this and Mother that, arranging her ornaments and putting her clothes in order, leaving nothing undone.

Yueniang, feeling very unhappy, went to her own room. Daian and Ping'an brought to her presents, money, rolls of silk, dresses and boxes, but Yueniang would not look at them. All she said was: "You rascals! Why have you brought that stuff here? Take it to the outer court."

"Father told us to bring it here," Daian said.

Yueniang told Yuxiao to take the presents and put them on the bed.

When Yueniang's brother, Wu the Elder, had had his second course, he went to pay a visit to his sister. She rose as soon as he came in and made a reverence to him. Then they sat down to talk.

"It was very kind of you to entertain my wife yesterday," said Wu the Elder, "and now my brother-in-law has done the same for me. My wife tells me that you have not been on speaking terms with your husband for some time, and I was thinking it would be my duty to remonstrate with you, when he happened to invite me here. Sister, if you persist in this course, you will lose all merit. There is an old saying that a man is a fool who fears his wife, but that a woman of gentle birth stands in awe of her husband. Obedience and virtue are the ordinary lot of woman. Whatever he does, you should not interfere. Take everything as a matter of course, and he will appreciate the good qualities that are in you."

"It is too late now to show him my good qualities," Yueniang said, "or I should not be treated with such contempt. Now, you see, he has a rich wife and I am treated as a maidservant, as if I didn't even exist. You need not worry. I shall put up with his treatment of me. He has changed his manner to me for some time now." She burst into tears.

"Sister," Uncle Wu said, "you are doing the wrong thing. You and I are not people of that sort. You must not behave like this. If you and your husband live together in harmony, it will redound to our credit."

He argued with Yueniang for a long time, and Xiaoyu brought him tea. When he had drunk it, a boy came from the hall to ask him to return to the party, so he took leave of his sister and went back. The feast continued until evening and then broke up. Li Ping'er gave each of the singing girls a handkerchief with a gold pattern, and five *qian*. They went away delighted.

Thereafter Ximen Qing spent every night with Li Ping'er. The others were quite happy about it except Jinlian, who secretly told stories to Yueniang about Li Ping'er, and to Li Ping'er about Yueniang, in the hope of stirring up trouble between them. Li Ping'er had no means of knowing the truth, so she fell into the trap, called Jinlian her sister, and became very intimate with her.

After his marriage with Li Ping'er, Ximen came into possession of more ill-gotten wealth, and was richer than ever. His house was refurnished, inside and out; rice and wheat were piled high in his barns; his mules and horses were in droves, and his maids and menservants would have made a small army.

Ximen Qing changed Tian Fu's name to Qintong. He bought two more boys, one called Qitong and the other Laian. He engaged Li Ming, Guijie's brother, to teach music to the maids. Chunmei was to learn the lute; Yuxiao, the cithern; Yingchun, the banjo; and Lanxiang, the four-stringed fiddle. Every day they dressed themselves beautifully and went to a room at the west side of the hall to study. Ximen gave Li Ming many meals and paid him five taels a month. He gave two thousand taels to Fu and Ben the Fourth, and instructed them to open a pawnshop. Chen Jingji, his son-in-law, kept all the keys and went out to collect the debts. Ben the Fourth kept the accounts and weighed the stock. Fu managed the medicine shop and the pawnshop, assayed the silver, and looked after the business generally. The medicine was stored in the loft above Jinlian's rooms. Shelves were made and put up in the loft over Li Ping'er's rooms, and on them were stored clothes, headdresses, curios, books and pictures from the pawnshop. Piles of silver came in every day.

Chen Jingji got up early every day and went to bed late. He was responsible for all the keys, and checked the accounts and the money. He was very clever at taking in and paying out, writing and making out accounts, and Ximen Qing was very pleased with him. One day when they were sitting together in the hall, Ximen said: "You have done very well since you have been here. If your father knew, he would be pleased. You know the saying that he who has a son must depend on that son, and he who has no son must depend on his son-in-law. If I have no child, this property will all come to you and your wife."

"Misfortune came upon me," Chen Jingji said, "and my family has had a very hard time. My father and my mother have both had to go far away, and I had to come to you. I have received the greatest kindness at your hands, and, whether I live or die, I can never hope to repay you. But I am young and inexperienced, and only ask that you will not be too severe with me. I dare not hope for anything beyond that."

Words of this kind were pleasing to Ximen Qing's ears, and he was more delighted than ever. Afterwards all the domestic affairs were entrusted to this young man. He dealt with the letters and present lists. Whenever Ximen's friends came to visit him, Jingji was invited to keep them company, and he was always about. Nobody could have suspected the treacherous villainy of this young man.

The time passed very quickly and it was soon the end of the eleventh month. Ximen Qing went to a party at Chang Zhijie's house. The party finished early, and, before it was time to light the lamps, he, with Ying Bojue, Xie Xida, and Zhu Shinian, got on their horses and started back. When they left the house, the snow clouds were very heavy.

"Brother," Ying Bojue said, "if we go home now there is nothing for us to do. It is a long time since we saw Guijie. It is going to snow. Let us go and see her, like Meng Hao-jan walking on the snow in search of Chunmei."

"It is a very good idea," Zhu Shinian said. "You give her twenty taels a month. If you never go there, she gets it all for nothing."

The three men badgered Ximen until he agreed to go to the house in East Street. It was dark when they got there. The maid was sweeping the floor in the hall. The old procuress and Guiqing came to greet them. They sat down.

"Guijie has enjoyed your hospitality," the old woman said, "and she thanks your Sixth Lady for the handkerchiefs and the flowers."

"I am sorry I treated her so shabbily," Ximen said, "but it was getting late, and, as soon as the guests left, I sent her home."

The old woman offered them tea and a maid set the table.

"Where is Guijie?" Ximen asked.

"She waited for you a long time," the old woman said, "but you did not come, and today, as it is her aunt's birthday, she has gone in a chair to wish her many happy returns."

As a matter of fact, Guijie had not gone to her aunt's. When she found that Ximen Qing did not come to see her for a long time, she welcomed the attentions of a gentleman called Ding Shuangqiao, the son of a silk merchant of Hangzhou. He had come with a thousand taels' worth of silk to sell, and was living at an inn. He defrauded his father and went to play in the bawdy house. He paid ten taels of silver and two dresses of heavy Hangzhou silk, and spent two nights with Guijie. He was, in fact, drinking in her room when Ximen suddenly arrived. The old woman sent them both to a secluded little room in the inner court to wait till he had gone.

Ximen Qing believed what the old woman told him. "If Guijie is not in," he said, "let us have some wine and we will wait for her." The old woman went to the kitchen and hastily got something ready. Guiqing played for them and sang a new song. They guessed fingers and drank.

Then something happened. Ximen Qing went to the back court to change his clothes and suddenly heard laughter coming from a room there. When he had done what he went to do, he crept to the window and peeped in. Guijie was drinking with a southerner who was wearing a square cap. Ximen could not contain himself. He went back again, threw over the wine table, and smashed all the plates and dishes to pieces. Then he called his four boys and told them to tear the curtains from the windows. His three friends tried to stop him, but Ximen was in a fury. He determined to tie the man and the girl together and throw them out of the door. Ding was not a very brave young man. When he heard the noise, he crawled under the bed and implored Guijie to save his life.

"Keep quiet," said Guijie, "Mother is here. It is quite a usual thing in our house. Let them make as much noise as they like, don't you stir."

The old woman saw Ximen devastating the place and still tried to lie and argue with him. He would not listen but urged his boys to break up the house. He would have struck the old woman, but fortunately for her his three friends prevented him. He made a great to-do, and swore that he would never enter the house again. Then he went home in the snow.

# CHAPTER 21
# Wu Yueniang Relents

The north wind pierces like an icy torrent
The powdered snow seems whiter
A steam of mist rises from the beasts
But it is warm within the silken curtains
Where dainty fingers tear apart fresh oranges
And pluck the lute strings.

Who goes to stand on guard?
A low voice asks.
The third night watch has sounded on the city wall.
It is better not to go. The horses slip upon the icy road
And there is no one now upon the way.

It was late when Ximen Qing set out for home. When he reached there, the boys opened the gate. He dismounted and, walking over the snow, found the door to the back court partly open. Everything seemed quiet and, thinking that this was strange, he stood there silently, hidden by the screen. As he waited, listening, Xiaoyu came from the room and set a table in the passage.

Since Wu Yueniang had ceased to speak to her husband, she had abstained from rich food three times a month, and, every day that had a seven in it, paid worship to her star and burned incense. This she did, imploring Heaven to change her husband's heart. Ximen Qing himself knew nothing of this. The maid set out the table, and, in a little while, Yueniang in her most beautiful dress came out and burned incense in the middle of the court. Then she bowed low towards the Heavens and prayed: "I am she who married Ximen Qing. My husband loves light women, and, though he is now of middle age, he has no son to carry on his name. He has six wives, but all are childless and there will be none to worship at our tomb. Day and night, my heart is heavy within me because I have no son to lean upon. Here then I swear: I will pray every night to the Three Great Lights of Heaven. I beseech you to save my husband. Make him amend his ways. Cause him to forsake things that are vain and turn with all his heart to the things of his own household. Let one of us six women, I care not which, soon bear a son that so our future may be secure. This is my only prayer."

> Secretly she went forth into the sweet night
> The courtyard was filled with fragrant mist
> And a strange light illumined the snow,
> There she prayed to Heaven,
> And paced in loneliness through the long night.

When he heard Yueniang's prayer, Ximen's heart was touched by shame. "Truly," he said to himself, "I have not appreciated her as I should. She loves me and is a true wife." He could hold back no longer. He came from behind the screen and took her in his arms.

Yueniang had not expected that he would come home while the snow was so heavy. She was startled and opened the door of her room, but her husband held her closely. "Sister," he said to her, "though I should die, I could never realize too well the goodness of your heart. You love me, and I have wronged you. I have made your heart cold. Now I am sorry."

"The snow is so thick it has made you mistake the door," Yueniang said. "This is not your room and I am not a respectable woman. What have you and I to do with one another? I have no wish to see you. Why should you come and bother me? Though I live for a thousand years I never wish to see your face again."

Ximen Qing carried her into her room. In the lamplight she looked even more beautiful. She was wearing a scarlet coat and a soft yellow skirt. There was a dainty ornament in her hair. He could not help loving her.

"I have been a fool for a long time," he said. "I have not taken your good advice and I have misinterpreted your intentions. I have been like those who did not recognize the jade of the Jing Mountain and thought it but a piece of common stone. Now I know that you are indeed a lady. You must forgive me."

"I am not she whom your heart desires," Yueniang said. "I do not know what you are talking about. What good advice have I ever given you? If you insist on staying here, please do not speak to me. Indeed I find your presence most distasteful. Kindly remove yourself at once, or I shall be compelled to call the maid to drive you out."

"Today," Ximen said, "I have had my fill of anger. That is why I came home though the snow was so heavy. I should like to tell you what the trouble was about."

"Trouble or no trouble," Yueniang said, "I have no desire to hear you. I do not live for you. Pray go and tell the person who does."

Finding that Yueniang would not condescend even to look at him, Ximen Qing knelt down, like a little boy, crying, "Sister! Sister!" all the time. Yueniang would have nothing to do with him. "You are an utterly shameless fellow. I shall call the maid," she cried. But when Xiaoyu came in, Ximen Qing stood up and began to think of a plan for getting rid of her.

"It is snowing," he said. "Hadn't you better bring the table from the courtyard?"

"I have already done so," Xiaoyu told him.

Yueniang could not help laughing. "You worthless rascal," she said. "Now you're trying to play tricks with my maid." Xiaoyu disappeared and Ximen Qing again knelt down. "If it were not for common humanity," Yueniang said at last, "I would have nothing to do with you, not for a hundred years."

Ximen rose, found a seat for himself, and ordered Yuxiao to bring some tea. Then he told his wife what had happened that afternoon in the bawdy house. "I have taken an oath never to go there again," he said.

"I don't care whether you go or not," Yueniang retorted. "You have poured out gold and silver like water to get that girl, and the moment you stay away, she sets out to find another lover. And with women of that sort you can never be sure of their hearts, even if you can make sure of their bodies. You can't put a seal on her, and seal her up."

"You are quite right," Ximen said. He sent the maid away, and began to undress, imploring Yueniang to be gracious to him.

"Today," she said, "I have allowed you to sit on my bed. That is enough. I am surprised you dare ask for any more. I shall certainly never allow it."

"Look at this fellow," Ximen said, making his intentions still more obvious. "He's another who is angry and won't speak. He opens his eye, but not a word has he to say for himself."

"You dirty rascal!" Yueniang cried. "Do you think I would look at you, even with my eyes half shut?"

Ximen Qing was not in a mood to bandy words. He set her white legs over his shoulders, and had his way. Their delight in each other was like that of the butterfly, as it sips the nectar from the blossom. Beauty and love were theirs in the fullest measure. Fragrance as of orchid and musk seemed to pass from one to the other. Ximen Qing, in the seventh heaven of delight, murmured, "Darling," and Yueniang answered him in a soft low voice. Soon they were sleeping, their faces close pressed together.

The next morning, Meng Yulou went to see Pan Jinlian. Before she opened the door, she asked if the Fifth Lady was out of bed. Chunmei answered: "My mistress has just got up and is dressing her hair. Please come in." Yulou went in and found Jinlian at her toilet before the dressing table. "I have news for you," she said. "Have you heard anything?"

"How should I hear anything," Jinlian said, "living, as I do, tucked away in a corner? What is it?"

"Last night," Yulou said, "his Lordship came home about the second watch, went to the upper room and made his peace with the lady who lives there. He stayed all night."

"Oh!" Jinlian said, "when we proffered our humble advice, she swore that, though she lived a hundred years, nothing would induce her to speak to him. And now with no excuse at all and nobody to act as peacemaker, she goes and makes friends!"

"I heard all about it just now," Yulou said. "My maid Lanxiang happened to be in the kitchen and she heard the boys saying that our master and Ying Bojue went yesterday to drink at Guijie's place. He caught the wench about some dirty business and smashed up the house. Then he came back, though it was snowing hard. When he got to the door leading to the inner room, she who lives there was burning incense. I fancy he must have heard something she said. Anyhow, he went to her and, the maid tells me, they talked all night. He went down on his knees and she behaved most scandalously. It is all very well for her to go on in this way, but if anybody else behaved like that, she would have a great deal to say."

"There are a great many advantages in being the first wife," Jinlian said. "I wonder what gave her the idea of burning incense. If she really wished to pray she could have said her prayers in secret. There was no need for her to go singing them out so that her husband might hear her. Well, she has become reconciled to him on the sly, without any assistance from anybody. I thought she would hold out, but it was evidently all pretence."

"I don't think so," Yulou said. "She really wanted to make friends with him all the time, but, being the first wife, she didn't care to talk to us about it. She thought that if she allowed us to intervene, we should take liberties afterwards. She ought to have realized that what goes on between husband and wife concerns others besides themselves."

"We must not let this opportunity slip. Hurry up and finish your hair dressing. I will go and see the Sixth Lady. You and I will contribute five *qian*, but I shall ask Li Ping'er for a whole tael, because it is really all her fault. We will buy some wine and a few delicacies and then we'll go and offer wine to them and afterwards have a feast to enjoy the snow. We'll spend all day over it. What do you think?"

"A very good idea," Jinlian said. "But he may be busy today."

"How can he be busy on a day like this? When I came past their door, everything was quiet. Xiaoyu was taking them some water."

Jinlian hurriedly finished dressing her hair and went with Yulou to see Li Ping'er. She was still in bed, but her maid went in to say that they had come.

"What a lazy woman you are," they said as they went in. "There you are, lying in bed like a lazy dragon."

Jinlian put her hand under the bedclothes and discovered a ball of perfume that had been used to make the bed sweet. "Ah," she said, "you have been laying an egg, Sister." She pulled off the coverlets and looked down at the white body.

Li Ping'er hastily jumped out of bed and began to dress. Yulou scolded Jinlian. "Hurry up and dress," she said to Li Ping'er, "we have something to tell you. The master and mistress of this house made friends yesterday. We are going to give five *qian* each, but it will be more for you because you're really responsible for all the trouble. It is snowing hard. We are going to have a feast; invite the happy pair, and enjoy the beautiful snow at the same time. Doesn't that seem good to you?"

"Excellent," Li Ping'er said. "How much do you want from me?"

"A tael," Jinlian said. "Get it weighed out at once, because we must go and collect something from the others in the back court."

Li Ping'er quickly dressed. Then, calling her maid, she opened a chest and took out a piece of silver. Jinlian weighed it and found that it was rather more than a tael. Then Yulou asked Jinlian to help the Sixth Lady to dress her hair, and she herself went to the back court to try to get some money from Sun Xue'e and Li Jiao'er. Meanwhile Jinlian sat and watched Li Ping'er complete her toilet. After a very long time, Yulou came back.

"If I had known what would happen," she said, "I would never have started this business. It is a matter in which we are all equally concerned, yet anybody would have thought I was begging money for myself. The little whore said to me: 'I am a poor downtrodden creature. My husband never comes near me. Where do you think I'm going to find any money?' I talked to her for a long time but all I got out of her was this silver pin. Weigh it and see how much it's worth."

Jinlian took the scales and found it did not amount to four *qian*.

"What did you get from Li Jiao'er?" she asked.

"First she said she didn't have any money," Yulou told them. "'Though every day the money passes through my hands,' she said, 'it is all checked carefully, and I have to give back every bit left over. I have nothing at all of my own.' I told her that none of us had any money to spare. 'It's a matter that concerns us all,' I said, 'but if you don't wish to give anything, don't.' I lost my temper and went out. That frightened her and she sent a maid to bring me back. Then she gave me something, but it's all most annoying."

When Jinlian weighed the silver that Li Jiao'er had contributed, it turned out to be a little less than five *qian*.

"What a cunning wench she is," she cried. "Even if you did everything you could think of, she'd give you short measure. Now we haven't sufficient."

"Yes," Yulou said, "but when she is measuring other people's silver, she uses a measure large enough. Getting money out of her is like getting blood out of a stone. I wonder how many times she has been cursed for it."

Jinlian and Yulou put all the money together. It came to just over three taels. They sent a maid to fetch Daian.

"Yesterday," Jinlian said to him, "you went with your master to Li Gui-jie's house. What happened there to make him so angry?"

Daian told them the whole story. "Father got very angry," he said. "He told us to break all the windows, doors and partitions, and he would have tied the pair together if Uncle Ying hadn't stopped him. He was still furious when he got on his horse, and on the way home he swore he hadn't done with the whore yet."

"The rascally strumpet!" Jinlian cried. "I always thought she acted like a woman with a jar of honey and held on to it tightly, but this time she's let it drop. Did your master really say so?" she said to Daian. The boy assured her that he had told the truth. Then she began to scold him.

"You young scoundrel," she said; "no matter how wicked she may be, she is your master's girl and you have no right to call her names. I remember once when I asked you to do something for me, you said you were very busy and hadn't any time. But when your master handed you some silver and told you to take it to that girl, you called her Auntie Guijie, and were as sweet as you could be. Now she is out of favor and your master is angry with her, you call her a whore. One of these days I will tell him what you said."

"Oho!" Daian said, "so you, Fifth Mother, are beginning to take her part now. That is indeed like the sun rising in the west. If Father hadn't called her a whore I wouldn't have, either."

"Just because your master says things like that, you need not think you can do so," Jinlian said.

"If I had known you would take it this way, Lady, I would never have said a word."

"Be quiet, you young scamp," Yulou said. "Here are three taels and a *qian*. You and Laixing must go and make some purchases for us. We are giving a snow feast to your master and mistress. If you can keep your hands off the things you buy for us, I'll ask the Fifth Lady not to say anything to your master."

Daian swore that he would never dream of stealing anything, and, calling Laixing, went off with him to do the shopping.

As Ximen Qing was dressing in Yueniang's room, he saw Laixing going to the kitchen with chickens and ducks and Daian carrying a jar of Jinhua wine.

"What are those boys doing?" he asked the maid.

Yuxiao told him that the ladies were going to give a party to Yueniang and himself. Then he asked Daian where he had got the wine, and the boy told him that Yulou had given him money to buy it. "Dear, dear," Ximen said, "why go out to buy wine when there is so much in the house already? Take a key and go and get some jasmine wine from the front court. We will mix it with this."

Curtains and screens had been set out in the hall; the winter season awning, with its design of Chunmei, had been put in position, and the stove well supplied with charcoal. Food and wine were daintily arranged. The ladies came and invited Ximen Qing and Yueniang to join them. Li Jiao'er poured wine into the cups while Yulou held the wine jar. Jinlian served the dishes. Li Ping'er knelt down and offered a cup of wine to Ximen Qing. He took it and said, laughingly, "This is very kind of you, my child. You are indeed a dutiful daughter. But an ordinary reverence is enough."

"Who do you think is paying reverence to you, you overgrown boy?" Jinlian said. "Like the onion that grows by the south wall, the older you grow, the hotter you get. Why, if it were not for the Great Lady, we shouldn't be paying any reverence to you today." They offered Yueniang a cup of wine. She thanked them pleasantly and said she had never expected such kindness.

"It is nothing at all," Yulou said, smiling. "We thought we should like to offer this poor repast to your honorable selves this wintry weather. Please sit down, Sister, and accept our reverences." Yueniang did not wish to do this without making equal reverence in return. But Yulou said they would remain on their knees forever unless Yueniang sat down. At last, after much friendly argument, they were content with half the prescribed salutation.

"Sister," Jinlian said, "we ask you to forgive him for our sakes this once. If he is ever rude to you again we shall not bother about him any more." Then she turned to Ximen Qing. "Why do you sit there like a fool? Come down at once from that place of honor, offer a cup of wine to the Great Lady, and make your apologies."

Ximen Qing laughed. The wine was passed around and afterwards Yueniang, bidding Yuxiao take the jar, herself poured out the wine and offered it to the ladies in return. Xue'e knelt down to receive her cup, but the others took theirs without doing so. Then Ximen Qing and Yueniang sat down in the place of honor, and all the other ladies, with Ximen's daughter Ximen Dajie, sat on either side.

"Sixth Sister," Jinlian said to Li Ping'er, "you ought to offer a special cup of wine to the Great Lady."

Li Ping'e rose and was about to do as she was told, but Ximen Qing stopped her. "Don't pay any attention to that little strumpet. She is teasing you. You have already offered us wine once and there is no need to do so again." Li Ping'er sat down.

Chunmei, Yingchun, Yuxiao and Lanxiang then brought their instruments and sang the song of the Thousand Blossoms of the Pomegranate, which is all about a second honeymoon. Ximen Qing asked them who had suggested that song, and Yuxiao told him that Jinlian had done so. Ximen looked at Jinlian and told her he did not know what she was thinking about. Yueniang suddenly thought of Chen Jingji and sent a boy to fetch him. When he came, he made reverence to them all and sat beside his wife. Yueniang had wine and food set before him and soon the whole family was enjoying a very merry time. Through the window Ximen Qing looked out upon the snow. It was as white as cotton wool and the falling flakes seemed like the whirling petals of the pear blossom. It was a very beautiful sight.

Snow like tender willow seeds
Snow like down from a goose's back
Falling softly with no more sound
Than a crab that creeps over the sand.
Piling up mountains of powdered jade
And dressing wayfarers with glittering spangles
Till they look like bees covered with pollen
And the palaces are covered deep.

The snowflakes whirl like a dragon of jade
Tossing his scales high in the air
The white powder scatters like the feathers
That fall from a stork
The lofty mansions are a mass of ice.
So cold is it that the body tingles
The earth shines like a silver ocean
And the flame of the candle seems like a flower upon it.

Yueniang noticed that the snow lay deep upon the mound in the garden. She sent a maid for a teapot and herself put snow in it, and, from the snow, made boiling water with which she made most fragrant tea for all of them.

They were drinking this tea when Daian came and said that Li Ming had come and was awaiting instructions. Ximen gave orders that he should be brought in. He came, made reverence, and stood before them. "You have come at a good time," Ximen said. "Where have you been?"

"I have been at Master Liu's by the Wine and Vinegar Gate. I give lessons to his children and today I have been to see how they are getting on. I heard that your maids know several tunes but that their time is perhaps not quite perfect, so I thought I would come and see if I could help them at all."

Ximen Qing poured out for him a cup of tea, telling him to drink it and then come and sing a song. Li Ming took his cup of tea and retired to drink it. Then he came back, tuned his zither, cleared his throat, and stood before them, his feet close together. He sang to them of winter in the capital. When he had done, Ximen Qing made Xiaoyu pour wine into a silver peach-shaped cup, and Li Ming, upon his knees, drank it. Then Ximen took four dishes from the table, set them on a tray and gave them to Li Ming, who went outside to eat. A little later, having wiped his mouth on a napkin, he returned and stood by the screen. Ximen Qing told him of the trouble there had been with Li Guijie.

"Of that I know nothing," Li Ming said. "It is some time since I was at my sister's house. But I cannot believe it was Guijie's fault. It must have been the old woman. Please do not be angry with her. I will go and see her."

All day until the first night watch, they drank wine together and the ladies enjoyed themselves immensely. Then Chen Jingji and his wife went to the front court, and they drank no more. Ximen Qing gave Li Ming a final cup of wine and told him that, if he should go to Guijie's house, he must on no account say that Ximen Qing was at home. Li Ming promised, and Ximen sent a servant to take him to the gate. The ladies went to their apartments and Ximen Qing again went to Yueniang's room.

The next day it had ceased to snow. Guijie and her mother were still afraid that Ximen Qing would seek vengeance, so they sent a roast goose and a jar of wine to Ying Bojue and Xie Xida, begging them to go and see Ximen and ask him to pay them a visit that they might express their sorrow for what had happened. Yueniang had just finished dressing and was eating cake with her husband when Daian told them that the two friends had come. Ximen Qing put down his cake and was about to go to them, but Yueniang said: "I can't think what has brought those two villains here today. Finish your cake and let them wait. Why should you hurry? I can't imagine where they think they are going to take you on a snowy day like this." But Ximen told a boy to take food to the front court and said he would eat it there with Ying Bojue and Xie Xida. Then he got up to go. "Don't go out with them when you have finished your cake," Yueniang said. "Remember we are going to celebrate Yulou's birthday this evening." Ximen promised and went to greet his two friends.

"Brother," Ying Bojue said, "you were very angry yesterday. So were we, and we told them what we thought about them. We said you had spent a great deal of money in that house in times past and that, just because they had not seen you lately, there was no reason why they should start to sing another tune. Yet they took that Southerner in. Unfortunately for them, you caught them. We asked how they could expect that you would not be annoyed. And not only you, we said, but we were angry too. We gave them a good talking to, until they felt very much ashamed of themselves. This morning they sent for us, and both mother and daughter knelt before us and sobbed bitterly. They are very much afraid of what you will do, so they have prepared a simple little feast and have asked us to persuade you to go to see them. They are anxious to apologize."

"I have no intention of doing them any harm," Ximen Qing said, "but I shall never go to that house again."

"Brother," Ying Bojue said, "it is natural that you should be angry, but, as a matter of fact, it really was not Guijie's fault. That young man Ding had no intentions upon her. He is one of her sister's old lovers. But there was another young man on his father's boat, a young fellow called Chen, a son of Privy Counselor Chen, and Ding thought he would like to spend ten taels and give him a party at Guijie's. The very moment he came to give them the money you suddenly arrived. They lost their heads and hid the Southerner in the back room where you discovered him, but he never so much as laid a finger on Guijie. This morning both mother and daughter swore this to us. They prostrated themselves before us and begged us to persuade you to go and see them so that the whole unpleasant business may be cleared up and you will not be angry any more."

"I have taken an oath," Ximen Qing said. "I have promised my wife that I will not go there again. I am no longer angry. Please tell them so, and that they need not trouble themselves on my account. I am very busy and cannot go to see them."

Ying Bojue and Xie Xida became excited. They knelt down. "Brother," they said, "if you refuse to go just for a few moments it will look as if you pay no attention to us. Do please go." They worried him so much that he finally gave way and, when they had eaten their cakes, told Daian to bring his clothes.

Yueniang was sitting talking to Yulou. "Where is your master going?" she asked the boy. But he said he did not know and that he had only been told to bring the clothes.

"You are lying, you young rascal," Yueniang cried. "It is the Third Lady's birthday today, and, if your master comes home late, you shall be whipped."

"Why should I be whipped?" the boy said, "I can do nothing."

"When he heard his friends had come," Yueniang said, "he dashed out as though his life depended on it. He was just having lunch, but he left everything. Where they'll take him, I can't imagine, or when he'll come back." She went on with her preparations for the evening.

Ximen Qing and his two friends went to Guijie's house. A table with refreshments had already been set out in the hall and two other singing girls had been brought in. Guijie and her sister Guiqing, dressed in their best clothes, went out to welcome the visitors, and the old procuress knelt on the floor to show how sorry she was for what had happened.

"You owe me a good deal," Ying Bojue said to Guijie. 'I have hardly any mouth left, I have had to do so much talking to persuade your young man to come. Now you give him wine and leave me without. If I hadn't dug him out you would have cried yourself blind and had to go singing in the street. You'd better talk nicely to me."

"Oh, Ying, you beggar," Guijie said, "you're such a loathsome creature, I can't find words bad enough for you. Why should I go singing in the street, begging?"

"You little strumpet," Bojue said, "you'd say your prayers, then beat the priest, would you? There was nothing you wouldn't do for me until he came, but now your wings are dry, I don't count any more. Come here and give me a kiss to warm me a little." He caught her by the neck and kissed her. Guijie laughed. "Look what you're doing, you've spilt the wine all over his Lordship."

"Oh, you little wretch! You love him so much you're afraid a drop of wine might fall on him. All your nice words are for him—there are none for me. I might be the son of a concubine."

"Well, you may be my son," Guijie said.

"Come here and I'll tell you a story," Bojue said. "Once upon a time a crab and a frog swore they would be brothers. They decided that the one who could jump over a certain brook should be the elder brother. The frog tried several times and at last succeeded. Just as the crab was about to see what he could do, two girls came up to draw some water from the brook. They tied a string to the crab, but, when they had got the water they had come for, they forgot to take the crab with them. The frog came back to the water's edge. 'Why don't you jump?' he said. 'Of course I can jump it,' said the crab, 'but just for the moment, I can't. Those two little whores have tied me up.' "

Guijie and her sister went and slapped Ying Bojue. Ximen Qing laughed heartily.

In Ximen's house, Wu Yueniang prepared a feast in celebration of Meng Yulou's birthday. Aunt Wu and Aunt Yang were there, and two nuns, and they all sat together in the upper room. They waited for Ximen Qing until sunset, but he did not come. Yueniang was much annoyed. Then Pan Jinlian took the hand of Li Ping'er and suggested that they should go to the gate and look out for him. Yueniang told them she wondered they had the patience to do so. Then Jinlian asked Yulou whether she would not go with them, but Yulou said she would wait until she had heard the nuns tell some stories. So Jinlian ceased to trouble them, though when they gathered around to hear the story, she asked the nuns not to waste any time. Nun Wang, who was sitting on the bed, told them one story, but when she had finished it, Jinlian said: "That's not much of a story, tell us another."

The nun told them another story. Then Jinlian, with Yulou and Li Ping'er, went to the gate to look for Ximen Qing.

"Where do you think he's gone today?" Yulou asked the others.

"I expect he's gone to that strumpet Guijie's house," Jinlian said.

"But he has sworn never to go there again," Yulou said. "I'm sure he hasn't gone there. What will you bet me?"

"Anything you like," Jinlian said. "Clasp hands on it. The Sixth Lady is the witness. I'm sure he has gone there today. The other day there was a row and that little scoundrel Li Ming came to see how the land lay. Those murderous ghosts Ying and Xie came here this morning and went off with him. They and that young strumpet have schemed to get him there so that they can apologize. Then he'll set the fire going in his old stove again. In my opinion, he'll stay there ever so long. Probably he won't come back at all today. It is silly of the Great Sister to wait for him."

"But if he doesn't come back," Yulou said, "he'll surely send a boy to tell us so."

While they were talking a seller of melon seeds came along, and they were buying some seeds from him when they suddenly caught sight of Ximen Qing, and all ran indoors. Ximen Qing was on horseback. He said to Daian: "Run and see who they are." Daian ran a little way, then came back and told Ximen that the three ladies were buying melon seeds. He got off his horse and went in by the second door. Yulou and Li Ping'er went to Yueniang's room and told her of Ximen's return, but Jinlian hid behind a screen, and, when Ximen Qing came up to it, jumped out and startled him.

"You frightened me, you little villain," Ximen cried. "What were you doing outside the gate?"

"Is that a question for *you* to ask?" Jinlian said. "You were late and we went to look for you."

Ximen went to join the ladies. Yueniang had everything ready and told Yuxiao to take the wine jar while she poured out wine for all of them. Ximen Qing was the first and then the others in their due order. They took their places and Chunmei and Yingchun played and sang for them. After a little while the things were cleared away and the birthday wine for Yulou was brought in, with forty different dishes. It was excellent wine, and of a color as exquisite as that of the clouds at sunset. Aunt Wu sat in the place of honor and they drank until the first night watch. By this time Aunt Wu could drink no more and went to her own room, but the others stayed, dicing with Ximen Qing, guessing fingers, and making up charades.

Yueniang suggested that they should take the title of a song and the name of a domino and make them fit with a line of the "Story of the Western Pavilion." Whoever happened to hold the domino that was named must drink a cup of wine as a forfeit. She herself began. "The Sixth Lady is drunk. Yang Fei dropped her eight jewels, and her hair is caught by the roses."

No one held the "eight jewels," and Ximen Qing began: "The lovely maiden Yu watched the battle between Chu and Han. The chief marshal was wounded and the noise of gongs and drums seemed like the heavens quaking." The lady who held the "chief marshal" had to drink a cup of wine. They continued till the turn came around to Yulou.

"A beautiful woman leans upon the scarlet rail, holding her silken skirt. She prays that the winds of spring may bring the moon within her net of gauze." She herself had the "scarlet rail," and Yueniang told Xiaoyu to pour a cup of wine for her.

"Drink three great cups," she said. "Tonight your bridegroom will spend the night with you." She turned to Li Jiao'er and Jinlian, "When we have finished our wine, we will all escort them to their room."

"Your word is law, and must be obeyed," Jinlian said. Yulou was very shy.

Soon afterwards Yueniang and the others took Ximen Qing to the Third Lady's room. Yulou asked them to stay a while, but they would not, and Jinlian said jokingly: "Sleep well, my child. Tomorrow your mother will come and see you. Now don't be naughty." Then, to Yueniang, "My daughter is still very young. I hope you will excuse her for my sake."

"You bad girl," Yulou cried, "you're like old vinegar. Wait till tomorrow and see what I'll do to you."

"I'm only like a go-between on her way upstairs," Jinlian said, "on tenterhooks as you might say." Then they all ran away.

As they came to the entrance to the inner courtyard, Li Ping'er slipped and fell. "Sister," Jinlian cried, "you're as bad as a blind woman. Just one slip and down you fall. I'd come and help you, but I'm over my ankles in the snow, and my shoes are in such a mess!"

"It is all this show," Yueniang said. "I've told the boys about it twice, but the thievish little scamps haven't cleared it away. Now the Sixth Lady has fallen down. Get a lamp," she said to Xiaoyu, "and take the ladies to their rooms."

Ximen Qing overheard this. "Listen to that little strumpet," he said to Yulou. "She gets into the snow and pulls the others after her. Then she talks about people treading on her toes. I'm surprised the others don't tell her what they think about her. Yesterday she said she never told the maids to sing that song, but I know she did."

"What did she mean by it?" Yulou asked.

"Well, she was trying to make out that the Great Lady deliberately burned incense in such a way that I was sure to find her doing it."

"She knows the meaning of all the songs," Yulou said. "The rest of us don't."

"Ah," Ximen said, "you don't realize how eager that woman is to score over others." They went to bed together.

Xiaoyu got a lantern and took Jinlian and Li Ping'er over the snow to their rooms. Yueniang went to her own place. Jinlian, who was already half drunk, took her companion by the hand. "Sister," she said, "I am tipsy and you must come to my room with me." Li Ping'er told her she was not drunk, but went with her and sent Xiaoyu back. Jinlian gave the Sixth Lady tea.

"You remember," she said, "how once you found it hard to join us here. Now we walk upon the same path. I had much to put up with for your sake and everybody had something to say about me. Still, my heart is in the right place, and I wouldn't have it otherwise. Heaven, at least, knows the truth."

"I realize how kind you have been to me," Li Ping'er said, "I shall never dare forget it."

"I only want you to understand," Jinlian said.

Chunmei brought tea. When they had drunk it, Li Ping'er said goodbye and went to her own room. Jinlian got into bed alone.

# CHAPTER 22
# Song Huilian

The next day the birthday celebrations were continued. Aunt Wu, Aunt Yang and old woman Pan spent the day with the ladies of the household in the inner hall.

Some time before, Laiwang's wife had died of a wasting sickness and Yueniang had found a new wife for him. This was the daughter of Song Ren, a coffin seller of the town, and her name, like the Fifth Lady's, was Jinlian. Originally, Cai, the Junior Prefect, had bought her for a maid, but she misconducted herself, had to leave, and ultimately married Jiang Cong the cook. This Jiang Cong often worked for Ximen Qing, and so it came about that Laiwang was frequently at his house on some errand or other. On such occasions he would drink wine and chat with the cook's wife, and they got on very well together. One day when Jiang Cong had been drinking, there was a quarrel among the cooks about the sharing out of certain moneys, and he was killed. The other cooks escaped over the wall. His wife then went to Ximen Qing and asked him to communicate with the authorities. This he did; the cooks were arrested and sentenced to death. Laiwang told Wu Yueniang that the young widow was a good needlewoman, and she gave him five taels of silver, two dresses, four rolls of black and red cloth, and some headdresses, and told him to marry the woman. But she changed her name to Huilian, for, there being already one Jinlian in the household, it would have been confusing to have another.

Song Huilian was twenty-four years old, two years younger than Pan Jinlian. She had a clear white skin, and her body was admirably proportioned, not too tall and not too short, neither too plump nor too slender. Her feet were even tinier than those of Jinlian. She was intelligent and wide awake, and had excellent taste in self-adornment. But she was indeed a captain among those who dally with men and a leader of those who disturb the harmony of households.

When she first came to Ximen Qing's place, she worked with the other maids and serving women in the kitchen, as plainly dressed as the rest. But, after a while, she noticed Meng Yulou and Pan Jinlian and began to copy them, dressing her hair high upon her head, with a long ringlet on either side. And when she served the ladies with tea or water, Ximen Qing gazed at her and gazed again. One day he formed a plan. He decided to send Laiwang to Hangzhou with five hundred taels to buy some dragon robes of ceremony for the Imperial Tutor, and other clothes for the family, an errand that would occupy him for about six months. It was about the middle of the eleventh month when Laiwang at last set off, and thereafter Ximen Qing never ceased to think of the delights that awaited him in Huilian's arms.

This day, Yulou's birthday, Yueniang and the others were enjoying a feast in the inner hall. Ximen Qing did not appear and Yueniang told Yuxiao to prepare a meal for him in her room. Through the lattice he chanced to see Huilian. She was wearing a double coat of red silk and a purple skirt. "Is that Laiwang's new wife?" he asked Yuxiao. "Why does she wear a red coat with a purple skirt? It looks very odd. Tell your mistress she must give her a skirt of another color."

"Even that purple skirt she borrowed from me," Yuxiao said.

The birthday passed, and on one of the following days Yueniang went to visit a friend. That day Ximen Qing drank heavily and went home in the afternoon. As he reached the second door, Huilian came out and they bumped into each other. Ximen Qing threw his arm around her neck and kissed her. "My daughter," he murmured, "if you do what I wish, you shall have all the ornaments and clothes you can desire." The woman made no reply but pulled her hand away from Ximen Qing and ran off to the other courtyard. He went to his wife's room and told Yuxiao to bring him a roll of blue satin.

"Take this to Huilian," he said to the maid, "and tell her that the other day I saw her dressed very unbecomingly. She must make herself a new skirt of this silk."

Yuxiao took the roll and Huilian looked at it. It was of bright blue satin, with the flowers of the four seasons as a design.

"If I make a new skirt," she said, "how shall I explain matters to our mistress?"

"You need not worry about that," Yuxiao told her. "Father will make any explanation that is necessary. He says if you do what he tells you in this matter he will buy you anything you like. The Great Lady is not at home and he wishes to see you. What have you to say about it?"

Huilian smiled, but for a long time she did not answer. At last she said: "When is he coming? I must clean my room."

"He says he will not come here," Yuxiao said. "He is afraid one of the servants might see him He wants you to go to the grotto beneath the artificial mound. It is very quiet there and an excellent place for you to meet."

"But if the Fifth Lady and the Sixth Lady hear of this, they will be angry," Huilian said.

Yuxiao assured her, saying that Yulou and Jinlian were playing a game with Li Ping'er and that she need not fear she would be disturbed. So the matter was settled and Yuxiao went back to tell Ximen Qing. He and Huilian went to the grotto, and Yuxiao kept watch for them.

Jinlian and Yulou were playing with Li Ping'er when a maid came and told them that Ximen Qing had come home. They separated. Yulou went to the inner court. Jinlian first went to her room to powder her face, then she, too, went to the inner court. When she came to the second door, she found Xiaoyu standing outside Yueniang's rooms. She asked the maid if Ximen Qing was there, but Xiaoyu only waved her hand in the direction of the outer court. Jinlian understood and went to the little gate near the artificial mound. There Yuxiao stopped her. Jinlian suspected that Yuxiao herself was carrying on a secret intrigue with Ximen and prepared to force her way in.

"You mustn't go in," Yuxiao cried in great confusion, 'Father is very busy."

"What if he is?" Jinlian cried. "What do I care?"

She went in and tried to find him. When she came to the grotto, matters were reaching a climax, but Huilian, hearing someone about, hastily set her clothes in order and came out. She flushed when she saw the Fifth Lady.

"What are you doing here, you scoundrelly slut?" Jinlian said.

Huilian muttered something about looking for Huatong and ran away like a streak of smoke.

Jinlian went into the grotto and found Ximen Qing hastily adjusting his girdle.

"Oh, you shameless object," she said angrily, "is this the way you behave with your slaves? In the daytime too! I would have boxed her ears, but she ran away too quickly. So you're Huatong, are you? She's been looking for you. Now tell me the truth. How often has this happened before? You must tell me, or, when the Great Lady comes back, I'll tell her all about it. If I don't have that strumpet's face beaten till it's as plump as a pig's, I shall know what to think of myself. You wait till you think we are amusing ourselves and then you play your games here. But you can't escape your old mother's keen eyes.

Ximen Qing laughed. "Be quiet, you funny little rogue. Don't let the whole world hear about it. I give you my word this is the first time."

Jinlian declared she did not believe a word he said, and Ximen Qing went off, laughing. When she went to the inner court, she found all the maids talking. They said their master had come home and sent Yuxiao for a roll of satin, and they wondered whom it was for. Jinlian realized it must have been for Huilian, but she said nothing to Yulou.

From that day onwards Huilian prepared soup and food for Jinlian every day and sewed for her. When she went to play chess with Li Ping'er, the woman would help her with advice. And, whenever there was a suitable opportunity, Jinlian helped Ximen Qing in his amorous adventure, hoping thereby to make herself more secure in his favor.

Ximen kept his promise to Huilian. He bought her clothes, ornaments, and perfumed tea leaves, and gave her silver that she spent on artificial flowers and powder. So, in course of time, she adopted a style of dress quite unlike that to which her poverty had originally constrained her. Further, Ximen told Yueniang that Huilian could make excellent soup and suggested that, in future, she and Yuxiao should not be sent to the common kitchen with the rest but that they should attend to the provision of tea and water at the smaller fire, and generally confine themselves to attendance upon Yueniang.

It was the eighth day of the twelfth month, and Ximen Qing had made an appointment with Ying Bojue to attend the funeral of one of their notable fellow citizens. He told the boys to saddle two horses and waited for his friend. Bojue was late and, meanwhile, Li Ming arrived. Ximen sat by the side of the fire in the great hall and looked on while Li Ming gave a music lesson to Chunmei, Yuxiao, Yingchun and Lanxiang, who were all dressed for the occasion. His son-in-law, Chen Jingji, sat beside him and talked. After they had heard one tune, Bojue came in with his boy Ying Bao, carrying a rug. Chunmei and the other girls were about to retire, but Ximen Qing said: "This is only Uncle Ying. There's no need to run away from him. Come and greet him properly." Then Ximen and Ying Bojue exchanged greetings and sat down, and the four girls came and kowtowed. Bojue rose quickly to acknowledge their greeting.

"Brother," he said, "what a lucky man you are to have four young ladies so beautiful as these, each more beautiful than the other. What a pity it is I left my house in such a hurry that I forgot to bring any money with me. One of these days I will give you something to buy some powder and things with." Chunmei and the others withdrew. Then Chen Jingji greeted Bojue and sat down.

"What makes you so late?" Ximen said.

"My eldest daughter has been very ill," Bojue said, "but she is a little better now, so my wife has decided to bring her home for a change. This has made me rather busy. I had to get a chair and buy one or two things before I could come."

"Well," Ximen said, "I have waited a long time. We had better have some gruel." He gave orders that some should be brought.

Li Ming greeted Ying Bojue, who asked what he had been doing lately. They all chatted while the table was being set. Four bowls of gruel were brought, with ten plates of other refreshments. The bowls were made of silver, and the gruel was mixed with nuts of various kinds and fruits with white sugar on the top. Ying Bojue finished off the gruel and drank a small cup of wine. As half the wine still remained in the jar, Ximen told a boy to take it with the dishes that were left and give them to Li Ming in one of the side rooms. Then he dressed, and he and Ying Bojue mounted their horses and rode to the funeral.

For a while after Ximen had gone, Yuxiao and Lanxiang went on with their music, but soon they stopped and went to the room where Ximen's daughter Ximen Dajie lived. Chunmei was left alone with Li Ming who was teaching her to play the lute. Li Ming had had too much to drink and, when his hand became entangled in Chunmei's broad sleeve, he freed himself with undue clumsiness.

"How dare you touch my hand, you thievish turtle!" the girl cried. "You must be anxious to die. You seem to have very strange ideas about the kind of girl I am. Every day you have good wine and good food, but today you must have taken leave of your senses. Would you dare touch my hand! You put your shovel in the wrong place. Before you do a thing like that, you should ask leave. I will tell Father the very minute he comes home and he will send you packing. Do you think you're the only person who can teach us songs? We can find a teacher anywhere, and we don't need you, you ugly turtle."

She used the word *turtle* very freely, and Li Ming gathered up his things and escaped as quickly as he could.

Chunmei was very angry and, still cursing Li Ming, went to the inner court. Jinlian, Yulou, Li Ping'er and Huilian were playing chess in Jinlian's room when the girl came in.

"Whom are you cursing?" Jinlian said. "Who has annoyed you?"

"Who but that disgusting little turtle, Li Ming?" Chunmei said. "When Father went out, he had the kindness to leave food and wine and gruel for him. Yuxiao and the other girls behaved most unbecomingly. They might not have had any modesty at all. They played there for a while and then went off to our mistress's room. When that turtle saw there was nobody in the room, he touched my hand and laughed at me—he was quite drunk— but I cried and cursed him and he took his things and went. What a pity I didn't box his ears! The thievish turtle doesn't choose the right people to play his tricks with. I am not the kind of girl to stand that sort of thing. I'll beat his turtle's face till it is green."

"You silly girl," Jinlian said, "there is no reason why you should study music if you don't wish to. Why allow yourself to become so angry that your face goes yellow? We will tell Father. He will send the rascal about his business, and that will be the end of it. We are not having you taught music to make money, and I won't have a rapscallion like that behaving in such a way to one of my maids. I know the turtle. He's full to the very brim of vice."

"He is the brother of the Second Lady," Chunmei said, "but that doesn't trouble me. She can hardly have me beaten to avenge her brother."

"He is a music master, and gives lessons here," Huilian said. "He has no business to make free with any of the girls. No matter how little he may be paid, he should treat us with the same respect as his own father and mother. Besides, he is always having his meals here."

"Not only that," said Jinlian, "we pay him five taels of silver every month. He will come to a bad end if he goes on in this way. Is there one of our boys who would dare to show his teeth to his master? Is there one who would dare to joke with him? They know that if they did they would get a cursing if Father happened to be in a good temper, and a beating if he were in a bad one. This turtle is playing with fire, and Father will teach him how hot the fire is." She turned to Chunmei. "Why didn't you come here as soon as your master went out? Why did you stay and give that turtle a chance to play tricks?"

"It was all because of Yuxiao and the others," the maid said. "They stayed, and would not come."

"Where are they now?" Yulou asked. Chunmei told her that they had gone to Yueniang's room. Jinlian rose and went to see them. Li Ping'er also went away and sent to fetch Yingchun. In the evening when Ximen Qing returned, Jinlian told him what had happened. He sent for Laixing and gave instructions that Li Ming was not to be allowed to enter the house again.

# CHAPTER 23

# Ximen Qing's Dalliance with Song Huilian

Winter at last gave place to spring. It was the beginning of a new year. Ximen Qing went to celebrate the festival with his friends, and Wu Yueniang paid a visit to her brother. In the afternoon Meng Yulou and Pan Jinlian played chess with Li Ping'er. When Yulou asked what should be the stakes, Jinlian said five *qian* of silver, three to be spent on wine, and the other two on a pig's head.

"We will ask Laiwang's wife to roast it for us," she said. "She can do it with a single faggot and make it very tender."

"But the Great Lady is not at home," Yulou said. "How can we do it in her absence?"

"We will save some for her," Jinlian said.

They began to play. They played three games and Li Ping'er lost. Jinlian told a maid to call Laixing, and gave him the money, telling him to buy wine, a pig's head, and four pig's trotters. When he had bought them, she said, he was to take them to Laiwang's wife, ask her to cook them and take them to the Third Lady's room. Yulou suggested another plan. "Sixth Sister," she said, "say that when she has cooked the head, she must put it in a container and bring it here. Li Jiao'er and Sun Xue'e will be there, and I am not sure we want them." Jinlian agreed.

After a while Laixing came back from his errand and took the pig's head to the kitchen. Song Huilian and Yuxiao were there, playing a game with melon seeds. "Sister Huilian," Laixing said, "the Fifth Lady and the Third Lady sent me to buy some delicacies. I have put them in the kitchen and the ladies wish you to cook them. When they are done, will you please take them to the Sixth Lady's room."

"I am busy now," said Huilian, "I'm making a pair of shoes for my Lady. Ask somebody else to attend to it. Why come to me?"

"Well, please yourself," Laixing said, "here they are. I've got other things to see about." He went away.

"We had better stop this game," Yuxiao said, "and you go and cook the things. You know what a sharp tongue the Fifth Lady has. Don't set it wagging."

Huilian laughed. "I wonder how she knows that I can cook pig's head?" She went to the kitchen, filled a cauldron with water, cleaned the pig's head and the trotters, found a suitable faggot and put it underneath the oven. Then she filled a large bowl with salt, put spices into it and mixed the ingredients together. She put the pig's head into a container. In less than an hour it was so tender that the skin began to peel. With all the flavor of the spices it smelled exceedingly appetizing. She set the head on a large tray and put the tray, with saucers of ginger and onion, into a large square box. This she carried to the Sixth Lady's room. Then she warmed the wine and took that in. Yulou chose some of the tastiest part, put it on a dish, set aside a jar of wine, and told a maid to take it to Yueniang's room. Then they all sat down to enjoy their feast.

Huilian came in smiling. "How do you like my cooking, Ladies?" she asked.

"The Third Lady," Jinlian said, "was just saying how clever you are. It is as soft and tender as can be."

"Is it really true that you only use a single faggot?" Li Ping'er said.

"Hardly that," Huilian replied. "If I did, it would be overcooked."

Yulou told a maid to pour some wine for the woman, and Li Ping'er picked out some meat and invited her to try some of her own cooking.

"I knew," Huilian said, "that you did not like things too salty, but I did not make it quite tasty enough. However, next time, I shall know exactly what you like." She kowtowed three times and stood beside them.

They drank till evening when Yueniang returned. Then they went together to receive her. Xiaoyu showed her the delicacy that had been put aside for her. "We have been playing chess today," Yulou said, with a smile, "and this is what we won from the Sixth Lady. We saved some for you."

"It is hardly fair," Yueniang said, "that one should pay for what all enjoy. I'll tell you what. We will have a kind of festival, and each of us in turn shall give a party to the rest and we will have Miss Yu here to sing. That seems to me a better plan than gambling. What do you think?" They all agreed, and Yueniang continued: "Tomorrow is the fifth of the month, I will begin. Li Jiao'er can take the sixth, Yulou the seventh, and Jinlian the eighth."

"That will suit me very well," Jinlian said, "for it is my birthday and I shall kill two birds with one stone."

They approached Xue'e, but she did not welcome the suggestion. Yueniang said they would not ask her again and Li Ping'er should take her turn. Yulou said that the ninth would be Jinlian's birthday and perhaps her mother and Aunt Wu would come. It was decided that Li Ping'er should entertain them on the tenth.

On the following day Ximen Qing went to visit a friend and Yueniang gave her party. Miss Yu, the singer, sang and played for them. Then came the turn of Li Jiao'er, Yulou, and Jinlian. On Jinlian's birthday old woman Pan and Aunt Wu came to spend the day. Then it was the turn of Li Ping'er. She sent Xiuchun twice to invite Sun Xue'e but, though she promised to come, she did not.

"I told you she wouldn't come," Yulou said, "there is no use asking her. She always tries to make out that we have all the money and she is as poor as an unshod donkey. Since she chooses to take that attitude, we'd better leave her alone."

"She is quite impossible," Yueniang said, "we won't bother about her any more." They all went to visit Li Ping'er. Miss Yu went with them to make music, and there were eight of them in all, including Ximen Dajie and Aunt Wu. Ximen Qing himself was not at home and Yueniang told Yuxiao that, if he should come in and ask for wine, she should see it was given him.

It was afternoon when Ximen returned. When Yuxiao took his clothes, he asked where Yueniang was, and she told him that all the ladies, with their guests, were with Li Ping'er, taking wine.

"What kind of wine are they drinking?" Ximen asked. When he was told, he called for a jar of Lily wine that Ying Bojue had brought, and told Yuxiao to open it. He tasted a little and said: "This wine is just what ladies like," and told the maids to take it to them. It happened that Huilian was serving wine to the ladies, and when she saw Yuxiao bringing the new jar, she very cunningly went to meet her. Yuxiao winked at her and pressed her hand so that she understood that Ximen had returned. Yueniang asked Yuxiao who had told her to bring the wine, and the girl told her. Then she asked how long Ximen had been back. "If your master wants anything to drink, set a table in my room. There is plenty to eat if he wants anything. You can wait upon him." Yuxiao went away.

Huilian stayed a while and then said she was going to the kitchen to make some tea. "There is some Liu'an tea in my room," Yueniang said, "use that." Huilian went to the inner court. There, Yuxiao was standing outside the door of the upper room, making a sign to her to go in. She pushed aside the lattice and went in. Ximen Qing was drinking wine. She went over to him and seated herself upon his knee, and they embraced each other lovingly. She fondled him with her hand until it became evident he was greatly stirred, and, from her mouth, she passed wine to his.

"Father," she said, "I have used all the fragrant tea leaves you gave me the other day; may I have some more? And have you any money? I owe some to Xue."

"There are a few taels in my purse," Ximen said, "you may take them." Then he would have unloosed her girdle, but she restrained him, saying she was afraid someone might come.

"If you stay in tonight," Ximen said, "we can enjoy ourselves." Huilian shook her head. "There are so many difficulties in the inner court. We had better go again to the Fifth Lady's room."

While they were amusing themselves Yuxiao kept watch for them outside the door. Xue'e happened to come into the court and heard the sound of laughing and talking. At first she thought it was Yuxiao talking to Ximen Qing, but then she saw the maid standing by the door. She stopped, and Yuxiao began to fear that she would decide to go in. "The Sixth Lady has sent for you several times," she said. "Why won't you go?"

Xue'e laughed contemptuously. "I am one of those women who never have any luck," she said. "However speedy the horse I ride, I can never catch up with them. How can I play with them? They can have ten parties, while I haven't even the undergarments I need."

Ximen Qing coughed and Xue'e went back to her kitchen. Yuxiao pushed the lattice to one side, and Huilian seized the opportunity and slipped away.

She went to the kitchen to make some tea, and soon Xiaoyu came and said that Yueniang wanted to know why the tea was so long coming. "It is just ready," Huilian said, "I am only looking for some nuts." She found the nuts and, with Xiaoyu carrying the tray, took the tea to the ladies.

"Why has it taken you so long to make the tea?" Yueniang said.

"Father is drinking wine in your room," the woman said, "and I did not venture to go in. I had to wait for your maid to get the tea for me and then I had to go to the kitchen for the nuts."

The ladies drank the tea and began to play. Huilian leaned over the table and made comments on the game until Yulou grew angry. "Why must you put in your word when we are playing?" she said. "It is not your place to speak here." Huilian was abashed. She blushed and did not know what to do with herself. Finally she went away.

The ladies drank wine until nightfall. Then Ximen Qing came in. "You all look very jolly," he said, laughing. Aunt Wu stood up and offered her place to her brother-in-law. "The place for you to drink is in the inner court," Yueniang said. "Why do you, a man, come and join a party of ladies?"

"Very well! I will go," Ximen said, and he went to Jinlian's room. She followed him. He was already half drunk.

"Little oily mouth," he said, taking her by the hands, "I want to ask you just one favor. I wished to enjoy Huilian in the inner court, but there was nowhere we could go. May we come here?"

ᴊ are a dirty creature," Jinlian cried, "and I can't find words bad ᴇnough for you. I don't mind what you do with that woman elsewhere, but there is no place for you here. Besides, even if I were willing, that young scoundrel Chunmei would object. Ask her, if you don't believe me. If she doesn't mind, I will raise no difficulties."

"Very well," Ximen said, "you won't do what I wish. I shall have to spend the night in the grotto. Please ask the maids to take some bedclothes and light a fire for me there. It is rather chilly."

Jinlian laughed. "Really, I can't tell you what I think of you. That slave's wife might be your mother and you might be Wang Xiang, carrying out the duties of filial piety in winter. Only you'd rather lie on a warm bed than on ice."

"Don't tease me," Ximen Qing said, laughing, "but tell the maids to light a fire." Jinlian agreed, and when the ladies separated that night, she told Qiuju to take bedclothes and a stove to the grotto under the artificial mound. Huilian, after escorting Yueniang, Li Jiao'er and Yulou to their apartments, asked if there was anything more she could do for them, and was told to go to her bed in the front court. She stood there for a short time and then, seeing that no one was about, went swiftly to the artificial mound.

Huilian thought, when she went into the garden, that Ximen Qing had not come yet, so she did not close the gate, but when she reached the grotto she found he was already there. She went in. It was very cold and the ground was covered with dust. She took two sticks of incense from her sleeve, lighted them and set them in the ground, shivering although there was a stove. She first covered herself with the bedclothes and pulled a sable cloak over her, then Ximen shut the door of the grotto, got on to the bed, removed his long gown and unloosed the woman's girdle. She placed herself upon him with legs outstretched. Then they came together and enjoyed the work of love to the full.

Jinlian heard them go to the garden, took off her headdress, and going very softly, opened the garden gate and went to the mound. She did not trouble whether the moss made her feet cold, or whether the branches of the shrubs tore her skirt. She stood quietly outside the door and looked in. The light was burning brightly. She heard the woman say laughingly, "Showering ice upon an icy bed! You are in no better case than a beggar. You can find nowhere else to go, so you come to this icy hell. You are like a man who swallows a long string so that when he comes to die of starvation somebody will pull him out." Then she went on: "It is so cold! Let us go to sleep. You do nothing but look at my feet though you know them perfectly well already. I have no new shoes. Will you buy some tops for me, and let me show you what beautiful shoes I can make?"

"My child," Ximen said, "of course I will. You shall have all colors tomorrow. Your feet are smaller than the Fifth Lady's."

"There is no comparison between hers and mine," the woman said. "I tried on her shoes yesterday and found I could get into them with my own shoes on my feet. But, so long as the feet are straight, it doesn't matter much whether they are large or small."

Jinlian heard all this and was anxious to hear more.

"Was your Fifth Lady married before she came here?" she heard Huilian say.

"Yes," Ximen replied, "she is one of the changeable kind."

"But how charming she is," Huilian said, "I don't wonder that she and you are like dew and water together."

Jinlian listened and was almost paralyzed. "If I allow this strumpet to carry on like this," she said to herself, "she will be the end of me." She would have gone at once and taxed the couple with their misdeeds if she had not been afraid of Ximen's hasty temper. She knew that if she let the matter pass too long he would refuse to admit it, and decided to leave something behind to mark the fact that she had been there. The next day she would confront him with it. She went back to the garden gate, and, taking a silver pin from her hair, put it in the latch. Then she went to her own room, in a very evil humor.

The next morning Huilian got up and went out, her hair hastily arranged. When she came to the garden gate, she was startled. The gate had not been locked, yet though she pushed, she could not open it. She had to go back to Ximen Qing, who called to Chunmei on the other side of the wall to come and open the gate. Then he saw the pin and knew that it belonged to Jinlian. He realized that she knew everything that had happened the night before. As for Huilian, it was as though she carried a ghost child in her womb. In the outer court she met Ping'an coming from the rooms on the east side. He looked at her and smiled.

"Why are you laughing at me, you young rascal?" she cried.

"Sister," Ping'an said, "what is the matter with you? I was only smiling."

"Why should you smile without any reason, and before breakfast, too?"

"Well, Sister, I'm smiling because you look as if you had had nothing to eat for three days. There is a hungry look about your eyes. I hear you weren't in your room last night."

Huilian flushed, and cursed the boy. "You thievish, gawpy, ghost-catching young imp! What night was I not in my room?"

"Your door is locked this very moment," the boy said. "I've just seen it. How do you explain that?"

"I got up very early to go to the Fifth Lady's room and I haven't been able to get back before now. Where have you been?"

"I suppose," the boy said, "that the Fifth Lady sent for you to salt crabs because you are so clever at anything to do with legs. And she sent you to the gate to find a basket seller because you are so good at putting one and one together."

Huilian snatched up a door bar and chased Ping'an around the court-yard. "You young rascal," she cried, "I'll tell my husband about this and he will treat you as you deserve. You are mad."

"Don't be angry, Sister. By the way, whom did you say you'd tell?" This made her still more angry and she ran after him again.

Daian, who happened to come from the shop, took the bar from her and asked her why she wished to beat the boy.

"Ask the wicked little chatterbox himself," Huilian cried angrily. "I haven't a particle of strength left."

Meanwhile Ping'an took advantage of the opportunity, and made off.

"Don't be angry, Sister," Daian said. "Go to your room and dress your hair."

Huilian took some small change from her pocket. "Will you buy me a large bowl of soup?" she said.

"Certainly," the boy replied. He took the money, washed his face, and then went to buy the soup. When he brought it, Huilian gave half of it to him. She dressed her hair, then closed her door and went to the inner court to wait upon Yueniang.

Then she went to see Jinlian. The Fifth Lady was doing her hair, and Huilian served her most attentively, holding the mirror, carrying hot water and doing one thing and another. Jinlian never so much as glanced at her.

"May I put your sleeping shoes under the bedclothes?" Huilian said.

"Please yourself," Jinlian said. "If it is too much trouble, I'll tell my maid." Then she called to Qiuju: "Where are you, you thievish slave?"

"She is sweeping the floor," said Huilian, "and Sister Chunmei is dress-ing her hair."

"Please do not concern yourself about my maids, but go away," Jinlian said. "I will have my own maids to attend to me. Besides, my dirty place will soil your shoes. Hadn't you better go and wait upon his Lordship? He likes to have women of your sort about him. He and I are the dew-and-water kind of husband and wife, and I am a twice-married woman. You, Sister, are of a very different kind; you came in a sedan chair. You are the real wife."

When Huilian heard these bitter words, she knew that all the happen-ings of the night before were known to Jinlian. She threw herself upon her knees. "Mother," she cried, "you are my true mistress. Unless you raise your hand, there is no place for me to stand. Without your kind aid, I should never have been able to do what my master wished. The Great Lady is only a shadow, but you are my benefactress and I shall always be faithful to you. Mother, you may watch me as much as you like, and if ever you find me deceiving you, may I not die peacefully in my bed."

"I do not like to have dust thrown in my eyes," Jinlian said. "If my husband wants you I shall not interfere, but I will not have you playing tricks and putting me in an invidious position. You must think twice before you decide to come between us."

"Mother," Huilian said, "question me if you will. I shall not dare deceive you. Last night you did not really hear what was said."

"I don't believe you," Jinlian said. "Let me tell you this. One woman can never bind a man, and your master not only has several wives here, but a host of lady friends outside. But he always tells me what he does. There was a time when the Great Lady had some control over him, and in those days he used to tell her things, and did not tell me. You have not the authority of the Great Lady."

There was nothing Huilian could say. She stood there for a while, and then went away. As she came to the passage by the second door, she saw Ximen Qing.

"Oh, you good man," she said, "you have let other people know all that we did last night, and I have had to suffer in consequence. You should keep to yourself the things we say to one another, until you forget them. Why should you let everybody know? Your mouth runs over like a water trough, and I will never tell you anything again."

"What's that!" Ximen cried, "I don't know what you're talking about." Huilian scowled at him and went away.

She was very careful and cunning in her dealings with other people in the household. If she was buying anything at the gate she would call Fu "Master Fu" and Chen Jingji "Uncle." Ben the Fourth was always "Old Fourth." Now that she had had this affair with Ximen Qing, she was much less sedate in her manner, and was often at the gate joking with some man or other. She would go after Fu and say to him, "Master Fu, I wonder if you would mind buying some powder for me?" Fu was a simple-minded fellow and looked out for the powder seller for her, but he was not altogether comfortable about it at heart.

One day Daian said jokingly, "Sister, you should have been out with your scales earlier. The powder seller has gone."

"You rascal," Huilian said, "the Fifth Lady and the Sixth Lady have asked me to buy some powder for them. What do you mean by talking of two measures of rouge and three of powder? They powder their faces many times a day. I shall tell them what you say."

"Oh, Sister!" the boy said, "you always try to frighten me by talking about the Fifth Lady."

Once she said to Ben the Fourth: "Old Fourth, please keep a lookout for the flower seller, and buy me two branches of plum blossom and a couple of chrysanthemums." Ben the Fourth waited about for the flower seller, neglecting his own business. When the man came, he told her, and, standing by the second door, she picked out the flowers she liked best, and two purple and gold handkerchiefs. She spent seven *qian* and more. She took a piece of silver from her purse and asked Ben the Fourth to weigh it for her. He was busy upon his accounts, but left them, weighed the silver, and was about to cut off the amount she wanted. Then Daian came up.

"I will cut off the silver you want," he said. He took the piece, but instead of cutting it, looked at Huilian.

"Well," she said, "you thievish monkey! Why don't you cut it? Why stand there looking at me? Did you hear the dogs barking the night I stole the money?"

"I don't say you stole the silver," Daian said, "but somehow or other it seems familiar. It is just like some Father had in his purse. The other day, he had a piece cut into two at the lantern market. One piece he gave to the goldsmith and this is the other. I remember it perfectly."

"Don't you know that many things in this world look alike? What should I be doing with your master's silver?"

Daian laughed. "I know what that silver paid for," he said. Huilian slapped him. He cut the silver and gave the money to the flower seller, but made no offer to give Huilian the change.

"You rascal," she said, "you must be a brave man to dare to take my money."

"I am not robbing you," the boy said, "I am only going to buy some fruit."

"You thievish monkey," Huilian cried, "give it back to me, and I will give you something." When Daian handed back the silver, she gave him a small piece and put the rest back in her purse.

After that she often stood at the gate to buy artificial flowers and handkerchiefs, sometimes spending several taels. She would buy four or five measures of melon seeds and give them to the maids and serving women. For herself she bought a pearl headband and a pair of bright gold earrings. She wore red silk trousers and a broad-sleeved gown in which she kept fragrant tea leaves. She carried several perfume boxes. Every day she spent at least two or three *qian*, all of which came from Ximen Qing.

After Jinlian knew of her relations with Ximen, Huilian went to the Fifth Lady's room every day and waited on her with the utmost diligence.

She served her with tea and water and sewed for her, doing many things that were quite unnecessary, and many things that she had no desire to do. She did not go to Yueniang even once a day, for all her time was spent with Jinlian, waiting upon her when she played chess or dominoes with Li Ping'er. Sometimes Ximen Qing would come in while they were playing, and then Jinlian would purposely ask Huilian to serve the wine. Sometimes they would sit and play together to please him.

# Chapter 24
# The Ladies Celebrate the Feast of Lanterns

Candles blaze in silver sconces
Wine is heated in the jars
The guests are merry and their laughter never ceases.
Untrammeled hips sway as the willows of Zhang Tai
Unpainted lips sing as the spring in the imperial gardens
From the fragrance of their attire we know their will with us
Flowers fall from their hair and are gathered in silence.
If it were not for the delights of love
Would Han be sober after drinking?

The day came when the moon shines in the heavens and lanterns shine upon the earth. Ximen Qing had all his lanterns set out and a splendid feast prepared in the great hall. On the sixteenth day of the first month the whole household assembled, with Ximen Qing and Wu Yueniang in the place of honor, and the other ladies all beautifully dressed. The four maids who acted as the musicians of the family played and sang many songs about the lanterns. A small table was laid specially for Chen Jingji. The food was exquisite and the fruits appropriate to the season. Four maids served the wine, and Laiwang's wife Song Huilian sat on a chair outside the door, chewing melon seeds, waiting for the wine to be brought from the kitchen. It was her duty, when wine was wanted in the hall, to send Laian and Huatong to the kitchen to fetch it. She said: "The rascals have all run away; there is no one here." Then Ximen Qing saw Huatong bringing the wine, and asked him where he had been, saying he deserved a whipping. When the boy came out of the hall, he complained to Huilian.

"Sister," he said, "why did you tell Father stories about me? I haven't been away at all."

"I can't help that," Huilian said, "they called for wine and you were not there. If you are not to blame, who is?"

"Sister," said the boy, "it is very nice and tidy here, yet you are throwing down melon seeds. If Father sees it he will be angry again.

"Don't you bother about me, you young rascal," Huilian said. "If you won't sweep them away, I'll tell one of the other boys, and if Father sees them, I'll take all the responsibility."

"Oh, don't make a fuss about it," the boy said. "I'll sweep them away for you."

Ximen Qing saw that his son-in-law Chen Jingji had no wine and told Pan Jinlian to give him some. She stood up quickly, poured out a cup of wine and smilingly handed it to Jingji.

"Brother," she said, "Father says I must give you some wine. Now you must drink it."

Jingji took the cup and looked slyly at Jinlian. "Fifth Mother, please don't trouble. I will drink it."

Jinlian, with the light between Ximen Qing and herself, squeezed Jingji's hand as he took the cup from her. He pretended to be paying attention to the others, but touched her tiny feet.

"What shall we do if Father sees us?" Jinlian whispered with a smile. They made love in front of the others, without anyone knowing what they were about. But Huilian, who was standing outside the window, saw quite clearly everything that passed between them.

"This woman," she thought, "is always trying to get the better of me, and here she is, behaving like this with that young man. Next time she treats me badly, I shall know what to say."

They had been drinking for some time when a message came from Ying Bojue inviting Ximen Qing to go with him to see the lanterns. Ximen told Yueniang to enjoy herself with the others, and he, with Daian and Ping'an in attendance, went to join Bojue.

Yueniang and her companions went on with their feast till the stars grew dim and the full moon, rising in the east, made the courtyard bright as day. Then some of the women went to their rooms to change their dresses; others adorned themselves in the light of the moon, and others put flowers in their hair in the lantern light. Meng Yulou, Jinlian, Li Ping'er and Huilian stood in front of the great hall to watch Chen Jingji set off the fireworks.

Li Jiao'er, Sun Xue'e and Ximen Dajie went with Yueniang to the inner court.

"He is out," Jinlian said to the others. "Shall we ask the Great Lady to let us go to the street?"

"If you go," said Huilian, "please take me with you."

"If you wish to go, you must ask the Great Lady," Jinlian said. "If she and the Second Lady would like to go too, we will wait here for them."

Huilian was about to go to the inner court, but Yulou said: "She will do no good. I will go myself and ask them." Li Ping'er said: "I am going to my room to find a warmer cloak. It will be cold as the night gets older."

"Sister," Jinlian said: "if you have a cloak to spare, bring one for me. It will save my going back to my room." Li Ping'er promised, and went away.

Only Jinlian was left to watch Chen Jingji setting off the fireworks. She went over to him and pinched him slightly. "Brother," she said, laughing, "don't you feel cold with such thin clothes on?"

A boy called Little Iron Rod was jumping about begging Jingji to give him some fireworks. The young man thought that here was an opportunity. He gave the lad a few fireworks and told him to go and set them off outside the gate.

"So you think my clothes are too thin," he said to Jinlian. "Have you anything warmer for me?"

"You are determined to get something out of me," Jinlian said. "You touched my feet, and I did not complain. Now you have the audacity to ask me for clothes. I don't belong to you. Why should I give you clothes?"

"If you won't give me any, well and good," Jingji said, "but why try to frighten me?"

"Oh, you're like the birds that gather on the city walls, always afraid of something."

They were talking when Yulou and Huilian came back. "The Great Lady," Yulou said, "says she will not go out because she is not very well, but we may go if we promise to come back in good time. Li Jiao'er has a bad leg and she doesn't feel like walking."

"Well," Jinlian said, "if they won't go, we must go with the Sixth Lady; then, if he comes back, we shall be the only ones to blame. Do you think we should take Chunmei, Yuxiao, your maid Lanxiang, and the Sixth Lady's Yingchun?"

Xiaoyu came up and asked if she might go, and Yulou said she might if she obtained her mistress's permission. This she did, and came back to them, smiling.

Then the three ladies set off with their maids. The two boys Laian and Huatong escorted them with lanterns. Jingji set off several fireworks on the mounting stone.

"Uncle," Huilian cried, "wait a moment for me. I am just going to my room for a second."

"We are off now," Jingji said.

"If you don't wait for me, I will never love you again," Huilian cried. She ran to her room and changed into a dress of red silk with a white skirt, set a red and gold kerchief on her head, pins and flowers in her hair. Finally she put on a pair of gold lantern-shaped earrings. Then she joined the ladies in their walk "to gain immunity from the hundred sicknesses." The ladies all wore white silk gowns. They had masses of pearls and flowers on their heads. With their white faces and red lips they looked like angels in the moonlight.

Chen Jingji and Laixing walked beside them, setting off fireworks as they went along. There were lotuses that slowly threw forth fire, golden thread chrysanthemum, and orchids ten feet high. When they came to the street, there was a never-ending stream of incense, and the revelers were as plentiful as ants. Crackers exploded with a sound like thunder and the lanterns were bright with a thousand different hues. Flutes and drums sounded wildly. It was a splendid festival.

When the people in the street saw a procession advancing with lanterns of various colors, they imagined that it must have come from some noble household, and gave way immediately. "Uncle," Huilian said, "light a rocket for me." And a little later: "Uncle, set off a full moon for me." First, her ornaments fell off; then she lost a shoe, and had to wait while someone helped her on with it again. She jumped about and joked incessantly with Chen Jingji. Yulou did not approve of this behavior.

"Why do your shoes keep coming off?" she asked.

Yuxiao said, "She was afraid of soiling her own shoes, so she put a pair of the Fifth Lady's over them." Yulou demanded that she should come and show her feet.

"She asked me yesterday to give her a pair of my shoes," Jinlian said, "but I never dreamed the scamp would think of putting them on outside her own."

When Huilian pulled up her skirt, Yulou saw that she was indeed wearing two pairs of red shoes, bound to her ankles by green laces. She said no more.

After a while they crossed the street and went to the lantern fair. "Let us go first to the Sixth Lady's house in Lion Street," Jinlian said to Yulou. She ordered the boys to take them there. Old woman Feng had gone to bed and two girls who had been entrusted to her to sell were asleep with her, but when the boys knocked at the door, she got up hastily and opened it, and the ladies went in.

The old woman opened the stove to boil some water, then took a jar and was about to go out to buy some wine, but Yulou told her they did not wish for any wine, they had had so much at home before they came. "But we shall be glad to have some tea if you will give us some," she said.

"If you invite people to take wine with you, you must give them something to eat," Jinlian said.

"Yes," said Li Ping'er, "and if you think of giving us wine, we shall want a couple of large jars. No small ones for us!"

Yulou told the old woman that they were only teasing her. "Don't go," she said, "just make some tea for us." Then the old woman decided not to go.

"Why is it so long since you came to see me?" Li Ping'er asked old woman Feng. "What are you doing, these days?"

"You see these two girls," the old woman said. "Who is there to look after them if I go out?" Yulou asked who was selling them.

"One is a maid belonging to a neighbor," the old woman said. "She is thirteen years old, and they only want five taels of silver for her. The other is the wife of a servant in the Wang household. Her husband ran away, so they sent her to me. They ask ten taels for her."

"I know someone who wants a girl, so there is a chance for you," Yulou said.

"Who is that, Third Lady?" the old woman asked.

"The Second Lady has only one maid," Yulou said, "and that, of course, is not enough for her. She needs someone rather older, so you can sell the older of the two to her. How old is she?" The old woman said that she was seventeen. Tea was brought and she served it to the ladies.

Chunmei, Yuxiao and Ximen Dajie went upstairs to look out over the street. Then Chen Jingji warned the ladies that it was getting late, and almost time to return. Jinlian told him to mind his own business. However, she called down Chunmei and the others, and they left the house. As the old woman was seeing them to the door Li Ping'er asked where Ping'an was.

"I haven't seen him all day," the old woman said, "but then I often have to wait till midnight for him."

Laian told them that the boy had gone with his master to Ying's house.

"Lock your door, and go to bed," Li Ping'er said to the old woman, "he will not be back tonight. Come and see me tomorrow and bring the maid for the Second Lady. You know you are like the Abbot of the Stone Buddha Temple: you never do anything unless you are made." They waited till she had locked the gate, and then went home again.

When they reached their own gate, they found a woman called Han, the wife of a Mohammedan, making a terrible to-do. Her husband was away on duty with a Chamberlain of the Royal Stables, and she had been out on the walk to cure the hundred illnesses. She had come home drunk. Now she said that somebody had broken open her door, stolen her dog, and a lot of things were missing. She was sitting at the side of the road and cursing everybody. The ladies stopped and Jinlian told Laian to bring the woman over to them to tell them what was amiss. The woman came, made reverence and told her story. The ladies gave her some money and fruits, and Yulou told Laian to ask Jingji to take the woman home. Jingji made fun of the whole affair and wouldn't do anything for the woman, so Jinlian bade Laian take her home. "Come and see me tomorrow," she said. "You can do some washing for me, and I will tell my husband and see that you get your rights." At this the woman Han smiled, thanked them repeatedly, and went home.

The ladies went on. When they came to the gate, Ben the Fourth's wife was standing there. She smiled, made a reverence to them, and invited them to take tea with her. Yulou told her that they had been delayed by listening to Madam Han's story, and that it was too late for them to accept her invitation, though they thanked her very much. But Ben the Fourth's wife pressed them and at last they went in. In her room there was an image of the Buddha of the Eight Calamities, and another of the sage Guan. A snow-flower lantern hung by the door. When they had all sat down, she told her daughter, a girl of fourteen years called Changjie, to greet the ladies and hand around the tea. Yulou and Jinlian each gave the girl two flowers, and Li Ping'er gave her a handkerchief and a *qian* of silver, with which, she said, she might buy some melon seeds. Ben the Fourth's wife was delighted and thanked them repeatedly. After a while they left. Laixing met them at the gate, and, when they asked whether Ximen Qing had come home, told them he had not. They stood at the gate for a few moments while Chen Jingji set off two large chrysanthemum fireworks, a large orchid, and a golden goblet with a silver stem. Then they retired. It was the fourth night watch before Ximen Qing came back.

At the festival Chen Jingji and Jinlian had been laughing and chatting with Huilian, and he had already begun to feel some attraction for the woman. The next morning he dressed, and, before going to the shop, went to the inner court to pay his respects to Yueniang. When he came to her room, Li Jiao'er, Jinlian and Aunt Wu were there, about to have some tea. Yueniang herself had gone to burn incense at the shrine of Buddha. The young man greeted them politely.

"You're a nice man, Brother Chen," Jinlian said. "When I asked you to take home that Han woman last night, you wouldn't move an inch, and in the end I had to get one of the boys to do it. You could think of nothing but joking and chattering with Huilian. I wonder what the understanding is between you. Wait till the Great Lady comes back. You'll see whether I tell her or not."

"How can you say such a thing?" Jingji said. "After all that long walk my back was nearly broken. How many miles do you think it is from here to Lion Street? Yet in spite of my tiredness you asked me to take that woman home. It was only fair that one of the boys should do it. I had had hardly any sleep and it was already nearly daybreak."

They were still wrangling when Yueniang came back. Jingji made a reverence to her, and she asked him what had been the matter yesterday when Han's wife was drunk and cursing all the world. Jingji told her that the woman had been to a party, and, when she came back, discovered that someone had stolen her dog, so she sat on the pavement and cried and shouted and insulted everybody. "When her husband comes back today, I imagine he'll give her a drubbing. She hasn't got up yet."

"If we had not pressed her to go home," Jinlian said, "Father might have seen her, and then there would have been a fine to-do."

Yulou, Li Ping'er and Ximen Dajie came to tea with Yueniang. Jingji joined them and afterwards went with his wife to their own room.

"You rascal," his wife said, when they were alone, "what do you mean by fooling with Laiwang's wife? If my father hears about it, it will be all very well for that strumpet, but you won't know where to find a hole to die in."

A few days later, Ximen Qing had slept in the room of Li Ping'er, and was dressing, when a certain Captain Jing, who had recently been appointed to the district, came to call upon him. Ximen hastened to the hall to greet him, telling Ping'an to bring them tea. The boy went to the kitchen. Huilian, Yuxiao and Xiaoyu were playing in the courtyard. Xiaoyu was riding on Yuxiao's back laughing, and crying, "You bad girl, you've earned a beating. Why won't you let me beat you? Come here, Huilian, catch her by the leg and see what I do to her."

Ping'an intervened. "Sister Yuxiao," he said, "Captain Jing is in the hall, and Father has ordered me to take them some tea."

Yuxiao paid no attention, but went on playing with Xiaoyu.

"Captain Jing has been here a long time already," the boy said.

"Go to the kitchen for your tea," Huilian cried, "don't come and bother us. We only make tea for the ladies. We have nothing to do with the hall."

Ping'an went to the kitchen. Laibao's wife was on duty, but she told him she was busy cooking, and that he must go to the inner court.

"I have already asked them in the inner court," Ping'an said. "They say they have nothing to do with the hall. Huilian says it is your business to provide tea for that part of the house."

"Oh, that strumpet!" Laibao's wife cried. "She thinks she only has to say that she serves the Great Lady. I seem to be the only one in the kitchen. I am cooking for several people already, and I have plain food to get ready for Aunt Wu. How many hands do you think I have? If you want me to make tea, well and good, but why try to make out that I alone have to work in the kitchen? You have no right to treat me as if I were the scullery maid. You won't get any tea from me."

"Captain Jing has been here for hours, Sister," Ping'an said. "Please make the tea or Father will be dreadfully angry." The boy was pushed from pillar to post. He had already wasted a long time. At last Yuxiao brought what was needed, and Ping'an took it to the hall. Captain Jing was preparing to take his leave. Ximen Qing urged him to stay but the tea was cold. Ximen scolded Ping'an and ordered him to change it, but, by the time the fresh tea had been brought, Captain Jing had gone.

Ximen Qing went to the inner court to find out who was responsible, and Ping'an told him that the scullery maid had made it. Then he went to his own room and told Yueniang what had happened.

"Go to the kitchen," he said, "and find out who made the tea. When you've done so, see that she has a beating."

Xiaoyu told her that it was the day for Laibao's wife to attend to the cooking.

"Oh, the wretch," Yueniang cried, "she must be eager to die, making tea like that."

She told Xiaoyu to fetch the woman. Laibao's wife came and knelt before Yueniang in the courtyard.

"How many blows do you want?" Yueniang said. Laibao's wife said the tea was cold because she had had to cook the dinner and also plain food for Aunt Wu. Yueniang scolded her for a time and then forgave her. Then she addressed all the maids and serving women. "Henceforth," she said, "whenever visitors come to the hall, Yuxiao and Huilian must make the tea, and those in the kitchen must see about the tea and food for our own people."

Laibao's wife went back to the kitchen in a fury. As soon as Ximen Qing had gone out, she went in a rage to the inner court. When she found Huilian, she shook her finger at her. "You abandoned, scoundrelly woman," she cried, "now you are satisfied. You have the luck. You do service for the mistress, and I am but the scullery maid. You told the boy to come to me for tea, and it was you who told him to call me scullery maid. Who are you to call me scullery maid? The cricket does not eat the flesh of a spotted toad, for they are akin. You are not one of the master's ladies, so why should you consider yourself superior to me? And if you were, I shouldn't be afraid of you."

"You are talking nonsense," Huilian said. "You made the tea badly, and Father didn't like it. What has that to do with me? Why vent your spite on me?"

This made Laibao's wife more angry still. "You thievish whore," she cried, "you wanted to get me a beating. You had a man on the sly when you were with the Cai family, and your wickedness is past all bounds. Now you come and play the same tricks here."

"Did you see me have a man on the sly?" Huilian said. "Well, dear Sister, you are yourself no virgin."

"No virgin?" Laibao's wife cried. "I'm better than you, anyway. You've had as many men as there are grains in a heap of corn. You can't set eyes upon a man without beginning your tricks. And you fancy nobody knows what you are up to. You have no respect for the ladies here, so why should you have any for us?"

"What are you talking about?" Huilian said. "In what way do I fail in respect to the ladies? Say all the nasty things you like. I don't care."

"No, you don't care," Laibao's wife shouted, "you don't care, because you have somebody behind you."

They went on quarreling until Xiaoyu asked Yueniang to intervene. "You rogues," Yueniang said, "instead of doing your work, you spend all your time squabbling. If your master hears of this, there will be more trouble. You have not been beaten yet, but you certainly will be. Do you wish to be beaten?"

"If I am beaten," Laibao's wife cried, "I will pull this woman's guts out. I will give my life to get even with her, and we will go together." She went back to the kitchen.

After this, Huilian was more arrogant than ever. Because of her relations with Ximen Qing, she thought the rest of the household unworthy of consideration. Every day she played with Yulou, Jinlian, Li Ping'er, Ximen Dajie and Chunmei.

A few days later old woman Feng brought the younger of her two maids, taking her first to Li Ping'er, and then to Li Jiao'er. Li Jiao'er paid five taels for the girl and kept her.

# CHAPTER 25
# Laiwang's Jealousy

The Feast of Lanterns was over and the Festival of Spring had come again. Ying Bojue came to ask Ximen Qing to go for a day in the country as the guest of Sun Guazui, and they went away together. Before the festival, Wu Yueniang had had a swing set up in the garden, and, while Ximen Qing was out, she took all the ladies to it that they might dispel that languor which the coming of spring seems to bring. The first to swing were Wu Yueniang herself and Meng Yulou, and, when they had done, she asked Li Jiao'er and Pan Jinlian to take their places. Li Jiao'er declined, saying she was not feeling well, so Yueniang asked Li Ping'er to be Jinlian's partner. Then Yulou cried, "Come here, Sister, and swing standing with me. But you mustn't laugh." They grasped the rope with their beautiful hands and stood on the board. Yueniang told Huilian and Chunmei to push the swing for them.

Jinlian laughed so much that Yueniang cried, "Don't laugh. It is dangerous. You will fall off." The words were hardly out of her mouth when Jinlian fell with a crash, for the board was slippery and she was wearing high-heeled shoes. But she caught the frame of the swing and saved herself from falling to the ground, though Yulou was nearly thrown off.

"Sister," Yueniang said, "I told you not to laugh. Now, you see, you've fallen." She turned to Li Jiao'er and the others.

"Never laugh when you're swinging," she said, "it makes the legs give way, and down you fall. I remember, when I was a girl, our neighbor Zhou had a swing in his garden. One spring holiday, his daughter and I and two or three other girls were swinging on it, and laughing just as the Fifth Lady was. Miss Zhou was thrown off. She fell across the board and broke her maidenhead. Later, when she married, people said she was not a pure girl, and she was divorced. Yes, it is a mistake to laugh, when one goes in for games of this sort."

"The Third Lady is no good," Jinlian cried, "I will swing standing with the Sixth Lady."

"Be careful, both of you," Yueniang said. She told Yuxiao and Chunmei to start them. Then Chen Jingji came.

"You are swinging, I see," he said.

"Yes," Yueniang said, "you have come at the right moment. You can push the swing for the ladies: the girls are not strong enough."

Jingji was as pleased as an old monk when the dinner bell goes. He gathered his clothes around him and hurried forward to offer his services. The first thing he did was to busy himself about Jinlian's skirt.

"Hold fast, Fifth Mother," he said, "I am going to push you." The swing flew up in the air so that the ladies looked like two winged angels. So high did it go that Li Ping'er was frightened.

"Brother," she cried, "I am falling, come and help me."

"Don't be alarmed, Lady, I will come in a moment," Jingji said. "If I am called first to one side and then to the other, I don't know where I am." He lifted Li Ping'er's skirts till her red trousers could be seen. Then he pushed the swing.

"Gently, Brother," Li Ping'er cried, "my legs are not very strong."

"Ah," said Jingji, "you shouldn't drink so much."

Then Jinlian complained that Li Ping'er was treading on her skirt, and they stopped swinging. Chunmei and Ximen Dajie took the places of the two ladies, and afterwards Yuxiao and Song Huilian swung standing. Huilian grasped the rope and, standing perfectly upright, danced upon the seat. She would have no one to push the swing for her, but herself drove it high into the air and down again. It was indeed a wonderful sight. Yueniang said to Yulou and Li Ping'er, "Just look at that woman. She certainly knows how to swing."

Laiwang had gone to Hangzhou to buy the clothes that were to be presented to the Imperial Tutor Cai. When they were ready, he had them packed in chests, and brought them back. As soon as he reached home they were unloaded, and he went to the inner court. Sun Xue'e was standing by the door of the hall. He made a reverence to her.

"Welcome home," she said, smiling graciously. "You must have had a very tiresome journey. It is only a short time since I saw you, but you have grown very stout."

"Where are my lord and my lady?" Laiwang asked.

"Your master has gone for a day in the country with Master Ying and the others," Xue'e said, "but your mistress and her daughter are swinging in the garden."

"Why do they play such games as that?" Laiwang said. Xue'e brought him a cup of tea and asked if he would like something to eat. "I will not have anything to eat," he said, "till I have seen the Great Lady, and I must go and wash first." Then he added: "I don't see my wife. Is she in the kitchen?"

Xue'e smiled sourly. "Your wife, indeed! Are you sure you still have a wife? She has become a great personage, and spends all her time playing chess and dominoes with the ladies. She doesn't condescend to come to the kitchen any more."

While they were talking Xiaoyu had gone to the garden to tell Yueniang that Laiwang had come. She came from the front court. Laiwang kowtowed and stood while she asked him about his journey. She gave him two jars of wine. Then Huilian came.

"You must be tired," Yueniang said. "Go to your room; wash and rest, and you can tell your master all about your business when he comes home."

Laiwang went to his room. Huilian gave him the key, and herself went to get him some water and unpack his luggage. "You black rogue," she said, "you have been away only a short time. What have you been eating to get as fat as this?" She helped him to change his clothes and prepared some food. When he had eaten something, he went to bed. The sun was setting when Ximen Qing came home. Laiwang got up and went to the front court to make his report.

"The birthday presents for the Imperial Tutor and the clothes for the members of his household are all in order," he said. "I had them packed, and brought them in four chests. They are at the customs office, and we must take porters to clear them."

Ximen Qing was pleased. Besides giving Laiwang money for the porters, and telling him to fetch the things next day, he gave him five taels of silver for himself and set him in charge of the buying department of the household. Laiwang had privately done a little business on his own account, and, secretly, he gave Xue'e two handkerchiefs, two pairs of silken trousers, four boxes of Hangzhou powder, and twenty cakes of rouge.

"Less than four months after you went away," Xue'e told him, "your wife began to carry on with his Lordship. Yuxiao was their go-between, and they made their nest in the Fifth Lady's room."

She told him how they had begun their naughty games in the grotto beneath the artificial mound, but had later made use of Jinlian's room, where they slept from morning till night and from night until morning.

"He has given her clothes," she said, "ornaments and artificial flowers, costing a lot of money, and she has been wearing them all the time. She is always giving the boys money and getting them to buy things for her, and she spends several *qian* of silver every day."

"No wonder her box is full of clothes and ornaments," Laiwang cried. "When I asked her where they came from, she said her mistress had given them to her."

"Mistress, indeed!" Xue'e said. "Master, more likely!"

Her words made a great impression on Laiwang. Wine helps a man to unburden his soul, and that night he drank deeply before he went to his room. He opened his wife's box, and found in it a roll of very handsome blue figured satin.

"Where did you get this satin?" he cried. "Who gave it you? Tell me the truth at once."

His wife did not know what was wrong, but she forced a smile and answered: "You funny old rascal. Why do you ask? It came from the inner court, and was given me to make a dress of. I haven't had time to make it up yet, so I put it in the chest. Where else do you think I could expect to get such a present?"

"You strumpet," Laiwang shouted, "don't try to keep up this pretense. Who gave it you, and where did you get these ornaments?"

"Pooh," said his wife, "you talk as if people had no relations of their own. Why, even if I had come out of a piece of stone, I should have come from somewhere. I borrowed these ornaments from one of my aunts. Where else do you think I got them?"

Laiwang struck her with his fist so that she all but fell. "Strumpet!" he cried, "you are trying to deceive me. I know for certain that you have been carrying on with that foul fellow. Yes, Yuxiao was the go-between. It was she who brought you this satin. You began in the garden, and afterwards amused yourselves all day long in the room of that whore Jinlian. Now, do you think you can deceive me any longer?"

"You wicked villain," Huilian cried, "you will come to a violent end, without a doubt. How dare you strike me? What have I done? You come and throw stones at me without the slightest cause. Explain yourself. Some backbiting sneak has been telling you a pack of lies about me, and you lay your hands on me. I assure you you shall not treat me as if I were dirt. If I am going to die, I will die clean. Ask anybody you like about the women of my family. If there is anything shady about me, my name is not Song. There is no reason at all for this fuss you are making. It's like a rainstorm without any wind. But there is something behind it, all the same. I suppose if it were suggested to you you would murder anybody?"

Laiwang did not know what to answer, and his wife went on: "I will tell you all there is to tell about this roll of blue satin. It was our mistress's birthday on the third day of the eleventh month, and she gave it me then because she saw me wearing a purple gown and skirt that I had borrowed from Yuxiao. She thought they did not suit me. I have been too busy ever since to make it up, and now I have put up with all this to-do. You have done me wrong. But I am not the sort to overlook a thing like this, and tomorrow you shall see. I'll let some of these people know what I think about them. My life is not worth living, and the sooner I find somebody to put an end to it, the better."

"If there is really nothing in it," Laiwang said, "there's no reason to make such a fuss. Get my bed ready."

"You scamp, you'll come to a bad end," Huilian said as she got the bed ready. "You go and drink a lot of wine and then come home and abuse your old woman instead of going quietly to bed." She hustled him off, and, in a very short time, he was snoring like thunder.

Unfaithful wives are always like this. However intelligent their husbands may be, with a few words their wives can twist things about in such a way that their husbands are completely hoodwinked. Such women are like the privy floor. They stink, but they hold their ground.

So Huilian made a fool of her husband and the night passed. Next day, she went to the inner court and asked Yuxiao who had been telling tales about her. As neither of them could fix upon the right person, she could only go about suspiciously, grumbling.

One day Yueniang wanted Xue'e and sent Xiaoyu to find her. Though the maid looked everywhere she failed to find her, until she went to the front court. There she saw Xue'e coming out of Laiwang's room. She supposed that the woman had been chatting with Laiwang's wife, but, when she reached the kitchen, Huilian was there, mincing meat. Meanwhile, in the front court, Ximen Qing had been talking to Master Qiao, who had come on behalf of a certain Wang Sifeng, a soda merchant of Yangzhou, who had been put in prison by the magistrate of that district. Qiao had brought two thousand taels of silver and wanted Ximen Qing to approach the Imperial Tutor, and secure the soda merchant's release. As soon as he had seen Master Qiao to the gate, Ximen called for Laiwang, who promptly came from his own room.

After this everybody knew that Xue'e and Laiwang were carrying on together.

One day when Laiwang had been drinking, he began to revile Ximen Qing before the servants in the front court. "When I was away," he said, "he got Yuxiao to take a roll of blue satin to my place and seduced my wife. At first, he had his way with her in the garden, but afterwards the Fifth Lady made a nest for them in her place. Let him look out for himself. If he falls into my hands, I will certainly kill him. My knife shall go in white, and it will be red when it comes out. Yes, and I'll kill that whore Pan as well, and get rid of the pair of them at the same time. You shall see whether I don't do as I say. I haven't forgotten how, when that whore Pan murdered her husband Wu Da, and her brother-in-law Wu Song brought an accusation against her, it was me they got to go to the Eastern Capital to get her off and have Wu Song banished. Now that she feels herself secure once more, she forgets all about the one who saved her life, and makes a whore of my wife. My hatred for her is as deep as the heavens. But there is a proverb which says that a man may as well be hung for a sheep as a lamb. I don't care whether I die or not, but I'll thrash his Majesty, even if I get chopped in ten thousand pieces."

Laiwang talked in this strain without realizing that anyone was eavesdropping, but Laixing overheard everything he said. Laixing was the servant to whom Ximen Qing had originally entrusted the business of buying and changing money for the household, but, after Ximen had fallen in love with Laiwang's wife, that business had been handed over to Laiwang. Since then Laiwang and Laixing had not been on the best of terms. So, when he had heard the kind of thing his rival was saying, Laixing slipped away to Jinlian's room. When he pulled up the lattice and came in, she was sitting with Yulou.

"What can I do for you?" she said. "Where is your master amusing himself today?"

"He has gone to a funeral with Uncle Ying," Laixing said. "Lady, I have something to tell you, but you must keep it to yourself, and not let anybody know I told you."

"If you have anything to say, let us hear it," Jinlian said.

"It is only this," Laixing said. "That rascal Laiwang got drunk somewhere yesterday, and made a fine hullabaloo, cursing everybody the whole day long. He wished to pick a quarrel with me but I came away and left him. In front of everybody he cursed Master, and you too, Fifth Mother."

"Why should the rogue curse me?" Jinlian said.

"I hardly like to tell you," Laixing said, "but since there is only the Third Lady here, and she is not a stranger, I will. He said Father had got him out of the way so as to be able to make love to his wife. He also said that you, Fifth Mother, had arranged everything for them, and allowed his wife to sleep with Father in your room from morning till night and from night till morning. He has got a knife to kill you both, and says it may be white when it goes in but it will be red when it comes out. He says you poisoned your first husband and sent him to the Eastern Capital to hush up the matter, and that though you owe your life to him, you only repay his kindness by injuries and help his wife to be unfaithful to him. I felt I ought to warn you. Fifth Mother, you must be continually on your guard against this fellow's plottings."

Yulou might have been plunged in a cold bath, she was so shocked when she heard this. Jinlian flushed beneath her powder and ground her silvery teeth. "The murderous villain," she cried, "I've never done him any harm in the past, and I'm not doing any now. If his master takes a fancy to his wife, what's that to do with me? That slave and I shall not both remain in

Ximen's household. How dare he say I got him to save my life? You may go now," she said to Laixing, "and if your master asks you any questions when he comes back, be sure to tell him what you've told me."

"Fifth Mother," Laixing said, "I have only told the truth. I have repeated exactly what I heard. If Father questions me, I can only tell him what I have told you." He went to the front court.

"Is it true that there is anything between his master and that woman?" Yulou said.

"Did you ever know that unprincipled scamp to lose an opportunity of getting hold of a pretty woman?" Jinlian said. "Now he has given himself into that slave's hands. The strumpet was once a servant in Cai's house, and there she and her mistress played the whore together till they were found out and she was sent packing. Then she married Jiang Cong. Was one man enough for her? No, indeed, she must have lovers like grains of rice. She is up to every trick you could think of. That wretched husband of ours, who is cunning enough to deceive even the spirits—he could play tricks on a spook—told Yuxiao to take her a piece of satin to make a gown of. I meant to tell you this before. Don't you remember the day the Great Lady went to a party at Master Qiao's house? We were all playing chess in the front court when one of the maids came and said, 'Father has come back.' We stopped our game and I went to the inner court. Well, when I got to the gate, Xiaoyu was standing in the passage and, when I spoke to her, she didn't answer. She made some sort of a sign with her hand. I went on, and when I reached the garden, that little scamp Yuxiao was standing at the corner gate. She was keeping a lookout for them. Still I didn't realize what the game was and was going on, but Yuxiao got in my way and wouldn't let me go farther. 'Father is there,' she said. I cursed her, because I had an idea that she was up to some trick of her own, but when I did get in, there he was in the grotto with that woman. She blushed crimson when she saw me, and ran away. He didn't know what to say, and he had to listen to a few remarks from me, the shameless fellow."

"Afterwards the woman came to see me. She knelt down and begged me not to say anything to her mistress. Then, in the first month, he was going to bring the whore to spend the night with him in my room, but I and Chunmei told him plainly what we thought about him. We said, of course, we would not allow him to do anything of the sort. The wretch tried to get me mixed up in the business, but I was not going to have that pretty little whore carrying on with him in my place. Even if I had been willing, young Miss Chunmei would never have allowed it."

"No wonder the wicked little wretch never stands up when we come in," Yulou said. "I should never have dreamed of anything of the sort. It is most improper on his part to want her when he can get a woman anywhere. Look at the opportunity to talk scandal he gives the slaves!"

"Yes," Jinlian said, "but it is tit for tat. If he has fallen in love with the slave's wife, the slave has done as much for him. There's a nice little exchange going on. That little thief Xue'e has had plenty to say about us, but now even if I give her a smack on the face, she will have to keep her mouth shut."

"Shall we tell him or not?" Yulou said. "The Great Lady will not do anything about it, and if that fellow really has made up his mind, and we keep silence about it, Father will know nothing, and, some time or other, the slave will get him. I think you ought to mention it to him."

"If that slave were my father," Jinlian said, "I might possibly forgive him, but he isn't, and nothing will ever induce me to do so."

Late that evening Ximen Qing came home. He found Jinlian in her room, her cloudlike tresses in disorder, her fragrant cheeks heavy with slumber, and her eyes red like two peaches from weeping. When he asked what was amiss, she told him that Laiwang had got drunk and was going about saying he was going to kill his master. "Laixing heard this with his own ears," she said. "While you were stealing that slave's wife, he was doing as much for you. If the wretch only intended to murder you, I shouldn't worry so much, but he means to kill me too. If we don't do something about it at once, sooner or later we shall fall into his clutches. We have no eyes at the back of our heads."

"Who has been telling tales?" Ximen said.

"It's no use asking me," Jinlian said. "Ask Xiaoyu. The slave said several nasty things about me. For one thing he said I poisoned my husband and, after you married me, we sent him to find somebody to save my life. This is the sort of thing he has been saying all around the place. It is a good thing I have no children. That slave's scandal-mongering would not make good hearing for them. 'When your mother first came to this house,' he would say, 'she was in a very unpleasant predicament. She had to ask me to get her out of it. I saved her life.' And if he goes around talking in that strain, what about your good name? It won't be any too glorious. If you are devoid of decent feeling, I'm not, and if that is the sort of life I've got to live, well, I just won't live."

Ximen Qing listened. Then he went to the front court, called Laixing to a quiet spot, and asked him many questions about the matter. Laixing told him in detail everything that had happened. Ximen Qing went back to the inner court and questioned Xiaoyu. Her account of the matter agreed perfectly with that of Jinlian. She told him how she had seen Xue'e coming out of Laiwang's room one day when his wife was out. It was a fact, she said.

Ximen Qing flew into a rage. He gave Xue'e a drubbing till Yueniang made him desist. He took away her ornaments and fine dresses and made her work in the kitchen with the maid servants, and forbade her ever to come out. Later, in the inner court, he told Yuxiao to bring Huilian to him in secret, so that he could hear what she had to say.

"Oh dear! Oh dear!" she cried. "Father, you mustn't talk like that. I am ready to swear by all I love that he never said anything of the sort. He may have been drunk, but no matter what state he was in, he would never have forgotten himself so far as to curse you. Why, how could he accept favors from Zhou Wang and then turn around and accuse Zhou Wang of being a scoundrel? He is dependent upon you for his livelihood. Don't believe everything people say to you, Father. Who told you this story?"

Ximen Qing shut his mouth firmly. He would not answer until the woman pressed him. At last he said: "It was Laixing."

"Father," Huilian said, "you gave Laixing's job to us and he credits us with having got him out of it. He can't make so much money as he used to. So he hates us and spits out slanders against us with his bloody mouth. And you believe him! If my husband were really plotting a thing like that, I would never forgive him. Father, do what I tell you. Don't keep him here. Give him a few taels and send him away somewhere to act as your agent. When he has gone, you and I can talk together whenever we feel inclined, and it will be much pleasanter for both of us."

Ximen Qing thought this an excellent idea. "You are right, my child," he said, "I think I'll send him to the Capital to see the Imperial Tutor about this business of Wang Sifeng. He can take the birthday presents at the same time. But he has only just come back from Hangzhou and I didn't think it was fair to send him off again so soon. I made up my mind to send Laibao instead. But now you suggest it, I will send him to the Capital and, when he returns, he shall have a thousand taels of silver and I'll send him to Hangzhou with someone else to act as a manager, and set him up in the silk business there. Will that suit you?"

Huilian was delighted. "Nothing could be better," she cried. Ximen Qing saw that there was no one about. He took her in his arms and kissed her. She slipped her tongue into his mouth, and they exchanged a long passionate kiss. "You promised me a new hairnet," Huilian said. "Why haven't you got it for me? If you don't get it now, I never shall have one. I shall have to wear this old one every day."

"Don't be impatient," Ximen said, "tomorrow I will give the silversmith eight taels of silver, and he shall make one for you. But your mistress will probably ask you where you got it. Then what will you say?"

"Don't worry," the woman said, "I shall find an answer. If anybody asks me, I shall say I borrowed it from my aunt. That will be all right." They talked a little longer and then parted.

Next day Ximen Qing took his seat in the hall and sent for Laiwang. "Get your clothes and luggage packed," he said. "Tomorrow is the twenty-eighth day of the third month, and you will start for the Capital to see the Imperial Tutor. When you come back, I am going to send you to do business at Hangzhou." Laiwang was very pleased. He bowed, and went back to his room to pack. Then he went out to buy a few things.

Laixing heard what was going on and went to tell Jinlian. She was told that Ximen Qing was in the bower in the garden and went there, but she could not find him. Chen Jingji was there, packing up the presents.

"Where is your father?" she said. "What is that you're packing up?"

"Father was here a moment ago," Jingji said. "He has gone to see the Great Lady and get the silver for that affair of Wang Sifeng. These are the presents for the Imperial Tutor."

"Who is going to take them?" Jinlian asked.

"I believe Father has told Laiwang to go," Jingji said.

As Jinlian was going down the steps towards the garden, she met Ximen Qing bringing the silver. She asked him to go to her room. "Whom are you sending to the Eastern Capital?" she said.

"Laiwang and Clerk Fu are going together," Ximen said. "You see, there are not only the presents, there's this silver to be spent for the soda merchant Wang Sifeng. Two will be safer than one."

"You always think you know best," Jinlian said. "Why don't you do what I tell you? You believe every word that strumpet tells you. There is not the slightest doubt she is thinking of her husband. Only a day or two ago that slave declared before all the servants in the house that you have taken his wife and he will have your money. If you lose your money, my good Brother, you will do so with your eyes open. You might as well make him a present of a thousand taels and have done with it. You want his wife. Very well. If you keep him here, it will be awkward, and, if you send him somewhere else, you won't be any better off. If you let him stay here, we shall never be safe against his evil designs, and if you send him away, he will run off with every penny of your money. So long as you are after his wife, he won't care a fig for anything you say. The best thing you can do is to get rid of him for good and all. You know the proverb: 'If you cut the grass, but do not pull up the roots, new shoots will spring up as before; but if you pull up the roots, there can be no new shoots to come up.' You would have no reason to be anxious, and you could do what you liked with the woman."

These words made Ximen Qing think.

# CHAPTER 26

# The Tragic End of Song Huilian

As Wu from Yue is parted, so I from my lord
Through the passing years the jade pillow marks our separation.
I climb the watchtower and look towards the north
I see but heavy mist and rain.
I turn again and cry to the moon hanging in the skies.

The night is dark and hides the spears beside the gate
I wander through the corridors and sleep alone.
I seek in vain for you in the inner chamber
My spirit goes to the waste lands and my soul to the waters.

After Pan Jinlian had talked to him, Ximen Qing changed his mind once more. The next day, though Laiwang, with his luggage all ready, waited for the order to start, noon passed, and still he received no word. At last Ximen Qing came and called Laiwang to him.

"During the night, I have been thinking the matter over," he said. "I remembered that you had only just come back from Hangzhou, and I decided that, instead of sending you to the Eastern Capital as I had intended, it would be too much for you, and I ought to send Laibao and give you a rest. Later on I will find something nearer home for you."

In matters of this sort, the master invariably has the last word. Laiwang could only acquiesce. Ximen gave the silver and the presents to Laibao and Clerk Fu, and, on the twenty-eighth day of the third month, they set out. Laiwang went back to his room in a temper, drank more than was good for him, and said all manner of foolish things, telling his wife he was going to kill Ximen Qing.

Huilian scolded him. "A dog that really means to bite never shows its teeth," she said. "You are talking nonsense. Remember the walls have ears. You are drunk again." She sent him to bed.

Next day, she went to Yuxiao's room in the inner court and asked her to go for Ximen Qing. They found a quiet place behind the kitchen wall where they could talk and Yuxiao kept watch for them by the door. Huilian was very angry.

"What a man you are!" she cried. "You promised me to let him go. Why have you changed your mind and sent somebody else instead? You have a mind just like a ball. It does nothing but bob up and down. You can't keep steady long enough to hold a candle. One of these days I shall build a temple in your honor and set up a banner pole, and bestow on you the title of Father of Lies. Never again will I believe a word you say. I did trust you, but evidently you don't care about me any more."

"Don't say that," Ximen Qing said, laughing, "it was not that I didn't want him to go, but I was afraid he didn't know his way about the Imperial Tutor's palace. That's the only reason I sent Laibao, and kept him at home. I'll see if I can't find some business for him here."

"What sort of business will you find for him?" Huilian cried. "Tell me."

"I will get a manager for him and set them up in a wineshop, not far away."

This delighted Huilian. She went back to her room and told Laiwang all about it. Then they waited for Ximen Qing's orders. One day Ximen called Laiwang to the front court. Lying on a table were six packets of silver. "My son," Ximen Qing said, "you must have had a very trying journey from Hangzhou. I did mean to send you to the Eastern Capital, but I thought perhaps you didn't know Cai's palace well enough, so I decided to send Laibao instead. Here are six packets of silver, three hundred taels altogether. Take them, find someone to act as your manager, and set up a wineshop somewhere not far away. You will bring the interest dutifully to me every month. That seems to me the best thing we can do for you."

Laiwang knelt down and kowtowed. He took the six packets of silver to his room. "He is using this business as a trap," he said to his wife. "He has given me these three hundred taels, and he says I am to find a manager and start a wineshop."

"You are a funny creature," his wife said. "It takes more than one shovel to dig a well; you must take your time. You have a business now and you will have to settle down, do your duty, and give up drinking so much wine. It's that which makes you talk so much nonsense."

"Well, I'm going to the street to find a partner," Laiwang said. He told his wife to put the silver in a chest. He went to the street but, though he looked about till late, he found nobody to suit him. Instead, he got very drunk and went home again. His wife sent him to bed, and, soon afterwards, Yuxiao called her away to the inner court.

Laiwang slept for a long time. It was the first night watch when he awoke. He was not yet sober and his head whirled. Suddenly he heard someone outside the window calling softly: "Brother Laiwang, why don't you get up and see what your wife is doing? That bad fellow has taken her to the garden again and, while you are asleep here, suspecting nothing, they are having a fine time." This made Laiwang wake up. He opened his eyes to see who was there. Huilian was not in the room. He decided that the voice must have been Xue'e's, and that she had come to tell him of something she had seen.

"You will be unfaithful before my very face, will you?" he cried, jumping out of bed in a fury. He opened the door and ran straight to the garden. He had just reached the garden gate when, suddenly, a stool was thrown out of the darkness and he was knocked down. At the same time a knife fell clattering on the ground. Servants came running from all directions, shouting: Thief! Thief!" and some of them pounced on him.

"It is only Laiwang," he cried. "I have come to look for my wife. Why are you seizing me?"

Nobody would listen to him, and he was dragged, struggling and fighting, to the great hall. There, among many brilliant lights, Ximen Qing sat, shouting, "Bring him in!"

"I woke up," Laiwang said, kneeling down, "and I couldn't see my wife anywhere, so I went to find her. What have I done to be seized and treated like a thief?"

Laixing produced the knife for his master to see. Ximen Qing cried angrily, "Animals one can deal with, but human beings are impossible. This fellow is a murderer. There was I, thinking he had just come back from Hangzhou, and giving him three hundred taels to set him up in business. Then, in the depth of night, he comes to murder me. If that was not what you were after," he said to Laiwang, "what were you doing with this knife?" He shouted to the attendants: "Take him to his room and bring me back my three hundred taels." The servants took Laiwang away.

Huilian was talking to Yuxiao in the inner court when she heard the news. She rushed at once to her room and, seeing what was happening, began to cry. "You went to bed drunk," she said. "What need was there for you to get up and start looking for me? Now you have fallen into a trap."

They opened the chest, took out the six packets of silver, and went back to the hall. Ximen Qing unwrapped the packets and examined the silver in the light of a lamp. Only one contained genuine silver, the others had nothing in them but tin.

"How dare you change my silver?" Ximen cried. "What have you done with my money? Tell me at once."

"Master," Laiwang sobbed, "you very kindly entrusted the silver to me so that I might set up in business. How could I think of cheating you and putting tin in its place?"

"You took a knife to murder me," Ximen cried. "Here it is. It is no use your trying to make excuses." He called forward Laixing, who knelt down and testified: "The other day, outside, didn't you say before a number of people that you were going to kill Master because he hadn't found anything for you to do?"

Laiwang gaped, his mouth wide open. "Now," Ximen Qing said, "the case is clear. The stolen property, the witness, the knife and the staves are all here. Chain him and put him into the gatehouse," he said to the servants. "Tomorrow I will write an accusation and send him before the magistrate."

At this moment, Huilian, her hair in disorder and her dress disarranged, ran into the hall and threw herself on her knees before Ximen Qing. "Father," she cried, "this is your doing. He was looking for me quite peacefully. Why should he be taken and treated as a thief? As for those six packets of silver, I was looking after them, and the original seal was never even broken. It cannot possibly have been changed. Though you may wish to get rid of the man, do not forget the justice of Heaven. What has he done? Why are you sending him to be beaten? Where are you going to send him now?"

Ximen Qing smiled sweetly upon her. "This has nothing to do with you, my good woman," he said. "Stand up. He has no regard for propriety, and he has been exceedingly impudent for some time. Now he has even attempted to murder me. But, of course, you know nothing about this. Be calm, you are not concerned in the matter at all." He said to Laian: "Take your sister very gently to her room, and see that she is not alarmed in any way."

Huilian, however, would not rise from her knees. "How stony-hearted you are, Father," she said. "If you will not listen to the priest's voice, at least hearken to the voice of Buddha. Won't you do this for me when I ask so earnestly? Though he did get drunk, he really would never have dreamed of doing a thing like this." Ximen Qing grew impatient and told Laian to pick her up and take her back to her room.

Next day Ximen wrote an accusation and told Laixing, as the witness, to take the papers and Laiwang to the court. "Upon a certain day," the accusation ran, "this man got drunk, and, in the middle of the night, made to kill his master with a knife. He is further charged with fraudulently changing money, etc." The party was about to set off for the court when Yueniang came into the hall. She pleaded earnestly with Ximen Qing. "If the slave has done wrong," she said, "we can deal with him here, and settle it ourselves without bothering the officers and disturbing the court."

"Woman," Ximen shouted, rolling his eyes, "you have no idea of what is fitting. This slave deliberately tried to kill me. Do you come here and ask me to forgive him?" He would not listen to her, and shouted to the servants: "Away with him to the court." Yueniang flushed and withdrew.

"What a cantankerous fellow the master of the house is," she said to Yulou and the others. "There is a nine-tailed fox at work somewhere.

I wonder whose advice he is taking in this business. He is sending the slave away quite unjustifiably. It is all very well for him to say the slave is a thief, but he must prove it. Putting a man into a paper coffin like this is no way to behave. He is an unprincipled tyrant." Then Huilian came and knelt down, weeping.

"Stand up, my child," Yueniang said, "they can't execute your husband when they have examined him. That villain has been drinking something to make him crazy; he won't listen to a word I say. His wife, it would seem, is about of as much account as a private soldier in the army."

"Just now, your master is in a temper," Yulou said to the woman. "We can only win him over by degrees. Don't worry. Go to your room."

Laiwang was taken to the court. Ximen Qing had taken the precaution of sending Daian with a hundred measures of rice to Magistrate Xia and Captain He. They accepted the present. They took their places in the hall of audience and Laixing presented the accusation. The magistrates were told that Laiwang had been given a sum of money with which to establish a business, but that the sight of the silver had put the idea into his head of replacing it by tin. Then, it was said, he became afraid lest his master should find out, and, in the middle of the night, he took a knife and went creeping to the hall to murder his master. The two officers angrily summoned Laiwang before them. He knelt down and pleaded: "If you, heaven-born officers, will permit me to speak, I shall be able to explain everything; but if you will not, I dare not say a word."

"Now, fellow," Magistrate Xia said, "the stolen property and the evidence are both here. It is no use your attempting to clear yourself. All we want from you is the truth. Then, perhaps, we shall not be so hard on you."

Laiwang began to tell how Ximen Qing sent a piece of blue satin to his wife, Huilian, and had seduced her. "Now," he said, "he has accused me of this crime, so that he can get me out of the way and enjoy my wife as he pleases."

Magistrate Xia shouted at him and ordered the attendants to strike him on the mouth.

"You slave," he cried, "this is all part of your plot to murder your master. If it were not for him, you would not have a wife, and now he has given you a business as well. Yet instead of trying to repay his kindness, you get drunk, sneak into his bedroom in the middle of the night, with murder in your heart. Why, if all servants were like you, nobody would dare to keep one."

Laiwang went on saying that he was innocent, but the magistrate called upon Laixing to give his evidence, and, after that, there was nothing more he could say.

The magistrate ordered his attendants to pick out the cruelest thumb-screws they could find and apply them to Laiwang. Then he ordered twenty strokes of the weightiest bamboos. The poor man's skin was broken and his flesh torn. Blood poured from him. After this the jailers were told to put him into prison. Laian and Laixing went home and gave Ximen Qing a full account of the affair. Ximen was delighted. He gave orders that none of the servants should take bedclothes to Laiwang or even so much as a scrap of food. Moreover, they were not to tell Huilian that her husband had been beaten. All they were to say was that he would be out again in a few days.

After Laiwang's arrest, Huilian refused to dress her hair or wash her face. She would do nothing but shut herself in her room and cry, taking neither tea nor food. This alarmed Ximen Qing, and he sent Yuxiao and Ben the Fourth's wife several times to reason with her.

"Don't worry about your husband," they would say. "He got drunk and talked wildly, but our master has only sent him to prison to cool his heels for a few days. He will have him out again soon." Huilian did not believe them. She sent Laian to the prison with some food, and questioned him when he came back. He told her the same story. "My brother came before the magistrates, but they did not punish him. He says you must not worry about him; he will be out in two or three days."

After this, Huilian dried her tears, and every day painted her eyebrows carefully, powdered her face, and resumed her old lively ways.

One day, when Ximen Qing passed her door on his way home from somewhere, Huilian, who was standing under the eaves, called to him: "There is nobody in my room, Father. Won't you come in and sit down for a while?" Ximen went in and talked to her.

"My child," he said, still keeping up the pretense, "your mind ought to be quite at ease now. For your sake I have written to the court, and he has not received a single blow. He must stay in prison a day or two to teach him a lesson, and then he shall come out and I'll set him up in business."

Huilian threw her arms around his neck. "Dearest," she cried, "if you love me, let him come out soon. I don't care whether you set him up in business or not, but when he comes out, I will see he keeps away from drink, and he cannot object if you decide to send him away. If that is not good enough, find another wife for him and all will be well. I have not belonged to him for a long time."

"Very well, my precious one," Ximen said, "I am going to buy the house across the road that belongs to Master Qiao, and I will set aside three rooms for you there. When you are established there, we shall have greater freedom to enjoy ourselves."

"Do just what you like, darling," the woman cried. When they had said what they had to say, she closed the door. In the summer months, she wore nothing but an open skirt without trousers, so that, whenever she came together with Ximen Qing, he had only to pull aside the skirt and proceed. Then the girdle was unloosed and the jade treasure of Chen Fei disclosed: eyebrows with all the fragrance of Han Shu were brought near together. They were like a pair of love birds flying shoulder to shoulder, or the meeting of clouds and rain.

Huilian was wearing a perfume satchel of fine silk, embroidered in silver. There were fir and cypress leaves in it, and some fragrant herbs, and on it were embroidered the four words: "delicate," "fragrant," "beautiful" and "seductive." She gave it to Ximen Qing. He was so delighted that his one regret was that he could not there and then make oath that he would live and die together with her. He took a few taels of silver from his sleeve and gave them to her to buy delicacies, saying several times: "Don't worry any longer, or you will make yourself ill. I'll write to his Lordship Xia tomorrow, and have him set free." They talked for a while, and then Ximen Qing became alarmed lest anyone should come, and hurriedly went away. Now that she had extracted this promise from him, Huilian went once more to the inner court and made merry with the maids and serving women.

Yulou heard of this and went to tell Jinlian. "Sooner or later," she said, "Father will set the fellow free. He is going to buy Master Qiao's house opposite, and install the woman there. She is to have three rooms and a maid, silver headdresses and nets. She will be as good as we are. Did you ever hear of such a thing? And the Great Lady will do nothing to prevent it."

When Jinlian heard this, she flew into a fury. A dark flush deepened the redness of her cheeks. "Don't you imagine," she said, "that he will be able to do exactly what he likes! Here and now I tell you that if I let that thievish whore become Ximen Qing's seventh wife . . . my name is not Pan."

"Our husband is a bad lot," Yulou said, "and the Great Lady does nothing to keep him in order. As for us, we cannot fly, we can only walk. What can we do to stop him?"

"You haven't a good enough opinion of yourself," Jinlian said. "Why do you think we are alive? To live a hundred years so that others can make a meal of us? No, if he doesn't do what I tell him, I shall kill myself, and he will be responsible. I'm not far from it now."

Yulou laughed. "I'm afraid I'm not very brave. I haven't the courage to make him angry. I'll watch and see whether you're clever enough to deal with him."

That night Ximen Qing was sitting in his study in the Hall of the Kingfisher, about to send for his son-in-law to write a letter to Magistrate Xia. Jinlian suddenly appeared in front of him.

"What letter is this you are going to get Brother Chen to write?" she asked, leaning over the table.

Ximen Qing could not hide anything from her. "I have decided to let Laiwang come out of prison, when he has been beaten," he said. One of the boys was going to fetch Chen Jingji, but Jinlian stopped him.

"You flatter yourself," she said to Ximen, "that you are a very fine fellow, but, actually, you steer your course according to the wind and go wherever the current takes you. You will not do what I tell you, but you listen to everything that thievish strumpet says. What do you think you're doing? You may feed her on honey and sugar every day, but it will be her husband she really thinks about. Now listen to me. If you set that slave free you won't find it such an easy matter to enjoy his wife. There will be nothing to prevent his making a scandal. If you keep her here she will be neither one thing nor another. How do you propose to treat her? If you make her your concubine, he will be here: if she is to remain his wife, you have already made her so conceited that her airs and graces are unbearable to us all. As for the plan of keeping her for yourself and finding another wife for him, what is going to happen when you are sitting somewhere together and he comes in to serve you? Can he be anything but furious? And, when she sees him, is she to stand up or remain seated?"

"The whole thing is most improper, and, if it gets about, I hardly need say that all our friends and kinsmen will think very badly of you. Indeed, the whole household will look down upon you. If the master beam is not in position, the rafters cannot be expected to keep their place. If you are in earnest about the matter, you must not stick at a little harshness. Finish off the slave. Then you can embrace his wife with an easy mind."

Ximen Qing changed his mind again. The letter he sent to the magistrate asked him to reopen the case at the end of three months, and to put Laiwang to the torture. The unfortunate man was hardly treated as a human being. The two magistrates, the prosecutor, the police, and the jailers had all accepted presents from Ximen Qing, and were severe in consequence. But among them was a scrivener who came from Xiaoyi in Shanxi, Yin Zhi by name, a man both humane and incorruptible. He realized that Ximen had manufactured this trouble so that he could take possession of Laiwang's wife, and he declined to make out the papers that would have brought Laiwang before the magistrates. Indeed, he went so far as to tell them what he thought, so that they found it difficult to proceed as they had intended, and finally compromised by giving Laiwang forty strokes more and banishing him to Xuzhou. They accounted the alleged stolen property as seventeen taels of silver and five packets of tin and ordered Laixing to return it to his master. An official wrote the reply to the accusation, saying that Laiwang was being banished that day.

The two magistrates made out a warrant and sent two runners to bring out Laiwang. He was severely beaten and put into sealed fetters, and the men were ordered to start immediately for Xuzhou, and leave Laiwang in charge of the governor there. Laiwang had been so long in prison that he was in a wretched condition. His clothes were falling to pieces. There was no one to whom he could appeal for help.

"Brothers," he said to the two runners, "now that I have been through this trouble, I have not a penny in the world. I should like to get some traveling money for you. Will you have pity on me and take me to my master's house? My wife is there. She will give me clothes and things and I will sell them for journey money, and so make things more agreeable."

"You don't seem to realize," the runners told him, "that this is all your master's doing. He will give you neither your wife nor your boxes. Isn't there anyone else whom you can ask? We don't mind overlooking it for Master Yin's sake, and taking you there to get a little money and rice for the journey. Don't worry about traveling money for us."

"Brothers," Laiwang again said, "for pity's sake, take me to my master's door first. There are one or two neighbors whom I will ask to say a good word for me. Probably I won't get much, but I may get something."

The two runners agreed. Laiwang went to see Ying Bojue, but Bojue pretended not to be at home. Then he persuaded his two left-hand neighbors, Jia Renqing and Yi Mianzi, to go and plead with Ximen Qing that he might be allowed to have his wife and his possessions. Ximen would not even come out to see them and ordered his servants to drive them away from the door. Jia and Yi were so greatly abashed that they did not know what to do. Huilian, Laiwang's wife, was unaware of all this. She never heard a word of it, because Ximen had given orders that any servant who mentioned it to her should be given twenty strokes.

The two runners took Laiwang to the house of his father-in-law, the coffin merchant Song Ren. Laiwang wept as he told his father-in-law the story, and Song Ren gave a tael of silver to the runners and a peck of rice to his son-in-law for food upon the way. So, weeping and bewailing, Laiwang set out on the highway for Xuzhou, leaving Qinghe at the beginning of the fourth month.

Day after day Huilian expected her husband to come. She gave the boys food to take to him, but they ate it themselves as soon as they were outside the gate. They came back and said: "Brother enjoyed that food and all is well at the prison. He would have been out before this but the magistrates haven't been to the court for a few days. In any case, he will be home in a day or two."

Ximen Qing deceived her. "I have sent to the court," he told her, "and he will be out very soon now." Huilian believed them, but, one day, she heard a rumor that her husband had been taken out of prison and had been begging at the door for his clothes. No one knew where he had gone. She questioned the boys time after time, but none of them would speak. One day, however, she caught Daian as he was coming back from waiting upon his master, and said to him: "How is your brother getting on in prison, and when is he coming out?"

"Sister," Daian said, "I will tell you. By this time he has reached the River of Shifting Sand." Huilian pressed him, and at last Daian, with a great show of reluctance, told her how Laiwang had been beaten and banished to Xuzhou. "Don't get excited about it," the boy said, at the end, "and above all, don't let anybody know I told you."

It was more than Huilian could bear. She shut herself in her room and sobbed bitterly. "Oh, my man," she cried, "how could you fall into the trap and let yourself be treated so? All these years you have served him, and now you have not even a single suit of good clothes to cover you, and they have driven you far away. How bitter it is! Buried away as I am, I do not even know whether you are alive or dead." She sobbed a while. Then taking a long kerchief, she fastened it to the lintel of the door and hanged herself.

The Beanpole, Laizhao's wife, lived next door to Huilian. As she was coming from the inner court, she heard the woman weeping in her room. Then she noticed that the sound stopped and she could only hear a kind of gasping. She knocked at the door but there was no answer. She was frightened and made Ping'an, one of the boys, climb through the window and get into the room. Huilian, with all her clothes on, was hanging from the lintel. The boy cut her down at once and opened the door. They brought ginger broth and poured it down her throat, then sent word to the people in the inner court. Wu Yueniang, Li Jiao'er, Meng Yulou, Li Ping'er, Ximen Dajie, and the two maids, Yuxiao and Xiaoyu, all came to see, and Ben the Fourth's wife also came to look. The Beanpole was sitting on the floor supporting Huilian who was sobbing soundlessly. Yueniang spoke to her, but she only hung her head. A froth came from her mouth.

"What a foolish child you are," Yueniang said. "If there was anything wrong, you should have told me. What sense is there in behaving like this?"

She told Yuxiao to help support her, and said again: "Huilian, my child, if anything is troubling you, tell me what it is." But though she spoke several times, Huilian did not answer. After she had questioned her for a long time, the woman began to cry, making a great noise and beating her hands together. Yueniang told Yuxiao to help her to bed, but she would not go. Then Yueniang and the others spoke firmly to her, and went back to the inner court, leaving Yuxiao and Ben the Fourth's wife to look after the woman.

After a while Ximen Qing pulled up the lattice and came in. Huilian was still sitting on the cold floor, and he told Yuxiao to put her to bed.

"My mistress has told her to go to bed," Yuxiao said, "but she won't go."

"What an obstinate child you are," Ximen cried, "you'll get cold there on the ground. If you have anything to say to me, say it, and don't behave in this silly way."

Huilian shook her head. "Father," she said, "you are a fine fellow, and you have deceived me splendidly. Why do you call me your child? I am no child of yours. You are an executioner in disguise: to bury a man alive means nothing to you. And not only are you ready to put him to death, you must needs see his funeral also. Day after day, you lied to me. One day you said: 'He will be here tomorrow,' and the next day you said: 'He will be here tomorrow,' and I thought he really would come. Why have you sent him away and said nothing to me about it? You did it secretly, and had him sent far, far away, while I knew not a thing about it. To do a cruel thing like that you can have no conscience at all. Even after you had done your worst, you still kept the matter hidden from me. If you wished to get rid of us, why didn't you get rid of us both? Why keep me here?"

"My child," Ximen said, "I have no quarrel with you. That fellow was a scoundrel and I had to send him away. Settle down quietly. I will look after you." He said to Yuxiao: "You and Ben the Fourth's wife spend the night here and look after her. I will tell one of the boys to bring you some wine." He went out, and, after Ben the Fourth's wife had helped Huilian to bed, she and Yuxiao tried to console her.

Ximen Qing went to the shop and asked Fu for a thousand cash. With the money he bought a roast and had it put on a tray with a jar of wine, and told Laian to take the tray to the woman's room.

"Father told me to bring you this," the boy said. When Huilian saw the tray, she cursed him.

"You thievish young rascal. Take it away at once or I will throw it on the floor."

"Do keep it, Sister," Laian said, "I can't take it away again or Father will beat me."

He lay the tray on a table. Huilian jumped out of bed and took up the jar of wine. She was going to throw it on the floor but the Beanpole stopped her. Ben the Fourth's wife looked at the Beanpole and put her finger on her mouth. They were sitting together when Ben the Fourth's son came in and said to his mother: "Father has come home and wants his dinner." The two women went out. When they came to the Beanpole's door, Ximen's daughter Ximen Dajie was there gossiping with Laibao's wife. They asked Ben the Fourth's wife where she was going.

"My man has come home and wants his dinner," she said. "I am going to see what he wants and then I'm coming back again. I did not mean to stay, but his Lordship pressed me, otherwise I shouldn't have been there as long as this."

"What did Father say to her?" Laibao's wife said.

"I should never have thought Huilian was so peppery," Ben the Fourth's wife said. "She gave Father a piece of her mind and no mistake. There are very few serving women who would dare to say as much."

"She is not like other women," Laibao's wife said. "She has received his Lordship's special favors. You can't expect the rest of us to do what she can do." She went away. The Beanpole said to Ben the Fourth's wife:

"Don't be long, Sister."

"You needn't trouble to say that," Ben the Fourth's wife said. "If I don't come back, Father will kill me."

Ximen Qing told Ben the Fourth's wife and the Beanpole to stay with Huilian, and late that night he sent Yuxiao to sleep there, hoping that the woman would gradually calm down.

"Sister," they said, "you are no fool. Why don't you take advantage of this opportunity while you have it? You are like a flower that has just blossomed. Our Master loves you and that is as Fate has decided. You cannot, of course, rank yourself among the ladies, but you are much better off than the rest of us. It will be far better for you to cast in your lot with Father than with a slave. Besides, he has already gone. You may feel a little sad—there's no harm in that—but if you keep on crying you will get in a bad way, and that will be just throwing your life away. There is an old saying: Strike the gong for a day, and be a priest for a day. After that, you need never bother yourself again about such things as virtue and chastity."

Huilian cried and sobbed. Days passed, and she still refused to take any food. Yuxiao told Ximen Qing and he sent Jinlian to talk to her. It was no use. Jinlian returned and said to him: "That whore can think of nothing but her husband. Everybody knows that after one night of marriage, the pleasure persists for a hundred nights; and lovers need walk but a hundred paces together for affection to remain with them forever. What hope do you think you have of capturing the heart of a woman as virtuous as this?"

Ximen Qing laughed. "Don't you believe it," he said. "If she is really so virtuous, why did she get rid of Jiang Cong the cook, and marry Laiwang?"

He sat down in the hall and sent for all the boys. He determined to find out who had told Huilian of her husband's banishment. "If the culprit confesses," he said, "he shall not receive a single blow, but if he doesn't, and I find out who he is, there shall be thirty strokes for him and he shall be sent away from the house."

Shutong knelt down. "The other day," he said, "when Daian came back with you, I heard my sister asking him questions in the passage. It was he who let it out and told her."

"Go and find Daian," Ximen cried in a rage. But Daian had already heard what was going on and had run away to take refuge in Jinlian's room. She was washing her face when the boy came in.

"Mother, save me! Save me!" he cried, kneeling before her.

"What do you mean by coming and frightening me like this, you little rascal?" Jinlian said. "What have you been doing?"

"Father is going to thrash me because I told Huilian about Laiwang's being sent away. Mother, you must go and pacify him. If he sees me when he is in such a temper, he will certainly kill me."

"You funny little rascal," Jinlian said. "You're as scared as a ghost. I thought it must be something serious enough to shake heaven and earth, and it's only some trifling thing connected with that strumpet. Stay here."

Daian hid himself behind the door.

Ximen Qing created a terrible uproar in the front court when Daian was not to be found. He twice sent boys to Jinlian's room, but each time she drove them away with curses. Finally, with a horsewhip in his hand, he came along, like a whirlwind.

"Where is the slave?" he cried.

Jinlian did not pay the slightest attention to him. He went round and round, searching, and at last dragged Daian from behind the door. He was going to thrash the boy, but Jinlian snatched the whip from him and threw it on the top of the bed.

"You shameless creature," she said, "you are not fit to be a master. That whore spends her time thinking about her husband, and goes and hangs herself, and you try to vent your spite by ill-treating this boy. What harm has he done?"

Ximen Qing rolled his eyes about, but Jinlian said to the boy: "Get off to the front court, and go on with your work. Don't be afraid of him." Daian slipped away and went to the front court.

Jinlian could see that Ximen Qing still cared for Huilian, and decided upon a plot. She went to the inner court and told tales to Xue'e. "Laiwang's wife," she said, "is telling everybody that you were in love with her husband and created such a scandal that Father was angry and sent Laiwang away. You remember how he struck you and took away your ornaments and dresses. It was all her doing."

So Jinlian touched a very sore spot. She saw the effect she had produced and went off to Huilian with a different story.

"Xue'e," she said, "has been saying nasty things about you in the kitchen. She says you used to be a slave in the Cais' household and that you are an expert at stealing other people's husbands and carrying on with men. I heard her say: 'If she has not been playing tricks of that sort with our husband, why did he send Laiwang away? She had better save her tears to wash her feet.' "

In this way Jinlian stirred up hatred in their hearts. One day it became obvious that trouble was brewing.

It was the eighteenth day of the fourth month, and Li Jiao'er's birthday. The old procuress and her daughter Li Guijie came to congratulate their kinswoman. Yueniang asked them to stay and entertained them with the other ladies in the hall. Ximen Qing had gone to a banquet. Huilian had taken some food, and, that morning, spent a few moments in the inner court. Then she went back to her room and slept till the sun was low. The maids came several times to call her but she paid no attention and would not leave her room. At last Xue'e, who was only waiting for the opportunity, went to see her.

"You must be a person of most surpassing beauty, Sister," she said, "since you cannot be persuaded to accept our invitations." Huilian did not answer. She was lying on the bed with her face to the wall.

"Are you thinking of your husband, Laiwang?" Xue'e said. "It would have been better if you had thought of him before. If it hadn't been for you, this would never have happened and he would still be in Ximen's household."

Huilian remembered what Jinlian had told her. She jumped off the bed. "Why have you come here," she cried, "with your lewd tongue and your filthy temper? Even if I was the cause of his being sent away, it is not for you, of all people, to come and tell me so. You did not get off scot-free yourself. You ought to be very thankful that some people did not say all they knew. You are the last person to give yourself airs and talk about other people's misdeeds."

Xue'e lost her temper. "You thievish slave, you loose woman," she cried, "how dare you insult me?"

"I may be a slave and a loose woman," Huilian said, "but at least I am not a slave's mistress. I may have carried on with Master, but that is better than carrying on with a servant. You stole my husband and now you come here and make a song about it."

Xue'e was now almost beside herself. She dashed forward and struck Huilian in the face. The woman was taken by surprise and her cheeks flamed scarlet.

"Will you strike me?" she cried, and made for Xue'e with her head. They closed with one another and fought, till the Beanpole separated them. Then Yueniang came and upbraided them. "You ought to be ashamed of yourselves," she said. "You never stop to consider whether there are visitors here or not. Wait till your master comes home and you'll see whether I tell him or not."

Xue'e went to the inner court, and Yueniang, seeing how Huilian's hair was all in disorder, said, "Go and attend to your hair. Then come and join us."

Huilian did not reply. She took Yueniang politely to the door and went back into the room. She locked the door behind her and cried bitterly. It was now getting dark and the people in the inner court were busy with the evening meal. Huilian could bear no more. She took two long ribbons, like those used for binding the feet, tied them to the lintel of the door, and hanged herself. She was only twenty-five years old.

Later that evening as Yueniang was taking old woman Li and Guijie to the gate, she passed Huilian's door. It was shut and there was no sign of life. She wondered what had happened. When she had taken leave of her guests, she came back and knocked at the door. There was no reply. This frightened her and she told some of the boys to climb through the window. They cut the ribbons and took the woman down. For a long time they tried to bring her back to life, for they did not know how long she had been dead.

When Yueniang found that it was impossible to revive the woman, she was greatly upset, and told Laixing to take a horse at once and go for Ximen Qing. Xue'e, for her part, was very much afraid that, when he came, he would try to find out how this had happened. She paced up and down the hall and finally knelt down before Yueniang and begged her not to tell her husband of the quarrel. She was in such a state of terror that Yueniang began to feel sorry for her.

"You are afraid now," she said. "Why didn't you have a little less to say before?"

Then Ximen Qing came home. They told him that Huilian had been thinking about her husband and had cried the whole day. Then, at a time when everybody was busy, she had seized the opportunity and hanged herself. Nobody knew exactly when she did so.

"Oh, the silly woman!" Ximen cried, "the Fates have treated her hardly." He sent a servant to report the matter to Li, one of the local magistrates. "The family were entertaining visitors," he was told to say, "and this woman, who was responsible for the silver, lost a silver cup. She was afraid her master would punish her, and killed herself." At the same time he was to make the magistrate a present of thirty taels of silver. The magistrate acted as was expected of him and only sent one of his officers with a few coroner's men to view the corpse.

Ximen Qing bought a coffin and applied for a certificate. Then Ben the Fourth and Laixing took the body to the cemetery outside the city.

They gave the firemen five *qian* of silver to burn the body. A heap of wood
had already been piled around the coffin and they were just about to set
fire to it, when Huilian's father, Song Ren the coffin dealer, suddenly came
up and stopped them. There was something mysterious about his daughter's death, he said, and he accused Ximen Qing of abusing his authority
and trying to seduce her. "My daughter," he said, "was an honest woman
and repulsed him. She had met her death at his hands. I am going to take
the matter to the Governor of the Province, so let no one presume to burn
her body."

The firemen were afraid to complete their task and went away. Ben the
Fourth and Laixing were obliged to leave the coffin in the temple. They
went back to tell their master what had happened.

# CHAPTER 27

# The Garden of Delights

Laibao returned from the Eastern Capital and made his report to Ximen Qing. "When I reached the Capital," he said, "I went to see the Comptroller of the Household and gave him your letter. Then I was taken to the minister. When his Eminence had looked at the list of presents, he accepted them. Then I explained the case. His Eminence said: 'I will send at once to the Governor of Shandong and ask him to liberate the salt merchant Wang Sifeng of Yangzhou and the others.' Master Zhai sent his greetings to you. He says he would like to have a talk with you and that you ought to go to the Capital for his Eminence's birthday on the fifteenth day of the sixth month."

Ximen Qing was satisfied. He sent Laibao to tell Master Qiao. While he was speaking, Ben the Fourth and Laixing came in, but seeing their master occupied, they stood aside until Laibao had gone. Then Ximen Qing said to Ben the Fourth: "I suppose you have come back from the funeral?" Ben the Fourth hardly dared to speak, but Laixing came forward and whispered: "Song Ren came to the funeral pyre, and refused to allow the body to be burned. He said it was extremely irregular. He said other things that I should not like to repeat."

Ximen Qing was very angry. "What a detestable, hateful creature!" he cried. He sent a boy at once for Chen Jingji, told the young man to write a letter to Magistrate Li, and sent Laian with it to the Town Hall. The magistrate dispatched two runners who bound Song Ren and took him to the court. He was charged with blackmail and attempting to use the dead woman as a means of extorting money. He was brought in fetters to the Hall of Audience and there given twenty strokes so severe that the blood flowed down his legs in streams. The magistrate then bound him over never again to be a nuisance to Ximen Qing. At the same time he ordered police and firemen to go with Ximen's servants to the place of burning and burn the body. Song Ren, his legs all beaten and bleeding, crawled home. He was so exasperated that he took a fever and died, bitterly lamenting his fate.

Now that he had finally disposed of Huilian, Ximen Qing got ready gold and silver to the value of three hundred taels and sent for Silversmith Gu and several others to make a set of silver figures for the birthday of the

Imperial Tutor. They worked beneath the awning at Ximen Qing's house. Each of the figures was over a foot high. They also made a pair of golden flagons with the character *Shou* engraved upon them. Ximen had bought two pairs of peach-shaped cups of jade, two sets of crimson robes from Hangzhou, and dragon cloaks embroidered in five colors. He still wanted two rolls of a particular kind of black cloth and some crimson dragon silk, but he could not find it at any price. Then Li Ping'er said to him, "I have some sets of dragon robes that have never been made up. They are upstairs in my place. Come and look at them."

Ximen Qing went with her and they picked out four sets, two of crimson silk and two of the special black cloth. They all were edged with gold braid, and embroidered with five-colored dragons. They were certainly much finer than anything they could have bought. Ximen Qing was delighted. He had them all packed up and Laibao and Clerk Fu left again for the Eastern Capital on the twenty-eighth day of the fifth month.

Two days later it was the beginning of the sixth month. The weather was very hot, and at noon the fiery sun was like a blazing umbrella in a cloudless sky. Not a particle of cloud was to be seen and it seemed hot enough to scorch the stones or to melt metal.

It was so hot that Ximen Qing did not go out. He stayed at home with his hair undone and his clothes unbuttoned, trying to keep cool. He sat in the bower by the Kingfisher Hall watching the boys watering the flowers. In front of the Kingfisher Hall there was a bowl of sweet-smelling daphne. He told Laian to take a little watering can, and watched him sprinkle the flowers.

Jinlian and Li Ping'er were both dressed in the lightest of silver silk, with skirts of dark red and a fringe of gold thread. Li Ping'er was wearing a short crimson cape and Jinlian had one of silver and red. Jinlian wore nothing on her head but a blue Hangzhou headdress, through which four braids of hair peeped out. On her brow were three flowers made of kingfisher feathers, which enhanced the beauty of her white face and glossy hair, her red lips and pearly teeth. The two women came smiling, holding each other's hands.

"You here, watering the flowers!" Jinlian cried, when she saw Ximen Qing. "Why don't you go and dress your hair?"

"Tell one of the maids to bring me some water," Ximen said, "and I will do my hair here."

"Put down your watering can," Jinlian said to Laian, "and send a maid with some water and a comb. Be quick about it." Laian bowed and went to do what he was told. Then Jinlian, seeing the sweet-smelling daphne, was going to pick some to put in her hair, but Ximen Qing stopped her. "Don't touch them, little oily mouth. I will give one to each of you." He had already picked a few blossoms and put them into a crackleware vase.

"Ah, my son," Jinlian said, "so you've been plucking the flowers, have you? What do you mean by hiding them there instead of offering them to your mother?" She snatched one up and set it in her hair. Ximen Qing gave one to Li Ping'er. Then Chunmei came with a mirror and comb, and Qiuju brought water. Ximen gave three flowers to Chunmei, for Yueniang, Li Jiao'er and Yulou, and said: "Ask the Third Lady to come and play her zither for me."

"Chunmei can go to the Great Lady and Li Jiao'er, and if you want Yulou, I'll go and fetch her," Jinlian said. "When I come back, I shall expect another flower, and, if I bring someone to sing for you, still another one."

"Go first," Ximen said, "and we'll see about that when you come back."

"My son," Jinlian said, "wherever can you have been brought up? What a naughty boy to think of trying to cheat me like that! If I go and fetch Yulou, I shall never get one. No, let me have it first, and then I'll go."

"You wicked little rascal," Ximen Qing said, laughing, "even in trifles like this you will have your own way." He gave her the flower. Jinlian set it in her hair, and went towards the inner court, leaving Li Ping'er alone with Ximen Qing.

Through the light silk skirt, Ximen could see her crimson trousers; the sun's rays made them so transparent that he could clearly distinguish the cool flesh beneath them. The sight aroused his passion, and finding that they were alone, he stopped dressing his hair, and carried Li Ping'er to a long summer couch. He pulled aside her skirt, took down the crimson trousers, and played with her the game that is called Carrying Fire over the Mountains. They played for a long time without his bringing matters to a conclusion, and their pleasure was like that of a lovebird and his mate.

Jinlian did not go to the inner court. She went as far as the corner gate and then decided to give Yulou's flower to Chunmei. She went back on tiptoe to the Kingfisher Hall. There, she stood listening outside the window, and, for quite a long time, could hear the lovers amusing themselves.

"My darling," she heard Ximen Qing say to Li Ping'er, "above all else I love your little white bottom. I shall do my very utmost to give you pleasure today."

After a pause, she heard Li Ping'er say softly, "My dearest, you must be gentle with me, for I am really not too well. The other day you were rough with me, and my belly hurt so much that only during the last day or two has it begun to feel better."

"You are not well?" Ximen cried. "What do you mean?"

"I will not keep it from you any longer," Li Ping'er told him. "For a month now, I have been cherishing a little one within me. Please treat me with some indulgence."

Ximen Qing was delighted beyond all measure. "Why, my precious one," he said, "why didn't you tell me before? If that is how things are, I will bring this game to an end at once." His happiness reached its culmination and his joy was complete. He set both hands upon her legs, and the evidence of his delight was overwhelming. The woman beneath him raised herself to welcome it.

After a while, Jinlian could hear Ximen breathing heavily, and his lover's gentle voice, like an oriole's, answering him. No sound escaped her as she stood beneath the window. Yulou came up suddenly from behind. "What are you doing here?" she asked. Jinlian signed to her to be silent, and they both went into the summerhouse. Ximen Qing was a little taken aback and did not quite know what to do.

"What have you been doing all this long time I've been away?" Jinlian said. "How is it you haven't washed, or combed your hair?"

"I am waiting for a maid to bring me some jasmine soap," Ximen said.

"I have no patience with you," Jinlian cried. "Why must you have that particular kind of soap? Is that why your face is cleaner than some people's bottoms?"

Ximen Qing paid no attention to this remark, but, when he had finished dressing, sat down beside Yulou. "What have you been doing in the inner court?" he said. "Have you brought your zither?"

"I have been making a pearl flower for the Great Lady to wear at a party. Chunmei is bringing the zither."

Soon Chunmei came. She said she had given the flowers to the Great Lady and the Second Lady. Ximen told her to set out wine, and a bowl of ice with plums and melons in it was brought. In the cool summerhouse Ximen Qing enjoyed the society of his ladies.

"Why didn't you tell Chunmei to ask the Great Lady to come?" Yulou said. "She does not care for wine," Ximen Qing said, "I thought there was no purpose in troubling her."

Then Ximen took the seat of honor and the three women sat down facing him. The exquisite wine was poured out for them and many delicacies were placed before them. Jinlian would not sit on a chair but took a porcelain stool for herself.

"Come and sit on a chair," Yulou cried, "you will find that stool too cold."

"Don't worry," Jinlian said, "I am getting old. I've no reason to fear an internal chill or anything of that sort. Why should I?"

The wine was passed around three times and Ximen Qing told Chunmei to give Yulou her zither, and a lute to Jinlian. "Play the tune 'The God of Fire Rules the World and His Glory Fills the Void.'" Jinlian refused.

"How well you must have been brought up," she cried, "to ask us to sing while you two sit there and enjoy yourselves. I will not play for you. Tell the Sixth Lady to play something."

"She doesn't know how to play," Ximen said.

"Well, even if she doesn't know how to play, she certainly knows how to count the beats," Jinlian said.

Ximen Qing laughed. "You little whore," he cried, "you always try to pick on something," but he told Chunmei to give Li Ping'er a pair of red ivory castanets. Then the two women began to play, spreading their exquisite fingers and slowly plucking the silken strings. They sang the song of "The Geese Flying Over the Sand," while Xiuchun stood at the side and fanned them. When the song was over, Ximen offered each of them a cup of wine. Jinlian went to the table, drank deeply of iced water, and ate some fruit.

"Why are you eating only cold things today?" Yulou said.

"Nothing of any particular interest is happening in my distinguished belly," Jinlian replied. "Why should I be afraid of cold things?"

Li Ping'er was so embarrassed that she became white and red in turns. Ximen Qing glanced sharply at Jinlian. "You little villain," he said, "you do nothing but talk nonsense."

"Brother," Jinlian said, "old women like me get nothing but dry meat to eat. We have to eat it sinew by sinew."

As they were drinking, the clouds began to gather. Far away the thunder rolled and suddenly a storm broke, drenching the flowers in front of the summerhouse.

In a few moments the rain stopped again. A rainbow appeared in the sky. The sun came out again, and in a twinkling the jasper steps glistened and a cool evening breeze freshened the courtyard. Xiaoyu came from the back court to call Yulou.

"The Great Lady wants me," Yulou said. "I have still some pearl flowers to finish. I must go now or she will be angry."

"I will go with you," Li Ping'er said. "I should like to see the flowers."

Ximen Qing said he would go with them too. He took the zither and asked Yulou to play. He beat time with his hands and they all sang together.

It is evening.
The storm has passed over the southern hall
Red petals are floating on the surface of the pool.
Slowly the gentle thunder rolls away
The rain is over and the clouds disperse
The fragrance of water lilies comes to us over the distance.
The new moon is a crescent

Fresh from the perfumed bath, decked for the evening
Over the darkening courtyard it wanes
Yet will not go to rest.
In the shade of the willow the young cicada bursts into song
Fireflies hover over the ancestral halls.
Listen. Whence comes this song of Ling?
The painted boat is late returning
The jade cords sink lower and lower
The gentlefolk are silent.
A vision of delight.
Let us rise and take each other by the hand
And tire our hair.
The moon lights up the silken curtains.
But there are no sleepers there.
The brave mandarin duck tumbles the lotus leaves
On the gently rippling water
Sprinkling them with drops like pearls.
They give forth fragrance.
A perfumed breeze moves softly over the flower beds
Beside the summerhouse
How can our spirits fail to be refreshed?
Why crave for the islands of the blessed, the home of fairies?
Yet, when the west wind blows again, Autumn will come with it.
Though we perceive it not, the seasons change.

So singing, they reached the corner gate almost before they knew it. Yulou gave her zither to Chunmei and went to the inner court with Li Ping'er.

"Wait for me," Jinlian cried, "I am coming too," Ximen Qing caught her by the hand and pulled her back.

"So you would run away from me, little oily mouth," he cried. "I shall not let you go." He pulled so hard that she almost fell.

"You funny creature," Jinlian cried. "They are both going. Why won't you let me go?"

"We will drink a little wine together," Ximen said, "and play Flying Arrows Beneath the Tai Hu Rock."

"We can play quite well in the summerhouse," Jinlian said. "Why stay here? And it's no use asking this young scamp Chunmei to bring any wine. She won't do it."

Ximen Qing told Chunmei to go. She handed the zither to Jinlian and went off with her head in the air. Jinlian strummed the zither for a while. "I have learned a few bars from Yulou," she said. She saw how freshly the pomegranate flowers were blooming after the rain, and laughingly plucked one and set it in her hair. "I am an old lady, wearing on my brow a 'starving-for-three-days' flower."

Ximen Qing seized her tiny feet. "You little villain," he cried, "if I weren't afraid of somebody seeing us, I'd make you die of delight."

"Don't get so excited, you naughty fellow," Jinlian said. "Let me put down this zither." She laid the instrument beside a flower bed. "My son," she said, "you have only just finished amusing yourself with the Sixth Lady. Why should you come and plague me now?"

"You are still talking nonsense," Ximen said, "I never touched her."

"My boy," Jinlian said, "you may try as hard as you like, but you will never succeed in deceiving the God who watches over Hearth and Home. What is the use of trying to hoodwink an experienced old woman like me? When I went to the inner court to take that flower, the pair of you wasted no time."

"Oh, do not talk such rubbish," Ximen cried. He set her down among the flowers, and kissed her lips. She slipped her tongue into his mouth.

"Call me 'darling,' and I'll let you get up," he said. Jinlian could not help herself. She called him darling, but, she added, "It isn't me you really love, so why do you bother me?"

They amused themselves for a while, and then Jinlian suggested that they should go and play Flying Arrows in the Arbor of the Vines. She took the zither into her lap and played.

They walked side by side. Soon they had turned by the shaded pool and passed the Hall of the White Rose. Then they went in front of the Kingfisher Hall and came to the Arbor of the Vines. It was a very beautiful place.

They came to the arbor. There were four summer stools there, and near them a vase for the game of Flying Arrows. Jinlian set down the zither and played the arrow game with Ximen Qing. Then Chunmei came with wine, and Qiuju carrying a basket of delicacies, with a bowl of iced fruits.

"You went off in a huff, young woman," Jinlian said. "What has made you decide to bring the things?"

"We have looked everywhere for you," Chunmei said. "How were we to know that you'd take it into your head to come here?"

Qiuju set out the refreshments and Ximen Qing opened the basket. There were eight rows of exquisite fruits and sweetmeats in it, a little silver jar of grape wine, two small Jinlian cups and two pairs of chopsticks. These they set upon a rustic table. Ximen and Jinlian sat down before it but went on with their game. They played Feathers through the Arch, The Geese Flying on their Backs, The Qiao Sisters Studying Their Books, and Yang Guifei Asleep in the Spring. Then they played The Dragon Entering His Cave and Pearls upon the Blind. Altogether, they had more than ten games. Then the wine went to Jinlian's head. The peaches began to bloom upon her cheeks, and her eyes lost their shyness. Ximen Qing thought he would like to drink the love potion known as the wine of the five fragrances, and told Chunmei to go and fetch it.

"Little oily mouth," Jinlian said, "you can do something for me too. In my room you will find a summer mat and a pillow. Bring them here. I feel very sleepy, and I think I shall lie down."

Chunmei professed to raise objections. "Oh dear," she said, "you give so many orders that nobody could possibly carry them all out."

"If you won't go," Ximen said, "send Qiuju. You bring the wine and we'll leave it at that." Chunmei went off, tossing her head. After a while Qiuju came back with the mat, the pillow and some coverlets. Jinlian ordered her to set them out. "Then fasten the garden gate and go to your room, and don't come back until I call you." Qiuju did as she was told, and went away.

Ximen Qing rose, and took off his jade-colored light gown. He hung it on the trellis, and went to wash his hands by the peony arbor. When he came back, Jinlian had already prepared the mat and its cushions inside the arbor of the vines, and had undressed till not a thread of silk remained upon her body. She lay flat on her back, a pair of crimson shoes still upon her feet, fanning herself with a white silk fan to gain some relief from the heat.

When Ximen Qing saw her, his wanton heart was quickly stirred, for the wine had not been without its effect upon him. He took off his clothes, and sat down on a stool, letting his toes play around the treasure of this beautiful flower.

Then proof of her pleasure oozed from her like the slime of a snail leaving its tortuous white trail. Ximen pulled off her decorated crimson shoes, loosened the ribbons that bound her feet and tied her ankles to the trellis, so that she looked like a golden dragon baring its claws. The gate of womanhood was open, its guardian was aroused, and a deep scarlet vale appeared.

Ximen Qing lay down and, taking his weapon in his hands, prepared to storm the breach, resting one hand upon the pillow, and proceeding to the attack as he had played Feathers through the Arch when at the Flying Arrow game. He strove with all his strength, till from the scene of combat a mist arose, spiraling, like an eel rising from the mud.

Jinlian beneath him never ceased to murmur, "Darling, my darling." Then, as he was just about to reap the fruits of victory, Chunmei came suddenly with the wine for which Ximen had asked. But when she saw them, she put down the jar of wine and fled to the top of the artificial mound, and there went into the arbor that was called the Land of Clouds. She rested her elbows on the chess table, and amused herself setting out the chessmen. Ximen Qing lifted his head and looked at her; then he beckoned her to come down, but she refused. "If you don't come down, I will make you," he cried. He left Jinlian and ran up the stone steps to the arbor. Chunmei fled down a tiny path to the right, through the grottos, till she reached a point halfway, where among the hanging foliage and flowers she tried to hide. Ximen Qing caught her there, and took her in his arms. "I've got you at last, little oily mouth," he cried. Then he carried her like a feather to the Arbor of the Vines.

"Have a cup of wine," he said, laughing, setting her on his knee, and they drank together mouth to mouth. Suddenly Chunmei saw that her mistress's feet were tied to the trellis.

"I don't know how you could do such a thing," she said. "It is the middle of the day, and if anybody should come in, what would they think of such goings on."

"Isn't the corner gate shut?" Ximen asked.

"Yes," Chunmei said, "I shut it when I came in."

"Now," Ximen said, "watch me. I'm going to play Flying Arrows with a living target. The game is called Striking the Silver Swan with a Golden Ball. Watch! If I hit the mark at the first shot, I shall treat myself to a cup of wine." He took a plum from the iced bowl, and cast it to the gate of womanhood. Three times he cast; three times he reached the inmost flower. One plum stuck there, but he neither removed it nor finished the work he had begun until the girl became faint and her distress from the effort was evident. Her starry eyes were half closed, and her body fell back limply upon the mat. "You are indeed a roguish enemy," she murmured. "You will be the death of me." Her voice trembled.

Ximen paid no attention to her, but told Chunmei to fan him, while he refreshed himself with wine. Then he lay down in an easy chair, and went to sleep. When Chunmei saw that he was asleep, she went softly over and touched him, then ran like a wisp of smoke to the Snow Grotto and so to the other side of the garden. There she heard someone knocking, opened the gate, and saw Li Ping'er.

Ximen Qing slept for an hour or so, and when he opened his eyes, Jinlian's white legs were still hanging from the trellis. Chunmei had gone. Again his passion was aroused.

"Now, you abandoned little creature," he cried, "I'll attend to you." He took out the plum, and gave it her to eat. Then, sitting on the pillow, he took from a pocket in his gown a case of love instruments. First he put on the clasp, and tied a sulfur ring about the root of evil. He refused to dismount her, but played so long about her entrance that she cried in fury. "My darling, my dearest, be a man quickly or I shall go mad. I see what it is. You are angry with me because of Li Ping'er. That is why you tease me like this. But now I have found how cunning you can be, I will never make you angry again."

"Ah," cried Ximen, laughing, "so you have learned your lesson. Well, speak nicely to me."

With one thrust he seemed to reach her inmost parts. Then he withdrew; searching in his pocket he found some of the powder that is called Delight of the Bedroom and Fragrance of the Penis, and applied it to the frog's mouth. He returned to the attack, and immediately a tall, proud warrior appeared, full of fire and fury; Ximen surveyed the struggle with admiration. She lay on the mat with half-closed eyes murmuring, "Oh my beloved darling! You don't know what you're putting into me. That thing has driven me to frenzy. Spare me, please." She spoke without shame, but Ximen instantly drove forward with full strength, his hands on the mat, tearing and digging, plunging into her depths a hundred times before withdrawing again. She wiped her wounds with a handkerchief, but in vain; the mat bore clear traces of battle, and the warrior, still erect and fierce, would not desist. "The time has come," cried Ximen, "the monk shall smite the timbrel." Suddenly he lunged, and reached the inmost citadel; for within the gate of womanhood there lies a citadel, like the heart of a flower, which, if touched by the conqueror, is infused with a wonderful pleasure. She felt pain and withdrew; but the sulfur ring broke inside her body with a crack.

She closed her eyes and her breath came faintly; only a faint murmur issued from her lips, the tip of her tongue became icy cold, and her body fell back apparently lifeless upon the mat.

Ximen Qing was alarmed. He hastily untied the ribbons, and removed the sulfur ring. It was broken into two pieces. Then he helped the woman to sit up, and at last her starry eyes began to gleam again, and she showed signs of life once more. In a caressing voice she said, "Darling, why did you treat me so cruelly today? You nearly killed me. You mustn't do this again. It is not simply fun. My head and eyes swim so that I hardly know where I am."

The sun was already setting. Ximen hastily helped her into her clothes, and then called Chunmei and Qiuju to come and take away the mat and the pillows. Then they supported her to her room. Chunmei came back to the garden to see that Qiuju removed all the empty cups. She was just shutting the garden gate, when suddenly Laizhao's little son Little Iron Rod jumped out of the summerhouse, and asked her to give him some fruits.

"What have you been doing, you young rascal?" Chunmei cried. She gave him a few peaches and plums. "Your father has been drinking," she told him, "and you had better run off, for he will certainly beat you if he sees you."

The little monkey took the fruit and disappeared. Chunmei fastened the garden gate, returned to her mistress and Ximen Qing, and helped them to retire.

# CHAPTER 28
# The Two Shoes

After Ximen Qing had taken Pan Jinlian to her room, he took off all his clothes. She wore only a piece of fine silk upon her breast. They sat down side by side and began to drink again. Ximen caressed her white throat with his hand, and they drank their wine, one from the other's mouth. They were profoundly happy in their love. Jinlian allowed her hair to fall about her; her delicate bosom was half disclosed, her eyes challenged him. She seemed like Yang Guifei inflamed by wine.

Her slender fingers played with the warrior between his thighs; it was exhausted after the battle. Still bound by the silver ring, it looked overworked but not quite spent. "Why don't you leave it in peace?" said Ximen. "It's your fault. You frightened it so much that it can hardly move."

"It can hardly move?" she replied. "What are you saying?"

"If it could move," said Ximen, "it would not be drooping like a fading flower, refusing to rise. Why don't you ask its pardon on bended knees?"

She looked at it and smiled. Then she squatted down, put her head on his thigh, undid his trousers and grasped the weary warrior. "You are he who raised his head so proudly, whose eye was so fierce that it terrified me. Now you pretend you are tired, and lie as if you were dead."

Meanwhile she played with it; she pressed it on her soft cheeks, caressed it with her hand, and then she brought it to her lips and kissed the frog's mouth. Immediately the warrior, boiling with passion, sprang up, its head was a talon, its eye was fire, its jaw bristled with hair, its body was stiff as iron.

Ximen Qing rested on a pillow and told Jinlian to go down on all fours, within the silken curtains, and put forth all her strength, the more to increase his pleasure. Immediately his passion blazed forth again, and again he engaged with the woman. "Darling," she pleaded with him, "you must spare me. Don't play with me again." That night their joy in each other was boundless.

The night passed. Next day Ximen Qing went out, and Jinlian got up about dinnertime. When she was ready to put on her shoes, she looked for the crimson pair she had been wearing the day before, but could not find them anywhere. She asked Chunmei where they were.

"When Father and I brought you back yesterday," Chunmei said, "Qiuju brought the coverlets and things."

Jinlian called Qiuju.

"I didn't notice you wearing any shoes when you came in," the maid said.

"Nonsense," Jinlian cried, "I didn't come in barefoot."

"Well, Lady, if you were wearing any shoes, they must be in your room."

"Don't be such a fool," Jinlian cried, "of course they must be here somewhere. Look for them."

Qiuju searched the different rooms, on the bed and under the bed, but could not find the odd shoe anywhere.

"There must have been a ghost in my room for my shoe to have vanished like this," Jinlian said. "Off my very feet too. What are you here for, you slave?"

"Probably you've forgotten, Mother, and left it somewhere in the garden," the maid suggested. "You weren't wearing it when you came in."

"You must be out of your senses," Jinlian cried. "Do you think I don't know whether I had my shoes on or not?" She turned to Chunmei: "Take the thievish slave with you and go and look in the garden. If you find it, well and good, but if it isn't found, she will have to kneel down in the courtyard with a piece of stone on her head."

Chunmei took Qiuju to the garden, but though they looked everywhere, and searched the Arbor of the Vines, they could not find the shoe.

After searching a long time they began to go back. On the way Chunmei scolded Qiuju. "You are like a go-between on the wrong track," she said. "What are you going to say now? You're as bad as old Goody Wang buying a mill. What's the good of it?"

"I'm sure I don't know who stole Mother's shoe," Qiuju said. "She wasn't wearing it when she came in. Perhaps you left the garden gate open and somebody got in and went off with it."

Chunmei spat in her face. "You slave," she cried, "you are frightened and you think you'll put the blame on me. Mother told me to open the door for her. What else could I do? Nobody could possibly have got in then. You brought the coverlets and you didn't take the trouble to look what you were doing. Now you make up a silly story like this."

She took Qiuju to her mistress and said that they had not been able to find the shoe. "Take her into the courtyard and make her kneel down," Jinlian cried.

The maid sobbed and cried. "Do let me go to the garden and look again," she begged. "Then, if I don't find it, punish me.

"Don't listen to her," Chunmei said, "she will never find it. We searched the garden so thoroughly that we could not have missed a needle."

"Why do you put in your spoke?" Qiuju cried. "If I don't find it, I'll ask Mother to beat me."

"Well," Jinlian said, "take her back once more, and let us see whether she finds it."

Chunmei took her to the garden. They looked beneath the artificial mound, around all the flowerbeds and under the evergreen hedges, but though they searched a long time, they found nothing. Qiuju began to get flustered. Chunmei boxed her ears twice, and began to drag her back to Jinlian.

"We haven't looked in the Snow Cave yet," Qiuju said.

"That is Father's summerhouse," Chunmei said. "Mother did not go there, and you will not find it there. You might just as well come with me and confess." But she went to the Snow Cave. Facing the door was a couch, and beside it a small table for incense. They looked around but saw nothing. Then they went to the bookshelves.

"Father's papers and visiting cards are on those shelves," Chunmei said. "It's no use looking there for Mother's shoe. You're just trying to put off the evil hour. If you upset those papers there will be more trouble, and you'll come to an evil end, for sure."

"Isn't this the shoe?" Qiuju cried. She pulled out a packet perfumed with incense and fragrant herbs, and gave it to Chunmei. "This must be it," she said, "and only a minute ago you were urging Mother to beat me."

Chunmei looked at it. There was no doubt about it, it was a crimson low-heeled shoe. "Yes," she said, "it is her shoe. How on earth did it get here? There's something very funny about this." They went back to Jinlian.

"Yes," she said, "this is my shoe, sure enough. Where did you find it?"

"We found it on the bookshelves in Father's summerhouse," Chunmei said. "It was among his visiting cards, wrapped up with sweet herbs and incense."

Jinlian took it in her hand and compared it with another of her shoes. They were both of crimson silk, embroidered with the flowers of the four seasons, the lower part white and also embroidered with flowers. The heels were green and the sides blue. The only difference between them was that the thread of the seam was green in one case and blue in the other, though, unless they were examined very carefully, it would have been impossible to tell them apart.

She tried on the shoe. It was a little tighter than her own. Then she realized that it must have belonged to Huilian. "This shoe belonged to Lai-wang's wife," she said to herself. "I wonder when she gave it to that scoundrel. He did not dare bring it to any of the rooms, so he hid it. Now the slave has fished it out." She gazed at the shoe for a while. Then she said: "This is not my shoe. Go and kneel down at once, you slave." She told Chunmei to find a piece of stone and put it on the girl's head.

"But whose shoe is it, if it isn't yours?" Qiuju said. She wept. "I've found your shoe, yet you are going to beat me just the same. I wonder what you would do if I hadn't found it."

"Shut your mouth, you thievish slave," Jinlian shouted. Chunmei brought a large piece of stone and put it on the maid's head.

Jinlian found another pair of shoes and put them on. The room was oppressively hot, and she told Chunmei to take the dressing case to the summerhouse. She went there to dress her hair.

The same morning, Chen Jingji had to come from the shop to get some clothes. When he reached the corner gate that led into the garden, Little Iron Rod was playing there. The boy saw that he was carrying a pair of silver necklets.

"What is that you've got, Uncle?" he said. "Let me have it to play with."

"They are necklets somebody has pawned," Chen Jingji said, "and I'm taking them back."

"Give them to me, Uncle," the boy cried, "I will give you something nice instead."

"You silly boy," the man said, "they don't belong to me, but, if you like, I'll see if I can find another pair for you. What's this pretty thing you're going to give me?"

The little monkey took a crimson embroidered shoe from his girdle and showed it to Jingji. "Where did you find this?" Jingji said.

"I'll tell you, Uncle," the boy said, laughing. "I was playing in the garden yesterday, and I saw Father in the Arbor of the Vines with Fifth Mother. He had tied her feet and they were shaking and jumping about. Then Father went away, and I saw Auntie Chunmei and asked her for some fruit. I picked this up in the Arbor of the Vines."

Chen Jingji took it in his hand. It was curved like the crescent moon and as red as a fallen lotus blossom. As he held it on his palm, it seemed no more than three inches long. He knew it must belong to Jinlian.

"Give it to me," he said to the boy, "and tomorrow I'll find a splendid necklet for you to play with."

"Don't try to cheat me," the boy cried, "I shall ask you for it tomorrow."

"I won't cheat you," the man said, and the little monkey ran away to play.

Chen Jingji put the shoe in his sleeve. "I have had some fun with that woman more than once," he thought, "but I have never made quite sure of her. Each time when it has come to the point, she has managed to escape me. Now the Fates have been kind enough to put this shoe in my hands, and today, I'll go and try my luck with her in real earnest. This time, I imagine, I shall get her."

With the shoe in his sleeve, Chen Jingji went at once to Jinlian's room. As he passed the screen, he saw Qiuju kneeling in the courtyard. "Young Lady, what's the meaning of this?" he said, laughing. "Are you practicing weight-lifting because you've joined the army?"

Jinlian was upstairs. She heard this remark. "Who is that talking about practicing weight-lifting?" she said to Chunmei. "Surely the little wretch hasn't put it down?"

"No," Chunmei said, "the stone is still on her head. It is Master Chen."

"Come upstairs, Brother-in-law," Jinlian cried, "there is nobody here."

The young man gathered up his clothes and hastened upstairs. Jinlian was sitting near the open window with the blinds pulled down, dressing herself before a mirror. He came to her side, sat down on a stool, and watched her doing her coal-black hair, so long that it nearly touched the floor. She dressed it with red silk ribbons, setting on it a headdress of silver thread, and arranging the hair beneath, till it seemed like a sweet-scented cloud. In her hair she placed rose petals, and made four braids of it. She looked as beautiful as the living Guanyin. She finished her hair and put away the dressing case. Then she washed her hands, completed her dressing and told Chunmei to bring some tea for Chen Jingji. The young man smiled.

"Why are you laughing?" Jinlian cried.

"I'm laughing because I'm sure you have lost something."

"If I have lost something, you short-lived rascal," Jinlian said, "what business is it of yours? And, anyway, who told you about it?"

"Well," Jingji said, "if that's the way you look at it, treating my kind heart as if it were the entrails of a donkey, and talking in that nasty tone, I may as well be off."

He rose and started downstairs. Jinlian pulled him back again. "Don't make such a to-do," she said. "Now that Laiwang's wife is dead and you haven't anybody else to make love to, you condescend to call on your poor old mother. Well, you've guessed right this time. I have lost something."

Jingji took the shoe from his sleeve and dangled it in front of her. "Whose is this?" he said, laughing.

"Ah, you pretty rogue," Jinlian cried, "so it was you who stole my shoe, making me send my maids all over the place to look for it!"

"Why should I steal your shoe?" Jingji said.

"Well, you're the only person who ever comes to my room. It was you, you rat, who stole it."

"You ought to be ashamed of yourself," Jingji said. "I couldn't possibly have stolen it. I haven't been to your room for several days."

"You wait," Jinlian cried. "I'll tell your Father you stole my shoe, and we'll see if you say I ought to be ashamed of myself."

"You can't terrify me by using Father's name," Jingji said.

"Oh, aren't you brave? Though you knew quite well he was carrying on with Laiwang's wife, that didn't prevent you from finishing his work for him. After that, of course, you are not afraid of anybody. However, the proverb tells us that when a man sees his own belongings, he is entitled to take them back again. If you even suggest that you will not give it back, I will kill you."

"Lady," Jingji said, "you are so clever you might be a Mongol. There is nobody about, and we have an excellent opportunity to discuss the matter. If you want your shoe, what are you prepared to give me in exchange? If you don't give me something, not even lightning shall get it away from me."

"It's my shoe, you wretch," Jinlian cried, "and you must give it to me. What right have you to ask for anything in return?"

Jingji laughed. "Fifth Mother," he said, "I will have that handkerchief you have in your sleeve. If you give me that, I will let you have your shoe, like a good, dutiful son."

"But your Father knows this too well," Jinlian said. "I dare not give you this one. I'll find another one for you tomorrow."

"No," the young man said, "a hundred other handkerchiefs will not satisfy me. This is the one I want."

Jinlian laughed. "Oh, what a practiced villain you are. Well, I haven't the strength to quarrel with you." She took the handkerchief from her sleeve and gave it to him. It was of fine lace, with white silk needlework, and attached to it were three silver characters. She gave everything to him.

Jingji bowed low and took the handkerchief. Jinlian told him to take good care of it. "Don't let your wife see it," she said, "she has too sharp a tongue." Jingji promised and gave her the shoe. He told her that Little Iron Rod had picked it up in the garden and given it him in exchange for a necklet.

Jinlian flushed with anger. "The dirty little slave has made it quite black. I will tell his master to give him a thrashing."

"If you do," Jingji said, "it will be the end of me, for whether the boy gets beaten or not, I shall get the credit for the business, for it was I who told you. For goodness' sake, don't say anything about it."

"I will forgive a scorpion sooner than that little slave," Jinlian cried.

They were talking when Laian came to find Jingji. "Father is in the outer hall," he said, "and he is asking for Master Chen. He wants a present list written."

Jinlian hurried the young man away. She went downstairs and told Chunmei to fetch a rod so that she might beat Qiuju. Qiuju objected strongly. "I found your shoe, Mother," she cried. "Why should you still wish to beat me?"

Then Jinlian showed her the shoe she had just been given by Chen Jingji. "You thievish slave," she said, "if the other was my shoe, what is this?" The maid stared at it open-mouthed, and said: "It is very funny. Where has this third shoe come from?"

"You impudent hussy," Jinlian cried, "you tried to palm somebody else's shoe off on me. You might as well call me a three-legged fox." She would hear no more, but made Chunmei give the girl ten strokes.

Qiuju tried to protect her bottom, crying all the while to Chunmei: "It was you who left the gate open, and let somebody get in and steal the shoe. Now you tell Mother to beat me."

Chunmei cursed her: "No, it was you who brought in the coverlets. You lost the shoe, and you try to put the blame on me, when Mother gives you a few strokes. All this fuss about an old shoe. I suppose if Mother misses an earring or a ring some day, you'll still blame everybody but yourself. Mother is very kind to let you off so lightly. If I were she, I would send for one of the boys, and make him give you twenty or thirty stiff strokes, and then see how you'd like it." Qiuju swallowed down her anger and was silent.

Ximen Qing had sent for Jingji to pack up a roll of silk and other presents for Captain He, who had just been promoted to be magistrate at Huaian, with full rank. His kinsmen and friends were giving him a send-off at the Temple of Eternal Felicity.

When Ximen had sent Daian with the presents, he and Jingji dined together in the hall. Then he went to Jinlian's room. Jinlian, with much ado, told him how Little Iron Rod had picked up her shoe.

"It is all your fault, you good-for-nothing," she said, "that that little slave—he deserves to be cut into a thousand pieces— got my shoe. He has taken it outside and by this time everybody must have seen it. I found out about it and got it back. If you don't give him a taste of a thrashing, he will always be spoiled."

Ximen did not wait to ask how she came to hear about it, but went off in a temper to the front court. The little monkey suspected nothing and was playing on the stone steps. Ximen caught him by the plaits of his hair, struck him with his fist and kicked him till the boy squealed like a pig being killed. When he let him go, the little monkey lay fainting on the ground for some time. Laizhao and his wife came running along to rescue their child. After a while the boy came to himself, though his nose was still bleeding. His parents carried him to their room and asked him what it was all about, and so learned that he had picked up a shoe.

The Beanpole was furious. She went to the kitchen and made a tremendous fuss. She poured forth streams of curses.

"You thievish, death-dealing whore, you young turtle, what has my boy done that you should bear a grudge against him? He is only ten years old. What does he know about your cunt? You have kicked up all this fuss for nothing, and got him beaten till the blood is pouring from his nose. If he dies, you whorish turtle, I'll make you suffer. It shall be the worse for you."

When she had finished cursing in the kitchen, she went to the front court and continued there. If she had gone on for a couple of days she would not have exhausted herself.

Jinlian was drinking with Ximen Qing in her room, and heard nothing of all this. That night, as they were together on the bed, he noticed that she was wearing a pair of green silk bed shoes, with crimson tops. "Why do you wear shoes like that?" he cried. "I can't bear the sight of them."

"I only had one pair of red ones," Jinlian said, "and that little slave has ruined one of them. Where do you expect me to get another in place of it?"

"My child," Ximen said, "you must make another pair tomorrow and put them on at once. They make me feel so loving when I see you wearing them. You know your sweetheart can't bear to see shoes of any other color."

"What a funny slave you are," the woman said. "And that reminds me. There was something I meant to tell you, but I forgot all about it." She told Chunmei to bring the shoe and said to him: "Do you recognize this?"

"No," Ximen said, "I haven't a notion whose it is."

"Don't look at it as if it frightened you, then," Jinlian said. "You can't deceive me. That was a nice trick of yours! Huilian's stinking hoof, kept in your summerhouse, among your visiting cards, as if it were some precious jewel, wrapped up in paper and incense! Pray, what makes it so precious? When that thievish whore died, she went to the lowest depths of Hell." She pointed to Qiuju. "That slave thought it was mine and brought it to me, so I gave her a beating. Throw it away," she said to Chunmei.

Chunmei threw it on the floor and said to Qiuju: "I'll make you a present of it. You can wear it."

Qiuju picked it up. "Mother's shoe is so small, I couldn't even get one of my toes into it," she said.

"You slave," Jinlian cried, "how dare you call that vile creature 'Mother'? She must have been your master's mother in a former life, or he wouldn't be guarding her shoe as jealously as if it were a precious heirloom, the low fellow."

Qiuju took the shoe and was going out with it, but Jinlian called her back and told her to get a knife. "I'm going to cut that whore's shoe into little pieces and throw it in the privy. That will banish the thievish strumpet forever beyond the hills of Hades, so that never again can she come to life."

She said to Ximen Qing: "If it distresses you so much to see me cut it, I will cut it all the more."

Ximen Qing laughed. "That's enough, you queer little slave," he said, "I don't feel in the least distressed."

"If you don't," Jinlian said, "take an oath on it. The whore is dead, and we don't know where she is. Why do you keep her shoe? Obviously because you like to look at it and remember her. I have spent many years with you but you don't really care for me. There is always another woman in your heart."

"You funny little strumpet," Ximen said, smiling. "Why do you say such things? She never did you any harm when she was alive."

He put his arm around her white neck and kissed her. Then the two once more did the work of clouds and rain.

# CHAPTER 29
# The Fortune-Teller

Next day Pan Jinlian rose early and set Ximen Qing upon his way. Then, taking her sewing basket, she went to the Kingfisher Hall, and, sitting down on the steps, began to design her shoes. She sent Chunmei to ask Li Ping'er to join her.

"What is that you're drawing?" Li Ping'er said.

"I am making a pair of crimson silk shoes with white flat soles, and on the toe I am going to embroider a cockatoo pecking at a peach."

"I have a piece of flowered crimson silk," Li Ping'er said. "I will copy your design, but I shall make my shoes with heels." She fetched her sewing basket and they sat down together. When Jinlian had drawn the pattern on one shoe, she asked Li Ping'er to draw the other. She said she was going to the inner court for Meng Yulou. "The other day," she said, "she told me she was going to make some shoes."

She went to the inner court and found Yulou in her room, bending over a table, putting the lining into a shoe.

"You are about early this morning," Yulou said.

"Yes," Jinlian said, "I was up early and saw Father off to Captain He's farewell party. Then I asked the Sixth Lady to come and work with me in the garden. It is cooler there. I have just finished drawing the pattern of one shoe and the Sixth Lady is doing the other for me. Now I've come for you. It will be jolly for us all to work together. What is that you're doing?"

"It is the mate to that black silk shoe I showed you yesterday," Yulou said.

"You do work hard," Jinlian said, "you have actually come to the lining already."

"I finished one yesterday and the other is half done," Yulou said.

Jinlian examined the shoe carefully. "What kind of a toe are you going to put on it?" she said.

"Oh, I am not like you two children," Yulou said. "You must have lots of flowers and pretty things. I am a staid old lady and shall simply have the toes of gilded sheep skin, bound around the edges with green thread. What would you suggest?"

"Oh, that will do well enough," Jinlian said, "but hurry up. Li Ping'er is waiting for us."

"Won't you sit down and drink a cup of tea first?"

"No," Jinlian said, "bring the tea with you, and drink it there."

Yulou told her maid to make some tea and bring it out to them. Holding hands, with the shoes in their sleeves, the two women went to the garden. As they passed Wu Yueniang, who was sitting under the eaves outside her own apartments, she asked where they were going. Jinlian told her that Li Ping'er had sent her for Yulou and that they were going to design some shoes. They went on to the garden. There they all sat down together, and looked at each other's work.

"Why do you always make crimson low-heeled shoes?" Yulou said to Jinlian. "They don't look nearly so pretty as the high-heeled ones. If you don't care for wooden soles, you can use felt, as I do."

"They are not walking-out shoes," Jinlian said, "they are for bedroom use. A little slave ruined my others, and Father told me to make some new ones."

"Speaking of shoes," Yulou said, "I hope the Sixth Lady will not think me a gossip, but yesterday you lost one of your shoes, and Father gave Little Iron Rod a beating. The boy fell down and lay in a faint for a long time. That upset Laizhao's wife, and she cursed like anything, up and down the back court. 'That whorish young turtle,' she cried, 'he has been telling tales about my boy and now the poor boy has had a thrashing. It's a good thing he didn't die, or that vile creature would have had to pay for it.' We couldn't make out whom she was cursing, but some time afterwards Little Iron Rod came along and the Great Lady asked him why Father had beaten him. 'I was playing in the garden,' he said, 'and I picked up a shoe. Uncle Chen came with a necklet and I asked him to give it to me for my shoe. I don't know who told Father and got me beaten.' Then he said he was looking for Uncle Chen so that he could get the necklet he had been promised, and ran off. You see the turtle in question is our brother-in-law. Fortunately, only Li Jiao'er was there, and not the Great Lady, or there would have been trouble."

"Why?" Jinlian said, "did the Great Lady have anything to say about it?"

"You may well ask that," Yulou said. "Indeed she had a good deal to say. She said: 'In this wretched household, there is now a nine-tailed fox who seems determined to rule the roost. I remember how comfortable everybody was when Laiwang came back from his journey to the south, until stories began to fly around. First that Laiwang's wife was flirting with his Lordship, then that he himself had got a knife and carried a club. All this ended in the poor man's being banished and his wife hanging herself. Now, all for the sake of a paltry shoe, she sets both heaven and earth in a turmoil. If she had been wearing the shoe in a proper and decent manner, it would not have been there for the boy to pick up. I suppose she was playing some dirty game in the garden with that man of hers, and drinking, and dropped her shoe. Now in order to keep the shameful business dark, she throws all the blame on the boy. After all, it is not a matter of any importance."

"She is talking out of her cunt," Jinlian cried. "What does she consider an important matter, I wonder. Surely murder is important enough, and the slave took a knife to murder his master." She turned to Yulou. "Sister, we have never had any secrets from one another. You remember how terrified we both were when Laixing came and told us, yet she, the first wife, talks in this strain. However, if it doesn't matter to her, it doesn't matter to me, and if the slaves like to kill their master, they may. That woman Huilian was one of her maids, but she never made the slightest attempt to control her, and the slave deceived her betters, and behaved badly to those beneath her. She flew into tempers first with one and then with another. Well, people must find somebody to let loose their hatred upon. If she is going to say nasty things about me, she will get as good as she gives. When that Huilian hanged herself, she didn't tell her husband the truth. She spent a lot of money hushing it up. If she hadn't done so, it would not have passed over so easily. She managed to scrape out of it, and now she puts on this high and mighty air. She accuses me of interfering with her husband. Well, if I don't make him kick out that slave and his wife, you can consider that I count for nothing. I don't intend to let myself be pushed down a well."

Yulou saw that Jinlian was growing purple with rage. "We are such firm friends, Sister," she said, "that I always tell you anything I hear, but when I do tell you things, you must keep them to yourself and not get so excited."

Jinlian did not take this advice. That night, when Ximen Qing came to her room, she told him the whole story. "Laizhao's wife," she said, "was screaming up and down the inner court that you had beaten her boy, and the first chance she got, you should pay for it."

Ximen Qing did not forget this. The next day he would have sent away Laizhao and his wife and child, but, fortunately, Yueniang persuaded him not to do so. Still, he would not keep Laizhao in the house, and sent him to take charge of the house in Lion Street in place of Ping'an whom he brought back and put in charge of the gate. Yueniang realized what had happened and was very angry with Jinlian.

One day Ximen was sitting in the front hall, when Ping'an came in and said: "Major Zhou has sent a fortune-telling gentleman, called Wu the Immortal. He is waiting at the gate to see you." Ximen gave orders that the man should be admitted, and, after looking at Major Zhou's card, he bade the fortune-teller welcome. Wu the Immortal was wearing a black Daoist hat, a long cloak, and straw sandals. He was girt by a girdle of yellow silk with two tassels, and carried a tortoiseshell fan. He stalked in with a majestic air. He seemed at least forty years of age. His spirit was as proud as the moon, and he was as venerable in appearance as the tall pines that grow upon the summit of Mount Hua.

There are always four marks by which an Immortal may be distinguished. His body is like the pine tree; his voice like a bell. When he is seated, he is like a bow, and when he walks, like the wind.

When Ximen Qing saw Wu the Immortal about to come in, he hurried down the steps to greet him and took him into the hall. The Immortal saluted Ximen with a religious reverence, and sat down. Tea was brought at once and Ximen said: "May I ask your Immortality's glorious and illustrious names? From what fairy country have you come, and how did you make the acquaintance of Major Zhou?"

The Immortal raised himself slightly. "I am called Wu," he said, "and my personal name is Shih. My name in religion is Shou Zhen. I was born in Xian Yu of Zhejiang, but while I was still a boy I went with my Master to the temple of the Purple Void on the Tiantai mountain. Afterwards, I wandered as a cloud over the earth, and have come at last to seek the Sacred Principle upon Taishan. On my way, I happened to pass through your esteemed city, and General Zhou was good enough to allow me to examine the eyes of his ladies. Then he bade me come to you to tell your fortune."

"Oh, Venerable Prince of the Immortals," Ximen Qing said, "to which school of magic do you belong, and what system of physiognomies do you follow?"

"I have a slight acquaintance with thirteen schools," the Immortal said, "and practice the method of Ma Yi. But I also understand the Liu Ren and the Magic Ke. I give my simples to cure people, but worldly wealth I never accept, knowing that I am upon this earth for but a short space."

Ximen Qing felt considerably more respect for his visitor. "You must indeed be a true Immortal," he said. He told his servants to prepare a table with monastic fare.

"But I have not yet performed my office," the Immortal said. "How can I eat your food?"

"Master," Ximen said, smiling, "you have come a long way, and I feel sure you have not yet breakfasted. There will be plenty of time afterwards for you to tell our fortunes." He sat down himself and shared the monastic fare with the Immortal. Then the table was cleared, and he called for writing materials.

"Sir," the Immortal said, "tell me first the eight words of moment in your honorable life, and I will relate the future for you." Ximen Qing told him the Eight Characters, saying that his animal was the Tiger, his age twenty-nine, and the hour of his birth noon on the twenty-eighth day of the seventh month. The Immortal silently made some calculations upon his fingers and said: "Sir, your horoscope would appear to show the year as *Wuyin,* the month as *Xinyu,* the day as *Renwu* and the hour as *Bingwu.* Now the twenty-third day of the seventh month is the Day of White Dew. We must therefore reckon your fate as from the eighth month. Taking the months in order, *Xinyu* is the controlling month, so obviously *Shangguan* is the controlling factor in your life. As Zi Ping says: wealth increases and riches multiply. You will obtain an official position. Then your luck will change again. Your fate depends upon *Shengong,* so your fortune starts from the seventh year *Xinyu.* Then at seventeen, it moves towards *Renxu,* at twenty-seven to *Guihai,* at thirty-seven to *Jiazi* and at forty-seven to *Yichou.* Your horoscope, Sir, as I see it, indicates that you will fill a position of authority and that you will be prosperous. Your Eight Characters are certainly clear and unusual. But though this is so, you are adversely affected by the Earth Element in *Wu,* seeing that you were born between the seventh and the eighth months, a fact that gives you too great physical vigor. Fortunately the day of your birth was *Renwu* and the Water Element of *Gui* comes between *Zi* and *Chou,* thus producing an equilibrium between water and fire, and putting beyond doubt the fact that you will profit by your abilities. The hour was *Bingwu,* and this fits in very well with *Xin,* so you may look forward to a career of great dignity: you will prosper, be happy, and at peace all your life. Your fortune will increase; you will obtain promotion, and you are destined to leave behind you an honorable descendant. Throughout your life you will be honest and fair dealing; when once you have made up your mind you will not change it. In joy you will be as agreeable as the breeze in spring, and in anger as terrible as the sudden thunder and the fierce lightning. You will enjoy many women, great wealth, and not a few of the insignia of office, and when at last you leave this world there will be two sons to speed you on your way. This year, *Ding* and *Ren* come together, and the fire of *Ding* will be in the ascendant. This means the coming of officials and ghosts, and certainly indicates your elevation to the clouds, or, otherwise, that you will receive an appointment and come into great wealth. Your fortune is now moving towards *Guihai,* so that the Earth of *Wu* moistened by the Water of *Gui,* and from the intermingling of water and earth, one naturally anticipates growth. I see the star of the Red Phoenix, and this is undoubtedly a sign of the coming of a son. Then, too, the controller of your life appears on horseback going towards *Shen,* so before the seventh month is out, these things will certainly come to pass."

"What about my life in the more distant future?" Ximen Qing said.

"Sir," the Immortal said, "I trust you will forgive me, but I am sorry to say that your Eight Characters do not go well with so much *Yin* water, and, when you reach the high tide of your fortune in the year *Jiazi,* the water will wash out the *Renwu* day, and the inconstant stars will then affect you. Before you reach your thirty-sixth year, you will suffer from sores, hemorrhage and wasting sickness."

"What then of the present?" Ximen said.

"This year you meet the five spirits of destruction. This means some slight trouble in your household. It will not be very serious, for the omens are favorable, and the trouble will pass away."

"Is there any great calamity in my life?" Ximen asked.

"Days lengthen into months, and months into years," the Immortal said, "it is hard indeed to prophesy."

Ximen Qing was satisfied. "Master," he said, "what do you read in my face?"

"Please turn your honorable countenance straight towards me," the Immortal said. Ximen Qing moved his chair slightly, and the Immortal said:

"What is this outward seeming? Without the mind it would be nothing, for outward seeming springeth from the heart. Whither the heart goeth, the appearance goeth also. I perceive that your Lordship's head is round, and your neck short. You are clearly a man favored by fortune. Your body is robust and your muscles strong, a sign that you are a man of heroic courage. Your brow is high and projecting, and all your life you will never lack raiment or wealth. Your chin is square and full, and in your old age you will fill an exalted office. Such are the good things I see. There are evil things also, but shall I venture to tell you these?"

"Pray tell me all, Immortal," Ximen said.

The Immortal asked Ximen Qing to take a few steps, and continued: "Your walk is like the shaking of the willow. It is a sign that you should outlive a wife, and if you do not do so, you will certainly suffer hurt. I trust you have already done so."

"I have," Ximen said.

The Immortal asked to see his hand, and Ximen Qing held it out. "Perfect wisdom," the Immortal said, "is always to be discerned by the skin and hair, and sorrow and happiness may be foretold by the hands and feet. Your hand is so fine and soft and firm, you are certainly destined by fortune for the enjoyment of wealth and happiness. Of your eyes, one is male and one female, a sign that you are wealthy and alert of mind. Each of your eyebrows has a fork, which shows that all through your life pleasure will mean much to you, but below them are three wrinkles, which mean that in middle age you will suffer a great loss. Your *Jianmen* is red; you will enjoy wealth and women all your life. Your brows are yellow, and in a few days you will receive an official appointment. There is red upon your *Sanyang,* and this very year a fine son will be born to you. One thing, which I hesitate to mention, is that your *Leitang* are thick and long, indicating a fondness for the flower maidens, but your nose, the star of wealth, would seem to promise a wealthy middle age. The *Zhengjiang* is hollowed, and from that we may foretell the fortunes and misfortunes of your next life."

The Immortal was silent. Ximen Qing asked if he would tell the fortunes of his ladies, and sent a servant to summon Wu Yueniang. She came with Li Jiao'er, Meng Yulou, Pan Jinlian, Li Ping'er, and Sun Xue'e, and they stood behind a curtain to listen. When the Immortal saw Yueniang, he quickly saluted her. He would not sit down in her presence, but stood to tell her fortune.

"Lady," he said, "your face is like the full moon, a sign that the household flourishes under your care. Your lips are like the red lotus, and so I know that you are prosperous and that you will have the dignity of motherhood. Your voice is sweet and fairy-like, and you will help your husband towards the attainment of happiness. Please show me your hands." Yueniang drew her delicate fingers from her sleeves. "Your hands," continued the Immortal, "are like dried ginger, a sign that you are well capable of controlling those under your charge. The hair upon your temples shines as does a mirror, which shows, according to the doctrine of Kun, that you are a very clever woman. These are the good points. There are others not so favorable, but these I hesitate to tell." Ximen Qing urged him to continue. "In your *Leitang* there is a mole, and if you were not so frequently ill, you would most certainly destroy your husband. There are wrinkles beneath your eyes, which show that your six relatives are as ice and as ashes."

> She stands erect, beautiful to see
> With footsteps slow and light, like a turtle coming from the water
> When she walks, the dust is not stirred. Her words are measured.
> The slender shoulders show that she must wed an honorable husband.

When Yueniang had withdrawn, Ximen Qing said: "There are still some ladies of lesser rank: will you see them?" Li Jiao'er came forward. The Immortal looked at her for a long time, and said: "This lady's brows are very abrupt, and her nose is small. If she were not a concubine, she would certainly marry three husbands. She is plump and well favored, a sign that she will want for nothing. She enjoys comfort and is a peaceable person. Her shoulders are high and her voice is shrill, so, unless she is an orphan, she is a person of low degree. The bridge of her nose is rather low, and she will be poor, or die young." He asked her to walk a few steps, and said:

The tapering brow, the sinuous back
Show that in youth she trod the path of wind and dust.
One of two things she must be, a girl from a house of evil fame
Or a woman who stands behind the screen.

Li Jiao'er went back to her place, and Yueniang said to Yulou: "Now it is your turn."

"This lady," the Immortal said, "has forehead, nose and chin all well proportioned. She will have no anxiety about material things. The six natural treasures are full to overflowing and she will have fortune and honor in her old age. She will suffer little from sickness, for her mouth is favored by a bright and dazzling comet, and in truth her *Niangong* is smooth and beautiful. Kindly walk a step or two, Lady."

Then he said:

Her mouth is like the character *Si*, her spirit pure and keen
Her gentleness and charm are like a pearl resting on a palm
Honor and dignity will be hers, wealth and prosperity.
She will outlive two husbands.

When Yulou had retired, Jinlian was asked to take her place, but she laughed and refused. Yueniang pressed her, and finally she went out. The Immortal raised his head and gazed at her for a long time. Then he said slowly: "This lady's hair is thick and uncommonly heavy at the temples, and her glance is not direct. This is a sign of a very passionate nature. Her cheeks are full of charm, her eyebrows arched, and, even when she is standing still, her body quivers. The moles upon her face mean that she will be the end of her husbands, and her upper lip, which is short, indicates that her own life will not be long."

Lightly and unrestrained she moves, craving the pleasures of love,
Her eyes, sparkling like fragments of lacquer, show that she is the
    cause of men's undoing
Beneath the moon, before the stair, never can she be sated
But, though she lives in a great mansion, her heart is not at rest.

Ximen Qing called for Li Ping'er, and asked the Immortal to predict her future. "Your complexion," the Immortal said, "is so sweet and fragrant that I know you for a maiden of high degree. Your bearing is modest, so that you may be told for a virtuous woman of high rank. Yet there is a sparkle in your eyes as though you had taken wine, and this suggests an engagement behind the mulberry tree. Your eyes are dark ringed, which shows that what happens to you each month gives trouble. Yet the sleeping silkworm is glossy and purple, and beyond a doubt you will bring forth a precious son. Your skin is white and your shoulders round, and your husband loves you dearly. You are often sick, for the roots are dark and deep, yet you constantly meet with omens of great joy, for the star of your fortune is bright and favorable. These are the points in your favor, but there are others not so favorable, and, Lady, you must be careful. The mountain root is black, and before your twenty-seventh year there are signs of tears, yet if you keep good counsel, you may survive the cock and dog years. Yet beware, beware!"

> Her countenance is like the flowers and the moon, yet she must guard
>     her plumage
> Close to her lover till life is done, like the phoenix and his mate.
> Trust in the wealth of the red doors
> And do not mix with humbler birds.

Li Ping'er withdrew, and Yueniang told Xue'e to take her place. The Immortal looked at her and said: "This lady's body is short and her voice shrill. Her brow is pointed and her nose small. Though she has come from the valley to the heights, her portion is of sneers and friendlessness. She manages her affairs well, and is not without guile, but she suffers from a fourfold "turn up," and it may be that disaster shall overtake her. The fourfold "turn up" is lips curling yet without an edge, ears curling yet without a curve, eyes turned up yet without a sparkle, nose turned up yet crooked."

> Her body is like a bird's, her waist like a wasp's. She is not of high
>     degree.
> Her eyes are like flowing waters; she is not chaste.
> She stands and leans upon the door
>  If she does not become a maidservant, worse things will befall her.

Xue'e withdrew, and Yueniang told Ximen's daughter, Ximen Dajie, to come and let the Immortal see her.

"This lady's nose is low and flat," he said; "she will bring discredit upon her ancestors and ruin upon her household. Her voice is like a cracked gong, and all her family wealth will be dispersed. Her complexion is coarse; she will die young and in distress. She walks like the hopping of a sparrow, and though she lives in her own home, she is in need of food and clothing. Calamity will fall upon her before she is twenty-seven."

Though she seems wise, she is not at peace with her husband
Only the food and clothes her parents give keep warmth in her
She is not handsome and honor will not visit her.
Even if violent death should be spared her, there are hard times in store.

Then Chunmei came to be examined. The Immortal opened his eyes wide as he looked at her. She was about eighteen years old, he saw. A silver hairnet was on her head, a white gown with a peach-colored skirt, and a fine blue silk wrap. She made a reverence to him when she came forward. The Immortal gazed at her for a long time. At last he said:

"This young lady has the five sense organs well developed. She is exquisitely made. Her hair is fine, but her eyebrows are thick. This is a sign of hot temper. Her spirit is volatile and her eyes round. This denotes that she easily becomes excited. Her nose is straight: she will marry an officer of high rank and bear him a son. Her brows are prominent: this is a sign that she will wear a pearl headdress while she is still young. She walks like a flying angel; her voice is clear and her spirit pure. She will bring wealth to her husband, and by the age of twenty-seven will assuredly receive high honor. Unfortunately her left eye is rather large. This means that she lost her father in her childhood. And the right eye is small, which shows that her mother died when she was one year old. The mole beneath the left corner of her mouth is the sign of a quarrelsome disposition, but the mole on her right cheek indicates that she will be respected and loved by her husband as long as she lives."

Her brow is high, the five sense organs as they should be
Her lips are red as though with rouge; her steps are light.
There will be wealth in plenty for her, and rich food
And men of rank and dignity will love her all her days.

When the Immortal had said this, the women bit their nails and thought over his words. Ximen Qing put five taels of silver into a packet and offered it to the Immortal. He gave five *qian* to the Major's servant, with a visiting card to express his thanks. But the Immortal would not accept the silver. "I wander over the earth as a cloud," he said. "I take my meals, exposed to the winds, and my bed is in the dew. What use is money to me? I cannot take it."

Then Ximen gave him a roll of cloth with which to make himself a habit. This the Immortal accepted, and told his young disciple to take it. He made a reverence to Ximen Qing and thanked him. Ximen took him to the gate, and there the Immortal proudly took leave of him.

When Ximen Qing came back to the inner court, he asked Yueniang and the others what they thought of what the Immortal had said.

"He was clever enough," Yueniang said, "but I think he was mistaken about three people."

"Which three?" Ximen said.

"He said that the Sixth Lady was ill, but that she would bear a son. She is with child now, so that he may be partly right. Then he said that there are hard times in store for our daughter. I don't see how he can make that out. He told us that Chunmei would have a son. You have probably done your part, but I see no signs of her having a child. And certainly I don't believe what he said about her wearing a pearl headdress and being a lady. We have nobody in this household of official rank, so I don't know where the pearl headdress is coming from, and even if there were one, it would not be for her head."

Ximen Qing laughed. "He said that I should rise from the ground to the clouds, that position and wealth would come to me, but really, I don't see where they are coming from. It seems to me that when you and Chunmei were standing together he got mixed up because of your dresses. She was wearing a silver hairnet, and he thought she was our daughter. He thought she would probably marry into some family of position and so would come to wear a pearl headdress. People have always said that it is better for us when the fortune-tellers are wrong. If our minds and our appearance had any relation to one another our mind would be different every time the appearance changed. But since Major Zhou sent him here, we couldn't very well refuse to let him try his hand."

Yueniang had a meal served in the hall, and they all took part in it. Afterwards, Ximen Qing took a palm-leaf fan and strolled about the garden. When he came to the pavilion of the Glorious Landscape, near the great arbor, he pulled down the blinds and curtains. Outside, the flowering shrubs and trees cast a refreshing shade. In the depth of the foliage, a band of cicadas were singing, and from time to time the breeze wafted the fragrance of the flowers towards him.

Ximen Qing sat on a chair and fanned himself. Laian and Huatong came to the well to draw some water.

"Come here, one of you boys," Ximen said.

Laian came. "Go to the inner court," Ximen said to him, "and tell your sister Chunmei to bring me a pot of plum juice."

Some time afterwards, Chunmei, wearing her silver hairnet, came to him with a pot of plum juice. She was smiling. "Have you had anything to eat?" she said.

"Yes, I had something in the inner court."

Chunmei pretended to be annoyed. "You do not come to see us," she said, "you only send to us when you want plum juice. Wait till I make it cool enough."

Ximen Qing nodded. When the girl had made it ready, she came and rested on his chair. She took the palm-leaf fan from his hand and fanned him.

"What did the Great Lady say?" she asked.

"She talked about Wu the Immortal."

"Oh, that absurd monk said I should wear a pearl headdress, and the Great Lady said that even if there ever was one in this household, it wouldn't be for my head. But the proverb says we should never judge by appearances, and the water in the ocean cannot be measured with a pint pot. Even when you can't use a lathe, it is always possible to use a knife. It is a most uncertain business foretelling what is going to happen to people. Do you imagine I shall always be a slave in your household?"

"Little oily mouth," Ximen said to her, "if you give me a son, you shall wear a headdress, certainly." He took her in his arms and fondled her. "Where is your mistress?" he said, "I haven't seen her for some time."

"She told Qiuju to heat some water for a bath," Chunmei said, "but she got tired of waiting, and now she is asleep on the bed."

"When I have drunk this plum water, I'll go and play a trick on her," Ximen said.

Chunmei took the pot from the ice, and gave it to him. He drank a mouthful. It was so cold that he could feel it in his bones. It went through his body and made his teeth chatter. It seemed like gentle dew dropping upon his heart. After a while, he finished the plum water and, resting his hand on Chunmei's shoulder, went to Jinlian's room. She was asleep on the mother-of-pearl bed that he had recently bought for her. It was facing the door. Li Ping'er had a bed similar to this one and Jinlian had asked him to buy one for her. It cost something like sixty taels of silver. It was a four-poster and the panels all around it were made of mother-of-pearl cunningly designed to represent flowers, grasses and birds. The curtains were of purple silk, with silver hooks.

Jinlian was completely undressed, except for a light, scarlet vest. The bedclothes were of the finest silk and there was a Yin Yang pillow beneath her head. She lay upon the summer mattress, fast asleep. Seeing her, Ximen Qing's desire was stirred. He told Chunmei to close the door and go away, and quietly took off his own clothes. Then he took away the gossamer coverlet, got upon the bed, and admired the sight of his body beside that of his beloved. Then he played a trick on her. He parted her legs, gripped his penis and put it between them. She opened her eyes wide in astonishment, but Ximen had already moved in and out ten times.

"You strange rascal," Jinlian said, laughing, "when did you come in? I was asleep and didn't see you. Yes, sleeping so sweetly, yet you came and disturbed me."

"Since it is I, no harm is done," Ximen Qing said. "If it had been a stranger, you would pretend you didn't know the difference."

"What can I say to curse you?" Jinlian said. "Who do you think would be bold enough to come into my room? Only a rude man like you would do a thing of that sort."

After Jinlian had heard Ximen Qing, in the Kingfisher Hall, saying how white and beautiful Li Ping'er's body was, she had made a mixture of the hearts of jasmine flowers, cream and powder, and had rubbed it into her skin all over her body to make it smooth and white, so that she might be favored as Li Ping'er had been.

Her body now seemed as white as snow, with only a pair of scarlet sleeping shoes upon her feet. Ximen Qing squatted on the bed, and holding fast to her legs, plunged forward with all his might. He looked down so that he might enjoy the sight of what he was doing.

"Why are you looking at me, you funny creature?" Jinlian said. "My body is black, and cannot rival the Sixth Lady's white skin. I suppose that is why you are looking at it. Now that she is with child, you love and think only of her, and I am considered fit for nothing but the rubbish heap. You think you can treat me as you like."

"I am told you are waiting for a bath," Ximen Qing said. "Is that so?"

"Who told you?"

"Chunmei."

Then Jinlian asked if he would like to join her, and told the maid to bring the water. The bathtub was set down, the water poured in, and the two got down from the bed to bathe in the fragrant water. They played about as merrily as fishes. When they had spent some time washing themselves, Ximen Qing set Jinlian on the bathing board and, holding her feet in his two hands, mounted upon her and thrust forward. They jumped up and down, and shook about, two or three thousand times, making a noise like a crab crawling in the mud. Jinlian was afraid that her hair would be disarranged, so she put one hand on her head, and supported herself on the edge of the tub with the other. She made herself as charming as could be.

They played in the water for a long time. Then Ximen Qing yielded, and they stopped. They cleansed their bodies, and the bathtub was taken away. Ximen put on a short thin cotton coat and got on to the bed. A table was placed on it so that they might eat some fruit and drink wine. Jinlian bade Qiuju bring some white wine, and gave him some fruit pastries, because she thought he must be hungry. After a very long time, Qiuju brought a silver pot of wine. Jinlian poured out a cup. It was as cold as ice. She threw the wine in Qiuju's face, and it splashed all over her.

"You slave!" she cried, "you are not fit to live. What do you mean by bringing this cold wine for your father? I don't know what you're thinking about."

She told Chunmei to take the girl to the courtyard and make her kneel down there.

"I was only out of the room for a moment," Chunmei said to Qiuju, "getting some ribbons for mother's feet, and you go and upset the whole place like this."

"The other day," Qiuju said, pouting, "they wanted iced wine. How was I to know that they would want something different today?"

Jinlian heard this and cursed her. "What's that you say, you thievish slave? Come here!" She said to Chunmei, "Give her a good slapping, ten times on each side of her face."

"Oh, Mother," Chunmei said, "you can't even see the skin on her face, and it would make my hands dreadfully dirty. Won't you make her kneel down, and put a piece of stone on her head?"

Without more ado, Qiuju was dragged to the courtyard and made to kneel down with a piece of stone balanced on her head. Then Jinlian told Chunmei to warm the wine, and she drank a few cups with Ximen Qing. When they had had enough, the table was removed; they pulled down the curtains and told Chunmei to shut the door. Then they put their arms around each other's necks and entwined their legs. They were very tired and soon went to sleep.

# CHAPTER 30
# The Birth of Guan'ge

After their bath, Ximen Qing and Pan Jinlian went to sleep. Chunmei settled herself under the eaves outside their room and busied herself making shoes. After a while Qintong came to the door in the corner, looking about him as though he were in search of someone. "What do you want?" Chunmei said. The boy looked at Qiuju who was kneeling in the court-yard with a piece of stone balanced on her head, and, instead of answering, pointed to the maid. Chunmei scolded him.

"What do you want, you young rascal? Why do you wave your hands about like that?"

Qintong did not stop laughing for a long time, but at last he told her that Zhang An, the grave keeper, had called to see Ximen Qing.

"Oh," Chunmei said, "only Zhang An! And you make as much fuss as if it were a ghost. Don't make such a noise. They are both asleep, and, if you wake them up, there will be trouble. Tell Zhang An to wait."

The boy did as he was told, but, after waiting a long time, he came again to look in at the corner gate and asked Chunmei whether his master was not yet up.

"You little rogue," the maid cried, "you frightened me, rushing in suddenly like that. It's nothing but a trifle, yet you dash about like a homeless spirit."

"Zhang An wants to see Master, but he has to go to town too, and he's afraid he'll be too late."

"Well, they're both sound asleep, and I dare not wake them. Tell Zhang An to wait, and, if he is too late today, he must wait until tomorrow."

At that moment Ximen Qing woke up, and, hearing voices, called out to ask Chunmei who was there. The girl told him. "I will get up," Ximen said. "Let me have my clothes." When Chunmei had brought the clothes, Pan Jinlian asked what Zhang An had come about.

"The other day," Ximen said, "he came to tell me that the widow Zhao, who owns the property next to our family graves, is anxious to sell it. She asks three hundred taels and I am prepared to give two hundred and fifty, so I told Zhang An to go and talk the matter over with her. There is a spring on the land with four places where water can be drawn. If I buy the place,

I shall join it up with our own and build a fair-sized arbor and a hall. I shall make an artificial mound, lay out gardens, put a cover over the well, and clear a space for practicing archery. I may make a ball ground where we can play when we feel like it. It will cost me quite a sum of money to do all I am thinking of doing."

"Buy it by all means," Jinlian said, "then we shall be able to have some fun when we go to visit our graves."

When Ximen Qing had gone to the outer court to see Zhang An, Jinlian got up, powdered her face and dressed her hair, and went to the courtyard to beat Qiuju. Chunmei went to bring Qintong with a rod.

"When I told you to bring your master some wine," Jinlian said to the maid, "why did you bring cold wine? One would think there was no discipline in the house at all. When I tell you to do anything, you stand there and argue, as brazen-faced as you can be.

"Give her twenty strokes," she cried to Qintong, "as hard as you can."

The boy had given the poor maid ten strokes when, fortunately, Li Ping'er came. With a smile, she bade him stop, and Qiuju was spared the ten remaining blows. Jinlian told her to kowtow to Li Ping'er, and then sent her to the kitchen.

"Old mother Pan," Li Ping'er said, "has come with a maid about fifteen years old, and our second sister has bought her for seven taels to wait upon her. She would like you to go and see her."

Together, they went off to the back court. Ximen Qing had given Li Jiao'er the money to buy a maid, who was given the name of Xiahua.

Laibao and Master Wu had set off upon their journey with the birthday presents. The weather was so hot that it was not an easy one. They ate when they were hungry, and when they were thirsty they drank, and so, after some days, came to the Eastern Capital. There they put up at an inn by the Gate of Ten Thousand Blessings. The next day they made ready their chests of presents and went straight to the Bridge of the Milky Way and the palace of the Imperial Tutor. Laibao, who had dressed himself in a suit of black clothes, asked Wu to look after the presents and went himself to the gate. He made a reverence to the gatekeeper who asked him whence he came.

"I am one of the household of Master Ximen who lives at Qinghe in Shandong. I have come with presents for the birthday of the venerable Imperial Tutor."

The gatekeeper upbraided him. "You scoundrelly rogue! What is Master Ximen to me, or Master Dongmen either? Let me tell you that my venerable lord has but one superior. All other men are far beneath him. I don't care what a man's position is. He may be a duke or a prince, but when he comes here, he does not dare to flaunt himself as you have done. Stand back, fellow!"

Fortunately, among the officers who were standing by, there was one who knew Laibao, and he came up and smoothed the matter over.

"Don't let this disturb you," he said to Laibao. "This gentleman has only just come here and he does not know you. Wait a few moments and I will ask the Comptroller, Master Zhai, to come and see you."

Laibao took a tael of silver from his sleeve and gave it to the officer.

"Really, there is no need for this," the officer said, accepting it, "but if I may make a suggestion, you might offer something to these other two gentlemen, and so you will avoid any difficulty on their part."

Laibao brought out two more taels of silver and gave them to the officers. At this, the faces of the officers became more pleasant.

"So you have come from Qinghe," the gatekeeper said. "Wait a few moments and I will take you to see Master Zhai. His Eminence has just returned from the Temple of Ether, Glorious and Indefectible, where he has been offering incense. He is resting in his study."

Some time later Zhai came. He was wearing light shoes, white socks, and a devotional robe of black silk. Laibao knelt down before him. The Comptroller greeted him, and Laibao handed over the list of the presents he had brought, while servants came forward with two rolls of Nanjing silk and thirty taels of white gold.

"My master, Ximen Qing, offers this to you with his best respects. He knows that he has nothing in any way worthy to repay your kindnesses, but you may be willing to distribute these trifles among your servants. You had so much trouble over the affair of Wang the Fourth, the salt-merchant."

"I really cannot accept this present," the Comptroller said, and a little later, "Well, perhaps I must."

Laibao presented the list of gifts that his master had sent for the Imperial Tutor. When the Comptroller had examined it, he handed it back to Laibao and told him to have the presents carried to the inner courtyard and to wait there. To the west of the inner door was an antechamber where all who had business in that place were entertained. Here an attendant brought tea for Laibao and Wu. After a while Cai, the Imperial Tutor, came to the hall, and after the Comptroller had told him of their visit, Laibao and his companion were summoned. They knelt at the foot of the steps while the Comptroller gave the present list to the Imperial Tutor. Then the two men brought in the gifts, vases of shining yellow gold, cups of finest jade, figurines and the multicolored dragon robe of ceremony. There was silk from Nanjing glimmering with green and gold. This was not all. Provisions of meat and wine had been carefully preserved, and were piled high beside fresh and seasonable fruits. The Imperial Tutor could not fail to be pleased.

"I feel quite embarrassed by such splendid presents," he said. "You must really take them away."

Laibao and Wu kowtowed and said, "Our master, Ximen Qing, knows only too well that he has no adequate means of expressing his filial devotion to your Eminence. He sends these trifles in the hope that you may at least think them not unworthy to be distributed among your attendants."

"Then I will tell my servants to remove them," said the Imperial Tutor. A host of attendants carried the presents away. "A little while ago," he said, "there was a little business about some salt merchants at Zangzhou. I think I wrote to the Governor on your behalf. Was the result satisfactory?"

"Thanks to your Eminence's gracious intervention," Laibao said, "as soon as your dispatch arrived, the whole party was set at liberty."

"Your master has been at great trouble and expense on my account," the Imperial Tutor said, "and I have no means of expressing my kindly feeling towards him. Has he any official position?"

"What position should he hold?" Laibao said. "He is only a simple countryman."

"Since he has not," the Imperial Tutor said, "I shall see that he is given an appointment as a law officer in Shandong. He shall be made Deputy Captain in He Jin's place. Only yesterday his Majesty placed a few appointments at my disposal."

Laibao kowtowed and thanked the Imperial Tutor. "I am most grateful," he said, "for your Eminence's extreme magnanimity. If all the members of my master's household should throw ashes upon their heads and dust upon their bodies, they could never repay such kindness."

The Imperial Tutor called for writing materials and filled up a blank warrant of appointment. Then he said to Laibao: "You two have brought me these presents at great inconvenience to yourselves. Who is that kneeling behind you?"

Laibao was about to say that this was his partner when Wu himself came forward and said that he was related to Ximen Qing, and that his name was Wu Dian'en.

"So you are related to Ximen Qing?" said the Imperial Tutor. "Well, you look a very respectable person." He called for another blank warrant and told Wu that he was appointing him an officer of the Imperial Post for the district of Qinghe. This made Wu so excited that, in his thanks, he beat his head upon the ground as though he were pounding garlic in a mortar. Upon another blank the Imperial Tutor inscribed the name of Laibao, appointing him tallyman at the palace of Duke Yun in Shandong.

They both kowtowed and thanked his Eminence, and the documents were handed to them. They were told that the next day they must go to the Boards of War and Civil Service, that their papers might be duly registered and their credentials made out, after which they should assume their offices in due course. Finally the Imperial Tutor instructed his Comptroller to entertain the two men with food and drink, and gave each of them ten taels of silver for traveling money.

In such manner was the administration brought into disrepute during the reign of the Emperor Huizong. Faithless ministers held posts of most responsibility, and the court was besieged by sycophants and men of deceit. Worst of all were Gao, Yang, Zong and Cai. Abusing their position at Court they bartered offices and accepted bribes for setting prisoners at liberty. The bribery was utterly barefaced. Appointments were given to men by the scales, and the price demanded was according to the rank of the appointment. Pushful men and those skilled in intrigue took hold upon all the offices of greatest worth, while those who were competent, wise, capable, and honest might wait for years, and still receive nothing.

Thus social morals became corrupt. Rapacious officials and their foul underlings overran the empire. Pressgangs and forced labor weighed heavily on the people. Taxation increased, so that the people were impoverished, and bandits and thieves multiplied. The Empire was completely demoralized. So, because of these faithless ministers and men in office, the people of the Middle Kingdom were drenched with blood.

Zhai took Laibao and Wu to a room at the side of the courtyard, and there entertained them so liberally that they had as much as they could eat. He said to Laibao: "I should very much like to ask a favor of your master, but I don't know whether he would care to do it or not."

"Uncle Zhai," Laibao said, "how can you say such a thing? You have done so much with his Eminence on my master's behalf that I am sure he will be only too glad to do anything you like to ask."

"I am always ready to do anything I can for him," Zhai said. "Now, I have only one wife, and I am getting on in years. My wife is always ill and she has not borne a child. What I should like to ask is this: if your master knows of a pretty girl about fifteen or sixteen years old, perhaps he will be good enough to send her to me. I will gladly pay whatever expenses he may be put to."

He gave Laibao a letter and some presents for Ximen Qing, and offered the two men each five taels of silver as traveling money. Laibao steadily refused to accept it. "We have had a present from his Eminence," he said, "so, Uncle Zhai, pray do not press this upon us."

The Comptroller insisted. "That was his Eminence's own affair," he said, "this is mine. Let us not stand too much on ceremony."

By this time they had finished their meal and Zhai told them that he would send someone to their inn who would accompany them next day to the Boards of War and Civil Service so that they might set their papers in order, and be able to start straight away without having to return to the Imperial Tutor's palace.

"The Boards will be more expeditious," he said, "if I send an order with you." He called an officer called Li Zhongyu and said to him: "Go with these two gentlemen to their respective Boards to register their appointments and secure the necessary papers. Then report to me."

Laibao and Wu Dian'en took leave of the Comptroller and left the palace with the officer. They went to a wineshop in the street near the Bridge of the Heavenly River, and there Laibao offered entertainment to Li Zhongyu, and gave him three taels of silver. They arranged that, next morning very early, they would go first to the Board of Civil Service and then to the Board of War. So indeed they did, registered their names and secured their papers, for, when the officers of these Boards knew that they had come from the Imperial Tutor's palace, they did not dare delay, but quickly prepared the documents, which were as quickly sealed by the responsible officer and sent down to the other part of the office. In two days everything was settled. Then Laibao and Wu Dian'en hired animals and set off as fast as they could to Qinghe, traveling day and night in their anxiety to tell the happy news.

One very hot day in the hottest part of summer, Ximen Qing was at home admiring the lotus flowers and drinking cooling wine in the great arbor. Wu Yueniang sat with him in the place of honor and the other ladies, with Ximen Dajie, sat on either side. Chunmei, Yingchun, Yuxiao and Lanxiang were there to sing and play for them.

The ladies were drinking together when they suddenly missed Li Ping'er. Yueniang said to her maid: "Why has your mistress gone to her room?"

"She has a pain and has gone to lie down," the maid told her.

"Go quickly," Yueniang said, "and tell her not to lie down there but to come and enjoy the music with us."

Ximen Qing asked Yueniang what she was saying, and she told him.

"Our sister is about eight months gone with child," she said to Meng Yulou, "and I don't wish her to do anything that may harm it."

Jinlian cried: "Oh, Great Sister, it is far from eight months yet." And Ximen Qing said:

"If her time is still some way off, we must send and tell her to come and listen to the music."

Soon Li Ping'er came back again. "You must not catch a chill," Yueniang said to her. "Drink a little warm wine and then you'll be all right."

Wine was poured for them all. Ximen Qing said to Chunmei: "Sing 'People All Dread the Summer Day' for me."

Chunmei and her companions had just touched the strings; they were opening their rosy lips and showing their white teeth, ready to begin: "All people . . . ," when Li Ping'er knitted her eyebrows in pain. She did not wait for the song to be finished, but went again to her room. Yueniang heard the song out, but she was uneasy about Li Ping'er and ordered Xiaoyu to go to her room. When the maid came back, she said that Li Ping'er was in severe pain and rolling about on the bed.

"I was sure her time had come," Yueniang said, excitedly, "and you said it was too soon. Send a boy to fetch the midwife."

Ximen Qing ordered Ping'an to run like the wind and fetch old woman Cai. They did not stay to finish their wine, but all went to the Sixth Lady's room.

"Sister," Yueniang said, "tell me how you feel."

"Great Sister, there is such a pain at the pit of my stomach and lower down that I feel as if all my insides were being dragged out of me."

"You had better get up," Yueniang urged. "Don't lie down any longer. It will not be good for the baby. I have sent for the midwife, and she will be here in a minute."

After a moment or two the pains grew worse and Yueniang asked anxiously: "Who has sent for the old woman? Why hasn't he come back?"

"Father told Laian to go," Daian said.

"You rascal," Yueniang cried. "Go and find him at once. What a silly thing to send a little slave on a business like this! Why, he doesn't know the difference between what is urgent and what is not."

"Get a mule quickly," Ximen Qing said to Daian, "and go yourself."

"Even when things are of the utmost urgency," Yueniang complained, "you go on in the same careless way."

Pan Jinlian was thoroughly annoyed when she realized that Li Ping'er was about to bear a child. She stayed in the room only a few minutes and then dragged Yulou out with her. They stood together beneath the eaves, where the breeze gave them a little coolness.

"How crowded it was in that room," Jinlian said, "it made the place so hot. Really, one would think they were watching an elephant laying galls, instead of an ordinary woman giving birth to an ordinary child."

At last Cai the midwife came. "Who is the mistress of the house?" she said.

"This is the Great Lady," Li Jiao'er said, indicating Yueniang.

The old woman knelt down and kowtowed, but Yueniang told her to waste no time on ceremony. "Why have you been so long?" she said.

"Kindly come and examine your patient at once."

The midwife went to the bed and carefully examined Li Ping'er. Then she said: "The time has come. Great Lady, have you got ready the paper that will be needed when the child is born?"

"Yes," Yueniang said. She sent Xiaoyu to bring what was needed.

When the midwife came, Yulou said to Jinlian: "Here is the midwife. Let us go in." But Jinlian would not. "If you wish to see," she said, "go by yourself. I don't want to have anything to do with it. She is going to have a child and she is a favored person in consequence. I don't want to see her. I said that I did not think she had reached the time, and the Great Lady was furious with me. Whenever I think about it, it makes me wild."

"I said I thought it was the sixth month," Yulou said.

"Then you are a fool too," Jinlian said. "Let me see. It was the eighth month of last year when she first came here. She was not a virgin. She married after her husband's death and did not remain any too chaste. She may have been gotten with child two or three months before she came here. Yet they are all quite sure that this child belongs to the family. What I say is: if this really is an eighth-month baby, it may possibly bear some resemblance to our family. But if it is a sixth-month child, even if we get upon a bench to make a god, we still can't get near it by a head. But when a young animal once gets away from its native place, there's no tracing it."

As they were talking, Xiaoyu came bringing paper bandages and tiny bedclothes. "These are things the Great Lady prepared for her own use," Yulou said, "now she is giving them to the Sixth Lady."

"Oh," Jinlian said, "one is great and one is small. They seem to have a competition in this baby getting. Rather than produce nothing they would be satisfied with any bit of rubbish. I'm one of those hens that never lays an egg, yet does anybody dare to eat me? Look at them there, stretching and pulling, like a dog gnawing at a bladder. All this fuss and delight over nothing at all."

"What are you saying, Fifth Sister?" said Yulou. But Jinlian did not answer. She hung down her head and played with the ribbons on her skirt. Xue'e, who had heard that Li Ping'er was about to bear a child, came bustling over from the back court, hurrying so that she did not notice the step and nearly fell down.

"Look at that little toady," Jinlian said. "Why can't she walk decently instead of dashing along like that? She might be running for her life. If she falls down and knocks her teeth out, it will cost some money. Just because the Sixth Lady has a baby, one would imagine this wretched woman would get a ceremonial hat."

At last, the sound of a cry came to them from the room. The midwife said someone must tell the master to get ready a present for her, because the lady had borne a son. Then Yueniang took word to Ximen Qing, who quickly washed his hands and burned incense in a full burner before the shrine of Heaven and Earth and of his Ancestors, and vowed that he would offer a solemn thanksgiving of a hundred and twenty degrees, with prayers for the happiness and prosperity of mother and child, and that the birth might be without danger and accompanied by good fortune.

Now that Jinlian knew that the child was born and saw everyone in the household happily engaged about the mother and the child, she became angrier still, went to her own apartments, shut the door, threw herself upon the bed and began to sob. It was the twenty-third day of the sixth month, in the fourth year of the reign period Zhenghe.

Madam Cai washed the child, cut the navel string, disposed of the after-birth, and then prepared soothing medicine for Li Ping'er. When all was done, Yueniang invited her to go to the inner court for refreshments. As she was about to go away, Ximen Qing gave her a piece of silver weighing five taels and promised that when she came again on the third day she should have a roll of silk. The old woman thanked him effusively and went away.

Ximen went to see the baby. It was very dainty and white, and he was delighted with his son. The whole household was elated. He spent that night in the apartments of Li Ping'er, and it seemed as though he could not take his eyes off his son. Before dawn he rose, had ten boxes made ready, and sent the boys to his neighbors and kinsmen with the noodles of good fortune.

As soon as Ying Bojue and Xie Xida received theirs and so learned that Ximen Qing had a son and heir, they set off, taking two steps in one, to offer their congratulations. Ximen entertained them in the arbor. When they had gone, he was about to send one of the boys to find a nurse, when old woman Xue came to introduce one. This was a woman of low degree, about thirty years old, who had lost her own child not a month before. Her husband was a poor soldier who was afraid that when he went to the wars there would be no one to look after his wife. He wanted no more than six taels of silver for her. Yueniang decided that the woman was clean and asked Ximen to pay the six taels and give her the charge of the newly born child. She was called Ruyi'er. Afterwards they sent for old woman Feng to work for Li Ping'er, promising her five *qian* of silver every month, besides her clothes.

They were all very busy when suddenly Ping'an came and told them that Laibao and Wu Dian'en had returned from the Eastern Capital. They were at the gate and had just dismounted. Soon they came in with the good news for Ximen Qing. When he questioned them, they told him all that had happened on their journey, and how the Imperial Tutor had given appointments not only to Ximen Qing but to themselves. Laibao produced the sealed documents that they had brought from the Boards of Civil Service and of War and laid them on the table.

Ximen Qing saw that there were many seals upon the papers, and it was clear that they had come from the court. He had been made a Deputy Captain. His brow lighted up and his face beamed. He took the document to show Yueniang and the others.

"The Imperial Tutor has been good enough to raise me to the position of a Deputy Captain, which is an appointment of the fifth grade," he said. "So now you are a real lady and must wear the ceremonial dress of your rank."

He told them also about the appointments that had been given to Laibao and Wu Dian'en. "Wu the Immortal," he said, "told us that I should be given a hat of ceremony and have the good fortune to rise from the ground to the clouds. Not more than half a month has gone by and two of his prophecies have come true already."

"The Sixth Lady has this boy," he said to Yueniang, "and he seems to be a good solid lad. After his washing on the third day, we will call him Guan'ge."

Laibao came in and kowtowed to Yueniang and the others. Ximen Qing told him to take the documents to Magistrate Xia the next day and told Wu to go to the town Hall. Then Laibao took leave of his master and went home.

The next day was the day for the solemn washing of the child. The neighbors and relatives all heard that Ximen Qing's wife had borne him a son and that he had been raised to official rank and they came, one and all, to offer their congratulations. All day long, people came and went without ceasing. As the proverb says: When fortune favors a man, so do other men; but when fortune departs, his friends depart too.

# CHAPTER 31

# Qintong Hides a Wine Pot

The next day Ximen Qing sent Laibao with the documents to the magistrate's court, and had a hat of ceremony made for himself. Then he sent for Zhao the tailor and gave him orders to make a colored cloak as quickly as possible. Several men were set to making girdles of office. That day Wu Dian'en went to call upon Ying Bojue and told him all about the appointment he had received. He begged Bojue to borrow some money for him from Ximen Qing so that he could expend whatever was necessary at his office. He promised to give Bojue ten taels for himself. So eager was he, that he knelt down before Bojue. Ying hastily raised him to his feet. "What could be more pleasant," he said, "than to do things for others? Thanks to Ximen's generosity, you have acquired this position, and this is no ordinary occasion. How much will you need?"

"I must own to you," Wu Dian'en said, "that, though my household manages to keep going, I have not a penny to spare. I shall have to give presents to my superiors in office and there must be a banquet. I shall need clothes and a horse. All this will cost seventy or eighty taels at least. I have made out a note, but without stating any definite amount. Do help me and I promise you shall be well repaid."

Ying Bojue looked at the note. "Brother Wu," he said, "I can't believe this is enough. You had better make it a hundred. I am sure that if I ask him, Master Ximen will not require interest from you, and you can pay him back in installments when you have taken up your duties. You will remember the proverb: Borrowed rice may be stored in the jar, but rice that has been begged will never find its way there."

Wu thanked his friend effusively and wrote a hundred taels upon the note of hand. They had tea and set off together to call upon Ximen Qing. Ping'an announced them, and as they went in they saw the tailors busy at their work. The Deputy Captain and his son-in-law were sitting under the eaves, watching a clerk writing visiting cards. The two visitors greeted them and then sat down to talk.

"Brother," Bojue said, "have you sent your papers to the office?"

"Yes," Ximen said, "I sent them to the courts this morning, and now

I am arranging for Ben the Fourth to take my card to the Prefecture at Dongping Fu and the District office here."

A boy brought tea. Bojue did not at once mention the business about which he had come, but went to watch the tailors at work upon the girdles. Ximen Qing saw him taking them in his hands and said with great pride: "What do you think of my new girdles?"

Bojue praised them: "Wherever did you get them, Brother? Each one seems to excel the other. Buckles as fine as these are not to be met with every day. And this rhinoceros horn; this button shaped like a stork's head! Why, you might take your money in your hand all around the Eastern Capital, and never be able to find anything like it. This is not flattery. Princes and nobles in the Capital have their girdles of jade and gold, but you would never find them with one of rhinoceros horn so good as this. And not the land rhinoceros ... this is the water kind, and ever so much more valuable. You know, the water rhinoceros they call *Tong Tian*. If you don't believe me, give me a cup of water. I will put the horn into it and you will see that it divides the water into two parts. It is indeed a priceless treasure. How much did you pay for it, Brother?"

Ximen Qing invited him to guess the price, but Bojue declared that such things had no definite price, and he could not possibly guess.

"I will tell you," Ximen Qing said. "It comes from the palace of the princely family Wang in the High Street. Yesterday someone heard that I was wanting a girdle and came to tell me about it. I sent Ben the Fourth, with seventy taels, to buy it, but they would not part with it for less than a hundred."

"Well," Ying Bojue said, "it would be a very difficult matter to find another so fine and beautiful. You will certainly look very grand when you go out in it, and your colleagues at the courts will fall in love with it." He went on in this strain for a long time and finally sat down.

"Have you taken your papers?" Ximen Qing said to Wu. Ying Bojue answered for him. "It was precisely because Brother Wu wishes to do so that he asked me to come here and trouble you. How extraordinarily kind to him you have been! You sent him to the Eastern Capital, and, though his appointment was actually given him by the Imperial Tutor, it really comes to him from you. It was a real piece of good luck. Whether he belongs to the first grade or the ninth, he is none the less an officer of the Court now. He has just told me that he wants to go to his office to make the acquaintance of his colleagues, but it will cost a lot of money to offer them a banquet and he doesn't know where to get it. One guest, Brother, does not inflict himself upon two hosts. For my sake, I want you to lend him a few taels so that he can enter upon his duties. Later, when he has taken up his appointment, there will be nothing too much for him to do for you. He has served your family long and well.

Brother, you help many people in the Capital and elsewhere. If you will do nothing for him, it will be very awkward indeed for him."

He turned to Wu. "Brother Wu, bring out that charm of yours, and let his Lordship see it."

Wu Dian'en quickly drew out the paper and handed it to Ximen Qing. The sum of a hundred taels was mentioned, Ying Bojue's name appeared as witness, and interest was promised at the rate of five percent each month. Ximen took a pen and crossed out the part about the interest. "Since Brother Ying is the witness," he said, "I shall not ask you to do more than repay the hundred taels. I had thought you would need some money." He put the document in his sleeve.

As he was about to go to the inner court to get the money, there came an underling with a card from Magistrate Xia. He sent twelve soldiers to await Ximen's orders. The clerk asked when Ximen Qing proposed to enter upon his duties and what titles he would use. All the officials of the district were anxious to come and to congratulate him, and bring their present. Ximen sent for the Master of the Yin Yang, asked him to find a suitable date, and it was arranged that upon the morning of the second day of the seventh month he should take possession of his office. Ximen sent a card in return to the magistrate, gave five *qian* of silver to the underling, and sent him back again.

Chen Jingji brought a hundred taels and Ximen handed them to Wu Dian'en, saying: "Brother, take this and repay me." Wu Dian'en took the money and kowtowed. "I will not detain you," Ximen Qing said, "you have business of your own to attend to. But, Brother Ying, I have something to say to you."

Wu Dian'en went happily away with his money.

Ben the Fourth, who had been to the office at Dongping Fu, now came back and Ximen invited him to take a meal with them. Besides Ying Bojue, Xu the Master of the Yin Yang was there. While they were eating, Uncle Wu came to congratulate Ximen Qing. Then the Master of the Yin Yang took his leave, and, shortly afterwards, Ying Bojue also went away. He went straight to see Wu Dian'en, who had ten taels of silver ready waiting for him. He held it out with both hands. "If it had not been for the clever way you spoke for me," he said, "he might never have lent me this money." Then he set about making his robes of ceremony and selected a day on which to assume office.

Li, one of the magistrates of the district, now joined with his colleagues in sending a present of sheep, wine and other things to Ximen Qing. In addition, he sent with his card a youth about eighteen years of age. This was a native of Changshou in Xuzhou, and his name was Little Zhang Song.

He had been one of the boys who waited upon the district officers. He was clear-skinned and good-looking. His face was white like powder, his teeth glistened, and his lips were red. He could read, write, and sing the songs of the south. He was wearing a gown of black silk with light shoes and white socks. Ximen Qing was very pleased to discover such an accomplished young man, and, sending a card of thanks to the magistrate, he at once took the boy into his service. He called him Shutong, and had new clothes, shoes, and a hat made for him. He decided that he would not have the young man to follow his horse like the other boys, but would use him rather as a secretary to take charge of his study, receive presents when they came, and take charge of the keys of the pavilions in the garden.

Zhu Shinian also recommended a boy to him. This one was only fourteen years old. Ximen Qing called him Qitong and appointed him to carry his visiting card case, and parcels, and to follow behind the horse with Qintong.

At last the day came when he was formally to take up his duties. A great banquet was given at the office and musicians were engaged from three of the bawdy houses. The party went on all day until sunset.

After this, Ximen Qing rode out every day upon a big white horse. He wore a black ceremonial hat and a robe of office with long-maned lions embroidered in five colors upon it. A girdle, four fingers broad, encircled his waist, and his feet were shod in white-soled boots. An escort of soldiers accompanied him and a large black fan was borne behind him. Men went before him, shouting to clear the way; others followed close upon his horse's heels. No less than ten were in attendance upon him. Up and down the streets he went.

As soon as he had left the office he went to see the Captain of the garrison and the various official personages of Qinghe. Then it was the turn of his kinsmen, friends and neighbors. It was a glorious occasion. Meanwhile, presents and visiting cards came to his house in shoals.

Now that he had definitely entered upon his duties, he went every day to the courts and took his seat in the great hall. There he examined official documents and attended to official business. The time passed very quickly.

Li Ping'er was now able to get up. Many ladies, both relatives and friends of the household, came with presents to celebrate the completion of the baby's first month of life. Li Guijie and Wu Yin'er, who had heard of Ximen's good fortune, made ready presents and came in their sedan chairs to congratulate him. Ximen Qing had a splendid feast prepared in the front hall for the ladies. Chunmei, Yingchun, Yuxiao and Lanxiang, all dressed in their most beautiful attire, served wine to the guests.

Every day as soon as Ximen Qing returned from the office, he took off his robes in the outer hall and Shutong took them, folded them, and put them away in the study. When he went to the inner court, he only kept on his hat. In the morning, he used to send a maid to the study to bring the clothes. A room at the side of the great hall had been specially arranged to serve him as a private room. There a bed, tables both large and small, chairs, screens, curtains, writing materials and books were set out, and, every night, Shutong slept at the foot of the bed. When Ximen slept in this room, he would send a maid in the morning to bring his clothes from the outer court. So, with all this sending backwards and forwards of clothes, Shutong, who was of very doubtful antecedents besides being taking in his ways and good looking, found plenty of opportunity to play tricks upon the maids from all the different rooms, and in particular, became a close friend of Yuxiao.

One day when this young man had just got up and was dressing his hair with red ribbon before a mirror on the windowsill, Yuxiao opened the door and came in. She saw that he was dressing his hair. "Ah, you young rascal," she said, "so you are still painting your eyebrows and your eyes. Father will be here as soon as he has finished breakfast."

Shutong paid no attention to her but went on dressing his hair.

"Where are Father's clothes?" she asked.

"By the side of the bed," the boy said.

"No, this is not the suit he wants today. He told me to ask you for the robe of black silk with the gold and embroidery down the front."

"They are in the cupboard," Shutong said, "I put them there only yesterday, and now he wants them again. Open the cupboard and get them yourself."

Yuxiao did not get the clothes. Instead she went over to the young man and watched him dressing his hair. "You funny thing," she said jokingly, "you are like a woman, putting red ribbons in your hair and making quite a headdress." She noticed that he was wearing a short coat of white material with two satchels for perfume, one of pink and one of green silk. "Give me the pink one," she said.

"You always want those things that people care most about," Shutong said.

"But you are a boy, and shouldn't wear such things," the maid said. "That pink one is much more suitable for me."

"That," Shutong cried, "is only a bag. What would you think if it were a husband?"

Yuxiao pinched him on the shoulder. "You young scamp," she said, "do not try to palm off your picture of the god of the door as if it were a genuine work of art." Without more ado, she broke the cord that held the two perfume bags and put them in her sleeve.

"Really," Shutong said, "your behavior is hardly becoming. You have broken my girdle."

Yuxiao slapped him playfully, but the young man was a little put out. "Sister," he said, "please do not play with me. I must finish doing my hair."

"Tell me," Yuxiao said, "have you heard where Father is going today?"

"Yes," the boy said, "he is going to say good-bye to Master Hua, the Deputy Assistant Magistrate for the district, for whom a farewell banquet is being given at Eunuch Xue's house. I expect he will be fairly late coming back as he is also going to Uncle Ying's to see about the payment for Master Qiao's house across the way. I should not be surprised if he drank wine there too."

"Well," Yuxiao said, "don't you go out. I may come and have a talk with you."

Yuxiao took the clothes, and went to the inner court.

Some time later Ximen Qing came. He told Shutong that he must not leave the house that day, and that he must write out twelve cards of invitation and put them in red envelopes. These invitations were all for gentlemen to come and celebrate Guan'ge's first month of life. Before he went out, Ximen Qing told Laixing to make all the necessary purchases, to engage extra cooks and, indeed, to do everything that was necessary. Daian and two soldiers were ordered to take out the invitations, and to engage singers. Qintong was to serve the guests with wine. After giving all these orders, Ximen Qing mounted his horse and set out.

Today was the ladies' party. Yueniang and her companions received their guests in the arbor. Tea was served there. The banquet was laid in the great hall, where gorgeous screens were set out, and cushions embroidered with lotus flowers. The four maids who were trained in music were told to be in attendance.

As soon as Ximen Qing returned in the afternoon, he had a box of wine and refreshments prepared, and asked Ying Bojue and Chen Jingji to go with him to Master Qiao's house, where he was to take seven hundred taels.

While the ladies were drinking, Yuxiao took a silver wine jar, a cup, and some pears, and went with them to the study. She expected to find Shutong. But when she opened the door, Shutong was not to be seen. She was afraid that someone might see her, so she quietly put down the things and slipped out again. Qintong, who was attending to the wine for the guests, saw her with his sharp eyes. He saw her go to the study and come back again. He thought that Shutong was there and ran to see him, but the young secretary, of course, was not there. Qintong spied a jar of warmed wine and some fruit at the foot of the bed. He hastily put the fruit into his sleeves, and, picking up the jar of wine, quietly made off with it to the Sixth Lady's room. The nurse Ruyi'er and Xiuchun were looking after the baby. Qintong asked where Yingchun was.

"She is serving wine in the hall," Xiuchun said. "What do you want with her?"

"I have something good here," Qintong said. "I want her to keep it for me."

"What is it?" Xiuchun said, but the boy would not show her.

At that moment, Yingchun came from the hall bringing a plate of hot goose and cakes made of rice flower and almonds for the nurse.

"What are you doing here, you young rascal?" she said. 'You ought to be attending to your duties in the hall."

Qintong brought the wine jar from under his clothes. "Sister," he said, "please keep this for me."

"But this is the jar we use for heating wine in the hall," Yingchun said. "Why did you bring it here?"

"Sister," the boy said, "Yuxiao took it to the study for Shutong. She stole it and some pears and took them to him, but, when there was nobody about, I slipped in and took it. I want you to keep it for me, and if anybody comes looking for it, let them go away without it. It was a real piece of good luck for me." He showed the pears and oranges to Yingchun.

"Well," Yingchun said, "if anybody starts looking for this jar and there is trouble about it, it will be your lookout."

"I didn't steal it," Qintong said. "There's no reason why I should be worried. Let those who did steal it be alarmed. I am out of it. It won't be my legs that get the beating." He went away in a most cheerful frame of mind. Yingchun put the wine jar on a table.

In the evening when the guests had all gone, the silver was checked and one wine jar was missed. Yuxiao went to the study to look for it, but it was nowhere to be found. When she asked Shutong, he said he knew nothing about it and that he had not been there. Then the trouble began. Yuxiao accused Xiaoyu, and Xiaoyu cursed her. "You silly strumpet," she cried, "I was making tea all the time. You were serving wine. If the jar is lost, what has it to do with me?" They looked everywhere, but still it could not be found.

When Li Ping'er went to her room, Yingchun told her that Qintong had brought the jar there and asked her to keep it for him.

"The young rascal!" Li Ping'er cried. "Whatever made him bring it here? There is a terrible fuss in the inner court about it. Yuxiao says it is Xiaoyu's fault, and Xiaoyu says it is Yuxiao's fault, and Yuxiao is taking all sorts of oaths and crying. You had better take it back at once or all the blame will be put on you."

While Yingchun was on her way to take the jar back to the inner court, Yuxiao and Xiaoyu had gone to see Yueniang, both talking away at one another as hard as they could.

"What," cried Yueniang, "are you still shouting? What were you doing to lose the jar?"

"I was serving wine in the hall," Yuxiao said, "and she was in charge of all the silver. Yet now the jar has been lost she says it is my fault."

"No," Xiaoyu said, "Aunt wanted tea, and I went to the inner court to take her some. You had the wine jar when it was lost. Your brains must have gone the way your dinner goes.

"There were no light-fingered people at today's party," Yueniang said. "Why should we lose a wine jar? We must wait till your master returns. When he hears what has been lost, certainly you will both get a beating."

In the middle of the squabble, Ximen Qing came in. He asked what the fuss was about, and Yueniang told him of the lost wine jar.

"You should keep calm," said Ximen. "What need is there for all this excitement?"

Jinlian interrupted. "If one jar is lost every time we have a party," she said, "you may be as rich as Wang the Millionaire, but you'll find that the early promise you seem to expect is not fulfilled."

In this way Jinlian was trying to be unpleasant. Li Ping'er had just borne a child and the losing of a wine jar at this particular time was of ill omen. Ximen Qing understood quite well what she meant, but he said nothing. Then Yingchun came in with the jar, and Yuxiao recognized it at once. When Yueniang asked where it had come from, Yingchun told them that Qintong had brought it to her mistress's room, but she did not know where he had found it. Yueniang asked where the boy was. Daian told her that it was his turn to go to the house in Lion Street, and he was there.

Jinlian sneered, and Ximen Qing asked what she was sneering about.

"Qintong," she said, "is one of her household, so it is natural that he should take the jar to her room. It must be plain to you what the jar was doing there. If I were you, I should send a boy to fetch that young slave, and beat him till the truth about the matter comes to light. If we blame these two maids, we shall be missing the mark completely."

This made Ximen Qing extremely angry. He glared at Jinlian. "I suppose you think the Sixth Lady coveted this jar for herself. Well, here it is. Let that be the end of the business. What need is there for you to try to make trouble?"

Jinlian flushed. "I didn't mean anything," she said. She went away in a very bad temper. When Chen Jingji came to discuss some business with Ximen Qing, she stood and talked bitterly with Meng Yulou.

"They will come to a bad end," she stormed. "The place is full of rogues and thieves. Why, she might have been going to die the other day. Now that she has this baby, she gives herself such airs one would think she had given birth to a prince. She looks like the goddess of Good Fortune whenever she meets us. She is too grand to condescend even to speak to us. And when she moves about, she opens her eyes as wide as two cunts and yells at everyone. We know she is rich. It seems to me she allows her boys and maids to carry on as they please, and if they rob all the rest of the household no one will hinder them."

Ximen Qing, who had finished talking to Jingji, went in the direction of the front court.

"You had better go," Yulou said. "He seems to be going to your room."

"Surely not," Jinlian said. "He finds it much pleasanter where the baby is. It is so cheerless where there is no baby."

At that moment, Chunmei came. "I told you he was going to your room," Yulou said, "and you wouldn't believe me. Now here is Chunmei come to fetch you!"

They called Chunmei and questioned her.

"I have come to ask Yuxiao for a handkerchief," she said.

"Where is your master?" Yulou said.

"He has gone to the Sixth Lady's room."

When Jinlian heard this, she became furiously angry. "The rogue," she cried. "May his legs be broken for a thousand years, and until the end of time he shall never cross my threshold again. May the rascal break the bones of his ankles."

"Why do you use these horrid words about him today?" Yulou said.

"You don't know that cheap bandit," Jinlian cried. "His mind is like a rat's belly, and his guts like a chicken's, not more than three inches long. We are all his wives. Why should he save all his favor for a woman who brings forth a seed wrapped in a bladder? Why should he raise one so high and kick the others into the mud?"

When Ximen Qing had gone to the front court, Eunuch Xue's servant came with a jar of rice wine, a sheep, two rolls of silk, a dish of lucky noodles and a dish of peaches. These were gifts to congratulate Ximen on the birth of his son, and his new appointment. Ximen gave a considerable present to the servant and dismissed him. Then he went to the inner court. Guijie and Wu Yin'er were about to go home. He asked them to stay.

"I have invited a number of gentlemen for the celebration," he said, "and there will be several performers of different kinds. I should like you two to serve the wine."

"If you wish us to stay," Guijie said, "I must arrange for someone to let my mother know so that she will not be anxious about us." Then she dismissed the two chair men.

The following day, the great hall was made ready for the feast. Silken screens were placed in position and embroidered cushions set around. Some time before, Ximen had made the acquaintance of Eunuch Liu, the controller of an Imperial brick manufactory. Both Liu and Xue had sent him presents, and Ximen, in return, had sent them cards of invitation. He had also asked Ying Bojue and Xie Xida to come and help him receive the guests. The two friends, dressed in suitable attire, came about dinnertime, and Ximen Qing asked them to sit down in the arbor and have tea.

"Whom have you invited today?" Ying Bojue said.

Ximen told them. "The two eunuchs Liu and Xue, Major Zhou, Jing Nanjiang, my colleagues, Magistrate Xia, Captain Zhang of the Militia and Captain Fan. My two brothers-in-law will be there too. Master Qiao has sent a man to say that he will not be able to come, so that, even including yourselves, there will be only a few guests."

The two Uncles Wu arrived. After greetings had been exchanged they all sat down. The servants set a table and served them with food.

When they had finished, Bojue said: "Has your young son been out yet, now that he is a month old?"

"Well," Ximen said, "the ladies were all anxious to see him. My wife thought we ought not to take him out lest he should catch cold, but the nurse said she did not think it would do him any harm, so he was wrapped up in a blanket and taken to my wife's room. This was just so that the day might be duly celebrated. He was taken back immediately."

"The other day," Bojue said, "you were good enough to send us an invitation, and my wife would have liked very much to come, but, unfortunately, she had a return of her old illness and could not get up. She was very upset about it, and before the guests arrive I take this opportunity of apologizing on her behalf. Won't you have your son brought here so that we may have a look at him?"

Ximen Qing sent word to the inner court that the baby was to be brought, but very carefully lest he should be frightened. "His two uncles are here," he said, "and also Brothers Ying and Xie, and they are anxious to see him."

Wu Yueniang bade the nurse Ruyi'er wrap the baby in a tiny shawl of fine red silk and take him to the corner door. There Daian received him and carried him to the arbor. They all looked at him. Guan'ge was dressed in a scarlet woolen vest. His skin was clear and his lips were red. He looked healthy. The guests paid him all sorts of compliments. The two Uncles Wu and Xie Xida each presented him with a stomach protector of figured satin with a small silver pendant attached. Ying Bojue had nothing better than a skein of five-colored threads and a few lucky coins. These things were all solemnly given to Daian for the child, and he was told to take Guan'ge back very carefully and be sure not to frighten him.

"The child looks very dignified and upstanding," said Ying Bojue. "He is obviously born to wear a hat of ceremony."

This pleased Ximen Qing immensely. He bowed in thanks to Ying Bojue.

Then news was brought that the two eunuchs had arrived. Ximen hastily put on his robes and went to the second door to welcome them. They were waiting, each in a sedan chair carried by four men. They were wearing robes with embroidered dragons, and were accompanied by a bodyguard with tasseled spears to clear the way. Ximen Qing asked them to go with him to the great hall. There he greeted them and offered tea. Then Major Zhou, Master Jing, Xia and the other military gentlemen arrived, all wearing their embroidered robes, with men attending them bearing staves and large fans, and runners shouting to clear the way. In a moment there was a crowd of attendants about the gate. Inside the courtyard there was a deafening sound of drums and instruments, and a never-ending succession of melodies and songs. Ximen Qing welcomed them in turn and introduced them to the two eunuchs Liu and Xue. At the upper end of the hall were twelve tables, and Ximen Qing, taking up a wine cup, prepared to put the guests in their proper places. The two eunuchs, Liu and Xue, repeatedly refused to take the places of honor. "Let others take them," they said. Major Zhou insisted that they should do so. "Most Worshipful Sirs," he said, "your age and dignity demand respect. As the proverb says: to be a Chamberlain at the Imperial Court for the space of three years confers more dignity than a barony. Obviously then, you must take the place of honor at once, and stand on ceremony no longer."

The two old gentlemen disputed for a long time over the first place. At last Xue said: "Brother Liu, since the other gentlemen will not take the upper seat, we must not be a nuisance to our host. Let us sit down."

They bowed politely to the guests. Liu took the left-hand place and Xue the right. Each placed a handkerchief on his knees and had a small boy to stand beside and fan him. When they had seated themselves, the others did so. Then the music blared in the courtyard, and food, exquisite and rare beyond description, was set before the guests. After the wine had gone around five times and three soup courses had been served, a troop of actors began their performance.

After the comedies, the two young singers, Li Ming and Wu Hui, came forward, one with a dulcimer, the other with a lute. Major Zhou raised his hand. "Most Worshipful Sirs," he said to the two eunuchs, "will you not tell these singers what songs they shall sing?"

"But only," Liu said, "when you have made your own choice."

"No," Major Zhou said, "it is right and fitting that you should give your orders first. Pray do not stand on ceremony."

"Well," Liu said, "I should like to hear 'Life Is Like a Dream.'"

Major Zhou demurred. "That is a song," he said, "for those who have withdrawn from the world and are weary of its enjoyments. This is a happy occasion for our excellent host Ximen. We are celebrating the birth of his son, and I really don't think it is suitable."

Liu tried again. "Can you sing," he asked the boys, "'Though He Is Not a Purple-girdled Minister of the First Eight Grades, He Governs the Young Ladies Who Wear Golden Pins in the Six Palaces'?"

Major Zhou objected again. "That alludes to Chen Lin and the dressing box, and is not suitable for an occasion like this."

"Send the two singers to me," Xue said, "and I will choose a song. Do you remember 'The World Is Full of Merriment, Yet Separation Is the Bitterest of All Life's Troubles'?"

Xia burst out laughing. "Most Worshipful Sir," he said, "that is worse still, for it speaks of separation."

"Well," Xue said, "we officials of the court are so wrapped up in our duties towards his Majesty that perhaps we don't know very much about songs and melodies. Let them sing what they like."

Xia, who was a magistrate and enjoyed such authority as a magistrate may claim, took advantage of his position and called for the thirty melodies. "Today," he said, "we are celebrating Master Ximen's appointment and at the same time the birth of his son. So let us have the song of the toy scepter."

"Why do you mention a 'toy scepter'?" Eunuch Xue said.

"Oh, Most Worshipful Sirs," Major Zhou said. "today our host's son is a month old. We have all been offering a little present in honor of the occasion."

"Is that so?" Xue said. "Brother Liu, we shall have to send a present tomorrow."

Ximen Qing thanked them. "This ignorant fellow has but a little dog. The occasion is not worthy of such honor, and I beg you not to trouble yourselves."

Daian was sent to the inner court to summon Wu Yin'er and Guijie to serve the wine. The two singing girls, as dainty as the flowers on the branches of a tree, kowtowed four times like a pair of candles. They took the wine jar and served wine to everyone and the two young musicians sang a new song. So delicate were their throats and so flexible, their voices echoed through the rafters.

That night with dancing and singing they enjoyed themselves immensely, and drank until the first watch of the night. Then Eunuch Xue stood up. "You have been exceedingly kind," he said, "and as this was a special occasion, we felt we ought to stay and enjoy ourselves, but now we must have outstayed our welcome and we will go."

"I have offered you the meanest of entertainments," Ximen said, "but you have condescended to visit me and my poor house has been illumined by your presence. I beg you, stay a little longer that my happiness may be complete." All the guests rose. "You have been extremely kind," they said, "but we really can drink no more wine." They bowed to Ximen Qing and thanked him. Ximen repeatedly urged them to stay, but in vain. So with his two brothers-in-law, he escorted them to the gate. The music rose to the skies, and outside the gateway on both sides, torches and lanterns blazed. The guests went away with men going before to guide them and men going behind to protect them. There was much shouting to clear the way.

# CHAPTER 32
# Li Guijie

After drinking their fill, the principal guests had gone away. Ximen Qing, however, pressed the two Uncles Wu, Ying Bojue and Xie Xida to remain. He told the musicians to go for their refreshment, bidding them come again next day. "I am entertaining the gentlemen from the District offices," he said, "and you must put on your best clothes. I will pay you for everything tomorrow."

The musicians answered: "Your servants will take the utmost care, and tomorrow we will dress ourselves in new clothes of the official type." They had food and wine, then kowtowed and went away. Soon afterwards, Li Guijie and Wu Yin'er came in side by side. They smiled and said: "Father, it is late and our sedan chairs have come for us. We must go."

"My children," Ying Bojue said, "your audacity surprises me. Here are two very worthy gentlemen, but instead of singing for them you just go off."

"Oh yes," said Guijie, "you would talk like that. We haven't been home for two days and mother will be wondering what has become of us."

"Why should she worry?" Bojue cried, "that yellow jade-colored old plum with a piece bitten out of her!"

"That is enough!" Ximen said, "let them go. They have had to work very hard these last few days. Li Ming and Wu Hui shall sing for us." He asked the two girls if they had had anything to eat. Guijie told him that Yueniang had given them refreshments. When they had kowtowed and were about to go away, Ximen Qing said: "I shall expect you the day after tomorrow. Bring another two girls with you. Han Jinchuan and Zheng Aixiang will do. I am inviting a few relatives and friends to dinner."

"You are lucky, you little strumpet," cried Ying Bojue, "you get away and do well out of it."

"I wonder what it is that makes you so clever," Guijie said. They laughed and went away.

"Whom are you going to invite, Brother?" Bojue said to Ximen Qing.

"Master Qiao, the two Uncles Wu, Brother Hua, Uncle Shen and the members of our brotherhood. We will spend the whole day enjoying ourselves."

"Though I realize that I am troubling you too greatly, "Bojue said, "I will come to assist you in receiving the guests."

Ximen Qing thanked him. Then Li Ming and Wu Hui came with their instruments and sang a few songs. Finally the men all went away.

The day when Ximen Qing had invited the officers from the District offices, Eunuch Xue was one of the first to arrive. Ximen offered him tea in the arbor. The eunuch asked whether his colleague Liu had sent a present. Then he asked to see the child that he might give him his blessing. Ximen Qing modestly deprecated such an honor, but at last told Daian to go to the inner court for the baby. The nurse brought the child to the corner gate where Daian received him and brought him to them. Xue looked at Guan'ge and praised him. "A very fine child!" he said. He called for his attendants. Two servants, dressed in black, brought a square gilt box, and from it took two packets of gifts. There was a length of royal silk, a roll of watered red silk, and four silver gilt coins, each with one of the lucky characters upon it: Good Fortune, Long Life, Health, and Peace. There was a small *Bo Lang* drum, painted in gold and various colors, and a set of amulets. "I am only a poor eunuch," he said, "and have nothing worth offering, but these trifles may serve to amuse your son."

Ximen Qing made a reverence to the eunuch and thanked him very heartily. When they had drunk tea, refreshments were served, but, before they had finished them, the expected guests were announced. Ximen Qing put straight his robes and went to the second door to welcome them. These were District Magistrate Li Datian, Assistant District Magistrate Qian Zheng, Chief Secretary Ren Tinggui, and Prison Governor Xia Tianji. They presented their cards and then went to the hall and greeted their host. Ximen asked Eunuch Xue to come and meet his guests, and the officers insisted that the old man should take the seat of honor. Among the guests was a graduate of the second degree named Shang.

When they had all taken their proper places, tea was served. After a while the sound of drums and music was heard in the courtyard. The actors came to offer wine to the chief guest and showed him their repertory. Eunuch Xue looked at it and bade them sing the song of Han Xiangzi attaining immortality. They danced to accompany this song. The performance was excellent. The eunuch was pleased and told his servant to give the musicians two strings of money. The party was very successful and did not break up until late.

Guijie went home. Now that Ximen Qing was an officer, she and her mother thought of a scheme for taking advantage of the situation. They bought four different kinds of presents and Guijie made a pair of shoes. The next day, she told her servant to put them in a box and, very early in the morning, got into a sedan chair and set off to ask Yueniang to accept her as a ward. She went in smiling, and kowtowed four times to Wu Yueniang, then to her and Ximen Qing together. Yueniang was greatly flattered.

"Only the other day," she said, "your mother sent me a valuable present and now you have gone to all this trouble to buy expensive gifts for me."

Guijie smiled. "Mother says that now his Lordship is an officer, of course he will not be able to come so often to see her. I have come to offer myself as his adopted daughter. Then there will be no difficulty about my coming here because we shall be relatives."

Yueniang told her to take off her long cloak and asked why Wu Yin'er and the others had not come with her.

"I spoke to Wu Yin'er about it yesterday," Guijie said. "I can't understand why she has not come. The other day, Father told me to bring Zheng Aixiang and Han Jinchuan. As I was coming along, I saw the chairs waiting outside their doors, so they are sure to be here before long."

Almost at that moment Wu Yin'er, Zheng Aixiang, and a young girl dressed in scarlet, came and kowtowed to Yueniang. They had brought their clothes in a bag. When Wu Yin'er saw Guijie sitting on the bed with her outdoor clothes already taken off, she said: "You are a fine friend, Sister Guijie. You would not wait, but came along without us."

"I was going to wait for you," Guijie said, "but when my mother saw the chair at the door she said: 'It looks to me as though your sister has already gone. You had better make haste.' I didn't realize you were not ready."

"She is not too late," Yueniang said, smiling. She asked the name of the newcomer. "She is Han Jinchuan's younger sister, Han Yuchuan," Wu Yin'er told her.

Yuxiao brought refreshments for the singing girls. Guijie, who was anxious to show that she was now the adopted daughter of Yueniang, sat on Yueniang's bed and helped Yuxiao to crack the nuts and put them into the fruit box. Wu Yin'er and the other girls sat together on a bench. Guijie lost no opportunity of making clear her new importance. "Sister Yuxiao," she would say, "would you mind giving me a cup of tea?" or "Sister Xiaoyu, may I have some water to rinse my hands?" Wu Yin'er and the others looked at her in astonishment, but Yueniang and Li Jiao'er were sitting opposite and they could say nothing.

"Sister Wu Yin'er," Guijie said, "you must get your instrument and sing a song for my mother. I have done my part already."

Again Wu Yin'er could not help herself. She picked up her instrument, and the four girls together sang the Eight Melodies of Ganzhou.

"What guests has Father invited today?" Wu Yin'er asked.

"They are all kinsmen and friends," Yueniang said.

"Are the two eunuchs coming?" Guijie said. Yueniang said no; that Xue had called the day before, but not Liu.

"His Lordship Liu is a fine man," Guijie said, "but Xue is always up to tricks. Sometimes he pinches me till I nearly faint."

"After all," Yueniang said, "he is a eunuch and there is something lacking about him. There is no harm in letting him have his little fun."

"You are right," Guijie said, "but sometimes I find him rather a nuisance."

Daian came for the box of fruits. When he saw the four girls sitting there, he said: "Half the guests are here already, and they are just about to take their places. Why do you not dress and go?"

Yueniang asked who had come, and Daian told her that Master Qiao, Uncle Hua, the two Uncles Wu and Uncle Xie were there. Guijie said: "What about Beggar Ying and Pockmarked Zhu? Have they come?"

"The ten gentlemen of the brotherhood are all here," Daian said. "Uncle Ying was here early and Father asked him to attend to a certain matter for him. He went away, but I think he will be back soon."

"Oh dear!" Guijie said, "every time I come into contact with those sharpers, I wonder how I shall be stung. I shall not go. I shall stay here and sing songs for Mother."

"You take too much upon yourself," Daian said. He took the fruit box and went back to the hall.

"Mother," Guijie said to Yueniang, "do you know that Pockmarked Zhu never allows his lips to stop moving when he is at a party? The others complain but he pays no attention. He and Greedy-Chops Sun have not an atom of shame about them."

"Yes," Zheng Aixiang said, "Pockmarked Zhu is always about with Ying. They came to our house the other day with Little Zhang the Second. Little Zhang had twenty taels and wanted my younger sister Zheng Aiyue. My mother told them that my sister had just been made a woman by a Southerner. It had only been a month before and the Southerner had not gone away yet, so we could do nothing for him. They would not listen to her, and my mother lost her temper, locked the door from the inside, and would have nothing to do with them. Young Master Zhang is very well off. He rides a great white horse and there are always four or five boys in attendance on him. Well, he simply sat down in our hall and refused to go away. Pockmarked Zhu knelt down in the courtyard and said: 'Old Lady, you must really come out and take this money. All we ask is to see Zheng Aiyue and have a cup of tea. Then we will go away.' This made us laugh like anything. He was like the man who comes to tell us about the floods. He's an utterly shameless fellow."

"That young Zhang," Wu Yin'er said, "once had the *dong* cat."

"Yes," Zheng Aixiang said, "and set fire to the tiger's mouth, and then the turtle broke with her."

She turned to Guijie. "Yesterday I met Zhou Xiao outside our door and he told me to tell you that the other day he and Nie Yue went to call upon you, but you were not at home."

Guijie glanced sharply at her. "Why, of course," she said, "I was here that day. It was my sister Guiqing he went to see."

"If there is nothing between you," Aixiang said, "why are you always so friendly?"

"You are as fond of your joke as old Liu the Ninth. Do you think Zhou means anything to me? I should be ashamed to have anything to do with that fellow. There was a row, and he told everybody he was coming to see me. He was very much annoyed because I wouldn't let his mother say so. Of course, I can't help his coming to our house. But I should be a piece of stone, whatever he had to do with anyone else. If I were so foolish, it would be like looking towards the South and driving a nail into my bosom."

They all laughed. Yueniang, who had been sitting on the bed listening to them, said: "I have not understood a single word of what you have been saying all this time. I do not even know what language you are speaking."

The guests in the front court had now all arrived. Ximen Qing, dressed in his robes of ceremony, served them with wine. Master Qiao was asked to take the place of honor and he offered the first toast to Ximen Qing. The three singing girls came from the back court. They wore glittering pearl headdresses on their heads and their bodies were exquisitely perfumed with musk. Bojue, as soon as he saw them, said, jokingly: "Where have you three odd things come from? Stop. You may not come in. Why is Guijie not here?" Ximen Qing declared he did not know.

Zheng Aixiang took the zither, Wu Yin'er the lute, and Yuchuan the castanets. They opened their red lips, showed their pearly teeth, and sang.

Besides Master Qiao, who sat in the place of honor, all the members of the brotherhood were present, with Fu, the manager of the shop, and Ben the Fourth. There were fourteen guests, and eight tables. Ximen Qing sat in the host's seat. It was a very splendid feast. Charming voices, exquisite dancing, wine like rolling waves, and food piled up mountains high. When the wine had been passed several times and three songs had been sung, Ying Bojue said: "Host, do not allow them to sing any more. They sing the same tune over and over again like a dog scratching at the door. I have no patience for any more of it. Won't you ask one of the boys to bring three chairs, so that they can sit down and serve wine for us? That would be much better than this singing."

"Leave them alone, you dog," Ximen said. "Why should you upset the whole party?"

"Oh, Beggar Ying," Aixiang cried, "you're letting off fireworks from your behind. You can't wait till evening."

Bojue rose in his place. "You marvelous little strumpet," he cried, "evening or not evening, what has it to do with you, you mother's cunt? Come here, Daian. Bring the thumbscrews, and let them have a taste. Then they may serve the wine."

"Oh, you scamp," Aixiang cried, "you have lifted me right off the ground."

"Listen!" Ximen cried, "we have not all the time in the world. Serve us with wine at once. I will wait no longer."

Wu Yin'er poured wine for Master Qiao, Zheng Aixiang for the elder of the Wu brothers and Yuchuan for the younger, then they went to the others in turn. When Wu Yin'er gave wine to Ying Bojue, he asked her why Guijie had not come.

"The Great Lady has accepted her as a ward," Wu Yin'er said. "I will tell you about it, Uncle, but please keep it to yourself. She is up to some trick. The other day, when we left here, we went home together and it was arranged that we should all come together early today. This morning I dressed and waited for her. I never dreamed she would buy some presents and come here by herself. The result was that we were all late. We sent our maid to call for her, and she was told that Guijie had gone. My mother was very angry. I don't see why she should not have told us that she was going to be made a ward. We couldn't do anything about it. But she made a great secret of it and, when we were in the inner court, she sat on the Great Lady's bed and fussed about to show off her new dignity. She cracked the nuts, set the fruit boxes in order, did this, that, and the other thing and kept us at our distance. I really don't know exactly how it all came about, but the Sixth Lady told me that Guijie had made a pair of shoes for the Great Lady, bought a box of fruitcakes, two ducks, a pair of large hams and two bottles of wine, and brought them with her in a sedan chair very early this morning."

"So now she will not come," he said. "Well, I will see that the little strumpet does come. It looks to me as though she had arranged all this with her mother. She knows that Ximen has been given an appointment; she is anxious now that he has become powerful, and afraid he may not go to their house quite so often. So, to make sure that their relationship continues, she gets herself made his ward. Isn't that it? Now here is some advice for you. She has persuaded the Great Lady to accept her as a ward. Tomorrow, get a few presents yourself and come here and ask the Sixth Lady to adopt you. You and she are connected through your relationship with your dead Uncle Hua, and it will be well for you to keep together. Don't let Guijie think you are annoyed."

"You are right," Wu Yin'er said. "I will tell my mother as soon as I get home."

She took the wine pot to the next guest. Yuchuan poured wine for Ying Bojue. "Sister," he said, "this is very kind of you. Pray do not make a reverence to me. What is your sister doing at home?"

"My sister has been at home for a long time," Yuchuan said. "She has not been out singing. Her time has been fully taken up."

"I remember," Bojue continued, "that I enjoyed your hospitality in the fifth month, but since then I have not seen her."

"The other day, Uncle, you came but you would not stay. You insisted on going away early."

"Well, as it happened," Ying Bojue said, "there was a little dispute that day, and I had some business with your uncle. Except for that I should certainly have stayed longer."

Yuchuan saw that Ying Bojue had finished his cup of wine and poured out another for him.

"It must be only a little," he said, "I dare not drink any more."

"Drink it slowly, Uncle," the girl said, "and when you have finished, I will sing you a song."

"Sister," Bojue said, "you seem to do just what I would have you do. I wonder how it is. You remember the proverb that says: We do not wish our children to make water of silver, or desire that their excrement should be of gold. All we ask is that they should be ready to act as the occasion demands. There can be no doubt that a girl like you need never be anxious about her livelihood. You are much more agreeable than that little strumpet Zheng Aixiang. That piece of mischief is simply trying to get out of singing."

"Beggar Ying, are you feeling ill?" Aixiang said. "How dare you insult me?"

"You dog," said Ximen Qing," you persuaded her to sing, and now you are teasing her,"

"Oh, that is all dead and done with," Bojue said. "She is serving the wine now. I was bound to ask her to sing. Now here I have three *qian* of silver. I will hire the little strumpet to turn the millstone like a ghost."

Yuchuan took up her lute and sang a short song. Then Bojue asked Ximen why he did not send for Guijie.

"She is not here today," Ximen said.

"But I have just been told that she is singing in the inner court. Why do you tell me such a lie?"

He told Daian to go to the inner court and fetch her. Daian made no move.

"Uncle Ying," he said, "you are mistaken. It was someone else who was singing for my mistress in the inner court."

"You rascally young oily mouth," Bojue cried, "so you too try to deceive me. Very well, I will go myself."

Zhu Shinian said to Ximen Qing: "Brother, please send for Guijie and ask her to serve wine to all of us. We will not ask her to sing, for I understand she has gone up in the world."

Ximen Qing was finally compelled to give way. He sent Daian to summon Guijie.

When the boy came to the inner court, Li Guijie was in Yueniang's room, playing the lute and singing for the ladies there. She asked Daian who had told him to come for her.

"Father said I was to ask you to come and serve one round of wine to his guests. Then you can come straight back."

"Mother," Guijie said to Yueniang, "you see Father is quite mad. I told him I would not go and yet he sends for me.

"The others urged him," Daian said. "They persuaded him to send me."

"You had better go, and serve them all with wine once, then come back," Yueniang said.

"If it is really Father who wants me," Guijie said, "I will go, but if it is that Beggar Ying, nothing he can do will ever persuade me, not if I live for a thousand years." She stood before Yueniang's mirror, repainted her face, and went to the hall.

The guests all gazed at her. Upon her head was a hairnet of silver thread; her pins and combs were gilt, and masses of pearls and emeralds were piled upon her hair. She wore a coat of "Lotus root" thread and a skirt of green satin. Her tiny feet were shod in scarlet shoes. She wore emerald pendants upon her cheeks. A strange fragrance came from her scented body.

Guijie kowtowed once towards the table, but it was carelessly done. She held a gilded fan before her face, assumed an air of modesty and dallied with her ornaments. Then she came and stood before Ximen Qing. He ordered Daian to place a chair with a cushion for her and asked her to pour a cup of wine for Master Qiao. But Qiao bowed hastily and said: "I must not trouble you, but will you not serve these other honorable gentlemen?"

"Of course she must begin with you," Ximen said.

Guijie lightly fluttered her silken sleeves and, taking a golden cup, raised it high in the air and handed it to Qiao.

"Most worthy Qiao," Bojue said, "pray be seated and let her stand beside you. These powdery-faced girls from the Li's house, it is their duty to serve wine. You must not indulge them."

"But, my dear Ying the Second," Qiao said, "this young lady is now the daughter of our honorable host. How can I trouble her? It would embarrass me."

"Do not worry yourself," Bojue said; "now that our honorable host has become an officer, she is not content to be a strumpet any longer; she must be his ward."

Guijie flushed. "Are you mad that you talk such nonsense?"

"But is this true?" Xie Xida cried. "I had heard nothing of it. Now all here, without exception, must all give five *fen* of silver to celebrate the occasion."

"It is a great thing to be an officer," Bojue interrupted. "Ever since the beginning of things people have never been afraid of officers in general, but only of those with whom they come into close contact. Now his Lordship has taken her as his ward, we shall have to sprinkle water on her body to wash the filth away."

"You talk the most arrant nonsense," Ximen Qing cried.

"Perhaps," Bojue returned, "but you can make an excellent knife out of barbarian iron."

Zheng Aixiang was pouring wine for Uncle Shen. "Beggar Ying," she said, "Sister Guijie is now his Lordship's ward. I advise you to become his adopted son, but, if you would rather, you can doubtless assume a more ambiguous relationship.

Bojue cursed her. "You little whore! Do you wish to die? Wait till I start on you, and then you'd better say your prayers."

"Curse him for me, Sister Aixiang," Guijie said.

"Don't worry about that looking-towards-Jiangnan tiger from the Ba Mountain, beshitten pants from the Eastern Hills."

"You little strumpet," cried Bojue. "Now you are even using the 'Confucius said' to curse me. I have said nothing. I am just a white ghost. I will tear the girdle that holds up your mother's trousers. Wait until tomorrow and see if I don't show you what I can do. Otherwise you will have no respect for me. You won't treat the general as a god."

"We had better not bother about him any more," Guijie said, "Little Brother's going to be angry."

Aixiang smiled. "Ah, dear Beggar Ying," she said, "you are like the devil in a cart with a lot of ugly-looking melons, so ugly that there are even none for you."

"You little crooked bone," Bojue said, "I can't deal with you all at once. I shall have to give way."

"You funny little pocketknife," Guijie said, "nice clean lips you've got. You have already broken everybody else's gums. Father, I'm surprised you don't beat him instead of sitting there, watching his naughty tricks."

Ximen Qing scolded him. "You dog, I asked her to come and pour wine, and you have no business to make game of her." He went over and slapped Ying Bojue.

"You thievish little strumpet. You simply depend upon your father's authority. Do you think I am afraid of you? Look at you, the heartfelt way you call him 'Father.'" Then he added: "Don't let her pass the wine. It is too good a job for her. Let us have the musical instruments and she shall sing a song for us. She has spent quite long enough in the inner court."

"Uncle," Yuchuan said, "you are like the soldier who came from Cao-zhou, managing everything the way you do."

So they drank wine and played and joked together.

After the birth of a son to Li Ping'er, Jinlian saw that Ximen Qing always slept in the Sixth Lady's apartments. She could not rid herself of her jealousy, and constantly thought of revenge. today she knew that Ximen Qing was entertaining guests in the front hall, and she stood before her toilet table painting her moth-like eyebrows carefully, dressing and redressing her hair, and putting a touch of color on her lips. Then she arranged her dress and went out from her room. As she passed Li Ping'er's room, she heard the baby crying. She went in and asked what was the matter with him.

"His mother has gone to the inner court," the nurse, Ruyi'er, said. "He wants her, and cries."

Jinlian smiled, went forward, and patted the baby.

"You are a real little man already," she said, "wanting your mother even at your age. Let us go to the inner court to find her."

"Fifth Mother," Ruyi'er said, "you had better not take him. He will make your clothes dirty."

Nonsense," Jinlian said, "I will put some more clothes on. It will be no trouble at all." She took the child to her breast, and went off with him to the inner court. When she reached the second door, she lifted him high in the air. Yueniang was sitting underneath the eaves, watching the maids and women cooking and changing the dishes. Jinlian looked at the baby, and smiled.

"Mother," she said, "what are you doing? The baby has come to look for his mother."

Yueniang looked at him. "Fifth Sister," she said, "what are you thinking about? His mother was not in her room, but you should not have brought him out. And why carry him up in the air like that? He will be frightened. His mother is inside, busy." She called to Li Ping'er and told her that her son had come to see her.

Li Ping'er hastily came out. When she saw Jinlian with the child, she said: "Oh, baby, you were quite happy with your nurse. Why should you want me? You will make your Fifth Mother's clothes dirty."

"He was crying," Jinlian said. "He wanted you, so I brought him along."

Li Ping'er opened her clothes and took the child. For a while, Yueniang played with him. Then she told his mother to take him to her own room, and be careful lest he should be frightened.

When Li Ping'er came to her own room, she said to Ruyi'er: "If the baby was crying, you should have done something to keep him quiet, and waited for me to come. Why did you get the Fifth Lady to bring him to the inner court?"

"I told her she should not do so," Ruyi'er said, "but she would not listen to me."

Li Ping'er watched the nurse feeding the child, and at last he went to sleep. Before he had been asleep very long, he woke from his dreams with a cry. In the middle of the night, he seemed first hot and then cold, and refused to take his nurse's milk. He would do nothing but cry, and Li Ping'er was alarmed about him.

When the party in the front court was over, Ximen Qing dismissed the four singers. Yueniang gave Guijie a dress of heavy silk and two taels of silver.

During the evening, Ximen Qing went to the rooms of Li Ping'er to see his son. The child was crying, but when he asked the reason, Li Ping'er did not tell him that Jinlian had taken him to the inner court.

"I don't know," she said, "what has made him cry and refuse to take his milk."

"Give him a few gentle pats," Ximen said. "That will make him sleep." Then he scolded the nurse. "You have not been careful enough of him. What have you been thinking about? You must have frightened him."

He went to the inner court to tell Yueniang. She, too, realized that the child had been frightened when Jinlian brought him to her room, yet she did not breathe a word of this to her husband. "I will send for old woman Liu tomorrow," she said, "she can look at him."

"You mustn't think of sending for that old rogue," Ximen said, "she will use the needle and the flame without hesitating. We must get the royal children's doctor to come and examine him."

Yueniang did not agree. "The child is only a month old," she said. "A doctor can't do him any good."

The next day, Ximen Qing went to his office and Yueniang told one of the boys to go for old woman Liu. The old woman said that the child had had a fright, and they gave her three *qian* of silver to make some soothing medicine for him. When he had taken the medicine, the boy slept quietly and kept down his milk. Li Ping'er smiled as though she felt like a stone that has come to rest at last upon the ground.

# CHAPTER 33
# Han Daoguo and His Wife

As soon as Ximen Qing reached home, he hurried to Wu Yueniang to ask if his little son was better. The doctor must be sent for at once, he said. But Yueniang told him that it was not necessary. She had sent for old woman Liu, and the baby, now that he had taken the medicine she had prepared, was sleeping peacefully and able to retain his food.

"I can't understand your faith in that old hag," Ximen cried. "She is far too ready with her lancings and cauteries. We ought to have the specialist who attends the children of the Royal House. If the child really is better, well and good, but if he is not, I'll have that old woman at the court and let her fingers feel the screws."

"How unreasonable you are with your scoldings and threats," Yueniang said. "I tell you the baby is much better now that he has taken her medicine. Why do you make all this fuss?"

A maid brought something to eat, and Ximen Qing was finishing it when Daian said that Ying Bojue had come. Ximen told one of the boys to take tea to the arbor and said he would join his friend there. He asked Yueniang to have the remaining dishes sent out to them. He sent for Chen Jingji to keep them company, saying that he himself would be there in a moment.

"Where did Ying the Second go for you yesterday, and what has brought him here again today?" Yueniang said.

Ximen told her. "Brother Ying knows a stranger from Huzhou called He who has five hundred taels' worth of raw silk and thread at an inn outside the city gate. He is in a hurry to go home and is prepared to sell his goods cheaply. I offered to pay four hundred and fifty taels and sent Laibao with Ying yesterday to let him see two bars of my silver as samples. The business was settled, and we are to pay for the goods today. The house in Lion Street is empty, and I propose to take two rooms on the street, set them in order, and open a shop there. Now that Laibao has got this appointment in Duke Yun's palace, I must look out for another manager, and arrange for him and one of the boys to keep the shop and look after the house at the same time."

Wu Yueniang agreed. Ximen said: "Brother Ying says he has a friend called Han who knows all there is to know about the thread business, but he has no money of his own and, for the moment, is out of work. Brother Ying says he is a capable business man, honest and straightforward; in fact, he recommends him very strongly. He is going to bring Han to see me, and we will fix up a contract."

He weighed the four hundred and fifty taels of silver and told Laibao to take them. Meanwhile Chen Jingji and Ying Bojue finished their meal in the arbor in a state of anxious impatience. They felt much happier when they saw the silver on the way. When Ximen Qing came, Bojue made a reverence to him and apologized for being late. He said that, after enjoying such hospitality the day before, he had found it hard to get up that morning.

"Well," Ximen said, "here are the four hundred and fifty taels. Laibao shall put them into a big sack. This is a day of happy omen, and I will hire a cart to bring back the goods, and put them away safely."

"You are very wise, Brother," Bojue said. "If we waste any time, I shouldn't be surprised to find that shifty fellow playing a trick on us. But if we get the stuff away, all will be well."

He and Laibao mounted their horses and went with the silver to the stranger's inn, and completed the transaction. As a matter of fact, Ying Bojue had made an arrangement of his own with He that the actual price should be four hundred and twenty taels, so that he got thirty taels for himself. He shared with Laibao the regular commission of five taels. They hired a cart and brought the merchandise to the city. They stored everything in the empty house in Lion Street, locked the door, and returned to give an account to Ximen Qing, who told Bojue to bring Han to see him on the next auspicious day.

Han was a short man, about thirty years of age, unguarded of speech and of a lively temperament. When Ximen Qing had made a contract with him, he and Laibao were given some money to engage workers to dye the thread. When everything was ready, the shop in Lion Street was opened, and there they dealt in threads of many colors, selling considerable quantities every day.

The time passed quickly. The sun and moon crossed and recrossed like the shuttles of a weaver. It was the fifteenth day of the eighth month, Wu Yueniang's birthday. A number of ladies had been invited, and Aunt Wu, Aunt Yang and old woman Pan were there. Two nuns were among the guests, and at night they used to recite the Buddhist scriptures for the edification of the others, continuing till the second or third night watch.

Ximen Qing, hearing that Aunt Wu was in Yueniang's room, did not go there, but to the apartments of Li Ping'er. She told him she was still anxious about the child, and suggested that he should go to Pan Jinlian instead. Ximen smiled, said he did not wish to be a nuisance, and did as he was told.

When Jinlian found her husband was coming, she was delighted. She might have discovered a hidden treasure. She hurriedly packed off her mother to sleep in one of the rooms belonging to Li Ping'er, lighted the silver lamp, delicately spread and smoothed the silken bedclothes, and perfumed her body daintily. She made the most intimate of preparations and awaited her master's pleasure.

That night they took their pleasure to the full. Jinlian was determined to gain possession of her husband's heart, so that he should go no more to the rooms of the others. He was like a wandering bee, stretching forth his proboscis among the tender petals that the winds of spring bestirred, or a flower-devouring butterfly, reveling by night within the deepest recesses of the blossoms.

When old woman Pan came, Li Ping'er asked her to come and sit on the bed, and told Yingchun to bring some refreshments. They talked till the night was late, and, the next morning, she gave the old lady a gown of white silk, two pieces of satin with which to make shoes, and a small sum of money. The old woman smiled and beamed delightedly. She took the things and showed them to her daughter. Jinlian said: "Mother, your eyes are too small and your skin too thin. How can you take gifts from her?"

"My good child," the old woman said, "other people are sorry for me and give me things. Why should you talk like this? What do you ever give me?"

"I have nothing to give you," Jinlian said. "You cannot compare me with the others. How can I possibly give you clothes when I have none to wear myself? But you go and accept favors from outsiders, and I shall have to get something ready—a few dishes and some wine, I suppose—and send them in return. If I don't, something will be said, and I can't have that."

She told Chunmei to prepare eight dishes, four boxes of fruits, and a jar of wine; then, seeing that Ximen Qing had gone, she ordered Qiuju to put them on a square tray and take them to Li Ping'er. "My mother and my grandmother," she was to say, "have nothing to do at the moment and would very much like to come and take wine with you."

Li Ping'er thanked her, and, in a few moments, Jinlian and old woman Pan came. When all three had taken their places, the wine was poured out and they talked together while Chunmei stood at hand to serve them.

Suddenly Qiuju came. "Brother-in-law is trying to find some clothes," she said to Chunmei. "He wants you to go and open the door of the room upstairs."

"When he has found the clothes," Jinlian said, "ask him to come here and take a cup of wine with us."

But when Chen Jingji had taken the clothes he wanted—they belonged to several different people—he hurried away, and Chunmei had to return to tell Jinlian that he would not come.

"He must come," the woman cried. She sent one of the maids for him. At last he did come and made a reverence to them.

Jinlian scolded him. "I was kind enough to send and invite you to take wine with us. Why wouldn't you come? Your luck will fail you." She told Chunmei to bring Jingji a large cup of wine. He put the clothes on the bed and sat down. Chunmei thought she would play a trick on him and brought a large bowl such as is used for tea and filled it to the brim with wine. Jingji was taken aback.

"Fifth Mother," he said, "if you insist upon my taking wine with you, I should much prefer a small cup. There are several people in the shop waiting for their clothes."

"Let them wait," Jinlian said. "I insist upon your drinking this large cup. A small cup will not do at all."

"Let our brother off with this one cup," old woman Pan said. "Perhaps his business is pressing."

"Don't believe a word he says," Jinlian cried. "What does he mean by being busy? He can drink good wine. If we gave him a pail of gold, he would drink it down to the second rib."

Jingji laughed and took the cup. Before he had drunk three mouthfuls, the old woman said to Chunmei: "Give your brother a pair of chopsticks. We can't have him drinking 'widow' wine."

Chunmei did not give him the chopsticks but, as a joke, took a couple of walnuts from the box and handed them to him.

"You think I can't crack them, do you?" he said, laughing, and putting them in his mouth, he broke them with one bite and ate them with his wine.

"You seem to have very good teeth still, young man," old woman Pan said, "I can't eat things that are at all hard, myself."

"There are only two things I can't eat," Jingji said: "stones like goose's eggs and ox horns."

Jinlian saw that he had finished his wine and told Chunmei to give him another cup. "The first cup was of my offering," said she. "You can't consider my mother and the Sixth Lady of less importance than myself. I don't wish to make you drink too much, so drink three cups and I will let you go."

"Really, Fifth Mother," Jingji said, "you must have mercy on me. I can't possibly drink any more. This cup I have already taken has made my face so red that I am afraid Father will be angry when he sees me."

"Are you afraid of your father?" Jinlian said. "I think not. By the way, where is he taking wine today?"

"He went to Master Wu's house this afternoon," Jingji said, "but now he is looking after the alterations that are being made in the house which used to belong to the Qiaos."

"They moved yesterday, didn't they?" Jinlian said. "Why haven't we sent them a present of tea?" Jingji told her that the tea had been sent that morning. Then Li Ping'er asked where they had gone. Jingji said that they had bought a very large house, as large in fact as Ximen's own, in the High Street. It had a frontage to the street of seven rooms and was five rooms deep. They went on talking and Jingji held his nose and swallowed another cup. Then, while Jinlian had her head turned away for a moment, he snatched the clothes from the bed and vanished like a cloud of smoke.

"Mother," Yingchun said, "he has gone off and forgotten to take the key." Jinlian took it and put it beneath her. "When he comes back to look for it," she said to Li Ping'er, "don't say a word. We will have some fun with him before I give it back."

"Don't tease him, Sister," old woman Pan said. "Give it to him."

Chen Jingji went back to the shop. He searched his sleeves and, of course, could not find the key. Finally he went back to Jinlian's room.

"Who's seen your old key?" she said. "What are you thinking about, putting it somewhere and then forgetting where you put it?"

"You must have left it in the room upstairs," Chunmei said.

"No," Jingji said, "I remember having it here."

"Ah, young man," Jinlian said, "the trouble with you is that a certain part of you is so large that you lose your brains when you really mean to get rid of something quite different. I wonder who it is, here or elsewhere, who makes you so absent-minded that your intelligence has got completely out of place."

"There are customers waiting for their clothes," Jingji said distractedly. "What shall I do? Father is not here, and I shall have to go and get a locksmith to force the door. Then we shall find out whether I left the key inside or not."

Li Ping'er could not help laughing. "Sixth Mother," Jingji cried, "you've picked it up. Do give it to me."

"I don't know what you're laughing about," Jinlian said. "You make it look as though we had his keys." Jingji became as excited as an ox prancing around a millstone. He looked at Jinlian and caught sight of the key string sticking out from beneath her.

"There's my key," he cried, but, before he could take it, she whipped it into her sleeve. She still refused to give it up.

"How can I possibly have your key?" she said. The young man was all of a flutter, like a chicken about to be killed stretching out its legs.

"They tell me," Jinlian said, "that you have a very sweet voice, and that you often sing for the boys in the shop. Why shouldn't you sing a song for me? Grandmother and the Sixth Lady are here, so you had better choose one of the latest and best. Then you shall have your key. If you will not sing, you may jump as far as the White Pagoda, but nothing shall induce me to give it to you."

So the young man was compelled to obey. "Very well," said he, "I do not propose to lose my life for it, so I will sing. As a matter of fact, I have such a stock of songs that I can sing you a hundred if you like."

"Boastful, short-lived rascal!" Jinlian said. She poured wine for all of them, saying to Jingji: "You had better take one more cup and then you will not be too shy to sing."

"No," Jingji said, "I'll finish the song first, and then I'll drink."

When he had done, he again asked Jinlian to give him the key. "Mother," he said, "give me the key now. I don't know what the clerks in the shop are doing, and Father may come at any moment."

"You think too much of yourself," Jinlian said, "and your tongue is too ready. If your father does come, and says anything to me about it, I shall tell him you got drunk, lost the key, and came here to look for it."

"Dear, dear!" cried Jingji "You might be an executioner, the way you play with your wretched victim." Then Li Ping'er and old woman Pan took pity on him and pleaded for him with Jinlian.

"If Grandmother and the Sixth Lady had not asked me," she said, "I would have made you sing till the sun went down. You have boasted that you know a hundred or two hundred songs, but so far you have only sung one. Yet you begin to spread your wings to take flight. I won't let you get the better of me."

Chen Jingji offered to sing another song. He had just finished it, and Jinlian was telling Chunmei to pour out another cup of wine for him, when Yueniang suddenly came from the inner court. Ruyi'er was sitting on the stone steps outside the door with Guan'ge in her arms. Yueniang scolded her.

"The baby is just getting a little better, and here you have him in a draft. Take him in at once."

Jinlian heard the voice and said: "Who is that?" One of the maids told her that Yueniang was coming. This put Jingji in a flurry. He hastily picked up the key and made for the door, but it was too late. The ladies were on their way to receive Yueniang.

"What are you doing here, Brother Chen?" she said.

Jinlian answered for him. "The Sixth Lady," she said, "was kind enough to entertain my mother, and brother-in-law came to look for some clothes.

We asked him to take a cup of wine with us. Great Sister, will you not sit down too, and drink something? The wine is very mellow."

"I must not stay to drink," Yueniang said. "My sister-in-law and Aunt Yang are getting ready to go. I came to ask after the baby. I am anxious about him. Sister, why don't you take better care of him, instead of allowing the nurse to have him in a draft? The other day old woman Liu told us that he had a bad chill. You really must be more careful."

"I was taking a little wine with Grandmother," Li Ping'er said. "I never dreamed the rascally slave would take him out."

Yueniang stayed with them a few moments and then went again to the inner court. She sent Xiaoyu to ask the two ladies and old woman Pan to come. Jinlian and Li Ping'er powdered their faces and went with the old woman to the inner court. They drank wine with the two aunts until sunset. Then Yueniang and the others went with their guests to the gate and saw them off in their sedan chairs.

As they were standing at the gate, Meng Yulou said: "Great Sister, Father is not at home. He has gone to a banquet at Master Wu's. Why should we not go and have a look at Qiao's house on the other side of the road?" Yueniang asked the gatekeeper for the key and was told that Laixing was in the house watching the laborers at their work.

"Tell them to withdraw," Yueniang said. "We wish to see it."

"Oh, Mother," Ping'an said, "just go over. They are all busy sifting the sand in the fourth big room." Yueniang and the others were carried across in their chairs. They went in, and found themselves in a large hall. The house had two stories, and Yueniang decided to go upstairs. She had hardly gone halfway—the stairs were very steep—when she missed a step. She slipped and cried "Ah!" Then she gripped the banisters on either side. Yulou was startled and asked what was the matter, grasping one of Yueniang's arms to prevent her from falling. Yueniang was frightened. She would go no farther, and the others helped her down the stairs again. Her face was as pale as wax. Yulou said: "What made you slip, Great Sister? Have you hurt yourself?"

"No," Yueniang said, "I didn't fall, but I wrenched my waist. It gave me such a fright that my heart is in my mouth even yet. It is because the stairs are so steep. I was thinking of those in our own house, and I missed one. Luckily I was able to take hold of the railing, or I don't know what would have happened to me."

"We really ought not to have gone upstairs with you in your present condition," Li Jiao'er said. They took Yueniang home, but, when they were back, she cried that the pains in her belly were so severe she could not endure them. Ximen Qing had not yet returned, and they told a boy to run for old woman Liu.

"I am afraid you have hurt the baby," old woman Liu said. "Indeed, in my opinion the damage is fatal."

"I am more than five months on the way," Yueniang said, "and now I have slipped on the stairs and given myself a wrench."

The old woman suggested that, as it was too late to save the child, Yueniang should take some medicine and get rid of it. When Yueniang agreed, the old woman gave her two big black pills and told her to take them with a little herb wine. Just before midnight the medicine took effect and the child was delivered into one of the pails used for the horses. They took a light to look at it and found that it would have been a boy. Indeed, it was already a boy. Its shape was that of a perfect male child.

Fortunately, Ximen Qing had decided to spend the night with Yulou. The next morning, Yulou came to see Yueniang and asked how she felt. Yueniang told her the whole story.

"It is very sad," Yulou said. "Does Father know?"

"No," Yueniang said. "After the party he came to my room. He was going to take off his clothes, but I told him I did not feel very well and asked him to go somewhere else. Then he went to you. I said nothing to him about it. There is still a little pain."

"Perhaps you have not got rid of all the blood," Yulou said. "I think, if we had some wine heated and you take some medicine to warm you, you will soon be well again. But you must be careful for a few days, Sister, and keep to your room. You see, these miscarriages take longer to recover from than a regular birth. You must take particular care not to catch cold or you will be really ill."

"You are quite right," Yueniang said. "Don't mention the matter to anybody, for, if you do, the news will be spread abroad; people will talk of my 'nest being empty,' and everybody will have some comment to make." Nothing was said to Ximen Qing about the matter.

Clerk Han, whom Ximen Qing had recently engaged, was anything but a reliable character. He was the son of a needy fellow whom people nicknamed Han the Bald, and his personal name was Daoguo. He was a poor man, though there had been a time when he had served in Duke Yun's guard, a post that his grandfather had held before him. Now he was constrained to live in a mean alley off East Street. Though he was nothing but a man of straw, he had a good deal to say for himself, did not spare his words, and was careful to watch which way the wind blew. Trying to get money out of him was as futile as grasping at a shadow, or trying to lay hold of the wind, but, when he himself was getting money from anyone else, his hand burrowed far into the sack. Now that he had secured a post with

Ximen Qing, he put on extra swagger. He had some clothes made, lifted his shoulders higher, and strolled jauntily through the streets. People changed his name to Show-off Han in consequence. His wife was a sister of Butcher Wang, the sixth in the family. She was tall, her face was dark and shaped like a melon seed; she was about twenty-eight years old. They had a little daughter. Han's younger brother, Han the Second, was known as Han the Trickster and belonged to one of the regular gambling sets. This young man had long made love to his brother's wife, and whenever Han Daoguo had gone to attend to the shop, he would come to the house and drink with his sister-in-law. He often stayed all night.

There were several high-spirited young fellows among the neighbors. They saw the woman painted and powdered, standing in her fine dresses at the door and ogling the passersby. Yet whenever they tried to make advances, they found her unkind and unresponsive. Indeed, she was so unsparing of her tongue that her young neighbors became irritated. In twos and threes they discussed the situation, and made up their minds to find out who was the favored suitor. It did not take them long to discover that it was her young brother-in-law.

Three rooms of the Hans' house looked upon the street; the rest of the house was bounded by the houses of the neighbors. At the back was a raised bank, and from this the young men watched, climbing upon the wall at night to look in. Sometimes, during the day, they would pretend to be catching butterflies on the bank, but actually they were trying to discover what was going on in the house. One day, Han the Second, knowing that his brother was out, bought some wine and took it to drink with his sister-in-law. They bolted the door and prepared to have a very merry time. But the young men were on the track, climbed over the wall, opened the back door, and all went in. When they burst open the door of the room, Han the Second tried to escape, but one of the young men knocked him down with a single blow. The woman was still upon the bed. She had no time to put on her clothes before one of the young ruffians was able to secure them. They bound the couple together with one cord. Before long the news spread all down the street and a crowd gathered before the door. While one asked what was amiss, another would go to have a look. In the crowd was an old man who, seeing the man and woman tied together, asked what was the matter. One of the more garrulous of the bystanders informed him.

"Venerable Sir," he said, "you may not know, but this is a case of unlawful relationship between a man and his elder brother's wife."

"Dear, dear," the old man said, nodding his head, "a younger brother and his sister-in-law indeed. I fear they will have their necks stretched when the matter comes before the courts."

Unfortunately, the garrulous fellow knew all about the old man's reputation. He had three daughters-in-law, and his relations with all of them had been such that he had been given a rude nickname in consequence.

"Venerable Sir," the fellow said, "doubtless no one is better acquainted than yourself with the law on such matters. As you say, their necks will be stretched. But I wonder what is the punishment dealt out to a man who carries on with his sons' wives."

The old man decided that the conversation was taking an inconvenient turn. He bowed his head and went off without another word.

That day it was not Han Daoguo's turn to stay late at the shop, and he left for home early. It was about the middle of the eighth month and he was wearing a light silk gown and a new hat. Whisking his fan about and walking along the street with an air of consequence, he stopped now and again to exchange a few words with his friends, babbling away like a flowing brook. Then he chanced to meet two of his friends, one a certain Zhang the Second, who kept a paper shop, the other Bai the Fourth, a silversmith.

"Brother Han," Zhang said, "it is quite a while since I last met you. I hear you are now set up in a splendid establishment belonging to his Lordship Ximen Qing. It shows, I fear, a great lack of courtesy on my part that I have been so remiss in offering my hearty congratulations. Pray forgive me." He invited Han to take a seat.

Han Daoguo sat down on a bench, lifted up his head and fanned himself importantly. "Indeed," he said, "I recognize my own little worth. I place all my confidence in the generosity of others. That is how I have entered the service of my gracious master Ximen. We share the profits in the proportion of three to seven. His wealth is truly immense and he has numerous establishments of one sort and another. He thinks much of me and treats me on a different footing from others."

"I was given to understand," Bai the Fourth said, "that you were selling thread for him."

Han Daoguo smiled. "You don't understand, my dear brother. The thread business is only a sideline. As a matter of fact, I am in charge, and all the money that comes in and goes out passes through my hands. His Lordship always takes my advice and falls in with all my suggestions. Whatever the fates have in store, whether good fortune or ill, we meet it hand in hand. Why, he can't exist a single moment without me. Every day, when he comes back from his official duties, he sends and asks me to dine with him. Without my company he has not the heart to eat. We spend our time in his retiring room, eating and chatting at our ease, till the night is very late and he goes to the ladies' apartments. It was his lady's birthday the other day, and my wife went in a sedan chair to the party. Ximen's lady kept her so late that it was the second night watch before she returned.

"Ximen and I, in fact, are bosom friends, and there are no secrets between us. Perhaps I should not say so, but he even goes so far as to tell me all that happens on the most intimate occasions. Such things, indeed, form one of the most frequent subjects of conversation between us.

"I must say, of course, that I have always acted strictly as a man of honor, and have never been guilty of any kind of indiscretion. My sole desire has been to assist a man of high standing to acquire more wealth, with the object of succoring those in need and rescuing the drowning and the afflicted. In money matters, no matter what their nature, my hands are clean. Long ago I made up my mind that all my actions in such affairs should be strictly in accordance with the highest standards of probity. Even Fu cannot disregard my wishes. Please understand: I do not mean this as a boast; all I do is to carry out my master's wishes."

The conversation was proceeding pleasantly when a man rushed up in a great state of excitement. "What, Brother Han," he cried, "are you still gossiping here? I have been to the shop for you but missed you." He dragged Han Daoguo to a quiet corner and told him all that had been happening at home. "You will have to bestir yourself," he said, "and find somebody to get the matter settled. They are to come before the courts tomorrow morning."

Han Daoguo changed color. He sucked his tongue and stamped about, only wishing he could take wing and fly away. "Old Brother Han," cried Zhang, "why are you going? We haven't finished talking." Han raised his hands. "His Lordship is waiting for me. We have some important business to transact, and I am afraid I must leave you." He hurried away.

# CHAPTER 34
# Ximen Qing Administers Justice

Han Daoguo hastened to the Town Hall to see what he could find out. There he discovered that his wife and brother had both been thrown into prison.

He rushed back to the shop to ask Laibao's advice. "If I were you," Laibao said, "I should go and ask Uncle Ying to speak to our master about it. If he sends a card to the magistrate, I'm sure everything will be well, no matter how serious the case."

Han Daoguo went straight to Ying Bojue's house. He was told that Ying was out and nobody knew where he had gone. Perhaps he was at Ximen's house. Han said this was not so, and asked for Ying Bao. Ying Bao had gone with Bojue. This was very disturbing. Han decided to go and look for his man in the bawdy house. He the Second, the brother of He of Huzhou, had invited Ying Bojue to a party at a house in the Fourth Lane, and there Han Daoguo found him, well filled with wine, and red in the face. He took him aside and told him all his troubles.

"You are in a very serious position," Bojue said. "I can't do less than go with you." He said good-bye to He, and went with Han to his house, where he asked for all the details of the story.

"I very much fear," Han Daoguo said earnestly, "that the case will come up tomorrow. I can see only one means of escape, and that is if you will go to my master and ask him for a card to the magistrate. If all goes well, I will not forget you." He knelt down before Ying Bojue.

"My good lad," Bojue said, pulling him up, "of course I'll see what I can do for you. Write out a petition and don't say anything that isn't necessary. Say that you are often away from home, and, during your absence, a number of young scamps among your neighbors are always throwing bricks and tiles, and insulting your wife. This enraged your brother and he had a row with them, but, unfortunately, they seized him, kicked, pulled, and beat him, and finally tied him and your wife together. Then ask his Lordship to send a card to the magistrate to ask that your wife shall not be compelled to appear before the court. I am sure all will be well."

Han Daoguo took brush and ink, wrote quickly, and put the paper in his sleeve. Then Bojue went with him to call upon Ximen Qing. When they reached the house, they asked Ping'an, the doorkeeper, if his master was at home. "He is in his study in the garden," Ping'an said. "Please go straight in." Ying Bojue's visits to the house were so frequent that the dogs had ceased to bark at him. They went in by the second door, passed through the hall, and came to the Kingfisher Hall. Here Ximen Qing was wont to seek coolness in the hot summer days. There were blinds and curtains on both sides, flowers everywhere, and bamboo trees spread a pleasant cool shade. Huatong was sweeping the floor. When he saw the two men, he cried: "Uncle Ying and Uncle Han are here." They pulled up the blind and went in. Shutong asked them to be seated. "My father has just gone to the inner court," he said. Then he told Huatong to go and find Ximen Qing.

The boy went first to Jinlian's room and asked Chunmei if his master was there. Chunmei called him a thievish, deceitful little slave. "Father is in the Sixth Lady's room on the other side. You know that well enough. Why do you come here and ask?" The boy then went to the other side of the court. The maid Xiuchun was sitting on the steps. "Uncle Ying and Uncle Han are here," he said. "They are waiting for Father to come and talk to them."

"He is in the room," Xiuchun said, "watching my mistress make some clothes for the baby."

Ximen had taken two rolls of material, one of scarlet linen, and the other of light parrot-green silk, so that Li Ping'er might make some little shirts, a little gown, a vest and a hat for Guan'ge. They had laid a cover on the bed. The nurse was there with the baby, and Yingchun was ready with an iron. Xiuchun went in and quietly pulled the other maid's sleeve.

"Don't pull me," Yingchun said, "I shall drop the iron." Xiuchun told her that Huatong had come to say Master Ying wished to speak with his master.

"You naughty little slave," Li Ping'er said, "if Uncle Ying is here, why didn't you come and say so instead of pulling Yingchun by the sleeve?"

Ximen Qing told the boy to ask the two men to wait: he would join them in a few moments. He watched the women finish cutting out the clothes, and went to the study in his ordinary dress. When he had greeted Bojue, they sat down to take tea. Han Daoguo sat facing them. At last Ying Bojue said: "Brother Han, you have, I think, something to say. Pray tell his Lordship what it is."

Han Daoguo had just begun to say that certain wicked neighbors of his, whose names he didn't know . . . , when Bojue interrupted him. "My dear boy," he said, "you are going the wrong way about it. You shouldn't wrap up the bones of the affair, and simply show the flesh. Be perfectly frank. Brother Han has been spending most of his time at the shop. There was no one to look after his house except his wife and his little daughter. The neighbors are not by any means what they should be, and, when they saw that there was no man in the place, they began to throw bricks and tiles, and play tricks generally. His worthy younger brother, Han the Second, found this sort of behavior to be too much. He came to the house and told the rascals what he thought about them. Then they all set upon him, beat him nearly to death, and finally seized him and shut him up in jail. Now he has to appear before the magistrate in the morning. Brother Han came to me and wept and asked me to beg you to send a card to his Worship so that his reputation might in some degree be saved. If only his brother goes before the magistrate, it will not be so bad, but his wife should not be allowed to appear." He said to Han Daoguo: "Let your master see the paper you have written. Then he will send a man to get the matter arranged for you."

Han hastily took the paper from his sleeve, and knelt down before Ximen. "I have had the good fortune to be employed in this household," he said. "Will you not, for Master Ying's sake, deign to do something for me, and I and all my house will not forget your kindness so long as the teeth are in our mouths."

Ximen Qing pulled him up and read the paper. "The accused woman Wang," it said, "implored you of your goodness, to withdraw the prosecution." "That is not how you should write it," Ximen said. "Mention your brother only." He said to Ying Bojue: "I will certainly send a card to the court, but I think a much better plan would be to arrange for the charge to be altered so that the young man appears before me."

"Brother Han," Ying Bojue said, "your master's idea is excellent. You should make a reverence to him." Han Daoguo knelt down again and kowtowed.

Ximen ordered Daian to go at once for the officer of the police on duty, and, in a little while, a policeman in black clothes was ready in attendance. Ximen Qing called him forward. "Go to Han's house and find out to which quarter of the town it belongs. Then go to the officer of that quarter and tell him that it is my order that he shall release Mistress Han forthwith. Afterwards, take the names of the young men concerned, make the necessary alterations in the charge sheet, and see that all the rascals are brought to my court tomorrow for examination.

The officer went away. "Brother Han," Bojue said, "you had better go with him and see after things. I have something else to talk to his Lordship about."

Han Daoguo repeatedly thanked them both and went home with the policeman.

Ximen Qing and Bojue sat in the Kingfisher Hall, and Ximen told Daian to go to the Great Lady and ask for the wine that Eunuch Liu had sent. He was to ask for the mackerel too. Hearing the word "mackerel," Bojue lifted his hands.

"Oh dear," he said, "I haven't thanked you yet. Those two mackerel you sent me yesterday were excellent. I sent one of them to my brother, and told my wife to send a portion of the other to our dear daughter. The rest she minced, put in sweet oil and preserved in a porcelain jar, so that I may have some to eat whenever I feel like it, and if a friend should call, he too may have a little and participate in your generosity."

Ximen told him how the fish had been given him. "Liu Bohu," he said, "Eunuch Liu's brother, has done pretty well out of the Imperial osier beds. A short time ago he built a house at Wulitian. Unfortunately, he used the imperial timber to build his house, and Magistrate Xia, who, as you know, is a colleague of mine, got to know about it. Not only did he propose to fine Liu a hundred taels but also to send the papers to the Provincial Courts. This was very distressing to Eunuch Liu, and he came to see me about it. He brought a hundred taels with him and said there was nothing he desired more than to see the matter ended. Now I don't mind telling you, I don't do so badly out of my business, and the money he offered was nothing to me. Eunuch Liu is a friend of mine: we see a good deal of one another and he often gives me presents. When he asked me to help him, I could hardly turn a deaf ear. But I wouldn't touch a penny of his money. I told them to pull the house down as fast as they could. Liu the Third's servant was beaten forty stripes and that was the end of the matter. Eunuch Liu was very grateful. He killed a pig and sent it with a jar of lotus wine of his own brewing, two fish, about forty *jin* in weight, and two rolls of flowered silk, with gold embroidery. He came in person to thank me, and each of us appreciated the advantages of friendship a little better than we had done before."

"Brother," Ying Bojue said, "money means very little to you, but Xia has been a soldier. He has never had anything of his own, and now he must make what he can. Have you had much to do with him since you have held your present post?"

"We have tried a few cases together, some great, some small. On the whole he is fair enough, but he is too fond of taking little presents. To him, so long as he gets his fee, all cases are of the same complexion, and the parties are set free. It is quite contrary to justice, and I have protested several times. We are both, as I tell him, officials of no very high degree, yet we represent the law and we should maintain its dignity."

When wine and dishes had been set before them, Ximen poured the lotus wine into a golden cup. They drank together and chatted till after the first night watch.

Meanwhile the black-robed policeman did as he had been told. Han's wife was set free and allowed to go home. The officer in charge of the records was sent for; the young men's names were taken down and they were ordered to appear before the court the following morning. Then they began to look at one another. They knew that Han Daoguo was employed by Ximen Qing, and realized that he had secured Ximen's help. They saw that Han the Second alone was detained, and began to think that the matter would end badly for them.

The next day, Ximen Qing and Xia took their places in the great hall and the police brought in the culprits. Han the Second came first and knelt down before the dais. Xia read the charge.

"Ox Hide Alley, in the fourth quarter of the first ward. officer of the Records Xiu Zheng reports a breach of the peace by the following, Han the Second, Che Dan, Guan Shikuan, Yu Shou and Hao Xian."

He asked Han the Second how the trouble began.

"My brother is a tradesman," Han the Second said, "and he is seldom at home. Only a young girl and myself were there. There are a number of young ruffians living about there, and they used to gather around the door and sing lewd songs. At night they used to throw bricks at us and insult us in every conceivable way. One day when I was at my brother's house, I found these insults more than I could stand, and said a few words to that effect. The scoundrels would not listen to me. They threw me on the ground, kicked, and struck me. And now we are all before you. I pray, Sir, that you will establish the truth of the matter."

Xia asked the others what they had to say. "Your Worship," they cried, "do not believe these cunning stories. Han the Second is a gambler and a rogue. When his brother was out, he made love to his sister-in-law. As for her, she is always trying to show how clever she is and insulting her neighbors. Yesterday we caught them in the act, and her trousers are here for evidence."

At this, Xia asked the policeman why Mistress Han was not before the court. The policeman did not dare to say she had been released, so he said her feet were so small that she could only walk slowly and would come later. Han the Second looked at Ximen Qing. A few moments later, Ximen bowed to Xia. "Your Worship," he said, "it seems hardly necessary to bring the woman before us. I suppose she is a pretty woman, and these young rascals hoped to have some fun with her and were disappointed. They probably plotted this in revenge."

He called Che Dan forward and questioned him. "Where did you catch Han the Second?" he asked.

"We caught him in the woman's room," the man said. Then Ximen said to Han the Second: "What relation are you to this woman?" A policeman said that she was his sister-in-law. Then he asked the police: "How did these fellows get into her room?" The policeman told him that they had climbed over the wall.

Ximen put on an air of great indignation. "You scoundrels!" he cried, "since he is her brother-in-law, they are near relations. Why should he not go to see her? What is his business to you, you scamps? How dared you climb over the wall? The husband was out, and she had only a little daughter in the house. It must have been one of two things. Either you intended to rob her, or you meant to rape her. Bring the rack," he shouted to the attendants, "rack each of them once, and give them twenty stripes with a heavy rod." Then they were all beaten and racked till their flesh was torn and the blood gushed forth. As none of them had been so punished from the day he left his mother's womb, they shrieked and yelled loudly enough to rend the skies and then lay groaning on the ground.

Ximen Qing did not give Xia an opportunity to speak, but ordered Han the Second to be taken away to await further examination. The other four were to be put in jail until they confessed. They bemoaned their fate, and their friends in the prison frightened them the more by saying that they would be banished and probably die in exile. This put them all in a terrible state, and, when their people sent food to them in prison, they secretly sent messages to their fathers or elder brothers to spend more money bribing the officials both high and low. Someone went and attempted to bribe Xia. "The woman's husband," said Xia, "is employed by his Lordship Ximen Qing. So long as he is concerned in the matter, I can do nothing. He is my colleague. You had better go and talk to him."

One of them thought of going to see Uncle Wu, but as for Ximen himself, they knew that he was very rich, and dared not offer money to him. So the fathers and brothers of the poor young men were greatly put about and finally held a conference.

"It is no use going to Master Wu," one said, "he can do nothing for us. But they tell me that Ying, the silk merchant's brother, is on very friendly terms with Ximen. We had better get together as much silver as we can, and ask him to plead with Ximen for us. Then we may have some success."

Che, the wineshop keeper, Che Dan's father, acted as spokesman. The others contributed ten taels apiece, so that they had forty taels in all; then they went to Ying Bojue's house to implore him to intercede with Ximen. Bojue accepted the money and sent them away.

"You have already worked for Han against these people," his wife said. "How can you take their money now and act for them? Han will be very angry."

"Do you think I haven't foreseen that difficulty?" Ying Bojue said. "I know what to do." He weighed out fifteen taels of silver, wrapped them up, put them in his sleeve, and set off for Ximen Qing's house.

Ximen had not yet returned, and Ying went into the hall. Shutong was coming from the study in the west wing. The boy was wearing a tile-shaped hat, with a pin fashioned like a lotus. His gown was of Suzhou silk with a jade-colored jacket, summer shoes, and white socks.

"Pray sit down in the guest's place, Uncle Ying," he said. Then to Hua-tong: "Boy, go at once and bring some tea for Uncle Ying. If you stay there playing knucklebones, I shall tell Father the moment he comes in." Hua-tong went to get the tea.

"Is your Father not back yet from the courts?" Ying Bojue asked.

"A message has just come to say that, after leaving the office, he went with his Lordship Xia to make a call. Is there anything I can do for you, Uncle?"

"I want nothing," Ying Bojue said.

"Uncle," the boy said, "the other day you came here on Clerk Han's business. Yesterday my master had those fellows beaten and sent to prison. Tomorrow the papers will be made out and they will be sent for trial."

Ying Bojue took the boy aside. "I will tell you one thing," he said, "their people have heard that they are to be examined further, and they are very much alarmed. Last night they came to me, cried and knelt down before me, and begged me to speak to your master for them. I realized that as I had already taken a hand in the matter, I could do nothing for them without upsetting Han, so I suggested that they should give me fifteen taels of silver, thinking that I might come to you, and perhaps you might think fit to mention the matter to your father, and we shall see whether he takes pity on them or not."

He took the money from his sleeve and handed it to Shutong. The boy broke open the packet. The silver was in four large and four small pieces.

"Uncle Ying," he said, "I will, of course do anything you command, but I think I should have five taels more. Then I will mention the matter to Father, though, naturally, I can't say whether he will be willing to listen. Uncle Wu was here yesterday and Father refused him point-blank. My influence is no bigger than a sesame seed, so what can I do? Really, Uncle, I cannot expect to succeed without some help. I shall have to lay out the money on the Sixth Lady, who has just borne a son. We must get to work indirectly."

"Very well," Bojue said, "I will add a word too, but remember: they want their answer tonight."

"I don't know when Father will be back," Shutong said. "They may have to wait until tomorrow."

Bojue went away, and Shutong took the silver to the shop, keeping a tael and five *qian*. This he spent on a jar of wine, two roast ducks, and two chickens, two *qian* on fruit pastries and delicate pastry, and one on sweet rolls. He ordered these things to be sent to Laixing's room, and then went to ask Laixing's wife to set them out for him.

Jinlian was not at home that day. Early in the morning she had taken a sedan chair and gone outside the city to celebrate her mother's birthday. Shutong borrowed a square tray and sent Huatong with the delicacies to Li Ping'er. He himself took the jar of wine.

"Who has sent these things?" Li Ping'er said. Huatong told her they were a present from Shutong. "The young rascal!" Li Ping'er cried. "What does he mean by this?"

Then Shutong came in. Li Ping'er was sitting on a gilt bed, playing with the baby and a tortoiseshell cat.

"You young scamp," she said, "for whom have you brought all these things?"

Shutong laughed, but did not answer.

"Why don't you answer instead of standing there laughing?" Li Ping'er said.

"If it is not for you, for whom do you imagine I have brought them?"

"You rascal," Li Ping'er said, "I don't suppose you are doing this without a reason. If you don't explain yourself, I shall not accept them."

Shutong opened the wine jar, set down the dishes on a small table, and asked Yingchun to bring a silver wine pot. Then he poured out a cup of wine and offered it to Li Ping'er with both hands.

"When you have drunk this, I will tell you," he said, kneeling before her.

"Say what you have to say before I drink it," Li Ping'er said. "Otherwise, you may kneel there a hundred years, but I will have none of it. Stand up at once and tell me."

Shutong told her how Ying Bojue had spoken to him about the four prisoners. "He had already done something for Han, and he did not see how he could work for the other side too. He suggested that I should come to you. If Father questions you about it, don't say I told you, but tell him that Uncle Hua sent someone to see you about it. Meanwhile I will go to the study in the front court and write a petition, and show it to him. I will tell him that you gave it to me, and perhaps you will say anything else that seems necessary. After all, Father has already had the men punished, so if you persuade him to make an end of the matter and let them go, it will be a very gracious action."

"If that is all," Li Ping'er said, "there need be no difficulty. I will speak to your master as soon as he returns. There was no need for you to get all these things for me. You rogue, I suspect you've made something out of them."

"I will not deceive you, Lady," Shutong said. "They gave me five taels for myself."

"You are a clever young rascal, making money in this way." She would not drink a small cup, but made Yingchun bring a large one shaped like a flower. After drinking two cups herself she poured one out for Shutong.

"I dare not drink," the boy said. "It would make my face red, and I should not like my master to see me."

"What does it matter if I give it to you?" Li Ping'er said.

The boy kowtowed to her and drank the wine at a breath. Li Ping'er took some of each of the dishes and made the boy eat some. He drank two more cups of wine, then dared not drink any more, for fear his face should be red. Then he went to the shop where he had left half the cakes and dishes he had bought. He set them on the counter, bought another jar of wine, and invited Clerk Fu, Ben the Fourth, Chen Jingji, Laixing and Daian to have some. The dainties vanished like a whirlwind or like melting snow. He forgot to invite Ping'an, the gatekeeper, who sat outside the gate pulling a long face.

It was afternoon when Ximen Qing came back from visiting his friends. Ping'an saw him coming but gave no warning. Shutong heard the shouts of the attendants clearing the road for their master before he had time to put away the things. He had to rush out in a great hurry to take Ximen Qing's clothes.

When Ximen asked if anyone had called to see him, Shutong said: "No." Ximen Qing took off his hat and cloak and, after putting on a cap, went into his study and sat down. Shutong gave him a cup of tea. When he had drunk a mouthful, Ximen put it down. He noticed how red the boy's face was. "Where have you been drinking?" he said.

Shutong took a paper from beneath the ink slab on the table and gave it to his master. "The Sixth Lady gave me this," he said. "She told me Uncle Hua had sent it. It is about the four prisoners, and she asked me to take it and bring it before you. She gave me a cup of wine, and that is why my face is red."

Ximen Qing looked at the paper. "The four accused implore your clemency," it said. When he had read it, he handed it back, and told Shutong to put it in the letter case and give it to the soldier-servant that he might be reminded about it next day. Shutong put the paper in the case, and came to stand beside his master.

After the wine he had drunk, the high color in his cheeks stood out in striking contrast to the fairness of his skin. Ximen could not resist the temptation. He drew the boy to his bosom, and kissed him passionately. Shutong had aromatic tea and some tablets of cinnamon in his mouth. His body was scented with a sweet fragrance. Ximen undid the boy's shirt, pulled down his multicolored trousers, and caressed him gently. "You must not drink so much wine," he said. "It will ruin your complexion."

"I will do your bidding in all things," the boy said.

Meanwhile, a horseman clothed in black rode up to the gate, dismounted, and bowed to Ping'an. "Is this the house of his Lordship Ximen Qing?" he said.

Ping'an was still sulking and pulling a long face, because Shutong had not invited him to the feast. He did not answer. The man waited a long time and finally said: "I have brought this letter from Major Zhou. Tomorrow there is to be a reception to General Xing Pingzhai at the Temple of Eternal Felicity. Three of the officers have given a tael of silver each towards the expenses, and I have come to see your master. Please be good enough to tell him. I will wait for his reply."

Ping'an took the paper and went in. Someone told him that Ximen was in the garden room, and he went into the garden past the pine tree grove. Huatong was sitting on the steps beside the window. He waved his hand and Ping'an suspected that something must be going on between his master and Shutong. He tiptoed to the window, peeped, and listened, and did not miss certain signs of agitation in the room. He heard Ximen Qing say: "Stand this way, my boy, and don't move." Then there was silence for a long time. At last Shutong came out to fetch water for Ximen Qing to wash his hands. When he saw Ping'an and Huatong standing at the window, he flushed, and hurried away to the inner court. Ping'an took in the subscription list and Ximen Qing set his signature to it.

"Go to the Second Lady for a tael of silver," he said. "Then get your brother-in-law to wrap it up and give it to the messenger." Ping'an went away.

When Shutong had brought the water, Ximen washed his hands and went to see Li Ping'er.

"If you would like something to drink, I will tell a maid to heat some wine," she said.

Ximen saw a jar of Jinhua wine underneath the table. "What is that?" he said.

Li Ping'er did not wish to tell him that Shutong had brought it. She said: "I thought I should like something to drink, so I sent a boy to the street to buy it. I opened it and drank a cup or two. Then I had had enough."

"We have plenty of wine in the outer court," Ximen said. "Why should you spend your money? I got forty jars of Heqing wine from Ding, the southerner, the other day. I haven't paid him for it yet, but the wine is all in the west wing. If you want any, you need only send a boy with a key to get some."

Plates of roast duck, chicken and fish were ready and Li Ping'er told Yingchun to prepare more. When the dishes were set on the table, she ate them with her husband. It did not occur to Ximen to ask where they had come from, for such things were plentiful in his house.

"Shutong has just given me a paper," he said as they were drinking. "He says you gave it him."

"Yes," said Li Ping'er, "Uncle Hua came and begged me to ask you to let those fellows go."

"Wu came yesterday about the same matter," Ximen said, "but I wouldn't promise him anything. I really intended to have the business still further examined but, since Hua has been here to ask, I will have them given another beating and set them free."

"Why beat them again?" Li Ping'er said. "You have already punished them till they opened their mouths and showed all their teeth. Really, a most repulsive sight!"

"I don't care whether they show their teeth or not," Ximen said. "My office is not conducted on those lines, as other people, of greater dignity than they, have found before now."

"Brother," Li Ping'er said, "you are an officer of the law, I know, yet your office does not forbid you to show mercy. To be merciful is to be virtuous, and you must lay up a stock of virtue for our child's sake."

"What do you mean?" Ximen said.

"In the future, do not rack and beat the people as you have been doing, and, when you have a chance to be kind, take it. So, you will certainly lay up for yourself a treasure in heaven."

"If I do my duty, I must not be too lenient," Ximen said.

They were still drinking when Chunmei thrust aside the blind and came in. It seemed to her that Ximen and Li Ping'er were sitting in a very affectionate position. "Here you are enjoying your wine," she said. "You have forgotten all about sending a boy to meet my mistress. She has gone a long way outside the city, and only Laian is with her. She will be very late, I fear, but that doesn't seem to worry you."

Ximen saw that the girl's headdress was disarranged and her hair tumbling down. He laughed, and said: "You've been asleep, little oily mouth." Li Ping'er told her that the kerchief on her head needed to be set in order and added: "This is beautiful Jinhua wine. Won't you have a cup?"

"Drink a cup," Ximen Qing said, "and I will send some of the boys for your mistress."

Chunmei, with one hand on the table as she leaned over to pull up her shoes, declined. "I don't feel very well," she said, "and I have only just got up. I don't want anything to drink."

"It is very good wine, little oily mouth," Ximen said. Li Ping'er said: "Your mistress is not at home; why make all this fuss over a cup of wine?"

"Please drink the wine yourself, Sixth Lady. It makes no difference whether my mistress is at home or not. If she were at home and I were asked to drink when I did not feel well, I should refuse."

"If you will not have wine, have some tea," Ximen said. "I will tell Yingchun to send a boy for your mistress."

He passed his own cup to her. Chunmei took it reluctantly, drank a mouthful of tea, and set the cup down.

"You need not send Yingchun," she said, "I have brought Ping'an. He is bigger than the others."

Ximen called through the window and Ping'an answered. "If you go," Ximen said, "who will attend to the gate?"

"I have told Qitong to look after the gate," the boy replied.

"Very well," said Ximen, "take a lantern and go to meet your mistress."

When Ping'an had gone halfway, he met the sedan chair. He knew the two bearers. One was Zhang Chuan, the other Wei Cong.

"I have come to escort my mistress," he said, going forward and taking hold of the shafts.

"Who told you to come?" Pan Jinlian said. "Your father?"

"Not so much my father as my sister," the boy said.

"I suppose your father has not come back yet from the office," Jinlian said.

"Not come back, indeed!" the boy replied. "He came back very early and is now drinking good wine in the Sixth Lady's room. If Chunmei had not fetched me and insisted that I should be sent with a lantern to meet you, I shouldn't be here now. I knew you had nobody with you but Laian, that the road was bad and you ought to have somebody bigger, so I came."

When you left the house, where was your master?"

"He was still in the Sixth Lady's room. He only sent me when Chunmei insisted."

Jinlian remained silent for a long time. Then she smiled, coldly. "The brigand seems to think I am a corpse already. He would spend every night in that strumpet's room if he could. She pins her faith to that water bladder of a baby, and I only hope she may not find out she has made a mistake. Zhang Chuan, you are one of the household and you have seen a good deal of the world. Why should they cut up a whole roll of silk to make clothes for that puling brat? Even Wang the millionaire wouldn't do a thing like that."

"Lady," Zhang Chuan said, "I should never have dared to mention the matter, if you had not done so, but you are certainly right. They should not. It is not the silk I am thinking about, but I am afraid they will spoil the baby. He has not gone through all his childish ailments yet, and he will not be reared without some trouble. I remember a sad case that happened last year. It was a very rich old gentleman who lived outside the Eastern gate, about sixty years old he was, living on a property that had belonged to his ancestors. He was as rich as rich could be, but he was childless. He kept his fast in the Eastern Temple and offered sacrifice in the Temple of the West. He made all manner of benefactions to religion, yet still no son was born to him. Then, suddenly, his third wife presented him with one and he was as delighted as our master has been. All day long, he would gaze upon that child and have him carried about in an embroidered silken cradle. He had three rooms for a nursery painted as white as driven snow. Three or four nurses were bought especially for the baby and, all day long, he was sheltered from the slightest breath of wind. Yet before he was three years old, he took the smallpox and died. I beg your pardon, but I can't help thinking it is better to bring up a baby a little more roughly."

"Roughly indeed!" Jinlian cried. "Their only trouble is that they can't keep him in a pile of gold."

"There is something else I have to tell you," Ping'an said. "If I do not, you will be angry with me when you hear about it. It is about that business of Clerk Han and the others. Father had the young men beaten and thrown into jail, and it was his intention to send the matter further. But this morning Uncle Ying came and had a talk with Shutong. I think he must have given Shutong a few taels, for he took quite a large packet of silver to the shop and had two or three taels cut off. He spent this on dainties that he got Laixing's wife to arrange, and took them, with a couple of jars of Jinhua wine, to the Sixth Lady's room. They drank some of the wine; then he went back to the shop and gave a party to his friends. When Father came back, the party broke up."

"Didn't he ask you to join the party?" Jinlian said.

"Ask me? Not he! He is the boldest of slaves and is not even afraid of you, so why should he bother about me? It is all Father's doing. I know that, for I caught the pair of them together in the study. He was once a servant at the officers' quarters, and you may be sure there is not much he does not know. If Father does not soon get rid of this slave, the whole household will suffer from his goings on."

"How long was he in the Sixth Lady's room, drinking?" Jinlian asked.

"A long time. When I saw him, he had evidently been drinking for a long time. His face was very red."

"Didn't your father speak to him about it?"

"My father's lips were sealed. How could he say anything?"

"Oh, the scoundrel! The shameless prince of all evil scoundrels!" Jinlian cried. "He must have a turn at everything. If ever you catch him and this slave playing their dirty games again, come and tell me at once."

Ping'an promised. "Please remember one thing," he said. "Don't let anyone know I told you." Then he went behind the sedan chair and they went on their way.

As soon as they reached home, Jinlian went to the inner court to pay her respects to the mistress of the house.

"What made you come back so soon?" Wu Yueniang said. "You might have spent another night."

"My mother asked me to stay," Jinlian said, "but one of my nieces was there, a girl about twelve years old, and I should have had to sleep in the same bed with her. Then, it seemed a very long way off, and I thought I had better come. My mother asked me to give you her compliments, and thank you for your kind presents."

She went in turn to the rooms of each of the other ladies, and finally to the front court. Ximen Qing was still talking to Li Ping'er.

When she came in, Li Ping'er quickly stood up and welcomed her with a smile. "Sister," she said, "you have come back very early. Won't you sit down and have a cup of wine?" She told Yingchun to give Jinlian a chair.

"I have had something to drink already," Jinlian said, "and, as for food, I've had enough for two. I won't sit down, thank you."

She turned and went out with her head in the air. Ximen Qing called her back. "What, you slave!" he cried. "Are you so bold that you decline to make your reverence to me when you return from your visits?"

"Make a reverence to you indeed!" said Jinlian. "If slaves are not bold, who should be?"

# CHAPTER 35
# The Favorite

Ximen Qing went early to his office. When they left the Great Hall, he spoke to his colleague Xia. "Che Dan and the others," he said, "have sent to me repeatedly to express their regret. I think we might be indulgent on this one occasion."

"I have had a number of visits too," said Xia, "but I hesitated to mention the matter to you. Since you have spoken of it, however, I suggest we have them before us, give them a beating, and let them go."

"An excellent idea, Sir," said Ximen.

They went back to the hall of audience and ordered the prisoners to be brought before them and made to kneel down. The unfortunate men were afraid of being punished again, and kowtowed. Ximen Qing did not give Xia time to speak, but said: "Why have you rogues sent so many people to us to plead on your behalf? I ought to send you for further trial, but this time I will forgive you. If ever you fall into my hands again, I shall send you to prison and there you shall die." He sent for Han the Second. The men, full of expressions of gratitude, ran off as though their lives depended on it. So this matter was happily settled.

Meanwhile Ying Bojue went to see Shutong and secretly gave him another five taels of silver. The boy put the silver into his sleeves, but Ping'an, who was watching from the gate, saw it. Shutong told Ying Bojue what he had done. Yesterday, he said, he had told his master about the whole affair, and the matter was to be settled that day.

"Their fathers and elder brothers told me," Ying Bojue said, "that they are very much afraid the rascals will have another beating."

"Do not worry," Shutong said. "I am prepared to promise that nothing more will happen to them."

Ying Bojue returned and told the good news to the young men's people. About midday, the four young men were all home again. They embraced their families and there was much weeping. They had lost more than a hundred taels of silver, and their legs were very sore. Never again did they give any trouble.

Before Ximen Qing came home, Shutong told Laian to sweep the study floor. From a box he took some delicacies that had been sent as a present and gave them to Laian. With a great show of secrecy and reluctance Laian said to Shutong: "Brother, there is one thing I wish to say to you. Yesterday, my brother, Ping'an, when he went to meet the Fifth Lady's chair, told her a long story of your misdeeds."

"What did he say?" Shutong asked.

"He said you took money from people and had the impertinence to buy presents of food that you gave to the Sixth Lady. When you were in her room, you drank for a long time and then went to the shop to eat, but didn't give him anything. He also said that you and Father had been playing tricks together in the study."

Shutong determined to remember this, but he said nothing. The next day Ximen Qing went early to a party that the officers had arranged at the Temple of Eternal Felicity to bid farewell to one of their number who was leaving for another post. He did not go to his office but returned early in the afternoon. When he dismounted, he said to Ping'an: "If anyone calls, tell him I am not at home." Then he went into the hall, and Shutong took his clothes. Ximen asked the boy whether there had been any visitors. "No," Shutong said, "but Mayor Xu has sent two baskets of crabs and some fresh fish. I gave his servant one of your cards. He gave me a *qian* of silver. And Uncle Wu has sent six invitations, one for each of the ladies, to a 'Third Day' party.'"

Ximen Qing went to the inner court and Wu Yueniang showed him the cards of invitation.

"You must put on your best clothes and go," Ximen said. Then he went back to the study and sat down. Shutong made haste to burn incense in the burner and, with both hands, offered Ximen a cup of tea. When he had taken the tea, the boy gradually came closer and stood beside the table. After a while, Ximen pursed his lips. This was a sign to the boy to make fast the door. Then he drew the boy to his bosom and with one hand stroked his cheeks. He put his tongue into his mouth; the boy passed him a sweetmeat and stroked his erect penis.

"My son," Ximen said to him, "are you being well treated by the people here?"

The boy seized his opportunity. "There is one thing, but except to you, Father, I would not dare to mention it."

"Tell me," Ximen said. "Keep nothing back."

Then Shutong told him about Ping'an. "The other day, when you and

---

* Uncle Wu's son, Wu Shunzhen, had married a young lady named Zheng, a niece of Master Qiao's wife. Ximen Qing had sent him some tea, and this was why invitations had been sent.

I were here together, he and Huatong were secretly spying through the window. When I went out to get water for you to wash your hands, I saw them. Besides that, he has treated me as a slave before outsiders, and bullied me in a hundred different ways."

Ximen Qing was very angry. "If I do not pull that slave's trousers down," he said, "I am not fit to be called a man."

Meanwhile Ping'an himself was not idle. He went quietly to Pan Jinlian and told her that his master and Shutong were again together. Jinlian ordered Chunmei to go at once to the front court and ask Ximen Qing to come and speak to her. As the maid passed the hedge, she saw Huatong making a pine tiger.

"What do you want, Sister?" he said. "Father is in the study."

Chunmei slapped his face. Ximen Qing, in the study, heard the rustling of skirts and knew that someone was coming. He hastily put Shutong aside, climbed upon his bed, and lay down. Shutong busied himself with the brushes and ink slabs on the table. Chunmei pushed open the door and went in.

"All very quiet," she said, "very quiet indeed! And the door shut too! Drawing the bonds of family closer, I suppose. My lady would like you to go and talk to her."

Ximen Qing did not move. "What does she want with me, little oily mouth?" he asked. "You go first and I will come in a moment. Let me have my rest."

Chunmei would have none of this. "If you will not come of your own free will, I shall have to drag you," she cried, and pulling and tugging, she forced Ximen Qing to go to Jinlian's room.

When they reached there, Jinlian said to her maid: "What was he doing in the front court?"

"He was with that boy in the study. They had the door shut, and everything was so quiet they might have been just on the point of catching a fly. I don't know what their little game was, but it looked to me as if there was something very close between them. When I went in, the boy was standing at the table pretending to write, and this one was lying on the bed. I had to drag him here, for he didn't want to come."

"Yes, he was afraid he would get into hot water if he did come," Jinlian said. "You shameless creature! Haven't you any self-respect left at all? In broad daylight, shutting yourself up in your study with that slave. What for? Just to make a beast of yourself with that mangy slave. And then, at night, you come to our place to sleep with us. A nice clean fellow!"

"You believe all that little oily-mouthed creature tells you," Ximen said. "I was simply lying on the bed and watching the boy write a visiting card."

"Why shut the door to write a visiting card?" Jinlian cried. "What secret, important words do you need for that? What three-legged Indra, or two-horned elephant, do you hide away in there that you are afraid someone may go in and see it? Tomorrow is Uncle Wu's birthday and we have all been invited to go there. Without making any bones about it, you can find something for me to offer when I go. If you will not, I will find some other husband who will. The Great Lady is going to give a dress and five *qian* of silver, and the others have flowers and ornaments to give. I am the only one who has nothing, and I had better stay at home."

"You may have a roll of fine red silk from the cupboard in the front court," Ximen Qing said.

"No," Jinlian cried, "I will not go at all if I have to take that red silk. Everyone will laugh at it."

"Be quiet and wait a minute," Ximen said. "I will go upstairs and get something for you. I am thinking about sending some presents to the Eastern Capital, some silk among them, and I will find something for you at the same time."

He went to the rooms of Li Ping'er, where he went upstairs and took two rolls of black silk woven with a gold thread, two of Nanjing colored silk, one of scarlet mixture, and one of kingfisher blue cloudy satin.

"I want to find a dress of taffeta for Jinlian to give as a present," he said to Li Ping'er. "If there isn't one, I must send a note to the silk shop and get one."

"There is no need to send to the silk shop," Li Ping'er said. "I have one, and a scarlet under-dress, and a blue skirt. There is no purpose in keeping one without the others, so she shall have them all." She took the clothes from a chest and herself carried them over to Jinlian.

"Sister," she said, "take either the under-dress or the skirt, whichever you like. We will wrap them up together and let the present be from both of us. That will save the trouble of going to the shop."

"But these are yours," Jinlian said, "1 cannot take them."

"Why say that?" Li Ping'er said. They argued pleasantly for some time, and at last Jinlian agreed. She asked Chen Jingji to write both their names on the card.

While this was happening, Bai Laiguang came to the gate.

"Is your master at home?" he said.

"No," said Ping'an, "he is not."

Bai Laiguang did not believe him and went into the house. There he found the window shut. "Well," he said, "it seems he really is not at home. Where has he gone?"

"He has gone outside the city to a farewell party," Ping'an said.

"Then he ought to be back soon," Bai Laiguang said.

"Uncle Bai," the boy said, "tell me what it is you wish to say, and I will give the message to my master when he comes back."

"Oh," Bai Laiguang said, "it is nothing very important, but I haven't seen him for a long time, so I thought I would call today. Since he is not here, I think I'll wait for him."

"I'm afraid he won't be back till very late," Ping'an said. "You will be tired of waiting."

Bai Laiguang paid no attention. He pushed open the door, went into the hall, and sat down on a chair. None of the boys did anything for him; they left him quite alone. But the Fates were kind to him. Ximen Qing and Yingchun, coming from the inner court with a roll of silk, passed the screen and came right upon him as he sat in the great hall. Yingchun put down the silk and hastily retired to the inner court.

"Isn't this my brother?" Bai Laiguang cried. "So you are at home after all."

There was no escape. Ximen Qing could only ask Bai Laiguang to be seated. Upon his head was a refurbished, remolded, ancient gauze hat, like those worn by the pilgrims to the summit of Taishan. He was wearing a white stuff gown that would hardly hold together and was fit only for the fire, the collar torn and the front all frayed. Upon his feet a pair of clapper-clopper black boots, out of shape and torn almost to shreds. And, inside the boots, socks like stirrups of yellow silk, which would not have imprisoned a fly.

They sat down, but Ximen Qing did not call for tea. Qintong was waiting beside him, and he ordered the boy to take the silk to the guestroom and ask Chen Jingji to wrap it up.

"I have not been to see you for a long time," Bai Laiguang said, waving his arms. "I am sorry."

"It is kind of you to remember me," Ximen Qing said. "Now that I have to go to the office every day, I have not much time to spend at home."

"What, Brother?" Bai Laiguang said. "Do you go to the office every day?"

"Yes," Ximen said, "I go twice every day and hear cases in the Hall. On the first and the fifteenth of every month I have to pay reverence to the tablets and to sign and stamp public documents and carry out public business, and attend to the police reports. Even when I get home, I have a great deal to do; I hardly have a moment's leisure. Today I have been outside the city with all the officers to say goodbye to Xu Nanxi, who has just been given a military appointment. The Governor of the Royal Estates, Eunuch Xue, has invited me to take wine with him tomorrow, but his place is so far away that I really shall not be able to get out there. The day after tomorrow

I have to go and welcome the new provincial governor, and the same day the fourth son of the Imperial Tutor in the Eastern Capital is to marry a princess. Then Grand Marshal Tong's nephew, Tong Tianyin, has recently been promoted to be the controller of the Palace Guards. All this makes me very busy, what with presents and so on, and, the last few days, I have been tired to death."

They talked for a long time, and, at last, Laian brought some tea. Bai Laiguang had taken only one mouthful when Daian hurried into the room with a red card in his hand. "His Lordship Xia is here," he said. "He is dismounting outside the gate."

Ximen Qing hastily went to the inner court to put on his ceremonial clothes. Bai Laiguang retired to a room in the wing, and from there looked through the lattice. He saw Xia come into the great hall and Ximen Qing, dressed in his robes of ceremony, come to receive him. They greeted one another and sat down in the places of host and guest. Qitong brought cups of tea.

"Yesterday," Xia said, "we were talking about the reception of the new governor. Today I have learned that his name is Zeng, and that he graduated in the third degree in the year *Yiwei*. His warrant has already reached Dongchang, and all our colleagues are going out to welcome him. Though you and I are military officers, there are administrative duties attached to our appointments, and it is one of our duties to enforce the law, which makes us rather different from mere soldiers. I think, therefore, that we should go the day after tomorrow and find a place a little distance from the town, where we may offer the new governor a dinner of welcome."

"That is an excellent idea," Ximen Qing said, "but pray do not trouble yourself about the matter. I will find some temple or private estate, and send servants and cooks to make all the necessary preparations."

"It is extremely kind of you," Xia said.

They drank another cup of tea and the magistrate took his leave. Ximen went to the gate to see him off. Then he came in again and took off his robes. Bai Laiguang had not gone. He came back into the great hall, sat down, and said to Ximen:

"For the last month or two, Brother, you have not been to our meetings, and the brotherhood is practically at an end. Sun is certainly old, but he has no capacity for organization, and Brother Ying does not trouble. In the seventh month, we went to the Temple of the Jade Emperor to celebrate the *Zhongyuan** and there were only three or four of us there including myself, and nobody with any money. All were empty-handed. We gave a great deal

---

*   The fifteenth day of the seventh month.

of trouble to Abbot Wu. He was very agreeable, and had engaged a story-teller specially for us, but he had to pay the man himself. The Abbot did not say anything, but we all felt most embarrassed. It was different when you were in charge. You always knew exactly what to do and how to do it. We hope it will not be long before you come and join us again."

"No, I think not," Ximen said, "the brotherhood had better be dissolved. I really have no time for things like that nowadays. If I can manage it, I will send a little offering to the Abbot as a thanks offering. But that must suffice. In the future you need not give me notice of any more of your meetings."

After this there was nothing for Bai Laiguang to say, yet he remained sitting there. Ximen Qing, seeing that he made no move, bade Qintong set a table in the side room. He had something to eat with Bai Laiguang, ordered wine to be warmed, and poured out several cups for him. At last, Bai Laiguang asked permission to leave. Ximen went with him only as far as the second door. "If you will excuse me," he said, "I will not go with you any far-ther. I have not my ceremonial hat and, in the circumstances, it would not be becoming that I should see you off." Then Bai Laiguang went away.

Ximen Qing returned to the great hall, pulled out a chair and sat on it. Then he shouted for Ping'an, over and over again. Ping'an came in and Ximen cursed him. "You thievish slave, how have you the audacity to stand there before me?" He called for his official attendants, and three or four men appeared immediately. Ping'an had no idea what was the matter, and was so terrified that his face became the color of wax. He knelt down.

"When I came home," Ximen Qing said, "I told you that if anyone called you were to say I was not at home. Why did you not obey me?"

"When Uncle Bai came," Ping'an said, "I told him you had gone out-side the city to a farewell dinner, and had not yet returned. He would not believe me and forced his way in. Then I followed him and asked if he would leave a message with me. He said nothing, but opened the door of the hall, went in, and sat down. Just at that moment, unfortunately, you came and met him."

"Don't try and deceive me with a lot of words," Ximen cried. "You are a coward. Where were you gambling and drinking, that when somebody came you were not attending to your duties at the gate?" He ordered the men to go and smell Ping'an's breath. They did so, but said: "We cannot smell any wine."

"You two, who can use the rod, give this slave a fair and honest finger-squeezing."

Two of the soldiers seized Ping'an, and one put the thumbscrews on the lad's fingers. They turned the screw till he could bear the pain no longer and screamed: "Indeed, I told him you were out. He forced his way in."

The soldiers released the screws and knelt before Ximen. "It is done," they said.

"Give him fifty stripes," Ximen cried. The number was counted; they went to fifty and stopped.

"Give him twenty more," Ximen said. They did so. The boy's skin was torn; the flesh was bruised, and blood poured down his legs.

"Stop," Ximen cried.

The soldiers removed the thumbscrews and the boy screamed shrilly.

"You rascally slave," Ximen said, "you said you were at the gate. It is my belief that you are always trying to get money out of people, and so, spoiling my good name. Let me hear not so much as a whisper of anything of the sort. If I do, you shall lose your legs."

Ping'an kowtowed, rose, and, pulling up his trousers, made off as fast as he could.

Then Ximen Qing saw Huatong standing beside him.

"Down with him," he cried to the soldiers, "and put the thumbscrews on him." The boy began to howl like a pig being killed.

Pan Jinlian was coming from her room to the inner court and, as she passed the door that opened into the great hall, she saw Meng Yulou standing behind the screen listening with all her ears.

"What is going on?" Jinlian said.

"I am listening to Father. He is having Ping'an beaten, and setting the thumbscrews on Huatong. I don't know why."

Qitong passed by. Yulou stopped him and asked what the punishment was for.

"Father is angry because Ping'an let Bai Laiguang come in," the boy said.

"Oh, that is not the real reason," Jinlian said. "The boy must have ruined something very precious or he wouldn't be beaten like that. What a shameless fellow Father is. He pulls a long face to show that he is the master of the house, but he is utterly without shame."

"What do you mean by saying that the boy must have ruined something very precious?" Yulou said, when Qitong had gone.

"I was going to tell you," Jinlian said, "but so far I have not had a chance. The other day, I went to see my mother on her birthday. While I was away, that little slave Shutong accepted several taels of silver from somebody, and went and bought two boxes of food and a jar of Jinhua wine and took them to the Sixth Lady's room. She and the young rascal drank there for a long time. Then he went away. When our shameless husband came back, he had not a word to say, but he and the boy went off to the study in the garden, locked the door, and goodness only knows what they did there. Ping'an had to take him a visiting card, found the door shut, and was standing by the window when Shutong opened the door and saw him. I imagine the young rascal must have told that shameless fellow all about it and today he is having the boy punished in revenge. I am very much afraid that in the future that young man will make mischief for everybody in the household, and be getting everybody into trouble."

"That is a nice thing to say," Yulou said, laughing. "Of course, in a household like this, some of us are wise and some are foolish, but not all of us have evil minds."

"No, you are quite wrong," Jinlian said. "Let me tell you this. At the present time there are only two people he really and truly cares for. One is a member of the household, and the other is not. His mind dwells continually upon those two. When he sees them, he laughs, he talks. But the rest of us are out of luck. He treats us like black-eyed chickens. The robber! He will never come to a natural end. He is fickle because the foxes have got hold of him, and he has become just like themselves. Sister, mark my words. There is going to be serious trouble in this household. Today, I have had a bother with him over the present. As soon as he comes in, he goes to his study. Today, I sent Chunmei to ask him to come and see me. Would you believe it, even in broad daylight that little slave had fastened the door. Chunmei pushed it open, went in and gave him a shock. He opened his eyes very wide and didn't know what to do. When he came to me, I cursed him well, but he simply protested and excused himself as best he could. He offered me a piece of red silk, but I would not have it. Then he went to the Sixth Lady's room to find something for me. The brigand knew he was in the wrong, so he took a dress of material woven with gold thread from her chest, and she brought it to me herself. I refused to take it. 'Sister,' she said, 'why think twice about it? Take the gown or the skirt, whichever you like best, and when you have made your choice, we will go to Brother Chen and get him to write a card for us.' At last I gave way, and she persuaded me to take the gown."

"Well," Yulou said, "that seems fair enough. I think she treated you very well."

"You don't understand," Jinlian said. "We have to yield place to her. In these days, the whole world fears the wide-eyed *Jin Gang*, and nobody bothers about the Buddha whose eyes are closed. In these affairs between husband and wife, if one gives the other the least bit of rope, he becomes like General Wang's orderly and looks upon you as one not worth the trouble of even the crudest affection."

"Really," Yulou said, laughing, "you are as hot as pepper."

They both laughed. Then Xiaoyu came to invite them to go to Yueniang's room to eat crabs. She told them she was going to ask Li Ping'er also.

Hand in hand, they went to the inner court and found Wu Yueniang and Li Jiao'er sitting beneath the eaves.

"What are you laughing about?" Yueniang asked.

"We are laughing at Father. He has been punishing Ping'an."

"No wonder I heard screams like those of a man running for his life," Yueniang said. "I didn't realize it was Ping'an being beaten. But why was this?"

"Because he broke something precious," Jinlian said.

"What was this precious thing?" Yueniang asked, seriously, "and how did he break it?"

Jinlian and Yulou broke into peals of laughter.

"I really don't understand why you find it so funny," Yueniang said, "or why you don't tell me what the joke is."

"Great Sister," Yulou said, "you do not know, of course. Father was beating the boy because he let Bai Laiguang come in."

"If that was all," Yueniang said, "well and good. But why did you talk about his breaking something precious? Really, I never heard of such a man. It would be far better if he sat on his behind in his own house instead of rushing into other people's houses when he has nothing to say worth saying."

"He came to see Father," Laian said.

"Nobody had fallen out of bed," Yueniang said, "and nobody is going to put up with behavior of that sort. It would be much nearer the mark to say that he came to fill his belly."

After a while, Li Ping'er and Ximen Dajie came. They sat in a circle and enjoyed the crabs. "There is some grape wine in my room," Yueniang told Xiaoyu. "Get it and warm some for the ladies."

"Oh, but when we eat crabs," Jinlian said, "we ought to have Jinhua wine." And, a little later: "It is a pity we have only this one course. How much nicer it would be if we had roast duck with our wine."

"It is late now," Yueniang said, "how can we have roast duck?"

Li Ping'er flushed. The words were meant for her, and they showed what was being thought of her. Yueniang was a simple-minded woman and did not appreciate the meaning of what was said.

When Ping'an had been beaten, he went outside. Ben the Fourth, Laixing, and the others hurried to discover why he had been punished.

"How should I know?" Ping'an said, weeping.

"I suppose Father was angry because you let Bai Laiguang come in," Laixing said.

"Well," Ping'an said, "I did all I could to stop him, but he insisted upon going in and then, unfortunately, Father came from the inner court and saw him. He had really nothing to talk about, but even after tea had been served he did not go away. Then his Lordship the Magistrate came and I was sure he would go, but he only retired to the wing room, and made no move to depart. Only when he had been given wine did he go. So I was punished like this. Father says I didn't stop him, but it was simply my bad luck that he would come in. Why should my poor legs be beaten for him? May heaven destroy this dog bone, may his sons become thieves and his daughters harlots! May the food he ate here break his backbone!"

"If his backbone breaks," Laixing said, "he will do well to dash in."

"May he choke and his gorge burst!" Ping'an cried. "Of all the shameless, faceless people in the world, there is none so shameless as this dog bone. He sneaks in so silently that the dog doesn't even bark: he shows his teeth and gobbles down our food. It was a beggar got him, and his rump will rot, the thievish turtle!"

"But if his rump does rot," Laixing said laughing, "none of us will ever know. He will tell us he is dribbling."

They all laughed.

"I suppose he has no rice to cook for his supper," Ping'an said. "How hungry his wife must be if he has nothing else to do but come to other people's houses to get food, and so save his own. This cannot go on. He had better let his wife keep another man on the quiet, and be himself a turtle. That would be more straightforward and he would not get himself cursed by the servants of other households."

Meanwhile Daian finished having his hair cut, paid the barber, and came away. To Ping'an he said: "I don't wish to say anything, but I can't help it. You are our master's servant. How is it you don't understand his temperament? You have no reason to complain. The proverb says: No one wants a boy to make water of gold and lay eggs of silver. What people do want is a boy who realizes what the situation is and acts accordingly. If Uncle Ying and Uncle Xie come, it is all right to let them come in whether Father is at home or not. They are good friends and have no secrets from one another, but as for the rest, if they come when our master has told you to say that he is not at home, why do you let them in? If he does not punish you, whom should he punish?"

Then Ben the Fourth made a joke. "Ping'an," he said, "you must learn how to be a little boy and play again. You see, he too knows how to play, and plays kickball all day."

They all laughed at this, and Ben the Fourth said: "You were punished for letting someone come in, but what had Huatong done? The fruit was not so tasty that you needed anyone else to help you enjoy it. When we have a banquet, we like to have others to keep us company, but I have never heard that the same thing is true when we are wearing thumbscrews."

Huatong rubbed his hands and cried. Daian said jokingly to him: "My son, stop crying. Your mother has brought you up too tenderly. Now somebody has given your fingers something to taste. Why don't you settle down to enjoy it?"

Ximen Qing watched Chen Jingji packing up the presents and the rolls of silk, and writing cards. The following day these gifts were to be sent to the Eastern Capital for their patrons there.

The next day, Ximen went to his office. Yueniang and the others, with pearls and jewels in their hair, and silk and embroidery upon their bodies, took sedan chairs to join the festivities at Aunt Wu's house. Laixing's wife, in a smaller chair, was in attendance upon them. Only Sun Xue'e and Ximen Dajie stayed at home to look after the house. In the morning, Han Daoguo sent a number of presents as a token of gratitude to Ximen. There was a jar of Jinhua wine, a teal, a pair of pig's trotters, four roast ducks, and four smoked fish. On the card that came with them was written: "The young student Han Daoguo kowtows and offers these." Because there was no one at home, Shutong did not accept them, and the boxes were set down. When Ximen Qing came back from the office, the boy showed them to him. Ximen bade Qintong go to the shop and bring Han Daoguo to him.

"What is this?" he said. "Why do you bring these presents? I cannot possibly accept them."

Han Daoguo made a reverence. "You have been extremely kind to me," he said. "You had compassion on me and avenged me. I and all my household are grateful to you. These trifles only express a tiny part of my gratitude. Take them, please, even if only as a joke."

"I cannot do so," Ximen Qing said. "You are associated with me in business, and that means that you are like one of my own household. Kindly send someone to take the things away."

Han Daoguo grew excited and insisted that Ximen Qing should accept them. After a long discussion, Ximen told one of the servants to take the ducks and the wine, but nothing more. The rest, he said, must all be taken back. Then he sent a boy with his card to invite Ying Bojue and Xie Xida. He said to Han Daoguo: "Tell Laibao to look after the shop this afternoon, and you come and join us."

"So besides not taking anything from me," Han Daoguo said, "you pile kindness after kindness upon me." He promised to come, and went away.

Ximen Qing bought many fresh fruits and dishes, and that afternoon, in the arbor by the Hall of the Kingfishers, they were all set out upon a square table. Ying Bojue and Xie Xida came early.

"Han has been at a great deal of trouble to buy presents for me," Ximen Qing said, "but I would not take them. He implored me to accept them, but I would only have the wine and ducks. I didn't wish to keep these all for myself, so I sent for you."

"He spoke about the matter to me," Ying Bojue said; "he said he was going to buy you some presents, but I told him you certainly would not accept them and that he should not take the trouble. Was I not right? I might have been in your very mind. You did refuse them."

They drank tea and played backgammon, and soon afterwards, Han Daoguo came. When they had greeted one another, he sat down. Ying Bojue and Xie Xida were in the places of honor, Ximen Qing in the host's seat, and Han Daoguo opposite. Four plates and four bowls were immediately brought in, with a host of dishes. Laian was told to open the jar of Jinhua wine, and heat it in a brass jar. Shutong was told to serve it.

"Go to the inner court," Ying Bojue said to Shutong, "and ask your mistress if she will not send some of her crabs for your Uncle Ying. Tell her I like them very much."

"You foolish dog," Ximen cried, "there are none left. Mayor Xu sent me a basket or two, but the ladies have eaten them all. We preserved the few that were left."

He told a boy to bring a few pickled crabs. "Today," he said, "the ladies have gone to a celebration at the Wus' house."

Before long, Huatong brought the pickled crabs. Ying Bojue and Xie Xida tried to see who could eat the faster, and ate them every one.

"Your Uncle Ying," Bojue said to Shutong, "never thinks of drinking wine without a song to it. You are always boasting of the way you can sing the songs of the South, but I have never heard you sing any. Let us have one today, and then I'll drink my wine."

Shutong began to beat time with his hands, and made ready to sing. Ying Bojue stopped him. "If that's the way you're going to sing, you may go on as long as you like, but I shan't pay any attention. When you play the part of a dragon, try to look like a dragon; and when you play the tiger, be a tiger. Off you go, get your face painted, and put on a girl's dress."

Shutong stood still, glancing at Ximen Qing to see what his master had to say to this. Ximen only laughed and cursed Ying Bojue, saying that he was just the kind of man who would seek to deprave a serving boy.

"Since he must have it so," he said to Shutong, "send Daian to the front court, and tell him to ask one of the maids for some clothes. Then go and paint your face."

Daian went first to Jinlian's rooms and asked Chunmei. She refused him. Then he went to Yueniang's apartments, and Yuxiao lent him four silver pins, a comb, a pendant, a pair of gilded imitation jade earrings, a scarlet double-fronted silk dress and a green skirt with purple trimmings. Then Shutong took powder and rouge to the study and dressed himself. So charmingly did he adorn himself that he looked exactly like a real girl. He went back to the table and offered a cup of wine to Ying Bojue with both hands. Then he cleared his throat and sang.

> Red withered leaves swirl down towards the water
> Though the plums are still young upon the branches.
> My brows lack color: who shall give it to them?
> Spring comes, and sorrow with it.
> Spring goes, but sorrow stays.
> Mountains and deep waters sunder us; we are together no more.
> I count the days until you come again
> And the tip of my brush is wounded by my grief.

Bojue applauded vigorously. "Anyone like you," he said to the boy, "need feel no shame when he eats his food. Your voice is as sweet as a flute, and the girls in the bawdy house simply cannot compare with you. Many, many times I have heard them sing, but there isn't one of them with a voice so sweet and rich as yours. Brother," he added, turning to Ximen Qing, "I don't wish to flatter you, but you really ought to be delighted to have such a boy in your household."

Ximen Qing smiled.

"Why do you smile?" Ying Bojue said. "I am perfectly serious. You must not undervalue this boy. You should regard him with unusual favor in all things. It was most fortunate that Li thought fit to send him to you. He did you a great favor."

"Yes, indeed," Ximen said. "Now, when I am out, this boy and my son-in-law are responsible for everything connected with the study. My son-in-law is mainly concerned with the shop."

Ying Bojue drank his wine and poured out two cups. "I shall be angry if you do not drink this," he said to Shutong. "Since I offer it to you, there is no reason why you should not."

Shutong looked at Ximen Qing.

"Since it is your uncle who offers it to you," Ximen said, "you had better drink it."

The boy knelt on one knee, gracefully bent his white neck, and sipped a mouthful, giving the rest of the wine back to Bojue. Then he turned to offer wine to Xie Xida, and sang another song.

"How old is this boy, Brother?" Bojue asked.

"Just sixteen," Ximen said.

Then Xie Xida asked the boy how many southern melodies he knew.

"Indeed, I know only a few," Shutong said. "I have sung for the amusement of Uncle Ying and yourself."

"You are certainly a clever boy," Xie Xida said, and he, in turn, offered Shutong some wine. Then the boy went to Han Daoguo, but Han Daoguo said: "How shall I take such a liberty in his Lordship's presence?"

"Today you are my guest," Ximen said.

"It is not to be thought of," Han Daoguo said, "your Lordship must drink first, and then perhaps I may make bold myself."

Shutong offered wine to his master, and again sang a song. When Ximen had drunk it, the boy went to Han Daoguo. Han stood up to take the wine. "Sit down," Bojue said. "The boy will sing for you." Han sat down, and Shutong sang again. Before the boy had finished his song, Han Daoguo had swallowed all his wine in one breath.

They were still drinking when Daian came and said: "Uncle Ben the Fourth is here, and would like to speak to you." Ximen gave orders that he was to be shown in. Ben the Fourth came in, made a reverence, and sat down. Daian brought chopsticks and a cup for him, and was told to go to the inner court for more dishes.

"How is the work getting on?" Ximen Qing asked Ben the Fourth.

"We are putting the tiles on the first story," Ben the Fourth said, "and yesterday we laid the foundations of the arbor. But we have not yet got the materials for the wings or for the back part of the living rooms. We are having to wait another five days for the flooring tiles: we cannot use any of the old ones. And we are still without some of the materials we need for the walls. We have earth enough to fill up the foundations and the artificial mound. Then we need a hundred cartloads of lime, and they will cost twenty taels of silver."

"Do not trouble about the lime," Ximen said. "When I go to the office tomorrow, I will order the lime burners to get it for you. Yesterday, Eunuch Liu of the brick kilns promised he would send me some. All you need to do is to tell him what you want and send a few taels, for this matter is as much one of friendship as of business. You will only need to buy the wood."

"Yesterday," Ben the Fourth said, "you told me to go outside the city to look at another place there. Early this morning Zhang An and I went. The place belongs to a noble family, but now the head of the family has died, and they are anxious to dispose of it. It is no use to us as it is, and I told them we should pull most of it down. They want five hundred taels for it but, in my opinion, if we decide to have it, we had better take some money with us and go to talk the matter over with them. We certainly ought to secure it for something like three hundred and fifty taels. Besides the wood, the tiles, bricks and mortar will amount to one or two hundred taels."

"Let me think whose house this is," Bojue said. "It must be Xiang the Fifth's. Xiang the Fifth was brought by somebody before the military court, and the case cost him a great deal of money. He used to keep Luo Cun there, and that is why he is so short of ready money. I'm sure he will be satisfied with three hundred taels. His hands are so cold that he will gladly welcome something to warm them."

"Tomorrow," Ximen said to Ben the Fourth, "you and Zhang An take two large bars of silver and go and talk to him. If he will accept three hundred taels, get on with the work."

After a while a bowl of soup and a plate of cakes were brought from the inner court. Ben the Fourth ate them, and then drank in company with the others. Shutong sang another song, and went away.

"It is very dull drinking wine like this," Ying Bojue said. "Won't you send for a dice box and let us have a game?"

Ximen Qing told Daian to go to the Sixth Lady's room and get a dice box. The boy brought it and set it down before Bojue. Then he went over and whispered to Ximen Qing: "Little Brother is crying, and Yingchun told me to ask you to send someone to fetch the Sixth Lady."

"Put down your wine jar," Ximen answered quickly, "and send a boy with a lantern at once. Where are the two boys?"

"Qintong and Qitong have already gone with lanterns to bring the ladies home," Daian said.

Ying Bojue noticed that there were six dice in the dice box. "I will cast a number," he said, "and I want the name of the tablet to agree with the number 1 throw. If there be anyone who cannot tell it, he must drink a cup of wine for forfeit, and the one next to him must sing a song. If he can't sing, he must tell a story instead."

"Ah, you funny dog," Ximen Qing cried, "you are too well versed in tricks."

"When the commander-in-chief lets forth a fart," Bojue said, "it must be obeyed as if it were the Emperor's command. It is no use your trying to keep me in order."

He said to Daian: "Pour a cup of wine as a punishment for your master, and then I will give my orders."

Ximen Qing laughed and drank the cup of wine.

"Listen, all of you," Bojue said, "I am going to give an order. If I make a mistake, I am ready to be punished for it. Here you are: 'Zhang Sheng got drunk and lay down in the Western Pavilion. How much did he drink? One large jar or two small ones?' Indeed it is a *yao* (one)."

Ximen Qing told Shutong to pour the wine, and Xie Xida had to sing.

Bojue drank the wine and passed the dice box to Xie Xida, that he might cast the dice. It was Ximen Qing's turn to sing. When he had thrown the dice, Xie Xida said: "Thanks be to Hong'er who helped me to bed. What time was it? The third night watch, and the fourth division thereof." Strangely enough, he really threw a four.

"Brother Xie," Bojue said, "that is four cups for you."

"Give me two," Xie Xida said, "I am no great drinker."

Shutong poured out two cups and Xie Xida drank one, then waited for Ximen Qing to sing. Meanwhile, he and Ying Bojue made short work of the nuts. Ximen Qing told them he could not sing, and would tell them a story, instead.

"There was once a man," he said, "who went to a fruit shop and asked the shopman if he had any olives. 'Yes,' said the shopman, and brought some out to show his customer. The man tasted a number of them. 'I am glad you like them,' said the shopman, 'but why don't you buy some, instead of popping them into your mouth like that?' 'I like them,' the customer said, 'because they are so soothing to the chest.' 'All you think about,' the shopman retorted, 'is soothing your chest. It never occurs to you that you are giving me a pain.' "

Everybody laughed. Ying Bojue said: "If you have a pain at the heart, order another two plates of nuts for us. I am like the old woman who went around picking up horses' droppings. The moister they are, the more drying they take."

Xie Xida drank the second cup, and it was Ximen Qing's turn to throw the dice. "I have left my gold pin and token behind. How much do they weigh? About fifty or sixty *qian*." He threw a five. Shutong poured out two half-cups of wine.

"Brother," Xie Xida said, "you are no poor drinker. If you drink only two cups it won't be fair, drink four. I offer them to you myself."

Then it was Han Daoguo's turn, but he asked Ben the Fourth to throw before him, for Ben the Fourth, he said, was older than he.

"I, too, cannot sing," Ben the Fourth said, "so I must tell a story." When Ximen Qing had drunk his two cups of wine, Ben the Fourth began. "Once upon a time a magistrate had to investigate a case of unlawful association. He asked the man how he set about the business. 'My head to the East,' said the man, 'and my feet to the East also.' 'Nonsense,' said the magistrate, 'whoever heard of going about sexual intercourse in that unsatisfactory way?' At that moment a man ran up and plumped himself on his knees before the magistrate and said: 'If you're in need of a clerk who knows how to be unsatisfactory, I'm the very man for you.' *

"Ah ha! Brother Pen," said Ying Bojue, "you don't intend to miss any chances! Your master is not an old man. You might be excused for anything else, but how can you think of getting a job like that which is evidently in your mind, in his household?"

Ben the Fourth was flustered. He blushed and said: "Uncle Ying, what do you mean? Such a thing never entered my head."

"What I said is like a scabbard made of sandalwood. The sword is gone and only the scabbard remains."

This made Ben the Fourth extremely uncomfortable, but he could not escape. He felt as though he were sitting on a cushion of needles. Ximen Qing finished his four cups of wine and it was Ben the Fourth's turn to throw the dice. Just as he was about to take them up, Laian came in and said that he was wanted by somebody from the tile works. Ben the Fourth was so anxious to get away that, as soon as he heard this, he ran off like a golden cicada breaking out of its chrysalis.

"Now that he has gone," Ximen Qing said, "it is your turn, Han." Han Daoguo took up the dice.

"I obey your orders," he said. "The old lady beat Hong Niang with a rod. How many blows did she administer? About forty or fifty."

"It is now my turn to sing," Bojue said, "but I shan't. I am going to tell a story." Then he said to Shutong: "Pour out wine for all of us, not excepting your master. Then listen to my story.

"Once a priest and his disciple went to a house to take some religious papers. When they came to their benefactor's door, they found that the pupil's girdle had become loose and the papers had fallen out. 'It looks as though you had no bottom,' the priest said to the young man. 'If I hadn't,' returned the pupil, 'you would not be able to exist for a single day.' "

"You dirty dog," Ximen cried, "but with a dog's mouth like yours, I suppose we must not expect elephant's teeth."

The party went on.

Daian went to the front court and called for Huatong. They set off with a lantern to Aunt Wu's house to find Li Ping'er. When they had told her that the baby was crying, she did not even wait to pay her respects to the young couple, but presented her gift and asked to be excused. The two Wu ladies would not let her go. "You must wait for the bride and bridegroom," they said.

---

* Pun on the word *Xingfang*, which means "sexual intercourse" when expressed with one character, and a kind of clerk when another character is used.

Then Wu Yueniang intervened. "Please excuse her," she said, "there is no one at home, and the baby is crying for her. We will stay, for we have no such reason for anxiety." So the Wu ladies allowed Li Ping'er to go. Daian left Huatong, and he and Qintong accompanied the chair on its way home.

After the bridal pair had received them, Yueniang and the others set off in their four chairs, but they only had one lantern to guide them. It was the twenty-fourth day of the eighth month and extremely dark. Yueniang asked where the other lantern was. "Why have we only one?" she said.

"I brought two," Qitong said, "but Daian and Qintong took the other when they went back with the Sixth Lady."

Yueniang said no more, but Jinlian took up the matter. "How many did you bring from the house?" she asked the boy.

"Qintong and I brought two, then Daian and Huatong came and took one of them. Daian left Huatong behind, and went off with Qintong after the Sixth Lady's chair."

"Didn't Daian bring a lantern with him?" Jinlian said.

Then Huatong answered. "We did bring one."

"If he had one, why did he take another?"

"That is what I told him," said Qintong, "but he took it by force."

"You see how it is," Jinlian said to Yueniang. "That rascally Daian is trying to curry favor with her. When I get home, I shall have something to say about this."

"Oh," said Yueniang, "how easily you get excited. They are only boys, and their master sent for her. Why shouldn't they take the lanterns?"

"Really, Sister," Jinlian said, "that is no way to talk. The rest of us might put up with it, but you are the chief among us, and you ought to see that discipline is maintained in the family. If it were not dark, it would not matter, but it is dark, and here we are with four chairs and only one lantern. Really there is no excuse for it."

At length the chairs reached the door. Yueniang and Li Jiao'er went to their own rooms; Jinlian and Yulou got out together. As they went in, Jinlian asked where Daian was. Ping'an was telling her that the boy was serving in the back court when Daian came out. Jinlian cursed him roundly. "You flattering young ruffian. You keep your eyes open and think you'll wait on those who are in favor. But mind your step. You had one lantern. That was enough. The way you go on will not do at all. You took another lantern by brute force, and you changed the boys. So she got two lanterns for her one chair and we, with four chairs, had only one lantern. Do you consider we are not your master's ladies?"

"Mother," Daian said, "you have no reason to blame me. When Father heard the baby was crying, he told me to take a lantern and come at once to bring the Sixth Lady home. He was afraid the baby might make himself ill, crying. If Father hadn't told me to do so, I should never have dreamed of doing such a thing."

"Don't try to deceive me, you rascal," Jinlian cried. "He may have told you to bring her home, but he did not tell you to take all the lanterns. Little Brother, you are one of those birds that always fly to the places where things are going best. Don't make a mistake. You should put your hand to the cold stove as well as to the hot one. I suppose you think our luck is out."

"How can you say that?" Daian said. "If such a thing ever entered my mind, one day when I am riding my horse, may I fall off and break my ribs."

"You deceitful young scamp," Jinlian said, "don't try to go too fast. I shall keep my eye on you." She and Yulou went to the back.

"I always seem to get into scrapes of this kind," Daian said to the other servants. "Father told me to go and fetch the Sixth Lady, and now the Fifth Lady turns and scolds me."

At the second door, Yulou and Jinlian met Laian. They asked him where Ximen Qing was. The boy told them that he was with Ying Bojue, Xie Xida and Han Daoguo, drinking wine.

"Brother Shutong," he added, "has dressed up as a singing girl and is singing for them. Wouldn't you like to go and see?"

The two ladies went and peeped through the window. Ying Bojue, already drunk, sat in the upper seat. His hat was on one side and his head was bobbing about as though it were pulled by strings. Xie Xida could not keep his eyes open. Shutong was still dressed as a girl, serving wine and singing Southern melodies. Ximen Qing told Qintong to put some powder on Bojue's face. Afterwards, the boy made a circlet of grass and, stealing behind Bojue, put it on his head. Yulou and Jinlian, standing outside, could not help laughing. "The scoundrel!" they said. "Sin will be his companion as long as he lives. He behaves just about as badly as anybody could do."

Ximen Qing heard the laughter outside and sent a boy to see who was there, but the two women slipped away to the inner court.

It was the first night watch before the party broke up. Ximen Qing went to sleep in the Sixth Lady's room. When Jinlian went to her own apartment, she said to Chunmei: "What did the Sixth Lady say when she came home?"

"Nothing," Chunmei said.

Then Jinlian asked: "Did that shameless creature go to see her?"

"After the Sixth Lady came back," Chunmei said, "Father went twice to see her."

"Did the child really cry so much that he sent the boys to bring her home?"

"Yes," Chunmei said, "he screamed terribly this afternoon. Whether he was carried about or put in his cot, it made no difference. He cried, and no one could do anything for him. So somebody went and told Father, and he sent a boy to fetch her."

"In that case," Jinlian said, "all right. I suspected that that shameless creature had made up the whole thing so as to get her back. Whose clothes is Shutong wearing?"

"Daian came to me," Chunmei said, "but I soon packed him about his business. Finally, he got some from Yuxiao."

"If they ever come again," Jinlian said, "give nothing for that boy to wear." She realized that Ximen Qing was not coming to her that night, and she fastened her door and went angrily to bed.

To return to Ying Bojue. He had noticed that Ben the Fourth was in charge of all the work that was being done, and apparently making money thereby. Tomorrow he was going to take money to buy Xiang's house and would make at least several taels of silver out of that deal. So he was glad of the chance to score off Ben the Fourth, when he was so indiscreet as to tell that story, and to point out his little weaknesses. He had meant Ben the Fourth to know what he was doing. Ben the Fourth was greatly perturbed, and, the next day, he packed up three taels of silver and took them to Ying Bojue's house. Bojue pretended to be greatly surprised. "I have done nothing for you," he said, "why should you do this?"

"It is a long time since I made you any present," Ben the Fourth said, "and all I ask is that you will speak well of me to my master. If you will, I shall be eternally grateful to you."

Ying Bojue took the silver, offered a cup of tea to Ben the Fourth, and escorted him to the door. Then he took the silver to his room.

"If a husband does not make his power manifest," he told his wife, "the wife will never get a new dress. It was I who introduced that son of a dog Ben the Fourth to Ximen Qing, and now he has his finger in every pie. And everything that comes in, he puts into his own bowl, and never thinks any more about it. Ximen leaves all the work on the estate to him, and now he is going to buy Xiang the Fifth's place. He has done well for himself. But at the party yesterday, my chance came and I took it and showed him up. That frightened him and, as I expected, today he came and gave me three taels of silver. Now we can buy some cloth, and make clothes for the children through the winter."

## CHAPTER 36

# Ximen Qing Entertains the Laureate

My heart is oppressed when I think of the distance before me
My spirit shrinks with fear before the journey I must take.
How can I not dread the hardship of the way?
Yet always I think of my duty to my country.
Ji Bu never forgot his promise
Hou Ying was faithful to his word.
In human hearts devotion always conquers
And men give up the thought of gold.

The next morning, Ximen Qing went with his colleague Xia to welcome the new governor. He also went to see his new property and distributed gifts to all the workmen to show his appreciation of their labors. It was late when he reached home. As soon as he came to the gate, Ping'an told him that a messenger from Dongchangfu had brought a letter for him from Zhai, the Comptroller of the Imperial Tutor's household. "I took the letter to my mistress's room," he said. "Tomorrow about noon the messenger will call for your answer." Ximen Qing hastened to the upper room, opened the letter, and read it.

To be delivered at the mansion of the most worthy Ximen [it read]. For long I have been hearing of your fame and great renown, but it is long too since I beheld your glorious countenance. I have often benefited by your most gracious kindness, and it is almost impossible for me to express my sense of indebtedness.

Some time ago, you were good enough to convey to me your instructions, and I have engraved them upon my heart. In every possible manner, I have done my utmost to serve you with his Eminence. So now, if I may trouble you about a trifle, there is a matter that I have already mentioned to your worthy attendant, and, doubtless, you have done what I desired. I take this opportunity of sending you my humble card together with ten taels of gold. Now I await your convenience. Meanwhile, may I present my best respects and trust that your high-mightiness will condescend to reply. Your kindness shall be ever in my heart.

The new laureate, Cai Yiquan, is His Eminence's ward. He has just received the Imperial Command to return to his native place to visit his parents. He will pass by your honorable mansion and I trust you may find it possible to entertain him. He will be grateful for any kindness you may show him.

From my heart, the day after the Autumn Day, your servant Zhai Qian at the Capital.

When he had read this letter, Ximen Qing sighed. "Send a boy for a go-between at once," he cried. "However did I come to forget all about this matter?"

"What are you talking about?" Wu Yueniang said.

"Comptroller Zhai, of the Imperial Tutor's household," Ximen said, "wrote to me the other day. He said he had no son and asked me to find a young girl for him. He does not care whether she is rich or poor, and expense is no object with him. He simply wishes to find a good girl who will present him with a son and heir. He said if I told him what I spent on wedding presents he would repay me in full. And he said he would do all he could for me with the Imperial Tutor. But I have been so busy going to the office and attending to one matter and another, that I had forgotten all about it, and Laibao has not reminded me, since he is at the shop every day. Now Zhai has been put to the trouble of sending someone all this way with a letter, and he asks me what has been done in the matter, and sends a present of ten taels. Tomorrow the messenger is coming for an answer. What can I say to him? He will be very angry. Send at once for the go-between and tell her to find a girl without delay. She need not trouble about the girl's family. She must be a good girl and somewhere about sixteen or eighteen years old, that's all. Whatever it costs, I will pay. Wait! Why shouldn't we send him Xiuchun, the Sixth Lady's maid? She is a pretty girl."

"You lazybones!" Yueniang said, "what have you been thinking about? He asked you to get him a really fine girl, and you ought to have done so. But you yourself have not left Xiuchun alone; we can't send her. You must treat this business as one of real importance. Sometime in the future Zhai may be very useful to you. If you let your boat drift into the rapids, how can you use your oars? It isn't like buying ordinary merchandise, where you go to the market with your money and carry off what you like. When you are buying a girl, you must wait and give the go-between a chance, and see one after another. Some girls are good and some are bad. You don't seem to realize that it is not a simple matter."

"But he wants an answer tomorrow," Ximen Qing said. "What am I to say to him?"

"Have you been a magistrate all this time and can't manage a little affair like this? Tell the boy to be ready for the messenger when he comes; give him plenty of journey money and a letter saying that you have found the girl, but that her clothes and things are not ready yet, and you will send her as soon as they are. When the messenger has gone, you can get someone to find a girl for you. There will be plenty of time. That's the way out of your difficulty, and you will have done a good day's work."

Ximen Qing smiled. "You are right," he said. He sent for Chen Jingji to write the letter. Next day when the messenger came, Ximen Qing himself went to see him and questioned him. "When does the Laureate's boat arrive? I must get ready to welcome him."

"When I left the Capital," the man said, "he had just left the court. Master Zhai said he feared the Laureate might be short of money for his expenses, and perhaps you would lend him some. Then, perhaps, you will write to Master Zhai, and he will repay you."

"Tell Master Zhai," Ximen Qing said, "that no matter how much the Laureate needs, I will gladly lend it to him." He told Chen Jingji to take the messenger to an anteroom and entertain him. When he was ready to leave, Ximen gave him a letter and five taels of silver for journey money. The man made a reverence and set out well pleased upon his long journey.

It may be remembered that some time before, An Shen had passed the examination in the highest place, but that the censors had objected that he was the younger brother of An Zhun, who had been the first minister in the last reign. As a younger son of an evil party, they declared, he must not be placed at the head of all the scholars. Consequently, Huizong could not do otherwise than put Cai Yun in the position. Cai Yun then went to the palace of the Imperial Tutor to be his ward. Later, he was appointed head of the office of Secret Archives, and given leave to go and visit his parents.

Wu Yueniang sent a boy for the two old women Feng and Xue, and another marriage maker. She told them to make a thorough search for a good girl, and to bring her full particulars when they thought they had found one.

One day Ximen Qing instructed Laibao to go to the river to see what he could find out about Cai's boat. Cai was traveling on the same boat as An Zhun, who had been given the third degree at the same examination as himself. An was so poor that he had not remarried. He seemed to be unlucky in every way. He had left the Court to try to find a wife in his native place, and so the two scholars came to be traveling together on the same boat.

Laibao took Ximen Qing's card and went on board. He had a dinner sent from the shore.

Before the Laureate had left the Capital, Zhai had told him that at Qinghe he would meet a certain Captain Ximen, one of the Imperial Tutor's clients. "He is a rich man," Zhai had said, "and a very pleasant fellow. It was through his Eminence's influence that he came into his present position. I am sure that he will entertain you most hospitably if you should go there."

The Laureate had not forgotten this and he was delighted when he found that Ximen Qing's servant had come so far to meet him, bringing such a handsome present.

The next day, he and An came to call on Ximen Qing who had arranged a feast in their honor. Ximen had seen a number of actors and singers from Suzhou, and now he sent for four of them. Cai offered a present of a silk handkerchief, a number of books, and a pair of shoes. An brought a gift of books and a handkerchief, with four bags of young tea and four Hangzhou fans. Both the scholars wore robes of ceremony and black hats, and sent their cards before them. Ximen Qing, wearing his ceremonial hat, welcomed them and invited them to go to the great hall. There they made reverences to one another; the two young men offered their presents to Ximen Qing, and they all sat down in the proper order of guests and host.

"My friend Zhai at the Capital," the Laureate said to Ximen Qing, "has spoken very highly of you. He says your honorable family is the most important in Qinghe. Consequently, I have been longing to see you for some time, but this is the first opportunity I have had. Now that today I have been permitted to enter your hall, I feel that Heaven has indeed been gracious to me."

"You are unduly kind," Ximen said. "I had a letter from Master Zhai the other day telling me that your worthinesses were about to visit us on your emblossomed boat. I should have been there to welcome you, but, unfortunately, my official duties would not allow me. I must most humbly beg your pardon. May I be allowed the honor of knowing from what enchanted country and glorious family you worthy gentlemen come?"

"The humble student before you," Cai said, "is a native of Kuanglu in Chuzhou, and his poor name is Yiquan. I had the good fortune to take the first place in the examination and to receive an appointment as head of the Department of Secret Archives. At the moment, I am on leave, and on my way to visit my parents."

"The humble student before you," An said, in his turn, "is a native of Qiantang of Zhejiang, and his undistinguished name is Fengshan. I have just received the appointment of Inspector of the Board of Works. I, too, am on leave and am returning to marry in my native place. May we know your own honorable second name?"

"I am only a poor military officer of low rank," Ximen Qing said. "How should I dare to allow myself to be called by my second name?" When they pressed him, he said at last: "My poor name is Siquan. I have frequently been favored by the kindness of his Eminence through the good offices of Master Zhai, and, in that way, was granted my present appointment as Captain. I perform certain legal duties but am really quite unfitted for the post."

"Honored Sir," the Laureate said, "you are not a man of mean ambition, and your reputation for delicacy has long been known. Do not let us stand on ceremony with one another."

Ximen Qing invited them to take off their robes of ceremony in the pavilion in the garden. But the Laureate said: "I am anxious to get home and our boat is at the wharf. Really I ought to go now. Yet, since I have basked in the sunshine of your company, I feel I cannot leave you so soon. What shall I do? What shall I do?"

"If you two noble gentlemen," Ximen Qing said, "do not disdain this snail's abode, pray let the banner of literature rest here a while. Take a little food with me, and let a small repast of celery prove the earnest of my goodwill."

"Since we are offered such exalted hospitality," the Laureate said, "we humble students can do no less than obey your commands." They took off their ceremonial robes and sat down.

The servants brought more tea. Cai looked about him. The garden, the pool, the pavilions and the flowers stretched so far and were so luxuriant that he could not see everything at a single glance. "This is fairyland," he said delightedly. A table was set and they played chess.

After a while, Ximen said: "I have brought a few actors here today for your amusement."

"Where are they?" An said. "Why not send for them?"

In a moment the four actors appeared and kowtowed.

"Which of you take the part of the hero and heroine?" Cai said. "And what are your names?"

One replied: "I take the hero's part; my name is Gou Zixiao. This is the heroine and he is called Zhou Shun. This one takes the second part: he is called Yuan Dan, and the other, the young man, is Hu Zao."

An asked them where they came from. Gou Zixiao said they were from Suzhou. "Good!" said An. "Now go and dress and then play for us."

The four actors went away to dress. Ximen Qing told someone to find women's clothes and ornaments for them. He told Shutong to dress up too. So, three women and two men, they played from *The Incense Sachet*.

At the upper end of the great hall two tables were set. The two scholars sat in the seats of honor, and Ximen Qing in the host's place. While they drank their wine the actors finished one act. An saw Shutong dressed as a girl and asked who he was.

"That is my boy Shutong," Ximen Qing told him. An called the boy to him and gave him some wine. "This boy excels all the boys I have ever seen," he said. Meanwhile Cai summoned the actors who had taken the parts of girls and gave wine to them. Then he called for the song of Chao Yuan. Gou Zixiao obeyed, and, clapping his hands, began.

> By the willows and the flowers
> The spider weaves a glistening web under the eaves.
> Beside the mountains and the waters
> The east wind is kind to the horse's back.
> But I must journey like a wandering spirit
> Dreaming about my home, whether I will or not.
> The geese are silent, and the fishes deep beneath the water
> And my heart is broken with the pain of separation
> The day is short. My mother, in the northern hall, wearies of her
>   dreams.
> When shall I come to the Ninth Palace of Gold?

Then An asked Shutong, if he knew the lines beginning: "The mercy of the gods is infinite" from *The Jade Bracelet*. "I do," Shutong said, and began.

> The mercy of the gods is infinite
> I met my father and my mother again
> It is a kindness man may seldom hope for.
> Fortune has given me a peaceful life, a worthy mate.
> I fly as the clouds fly in the wind
> My love to me is like a female phoenix to her mate.
> True it must be that not in this life marriages are made
> And, in my last life, I must have set the jade in Lantian.

An, who was from Hangzhou, was fond of boys. He was delighted with Shutong's singing, held his hand, and took wine from his mouth.

After a time they had all had wine enough, and Ximen Qing took his guests to look at the gardens. They played chess in the summerhouse. Ximen told the boys to bring two boxes filled with every kind of delicacy to eat with their wine.

"This is the first time we have met you," the Laureate said. "We must not place too great a strain upon your hospitality. It is late and we should go."

"Noble Cai," Ximen cried, "how can you think of going yet? Are you really thinking of going back to your boat?"

"I propose to spend the night in the Temple of Eternal Felicity, outside the walls," Cai said.

"It is too late for you to go outside the city now," Ximen Qing said. "Keep one or two of your attendants here and let the rest return tomorrow for you. Then we shall all be content."

"I greatly appreciate your kindness," Cai said, "but I hesitate to give you so much trouble." Nevertheless, he and his companion told their servants to go to the temple and spend the night there, and come again in the morning with their horses. They played two games of chess in the summerhouse, and the actors performed till it was late. Then Ximen paid and dismissed them. Shutong alone remained to serve wine and other things.

They drank till it was dark and the lamps were lighted. Then they went to change their clothes. The Laureate took Ximen Qing's hand and said to him:

"I am going home to see my parents, and I am a little short of money."

"Please do not let that trouble you," said Ximen, "I shall be only too glad to do what Master Zhai suggested."

He asked the scholars to go into the garden with him and led them around the white wall till they came to the Cave of Spring and into the Snow Cavern. There the lamps and candles were lighted. The place was comfortable and warm. A table was set with fruits and wine, and couches were arranged, with books and musical instruments. There they drank wine again and Shutong sang for them.

"Do you know the song about the Fairy Peaches touched with red?" the Laureate asked Shutong.

"Yes, I think I remember it," the boy answered, "it goes to the tune of the 'Moon in the Hall of Tapestries.'" He poured wine for them, then clapped his hands and began to sing.

An's feelings were indescribably moved. "The boy is perfectly adorable," he said to Ximen Qing. He emptied his cup.

Shutong was wearing a green gown with a red skirt, a golden ribbon at his waist. He raised the jade cup high in the air to offer wine to them, and then sang another song. They enjoyed themselves until far into the night. At last they were ready to go to bed. Ximen Qing had had silken coverlets prepared for them in the Cave of Spring and the Kingfisher Hall. He told Shutong and Daian to wait on them. Then he said good-night and went to the inner court.

The next morning the servants came for the two scholars, bringing horses and sedan chairs. Ximen Qing had food made ready in the great hall, and refreshments for all the attendants. Two boys brought in square boxes of presents. To the Laureate Cai he offered a roll of gold silk, and silk for making collars, perfume and a hundred taels of white gold. He gave to An a roll of colored satin, one piece of silk for collars, perfume, and thirty taels of white gold. The Laureate at first refused to accept it. "Ten taels will be quite sufficient for my needs," he said. "Why should you give me so much? You are too generous."

"Brother Cai," An said, "you accept, but I dare not."

Ximen Qing smiled. "These trifling things are nothing more than a token of my regard for you. You are going home and you are about to take a wife. I should like to help you to get a little tea."

The scholars rose and thanked him. "We shall never forget your kindness," they said. Then they bade their servants remove the presents. "We must go," Cai said to Ximen Qing, "and renounce the benefit of your instruction for a while. But before long we shall be returning to the Capital. Then, if a slight measure of advancement should come to us, we shall do something to return your kindness."

"I hope to behold the glory of your dignity again," An said.

"Indeed," Ximen said, "I only hope your honor has not been tarnished by this stay in my snail's nest. I beg your indulgence for all that has been done amiss. I would come to see you on your way, but, unfortunately, my duty calls me and I can only say good-bye."

He took them to the outer gate and watched them mount their horses.

# CHAPTER 37

# Wang Liu'er

Though she be dressed in rags, such is her charm
It makes its presence known.
The flashing eyes reveal the ardor of her love
And he who listens to the music of her soul
Must yield himself her prisoner forever.

They meet within the hall of flowers
The breeze is gentle and the moon is calm.
Softly they talk, and tenderly they smile,
Draw near the bed with phoenixes in flight
Embroidered on its curtains.
Then silently unloose the scented girdle.

After saying good-bye to his guests, Ximen Qing went out on horseback, wearing shades upon his eyes. Soldiers cleared the way for him. In the street he met old woman Feng and told one of the boys to stop her.

"What about this finding a girl for me?" he said. "How is it I have heard nothing from you before this?"

"During the last few days," the old woman said, "I have inspected several girls, but they all turned out to be the daughters either of butchers or of hawkers. Of course, they were out of the question. Then, fortunately, Heaven granted me a miracle, and I remembered a girl who lives quite close to me. She is a beauty of the very first order, and is but fifteen years old. Her animal is the Horse. If I had not happened to pass her door, and she had not invited me to call, I should not, even now, have thought of her. She has just reached the age for her hair to be dressed. She is as upright as the holder of a brush; her feet are tiny, and she knows how to paint her face most charmingly. Her little mouth is so dainty she might be an elf. Her mother says she was born on the fifth day of the fifth month. I think she is beautiful, and I'm sure you will fall in love with her yourself as soon as you set eyes on her."

"You crazy old woman," Ximen said, laughing, "I don't want to fall in love with her. I have plenty on my hands without her. As a matter of fact,

Zhai, the comptroller of the Imperial Tutor's household in the Eastern Capital, is anxious to ensure the continuance of his family, and he has asked me
to find a girl for him. If you only find the right one, so much the better for
you. Who is the girl? You must send me the necessary papers."

"She lives not a thousand miles away," the old woman said. "In fact,
there is hardly a brick between us at this moment. She is the daughter of
Han Daoguo who looks after your thread shop. If you wish, I will get her
father to have the necessary papers made out, then we can fix a day and you
can go to look her over."

"Very well," Ximen said, "go and see him, and if he has no objection,
get him to give you the papers and bring them to my house."

Two days later Ximen was sitting in the great hall when old woman Feng
came with the papers. In them the girl was described as "the maiden Han,
fifteen years of age, whose birthday is the fifth day of the fifth month."

"I told her father what you said," the old woman began, "and he said
that, thanks to your generosity, the girl has certainly a great future in store
for her. But he is afraid that, being a poor man, he cannot provide what is
necessary for the marriage."

"Go and tell him," Ximen said, "that I don't want a single thread from
him. Everything she needs—clothes, ornaments, toilet boxes and everything
else—shall be prepared here. Moreover, I will make him a present of twenty
taels. If he provides her with shoes and socks, that will be all that is needed.
As soon as everything is ready, we shall ask him to escort her to the Eastern
Capital. You see, she is not going to be an ordinary concubine. The comptroller hopes that she will bear him a son and he will treat her as his wife.
So long as she furnishes him with a boy or even a bit of a daughter, she will
have nothing to worry about."

"When will you go and see her?" the old woman asked. "They would
like to know so that they can make preparations."

"Since he has agreed, I may as well go tomorrow. Zhai is in a hurry for
her. But tell Han not to make any preparations on my account. He need
only offer me a cup of tea. Then I shall take my leave."

"Oh dear," the old woman cried, "it is not very often you condescend
to go and see anyone. You may not want anything, but you must not rush
away. He is one of your people; he can't allow you to go away with an
empty stomach."

Ximen Qing explained that he was very busy, and the old woman went
off to tell Wang Liu'er, Han Daoguo's wife, all that he had said.

"Don't tell stories," Wang Liu'er said.

"Indeed, he did say so," the old woman said. "Why should I deceive
you? You know how busy he is, with people coming and going at his house

all the time." Wang Liu'er gave the old lady some food and wine. Then she went away, promising to come the next morning to await the master.

That night, when Han Daoguo came home, his wife talked to him and they discussed the whole matter. In the morning he got up early, went to the High Well for some sweet water, and bought the finest nuts he could find. These he left at home, then went to the shop to attend to the business. His wife, alone in the house, dressed herself in her prettiest clothes, powdered her face, and made herself look very charming. She washed her hands, cleaned her fingernails, polished the teacups, cracked the nuts, and made some excellent tea. Then old woman Feng came and helped the woman to put everything in order.

Ximen Qing, when he came back from the office, put on plain clothes and set out on horseback. Daian and Qintong followed him. When they came to Han's house, he dismounted and went in. Old woman Feng received him and took him into the sitting room. He sat down. Soon Wang Liu'er and her daughter came to see him. Ximen Qing did not look at the girl; he could not take his eyes from the mother. She was wearing a coat of purple silk, a scarf of black and gold upon her shoulders, and a jade-colored skirt, beneath which Ximen could see two perfect little feet. She was tall, and her face, shaped like a melon seed, had a high color.

Ximen Qing was almost beside himself. He decided that, seeing what manner of woman Han Daoguo's wife was, it was not surprising that the young men who lived near her had been inclined to play tricks. The girl was very beautiful too, but this did not surprise him when he had seen the mother.

Wang Liu'er made a reverence to him and called her daughter forward. The girl kowtowed four times before Ximen, bowing as gracefully as a bunch of flowers before the wind. Then she rose and stood before him, and the old woman went to bring tea. Wang Liu'er rinsed the cup before she would allow the old woman to hand it to Ximen. Then Ximen looked the girl over from head to foot. The black hair was piled gracefully upon her head and her cheeks were delicately powdered. She seemed like a lonely flower, with a kind of quiet fascination. Her skin was like the purest jade, tender and fragrant.

Ximen told Daian to take from a box two silken handkerchiefs, four gold rings and twenty taels of white gold. He told the old woman to put them on a tray. From it Wang Liu'er took a ring that she set on her daughter's finger. The girl again made reverence to Ximen Qing, and withdrew.

"In a day or two," Ximen said, "I will ask you to bring your daughter to my house so that the necessary clothes may be prepared for her. Meanwhile, perhaps, you will be good enough to use this money to provide her with shoes and socks."

"All that we have upon our heads and all we wear upon our feet," Wang Liu'er said, kneeling down, "we owe to you. Now you have been kind enough to arrange this marriage for my daughter. Even if my husband and I laid down our lives, we could never sufficiently repay you for your kindness. Again I thank you for your precious gifts."

"Is your husband not at home?" Ximen said.

"No," the woman said, "this morning he told me what I must do in this matter, and then went to the shop. I will tell him to come and kowtow to you."

Ximen thought that the woman talked very charmingly. She called him Father in nearly every sentence. He was touched. "I must go now," he said, rising. "Please tell your husband what I have said."

Wang Liu'er pressed him to stay longer, but he would not. He went straight home to report the business to Wu Yueniang.

"Really," she said, "the marriage cord unites people, even when a thousand miles lies between them. Since you say this girl is very beautiful, we have not spent our labor in vain."

"As soon as possible," Ximen said, "we will bring her here so that her clothes may be made. I will take ten taels of silver at once and have them made into ornaments, rings, pins and other things."

"The sooner the better," Yueniang said, "then we will ask her father to go with her to the Eastern Capital. We need not send anyone else."

Ximen Qing thought it would be better to close the shop for a few days and let Laibao go too. He wished, he said, to make sure that a present he had recently sent had been safely delivered.

Two or three days later Ximen sent a boy to escort the girl. Her mother, Wang Liu'er, came with her, bringing a few small presents. When they came in, they kowtowed before Yueniang and the others.

"Father and Mother," Wang Liu'er said, "and you other ladies, I thank you for the kindness you have shown my daughter. My husband and I will be eternally grateful to you."

They took tea in Yueniang's room and then were entertained in the great hall. Li Jiao'er, Meng Yulou, Pan Jinlian and Li Ping'er joined them. Ximen Qing had provided rolls of red and green silk, material for undergarments, and Tailor Zhao had made two dresses of gold and silver-figured silk and a scarlet satin long gown. Wang Liu'er said a few words to reassure her daughter and went home.

Ximen bought for the girl a small suite of furniture, a gilded chest, a dressing mirror and a hand mirror, boxes, jars, and vessels of bronze and pewter, even a pail to serve a purpose we need not mention. In a few days, everything was ready; a letter was written to go with the party, and the tenth day of the ninth month appointed for the start.

Ximen borrowed four men and two non-commissioned officers from the local police office to act as escort. Han Daoguo and Laibao hired four horses, and, riding behind the wagons and the sedan chair, set off for the Eastern Capital.

Wang Liu'er was left alone. She felt very lonely as she went about her daily duties. For some days indeed, she wept nearly all the time.

One day, when Ximen Qing had nothing particular to do, he mounted his horse and rode down to Lion Street to see what was happening at the house there. Old woman Feng met him and brought him tea.

"I was very satisfied with the way you managed that little business the other day," he said. "Here is a tael of silver for you to buy some cloth." The old woman kowtowed and thanked him.

"Have you been to Han's house lately?" Ximen said.

"Oh yes," the old woman said, "I go every day to cheer up his wife. Now that her daughter has gone she is all by herself. She has never been separated from the girl before, and until the last day or two, she has been crying all the time. 'You have been to a good deal of trouble over my daughter's marriage,' she said to me. 'Has his Lordship given you your fee?' I told her you had been very busy, and I had thought it better not to trouble you. I said I knew it would be safe to wait, and, doubtless, when her husband returned, there would be something coming to me from that quarter."

"Of course that will be so," Ximen said. He looked cautiously around. Seeing there was no one about, he whispered: "When you have an opportunity, just let her know that I should very much like to call and see her. Tomorrow tell me what she says about it."

The old woman put her hand over her mouth and chuckled knowingly. "Now that your shovel has dug you up a golden baby, you want to dig again and find the mother. Well, this very evening, I'll see if I can do anything for you. I suppose you know who she is? She is a sister of Butcher Wang in the back street, the sixth of her family, and about twenty-nine years old. She dresses in smart clothes and may look rather forward, but, to the best of my knowledge, she is virtuous. If you like to come here tomorrow, I will see if I can't have some news for you." Ximen agreed, mounted his horse, and rode home.

When old woman Feng had dined, she locked up the house and set out to see the woman. Wang Liu'er opened the door and asked her to go in. "I cooked some noodles for you yesterday, and waited," she said, "but you never came."

"I meant to come," the old woman said, "but I was obliged to go and see someone else. What with one thing and another, I couldn't manage to get here."

"Well," Wang Liu'er said, "I have a rough meal ready. Will you have something?"

The old woman said she had just had dinner, and would have nothing but a cup of tea. Wang Liu'er made a cup of strong tea for her and ate her own dinner while the old woman sat and watched her.

"I feel very lonely," the woman said. "Always before, I have had my child to fall back upon. Now she has gone the place seems empty, and I have to do everything for myself. My face gets dirty, and everything is horrid. I'd rather die than live like this. She has gone so far away, and if I want to go and see her, I can't. How can I help being upset?" She began to cry.

"It has always been the same," old woman Feng said. "When there are boys in a family, it is always busy, but with girls, it is always lonely. For a girl, if she lives long enough, sooner or later will leave the home and go elsewhere. Things seem bad to you now, but you must remember that, when your daughter settles down in that palace and has borne a son or even a daughter, you and your husband will reap the benefit. When that time comes, you will have nothing to complain of."

"In families of rank," Wang Liu'er said, sadly, "there are always ups and downs. How can we ever say what will happen? Even if she prospers, how am I to know where my bones will be rotting, when that time comes?"

"Oh, don't talk like that," the old woman cried. "Your daughter is certainly not a bigger fool than anybody else. She is a clever needlewoman, and everybody has the fortune that is his due. There is nothing for you to worry about."

They chatted for a long time in this strain, and at last the old woman decided to broach more serious matters. "I hope you won't think I'm talking nonsense," she said, "but now that your husband is away, don't you feel lonely during the night?"

"Do you ask that?" Wang Liu'er cried. "Why, you're the very one who has made me so. Indeed, since you are responsible, I am expecting you to come and keep me company in the evenings."

"I'm afraid I can hardly do so," the old woman said, "but perhaps I know someone who can. You may not care about it, though."

"Whom do you mean?" Wang Liu'er said.

Old woman Feng put her hand before her mouth and laughed. "One host suffices for a single guest," she said. "I mean our master. Yesterday, he came to see me, and said you must be very lonely now that your daughter has gone away, and he would like to come and try to console you. What do you think? No one else is concerned in the matter, and if you are kind to him, you need never worry again about a livelihood. Indeed, if he comes often, he will probably buy you a house, and you will find it much more pleasant than living in a hole like this."

Wang Liu'er smiled. "He has already many ladies of his own, beautiful enough to be the wives of the gods. What can he want from an ugly thing like me?"

"You must not say that," the old woman said. "There is an old proverb that says: Beauty springeth from the lover's eyes. Fate has decided this for you. If he had not taken a fancy to you he would not have come to see me yesterday. He gave me a tael of silver, and said it was for arranging your daughter's marriage. Then, seeing there was no one to hear him, he spoke to me about yourself, and now he is only waiting for your answer. After all, it is like selling a field: a piece of business that depends solely on the will of the two parties concerned. It has nothing to do with me."

"Well," the woman said, "if he would really like to come, tell him I shall expect him tomorrow."

Old woman Feng, now that she had gained her point, stayed a little longer and then took her leave. The next day Ximen came again to see her and she told him the result of her visit. He was delighted and gave her another tael of silver to buy wine and food.

When Wang Liu'er knew that Ximen was coming, she swept out her room, burned fragrant incense, set clean hangings around the bed, and prepared some special tea. Old woman Feng came first, with a basket full of fresh vegetables and fruits. She went into the kitchen to prepare them. Wang Liu'er washed her hands, cleaned her nails and prepared some food. In the sitting room, she scrubbed and cleaned the tables and chairs till they shone.

It was afternoon when Ximen Qing came, dressed in his civilian clothes, and wearing shades upon his eyes. Daian and Qitong followed him. When Ximen had dismounted, he gave orders that the horses should be taken to the house in Lion Street and brought again that evening. He only kept Daian with him. Wang Liu'er, exquisitely dressed, came to the sitting room to welcome him.

"It was very kind of you to take so much trouble over my daughter's wedding," she said. "It is hard for me to find words to express my gratitude."

"Not at all," Ximen said politely, "I must ask you and your husband to pardon me for what I failed to do."

"What complaint could we possibly make," the woman said, "since everyone in our household is so much in your debt?" She kowtowed to him four times. Old woman Feng brought tea, and Wang Liu'er handed it to Ximen Qing. Meanwhile Daian saw the horses taken away, and bolted the gate.

Ximen Qing and the woman sat for a while, and at last she invited him to go and see her own room. The windows and doors were papered; there were a long bed and a few chests. On the wall were four pieces of tapestry that depicted Zhang Sheng meeting with Ying Ying, and bees and flowers. There were tables and tea tables, large mirrors and small, boxes and pewter, all set out in their proper places. A stick of incense was burning. In the place of honor was a chair, in which Ximen Qing sat down, while the woman again prepared some tea with walnuts and offered it to him, taking the cup when he had finished it.

Wang Liu'er sat down on the edge of the bed and chatted about matters of no particular importance. Ximen saw that she brought in all the trays herself.

"You ought to have someone to wait on you," he said.

"Ah," the woman said, "now my daughter has gone, things are certainly difficult. I have to do everything myself."

"You must not put yourself out," Ximen said. "I will arrange with old woman Feng to find a girl about thirteen or fourteen years old for you. She may be able to save you a little."

Wang Liu'er suggested that she must wait until her husband came back, but Ximen hastily assured her that not only would he make all the arrangements, but he would also pay the expenses.

"Have I not troubled you enough already?" the woman said.

Ximen Qing was delighted to discover how intelligent the woman seemed. When old woman Feng came in to set the table, he spoke to her about the girl.

"You must thank his Lordship," the old woman said. "Sister Jiao, down in the South of the city, has just the girl you need, thirteen years old, and she only asks four taels for her. In my opinion, that is the girl you should ask his Lordship to buy for you."

Wang Liu'er bowed to Ximen. Then the food was brought, and the wine heated. She poured out a full cup of wine and presented it to him with both hands. She was about to kneel before him, but he would not allow this.

"You have already made one reverence to me," he said; "there is no need for you to repeat it."

The woman smiled, and sat down upon a small bench. Old woman Feng brought the dishes from the kitchen, one by one, and finally a kind of savory paste. Wang Liu'er selected the tastiest morsels of meat, took some of the vegetables, rolled them up in the paste and handed the roll to Ximen on a small plate. They passed their wine cups to one another and drank together. Meanwhile old woman Feng offered Daian a chair in the kitchen, and saw that he was well fed.

When they had taken a few cups together, the woman moved her seat nearer to Ximen's, and they passed their wine from mouth to mouth. After making sure that there was no one about, Ximen threw his arms around her, kissed her and caressed her tongue with his own. She took the jade scepter into her hand. Their passions were stirred into flame. They drank no more, but saw to the fastenings upon the door. Then both took off their clothes, and the woman prepared the coverlets upon the bed. It was the hour before sunset. The wine had set Ximen Qing on fire. He took the silver clasp from its case, and put it in position, while the woman fondly touched him with her slender hands. She thought his weapon looked magnificent; the veins swelled with dark red blood, and the flesh was firm and powerful. She sat on his knees; they threw their arms around each other's necks, and kissed again. Then she raised one of her legs, and, with her hand, helped that sword to find its scabbard. For a while they jousted together. Ximen Qing allowed his hands to wander over the woman's body. It was very soft but firm. The hair was fine and delicate. Eventually he told her to lie on the bed; he pulled her legs around his body and threw himself fiercely into the struggle.

> The god of battle now holds sway over the green-clad bed.
> The coverlets, with silk-embroidered love birds, feel the press of strife.
> Heroes display their prowess on the coral pillows
> Striving for victory within the silken curtains.
> The hero dashes madly to the fray, plunges his spear with fury home.
> The heroine's heart beats wildly. She yawns and gapes and fain would all devour him.
> Then up he brings his pair of culverins, and lets them loose upon the enemy skulking in the trousers.
> The other raises her shield to meet the mad attack of the great general stationed beneath the navel.
> One plays the golden cockerel, standing on single leg, raising the other high, to show his mettle
> The other, like a stripped tree, with roots that spread in all directions, thrusts forth to meet the foe.
> When they have fought a while, the shining eyes are dimmed
> A single movement makes them squirm and quiver.
> Though their limbs tremble, they still fight on
> Clashing a hundred times, they cannot break away,
> Then, letting loose the dam, the captain of the scanty hair would drown his enemy in the flood.
> The general in black armor feigns to make a thrust, but turns aside and seeks to fly.
> The warden of the navel is unhorsed, thrown down and ground to dust in but a moment.

Lord "warm and tight" now plays the fool, tumbling he falls to the far
   depths of the abyss.
The heavy mail is broken into pieces, like faded blossoms when the
   storm breaks on them
The silken cap gives way beneath the strain, like fallen leaves before
   the raging winds
And Marshal "sulfurous," his crest awry, can find no place to flee.
Prince "Silver Armor" holds his ground, and swears he'll stand till death.
The skies are hidden by a sad dark cloud
The warriors roll stricken on the field.

Wang Liu'er liked one game more than any other. When she had joined
with him as lovers do, she wanted him to enjoy the flower in her bottom
while she played with the flower in her womb. Satisfied in this way, she
reached the blissful oblivion that is the aim of lovers. She used to practice
this game so often that in thirty days Han Daoguo would take his pleasure
at the front gate no more than three times. Apart from this, she titillated his
ivory scepter with her lips and fondled it all night with never-failing desire;
if its master flagged, her lips returned his strength.

Nothing could have given Ximen Qing greater pleasure. All that day
they played, till the watchman gave his first warning. Then he went home.

Before Ximen left her, Wang Liu'er asked him to come again the next
day, and to come early. She promised that if he did so, he should not go
away unsatisfied. Ximen could have asked for nothing better.

The next day he went to the thread shop in Lion Street, and took four
taels of silver. These he gave to old woman Feng, and told her to purchase
the maid. Two days later, Ximen, who could not forget the sweetness of his
last visit, went again to visit Wang Liu'er. Qitong and Daian went with him.
When they reached the house, he told Qitong to take his horse to Lion
Street. Old woman Feng came to attend to the wine and other things, and
set them out. By such small services as these, she hoped to enrich her belly
with oil and vegetables.

This time, Ximen Qing gave to Wang Liu'er a few taels of silver for
household expenses. It was day when he arrived, and night when he went
away. Not one word of the matter did he mention to any member of his
own household.

Old woman Feng went every day to work for Wang Liu'er, so she seldom
had time to go to Ximen Qing's house. Li Ping'er sent a boy two or three
times to summon her, but she was far too busy to come. Often, indeed, she
locked her door and stayed out all day. One day, Huatong ran across her in
the street and made her go with him to Li Ping'er.

"Now, old woman," her mistress said, "for some days I have not seen even your shadow; what game is this you're playing? Every time I have sent after you, you have been out. It looks as if you didn't wish to come. Here I have been, as busy as could be, with a pile of clothes and the baby's bedclothes, all waiting for you to come and help the maids to wash them. And you never came."

"It is easy for you to talk, my lady," the old woman said, "but I have been like a scrivener running after a deserter. I am as busy as anybody can be. One day I seem to be a salt seller, and the next I have to turn myself into a carpenter. I don't have a moment."

"It is all very well," Li Ping'er said. "When I ask you to come, you say you are too busy, but I should like to know where you have been earning your daily bread these last few days."

"I am like a vase whose ears the wind has blown away; it can't get them back with its mouth.* I have not earned anything. You are angry with me, I see, but I simply have not had a chance to come and see you. I have been too busy to know where I am. The other day, the Great Lady gave me some money to buy her a cushion for her prayers, and I forgot all about it. When I did remember, yesterday, the rogue of a cushion seller had taken himself off, and I don't know what to say to her."

"Do you mean to say you have come without the cushion?" Li Ping'er said. "I should advise you to see if you can't find some monkey to run off with you. She gives you the money; you come empty-handed, and then pretend you don't know what you're about."

"I am going to give the Great Lady her money back," the old woman said. "Yesterday I went for a ride on a donkey and nearly fell off."

"If it happens again," said Li Ping'er, "you will certainly be killed."

Old woman Feng went to the inner court to see Wu Yueniang, but first she called at the kitchen. Yuxiao and Laixing's wife were sitting together. When they saw her, one of them said: "Why, here is old woman Feng! Well, honorable madam, and where have you been? The Sixth Lady is ready to eat you up."

The old woman greeted them. "I have just come from her," she said, "and a nice to-do she made."

"My mistress wants to know whether you have bought her cushion," Yuxiao said.

"Yesterday," the old woman said, "I took the money and went outside the city, but the cushion seller had sold his stock and gone home. He will

---

*   i.e. I am not in a position to argue with you.

not be here again before the third month next year. Here is the silver. Please take it, Sister."

"You marvelous old woman," Yuxiao said. "At the moment our master is weighing some silver. When he has gone, you had better see our mistress for yourself. Meanwhile, please sit down. By the way, it seems a long time since Han went off with that daughter of his. He ought to be back now, surely. When he does come, you will be in luck. He will certainly have to give you something."

"Something or nothing," the old woman said, "that is his concern. But he has only been gone about eight days. I don't see how he can be back before the end of the month."

Ximen Qing finished weighing the silver and gave it to Ben the Fourth to spend on the estate. Then he went out, and the old woman went to the upper room to see Wu Yueniang. She did not produce the money but said that the cushions which the merchant had were not good enough. The better ones were sold, and he had gone home to fetch some of an especially good quality. Yueniang was simple and unsuspecting. She said: "That is all right. Keep the money and bring me two cushions next year." She gave the old woman some cakes and old Feng then went back to see Li Ping'er.

"Did the Great Lady scold you?" Li Ping'er said.

"No," said the old woman. "I told her something that made her very happy and she gave me some tea and a few cakes."

"The cakes have come from the Qiao family," Li Ping'er said. "It was the day of the first full month for them yesterday. Well, old woman, your mouth has been stopped. You are like the mosquitoes that come in the fourth month, those that have such a deadly bite. Anyhow, now you are here, you must stay and wash some clothes for me."

"Put the things in soak," the old woman said, "and I will come early tomorrow. This afternoon, I have to go and do some business for a very special client of mine."

"Oh, you old rogue," Li Ping'er said, "you always find some excuse. If you do not turn up tomorrow, you shall see what happens."

The old woman laughed. She stayed a little longer talking with Li Ping'er, and then prepared to go. Her mistress asked her if she would have some food before she went, but she said she was not hungry, and would not stay. Really, she was wondering whether Ximen Qing might not be going to see Wang Liu'er, and she scuttled away as fast as her old legs would carry her.

# CHAPTER 38

# Pan Jinlian Is Melancholy

When old woman Feng came to the door beside the great hall, Daian was standing there with a tea tray in his hands, waiting. He looked at the old woman, made a face and said: "You go first. We shall start as soon as Father has finished talking to Uncle Ying. Qitong has already gone with the wine." The old woman quickened her pace and hurried away.

Ying Bojue had come to say that Li Zhi and Huang the Fourth, the contractors, had secured orders for the provision of thirty thousand lots of incense and wax for the annual contribution to the Emperor, in value about ten thousand taels. "Of course, there will be interest," he said, "and they are to be paid the money in Dongpingfu when the contract is completed. I have come to see what you think about it, and whether you would like to take a hand."

"Why should I?" Ximen said. "These contractors are all rogues. They will bribe the officials so as to get some advantage for themselves. Now that I am an official myself, I must not get mixed up in affairs of that sort."

"Brother," Ying Bojue said, "if you feel you cannot, I must ask somebody else. But I venture to ask you to lend two thousand taels, with interest at five per cent. to be paid monthly, and the capital to be repaid when they get their money. What do you say to that?"

"Since it is you who come to ask," Ximen said, "I think I might manage a thousand taels for them, but I am spending a great deal of money on my estate and have not much to spare."

Ying Bojue, seeing that his friend showed less disinclination in this matter, said: "If you can manage it, why not add five hundred more and make it fifteen hundred? They will not dare to be late with their payments."

"If they are late," Ximen said, "I shall know how to deal with them. Just one word, Brother Ying. If I let them have this money, I won't have them going here there and everywhere, using my name and doing dirty work under my banner. If I hear of anything of that sort, they will discover that the local jail is a most uncomfortable lodging."

"You should not say that, Brother," Ying Bojue said. "If they have responsibilities, they must carry them out. If they go about using your name, it will be all right for them, but if they do anything wrong, what shall

I do? Please do not think any more about that, Brother. If there is anything wrong, I will answer for it. Now that you have made up your mind, I will bring them tomorrow to sign the document."

"Don't bring them tomorrow," Ximen Qing said, "I shall be busy. The day after will be more convenient."

Bojue went away, and Ximen Qing told Daian to saddle his horse. He put on his eyeshades and asked if Qitong had gone. "He came and took the net for the wine jar and went off with it," Daian said. He helped Ximen Qing on to his horse, and they set out for Ox-hide Alley.

One day Han the Second, Han Daoguo's younger brother, the ne'er-do-well, lost all his money gambling, drank till his eyes almost came out of his head, and then went to his brother's house to ask Wang Liu'er to give him some more wine. He took some little sausages from his sleeve and said: "Sister-in-law, my brother is away and I am going to drink a jar of wine with you."

The woman was afraid. She knew Ximen Qing was coming, and old woman Feng was in the kitchen. She would have nothing to do with him.

"I'm not going to drink," she said. "If you wish to, go and drink by yourself. I have no patience with you. Your brother is not at home. Why do you come here and bother me?"

Han the Second glared with his greedy eyes and refused to go away. Then, underneath the table, he saw a jar of wine, sealed and with a label of red paper. "Sister-in-law," he said, "where did you get that wine? Open it and have a pot warmed for me. You know how to enjoy yourself."

"You must not touch it," Wang Liu'er cried, "it came from the Master's. Your brother has not seen it yet, but when he comes back, you shall certainly have some of it."

"Why should I wait for my brother?" Han the Second cried. "I don't care if it belongs to the Emperor. I am going to have a cup."

He was going to remove the seal, but the woman snatched it out of his hand, and took it to her room. As she did so, she pushed Han the Second, and he fell to the ground, his face upturned to the skies. He had considerable difficulty in getting to his feet again, and his shame was turned to anger.

"You thievish whore!" he mumbled. "I am kind to you and bring you something to eat. I remember that you are lonely and come to have a drink with you. But instead of taking any interest in me, you knock me down. Let me tell you this. Don't you get on any high horse. I know you have a rich lover. That is why you won't have anything to do with me. You want to get me out of the way, so you insult me and push me about. You took very good care not to let me know. If you had done, you worthless wretch, you would have seen my knife go in white and come out red."

When Wang Liu'er heard him talking so unpleasantly, the color came into her cheeks and spread from her ears until her whole face was crimson. She took a dolly pin in her hand, beat him, and cursed him. "You starving thief! Where did you get drunk before coming here to spread your wild fire? I will never forgive you." Han the Second, mumbling and calling her evil names, finally went out, still cursing.

At that moment, Ximen Qing arrived. He saw what happened and asked who the man was. "Who is he, indeed?" Wang Liu'er cried. "Why, that Han the Second. He knew his brother was not at home, so when he had lost his money gambling, he got drunk and came here to knock me about. His brother often had to give him a thrashing when he was here."

When Han the Second saw Ximen Qing, he was off like a streak of smoke.

"The beggar!" Ximen Qing said, "tomorrow I will give him a little moral instruction at my office."

"I am sorry he made you angry," Wang Liu'er said.

"You don't know," Ximen said. "With fellows like that, one must not be too indulgent."

"You are right," the woman said, "it never pays to be generous with some people."

She asked Ximen Qing to go in and sit down. He told Qitong to take back his horse, and said to Daian: "You stand at the door, and, if you see even so much as that rascal's shadow, tie him up, and I'll have him before me at the office tomorrow."

"When he knows you are here," Daian said, "his spirit will not know where to hide itself."

Ximen Qing sat down, and Wang Liu'er made a reverence to him. Then she bade her young maid bring some tea with nuts for him. She told the girl to kowtow.

"She seems a good girl," Ximen said. "You must use her as you think fit." Then he added: "Old woman Feng is here. Why doesn't she bring the tea?"

"The old lady is in the kitchen," Wang Liu'er said. "She is doing some work I told her to do, and busy at the moment."

"That wine I told a boy to bring you," Ximen said, "was presented to me by a eunuch. It is 'Bamboo Leaves' wine, which has a good many drugs mixed with it and is very potent. The other day I found that the wine you have is not good enough for me, and so I sent this jar."

Wang Liu'er again made a reverence to him. "Thank you for the wine," she said. "We are unpretentious people, and live in this hole-and-corner street where there is no good wineshop at which I can get any of the best wine. If I want it, I have to go to the High Street to buy it."

"When your husband comes back," Ximen said, "I am going to arrange with him to buy a house in Lion Street, and then you can go to live there. It is near our own shop and in a good district for buying things."

"How kind of you, my lord, to think of me like that. I have been anxious for a long time to get away from this place. If we move, it will be easier for you to come and see me, and we shall escape people's chatter. Of course, my behavior is perfectly correct, and I don't care what they say. Father, do whatever seems good to you, whether my husband is at home or not."

They talked for a while, then Wang Liu'er set out a table in her own room, and invited Ximen to go in and take off his cloak. Wine and dishes were brought, and she poured wine for him and drank with him. She sat upon his knees, and so they drank. When they had had wine enough, they took off their clothes and went to the bed, where they played together merrily and without constraint. Wang Liu'er had placed soft bedclothes on her bed, and perfumed them with most powerful scent. Ximen Qing had discovered that she was well skilled in the arts of love, and was anxious to show her that he himself was no mean performer.

In his sleeve he had a silken kerchief. He opened it. Inside were a silver clasp, a lover's cap, a sulfur ring, a white silk ribbon with medicinal properties, and all manner of things for increasing passion. Wang Liu'er set her head upon the pillow.

She lifted her ivory-white legs to show her cock's tongue. Ximen asked whether he could put his medicine into it; he attached the silver clasp to the root of his penis, added the sulfur ring and smeared his belly with ointment from the navel downwards. She grasped his treasure and put it deep inside her, embracing him hard and long.

"Are your legs tired?" said Wang Liu'er. "Hold the bed; I'll move my body." And again, "I hope you're not in pain. Shouldn't I lift my legs higher?"

Ximen tied her leg to the bed and pressed down with his body. The juice of love flowed continually from her body like snail's slime. Something white came out too, and Ximen asked, "Why have you got so much of this?"

He was about to clean himself, but Wang Liu'er said, "Wait, I'll clean you in my own way," knelt down, and licked him clean with her sensuous tongue.

Then Ximen, again fired with desire, turned her over and started on the flower in her bottom. But the sulfur on his penis proved sticky, so progress was difficult and she grimaced with pain. He made little headway, and Wang Liu'er, feeling about with her hand, found that he had gone only halfway. She turned around and said, with a winning look, "Darling, please go in slowly. The root of your prick is bigger than I can take." Ximen lifted his legs so that he could see himself going in and out.

"Wang Liu'er, my daughter," he said, "there is nothing I enjoy more than this. It is well that I met you: you please me greatly. I will never leave you."

"Dearest," Wang Liu'er said, "my only fear is that you will tire of me and put me aside."

"If you had known me longer, you would know that I am not that kind of man."

They talked and sported together for a long time. "Unless you speak lovingly to me," Ximen said at last, "I will not yield to you." Then Wang Liu'er raised herself upon her hands to receive the stream of life. Ximen had such an orgasm that the liquid flowed like a torrent. He withdrew, still wearing the ring. Wang Liu'er washed him orally, and they lay down together.

Ximen Qing and Wang Liu'er embraced, and lay together till the second night watch. Then a boy came with a horse, and he went home.

The next day, when he reached his office, he sent two policemen to seize Han the Second. The young man was treated as a footpad, and, without any trial, the screws were put upon him and he was given twenty stripes. The blood ran down his legs. For a month he had to keep his bed. Indeed, he nearly died. This frightened him so much that he never again passed anywhere near the woman's door.

The days passed. Laibao, Han Daoguo and the others came back from the Eastern Capital and gave an account of their journey to Ximen Qing. "Comptroller Zhai," Han Daoguo said, "was very pleased with my daughter, and told us to thank you very much. We stayed a few days with him. Then he gave me a letter of thanks, and sent you a black horse as a present. Clerk Han got fifty taels of silver, and I got twenty as journey money."

"Money enough," said Ximen Qing. He read the letter of thanks. Ever afterwards, Zhai and Ximen Qing regarded one another as kinsmen and addressed each other as such.

Han Daoguo kowtowed to Ximen Qing and made ready to go. "Han," Ximen said, "the money is yours. A daughter like that is worth it."

Han Daoguo hesitated to take it. "Only the other day," he said, "you were good enough to lend me money. How can I take this now? I have already troubled you enough."

"If you do not take it, I shall be annoyed. Take it home with you, but do not spend it. I will tell you why later."

Han Daoguo expressed his gratitude and went away. His wife was very pleased to see him. She took his luggage, cleaned the dust from him, and asked him question after question about her daughter's affairs. Han Daoguo told her about the journey.

"It is an excellent household," he said. "When our daughter arrived, she was given three rooms for herself, and two maids to wait on her. As for clothes and jewels, they were too many for me to give you any idea of them. The day after her arrival she went to pay her respects to the Lady, and Comptroller Zhai was delighted with her. He asked us to stay a day or two, and entertained us so well that, even with the servants, there was too much for us. He gave me a present of fifty taels that I did not mean to keep, but our master would not have it, and told me to keep it."

He gave the money to his wife. She was as delighted as a piece of stone when at last it comes to rest upon the ground. "We must give a tael to old woman Feng," she said. "She has very kindly come here all the time you have been away. Our master has already given her one tael."

As they were talking, the little maid brought them tea. "Who is this?" Han Daoguo said.

"I have just bought her," his wife said, "and her name is Jin'er." Then she said to the girl: "Come here and kowtow to your father." The little girl did so and then retired to the kitchen.

Wang Liu'er told her husband all about her dealings with Ximen Qing. "Since you have been away," she said, "he has been here three or four times. He gave me four taels of silver to buy this little girl, and, every time he comes, he gives me a tael or two. That younger brother of ours, who does not know the difference between high and low, came piddling around. Master Ximen happened to see him, and he was haled to the office and well beaten there. Since then he has never dared to show his face again. Our master says this place is not very convenient, and he has promised to buy a house in the main street, and let us go there."

"I see now why he would not take the silver," Han Daoguo said, "but asked me to take it and not to spend it. Now I understand what he was thinking about."

"Well," Wang Liu'er said, "here are fifty taels. We will add a few more, and buy a really fine house. Then we shall have a comfortable life, good eating and fine clothes. It is obviously worth while my letting him have me."

"Tomorrow," Han Daoguo said, "if he should happen to come when I have gone to the shop, pretend that I know nothing about it, and don't treat him unkindly. Do everything he would have you do, for it is no easy matter making money nowadays, and I know no better way than this."

Wang Liu'er laughed. "You rascal. It is easy money for you, but you don't know the sufferings I have to endure." They both laughed heartily. She prepared supper, and they went to bed.

The next day Han went to Ximen's house to get the key, then opened the shop and gave old woman Feng a tael of silver for her pains.

*       *       *

One day Magistrate Xia and Ximen Qing left the office together. Xia saw that his colleague was riding a big dappled black horse. "Why don't you ride your white horse now, but this black one? This is a fine horse, but I am not so sure about his mouth."

"I am letting my white horse have a few days' rest," Ximen said. "This one was sent to me by my kinsman Zhai at the Eastern Capital. He got it from General Liu of Xixia. It has good teeth, and is not too fast or too slow, but it has one slight defect; it won't let any other horse get near the manger. When I first had it, it lost its sleekness for a while, but it has been eating better these last few days."

"It seems to me to go very well," Magistrate Xia said, "but if I were you, I should keep it for riding about town and not take it too far. A horse like that would cost seventy or eighty taels to buy here. There has been something wrong with my horse, and before I could come to the office today, I had to borrow this one from a relative. It is a very poor beast."

"Don't let that upset you," Ximen Qing said. "I have another one at home, a chestnut. You shall have that."

Magistrate Xia bowed. "If you are really so kind, I must pay you, of course."

"Don't think of such a thing," Ximen said. "As soon as I get home, I will have it brought to you." They came to West Street and there separated.

When Ximen reached home, he told Daian to take the horse to his colleague Xia. The magistrate was very pleased and gave the boy a tael of silver. "Thank your master for me," he said, "and I will thank him myself when I see him at the office."

Two months went by. Magistrate Xia made some chrysanthemum wine, engaged two young actors, and invited Ximen Qing. Ximen dined at home, attended to some business, and then went to the party. Xia had prepared an excellent repast especially for Ximen Qing, and was very pleased when he arrived. He came down the steps to welcome his guests, and they greeted each other in the hall.

"Why have you been to so much trouble on my account?" Ximen said.

"I have simply made a little chrysanthemum wine," said Xia, "and thought I might perhaps invite you to my poor house for a talk. I have not invited anyone else." They took off their ceremonial clothes, and sat down in the places of guest and host. After tea, they played chess. Then they sat and drank wine while they talked. The young actors played and sang for them.

For a long time, Ximen Qing had not been to the apartments of Pan Jin-lian. She felt the loneliness of her curtained bed, the coldness of its dainty coverlets. One day, she opened the corner gate and lighted the silver lamp in her room. She leaned upon the screen and played her lute. It was about midway between the second and the third night watches. Several times, she sent Chunmei to look for her husband, but Chunmei could never see him.

Through the long night she played her silver lute, but the room seemed so lonely that she could not bear to continue. Then she took the lute and laid it upon her knees. She played softly to herself and sang

> I rested sadly on the lattice
> Then sought my rest without undressing.

Suddenly, she thought she heard a sound on the gong outside and imagined it was Ximen's signal. Hastily, she bade Chunmei go out to see. "You were mistaken, Mother," Chunmei said when she returned, "it was only the wind. It is going to snow." Then Jinlian sang again.

> I hear the sound of the wind
> The snow is fluttering against my window
> And the ice flowers drifting one by one.

The lamp grew dim, and the incense burned out. She would have drawn the wick, but there was no sign of Ximen Qing. She could not summon energy enough to touch it. She sang again.

> I am too languid to trim the jeweled lamp
> I am too languid to light the incense
> I make shift to pass the night
> Dreading the morrow that must come.
> When I think of you, how shall my sadness end?
> When I think of you, my mind is consumed.
> You have despoiled my tender years, the flower of my youth
> You have deserted me.
> You have not fulfilled the promise you made in days gone by.

About the first night watch, Ximen Qing returned from Magistrate Xia's house. As he rode along, the sky was dark and lowering. The sleet covered his cloak and melted where it fell. He pressed his horse homeward. The boys carried lanterns for him. He did not go to the inner court but straight to the room of Li Ping'er. Li Ping'er welcomed him, brushed off the snow, and took his clothes. Dressed only in his silken gown, he sat on her bed and asked if the baby was asleep. "He has been playing for some time and now he has gone to sleep," Li Ping'er told him. Yingchun brought tea.

"Why have you come back from your party so early?" Li Ping'er said.

Ximen Qing said: "Some time ago, I gave Xia a horse, and today he gave a feast especially for me, and engaged two young actors. I saw that it was going to snow, so I came back in good time."

"Would you like to drink again?" Li Ping'er said. "I will tell the maid to heat some wine for you. You came back through the snow and you must not catch cold."

"We have some good grape wine," Ximen said. "Heat some of that for me. The wine I drank at Xia's place was homemade chrysanthemum wine, but I do not care much for its strong odor and I did not have enough to drink."

Yingchun set out a table with refreshments and fruits. Li Ping'er sat down on a little bench opposite Ximen. There was a small charcoal burner under the table. They sat together drinking. Meanwhile, Jinlian was cold and lonely in her room. She sat on the bed with her lute still upon her knees. The lamp had gone out, and the candles were dim. She would have gone to sleep, but she still hoped that Ximen might come. She was sleepy and cold. At last, she took off her headdress, tied her hair carelessly, pulled down the curtain, and sat on the bed with the bedclothes huddled over her.

> I cast myself upon the embroidered bed
> too sad to sleep.
> I draw the silken curtains.
> But there is only emptiness within them.
> Would that I had known his faithlessness before
> My trusting heart meets with an ill reward.

Again she sang:

> I hate him for his cruelty, so lightly he deserted me.
> In hours of idleness, our separation tortures me.

Once again, she bade Chunmei go outside to look for Ximen. "Go once more to see if Father is coming," she said. "Come back quickly and tell me."

The maid soon returned. "Mother," she said, "are you still thinking that Father is not back? He came back a long time ago and he is drinking in the Sixth Lady's room."

This was more than Jinlian could bear. It made her suffer as though her heart had been pierced by knives. Over and over again she cursed him for a fickle-hearted rogue. Tears rolled down her cheeks. She lifted her lute and sang.

My heart aches. I cannot comfort it
Sorrow and misery consume me utterly
He casts aside the tender peach and seeks a bitter fruit.
He, whom I made my guide, led me astray.
When I think of you, my mind is consumed.
You have despoiled my tender years, the flower of my youth
You have deserted me.
You have not fulfilled the promise you made in days gone by.

Ximen Qing suddenly heard the strains of the lute. "Who is playing the lute?" he asked.

"It is the Fifth Lady," Yingchun said.

"Hasn't the Fifth Lady gone to bed yet?" Li Ping'er said. "Go at once," she said to Xiuchun, "and ask her to come and take wine with us. Tell her I ask her to come."

Xiuchun went out, and Li Ping'er told Yingchun to place another seat for the Fifth Lady and to set out cup and chopsticks. When the maid came back, she said Jinlian would not come, she had gone to bed. "You go and ask her," Li Ping'er said to Yingchun. But Yingchun came back with the same story.

"The Fifth Lady has fastened the corner gate and blown out her lamp. She has gone to bed."

"Don't believe the little strumpet," Ximen Qing said. "Let us go and drag her out. We will make her come and then we will play chess with her."

He went with Li Ping'er to the corner gate. After they had knocked for a long time, Chunmei came and opened it. Ximen Qing took Li Ping'er by the hand, and they went together into Jinlian's room. She was sitting inside the bed curtains, with the lute beside her.

"You funny little strumpet," Ximen said, "why do we have to send for you three times, and still you won't come?"

Jinlian sat on the bed and did not make the slightest show of moving. She looked sulky. After a long wait, she said: "Unlucky people like me are only fit to be left in the cold. Let me live my own life. Don't trouble about me. Don't try to be kind to me. Save all your attentions for others."

"You marvelous little slave!" Ximen said, "you are like an eighty-year-old woman who has lost her teeth but can still make shift to chatter without them. Your Sixth Sister wants to play chess, and we have waited for you a long time."

"Yes, Sister," Li Ping'er said. "I have set out the chess, and we have nothing better to do. Let us play and win some wine to drink."

"Sister," Jinlian said, "please go away. I shall not come. You don't seem to realize that I am not very well. I need sleep. I have more to worry me than you have. These last few days I have had a wandering fit. Who but I would have to taste yellow soup and plain water? I have had to spend my days looking at my own face."

"There is nothing at all the matter with you," Ximen Qing said. "Why do you pretend to be ill? If you really are, tell me, and I will send for the doctor."

"You don't believe me, do you?" Jinlian said. "Chunmei, bring me my mirror and let me look at myself. I have been growing thinner and thinner day by day."

Chunmei brought her a mirror and she looked at her reflection in the lamplight. Ximen took the mirror from her and looked at himself in it. "I am not very thin," he said.

"You don't expect me to look like you, do you?" Jinlian said. "You drink wine day after day, and gobble down huge slices of meat. You have grown fat. Now you are making fun of me."

Ximen Qing said no more, but seated himself beside her on the bed. He put his arm around her neck and kissed her. He would have stretched out his hand to smooth her body, but she was still wearing her clothes. He put both hands around her waist. "My daughter," he said, "you really are thinner."

"How cold your hands are, you funny creature," Jinlian said. "You make me feel like ice. Did you think I was trying to deceive you? Nobody cares if I am sad, and my tears flow down to my own stomach."

She resisted for a little longer, but Ximen Qing dragged her bodily to the room of Li Ping'er. There they played chess and drank wine. When Jinlian had to go away, Li Ping'er noticed that her face was sour, and urged Ximen Qing to go with her.

# CHAPTER 39

# The Temple of the Jade Emperor

Ximen Qing stayed the night in Pan Jinlian's room. It seemed to her detestable that she could not unite herself even more completely with her lover. In a thousand delightful ways she made love to him: in ten thousand different manners she sported with him. Her tears fell softly on the silken coverlets, and her words were warm and gentle. She wished, more than all else, to win her husband utterly for herself.

She did not know, however, that Ximen was on such intimate terms with Wang Liu'er. He spent a hundred and twenty taels of silver on a house east of the stone bridge for Wang Liu'er to live in. Two rooms stood upon the street, and it was four rooms deep. There was a guest room, a shrine for the worship of Buddha and the ancestors, a bedroom, and a kitchen. When they removed there, the neighbors knew that Han Daoguo was Ximen Qing's clerk, and no one dared to behave other than kindly. Many sent boxes of tea and presents to celebrate the housewarming. They called Han Daoguo Brother Han or Son-in-law Han, and the young people addressed them as Uncle and Aunt.

Whenever Ximen Qing came to the house, Han Daoguo would sleep at the shop so as to allow complete freedom to his wife and her lover. Ximen came in the morning and went away in the evening and all the neighbors knew of it. Yet they were so in awe of his power and wealth that none of them dared to say a word. In less than a month, Ximen Qing visited the woman at least three or four times, and their passion for each other was as fiery as burning charcoal.

The end of the year was approaching, and Ximen was busy arranging to send presents to the Eastern Capital. He also prepared gifts for the civil officers of the district and those of his own department. About this time, Abbot Wu of the Temple of the Jade Emperor bade his novices take to Ximen Qing four boxes of gifts, "Heaven and Earth" pictures, charms for the coming spring, and prayers to the God of Fire. Ximen Qing was taking a meal in his wife's room when Daian brought a card upon which was written: "The unworthy priest, Wu Zongjia, offers these things with his most respectful compliments." Ximen Qing read it.

"This priest," he said, "has troubled himself on my account again." He told Daian to ask Shutong to give a tael of silver with his card to the young novice.

"He is a priest," Wu Yueniang said, "and every new year and every festival you take presents from him. You would do well to make the sacrifice you promised when the Sixth Lady's baby was born."

"Thank you for reminding me," Ximen Qing said. "I did promise to make a first-class sacrifice, but I had forgotten all about it."

"You are a splendid example of gratitude," Yueniang said. "Whoever heard of anyone forgetting a promise of that kind? Your mouth makes promises readily, but your mind is elsewhere at the time. The gods do not forget. No wonder the baby is always cross. It must be because you have not kept your word."

"If you think that," Ximen said, "we will have the sacrifice at Abbot Wu's temple at the beginning of the new year."

"The Sixth Lady told me yesterday that the boy had not been very well," Yueniang said. "She was thinking about giving the boy a name."

"Well, we have the very place," Ximen Qing said. "We will enroll him at the Temple of the Jade Emperor." He said to Daian: "Who has come from the temple?"

"The novice Ying Chun," Daian told him.

Ximen Qing went out to see the young man. The novice kowtowed and said: "My master sends his compliments to you. He has nothing worthy to offer you, but ventures to send these trifles. They are for you to distribute among your servants."

Ximen Qing made a moderate reverence to Ying Chun, and asked him to thank the Abbot for his gifts. Then he invited the young novice to take a seat. Ying Chun bowed. "How dare I sit in your presence?" he said. But Ximen made him sit down, saying that he wished to talk to him. The novice was wearing a small hat and a long black gown. He was very modest in his bearing, and only after much hesitation was persuaded to take a chair and sit down. "What are your commands?" he asked. "In the first month of the new year," Ximen Qing said, "I wish to make a sacrifice, and would venture to ask your master to make the necessary arrangements. And I wish, too, to enroll my son's name in the register of your temple. But perhaps your master is too busy?"

The novice rose hastily. "Since such is your desire," he said, "even if we had other religious duties on that day, we should put them off."

"Then what about the ninth day?" Ximen Qing said. "Isn't that the birthday of the Gods?"

"Yes, that is the birthday of the Gods," the young priest said, "and it is written in the *Book of the Jade Casket* that upon that day we should pray the

Gods to bless us, and the five blessings will descend together. It is an excellent day for fasting and worship. May I ask how many degrees of sacrifice you will require?"

"My son was born in the seventh month," Ximen Qing said. "At that time I vowed to make sacrifice of a hundred and twenty degrees."

"How many priests do you wish to take part in the sacrifice?"

"Let there be sixteen," Ximen Qing said.

A table was set, and the young priest was offered tea. Ximen gave him fifteen taels of silver for the expenses of the sacrifice, and one tael in return for the Abbot's gift. "There is no need for your master to prepare things," he said to the novice. "I myself will send paper offerings, incense and candles."

The young priest was so delighted that he completely forgot himself. He pissed himself and farted like thunder. He thanked Ximen Qing over and over again.

On the eighth day of the first month, Daian was sent to the temple with a measure of fine rice, a supply of paper money, and ten catties of official candles. He also took with him five catties of incense, and sixteen rolls of unbleached material for other things that were needed by the priests. In addition, Ximen Qing sent two rolls of brocade, two jars of Southern wine, four live geese, four live chickens, a set of pig's trotters, a leg of mutton and ten taels of silver. All this was for the enrollment of the baby's name.

Cards of invitation to the ceremony were sent to Uncle Wu, Uncle Hua, Ying Bojue and Xie Xida. Chen Jingji, on horseback, went to the temple to see that everything was in order.

The ninth day came. Ximen Qing did not go to his office, but rose very early, dressed, then mounted a great white horse and set off by the East Gate to the Temple of the Jade Emperor. Attendants marched before and behind him. Even from a far distance they could see the banners, decorations and arches that had been set up. Soon they reached the temple gate and Ximen dismounted.

Passing through the first gate, he came to another, the Gate of the Meteor, on either side of which were scarlet boards, seven feet long, with these words written upon them.

Then Ximen Qing came to the main sanctuary. There, written in twenty-four characters, they saw a sign:

In gratitude to Heaven and Earth we offer our treasures.
May our land be blessed and our benefactors rewarded.
We take an ally to ourselves, and enroll his name.
May all good fortune descend abundantly upon our altar.

On either side were scrolls, bearing the inscriptions:

Established before the Heavens
May we behold the majesty of DAO
And manifest our singleness of heart

and

Here is the honorable dwelling of the Most High,
Here can we behold the glory of the Pure Cultivation,
Here would we show our gratitude for every blessing.

Ximen Qing went up to the shrine. Before the table of incense stood a boy, with a ewer, in which Ximen Qing washed his hands. Then an acolyte knelt down and invited him to burn incense. Ximen Qing prostrated himself before the altar. Abbot Wu was wearing a hat of the Nine Yang Thunder, with rings of jade and a sky-blue vestment, broad-sleeved and embroidered with the crane and the twenty-eight stars. A silken girdle was about his waist. He came down from the lectern and made a priestly reverence to Ximen Qing.

"Unworthy priest that I am," he said, "your misdirected kindness has often made me its object, and I have frequently received precious gifts from you. Consequently I feel that if I refuse them, I shall not be truly sincere; and if I do accept them, I must be ashamed. It is my duty to pray that your son may have length of days. Why should you send me such valuable presents? I am truly embarrassed. Besides, your gifts for the purposes of the sacrifice have been far too generous."

"But it is I who feel grateful for the trouble you have taken," Ximen Qing said. "I have done nothing to repay you. These things are a very slight token of my appreciation, and nothing more."

After these polite exchanges, the priests who stood on either hand came to greet Ximen Qing, and he was invited to go to the Abbot's cell. This was a large hall, three rooms wide, called the Hall of Pine Trees and of Cranes. There tea was served.

Ximen Qing sat down and told Qitong to take a horse for Ying Bojue. "I don't think he can have a horse, so that is why he has not arrived yet."

"The donkey that Brother-in-law Chen rides, is here," Daian said.

"Very well," Ximen said, "let him take that." Qitong went away.

When the Abbot had finished his reading of the sacred books, he came to offer tea to Ximen and then sat down to talk. "Realizing the keenness of your desire to worship Heaven," he said, "I rose this morning at the fourth watch and read many sacred texts at the altar for you. Today is the third dawn and the ninth revolution, and I performed all the necessary exercises for the worship of the Jade Pivot. I also prepared a document with your son's birthday and his eight characters, and presented the name to the Three Most Mighty Ones. The name I chose for him was Wu Yingyuan, calling upon him every blessing, continual prosperity and strength of body. I made ready a sacrifice of twenty-four degrees to offer to Heaven and Earth, twelve more for the glory of the gods, and still another twenty-four for the dead. So we have a hundred and eighty degrees in all."

Ximen Qing thanked the Abbot. After a while the drum was heard, and he was asked to go to the altar to see the document of enrollment. He dressed himself in a scarlet robe of ceremony with a five-colored badge of rank. Then he fastened about himself the girdle with the buckle of gilded rhinoceros horn. When he came to the altar, a lector, robed in purple, began the reading of the sacred purpose.

> The devout Ximen Qing, dwelling in Xianpaifang of Qinghe in the Province of Shandong, venerating the sacred Principle, comes to implore a blessing, to offer sacrifice, and to pray for peace. He was born at the hour of midnight, on the twentieth day of the seventh month of the year *Bingyin.* His wife Wu was born at the hour of midnight, on the fifteenth day of the eighth month in the year *Wuzhen.*

There the lector stopped. "Have you," he said to Ximen Qing, "any other members of your household whom you would wish me to include?"

"Simply write this," Ximen said. "Li, born at the hour of dawn on the fifteenth day of the first month in the year *Xinwei,* and the boy Guan'ge, born at the hour of *Shen* on the twenty-third day of the seventh month in the year *Bingshen.*"

The lector repeated this after him and returned to his reading.

> This day, I, Ximen Qing, and all my household come to fulfill our humble duty and to do worship before the Mighty Creator. My life is but a particle of dust from the lowest order of the Three Forces. Yet when I go out and come in; when I rise from my bed or seek it, I am ever indebted to the protection of the Dragon Heaven. Seasons change from hot to cold, yet the mercy of the Almighty never faileth me.
>
> I have an appointment among the soldiery and a post in the Imperial Guard: I bask in the sunshine of the Emperor's favor; wealth and riches have come to me.

Therefore, with humble devotion, I make this sacrifice towards the twenty-four regions in thankfulness for the great mercies bestowed on me by Heaven and Earth and to acclaim the benefits of the Kingly One. Twelve sacrifices I offer in honor of the True God whose birthday we celebrate this day.

May I be blessed by the Five Fortunes, may I prosper and the gifts of Heaven descend upon me.

On the twenty-third day of the seventh month last year, my second wife Li bore me a son, Guan'ge. At that time I prayed for her safe delivery and that good fortune might be with the child. This son, Guan'ge, I pray may be received into the religious life in the sanctuary of the Three Holy Ones, receiving the name Wu Yingyuan.

I vowed that I would make sacrifice of a hundred and twenty degrees that my seed may be continued after me and that this my son may enjoy length of days.

I desire to do worship to the spirits of three generations of the House of Ximen, to my grandfather Ximen Jingliang, to my grandmother Li, to my father Ximen Da and my mother Xia, to my late wife Chen, and all those who have died, one after the other. Whether they have ascended to Heaven I know not, or whether they have gone down to the place below. I offer twelve sacrifices that the omnipotent DAO may set them all upon the way of life. In all I offer a hundred and eighty degrees of sacrifice. Look graciously upon this petition and grant these blessings.

Upon this the ninth day of the first month in the third year of the reign Xuan He, the feast of the birthday of the Gods, in humble duty I come to the sanctuary of the Most Beneficent Jade Emperor, here, by the ministry of the priests, to give thanks to Heaven and Earth, and to pray that the Gods may bestow their blessing upon me and give me peace. Here I have enrolled the name of my son and recited the sacred scriptures that blessings may be multiplied. I have kept the great fast for a day and a night to invoke the glory of the Three Worlds and to welcome the Chariot of the God of Ten Thousand Heavens.

May He grant lasting peace to all my household and ensure that the Four Seasons shall be harmonious and fruitful.

For this I place my trust in the power of DAO and pray that manifold blessings may be bestowed.

This have I set down with faithful care.

When this had been read, the priests brought many talismans, petitions and papers and asked Ximen Qing to look at them one by one. There were between a hundred and eighty and a hundred and ninety of them, all well done and in excellent order. Then they showed him the talismans, petitions and papers for the enrollment of the child's name under the protection of the Three Holy Ones. The task was too great for Ximen Qing. He had observed the great care that the Abbot brought to his duties, so he contented himself with offering incense and signed the documents. He called for a roll of silk to be brought and given to Abbot Wu. The Abbot refused it for a long time, but finally bade a boy receive it.

Then a priest at the corner of the sanctuary beat the drum with a roaring like spring thunder and the others played their instruments. The Abbot vested himself in a scarlet robe with embroidery of the five colors, and red shoes. He took up an ivory scepter. Then he dispatched all the documents and went to the altar to await the coming of the Gods, and a bell was rung on either side. Ximen Qing was escorted to the altar, and there offered incense on both sides of the sanctuary of the Three Holy Ones. He opened his eyes wide and gazed at them. Ximen Qing went around the altar and offered incense. When he was done, the servers invited him to go to the Hall of the Pine Trees. In the innermost room, a fine carpet had been laid and animal charcoal was burning in the brazier. After a while Ying Bojue and Xie Xida arrived. They greeted Ximen Qing and each of them offered a star of silver as tea money. "We should have liked to send some tea," they said, "but it is a long way, and we offer this trifle instead."

Ximen Qing would have none of it. "Really," he said, "I have no patience with you. I invited you. Why should you do this? My relative Wu will bring something for tea, and that will be enough for all of us."

Ying Bojue hastily made reverence and said: "If you insist, we must take it back." Then he looked at Xie Xida. "It is your fault," he said, "I told you our brother would not accept it. Now, you see, he upbraids us."

Then Wu and Hua came, and each of them brought two boxes of fine cakes to have with tea. Ximen Qing asked Abbot Wu to accept them. After tea a vegetarian meal was prepared, and Ximen Qing and the others took part in it. The Abbot had engaged a storyteller, who told them all about Hong Men of the Han Dynasty.

When the Abbot had finished attending to the papers, he came in and sat down with them. He asked if Guan'ge himself was to be brought that day.

"No," Ximen Qing said, "he is very small, and my wife was afraid that the distance might be too much for him. But this afternoon his clothes are coming and we will offer them before the Three Holy Ones. I imagine that will have the same effect."

"I agree," Abbot Wu said, "it is the best thing you could do."

"In every other respect," Ximen Qing said, "the child is getting along very well, but he is much too easily alarmed. I have three or four maids and a nurse to look after him, but something is always disturbing him. We dare not let dogs or cats come anywhere near him."

"Rearing a child is no easy business," Uncle Wu said. Then Daian came and said that Li Guijie and Wu Yin'er had sent Li Ming and Wu Hui with tea. Ximen Qing ordered them to be brought in. The two boys came, carrying boxes, which they presented on their knees. When the boxes were opened, it was seen that they contained all kinds of delightful cakes, and tea with rose petals. Ximen Qing asked Abbot Wu to accept them.

"How did you come to know about this?" he asked Li Ming. "This morning," Li Ming said, "I met Uncle Chen riding along the street. He told me that you were performing your devotions here today, and I went home and told Guijie's mother. She told Wu Yin'er, and they asked us to come and bring you their best wishes. Really they would have come themselves, but it would have been hard for them to get here. These poor cakes are to be given to your servants."

Ximen Qing said that the two boys must have food, and the Abbot sent them to a room aside. Even the porters who had come with them were given a meal.

In the afternoon there were further devotions. The Abbot had prepared a large table of food, a jar of Jinhua wine, and, for the baby, a Daoist hat of black silk, with trimmings of gold, a black Daoist gown made of linen, and another of green cloudy silk. There were tiny black silk shoes and a yellow girdle, a yellow cord from the shrine of the Three Holy Ones, a purple cord from the Patroness of Children, and a silver necklet, on which was engraved: "Gold and jade fill the hall. Long Life, Honor and Riches be thine." There was a talisman of yellow silk with red characters to drive away devils. This bore the inscription: "God said the word" and "Long Life and Health." The parcels were tied with yellow string and set upon a square tray. Plates of fruit were on the table.

A boy was told to take from a bag copies upon red paper of all the texts they had been reciting, and the Abbot asked Ximen Qing to look at them. The papers were then put into boxes, and in all there were eight bundles to be sent to Ximen's house. Ximen was very pleased. He told Qitong to go at once and tell the people at home that the messenger must be given two handkerchiefs and a tael of silver.

This day was Pan Jinlian's birthday. Aunt Wu, old woman Pan, Aunt Yang and Miss Yu were sitting in Yueniang's room when the presents came from the temple. They set them on four tables, but even so there was not room for all. The ladies came to look at them.

"Come quickly, Sixth Sister," Jinlian said to Li Ping'er, "your baby's teacher has sent him some presents. Here is a little Daoist hat and robes. Oh, look! There are some little shoes too."

Yulou went forward and took the little shoes in her hands. "See how very careful those priests are," she said. "These little shoes with their white silk heels are done in *Daokou* work, and the laces in *Fangsheng*. The clouds are very well done. The priest who did this must have a wife. He could never do such good needlework himself."

"Nonsense," Wu Yueniang said, "if he is a monk, how can he have a wife? He must employ someone to do the work for him."

"If the Daoist monks have wives," Jinlian said, "Nun Wang here and the Abbess can make excellent girdles; must we assume that they have husbands?"

"Oh, the monks," Nun Wang said, "can go anywhere in those hats of theirs, but we of the Buddhist persuasion are recognized wherever we go."

"They tell me," Jinlian said, "that your convent, the Temple of Guanyin, is opposite the Daoist monastery. You remember the saying: ' When a house of nuns stands near a house of monks, something is bound to happen.' "

"The Fifth Lady loves to talk nonsense," Yueniang said.

"Ah," Jinlian said, "here is the purple cord talisman. With this the priest dedicates the child to Guanyin. And here is a silver necklet with a medal attached, and eight characters engraved upon it. How nice the baby will look when he puts it on. And on the back is the child's name—Wu—something —Yuan."

"That is the name the priest gave him," Qitong said. "Wu Yingyuan."

"Yes, the character is Ying," Jinlian said. "But the priest is certainly impertinent to change the baby's surname."

"That's what you think," Yueniang said. She asked Li Ping'er to bring Guan'ge, that they might see him dressed in his monastic habit. But Li Ping'er said: "He has just gone to sleep and I don't like to disturb him."

"It will do him no harm to wake him up," Jinlian said, and Li Ping'er then went to bring her son. Jinlian, who could read, took the parcels of red papers, pulled out the texts, and in one of the documents discovered that after Ximen Qing's name, only those of Wu Yueniang and Li Ping'er were mentioned. There were no others. This made her jealous.

"Look how that obstinate scoundrel arranges people in ranks and classes. Isn't it clear that he has his favorites. This paper mentions only one and the rest of us are left out. We don't count. We are pushed on one side."

"Is the Great Lady mentioned?" Meng Yulou asked. "Oh, it would be a joke if she were not there," Jinlian said.

"There is nothing the matter with it," Yueniang said. "If it mentions one of us, that is enough. Just because we have a regiment of women in the house, there is no reason why everybody's name should go down. The priests would laugh."

"We are no worse than anybody else," Jinlian said, "we all took the same length of time to come into the world."

Then Li Ping'er brought Guan'ge.

"Give me the clothes and I will dress him," Yulou said. Li Ping'er held the child while Yulou put on him the hat, the necklet and the two strings. The baby was frightened, closed his eyes, and, for a long time, held his breath. Yulou put on the little monastic dress.

"Take these papers and some paper money," Yueniang said, "and go to our domestic chapel and burn them there." Li Ping'er did so.

Yulou held the baby and played with him. "Now that you are wearing these clothes," she said to him, "you are a little priest."

"A little priest indeed!" Jinlian said, "rather the Great Omnipotent himself."

"Why do you say a thing like that?" Yueniang said seriously. "You must not talk in that way in the child's presence." Jinlian was abashed and said no more.

The wearing of these new clothes seemed to frighten the child and he began to cry. Li Ping'er came back, took him and undressed him. While she was doing so, he soiled her dress.

"Oh, you good little Wu Yingyuan," Yulou said, laughing, "if you're going to make messes, you must have something to sit on."

Yueniang bade Xiaoyu take paper, and put things to rights. Then the child lay on his mother's breast and went to sleep. Yueniang distributed all the cakes and invited Aunt Yang, Aunt Wu, and old woman Pan to come and eat the food that had been sent from the temple. It was growing dark.

The day before, Ximen Qing, in preparation for his sacrifice, had taken no meat or wine. Now, Jinlian, who had been unable to celebrate her birthday at the proper time, waited for him to come back from the temple that she might offer wine to him. She went and stood at the gate. About sunset, Daian and Chen Jingji came riding back. Jinlian asked Jingji if Ximen was returning.

"I don't think so," Jingji said. "When we left, the service was not over. They had only begun it, and I don't see how they can finish before the first night watch. Priests never let people go without a struggle. They want to thank the Gods and drink a cup of wine."

When Jinlian heard this, she said nothing but went to Yueniang's room in a bad temper. "I have just come from the gate," she said. "There I saw Brother-in-law Chen come back on horseback. He says that Father will not be here yet because the service is not finished. He himself came back before the others."

"That is all right," Yueniang said, "we shall be more at our ease. Tonight we will listen to these two nuns talking about religion and singing hymns."

Chen Jingji pulled the lattice aside and came in. He was a little tipsy.

"I have come," he said, "to pay my respects to Fifth Mother." He turned to his wife and asked her for a cup.

"Why should I get you a cup?" his wife said. "Kowtow to the Fifth Lady and I will offer the wine for you. Look at you! You are drunk! It is clear you found this sacrifice a splendid excuse for drinking. Coming back in a state like this!"

Yueniang asked him whether Ximen Qing was really not coming back, and whether Daian had returned.

"Father saw that the service would not be finished for some time," Jingji said, "and as he knew there was no man in the house, he told me to come back, and Daian to stay and wait upon him. The Abbot would not let me go. He pulled me and dragged me about, and gave me two or three great cups of wine. Then, at last, I got away."

Yueniang asked him how many people were at the temple. "Uncle Wu, and Uncle Hua, who lives outside the gates, Uncle Ying and Uncle Xie. The two young actors Li Ming and Wu Hui are there too. When the party will come to an end, I don't know. I only know that Uncle Wu was going home, and that Uncle Hua was not allowed to do so. In my opinion they will spend the night there."

Jinlian saw that Li Ping'er was not there.

"Why do you call him Uncle Hua?" she said to Chen Jingji. "What relation was he to the departed? You ought to know that he should be called Uncle Li."

"Fifth Mother," Jingji said, "you should take a lesson from the country girl who married Zheng En. Keep one eye open and the other shut."

"Kowtow and be off, you scamp," his wife said. "Don't come here with your scandalous talk."

Jingji asked Jinlian to take the proper position. He kowtowed four times, drunkenly, then went to the outer court.

After a while, candles and lamps were brought and the tables were set. They all ate noodles and wine, and then everything was cleared away. Yueniang told Xiaoyu to close the second door and put a small table on the bed. They all sat in a circle with the two nuns in the middle. They burned incense; then, with only two candles burning, listened to the two nuns telling religious stories. First the chief nun began. She told how the Thirty-second Sage came down from the Western Heaven to the Eastern World. Here he preached the teaching of the Buddha, the sacred doctrine of the Master, and the principle of retribution. She told the story of Master Zhang, a very wealthy man, giving one episode after another, very slowly. She spoke of the nobleman who was converted to the teaching of Buddha, left his house, his garden, and his belongings and went to lead a religious life in the Temple of the Yellow Plum.

When she had finished these stories, Nun Wang chanted a psalm. Then Yueniang said: "Teachers, you must be hungry, we had better have something to eat." She bade Xiaoyu bring four plates of vegetarian food and another four plates of buns and cakes, and asked Aunt Wu, Aunt Yang, and old woman Pan to join the two nuns.

"I have just had something to eat," Aunt Wu said. "Ask Aunt Yang. She has been fasting."

Yueniang put the cakes on small gilded plates and offered them first to Aunt Yang and then to the two nuns. "Take some more, old lady," she said to Aunt Yang, but the old lady protested that she had had enough.

"There are some bones on the plate," Aunt Yang said. "Please, Sister, take them away. I might put them in my mouth by mistake." This made everybody roar with laughter.

"Old Lady," Yueniang said, "this is vegetarian food made to look like meat. It has come from the temple, and there can't possibly be any harm in eating it."

"If it is really vegetarian," Aunt Yang said, "I will taste it. My eyes are so bad I thought it was meat."

As they were eating, Laixing's wife, Huixiu, came in.

"What do you want, you rogue?" said Yueniang. Huixiu said she had come to hear the nuns sing.

"How did you manage to get in, since the second door is closed?" Yueniang asked.

Yuxiao answered. "She was in the kitchen, putting out the fire."

"Then no wonder your nose and mouth are so black. You look like a spiritual drumstick. What use is there in your coming to listen to religious admonitions?"

The ladies and the maids still sat around the two nuns. When the cakes were done with, everything was cleared away; the lights were trimmed, and more incense burned. The two nuns beat small gongs and began their chanting again. They told how the nobleman Zhang, in the Temple of the Yellow Plum on the mountainside, spent all his days upon his knees listening to the sutras, and all his nights in meditation. They told how the Fourth Sage perceived that Zhang was no common man, so he took the nobleman among his disciples, gave him three precious favors and bade him go to the bank of the River of Foulness, there to find a womb wherein he might be born again. Then they told how the Virgin of a Thousand Pieces of Gold was washing clothes on the bank of the River of Foulness. She met a monk who begged for a place in which to live, and when she did not answer, the monk jumped into the river.

Jinlian was very sleepy, and her head kept nodding. After a while she went to her room to bed. Then Xiuchun came to tell Li Ping'er that Guan'ge had waked up, and she, too, went away. Only Li Jiao'er, Meng Yulou, Sun Xue'e, old woman Pan and the two aunts remained to listen to the end of the story.

They were told how, from the river, there came a big scaly fish, and the maiden ate it. Then she went home, and bore a child after ten months.

By this time Yueniang noticed that her stepdaughter had gone to bed, and Aunt Wu, who was lying on Yueniang's bed, was fast asleep. Aunt Yang was yawning and the candles had already been renewed twice. She asked Xiaoyu what time it was. "It is the fourth watch," Xiaoyu said, "and the cock has crowed."

Yueniang told the two nuns to take their books. Aunt Yang went to Yulou's room and Miss Yu to the inner court to sleep with Xue'e. The Abbess slept with Li Jiao'er, and Nun Wang remained with Yueniang. They waited for Xiaoyu to make them some tea and then went to bed. Aunt Wu slept in the inner room with Yuxiao.

"How did the Fifth Sage grow up?" Yueniang asked Nun Wang. "Did he become a true Immortal?"

Nun Wang told her how the maiden's parents drove her from their home, and how she went to Xianrenzhuang where the Fifth Sage was born. When he was six years old, he went to the River of Foulness, recovered his three precious gifts and returned again to the Temple of the Yellow Plum to listen to the teaching of the Fourth Sage. Afterwards he became an Immortal and took his mother with him to Paradise. Yueniang heard the whole story from beginning to end, and afterwards believed even more fervently in the teaching of Buddha.

# CHAPTER 40

# Wu Yueniang and the Nun

Nun Wang and Wu Yueniang lay together upon the same bed. "Lady," said the nun, "has any sign of good fortune yet been granted you?"

"Good fortune!" Yueniang said. "In the eighth month of last year we bought the house belonging to the Qiao family, on the other side of the street from here. I went to look at it, but I slipped on the stairs, and the child, which was about six or seven months on the way, came from me. Since then there has been no sign of another."

"If it was seven months on the way," the nun said, "it must have been well formed."

"It fell into the pail in the middle of the night," Yueniang said, "and when the maid brought the light near I saw it was a boy."

"What a sad affair," Nun Wang said. "But it seems to me not that you strained yourself, but that your womb is not so strong as it might be. It would be much better for you to have a child than any of the other ladies. The Sixth Lady has been here only a little while, and see how happy she is with her child."

"Heaven decides whether we shall bear children or not," Yueniang said.

"Never mind," the nun said, "I have a friend called Xue who makes excellent charms and medicine. Last year there was Secretary Chen's wife. She was well on in years and had never borne a son, though she had several miscarriages. After she had taken my friend Xue's charms, she had a very fine boy. Everybody was so pleased. But one of the ingredients is very difficult to get."

"What is that?" Yueniang asked.

"First we need the afterbirth of a boy. This must be washed in wine and burned to ashes. Then the ashes must be mingled with the charm and medicine, and, on the *Renzi* day, in absolute secrecy, so that no evil spirit may interfere, you must swallow them with a little yellow wine upon an empty stomach. After that, all you have to do is to make a note of the date, and you will find that in exactly one month you will conceive. It is always so."

"Is your friend a monk or a nun?" Yueniang said, "and where does he or she live?"

"She is a nun about seventy years old," Nun Wang replied, "and once she lived at the Dizang Temple. Now she has gone to be the Abbess of the Fahua Temple. She is wonderfully learned. She knows all the religious texts and stories and can preach upon the Diamond Sutra and the sacred doctrine of Cause and Effect. She can talk for a month without exhausting her stock of learning. She only visits families of distinction, and, sometimes when they get hold of her, they will not let her go for ten days or a fortnight.

"Will you go tomorrow and ask her to come here?" Yueniang said.

"I will," said the nun, "and, moreover, I will ask her for the charms and medicine you need. There is only the one thing that is difficult to get, and I don't know what we can do about that. I think we had better dig up the Sixth Lady's and use that."

"Why should I hurt others to benefit myself?" Yueniang said. "I will give you some money, and you must try to get another one for me somewhere."

"For things like that we must go to the midwives," the nun said. "I will get the medicine for you, and, if you take it, I give you my word that you will have a baby like a moon that not even ten bright stars can outshine."

"Don't mention the matter to anyone," Yueniang said.

"What are you thinking about, my good Lady?" the nun said. "I should never dream of mentioning it."

At last they went to sleep.

Next day, when Yueniang had just got up, Ximen Qing came back from the temple. Yueniang was dressing her hair. Yuxiao took his clothes and he sat down.

"Yesterday," Yueniang said, "the Fifth Lady wished to offer wine to you on her birthday. Why did you not come back?"

"The sacrifice was not over," Ximen Qing said, "and kinsman Wu had arranged to entertain us to dinner. We stayed all night drinking. Brother Hua, Ying Bojue and Xie Xida were there, and two young actors sang to us. This morning when I came back, Brother Ying and the others were still drinking there."

Yuxiao brought tea. That day Ximen did not go to the office. He went to his study, lay on the bed and slept. Pan Jinlian and Li Ping'er dressed their hair and went with the baby to Yueniang's room.

"His father has been back some time," Yueniang told them. "I asked him to have something to eat, but he would not. Now dinner is ready. Dress the baby in his Daoist robes; then take him to the front court and show him to his father."

"Let me put on the baby's clothes," Jinlian said. "I will go with you."

They dressed the child in his Daoist hat with its gold bands, the Daoist habit, with the necklet, the medals and the tiny shoes and socks. Jinlian wished to carry the baby, but Yueniang said: "Let his own mother carry him. Your yellow embroidered skirt might easily be soiled. If the baby wets it even a little, it will be ruined."

So Li Ping'er carried Guan'ge, and Jinlian went with them. When they came to the room in the wing, Shutong pulled aside the lattice and came out. Jinlian saw Ximen Qing asleep, his face turned to the wall.

"How soundly you sleep, you old beggar," she cried. "Here is a young priest come to pay you a call. Dinner is ready in the Great Lady's room, and he has come to ask you to go. Get up at once. Don't stay there sleeping."

Ximen Qing had been drinking all night, so that when his head touched the pillow he forgot how high the sky is and how thick the earth. He snored like thunder. Jinlian and Li Ping'er sat down on either side of the bed and put down Guan'ge before Ximen Qing's face. When he opened his eyes, there was Guan'ge dressed in his priestly robes. Ximen was so delighted that he opened his eyes wide and smiled. He took the child in his arms and kissed him.

"What a nice clean mouth to kiss the baby with!" Jinlian said. "Now little Master Priest, Wu Yingyuan, spit in his face and ask him over what field he has been toiling like an ox that he is so sleepy he would sleep all day. Yesterday poor Fifth Mother waited and waited for him. But he is so grand he would not come and kowtow to Fifth Mother."

"The service finished very late," Ximen said. "I had to thank all the gods, and we were drinking all through the night. My head is still heavy with wine and I should like to sleep a little longer because I have to go to a party at Master Shang's."

"You ought to have done with drinking for a while," Jinlian said.

"He sent me an invitation yesterday, and, if I do not go, he will be annoyed."

"Well, if you do go, you must come back at once. I shall expect you."

Li Ping'er said: "The Great Lady has had dinner prepared, and some bitter bamboo shoots specially for you. She wants you to go and have some."

"Really I don't feel like eating anything," Ximen Qing said, "but I will go and have some soup." He got up and went to the inner court.

When he had left, Jinlian sat on the bed and put her feet on the warmer below the floor. "This is indeed a warm bed," she said. Then she touched the mattress and cried: "The bed is quite hot." On a table was a small stove made of tiles, with a guard about it. She took it in her hands. Then she said: "Sixth Sister, there is a box on that table with some fragrant tablets in it. Give it to me." She opened the box, took out a few tablets, and, wrapping them in her skirt, put them between her legs to perfume her body.

They sat there a long time till Li Ping'er said: "Let us go. He will be coming back in a moment."

"What if he does?" Jinlian said. "I don't care." But they took Guan'ge and went to the inner court.

When Ximen Qing had finished his dinner, he ordered a servant to get ready his horse. Then he went to Master Shang's house for the party. Old woman Pan left that afternoon. When Nun Wang was about to go, Yueniang told her she must not speak to the Reverend Mother about the arrangement between them. She gave the nun a tael of silver and asked her to remember the charms and the medicine. Nun Wang took the silver. "I cannot come before the sixteenth," she said, "but then I will bring what you wish for." Yueniang promised that she should have more silver, and the nuns went away.

My dear readers: monks, nuns and go-betweens should never be allowed to enter the palaces and dwellings of the gentry where there are ladies. They pretend to talk of religion and to tell edifying stories, but secretly they do all manner of mischief.

In the evening, Jinlian stood before her dressing table, dressed her hair in simple braids, powdered her face till it was as white as snow, and freshly painted her lips. She put on two earrings like tiny lanterns, set ornaments upon her cheeks, and bound her hair with a ribbon of purple and gold. Then she took a gown of scarlet woven with gold, and a skirt of blue satin. She dressed up like a maid, to make fun with Yueniang. She sent for Li Ping'er, who laughed until she shook.

"Sister," Li Ping'er said, "you look exactly like a maid. I have a red handkerchief in my room, and you shall have it to put over your head. Then I'll go to the back court and tell them that Father has bought a new maid. They will certainly be taken in."

Chunmei took a lantern and they went to the front court. When they came to the second door they met Chen Jingji. He laughed. "I should never have dreamed it was the Fifth Lady," he said.

"Come here, Brother-in-Law," Li Ping'er said, "I'll tell you what to do. You go in first and say so and so."

"Oh, I'll deceive them," Chen Jingji said.

He went before them to Yueniang's room. The people there were sitting on the bed drinking tea.

"Mother," said Jingji, "Father has gone and told old woman Xue to buy a maid for sixteen taels of silver. She is twenty-five years old and knows how to play and sing. She has just come in a sedan chair."

"Indeed?" Yueniang said. "Why didn't Xue come and tell me?"

"She was afraid you would scold her, so she only brought the sedan chair as far as the gate and then went away. The servants received the maid."

Aunt Wu was silent. Aunt Yang said: "He has so many wives already that I should have thought he had enough without buying another girl."

"My good Lady," Yueniang said, "you don't understand. If a man is rich, he may buy a hundred women and still not be satisfied. We are like a regiment of women soldiers."

"I will go and have a look at her," Yuxiao said. She went out, and saw Chunmei coming along in the moonlight, a lantern in her hand. Chunmei gave the lantern to Laian, and she and Li Ping'er assisted the new maid. The girl's head was covered with a red cloth, and she wore a scarlet gown. Yulou and Li Jiao'er were greatly excited. They came out to see. The maid came in. Yuxiao stood beside Yueniang.

"This is our mistress," she said to the maid. "Kowtow to her."

She took off the cloth that covered the new maid's head, and Jinlian gracefully kowtowed to Yueniang. But she could not help laughing.

"You maid," Meng Yulou said, "what do you mean by laughing instead of making your reverence?"

Yueniang laughed too. "Fifth Sister," she said, "you might have been a spirit, you deceived us all so well."

"She didn't deceive me," Yulou said.

"How could you tell?" said Aunt Yang.

"Because the Fifth Lady always kowtows in this way. She went backwards two steps and then bowed her body."

"You are quite right," Aunt Yang said, "but she certainly deceived me."

"She deceived me too," Li Jiao'er said. "I should never have recognized her with that cloth on her head, or until she laughed."

Qintong came with the wrapper and said his master had come.

"Hide yourself in the other room," Yulou said to Jinlian. "We will have some fun with him." Ximen Qing came in.

"Today," Yulou said to him, "Xue brought a maid in a sedan chair. She said you told her to buy her. You are not young, and the burden of the household is upon your shoulders. Why do you play games like this?"

"I never told her to buy a maid," Ximen said, laughing. "Do you believe everything that old rascal tells you?"

"Ask the Great Lady whether I am telling the truth or not," Yulou said. "The maid is here now. If you don't believe me, send for her." She said to Yuxiao: "Go and bring the new maid to see your father."

Yuxiao laughed and put her hand before her mouth, but she did not go. She took a few steps forward, then came back again. "I don't think she will come," she said.

"You are a brave maid to disobey your master's orders," Yulou said. "I will go for her. If she will not do what she is told, she will be no use as a maid."

She went into the next room. Then they heard: "You wonderful creature. I won't go. And don't pull me about like that."

Then Yulou said: "You slave, where were you brought up? Wherever did you learn to be so stubborn as to refuse to do reverence to your master?" Jinlian was dragged out.

In the light of the lamp, Ximen saw that it was Jinlian dressed as a maid, her hair done as a servant's. He laughed till he could not open his eyes. Jinlian took a chair and sat down.

"You bold maid," Yulou said, "you have only just come to the house, and yet you take such liberties that you even dare to sit in your master's presence."

"This is your master," Yueniang said. "Kowtow to him."

Jinlian did not move. After a while, she went to Yueniang's room, took off her ornaments and redressed her hair. They all laughed.

"Today," Yueniang said to Ximen Qing, "the Qiaos have sent six cards of invitation asking us to go on the twelfth and see the lanterns. I think we ought to send them some presents first."

"Tell Laixing to buy some food and a jar of Jinhua wine. That will be enough. We will send invitations to Madam Qiao, Madam Zhou, Madam Jing, Madam Xia and Madam Zhang for the fourteenth. Aunt Wu will be able to stay until then. I will tell Ben the Fourth to get the firework makers to make some fireworks for us. We will engage the young actors from the household of the Wangs, and Li Guijie and Wu Yin'er can come. You can all stay at home, see the fireworks, and drink wine, and I, Brother Ying, and Brother Xie will go to a wineshop in Lion Street."

The tables were set and wine was brought. Jinlian served the wine and all the ladies drank her health. Ximen Qing thought how pretty she had looked in the lamplight, dressed as a maid, and his heart grew warm towards her. He looked meaningly at her. Jinlian realized what was in his mind and went to her own room. She dressed herself again, doing her hair after the manner of Hangzhou. She painted her lips and powdered her face. Then she prepared some especially dainty dishes, set out wine, and waited for her husband.

Before very long Ximen Qing came. He noticed that she had dressed her hair again, and was pleased. He sat down on a chair and took her upon his knee. They laughed and talked, and Chunmei brought in food and wine. Jinlian again offered wine to him.

"Little oily mouth," Ximen said, "you have offered me wine already in the outer court. Why do you take the trouble to do so again?"

Jinlian smiled. "That was nothing," she said. "There, you were drinking with the others. This is my special offering to you and to no one else. Year after year you have been good enough to spend your money on me, and I trust you have no reason to complain."

This speech delighted Ximen. He took the wine immediately and set the woman on his knees. Chunmei served the wine, and Qiuju served the dishes.

"The Qiaos have asked us all to go to their place on the twelfth," Jinlian said, "but I think only our Great Lady ought to go."

"Since you have all been invited," Ximen Qing said, "why shouldn't you all go? I will tell the nurse to take the baby, so that he will not cry for his mother."

"The Great Lady and the others all have dresses," Jinlian said. "I am like an old priest: I only have old ones. Not one of them is fit to be seen. Won't you give me some of the new clothes you have just had made in the South, or some material so that I can make a dress for myself? There is no sense in your hoarding it up. Surely you don't expect it to increase and multiply! When it is our turn to give a party, and all the honorable ladies come, I shall have to dress properly to receive them or they will laugh at me. I have spoken to you about it several times, but you never pay any attention."

Ximen Qing laughed. "I will send for the tailor tomorrow, and he shall make you some clothes."

"It will be too late tomorrow. There are only two days left."

"I will tell him to bring more tailors with him and make two or three dresses for you at once. The rest can be done more slowly."

"I have mentioned it before," Jinlian said. "This time I shall expect some first-class material. All the others have beautiful clothes, and I have none. You have never bothered about clothes for me."

Ximen Qing laughed. "Ah, little oily mouth," he said, "you always insist on having the best of everything."

They talked and drank till the first night watch. Then they went to bed, and were like the love bird and his mate beneath the bedclothes, or a couple of phoenixes behind the curtains. They sported wildly for half the night.

The next day, when Ximen Qing came back from the office, he opened his boxes and took out some rolls of southern silk, enough to make a long gown, a suit of figured satin, and another embroidered suit. For Yueniang he ordered two long-sleeved scarlet satin gowns and four embroidered dresses. Then, sitting under the arbor, he ordered Qintong to go for the tailor. The tailor came and kowtowed. He took his tape and scissors, covered the tables, and cut out the material. First he cut out the long-sleeved satin gown of five colors; then another with a stomacher embroidered with the head of a wild beast; a black cloak with the five colors and gold ribbons, with designs of gourds and flowers intertwined; a gown of scarlet satin woven with gold, and another stomacher with the head of a wild beast; and a skirt of light blue woven with gold. Then he prepared a gown with a stomacher of sandalwood color, with embroidered flowers, and a scarlet skirt to match, of the hundred flower design, and all the flowers had gold branches and green leaves. These were for Wu Yueniang. For Li Jiao'er, Meng Yulou, Pan Jinlian and Li Ping'er, a long-sleeved satin cloak of scarlet with the five colors, embroidered with flowers and birds, and two dresses of embroidered silk. There was no cloak for Sun Xue'e, and only one dress.

The tailor cut them out very quickly, though there were more than thirty pieces in all. Ximen Qing gave him five taels of silver, and then he brought another ten tailors to make up the clothes in his house.

# Chapter 41

# The Baby Guan'ge Is Betrothed

Ximen Qing watched the tailors as they hastily made up the dresses, and the work was finished in two days. On the twelfth, a messenger came from the Qiao household to renew the former invitation. That morning Ximen Qing had sent presents. Wu Yueniang, Aunt Wu, and the others set off together in six sedan chairs, leaving Sun Xue'e behind to look after the house. The nurse, Ruyi'er, took Guan'ge, and Laixing's wife, Huixiu, went with them to act as tiring maid. They too went in sedan chairs. At home Ximen Qing watched the firework makers making their fireworks, and superintended the hanging of the lanterns in the great hall. He sent a boy with his card to the house of the princely family of Wang to engage the actors.

In the afternoon he went to Pan Jinlian's room. Jinlian was not there, and Chunmei gave him something to eat.

"I have invited several ladies to come on the fourteenth," he told her. "You four girls must wear your best clothes when you wait upon them."

Chunmei leaned over the table. "You should say that to the other girls. There will be no dressing for me."

"Why?" said Ximen.

"The ladies will all be dressed in their new clothes," Chunmei said. "They will be very smart, and we shall look like burned paper. Everybody will laugh at us."

"But you all have dresses and ornaments, and pearls and flowers," Ximen Qing said.

"The ornaments are all right, but we have no clothes," Chunmei said. "I have only two old dresses and I am not fit to be seen."

"I see," Ximen said, laughing. "I have had clothes made for the ladies, and you are jealous, little oily mouth. Never mind. I am going to tell the tailor to make three dresses for my daughter, and you four girls shall each have a suit and a short dress of figured satin."

"Don't put me in the same class with the rest," Chunmei said. "I want a white silk coat and a scarlet-figured silk wrapper."

"If it were only for you," Ximen said, "it would be all right; but if you have one, my daughter will have to have one."

"Your daughter has one already," Chunmei said. "I have not. I don't see how she can object."

Ximen Qing took the keys and went upstairs. He chose enough material for five dresses and two figured satin wrappers, and took a roll of white silk for two double-breasted white cloaks. The wrappers for his daughter and Chunmei were scarlet; those for the other three maids were bluish green. There were scarlet satin short coats and light blue skirts for all of them, seventeen pieces of material in all. Ximen told the tailor to make the clothes, and gave him a roll of thin yellow silk for the tops of the skirts, and Hangzhou lining silk for the linings. Chunmei was satisfied. She laughed and talked all day with Ximen Qing and served him with wine when he wished for it.

Madam Qiao had invited several ladies to her party. There was the wife of Master Shang, Censor Song's wife, a young woman named Cui who was connected with the family, two nieces, Miss Duan and Wu Shunzhen's sister-in-law Zheng. She had engaged two singing girls to play for them. When Wu Yueniang, Aunt Wu, and the others arrived, Madam Qiao went to the second door to welcome them and took them to the great hall. There they exchanged greetings. She called Yueniang Aunt, and the others Second Aunt, and Third Aunt, and so on. Then she introduced the other ladies and took their places in due order. The maids brought tea, and Master Qiao came to greet the ladies. When they had greeted him, he told his wife to ask them to go to the inner room to take off their cloaks. A table was set, tea brought, and they all sat down to drink it. Ruyi'er and Huixiu looked after the baby and were entertained in another place.

After tea they came back to the great hall, where handsome screens were placed about and cushions embroidered with lotus flowers. Four tables were set and Yueniang was asked to take the place of honor. The eleven ladies all sat at one table, except for Miss Duan and Miss Zheng, who were at a table apart. The two singing girls sang for them. When soup and rice had been served, the cooks served up a crystal goose. Yueniang gave them two *qian* of silver. Then stewed trotters were served, and Yueniang gave the cooks another *qian*. Then came roast duck and again Yueniang gave the cooks a *qian*. After this course Madam Qiao rose and offered wine, first to Yueniang and then to Master Shang's wife. Yueniang left the table and went to the inner room to change her clothes and powder her face.

Yulou went to Madam Qiao's room, where Ruyi'er had the baby Guan'ge. He was in a small crib placed on the bed, and, lying beside him, was the little girl baby of the Qiaos. The two babies were playing together, putting out their hands to touch one another. This delighted Wu Yueniang and Meng Yulou. "These two babies," they said, "are like bride and bridegroom." Aunt Wu came in, and they said to her: "Come here, Aunt Wu, and look at this young couple."

"Yes," Aunt Wu said, smiling, "they are stretching out their hands and kicking their little heels, touching one another, just like a young husband and wife."

Madam Qiao and the other ladies heard what Aunt Wu said. "How might an inconsiderable family like mine," Madam Qiao said, "aspire so high as to ally itself with that of my aunts?"

"You are very kind," Yueniang said, "but indeed what manner of lady are you, and Miss Zheng too? I should very much like to enter into an alliance with this household, if only my son will not make your house ashamed. Do not say that."

Yulou pushed forward Li Ping'er. "Sister," she said, "what have you to say?" Li Ping'er smiled but said nothing.

"If Madam Qiao does not agree," Aunt Wu said, "I shall be very disappointed."

Master Shang's wife and the Censor's lady both said together: "For the sake of your kinswoman, Lady Wu, you must not stand too much on ceremony. Your Zhangjie was born in the eleventh month of last year."

"And our baby," Yueniang said, "was born on the twenty-third day of the sixth month. He is just five months older. Their ages could not be more suitable."

The others would allow no further parley. They urged Madam Qiao, Wu Yueniang and Li Ping'er to the great hall. There, pieces were cut from the bosoms of their dresses. The two singing girls sang for them and Master Qiao was told. He brought out fruits, three pieces of red cloth, and offered wine. Yueniang told Daian and Qintong to go home and refer the matter to their master. In a short time, two jars of wine, three rolls of silk, red and green thread, flowers of gold wire, and four large boxes of cakes and fruit were brought from Ximen's place, and the two households together hung up red charms and drank wine to celebrate their union.

Tall silver candlesticks blazed with light in the hall. Flower-shaped lamps burned brightly. Incense filled the air with delightful perfume. Smiling serenely, the two singing girls opened their ruby lips, showed their white teeth and gently plied their jade plectrums. They held their lutes in one hand and sang. The ladies put flowers and red talismans on the heads of Yueniang, Madam Qiao, and Li Ping'er. When wine had been served, the ladies made reverence to one another and began their banquet again. As the first course, the cook brought in a snowflake pie, filled with mincemeat. The word "Long Life" was fashioned upon it. There was lotus-seed soup, which looked as delightful as a pool, the seeds floating side by side upon its surface. Yueniang sat in the place of honor; she was very happy. She told Daian to give the cook a roll of silk, and each of the singing girls a roll of silk also. They all kowtowed to thank her.

Madam Qiao would not allow the ladies to go. She took them to the inner court, where she had prepared all kinds of delightful refreshments for them. It was not until the first night watch that Yueniang was able to leave.

"My dear relative," she said to Madam Qiao, "you must come to our poor house tomorrow."

"You are very kind," Madam Qiao said. "My husband has spoken to me of your invitation, but I fear I am no fit person to come to your party just now. Perhaps you will allow me to come some other time."

"There will be no strangers present," Yueniang said. "Please do not stand on ceremony." Then she said to Aunt Wu: "There is no reason why you should leave when we do. You will be coming with Madam Qiao tomorrow."

"Madam Qiao," said Aunt Wu, "if you do not care to go tomorrow, any other day will serve as well, but the fifteenth is your new kinswoman's birthday, and that day you must not fail to go."

"Oh," Madam Qiao said, "if it is my relative's birthday, how should I dare not go?"

"If Madam Qiao does not come to see me, I shall blame you," Yueniang said to Aunt Wu. Then, leaving Aunt Wu behind, she said good-bye and got into her chair. Two soldiers carried a large red lantern before the sedan chair, and behind it were two boys with lanterns. Yueniang was at the head of the procession, then Li Jiao'er, Meng Yulou, Pan Jinlian and Li Ping'er each in her place. Then came the chairs with Ruyi'er and Huixiu. The nurse had Guan'ge closely wrapped in a red silk coverlet, and as still further protection against the cold, she had a brass warming pan in the chair. Two more boys followed her.

When they came to their gate and got out of their chairs, Ximen Qing was drinking in Yueniang's room. Yueniang and the others came in and made reverence to him. Then Yueniang sat down and all the maids came to kowtow to her. She told her husband about the betrothal. He asked what ladies had been present. She told him.

"This marriage," he said, "is all very well, but the families are not of equal rank."

"It was my sister-in-law's doing," Yueniang said. "She saw the Qiaos' baby lying on the same bed as Guan'ge, covered with the same bedclothes, so that the children looked like two young lovers, and she called to me to look at them. When we were having supper, we could not help talking about it, and it was arranged. I sent the boy to tell you and get you to send the boxes of fruits."

"Now that it has been settled," Ximen Qing said, "it doesn't matter, but there is a certain inequality of position. Qiao has some property, but he is only a private citizen, while I am an officer and have duties at the courts. If we have to ask him to a party here, he will wear an ordinary hat, and I don't see how I can invite him to sit with me. It will be most awkward. Only the other day Jing Nangang sent one of his people to try to arrange a marriage. His daughter was five months old, the same age as our own child, but I did not care much for the arrangement because the baby's mother is dead. Besides, she was not the daughter of the first wife. So I would make no promises. Now, without my knowing anything about it, you have gone and settled everything yourself."

"If you did not care for that child because she is a second wife's daughter, what are you going to do now?" Jinlian said. "The Qiao baby is a second wife's daughter too. It seems to me like Xian Daoshen and the God of Long Life, one complaining that the other is too tall, and the other objecting that the first is too short."

This made Ximen Qing very angry. "You strumpet," he shouted, "why don't you take yourself off? We are talking, but nobody asked you to put in your word."

Jinlian flushed and went out of the room. "Of course," she said, "I have no right to speak in this place, or in any other place, for that matter."

When, at the party, Jinlian saw the arrangements being made between Madam Qiao and Yueniang, and Li Ping'er wearing flowers and red charms upon her hair, it had made her very jealous. Now that Ximen Qing spoke angrily to her, she was still more upset and went to cry in Yueniang's inner room.

"Why has Aunt Wu not come back with you?" Ximen Qing asked Yueniang.

"Madam Qiao said she would not come tomorrow because we have ladies of rank coming, so I left Aunt Wu there, and they will come together."

"I told you there would be difficulties about precedence," Ximen said. "I don't know what you are going to do about it."

Some time later, Yulou went into the inner room and found Jinlian in tears. "Why are you so upset?" she said. "Let him say what he likes."

"You heard what I said to him," Jinlian cried. "It was nothing wrong. He said that child was not born in proper wedlock, and I said that neither was the Qiao baby. There is nothing there to complain about. But that bandit—he will come to a bad end—glared at me and swore without rhyme or reason. What does he mean by saying I had no right to speak? He has changed his tune completely. I'll see he gets paid back for it. There is that baby, a miserable, puny little thing that can do nothing but piddle, and they begin arranging a marriage for him. It is because they have so much money they don't know what to do with it. May he tear his coverlets and have nothing to cover him! May he be like a dog snapping at a bladder and get no joy out of it.

"Today the prospects of this marriage seem rosy. Let us hope they won't look different in time to come. They are behaving just like a man who puts out the light, blinks his eyes, and wonders what on earth is going to happen next. They think this is a good house to marry into; we shall see what they think in four or five years' time. This is the only child he has."

"In these days, people are always trying to be clever," Yulou said. "I don't care much for this sort of behavior, myself. It seems to me too early. The baby is so young. They might have dispensed with the cutting of the cloth. But perhaps they only want to be friendly and do this sort of thing for fun."

"If it is meant for fun, well and good," Jinlian said, "but why should that rascal curse me?"

"You shouldn't have said what you did say," Yulou said. "He couldn't help himself."

"I find it hard to say all I think about it," Jinlian said. "That woman is not a second wife any longer. She is the lady of the house. But even if Qiao's baby is the daughter of a second wife, there is no doubt she has old Qiao's blood in her veins. Whereas, in our household, people have not always gone straight, and who knows whose blood runs in our baby's veins?"

Yulou said nothing. They talked a while longer, then Jinlian went to her own room. Li Ping'er waited until Ximen Qing had gone away, then she kowtowed most gracefully to Yueniang.

"I am grateful to you," she said, "for all that you have done for my child today."

Yueniang smiled and returned her reverence. "It is you who are to be congratulated."

"You also, Sister," Li Ping'er said. She stood up while Yueniang and Li Jiao'er sat down to talk. Sun Xue'e and Ximen's daughter came in and kowtowed to Yueniang, making an equal reverence to Li Ping'er. Xiaoyu brought tea. While they were drinking it, Xiuchun came and said the baby needed his mother. Ximen Qing had told her to come.

"It was thoughtless of the nurse to take the child to my room," Li Ping'er said. "I ought to have gone with them, for I don't suppose there was a light."

"When they came home," Yueniang said, "I told Ruyi'er to take the child to your room. It was so late."

"I saw Ruyi'er with the baby," Xiaoyu said. "Laian was carrying a lantern for them."

"That is all right, then," Li Ping'er said, and went to join her baby. She found Ximen Qing in her room and the baby asleep at his nurse's breast.

"Why didn't you tell me you were going to bring the child here?" she said to the nurse.

Ruyi'er told her that Yueniang had seen Laian with a lantern and told her to bring the baby to his mother's room. "Young Master cried for a while," she said, "but I have got him to sleep now."

"Yes," Ximen Qing said, "the baby wanted you for a while, but he has gone to sleep now."

"He has been betrothed today," Li Ping'er said, "and I must kowtow to you." She knelt down. Ximen was very pleased with her and beamed with delight. He quickly raised her to her feet and sat beside her. They told Yingchun to set a table, and they drank together.

Jinlian went to her room in a most vicious temper. She knew that Ximen Qing was with Li Ping'er and, when Qiuju was a moment slow in opening the door for her, she boxed her ears and cursed her loudly.

"You thievish slave," she cried, "why did I have to knock so long before you opened the door? What are you here for? I shall not speak to you again." She went into her room and sat down. Chunmei came and gave her some tea.

"What was that thievish slave doing?" Jinlian said. "She was sitting in the courtyard," Chunmei said. "I told her to open the door for you, but she didn't pay any attention."

"Oh, I know," Jinlian cried; "just because he and I have had words, she is like Grand Marshal Dang eating a tablet. She thinks she will put on airs and annoy me."

Jinlian would have liked to give Qiuju a beating, but she was afraid Ximen Qing might hear. She said no more for the moment, but she was angry nonetheless. Then she undressed. Chunmei prepared her bed. She got into it and went to sleep.

Next day, when Ximen Qing had gone to his office, Jinlian made Qiuju balance a piece of stone on her head and kneel down in the courtyard. When she had finished dressing her hair, she told Chunmei to take down Qiuju's trousers and beat her with a thick stick.

"I shall soil my hands if I take down your trousers," Chunmei said to her fellow maid. She went to the front court and called for Huatong. The boy took down the girl's trousers while Jinlian stood by and cursed her.

"You thievish slave," she cried, "where did you learn to give yourself such airs? Others might forgive you, but I never will. Sister, you know I understand your little ways, and you would do well to restrain yourself. Who are you to put your face forward and show what a great person you are? Sister, don't count on getting help from any other quarter. I shall keep my eyes skinned and watch you." She struck and cursed her and cursed and struck her till Qiuju squealed like a pig being killed.

Meanwhile Li Ping'er had got up. The nurse was trying to rock the baby to sleep, but he kept on waking. She could hear Jinlian cursing Qiuju, and recognized all the references to herself in what was said. But she said nothing, and only covered Guan'ge's ears with her hand.

"Go and ask the Fifth Lady not to beat Qiuju," she said to Xiuchun. "Tell her the baby has just had his milk and is going to sleep."

Xiuchun gave the message, but Jinlian beat Qiuju more severely still. "You thievish slave," she cried, "you shout as loudly as though someone were sticking ten thousand knives into you. But I am a queer person; the louder you cry, the more I shall beat you. I did not expect outsiders to interfere because you were having a beating. Why do you come to have a look? My good sister, you ought to tell our husband to get rid of her."

Li Ping'er heard all this, and knew that the curses were aimed at her. She was so angry that her hands were as cold as ice, but she swallowed her anger and did not show any temper. That morning she had no tea. She carried Guan'ge in her arms and rocked him to sleep.

When Ximen Qing came back from his office, he went to see his son. The Sixth Lady's eyes were red with weeping, and she was lying on the bed.

"Why have you not dressed your hair?" he asked her. "The one in the upper room wishes to see you. And why are your eyes red?"

Instead of telling him about her trouble with Jinlian, Li Ping'er said she was not very well. Ximen told her that the Qiaos had sent some birthday presents for her, a roll of silk, two jars of southern wine, a plate of longevity peaches, another plate of noodles, and other dishes. "They have sent something for the baby too," he said, and told her all the different things that had come. "We have done nothing for them," he added, "and now they have sent all these things for your feast day. That is why the one in the upper room wishes to talk to you. They sent old woman Kong and Qiao Tong with the presents. Aunt Wu has come back. She says Madam Qiao cannot come until the day after tomorrow. She has a relative, Lady Qiao the Fifth, who is related in some way to the royal family. This Lady has heard about the betrothal and is very pleased. She is coming on the fifteenth too, so we must send a card to her."

Li Ping'er got up and slowly dressed her hair. Then she went to the inner court to see Aunt Wu and old woman Kong. They were having tea in Yueniang's room. The presents were set out there. She looked at them all. The cases were returned, and old woman Kong and Qiao Tong were each given two handkerchiefs and five *qian* of silver. When a card of thanks had been written out, they went away.

## Chapter 42
# Ximen Feasts in Lion Street

Stars and moon make glorious the sky
Ten thousand candles burn on earth.
Heavens and Earth make festival today.
Spring is the season of harmony.
Now people wear their finest clothes and even their horses are proud.
The days pass quickly: we must not spend them idly
White hair is a judge who spares no man.
Fools spend a thousand pieces of gold to buy a moment's happiness
And bid the watchman strike the night drum softly.

When the messengers from the Qiao family had been sent away, Ximen Qing went to the upper room to discuss matters with Wu Yueniang, Aunt Wu, and Li Ping'er.

"We must, of course, send them something in return for these presents," Yueniang said, "and something for the baby too, to show that we consider the betrothal definite. Besides, we do not wish to show ourselves behind them in courtesy."

"Yes," Aunt Wu said, "and we must send a marriage maker."

"They sent old woman Kong," Yueniang said. "Whom shall we send?"

"One guest never troubles more than one host," Ximen Qing said. "Old woman Feng is good enough for us." He had eight cards of invitation written; then he sent for old woman Feng, and told Daian to take the presents and the cards.

The invitations were for the fifteenth day. All the ladies who had been present at the Qiaos' party, and Lady Qiao the Fifth, were invited to celebrate the birthday of Li Ping'er and to enjoy the Feast of Lanterns. Ximen ordered Laixing to buy cakes and buns and fruits and food, two suits of silk clothes, a little scarlet cloak, a silk hat with golden ornaments, two lanterns made like sheep's horns, that came from Yunnan, a box of ribbons, a pair of tiny gold bracelets, and four gold and jade rings. These things were all packed up on the morning of the fourteenth, and Chen Jingji and Ben the Fourth were told to put on their black clothes and take them to the Qiaos.

Master Qiao received them well, and gave them presents of some value in return, particularly little things for the baby. While they were busying themselves with the presents, Ying Bojue came to talk to Ximen Qing about the money that had been lent to Huang the Fourth and Li Zhi. Seeing them so busy, he asked what it was all about. Ximen Qing told him about the betrothal.

"On the fifteenth," he said, "you must ask your Lady to come and spend an hour or two here."

"Your lady has only to give the command," Bojue said, "and my wife will come."

"A number of ladies are coming," Ximen said, "and I think we men had better go to Lion Street to see the lanterns." Ying Bojue agreed, and went away.

The same day Wu Yin'er brought four boxes of birthday presents to Li Ping'er and asked to be adopted as her ward. Li Ping'er accepted the presents and sent away the sedan chair. When, next day, Li Guijie came and found Wu Yin'er already there, she asked Wu Yueniang why she had come. Yueniang told her what had happened. Guijie made no comment but, all that day, she was sulky and would not speak to Wu Yin'er.

From the princely family of Wang there came a troop of twenty actors with two managers to direct the performance. They brought their chests of costumes. When they came and kowtowed to Ximen Qing, he told them to use the rooms in the west wing as their dressing rooms, and there they had their meals.

Major Zhou's wife, General Jing's mother and Captain Zhang's wife came. They all had soldiers to clear the way before their sedan chairs, and a number of attendants and serving women. Yueniang and the others, dressed in their long cloaks, came out to welcome their guests, and took them to the great hall where they exchanged greetings. Then they sat down and drank some tea, but not ceremonially, for they were waiting for the wife of Magistrate Xia. They waited a long time but she did not come. Two or three times they sent boys to see if she was coming. At last she came with soldiers to clear the way for her, and a number of attendants, with a woman to carry her dressing case. When she came into the great hall, she was received with music. There she greeted the other ladies, and they took their places according to their rank. They had tea under the awning and then went to the great hall, where Chunmei, Yuxiao, Yingchun, and Lanxiang, all exquisitely dressed, served them with tea and wine. The actors performed the *Story of the Western Pavilion*. It was a most brilliant scene.

Ximen Qing waited until the ladies had had tea, then mounted his horse, and went to the house in Lion Street. He had told Ying Bojue and

Xie Xida to meet him there. Some of his men had been told to take one of the four great fireworks to Lion Street and set up two for the entertainment of the ladies. The cooks were ordered to send two boxes of food and two jars of Jinhua wine. Two singing girls had been engaged, Dong Jiao'er and Han Yuchuan, and Daian had taken a sedan chair for Wang Liu'er.

"Aunt Han," Daian said when he met her, "Father has sent me to take you to see the fireworks this evening."

"But I don't know that I ought to go," Wang Liu'er said, smiling. "What do you think your Uncle Han will say about it?"

"Father has spoken to him already," Daian said. "He says you must dress and go. There are only to be two singing girls there, no one else."

Wang Liu'er did not move. Then Han Daoguo himself came in.

"Here is Uncle Han," Daian said. "Your wife will not believe what 1 say."

"Do you really wish me to go?" Wang Liu'er said to her husband.

"Well," he said, "his Lordship said that there is no one to look after the two singing girls. That's why he wants you. And you will see the fireworks this evening. Hurry up and dress. He told me to shut the shop and go there myself. We shall have a good time. Laibao has gone home already. It is his turn to watch the shop tonight."

"I don't know how long it will last," Wang Liu'er said. "We will go and stay a while and then come home. We can't leave the house without anyone to look after it and, besides, this is your day off and you must have some sleep."

She dressed and went with Daian to the house in Lion Street. Laizhao's wife, the Beanpole, was there. She had dusted the beds, changed the bed-clothes and the curtains, burned incense to sweeten the rooms, hung up two lanterns, and put a brazier in the room. Wang Liu'er went in and sat down on the bed. The Beanpole made reverence to her and brought her tea.

When Ying Bojue and Ximen Qing had seen the lanterns, they came in and played backgammon in the upper room. Six windows were opened and the shades hung out before them. Below them they could see the lantern fair. It was a picture of gaiety and merriment. After playing a while, they had some food. Then they sat down to look at the lanterns through the blinds. While they were watching the crowd below, Ximen Qing suddenly saw Xie Xida, Zhu Shinian, and another man, who wore a scholar's hat, standing beneath the arch of lanterns. He pointed to them and said to Ying Bojue: "Do you know that fellow wearing a square hat?"

"He seems very familiar to me," Ying Bojue said, "but I don't know him."

Then Ximen Qing said to Daian: "Go down and ask your Uncle Xie to come, but don't let Pockmarked Zhu or the other man see you."

Daian crept downstairs like a young pickpocket and went out into the crowd. He waited till Pockmarked Zhu and the stranger were out of the way for a moment, then pulled Xie Xida by the sleeve. Xie Xida turned quickly and recognized Daian.

"Father and Uncle Ying would like to see you," the boy said.

"Very well, I understand," said Xie Xida. "Now slip away. I will go with these two as far as the place where the Plum Flowers are, and then I'll come to see your master."

Daian made off like a streak of smoke. Xie Xida, when he came to a more crowded place, turned aside and left Zhu Shinian and the other man looking for him. He went to the room where Ximen Qing and Ying Bojue were sitting, and made a reverence to them.

"I see you have come to look at the show, Brother," he said. "Why didn't you send me a message this morning?"

"There were a number of guests at my place all the morning," Ximen said, "and I couldn't find an opportunity to send you word. I did tell Brother Ying to invite you, but you were not at home. Did Pockmarked Zhu see you come here? Who is the man with the scholar's hat?"

"The man with the square hat," Xie Xida said, "is Wang the Third, of General Wang's family. He and Zhu came to see me because Wang is trying to borrow three hundred taels. He asked me, old Sun, and Pockmarked Zhu to be his guarantors. He is going to take a course of study at the military academy, and qualify for official rank. I was not interested in his business. I simply came with him to see the lanterns. When I heard you wished to see me, I went with them as far as the place where the Plum Flowers are and gave them the slip." He asked Bojue how long he had been there.

"Brother told me to come, to your house," Bojue said, "and I did so, but you were not at home. Then I came here. We have been playing backgammon."

"Have you had anything to eat?" Ximen Qing asked Xie Xida.

"When I left your place this morning," Xie Xida said, "I met those two, and I have had nothing to eat all day."

Ximen told Daian to go to the kitchen and ask for some food to be prepared. Before long it was brought. It was a very substantial meal, but Xie Xida soon disposed of it, cleaning up both inside and outside of all the dishes. The little soup that he had left, he put into his rice bowl, and so finished off everything. Daian cleared away, and Xie Xida went to stand beside his two friends. They were now playing backgammon again.

Meanwhile the two singing girls arrived, and the sedan chair men carried in their clothes. They came in smiling. Ying Bojue saw them through the window.

"What makes those little whores so late?" he said. Then to Daian: "Don't let them go to the inner court. Tell them to come up here and see me."

Xie Xida asked who they were. Daian told him, then ran downstairs and said to the singing girls: "Uncle Ying wants to see you." The two singing girls paid no attention, but went on to the inner court. They made a reverence the Beanpole, who took them to the inner room where Wang Liu'er was sitting, wearing a new-fashioned net upon her hair, a purple silk dress, a long black cloak, and a white ribboned skirt. Below the skirt her two tiny feet peeped out. Her hair came down rather low upon her cheeks, and her face was bright but not too highly painted. She looked like a person of the middle class. She was wearing two earrings, shaped like cloves.

They made the usual reverence to her and sat down on the bed. Little Iron Rod brought tea and Wang Liu'er drank it with them. The two girls looked at the woman from head to foot. After they had examined her well, they laughed. They had no idea who she was. Then Daian came and the girls secretly asked him. Daian did not know what story to tell. Finally he said: "The lady comes from my father's sister-in-law's. She has come to see the lanterns."

When the two girls heard this, they went back into the room.

"We did not realize you were our aunt," they said to Wang Liu'er, "and so we did not make the correct reverence to you. Please forgive us." Then they knelt down and kowtowed to her. Wang Liu'er hastily made a half reverence in return. Soup and dishes were brought and she ate with them. Afterwards they took their instruments and sang for her."

When Ying Bojue had finished his game of backgammon, he went downstairs to wash his hands. Hearing the sound of music coming from the inner court, he called Daian and said to him: "Tell me: to whom are those girls singing?" Daian laughed but did not answer for some time. At last he said: "You might be the Captain of Caozhou, the way you poke your nose into everything. Whether there is singing or not, it is no business of yours."

"You thievish young rascal," Ying Bojue said, "whether you tell me or not, you know I shall find out."

"Then why ask me?" Daian said, laughing.

Bojue went upstairs again. By this time, Ximen Qing and Xie Xida had played three games of backgammon. Then Li Ming and Wu Hui came in and kowtowed.

"Good!" said Ying Bojue, "you have come just in time. How did you know we were here?"

Li Ming, still upon his knees, said: "We went to his Lordship's house and there they told us that he was having a party here, so we came on to await his pleasure."

"Excellent!" Bojue said. "Stand up."

Then he said to Daian: "Go and ask your Uncle Han to come." Han Daoguo came, greeted them, and sat down.

The tables were laid; dishes appropriate to the season were brought in, and Qintong served wine. Ying Bojue and Xie Xida sat in the seats of honor—Ximen Qing in the host's place, and Han Daoguo opposite. When the wine had been heated, Daian was told to bid the singing girls come. The two girls, Dong Jiao'er and Han Yuchuan, came in, slowly and gracefully. They kowtowed, but not exactly in the direction of the two guests.

"I wondered who was here," Ying Bojue said. "Now I see it is only you two little whores. Why didn't you come when I sent for you? You are getting far too independent. If I don't take you in hand, you will become quite unbearable."

Dong Jiao'er laughed. "Brother," she said, "you are like a ghost playing his ghostly tricks on the other side of a wall. But you won't frighten me to death."

Han Yuchuan said: "You know, my dear slave, that you are like an animal's head picked up by the city wall, a fine specimen of an unwanted baby."

"Brother," Ying Bojue said to Ximen, "you have done more than you need today. Li Ming and Wu Hui are here, and that ought to be enough. What need have you of these two whores? Why not send them about their business at once? Tonight is the Feast of Lanterns, and they will have plenty of opportunity to go and beg elsewhere. But don't make them too late. Nobody will have them if they are too late."

"Brother," Yuchuan said, "how can you be so shameless? It wasn't you who sent for us, but Father. What business is it of yours?"

"Foolish little bone," Bojue said. "I happen to be here and you will have to wait on me whether you like it or not."

"You are like Tang, the fat man, who fell into a jar of vinegar and was sour all over," Yuchuan said.

"It is your heart that is sour, you thievish little strumpet," Bojue said. "But wait a while. I will show you something when you go home. I have two scores against you now, and you shall not escape me."

"What do you mean?" Dong Jiao'er said. "Tell me."

"I shall tell the policeman that you are breaking the law by night. He will arrest you and put the thumbscrews on you. And if that is not enough, I will spend a few coins on white wine and make your chair men drunk, and then you will wander all over the place, get home late, and have a beating waiting for you when you do get there."

"If we are late," Han Yuchuan said, "we shall not go. We shall stay here, or we shall ask Father to send us home and give mother a hundred cash. But it has nothing to do with you anyway. I like your impertinence!"

"Yes," Bojue said, "I suppose it is I who am the slave. Everything is topsy-turvy nowadays. I lose."

They laughed and talked. The two singing girls sang the songs of spring, and the men dined. Then Daian came and said: "Uncle Zhu is here." No one spoke. Zhu Shinian came upstairs and saw Ying Bojue and Xie Xida sitting in the places of honor.

"Ah!" said he, "a fine pair you are, stuffing yourselves with good food, but do you call yourselves men?" He turned to Xie Xida. "Brother, you are given an invitation and, without a word to us, you run away. We were looking for you everywhere, there by the Plum Flowers."

"It was quite by chance," Xie Xida said, "that I saw his Lordship and Brother Ying playing backgammon. I came up to greet them, and his Lordship made me stay."

Ximen Qing told Daian to bring a chair and invited Zhu Shinian to sit down. Cup and chopsticks were brought; Zhu sat down in the lower seat, and the cook brought something for him to eat. Ximen Qing had only one pie and a mouthful of soup. Li Ming was standing beside him, and he gave everything that was put before him to the young man to take away and eat. Ying Bojue, Xie Xida, Zhu Shinian and Han Daoguo each had a large bowl of soup, three large pastries, and four peach-blossom buns. They left one pie as ballast for the plate. Then all the food was cleared away and more wine was brought.

"Where did you leave him?" Xie Xida said to Zhu Shinian. "And how did you know I was here?"

"I searched everywhere for you," Zhu Shinian said, "and when I couldn't find you, I went to old Sun's place with Wang the Third. We met Master Xu Buyu. He borrowed the three hundred taels, but old Sun made a mistake in the contract."

"You must not put my name on it," Xie Xida said. "I will have nothing to do with it. You and old Sun are the guarantors and the commission will come to you. What mistake did you make?"

"I told him to write out the contract more or less indefinitely and make three conditions for repayment, but he didn't do so, and I made him write it out again."

"What were the three conditions?" Xie Xida said.

"First, when the wind blows away the stone roller and kills a single goose in the sky. Secondly, when a fish jumps from the bottom of the river to the bank; and thirdly, when the stones in the riverbed are so waterlogged that they fall to pieces. When those three things happened, he was to pay his debt."

"Well," Xie Xida said, "if he wrote that, it was indefinite enough."

"It is not so indefinite as you think," Zhu Shinian said. "One day, if the weather is fine and the water low, and the authorities think fit to dig up the river, and the stones in the bed are broken by the workers with their tools, he will have to pay."

Everybody laughed. It was now growing dark and Ximen Qing told the boys to light the lanterns. They were sheep's horn lanterns, and very wonderfully made.

Yueniang sent Qitong and some soldiers with four boxes full of dainties. Ximen asked the boy if the ladies had finished their party, and who had told him to bring the things. "Great Mother told me to bring them for you to eat with your wine," Qitong said. "The ladies have not gone yet, and four acts of the play have been performed. My lady is entertaining her guests in the great hall. They are drinking there and watching the fireworks."

"Has anybody come to see the fireworks?" Ximen said.

"There is a crowd at the gate," the boy told him.

"I told four black-garbed soldiers to take their staves and keep order and not to allow the people to push one another about."

"Ping'an and the soldiers are keeping guard over the fireworks," Qitong said. "There is no disorder."

Ximen Qing gave orders that the table should be cleared and the boxes brought in. The cook brought some excellent fruit pasties. The two singing girls served wine. Ximen told Qitong to go home again. Then he and the others drank the warm wine, and enjoyed the delicacies Yueniang had sent. He told Li Ming and Wu Hui to sing the song of the lanterns. When the song was ended, they ate the pasties.

Han Daoguo was the first to go home. Ximen Qing told Laizhao to pull up the blinds downstairs and take out the fireworks. Ximen and his friends watched from the upper room, and sent word to Wang Liu'er, the singing girls, and the Beanpole to look on from below. Daian and Laizhao carried the firework to the middle of the street and there set light to it. People came crowding to see, shoulder to shoulder, for they were told that Ximen Qing was responsible for it.

Ying Bojue saw that Ximen Qing was a little tipsy. When the firework was burnt out, he went downstairs. Wang Liu'er was washing her hands. He dragged Xie Xida and Zhu Shinian away, without even waiting to say goodbye to his host.

"Where are you going, Uncles?" Daian said to him.

"Foolish boy," Ying Bojue whispered. "I have told you before. If I don't go, they will stay and stay, and it will be awkward. If your father asks for me, say we have all gone."

When the fireworks were done, Ximen Qing asked where Bojue was. "Uncle Ying and Uncle Xie have both gone," Daian said. "I tried to stop them, but they would not stay. They told me to thank you for them."

Ximen Qing said no more. He gave a great cup of wine to Li Ming and Wu Hui. "I am not giving you money today," he told them. "Come to me on the morning of the sixteenth. I am going to ask Uncle Ying and some of my friends that day."

"I must tell you, Father," Li Ming said, kneeling down, "that on the sixteenth, Wu Hui, Zuo Shun, Zheng Feng and I are all going to his Lordship Hu's place. Hu is the newly appointed governor of Dongpingfu. I am afraid we shall not be able to come until the evening."

"That is all right," Ximen said, "we are going to have our party in the evening, anyway. But you must not be too late."

The two boys promised. Then the two singing girls came to say goodbye. Ximen Qing said to them. "Tomorrow I am giving a party at my house to some ladies. Li Guijie and Wu Yin'er will be there, and I want you too." The two singing girls agreed, and went home.

Ximen Qing told Laizhao, Daian, and Qintong to clear everything away and blow out the lanterns and the lamps. Then he went to the back court. Little Iron Rod, who had been watching the fireworks, saw him come in. He ran upstairs, where his father was putting some food on a plate, with a jar of wine, and some pasties. These he took to another room. The boy asked his mother to give him some. But she boxed his ears twice and drove him out to play in the courtyard. He heard the sound of laughter coming from one of the rooms and thought it must be the singing girls. The door was shut, but he peeped through a crack. The room was brightly lighted by lamps and candles, and he could see Ximen Qing and Wang Liu'er busily engaged upon the bed.

Ximen leaned the woman over the edge of the bed, stripped off her underwear, put the clasp over his thing and began work on the flower in the back court. Back and forth, in and out—how could he stop after only a few hundred thrusts? The sounds of their banging away were clearly audible. From their rapid breathing and their behavior it looked as though they wished to break the bed in pieces.

The boy was looking on, when his mother caught him. She pulled him by the hair and dragged him to the front court. There she boxed his ears and cursed him. "You root of trouble, you little slave!" she cried. "Do you wish to die that you stand there and watch them?" She gave him some fruits and sweets and kept him carefully indoors. The boy was frightened, climbed into his bed, and went to sleep.

Ximen Qing and Wang Liu'er enjoyed themselves for a long time. Daian gave food and wine to the sedan chair men, and they took Wang Liu'er home. Then he and Qitong lighted their lanterns and went home with Ximen Qing.

# CHAPTER 43

# The Lost Bracelet

Sadness fills my heart
The love that came so lately soon has gone again
The past is past and nothing can bring it back.
Yellow chrysanthemums beside the fence
I know not whom your blossoms will delight
Wine for a time can banish sorrow
But sorrow returns before the wine is done.
I have waited long beside the balustrade.
The golden moonbeams slowly pass
And pure dew falls upon the dark green moss.

It was the third night watch when Ximen Qing returned. Wu Yueniang had not gone to bed. She was talking to Aunt Wu and the other ladies. Li Ping'er was there and offered wine to him. When Aunt Wu saw that Ximen had come, she went to her own room. Yueniang realized that Ximen was a little tipsy, but she took his cloak and told Li Ping'er to kowtow to him. Then they sat together for a while. He asked about the party, and Yuxiao brought tea. Then, seeing that Aunt Wu was staying in Yueniang's room, he went to sleep with Meng Yulou.

The next morning the cooks came early to prepare for the banquet. Ximen Qing went to his office to attend to the documents that needed to be dealt with. There Magistrate Xia thanked him. "My wife," he said, "enjoyed your very kind hospitality yesterday."

"I fear, the entertainment we could offer her was very poor," Ximen said, "I really should apologize." Then he went home.

Old woman Kong came before Lady Qiao the Fifth, and brought her presents. Ximen accepted them and gave a meal to all the servants. Old woman Kong went to rest in Yueniang's room. Then Miss Zheng came. She made a reverence to all the ladies and sat down to have tea.

Li Zhi and Huang the Fourth, having secured payment for their supplies of incense and wax, together with Ben the Fourth, brought the money from Dongpingfu. Ying Bojue was told of this and came with them to be present at the repayment of the debt. Ximen Qing told Chen Jingji to take a balance to the great hall and measure the silver. This was done and Ximen took the money. Huang the Fourth produced four gold bracelets weighing about thirty taels, and these were accepted as equal to a hundred and fifty taels of silver. They still owed Ximen about five hundred taels and asked to have their contract altered. "Come back after the festival," Ximen said to them, "and we will see about it. I am busy now." Li Zhi and Huang the Fourth addressed Ximen as "Old Father", thanked him very heartily, and went away.

Ying Bojue had not forgotten that the two men had promised him something for himself, and he thought this a very suitable opportunity to remind them of the fact. He was going out after them when Ximen Qing stopped him.

"Why did you three go away last night without saying a word to me?" he said.

"You were very hospitable yesterday," Bojue said. "I had a great deal to drink, and so had you. I knew you were going to have a party here today and that you would be wanted at home to make arrangements, so I thought we had better go. Today I suppose you have not been to your office; you must be very tired after your exertions."

"It was the third night watch when I returned," Ximen said, "but this morning I did go to the office to attend to some papers. I had a good deal of business there, and now I am hard at it getting ready for the banquet. I still have to go to the temple to offer the sacrifice appropriate to the festival and, after that, I have to go to Zhou Nanxuan's place for a party. I don't know how long it will take me."

"What powers of endurance you have," Ying Bojue said. "You really are a lucky fellow. I don't wish to flatter you, but I know no one else who could get through what you do."

They talked a while, then Ximen Qing invited Bojue to have a meal with him. Bojue excused himself.

"Why has your wife not come yet?" Ximen said.

"I ordered a sedan chair for her," Bojue said. "She must be on her way now." He made a reverence and went after Huang the Fourth and Li Zhi.

Ximen Qing examined the four golden bracelets and liked them very much. He thought of the luck that had lately come to him. Li Ping'er had borne him a son; he had been given an official appointment; he had betrothed his son to the baby Qiao, and now he had done an excellent piece of business. He put the gold bracelets in his sleeve and went to see Li Ping'er. As he passed Pan Jinlian's room, she came out.

"What have you there?" she called to him. "Come here and show me."

Ximen said he would be back in a moment and went on to see Li Ping'er.

Jinlian was disappointed when she found that he would not stop. "I wonder what treasure he has there to make him so excited," she said to herself. "Well, if you won't show me, all right. You little whippetysnip of a rogue, you'll break your leg if you don't look out. And if you go to her room, may you break both legs!"

When Ximen Qing came to her room, Li Ping'er had just finished dressing her hair and the nurse was playing with the baby. Ximen let the child play with the bracelets.

"Where did you get them?" the Sixth Lady said. "Take care the baby doesn't make his hands cold."

"I got them from Li Zhi and Huang the Fourth," Ximen said.

Li Ping'er was afraid they would make the baby's hands cold, so she took an embroidered handkerchief, wrapped them in it and then allowed him to play with them.

Daian came. "Yun has brought some horses for you to see," he said to his master.

"Where have they come from?" Ximen asked.

"He says his brother, Colonel Yun, has sent them."

Then Li Jiao'er, Meng Yulou, Aunt Wu and Miss Zheng came to see Guan'ge. Ximen Qing left the four bracelets and went to look at the horses. When all the ladies came in, Li Ping'er asked them to sit down and made a reverence to them, forgetting that the baby was still playing with the bracelets. After a while she discovered that one of them was missing. The nurse, Ruyi'er, said to her: "Have you one of those ornaments? I can only find three."

"No," Li Ping'er said, "I haven't one. I wrapped them all together in the handkerchief."

"Here is the handkerchief on the floor," Ruyi'er said, "but the other bracelet is not there."

There was immediately a terrible to-do. Ruyi'er questioned Yingchun, and Yingchun questioned old woman Feng.

"Ai ya, ai ya!" old woman Feng cried. "May I lose my sight if I have ever set eyes on them. All these years I've been coming here, I have never so much as touched a broken needle or a snapped thread. Your mother knows that I have never been greedy for gold. You are in charge of the baby. Why do you try to put the blame on me?"

Li Ping'er laughed. "Don't be so silly, old lady. But we have lost some gold ornaments." She turned to Yingchun. "Why are you making so much fuss about it, you rascal? We must wait until your master comes back. Probably he took it with him. But it is strange that he should only take one."

"What are you talking about?" Yulou asked.

"Our husband brought some gold ornaments here," Li Ping'er told her, "and he gave them to the baby to play with. That is all I know."

Ximen Qing went to the gate and looked at the horses. The servants were there, and he told the boys to put them through their paces.

"They may be Eastern horses," Ximen said, "but I don't think much of their condition. Besides, their action is anything but good. They can only walk. How much does your brother want for them?"

"Only seventy taels for the pair," Yun Lishou said.

"It is not a great amount," Ximen said, "but they can't trot. Take them back and wait till you get something with more style. Then let me know. It's not a question of price."

He went back to the house. A boy asked him to go and see Li Ping'er.

"Did you take away one of those gold ornaments?" she asked him. "There are only three here."

"I went to look at the horses," Ximen said, "I didn't take anything."

"Well, if you didn't, where has one of them gone? We have been looking for it everywhere."

"It was old woman Feng who took it," the nurse said. Old woman Feng began to cry and swore she had done nothing of the sort.

"Who did take it, then?" Ximen said. "Have another look for it."

"Aunt Wu and her sister-in-law came," the Lady of the Vass said, "and I asked them to sit down, forgetting all about the ornaments. I thought you must have taken it with you. So I never found out for a long time and, when I did, the ladies were upset and went away." She gave the other three bracelets to Ximen Qing.

Ben the Fourth came and gave a hundred taels to his master and Ximen went to the inner court to put the money away.

When she heard of the trouble in Li Ping'er's room, Jinlian, who could never leave ill alone, went to Yueniang and told her what she thought about it.

"Sister," she said, "see how that foolish thing behaves. No matter how rich he is, he should not give gold bracelets to the baby to play with."

"I have heard that a bracelet has been lost," Yueniang said, "but that's all. I have no idea what happened."

"Nor has anyone else," Jinlian said. "You didn't see him. I did. He came from the front court with those gold ornaments in his sleeve, looking like the eight barbarians on their way to pay tribute. I asked him what he had got there and would have looked at them, but he did not even turn his head. He dashed off to the Sixth Lady's room. Afterwards, I heard everybody talking about one of the things being lost. He had missed one and set them all looking for it. Even if he were as rich as Wang the Millionaire, he could not afford to throw gold away like this. Why, it must weigh ten taels and be worth at least fifty or sixty taels of silver. There will be a row about it yet. It is like a turtle escaping from a jar. The people in her room were all her own people, and she must take the responsibility for them."

As they were talking, Ximen Qing came in to give to Yueniang the hundred taels that Ben the Fourth had brought and the three remaining bracelets.

"I got these," he told his wife, "from Li Zhi and Huang the Fourth. There were four of them, but I gave them to the baby to play with and one is lost. I want you to send for all the maids in the house and question them. I am going to send a boy to the street for a piece of wolf's sinew. If the missing piece of gold is produced, well and good. Otherwise, I shall make good use of the wolf sinew."

"You ought never to have given the gold to the baby," his wife said. "It is cold and heavy, and it might have hurt the baby's hands or feet."

"No, you ought not to have given it to the child," Jinlian said, "but you could think of nothing but getting it to her room. I spoke to you and you wouldn't look at me. Just like a red-eyed soldier with some loot that he didn't wish anybody to see. Now that you have lost a piece of gold, you have the nerve to come here and tell the Great Lady about it. You ask her to examine all the maids. Well, if the maids don't laugh at you with their mouths, they will laugh at you with their cunts."

This made Ximen Qing angry. He took Jinlian by the hair and threw her on Yueniang's bed. He raised his hand threateningly and said: "I hate you. If it were not for what people would say, I would beat you to death, you bad little bone. You are always trying to show off your sharp tongue and interfering in matters that do not concern you."

Jinlian made a show of tears. "Because you are powerful and rich," she sobbed, "you have become cruel. You only think about being brutal to me. Your words are brave; you don't care whether you murder anybody or not. Go on, beat me, there is no one to hinder you. So long as I don't stop breathing, it will be all right, but if I do, my old mother will certainly come and ask you a few questions. No matter how rich and powerful you are, if my mother goes to the court and accuses you, you needn't think you will escape, just because you happen to be an officer. The post you hold is nothing very glorious and your ceremonial hat is a miserable thing. You can't stand a charge of murder against you. Even the Emperor has no right to murder his subjects."

Ximen Qing laughed. "Oh, how cleverly you talk, you bad little bone. You say that my position is of no account, and that my ceremonial hat is in rags.

I will tell a maid to bring my hat, and then you'll see whether it is in rags or not. Go and ask the people in Qinghe if I owe anybody any money. You say I owe money."

"Why did you call me a bad little bone?" Jinlian lifted one of her feet. "What is wrong with my feet? Why should you call me names like that?"

"You two are like a brass bowl and somebody banging it with an iron broom handle," Yueniang said. "There is a proverb that says that the devil-ish man has a devil of his own, and, when he meets another devil, there is nothing he can do. The stronger-mouthed always comes out on top. Sister, your mouth is all you have to count on. If it were not quite so sharp, you would be done."

Ximen Qing realized that there was nothing he could do, so he put on his clothes and went out. On the way, Daian said to him: "A messenger has come from Major Zhou asking you to go there after the sacrifice."

"Tell Jingji to take a horse and go to the sacrifice for me," Ximen said. "I will go to Major Zhou's now."

The two stage managers and the actors from the princely family of Wang came and kowtowed to Ximen Qing. He told Shutong to arrange for them to have something to eat. "Amuse the ladies well," he said to them, "and I will see that you are suitably rewarded. Do not open your boxes in the upper room."

The two managers knelt down and said: "If we do not play our parts well, we shall ask for no reward."

"This will make the second day they have played for us," Ximen said to Shutong. "You may give them five taels of silver." He mounted his horse and rode away.

Jinlian was sitting in Yueniang's room. "Why don't you go to your room and powder your face?" Yueniang said to her. "Your eyes are all red, and you will not be fit to see the guests when they come. Really, you ought not to provoke him. I did the best I could for you. If I hadn't stopped him, you would certainly have had a beating. There is always dog's hair on a husband's face. He doesn't distinguish between the rights and the wrongs of a case, but is always ready to trounce somebody. Why did you make trouble with him just now? He lost his gold. Well, what if he did? It is no business of yours whether he looked for it or not. It didn't happen in your room, and there was no call for you to start arguing with him. You must learn to keep your temper."

She calmed Jinlian, who went to her room to powder her face.

Shortly afterwards, Li Ping'er and Wu Yin'er, dressed for the party, came to Yueniang's room.

"How did the gold come to be lost?" the Great Lady said. "The Fifth Lady and he quarreled about it and nearly came to blows. I stopped them, and now he has gone out to a party somewhere. But he has sent a boy to buy a wolf's sinew and when he comes back tonight the maids will all be punished. What were the maids and serving women in your room about? They were supposed to be looking after the baby and they must have lost the gold. A piece of gold is not like a penny,"

"He gave the baby the four pieces of gold to play with," Li Ping'er said, "and I was busy entertaining Aunt Wu and Miss Zheng and the two other ladies. It was then one of the ornaments was lost. The maids say it was the nurse's fault, the nurse blames old woman Feng, and old woman Feng cries and says she is going to kill herself. It really is a most mysterious business, and I don't know whom to blame."

"I often play with the baby," Wu Yin'er said, "but thanks be to Heaven, I was dressing my hair in another room and kept out of it all. Otherwise, I should have been dragged into it and, even if you had said nothing, I should have felt very uncomfortable. People often lose money, but in such a household as yours it is most regrettable for such a thing to happen. If people outside hear about it, it will bring shame upon the household."

While they were talking, Han Yuchuan and Dong Jiao'er came, bringing their dresses with them. They kowtowed to Yueniang, Aunt Wu, and Li Ping'er and, rising, made a reverence to Wu Yin'er.

"You did not go home yesterday, Sister," they said to her.

"How did you know?" said Wu Yin'er.

"We went to the house in Lion Street," Dong Jiao'er said, "where the Feast of the Lanterns was held, and Father told us to come here today."

Yueniang asked them to sit down and Xiaoyu brought them tea. The two girls stood up to take the tea and made a reverence to Xiaoyu.

"At what time did you finish singing last night?" Wu Yin'er asked them.

"It was the second night watch when we reached home. We went with your younger brother, Wu Hui."

After they had talked for a short time, Yueniang said to Yuxiao: "See that they have their tea in good time." She was afraid it would be awkward if the guests arrived before they had had it. The table was set. There were two plates of spring dishes and four boxes of cakes. "Go to the Second Lady's room," Yueniang said to Xiaoyu, "and ask your sister Li Guijie to come and have tea."

Guijie and her aunt came in together. When they had made a reverence to everybody present, they sat down and had tea, and then the things were all cleared away. Yingchun, specially dressed for the occasion, came in carrying Guan'ge. The baby was wearing a silken cap of Good Fortune, with a gold brim, a long red gown, white silk socks and shoes. On his chest hung the cords and medals and on his wrists were little golden bangles.

"Well, my young lord," Li Ping'er said, "what have you come for? Nobody invited you." She took the child and set him on her knees. The baby saw that the room was full of people and looked at them one after another. Guijie, sitting on the bed, played with him. "Brother," she said, "you look at me so hard you must wish me to carry you." She held out her arms to him and the baby nestled to her breast.

"Ah," Aunt Wu said, laughing, "even a baby of his age seems to know the meaning of love."

"Think who is his father," Yueniang said. "When he grows up, he will assuredly be a very gay young man."

"If he is anything of the sort, I shall ask you to beat him," Yulou said.

"Baby," Li Ping'er said, "Sister is carrying you, and you must not soil her clothes. If you do, I shall beat you."

"I don't mind whether he does or not," Guijie said. "I love to have him in my arms and play with him."

Dong Jiao'er said: "We have been here a long time but we have not yet sung for the ladies." Han Yuchuan took her lute and Dong Jiao'er her zither: Wu Yin'er sang. She sang the song "Splendor of Riches Like the Moon at the Full. The Golden Chain Hangs on the Wu T'ung Tree." Her voice echoed through the rafters and stirred the dust there. It seemed powerful enough to pass through rocks and mount even to the skies.

Guan'ge was frightened. He lay still against Guijie's breast and dared not lift his head. Yueniang saw this. "Take the child," she said to Li Ping'er, "and let Yingchun take him to your room. What a delicate child he is. Look at his pale face." Li Ping'er took the baby. She bade Yingchun cover his ears with her hands and take him out.

The girls were still singing when Daian came in. "I have been to Mistress Qiao's," he said. "Mistress Chu and Master Shang's wife were ready; they were only waiting for Lady Qiao the Fifth. They will be here in a few moments. The musicians are ready both at the gate and in the hall. Ladies, you will do well to expect them at any moment."

Yueniang saw that many beautiful things were set about in the back hall, and the chairs put in their proper places. The lattices were suspended by golden chains and the air was sweetly perfumed. Chunmei, Yingchun, Yuxiao and Lanxiang were dressed in their new clothes. All the maids and serving women wore ornaments of gold and silver, and, in their dresses of green and gold, waited to do honor to the new relative of the household.

The first person to arrive was Ying Bojue's wife. Ying Bao was in attendance upon her. Yueniang welcomed her and took her to her room. Madam Ying made reverence after reverence to Yueniang. "We are always troubling you," she said, "troubling you beyond all reason."

"Not at all," Yueniang said, "it is we who are always troubling your worthy husband."

Soon they heard the shouts of men clearing the way; then the musicians in the outer hall began to play. Ping'an came and announced Lady Qiao's sedan chair. A host of people surrounded the five sedan chairs that had stopped outside the gate. The first was that of Lady Qiao the Fifth. It was covered with a canopy of sky-blue and had a double gold fringe around it. The men who cleared the way carried rattans. Behind the large chair were smaller ones for the maidservants. Then four soldiers with dressing cases and braziers. Then two black-robed attendants riding on ponies. After Lady Qiao the Fifth came Mistress Qiao, then Mistress Zhu, Master Shang's wife and Miss Duan, a sister-in-law of an officer named Cui.

Ximen Qing's six ladies, most exquisitely dressed and looking like jade carvings, came to the second door to welcome their guests and escorted Lady Qiao the Fifth to the hall. Lady Qiao was about seventy years old. She was not very tall. She wore a headdress of pearls with many precious stones and a scarlet gown embroidered in the palace fashion. Her hair was perfectly white and her eyebrows like two strips of snow. Her eyes were like autumn water, perhaps rather dark. Hair like a bundle of silk fell, not in too great abundance, over her temples. It was like the cloud resting on the Chu Mountain.

When they came to the hall, she made a reverence first to Aunt Wu, then to Wu Yueniang and the others. Yueniang asked Lady Qiao to accept a reverence from her, but the old lady refused. Even after much discussion, she would only accept a half reverence. Then Yueniang greeted Mistress Qiao in the manner appointed for relatives. After the greetings they thanked one another for the presents that had been exchanged. Then they took their seats. Lady Qiao the Fifth sat upon a chair with an embroidered cushion in front of the screen. Yueniang asked Mistress Qiao to sit next to her, but she said: "I must not sit next to the Fifth Lady, for I am her niece." Mistress Zhu and Master Shang's wife were invited to take the next places. They made a show of hesitation and the matter was settled after much discussion, with Lady Qiao the Fifth in the most honorable place and the others according to their rank.

In the midst of the hall was a great square stove with fire burning. It made the room as warm as though it were spring. Chunmei, Yuxiao, Yingchun and Lanxiang, dressed in their best clothes, served the wine.

"Will you not introduce me to your distinguished husband?" Lady Qiao the Fifth said. "I should like to salute him in accordance with the rites between relatives."

Yueniang told her that Ximen Qing had gone to his office and had not yet returned.

"What office does he hold?" Lady Qiao asked.

"He was only a private citizen," Yueniang said, "but the Imperial Court was gracious and made him Captain of a Thousand Families, and he has duties at the law courts. I fear that this betrothal will lower the prestige of your house."

"What is that you say?" Lady Qiao the Fifth said. "We are quite content to be allied to one of such high rank as your worthy husband. My niece told me the other day about the matter and I was delighted. That is why I have come to see you today, and I trust that in future we shall see more of each other."

"My only fear," Yueniang said, "is that we shall damage your reputation."

"Do not say that," Lady Qiao replied, "even an Emperor sometimes marries the daughter of a commoner. If you do not mind my telling you rather a long story, I will explain to you that the present Empress of the Eastern Palace is a niece of mine. Her parents died and I looked after her. When my husband was alive, he succeeded to the post of High Commander. But he died, alas, when he was only fifty. I have no children and have always lived with my nephews, of whom none is wealthy but this one. Though he has no great position, he is able to live very comfortably, and I don't think your family need be ashamed of him."

After they had talked for a while, Aunt Wu said to Yueniang: "Send for the baby and let her Ladyship see him and give him her blessing." Li Ping'er at once bade the nurse take the baby and kowtow to the old lady. Lady Qiao the Fifth admired Guan'ge and said he was a very fine boy. She told her servants to open her bag, and from it took a piece of yellow silk shot with purple, such as is used at the Court, and a pair of golden armlets. These she presented to the child. Yueniang thanked her. Then she asked her to go to an inner room to change her clothes.

In the outer court four tables were laid and tea was waiting. Upon each table there were forty dishes and every kind of delicacy imaginable. After tea Yueniang took them to see the gardens.

By this time Chen Jingji had come back from the service at the temple, and, when he had taken a religious meal, he, with Shutong and Daian, arranged the tables in the outer hall. Then the ladies were invited to come to dinner, and a very magnificent banquet they had.

Musicians and singers were posted near the tables. Wu Yueniang and Li Ping'er themselves served wine, while, outside the door, the musicians played. Then Mistress Qiao and the other ladies offered wine to Li Ping'er in celebration of her birthday and, afterwards, all took their places again. Guijie, Wu Yin'er, Han Yuchuan and Dong Jiao'er stood before them and sang the song "Long Mayest Thou Live Like the Southern Mountain."

The actors brought the list of their plays, and Lady Qiao the Fifth asked them to play the drama "On the Night of the Feast of Lanterns, Wang Yueying Lost a Shoe." The cooks brought in small slices of roast goose, and were rewarded with five *qian* of silver. Five courses of meat were served and three of soup. The fourth act of the play was ended, and it began to grow dark. The candles in the hall and all kinds of lanterns were lighted. They looked like embroidered ribbons floating, like strings of color waving in the air. Then the full moon rose and the moonbeams mingled with the lights within the hall. The musicians took their instruments and played the melody of the lanterns.

When the music was done, Lady Qiao the Fifth and Mistress Qiao gave two taels of silver to the actors and two *qian* to each of the four singing girls. In the hall of the inner court, Yueniang had arranged for more tables to be prepared with fruits and other things. Now she asked the ladies to go there. The four tables were piled high; the singing girls sang, and the musicians played. They drank again.

Several times Lady Qiao said, "It is late, and I must go." At last Yueniang and the others were unable to dissuade her any longer, and they escorted her as far as the great gate. There they again offered her wine and stayed to see the fireworks. On both sides of the street, people were crowding, as close together as the scales on a fish, or as bees in a swarm. Ping'an and the soldiers kept the crowd back with their sticks, but still the people pushed forward. Then one of the fireworks was burnt out, and the people began gradually to drift away.

Lady Qiao and her companions said farewell to Yueniang, got into their chairs and departed. It was about the third night watch. Ying Bojue's wife went away too.

Yueniang and the others then went to the inner court and told Chen Jingji, Laixing, Shutong and Daian to see to the clearing away of everything and to give the actors and their two leaders refreshments, pay them five taels of silver for their performance, and dismiss them.

Yueniang said that some food and half a jar of wine that was left should be given to Clerk Fu, Ben the Fourth and Chen Jingji. "They have worked very hard," she said, "and it is only right that they should have a cup of wine." A table was set in the great hall. "I do not know when the master will return," Yueniang told them, "so do not put out the lanterns."

Clerk Fu, Ben the Fourth, Chen Jingji and Laibao sat in the upper seats, Laixing, Shutong, Daian and Ping'an in the lower. The wine was poured out.

"You had better put a man at the gate," Laibao said to Ping'an. "If our master comes home, there will be no one to receive him."

"It is all right," Ping'an said. "I have already posted Huatong there."

Then they amused themselves playing Guess Fingers and drinking wine.

"Don't let's guess fingers," Jingji said, "we must choose a quieter game. We shall be heard in the inner court if we make so much noise. Let each one recite a line of poetry. If he can do so, well and good, but if not, he must drink a large cup of wine. Now, Clerk Fu, you begin."

"At the Feast of Lanterns, I laughed at the streamers," Clerk Fu said. "Happiness in life is only for dreamers," added Ben the Fourth. "The moonlight and the lanterns are our joy today," said Jingji. "So we'll enjoy life as long as we may," said Laibao. "I invited my girl, why isn't she here?" said Laixing. "I, like the Great Lady, inspire with fear," Shutong continued. Then Daian said, "Though the wine has been left us, the lanterns are dim." "And the cup of enjoyment is full to the brim," Ping'an said.

They all laughed very merrily.

# CHAPTER 44
# The Thief Is Discovered

Chen Jingji and the others drank their wine in the outer court. Aunt Wu's sedan chair came for her. She got her things together and prepared to take her leave, but Wu Yueniang begged her not to go.

"Sister-in-law," she said, "please stay tonight. Go tomorrow instead."

"But I have stayed here and with the Qiaos for three or four days. There is no one at home, and your brother's business keeps him busy at the office. I hope you will all come to see me tomorrow, and in the evening we will walk off the hundred illnesses."

"We will gladly come," Yueniang said, "but it must be in the evening."

"No," Aunt Wu said, "come early in your sedan chairs, and you can return on foot in the evening."

Yueniang filled one box with the pasties that are made for the Feast of Lanterns and another with spiced cake, and ordered Laian to accompany Aunt Wu. Then Li Guijie and the other singing girls kowtowed to Yueniang and made ready to leave.

"Why are you in such a hurry?" Yueniang said. "You must wait for your father. He told me not to let you go before he came back. I fancy he has something to say to you, and I dare not let you go before he comes."

"But Father has gone to a party," Guijie said, "and there is no telling when he will return. I don't think we can wait for him. So please, Lady, let Wu Yin'er and me go. The others can stay. They only came today, but we have been here two days already, and I am sure my mother is anxious about me."

"I only want you to stay one night more," Yueniang said.

"Mother," Guijie said, "it is very kind of you, but there is no one at home. My sister is engaged elsewhere. I will sing a song for you, and then you will let me go, won't you?"

While they were talking, Chen Jingji came in to give an account of the money that he had spent on the servants. "I gave the sedan men one *qian* of silver apiece, so, in all, I paid out about ten packets, about three taels. Here are ten packets left." Yueniang took the silver.

"Uncle," Guijie said, "may I trouble you to go and see whether my sedan chair has come yet?"

"The chairs have come for the other girls," Jingji said, "but yours and Wu Yin'er's are not here. I don't know, but it is possible they may have been sent away again."

"Uncle," Guijie said, "either you have sent them away yourself, or you are deceiving us."

"If you don't believe me," Chen Jingji said, "go and see for yourself."

Then Qintong came with the wrapper and told them that Ximen Qing had returned. "It is a good thing you didn't go," Yueniang said. "There is your father."

Ximen Qing came in. He had drunk a great deal of wine. He sat on the upper side, and Han Yuchuan and Dong Jiao'er kowtowed to him.

"Have our guests gone?" Ximen asked his wife. "Why don't you make the girls sing?"

"They were just thinking of going home," Yueniang said.

"You and Wu Yin'er must not go away until the festival is over. The other two girls can go."

"There!" Yueniang said. "You wouldn't believe me. I might be always telling stories. You hear what he says." Guijie bent her head and said nothing.

Ximen Qing asked Daian if the sedan chairs had come for the girls. The boy told him that those for Dong Jiao'er and Yuchuan were waiting.

"I will not have any more wine," Ximen said, "but take your instruments and sing for me. Then two of you may go."

The four singers took their instruments and sang the twenty-eight verses from *Ten Bolts of Brocade*. The ladies sat and listened. Afterwards, Ximen Qing gave some silver to Yuchuan and Dong Jiao'er and let them go. The two other girls stayed.

Suddenly there was a great to-do in the outer court. Daian and Qintong, shouting, dragged in Xiahua, Li Jiao'er's maid.

"We had taken the two singing girls to the gate," they said, "and had our lanterns with us. When we passed the stable to give some hay to the horses, we found Xiahua there, hiding under the manger. We had no idea what she was doing there, and we were startled. We spoke to her, but she made no answer."

Ximen Qing went outside and sat down on a chair underneath the eaves. He summoned Qintong, and the boy brought out the girl. She knelt down.

"What were you doing in the outer court?" Ximen asked her. The maid was silent.

"I didn't send you to the stable," Li Jiao'er said. "Why did you go there?" The maid was frightened. Ximen Qing was determined to know what it was all about and told the boy to search her. Qintong pulled the girl down; there was a tinkle, and something fell to the ground. Daian picked it up. It was the gold bracelet. Ximen Qing looked at it in the light of the lantern and recognized it as the missing piece of gold.

"You slave!" he cried. "You stole it!"

"I picked it up," said the girl.

"Where did you pick it up?"

The girl made no reply. Ximen Qing was very angry. He sent Qintong for the thumbscrews. They were put on the girl's hands and turned till she screamed like a pig being killed. Again the screws were turned, and twenty times they ground her fingers. Yueniang did not dare to try to stop her husband, for she knew that he was drunk. When the girl could bear no more, she cried. "I picked it up in the Sixth Lady's room."

Ximen Qing had the thumbscrews removed, and told Li Jiao'er to take the girl away. "Tomorrow," he said, "I will send for the go-between and sell the slave. I won't have her here any more."

Li Jiao'er dared raise no objection. She said to the girl: "You thief! Who told you to go to the outer court? I know nothing of this. If you picked up the gold, why didn't you tell me at once?" Xiahua sobbed. "You may well cry," Li Jiao'er said. "You ought to be beaten to death."

"Stop!" Ximen Qing said. He gave the piece of gold to Yueniang and went to the apartments of Li Ping'er.

Yueniang told Xiaoyu to fasten the second door. "When did that maid go to the outer court?" she asked Yuxiao.

"When the Second Lady and the Third Lady went to the Sixth Lady's room," the maid answered, "Aunt Wu and our young lady went with them. That is when she went. Who would have dreamed of her stealing that piece of gold? She heard you say that Father had sent a boy to buy a piece of wolf sinew and she was frightened. In the kitchen she asked me what wolf sinew was. Everybody laughed, and we told her that wolf sinew was a part of the wolf's body. We said that when a person steals anything and won't give it up, a piece of wolf sinew is used to bind the thief's hands and feet. When she heard this, she must have become alarmed. So, when the two singers went away, she went out too. Seeing people at the gate, she must have hidden herself in the stable where the boys found her."

"It is very, very hard ever to know what people are really like," Yueniang said. "A young maid like that with such a thievish head and a rat's brain! It is disgraceful."

Li Jiao'er took Xiahua to her room. Guijie reproved her. "What a fool you must be," she said. "You are sixteen years old and you ought to know what you're about. How could you have been such an idiot? When you picked that thing up, you should have brought it here and given it to your mistress. Then, if it had been found out, she could have done something for you. Why didn't you tell her about it? Do you enjoy having thumbscrews put on you? You are an absolute fool. You know the proverb: 'A black-clothed man will stand beside a black pillar.' If it were not that you belong to these apartments, we shouldn't bother about you. But you do belong here, and now that you have been punished it brings shame upon us all."

Then she reproached her aunt. "You are no good either," she said. "If I'd been in your place, I shouldn't have allowed my maid to be punished. I should have dragged her to my room and punished her myself. Why are thumbscrews never put on other people's maids? Why is your maid picked out? You are too soft, and your nostrils have no breath in them. If they send your maid away, I suppose you will still say nothing. But if you won't say anything, I will. I am not going to have this girl turned out and everybody laughing at you. Meng Yulou and Pan Jinlian are like a couple of wolves. You can never hold your own against them."

She turned to the maid. "Do you wish to be sent away?" she said.

"No," said the maid.

"Well, in the future, you must consider nobody but your mistress. You must do everything she wants you to do. Then we will do our best for you."

"I will do everything you say," Xiahua said. When Ximen Qing came to Li Ping'er's room, he found her sitting on the bed with Wu Yin'er. He was going to take his clothes off and go to bed, but Li Ping'er said: "Wu Yin'er is here, and there is no room for you. Please go somewhere else."

"Why is there no room for me?" said Ximen. "One of you can sleep on one side, and one on the other, and I'll sleep in the middle. That will be all right."

Li Ping'er looked at him. "What bright ideas you do have," she said.

"Where shall I go, then?" said Ximen.

"Go and spend the night with the Fifth Lady," Li Ping'er said. Ximen Qing did not move for some time, then he said: "Very well, I don't want to trouble you. I'll go." He went to Pan Jinlian's room.

He might have been an angel from Heaven. Jinlian took his clothes and girdle. Then she arranged the bed and put silken bedclothes on it. She made tea and afterwards they went to bed.

When Ximen Qing had left, Li Ping'e and Wu Yin'er set out chessmen to play Elephant Chess. Li Ping'er told Yingchun to bring a box of fruits and heat a jar of Jinhua wine so that she might drink it with Wu Yin'er. "If you would like some food," she said to the girl, "I will have some prepared for you."

"I am not hungry, Mother," Wu Yin'er said. "Please don't trouble my sister."

"Your sister Wu Yin'er is not hungry," Li Ping'er said to Yingchun. "Bring her some fruit cakes on a tray." After a while the tray was brought and set beside them.

Li Ping'er and Wu Yin'er played one or two games. Then the wine was heated, and they drank together in silver cups.

"Give me my lute," Wu Yin'er said. "I will sing Mother a song."

"Perhaps you had better not sing," Li Ping'er said. "The baby is asleep and, besides, Father might hear and he won't like it. Let us play dice instead." She told Yingchun to bring the dice, and they threw the dice with wine for the wager. When they had played for some time, Wu Yin'er said to Yingchun: "Go to the other room and ask the nurse to come and have some wine with us."

But Yingchun said: "She is in bed with the baby. He has gone to sleep."

"Yes, she must look after the baby," said Li Ping'er. "Take a jar of wine to her. You don't realize how knowing the baby is. If he is left, he wakes up at once. One day, we three were asleep on the bed. His father moved slightly and the baby opened his eyes at once. He might have known. The nurse came and took him away, but he cried and would insist on having me to nurse him."

Wu Yin'er smiled. "Since you have had the baby, it must be awkward for you and Father. How often does he come to you?"

"He doesn't come very often," said Li Ping'er. "Sometimes several days pass and he only comes once or twice. But he often comes to see the baby. And sometimes my belly nearly bursts with anger, for now both he and the child get nothing but secret curses from some members of the household, not to speak of the curses I get. This has made me suffer a great deal, but I can't help it. I sometimes wish he didn't come at all, because, after he has spent the night here, the next day there is much raising of eyebrows and ugly looks, as much as to say that I monopolize him. That's why I urged him to go away just now.

"You don't know how it is, my dear. There are many people in this house and that means many tongues. Look at that business of the gold today. Someone who is jealous asked the Great Lady how it could be lost in my room. Luckily it turned out that Xiahua had taken it, so there was no mistaking green for red or black for white. Otherwise they would have said that one of my maids or my nurse or old woman Feng had taken it, as if they had caught a ghost. As it was, they made old woman Feng cry and talk about killing herself. She said she would not go away if the gold wasn't found. Now that it has been found, she has just taken a lantern and gone."

"Mother," said Wu Yin'er, "you must look well after the baby for Father's sake, and let people do what they like. The Great Lady never talks in this way. It is only the others who are jealous because you have a child. I only hope that Father will do what he thinks fit."

"If it hadn't been for your father and the Great Lady," Li Ping'er said, "the child would never have lived until today."

They talked and drank until the third night watch. Then they went to sleep.

# CHAPTER 45
# Beggar Ying and Wu Yin'er

The next day Ximen Qing did not go to his office. When he got up in the morning, he went to the front court and told Daian to take two presents of food to the Qiaos' house, one for Lady Qiao the Fifth and one for Mistress Qiao. Lady Qiao the Fifth gave the bearers two handkerchiefs and three *qian* of silver. Mistress Qiao gave them a roll of black cloth.

When Ying Bojue left Ximen, he hastened to Huang the Fourth's house. Huang had prepared and sealed ten taels of silver for him.

"His Lordship," he said, "told me to go and see him again after the festival. I think it will be all right about the five hundred tael contract, but what about the land tax?"

"How much will you need?" Bojue asked him.

"Brother Li," said Huang the Fourth, "does not understand. He talks about borrowing from some eunuch or other. But it seems to me that anywhere we shall have to pay five percent interest. We might as well do all our borrowing here and so save a good deal of commission. I want fifty silver ingots. In other words, I must borrow a thousand taels. I am prepared to pay interest monthly."

Ying Bojue nodded. "Don't worry," he said, "I will see about that. But there are six of you. How much do you propose to give me?"

"I will tell Brother Li that each of us must give you five taels."

"I think I can save that five taels for you by my cleverness," Bojue said. "One word from me will do all you require. My wife has gone to his Lordship's place today, so I shall not go now. But he has invited me to go tomorrow evening and see the lanterns with him. You two get up early, have some excellent dishes prepared and buy a jar of Jinhua wine. Don't engage any singing girls, because Li Guijie and Wu Yin'er will be there, but arrange for six musicians from the bawdy house. I will take everything for you. He is sure to invite you to his party. When we are all together, I shall only need to speak a sentence, or even half a sentence, and, I promise you, that will do the trick. You will get five hundred taels and make out your contract for a thousand. You pay thirty taels a month interest. It won't cost you any more than keeping a woman. The proverb says: Forgery is not one of the recognized fine arts, yet there is no genuine lacquer to be found anywhere.

When you pay your tax, put plenty of wood in the incense and mix enough pine oil with the wax. Nobody is going to find out. We have no ambition to catch any fish; all we hope to do is to stir up the water a bit. A man who wants to borrow money has only to establish a reputation, and then everything is plain sailing."

They agreed upon this plan. The next day Li and Huang bought the presents and Ying Bojue got two boys to carry them to Ximen's house. When they arrived, Ximen was having the tables made ready in the outer court. Bojue made a reverence. "Yesterday," he said, "my wife must have greatly inconvenienced you. She came home quite late."

"I went to a party at Zhou Nanxuan's place," Ximen said. "It was the first night watch when I came back, so I didn't see any of my new relatives. They had left early. Today I am taking a holiday. That is why you don't find me at the office." They sat down. Bojue summoned the boys and told them to bring in the presents. The boxes were carried in and set down inside the second door.

"Brother Li and Brother Huang," said Bojue, "have repeatedly told me how grateful they are to you. They have nothing worthy to offer you, but they have bought these trifling things, and send them for you to dispose of among your servants." The two boys came forward and kowtowed.

"I have done nothing to deserve these gifts," said Ximen Qing, "and I can't possibly accept them. They must go back." "Brother," Bojue said, "if you will not accept the things, if you make the boys take them back again, my friends will die of shame. They were going to engage singing girls, but I told them not to. They have sent some musicians who are waiting outside for your orders at this moment."

"Well," said Ximen, "since they have sent the things, I can't very well send them back. I suppose we had better ask them to come and join us."

Ying Bojue immediately told Li's boy to go back to his master. "Tell him that his present has been accepted," Bojue said. "We are not sending anyone especially to invite him, but ask him and Uncle Huang to come here at once."

The boy brought in the presents. Ximen Qing told Daian to give him two *qian* of silver. Then he kowtowed and went upon his errand. The six musicians still waited for orders. Qitong brought tea, and Ximen and Ying Bojue drank it together. Then Ximen asked Bojue to go to the rooms in the eastern wing. "Have you seen Xie Xida today?" he asked.

"No," said Bojue, "I got up early this morning and went to Li's place to see about the presents, and I have been too busy to see him." Ximen Qing told Qitong to go at once and invite Xie Xida to join them.

Shutong set the table, and dinner was served. They ate it together, and afterwards everything was cleared away. They played double sixes for wine.

Ying Bojue decided to speak before Xie Xida came. "How much can you give Li and Huang?" he said.

"I shall take back the old contract and give them another for five hundred taels."

"You can do that, of course," Ying Bojue said, "but it would be better to make the amount a thousand taels. It is easier to calculate the interest. Then, too, you have no use for that gold they brought you. Let them have it back, and count it as a hundred and fifty taels. If you do that, only a little more will be needed to make up the thousand."

"That is a good idea," Ximen said. "I will let them have another three hundred and fifty taels and make out the contract for a thousand. It is better than keeping gold where I have no use for it."

They were playing double sixes when Daian came in. He said: "Ben the Fourth is bringing a large marble screen with a shell base, two sets of bronze gongs, and some little bells. Their Highnesses, the Bai family, propose to pawn them with us for thirty taels, and Ben the Fourth wishes to know whether you are satisfied."

Ximen gave orders that the things should be brought in. Ben the Fourth and two other men carried them and set them down in the great hall. Ximen Qing and Ying Bojue stopped their game and went to see them. The screen was three feet wide and five feet high, made of a single piece of marble the size of a table. The frame had a pattern of conchs and was gilded, and the black and white markings in the marble were exquisitely delicate.

Bojue looked at it. After a while he said quietly to Ximen Qing: "Brother, if you look at it closely, you will see that the markings are exactly in the shape of a couching lion keeping guard over the house." They examined the bronze gongs and drums, decorated in gold and colors, and engraved with a cloud design. They were very handsome.

"I should have them if I were you, Brother," said Bojue. "You could not buy a screen like this for fifty taels, without taking the other things into account."

"But they may be redeemed," Ximen Qing said.

"Don't trouble about that," said Bojue. "It is like rattling down a steep hill in a carriage. If, after three years, they redeem them, the interest will amount to a tidy sum."

"Very well," Ximen said. "Tell Jingji to get the money ready for them."

Ximen Qing had the screen cleaned and put at the upper end of the great hall. He looked at it from all angles, and, indeed, the gold and green made a very harmonious and brilliant effect. He asked if the musicians had yet had their meal. One of the servants told him they were still eating. "When they are done, tell them to come and play for us," he said.

The big drum was taken out of the hall and a bronze gong and drums were set down under the eaves. When they were sounded, the noise went up to the skies, and the reverberations startled the birds of the air and the fishes under the water. Meanwhile, Xie Xida was announced. He came in and greeted his two friends.

"Come here, Brother Xie," Ximen Qing said, "and tell me how much you think this screen is worth." Xie Xida examined it carefully. He had nothing but good to say of it.

"Brother," he said, "you have a bargain here. It must be worth at least a hundred taels."

"Well, this," said Ying Bojue, "the two sets of drums and gongs and the bells have all been pawned together for thirty taels." Xie Xida clapped his hands.

"Buddha!" he cried. "What a bargain! Thirty taels! Why, it wouldn't buy the two sets of bronzes, not to mention the screen. Look at those two sets. How elaborately they are made. The red lacquer is all of the finest quality and there must be at least forty *jin* of musical bronze in them, and that is worth a lot of money. Really, everything comes in time to its proper owner. How lucky you are, Brother, to get these beautiful things so cheaply."

Ximen Qing asked them to go to the study. By this time Li and Huang had arrived. "Why did you trouble to give me those presents?" Ximen Qing said. "It really embarrassed me to accept them."

"We were ashamed to offer anything so trifling," said Li and Huang. "They were only intended for you to give your servants. We received your order to attend here and did not dare to disobey."

They sat down opposite. Huatong brought five cups of tea, and they drank together. Then Daian came and asked Ximen Qing where he wished to have the table placed. "Here," Ximen said. Daian and Qitong brought a square table and placed a small brazier beneath it. Ying Bojue and Xie Xida took the seats of honor. Ximen Qing took the host's seat, and Li and Huang sat opposite. There was an abundance of wine, and of food appropriate to the season, and every kind of delicacy. The musicians played outside the window. Ximen sent for Wu Yin'er to serve the wine.

Later that day there came a man from Li Guijie's house and the maid from Wu Yin'er's house, with sedan chairs to take the girls home. When Guijie heard that the man had come, she hurriedly went out and talked to him in a whisper for a long time. Then she went back to Wu Yueniang's room and said she must go home. Yueniang objected. "We are all going to Aunt Wu's house," she said, "and I want you to come with us. You will be too late to go home today. We shall come back without our chairs, for we are going to take the walk to banish the hundred illnesses."

"Mother," Guijie said, "let me explain. There really ought to be some-one at our house. My sister is away. My fifth aunt has come, and there will be several other guests. They expect me. If they were not anxious to have me back, they would not have sent the man for me. If I were not engaged, I should be only too glad to stay for several days."

When Yueniang saw that Guijie was determined to go, she told Yuxiao to fill a box with the pasties specially made for the festival and another with sweet things. These were given to the man to carry. Then she gave Guijie a tael of silver and let her go.

Guijie said good-bye to Yueniang and the others, then went to see her aunt. Li Jiao'er went with her to the outer court and told Huatong to carry her things. When they came to the study door, the girl told Daian to ask Ximen Qing to come out. Daian slowly lifted the shutter and went in. "Guijie is going home and would like to speak to you," he said to Ximen.

"Guijie, you little whore!" Ying Bojue cried. "Are you still here?"

"She is just going," Ximen Qing said. Then he went out. Guijie kow-towed four times to him and thanked him for allowing her to come. "Can't you stay until tomorrow?" Ximen asked.

"My mother has sent a man with a sedan chair for me. She really needs me. But there is one thing I want to say to you before I go. It is about my aunt's maid. You really mustn't get rid of her. Last night my aunt gave her a very severe beating. She is so young, she really does not understand what she is doing. I gave her a good talking-to and told her she must change her ways, and she promised she would never do such a thing again. It will upset my aunt terribly if you send her away during this festival. She would have no maid, and, if the only poker you have is a wooden spoon, and a short one at that, it is still better than using the fingers. For my sake, Father, don't turn the girl away."

"If you wish it so much, I will allow her to stay," Ximen Qing said. He bade Daian tell Yueniang not to send for the go-between. Daian saw Hua-tong carrying Guijie's things.

"Give them to me," he said to the boy, "and you go to the inner court with the message." Huatong did as he was told. When Guijie had finished speaking to Ximen Qing, she went to the window.

"Beggar Ying," she called, "I have made no reverence to you, and now I, your mother, am going home."

"Drag the little creature back," cried Bojue. "Don't let her go until she has sung a song for me."

"You must wait," Guijie said. "When your mother has nothing to do, she will sing a song for you."

"What do you mean by going home in the middle of the day?" Ying Bojue said. "You must be expecting good fortune in the shape of a lover or two this evening."

"You dirty beggar," Guijie cried. She laughed and went away.

Daian went out with her and helped her into her sedan chair.

After Ximen Qing had spoken to Guijie, he went to the inner court to change his clothes. "That little whore Guijie is just like a thief who has escaped from jail," Ying Bojue said to Xie Xida. "She is more cunning than ever. On an occasion like this, you would expect her to stay, instead of which off she goes. I wonder who is waiting for her."

"I will tell you," Xie Xida said. He whispered something to Bojue.

"Don't speak too loud," said Bojue when he had heard a sentence or two. "Our brother knows nothing of this." They heard Ximen's footsteps and the conversation ended.

Ying Bojue embraced Wu Yin'er and drank wine with her mouth to mouth. "This is the daughter for me," he said. "Soft and gentle, a hundred times nicer than that little strumpet Guijie, whom even a dog will have nothing to do with."

Wu Yin'er laughed. "When it comes to bad language, Uncle," she said, "you are a master. When you say one you mean one, and when you say a hundred you mean a hundred. There are wise and foolish people everywhere, and we do well not to make comparisons. My sister Guijie has annoyed you."

"Don't talk to him, the dog," Ximen Qing said. "He is always grumbling about something."

"Don't pay any attention to him," Bojue said. "Don't you interfere with her. She is my little daughter. Come here, daughter, take your lute and sing me a song."

Wu Yin'er slowly stretched her jade fingers, gently touched the strings, and softly sang the song "The Willows Are Like Golden Tassels." She served wine to Ying Bojue, then to Xie Xida, and sang another song.

Meanwhile Huatong had gone to the inner court. All the ladies and the nuns were there, except Pan Jinlian. When the boy came, Yueniang was just about to tell old woman Feng to sell Xiahua. "Father bade me tell you not to send the girl away," Huatong said.

"But he told me to sell her," Yueniang said. "What has made him change his mind? Tell me. Who has been talking to him to make him change his mind like that?"

"I was helping Guijie to carry her things," the boy said. "It was she who told my father to keep the maid. Father told Daian to come and tell you, but instead of coming himself he made me come, and he went to the gate with her."

Yueniang was annoyed. "Daian is one of those slaves who try to be in with both sides," she said. "When I was angry and wouldn't send for the go-between, he told me his father insisted upon it. Now he is up to some trick or other. He has gone off with the girl. When he comes back, I will have a reckoning with him."

As she spoke, Wu Yin'er, who had finished singing, came in. "Your maid has come for you," Yueniang said to her. "Guijie has gone. Are you going too?"

"Mother," Wu Yin'er said, "I will stay if you like. Otherwise, you might think I did not appreciate the claims of courtesy." She asked her maid who had sent for her.

"Your mother sent me," the maid told her.

"Is there anything at home that calls for my presence?" said Wu Yin'er.

"No," replied the girl.

"Then, if not, why did you come for me? Go back. The lady here wishes me to stay. I am going to take the walk of the hundred illnesses with her and I will come home after that."

The maid was going away when Yueniang asked Wu Yin'er to call her back, that she might have something to eat. "The Great Lady is going to give you some food," Wu Yin'er said, "so wait. I want you to take my clothes with you. When you get home, tell my mother not to send a sedan chair for me. I shall come back on foot. Where is Wu Hui?"

"He has had some trouble with his eyes," the girl told her.

Yueniang told Yuxiao to take the girl to the back court. There they gave her two bowls of meat, a plate of bread and a jar of wine. Then they filled her boxes with pasties and tea cakes.

Wu Yin'er's clothes were in the rooms of Li Ping'er. Li Ping'er had taken a dress of fine silk woven with gold, two gold-fringed kerchiefs and a tael of silver, and these were all wrapped up together and given to Wu Yin'er. She was delighted. "Mother," she said, "don't give me these clothes." She smiled. "Really, I only want a white gown, so keep these silken dresses and give me an old white gown. I don't mind how old it is."

"My white gown is very big. It won't fit you," said Li Ping'er. She said to Yingchun: "Take the key, go to my large chest, and take from it a roll of white silk for your sister Wu Yin'er." To Wu Yin'er she said: "You must ask your mother to get the tailors to make two good gowns for you. Would you rather have figured or plain silk?"

"I should prefer plain, Mother," said Wu Yin'er. "Then it will match my wrapper." She smiled and said to Yingchun: "Sister, I have troubled you to go upstairs again for me. I have nothing with which to reward you, but I will sing you a song."

After a while Yingchun came down with a roll of plain white silk made on the broad looms of Songjiang. There was a label upon it that said: "Thirty-eight taels' weight." She gave it to Wu Yin'er, who kowtowed four times to Li Ping'er. Then she stood up again and made reverence several times to Yingchun.

"Wu Yin'er," said Li Ping'er, "take the other silken clothes too. Sooner or later you will need them when you are serving wine."

"You have already given me the white silk to make a dress. How can I accept these?" She again kowtowed to Li Ping'er.

After a while her servant had finished her meal, and Wu Yin'er gave her the clothes to carry home. "Why are you so pleased?" Yueniang asked her. "Don't imitate Guijie, who is full of self-conceit. Both yesterday and this morning, that girl has been like a raging tiger. She insisted on going home, and nothing we could do would stop her. She was so anxious to get away she didn't even sing properly, and, when her people came for her, she wouldn't wait to eat anything. Sister Wu Yin'er, you must not follow her example."

"Good Lady," Wu Yin'er said, "your palace is no ordinary house. We must remember the difference and, though we may give ourselves airs elsewhere, we should not do so here. Guijie is very young. She doesn't understand the ways of the world. Please, Lady, do not be angry with her."

While they were talking, a boy came with a message from Aunt Wu. "My mother hopes," he said, "that all you ladies, and Guijie and Wu Yin'er, will come early. She would like Lady Sun Xue'e to come too."

"Go home and tell your mistress," Yueniang said, "that we are now dressing. The Second Lady has a painful leg and she will not be able to come. My husband is entertaining some friends in the outer court today, so the Lady in charge of the kitchen will not be able to come either. Guijie has gone away, so, with my stepdaughter and Wu Yin'er, there will be six of us. Tell your mother she must not make any special preparations: we shall be quite content just to spend the evening with her." She asked the boy who was going to sing for them. The boy, Laiding, told them that it was Miss Yu. Then he went away.

Wu Yueniang, Meng Yulou, Pan Jinlian, Li Ping'er, her stepdaughter, and Wu Yin'er then set off. Before she went, she said to Ximen Qing: "I have told the nurse to look after the baby." They went to their sedan chairs, with the three boys, Daian, Qitong and Laian, and four soldiers. So they came to Aunt Wu's house.

# CHAPTER 46
# Daian in Trouble

Gongs and drums beat everywhere
In every house there is the sound of pipes and strings.
People go singing through the streets in bands
Young men and women play sweet melodies of the dance.
A mount of paper with gay colored streamers
Towers into the blue sky.
Incense from the royal palace rings its way heavenward over the
    assembled people
The precious moon sheds its soft brilliance within the courtyard and
    without.
Everywhere the scene is lovely.
This is the most glorious festival of the year
When we celebrate the first full moon.

Ximen Qing sent off Wu Yueniang and the others to the party at Aunt Wu's house. About sunset, Li Zhi and Huang the Fourth stood up to take their leave. Ying Bojue went out with them. "I have managed that business for you," he said, "and tomorrow you will get your five hundred taels." Li Zhi and Huang the Fourth bowed to him repeatedly and went away. Ying Bojue went back and drank wine with Xie Xida and Ximen Qing. Then Li Ming came in. "Here is young Li," Bojue said. Li Ming knelt down and kowtowed to them.

"Why has Wu Hui not come?" Ximen Qing asked him.

"He has not been able to go even to Dongpingfu," Li Ming said. "There is something wrong with his eyes. But I have brought Wang Zhu."

Wang Zhu was called in and, after he had kowtowed to Ximen and the others, he and Li Ming stood beside them.

"Your sister Li Guijie has just gone home," Ximen said to the boy. "Did you know?"

"I have only just returned from Dongpingfu," Li Ming said. "I came here as soon as I had washed my face, so I have heard nothing about her."

"I fear that these two boys have had nothing to eat," said Bojue. "Will you give orders for them to have some food?"

"Uncle," Shutong said, "a meal is being made ready for the musicians, and if these two wait a while they can eat with them."

Bojue told Shutong to bring a tray. He picked out some of the dishes and handed the food to Li Ming, telling him to take it away and eat it with his companion. Then he said to Shutong: "You foolish boy. People, like things, all belong to some definite class or other. You do not understand that, though they may come from the bawdy house, they are not on the same footing as the musicians. We cannot treat them in the same way, or it would look as though we were lacking in a sense of the fitness of things."

Ximen Qing tapped Bojue on the head. "You dog," he said, "you always look after actors because they belong to the same class as yourself and you know what they have to put up with."

"Stupid dog yourself!" Bojue said. "What do you know about it? Have you lived so long as a gay young man and still don't know the jingle: 'Be tender with the jade and loving to the flowers'? The more you love them, the more you get out of them, but treat them harshly and they wither away and die."

"Oh yes, my son," Ximen said, laughing, "no doubt you know all about that."

When Li Ming and Wang Zhu had finished their meal, Ying Bojue called them and asked them to sing a song he named to them. Wang Zhu took his lute and Li Ming his zither: they cleared their throats and sang. When they had finished, it was nearly evening.

Ximen Qing ordered the things to be cleared away and sent for Clerk Fu, Han Daoguo, Ben the Fourth and Chen Jingji. A great screen was set at the gate; two tables were placed there, and two sheep's horn lanterns hung. Food was piled abundantly upon the tables. Ximen Qing and Ying Bojue sat in the place of honor, and the clerks and managers on either side. On each side of the door hung twelve golden lotus lanterns. There was a small set piece of firework. This, Ximen said, was to be lighted when the ladies returned. The six musicians carried the bronze gongs and drums to the great gate. There they beat them for a short time, and then played their instruments. Delicate sweet strains came from them. Li Ming and Wang Zhu, the two young actors, played and sang the songs of the lanterns. And, of the people who passed along the street, none dared to raise his head to look. Ximen Qing was wearing a *zhongjing* hat, a velvet cloak and a white silk gown.

Daian and Ping'an set off the fireworks in turn, while two soldiers with rods kept back the crowd and would not allow them to push forward. In the cloudless sky the full moon appeared. There was great excitement in the street.

\*         \*         \*

The four maids, Chunmei, Yingchun, Yuxiao and Lanxiang, knowing that Yueniang was not at home and hearing the drums and music at the gate, and the fireworks, dressed themselves and looked out from behind the screen. Shutong and Huatong were heating wine at a brazier on the other side. Yuxiao and Shutong were old friends, and were always playing together. Now they had a struggle to see who could steal the other's melon seeds. Without caring what they were doing, they upset the wine jar on the fire. The fire sent forth a great flame, filling the whole place with smoke. Yuxiao laughed and Ximen Qing heard her. He told Daian to go and see who was laughing and what had caused the smoke.

Chunmei was wearing a new white cloak with a scarlet wrapper. When the wine jar was upset, she was sitting in a chair watching Yuxiao and Shutong playing together. Now she cursed her fellow maid. "Whenever you set eyes on a man, you lose your senses," she cried. "It was bad enough for you to upset the wine, without laughing. I don't know what there is to laugh about. You've put the fire out, and the ashes are coming down all over my head."

Yuxiao said nothing. She went to the back court. Shutong was rather anxious. He went to Ximen Qing and said: "I was warming the wine over the fire and the jar fell in." Ximen Qing asked no more questions, and that was the end of the matter.

Before the festival, Ben the Fourth's wife had learned that Yueniang would be away. She knew that the four maids, Chunmei, Yuxiao, Yingchun and Lanxiang, were all favorites of Ximen Qing, so she prepared some dainty dishes and told her daughter to go and ask the four maids to come and see her. The little girl was taken to Li Jiao'er. "I have no say in the matter," Li Jiao'er said. "I can do nothing; you must go and see what your master thinks about it." Then they went to Sun Xue'e, but she did not dare to take the responsibility. When the lanterns had been shown, Ben the Fourth's wife sent again to invite the four maids. Then Lanxiang urged Yuxiao, and Yuxiao urged Yingchun, and Yingchun urged Chunmei to go and plead with Li Jiao'er to ask Ximen Qing's permission. Chunmei refused to move. She was still angry with Yuxiao.

"You are like some poor beast who has never seen any food. You have never been to a feast and now you are anxious to have a sniff at one. It doesn't matter to me whether we go or not. I'm not going to ask anybody to help us. You are all fussing about like a lot of ghosts, and I'm sure I don't know what all the fuss is about. I have nothing but contempt for the lot of you."

Yingchun, Yuxiao and Lanxiang had all dressed in their best clothes, but they dared make no move. Chunmei sat still. Then Shutong came and said: "Ben the Fourth's wife has sent her little girl for you again. I don't mind if

Father scolds me: I'll go and speak to him." He went to Ximen Qing and whispered, "Ben the Fourth's wife has sent an invitation to my four sisters, and they have sent me to ask if they may go."

"Tell them they may go," Ximen said. "But they must come back in good time, for there are not enough people to attend to the household."

Shutong hurried back. "I have managed that little business very well," he said. "One word from me, and you get permission. Father says you may dress up and go. But you must come back early."

Chunmei, at this, went slowly to her room to dress. Then, all together, the four girls came out. Shutong pulled the screen partly back for them so that they could pass. They came to Ben the Fourth's house and, to Mistress Ben, they might have been angels from Heaven. She took them to her room. Several snowball lanterns had been hung there and a table was spread with excellent food. Mistress Ben, when she spoke to them, addressed them as First Aunt, Second Aunt, and so on. They made reverences to one another. Han Huizi's wife had also been invited.

Chunmei and Yuxiao sat in the places of honor; Yingchun and Lanxiang sat opposite them. Mistress Ben and Mistress Han sat on either side. The little girl, Changjie, went backwards and forwards to heat the wine and serve the dishes.

Ximen Qing told the musicians to play the tune "The East Wind Is So Gentle That We Know Fair Weather Is Here."

Little cakes, made with roses, were brought and everybody ate some. They were sweet, fragrant and delicious, and melted as soon as they were put into the mouth.

Li Ming and Wu Hui took their instruments and sang the song. Their voices were melodious and their rhythm excellent.

Daian and Chen Jingji put some fireworks in their sleeves and called for two soldiers with lanterns to go with them to Aunt Wu's house. They were to escort Yueniang and the others on their way home. The ladies were drinking wine in the hall when Jingji arrived and, as the elder Wu was not at home, Jingji was invited to take wine with the younger brother. A table was set and the two men took cakes and wine together.

Daian went forward and said to Yueniang: "Father has sent me to escort you home. He wishes you to go home early. He thinks the streets will be crowded tonight."

Yueniang was still displeased with Daian, and would not speak to him. Aunt Wu told her servant Laiding to give the boy some food. "Wine, meat, soup and rice are all ready in the front court," Laiding said.

"Don't hurry," said Yueniang. "Why should you give him food as soon as he arrives? Let him wait in the front court until we are ready to go."

"Are you really so busy these days?" Aunt Wu said to Yueniang. "This is a great festival and it is well that we should sit together and enjoy ourselves. The Second Lady and the other lady are at home and there is nothing for you to be anxious about. Why should you think of going away so early? If we did not belong to the family, it would be another matter." Then she said to Miss Yu: "Sing a good song for the ladies." Yulou spoke. "The Sixth Lady is not at all pleased with her: she did not come to the birthday party." Miss Yu stood up and kowtowed four times to Li Ping'er.

"I have been ill," she said. "When this good lady invited me yesterday to come here, I was only just able to come. If I had not been ill I should certainly have come to kowtow to you."

"Miss Yu," Jinlian said, "since the Sixth Lady is displeased with you, you must sing a particularly good song. Then she may forgive you."

Li Ping'er laughed but said nothing. "Certainly," Miss Yu said. "Give me my lute and I will sing." Aunt Wu bade Miss Zheng pour out wine for the ladies. "They have not had any for a long time," she said.

Miss Yu took her lute and sang "There Is a Storm upon the River." While she was singing, Yueniang said: "Why do I feel so cold now?"

"It is snowing," Laian said.

"Sister," Yulou said, "you should not be wearing such thin clothes. I have brought my heavy cloak."

"It is snowing," Yueniang said, "and we had better send the boys home for our fur coats."

Laian hurried out. He said to Daian: "The mistress says you are to go home and bring furs for the ladies."

Daian said to Qintong: "You go and get them. I'll stay here." Qintong did what he was told, without a word. After a while, Yueniang remembered that Jinlian did not possess a fur coat. She said to Laian: "Who has gone to get the coats?" Laian told her that Qintong had gone. "Why did he go without coming to me first?" Yueniang said.

Yulou said: "He has slipped off without a word. The Fifth Lady has no furs. We ought to have told the boy to bring the Great Lady's and not to bother about ours."

"Oh, we have a fur that someone has pawned," Yueniang said. "We will use that, and send for furs for everybody." Then she added: "Why did Daian send Qintong instead of going himself? Send him here."

When Daian came in, Yueniang scolded him severely. "You slave," she said, "what do you mean by ordering other people to do your work for you? You sent that slave away without asking my permission. You behave just like a cabinet minister. You are afraid you might disturb the set of your hat and so you tell someone else to go."

"You have no reason to be angry with me, Mother," Daian said. "If you had sent word for me to go, of course I should not have dared to disobey. Laian simply said that one of us must go."

"How brave Laian must have been to give you orders," said Yueniang. "Why, even I, who am the First Wife, do not venture to tell you to do anything. The truth is, we are too kind to you slaves, and you give yourselves airs in consequence. Your master has a picture of Buddha that was blackened by smoke and hung upon the wall. There are monks like that and there are benefactors like that. Your game is to curry favor with both sides at once, and you are so clever at it that your tongue might have been brought to a sharp point. You keep on the right side of those in the house and ally yourself with those without. You are idle, yet you must have your food. You are up to all kinds of dirty games on the sly, but don't think you deceive me. The other day, your master never told you to take Guijie home. What right had you to do so? One of the other boys was carrying her things and you snatched them out of his hands. It was none of your business whether we kept our maid or did not keep our maid. Why should you mix yourself up in that business? It was simply because someone suggested that you should. You thought you would get something out of it. You told someone else to come to me, because you thought that, if I had anything nasty to say, the one you sent would get it and not you. Now, can you say you don't play games like this?"

"That is Huatong's story," Daian said. "Father saw Huatong carrying her things, and he told me to see her home and Huatong to come back. You say, Mother, that whether you kept the maid or not was no business of mine. That is true. Why then should I bother about it?"

Yueniang was very angry and cursed him. "You thievish slave! Are you trying to argue with me? I have too much to do to say any more to you. You go too far. I tell you to do something: you don't do it; then you try to put me off with some cock-and-bull story. Wait! You shall see if I don't tell your father to treat you like a moldy sheep's head."

"Daian," Aunt Wu said, "go at once and bring your mother's fur cloak." Then she said to Yueniang: "Sister, tell him which one you wish him to bring for the Fifth Lady."

"Don't send him," Jinlian said. "I don't want any fur coat, and, if he does go home, let him bring my cloak. The fur coat is one that someone or other has pawned and I know nothing about it. If it is yellow dog's skin, people will laugh at me for wearing it. Besides, I can't keep it long; it will be redeemed."

"The fur coat I am thinking of is not one that has been pawned," Yueniang said. "It was brought in payment of debt by Li Zhi, who owed us sixteen taels of silver. It is the one Li Jiao'er wears that was pawned by General

Wang's people." To Daian she said: "The fur coat is in the large chest. Ask Yuxiao to get it for you and bring my stepdaughter's coat too."

Daian went out with a very angry face. Chen Jingji asked him where he was going. "Such nasty temper!" said Daian. "Now all the work has to be done over again. Late though it is, I must run home." He went out. When he reached the house, Ximen Qing was still drinking at the gate. Fu and Yun had gone, but Ying Bojue, Xie Xida, Han Daoguo and Ben the Fourth were still there.

"Have the ladies come?" Ximen Qing asked.

"No," said Daian, "they have sent me for their fur coats." He went to the inner court.

Qintong arrived before Daian and went to the upper room for the furs. Xiaoyu was sitting sulkily upon the bed. "Those four strumpets," she told the boy, "have gone to Ben the Fourth's wife's to drink wine. I don't know where the fur coats are. You had better go there and ask them."

So Qintong went to Ben the Fourth's house. He did not knock at the door but stood quietly outside the window. Ben the Fourth's wife was saying: "My dear eldest aunt, and you, Second Aunt, is it because you despise the preparations I have made for you in this small mean hovel that you have had no wine for so long?"

"Fourth Sister," Chunmei said, "really we have had wine enough."

"Oh, how can you say that?" Mistress Ben said. "Why must you stand so much on ceremony here?" Then she said to Mistress Han: "You are my near neighbor and I look upon you as a second hostess. You must urge the Third and Fourth Aunts to drink. Don't sit there like a guest." She said to her little daughter: "Heat some wine and pour it out for your Third Aunt. But don't fill it quite full for your Fourth Aunt."

"I never drink wine," Lanxiang said.

"Ladies," said Mistress Ben, "you have gone hungry today because I have no good food to offer you. Please don't laugh at me on that account. I would have sent for some blind singers, but I was afraid the noise would disturb his Lordship. This is such a tiny place. Dear, dear! What a hard life poor people have!"

Qintong knocked at the door. The little girl went to see who was there. Qintong looked at her and smiled, but said nothing. "You funny creature," Yuxiao said, "what is it you want, standing there showing your teeth and grinning? Why don't you speak?"

"The ladies are drinking at Madam Wu's house," Qintong said. "When they saw it was snowing, they sent me for their furs. They all want them."

"They are in the gilded chest," Yuxiao said. "Ask Xiaoyu to give them to you."

"Xiaoyu told me to come here and ask you," Qintong said.

"Don't pay any attention to that little whore," said Yuxiao. "She knows well enough where they are."

"Your ladies have fur coats," Chunmei said, "and you must go and get them. My lady has none, so I can stay where I am."

"Go and ask Xiaoluan for the Third Lady's coat," Lanxiang said.

Yingchun gave Qintong a key. "Ask Xiuchun," she said, "to open the door of the inner room, and give you the Sixth Lady's fur coat."

Qintong went back to the inner court. Xiaoyu and Xiaoluan wrapped up the fur coats belonging to the Great Lady and Yulou and gave them to him. As he was coming away, he met Daian and asked what he had come for. "You may well ask," Daian said. "It was all your fault that I got a scolding from the Great Lady and was told to come and bring a coat for the Fifth Lady."

"I am going for the Sixth Lady's coat," Qintong said.

"Well," said Daian, "when you have got it, wait here for me and we will go together. If you go back before I do we shall have another taste of the Great Lady's temper." Daian went to the upper room. Xiaoyu was still sitting on the bed, warming her hands at the fire and biting melon seeds.

"Ah, Daian," she said, "so you have come too?"

"Yes," said the boy, "and I have a bellyful of anger. The Great Lady complains that I order other people about too much. She has sent me for the fur coat that Li Zhi brought in payment of a debt, because the Fifth Lady has none of her own. It is in the great chest."

"Yuxiao keeps the keys of the inner room," the girl said. "She and the others have gone to drink wine at Ben the Fourth's place. You will have to go to her."

"Qintong has gone to the Sixth Lady's room to get her furs," said Daian. "He will be back soon and he can go to Yuxiao. I am going to rest and get warm."

Xiaoyu invited Daian to sit on the bed. They sat close together and warmed their hands at the fire. "There is some wine in the jar," Xiaoyu said; "Would you like a drink?"

"You are very kind," said Daian. Xiaoyu got down from the bed, took the wine jar and set it on the fire. She opened the cupboard and took out a plate of preserved goose. There was nobody else about, and they kissed one another.

While Daian was drinking his wine, Qintong came back. Daian gave him a cup of wine and told him to go to Yuxiao to ask for a fur coat for the Fifth Lady. Qintong left the other coats behind and went again to Ben the Fourth's place. Yuxiao cursed him. "You young jailbird!" she said. "What has brought you back here?" She refused to come with him, but gave him the keys. The boy returned and asked Xiaoyu to open the door. Xiaoyu did so and picked up the bundle of keys. For a long time she tried to open the chest, but without success. Again Qintong went to Ben the Fourth's place to Yuxiao. "These are not the keys," Yuxiao said. "The key of the chest is under the bed in the Great Lady's room."

When the boy returned this time, Xiaoyu began to curse. "The whore might be nailed there," she said. "Instead of coming herself, she lets me have all the trouble." She opened the chest, but the fur coat was not inside it. Qintong had to run backwards and forwards, and he too cursed. "If I am going to die," he said, "it will take me three days and three nights to do so. These young ladies are like the ghosts of some infectious disease. I'm almost exhausted." He said to Daian: "What a fine scolding we shall get from the Great Lady when we get back. She won't have a word to say against the maids. We shall have to take the blame for being late." He went back to Yuxiao. "There is no fur coat in the chest," he told her.

Yuxiao thought for a while. Then she laughed. "I forgot. It is in the chest in the other room."

Qintong went back again. "The whore is crazy," cried Xiaoyu. "Her naughty lover has been too much for her. First she tells us it is in one place and it is not. Then she tells us to look somewhere else." However, she found the coat and wrapped it up with Ximen Dajie's. She gave them both to Daian and Qintong, and the two boys took them to Aunt Wu's house.

Yueniang scolded them again. "You two thievish slaves have been putting your heads together. You didn't want to come."

Daian did not dare to say anything, but Qintong said: "We got all the other coats, but had to wait until the maid found this one." He produced it and Aunt Wu looked at it.

"This is a splendid coat," she said. "Why did you call it a yellow dog's skin, Fifth Sister? I should be very glad to have one like it."

"It is really new," Yueniang said. "A little worn, perhaps, at the front. We will replace that part by a golden stomacher and then it will be perfect."

Yulou said jokingly to Jinlian: "Come here, my child, and put this yellow dog's skin on you. Let mother see whether it suits you or not."

"I shall have to ask my husband for one," Jinlian said. "I don't care to wear other people's old clothes."

"You are too clever," Yulou said, laughing. "You ought to thank Buddha you have a coat like this." She put it on Jinlian. It was very large and cozy. Jinlian was somewhat appeased. Yueniang, Yulou and Li Ping'er put on their fur coats, all of which were made of sable. Then they said good-bye to the Wu ladies, and Yueniang gave Miss Yu two *qian* of silver.

Wu Yin'er said she too must say farewell. She knelt down and kowtowed to all the ladies. Aunt Wu gave her a set of silver flower ornaments; Yueniang and Li Ping'er each gave her a tael of silver. She again kowtowed and thanked them.

The two aunts and Miss Zheng would have taken the ladies to the gate, but Yueniang would not let them because it was snowing.

"A little while ago it was snowing very heavily," Qintong said. "Now it is more like rain. I am afraid the ladies' clothes will get wet, and I suggest borrowing umbrellas from our aunt." The younger uncle Wu quickly found some umbrellas and Qintong took them. Two soldiers with lanterns led the way. After passing through a few lanes, they came to the main street. Chen Jingji set off fireworks all along the road. He said to Wu Yin'er: "Sister Wu Yin'er, your home is not far away. Let us take you home."

"Where does she live?" said Yueniang.

"You go down this street," Jingji said, "and halfway down you come to a house with a high gateway. That is where she lives."

"I must say good-bye to you, ladies," Wu Yin'er said.

"Go straight home," Yueniang said. "Don't stop to make reverence to us. You have done so already, and the ground is wet. I will send a boy with you to see you to your door." She told Daian to go with the girl.

Then Jingji said: "Mother, I think I ought to go with Daian."

"Very well," said Yueniang, "you can both go with her." This was what Jingji was hoping for: he and Daian went off together.

Yueniang and the others went on their way. Jinlian said to Yueniang: "Mother, you talked about our taking her home. Why didn't we?" Yueniang laughed.

"What a child you are! I was only joking, and you took every word I said seriously. What kind of a place do you imagine this 'Home of Spring's Delights' to be? We could not possibly go there with her."

"But when men go to amuse themselves at such places," said Jinlian, "I have heard of their wives going after them and making a disturbance."

"Then, next time our lord goes there," Yueniang said, "you go and look for him. The chances are you will be driven out by another man who will take you for one of the ladies there."

They came to East Street. Outside the Qiaos' house, Madam Qiao herself and Miss Duan were standing. When they saw Yueniang and the others coming, they came forward and invited them to go in. Yueniang thanked them. "It is very kind of you," she said, "but it is late and we must not stay." Madam Qiao begged them not to stand on ceremony, and insisted that they should go in for a while. In her room, lanterns were hanging, and wine and fruit were set out upon the tables. Two singing girls were there to entertain the company.

At the gateway, Ximen Qing and his friends at last had wine enough. Ying Bojue and Xie Xida had been eating all day, and now the food had reached so high a point in their throats that they could not swallow another morsel. They saw that Ximen Qing was nodding in his chair and, not to miss a chance, they emptied the plates of fruit into their sleeves and went off with Han Daoguo. Only Ben the Fourth remained. He helped Ximen Qing to pay the musicians, told the boys to clear away, saw that the lanterns and candles were blown out and assisted Ximen Qing to the inner court.

Ping'an went to Ben the Fourth's place and said to the maids there: "Father has gone to the inner court. Why don't you come?"

When they heard this, Yuxiao, Yingchun and Lanxiang hurried away as fast as they could without even saying good-bye to Mistress Ben. They were off like a streak of smoke. Chunmei alone thanked Mistress Ben, and went back in a leisurely way. She overtook Lanxiang, who had been left behind because her shoe had come off. Chunmei scolded her. "You are like someone who steals a coffin for her own funeral," she said. "What kind of manners are these, letting your shoe fall off like that?"

When they came to the back court, they found that Ximen Qing had gone to Li Jiao'er's room, and all went in to kowtow to him. When the nun saw him come in, she left that room and went to Yueniang's room where she sat with Xiaoyu. When Yuxiao came in, she made a reverence to the nun.

"Sister," Xiaoyu said to her, "when Mother sent a boy for the ladies' furs, why didn't you come and look for them yourself instead of making me do so? I didn't know which was the key of the chest, and when I opened it, there was no coat inside. In the end, I found it in the great chest in the other room. You put the fur there, and you must have known where it was. You must have been off your head. You had food enough at Mistress Ben's, and now you are fatter than ever."

In truth, Yuxiao had had a good deal to eat, and her face was red. "You little whore," she cried, "what do you mean by behaving like a mad dog? If she didn't invite you, that's no reason why you should be angry with me. Do you think I wanted the whore to invite me?"

"Sisters," said the nun, "be calm, and do not let your master hear you. The ladies will be back in a moment and you had better have tea ready for them."

Then Qintong came with the wrappers. Yuxiao asked if the ladies had returned. The boy told her that Madam Qiao had kept them, and that they had gone in to take a cup of wine with her. They would probably be back soon, he said. The two maids stopped quarreling.

Before long, Yueniang returned from Madam Qiao's. When she reached the gate, Ben the Fourth's wife came out to welcome her. Then Chen Jingji and Ben the Fourth brought a small set of fireworks and set it off outside the gate. Afterwards, Yueniang went in, and Li Jiao'er and the nun came and made reverence to her. Xue'e kowtowed.

"Where is his Lordship?" Yueniang said to Li Jiao'er.

"He came to my room," Li Jiao'er said, "and I helped him to bed." Yueniang said no more.

Yingchun, Chunmei, Yuxiao and Lanxiang came to kowtow to their mistress.

"Madam Ben the Fourth sent these four maids an invitation," Li Jiao'er said. "They stayed a while and then came back."

For some time Yueniang did not speak. Then she said: "You wonderful little bitches. What do you mean by going? Who told you you might go?"

"They asked their master's permission before they went," Li Jiao'er said.

"Asked his permission!" said Yueniang. "What is the use of asking him? This house is like a temple where the doors are opened early on the first and fifteenth days of every month so that all the little ghosts can run away."

"Lady," the nun said, "these sisters are just like pictures; how can you speak of them as little ghosts?"

"They look like half-painted pictures to me," Yueniang said. "What right have they to go out for others to feast their eyes upon?"

Yulou saw that Yueniang was not in the best of tempers, and was the first to leave. Jinlian, Li Ping'er and Ximen Dajie went after her. Only the nun remained. She went to bed with Yueniang. The snow did not stop until the first night watch.

Next day, Ximen Qing went to his office. About midday, Yueniang, Yulou and Li Ping'er said good-bye to the nun. At the gate they saw an old country woman telling fortunes. She wore a pleated gown and a blue cloth skirt; there was a piece of black cloth over her head, and on her back she carried a bundle. She was walking along the street. Yueniang told a boy to go and bring her inside the second door to consult the divining diagram.

The old woman set out the spirit tortoise, and they asked her to tell their fortunes. She knelt down and kowtowed four times. "Lady, how old are you?" she asked Yueniang.

"Tell the fortune of a woman whose animal is the dragon," Yueniang said.

"If you speak of the great dragon," the old woman said, "the age is forty-two, but if it is the lesser dragon, it must be thirty."

"I am thirty," Yueniang said, "and I was born at midnight on the thirteenth day of the eighth month."

The old woman cast the spirit tortoise. It turned once, and she took up one of the divining cards. On it was a picture of a man and a woman in the place of the master, and a number of servants, some sitting, some standing. They were all watching gold and silver and treasure being put in safety.

"Lady," the old woman said, "you were born at the lucky hour of the *Wu* period. Now *Wu* and *Ji* together are like a great forest, and your being born in their conjunction means that you are a woman of benevolence and justice. You are generous and kind-hearted. You are charitable and devout and a supporter of the religious orders. You are, in fact, given to good works of every sort. All your life you have done your duties as a housewife; you are prepared to take the blame that others should have, and keep silence. Happiness and anger are both natural to you. But you do not manage your servants with great discretion. When you are pleased, you laugh long and heartily, and, when you are angry, you make a terrible to-do. In the early morning, when others are asleep, you burn fresh incense and wash the tripods. This while others sleep till the sun is long risen. Although by nature you are very quick, like wind and fire, yet you forget about a thing in a twinkling and you are ready to talk and laugh with anybody. There is a star of ill omen in the palace of diseases. You have to suffer from the babble of others. But you have a good heart, and so can overcome this, and you will live till you are seventy."

"Tell us whether this lady will have a son," Yulou said.

"I am sorry," said the old woman, "but there is something uncertain about the sign for children. I seem to see that she will have a son in a religious order to see her soul into the next world. But I doubt whether any other children she may have will live, no matter how many they may be."

"Your Wu Yingyuan is a priest already," Yulou said to Li Ping'er, smiling.

Yueniang said to Yulou: "Let her tell your fortune."

"Tell the fortune," said Yulou, "of a woman aged thirty-four, born at the hour of the tiger on the twenty-seventh day of the eleventh month."

The old woman again set the cards in order and cast the spirit tortoise. It stopped at the Star of Fate. She picked up a card on which was depicted a woman and three men. The first man was dressed as a traveling merchant, the second wore a red robe of ceremony, the third was a scholar. There was a room of gold and silver, and many servants stood on either hand.

"This lady was born in the year *Jiazi*," the old woman said, "and when *Jiazi* comes into conjunction with *Yichou*, it is like gold in the ocean. But there are three deaths and six injuries indicated by Fate. All will be well when you have been a widow."

"I have already been a widow once," Yulou said.

"You are gentle, kind and good-tempered," the old woman continued. "Nobody can tell whom you like and whom you dislike, because you never show it. You are respected by those below and loved by your husband, but, in spite of your kindness to others, you never win people's hearts. You must take the blame for what others do, and backbiters will make trouble for you. Though you suffer this, no one will admit that you are kind. But you are good-hearted, and though you will have to put up with troublemakers, they will do you no real harm."

Yulou laughed. "Only a moment ago," she said, I asked for some money for the boys and there was trouble. I think that is what you must be thinking of when you talk about my being blamed for what others do."

"Can you tell us whether this lady will have a son?" Yueniang said.

"At the best, she will have a daughter," said the old woman. "Certainly not a son. But she will live long."

"Now tell this other lady's fortune," Yueniang said to the old woman. "Sixth Sister, tell her your eight words."

Li Ping'er laughed. "I am a sheep," she said.

"If you are a lamb," the old woman said, "you must be twenty-seven years old and you were born in the year *Xinwei*. What was the month?"

"Noon on the fifteenth day of the first month," Li Ping'er said.

The old woman spun the turtle. When it came to the Star of Fate, it stopped dead. She picked up a paper on which was a picture of one woman and three men. The first was wearing red, the second green and the third black. The woman was carrying a child. In a room filled with treasures of gold and silver there stood a demon with black face, long fangs, and red hair.

"This lady," the old woman said, "shows *Gengwu* in conjunction with *Xinwei*. It is as earth by the roadside. She is of high position and great wealth. She has food and clothing in plenty, and all her husbands are men of standing. There is virtue in her heart, and she does not care for money and treasure. Should she be robbed of them, she is happy nonetheless. Indeed, she will be angry if she is not. But she is plagued by people of little worth, and such people return her evil for good. Such evildoers disturb her peace, and begin their cunning tricks as soon as they have turned their eyes away from her. It is better to meet a tiger in a place where three roads meet, for then we can escape one way, than a man with a sword whose blade is double-edged.

"Lady, I hope you will forgive me. You are like a roll of fine red silk, yet one, alas, of no great length. You must exercise great self-control, and be on the lookout for danger to your child."

"My child has been enrolled at the Daoist Temple," Li Ping'er said.

"All to the good," the old woman said, "but I must warn you that this year you are under the spell of the *Jidu* star and there are signs of blood. You must be particularly careful in the seventh and eighth months. Then you must not see anything that might disturb you."

When the old woman had finished, Li Ping'er gave her five *fen*, and Yueniang and Yulou each gave her fifty coins. Then she was dismissed.

Jinlian and Ximen Dajie came. "No wonder I could not find you in the back court," Jinlian said, laughing. "You were all here."

"Yes," Yueniang said, "we came to say good-bye to the nun, and then we had our fortunes told. If you had been a little earlier, you too could have had your fortunes told."

"I don't want my fortune told," said Jinlian. "There is a proverb: 'Fortunes may be foretold, but not our conduct.' You remember how, some time ago, that priest said I had not long to live. It made me very depressed. But I don't care. If I die in the street, bury me there. If I die on the road, bury me there. If I fall into a ditch, the ditch will serve as a coffin."

She went with Yueniang to the inner court.

## CHAPTER 47
# The Villainy of Miao Qing

In the city of Guangling in Yangzhou in the province of Jiangnan, there lived a gentleman of standing in the official service whose name was Miao Tianxiu. He was extremely wealthy, a lover of poetry, and devoted to the Rites. He was now about forty years old, and his only child was a daughter, still unmarried. His wife suffered from a chronic wasting sickness, and the affairs of his household were entrusted to his favorite concubine, Diao the Seventh, who had originally been a woman of no great virtue. Master Miao had paid three hundred taels for her and was extremely fond of her.

One day, an old monk came to beg alms at the gate. He said that he came from the Temple of Thankfulness at the Eastern Capital. The monks there had determined to secure a golden Lohan, and he was traveling about begging for contributions.

Master Miao was no miser. He gave the monk fifty taels of silver.

"This is really more than I need," the old monk said. "Half of this amount will be sufficient for me."

But Miao said: "Don't say that, Master. If there is more money than you need for the image, let the rest be spent on sacrifices."

The monk made reverence to him and thanked him. As he was about to go away, he said, "Sir, beneath your left eye there is the sign of death. This presages great danger for you. You have been so generous to me that I can do no less than warn you. If you have business to do, on no account leave your native place. Be on your guard, be on your guard." He went away.

A few weeks later, Master Miao happened to go to his garden and there found his servant Miao Qing talking to his concubine Diao the Seventh beside a summerhouse. They had not expected that he would come upon them so suddenly, and so he caught them. Master Miao said nothing, but he gave his servant a tremendous thrashing and swore he would get rid of him. Miao Qing was greatly alarmed and went about asking his relatives and neighbors to intercede for him. In the end he was allowed to stay, but, ever afterwards, he hated his master.

Master Miao had a cousin named Huang Mei, a graduate from Yangzhou. This man was a secretary at Kaifengfu, the Eastern Capital. He was a man of great learning and wide reading. One day he wrote to Master Miao

suggesting that he should make a journey to the Capital, both for amusement and in the interests of his future career. Miao was delighted with the
idea. He said to his wife and his concubine: "The Eastern Capital is the
place for people of high standing, and there are hosts of interesting and
beautiful things to see there. For a long time I have wanted to go there, but
there was no particular reason why I should. Now my cousin sends me an
invitation, and it is exactly what I should most enjoy."

"The other day," his wife said to him, "the monk told you that you
were in grave danger and that you must not leave this place. It is a long
way from here to the Capital, and there is plenty to busy you here at home.
If you go away, you leave an invalid wife and a young daughter at home,
and what we shall do if you go, I can't imagine. I think you ought to stay."
But Master Miao did not agree. Indeed he almost lost his temper. "A man
who lives in this world," he said, "should carry bow and arrows. It is a disgraceful thing if a man cannot wander over the world to see the glory of
his native land. I have a heart in my bosom and something in my pocket,
and I am sure to acquire both renown and a position. My cousin must
have something good in store for me. Please say no more about it." He
told Miao Qing to pack his clothes and get ready his baggage. So, with two
chests of gold, silver, and other treasure, they had enough to load a boat.
With a boy, Antong, and Miao Qing, he set off for the Eastern Capital. It
was about the end of autumn and winter was near at hand, when he com-
mended his household to the care of his wife and concubine, and chose a
day to start upon his journey. Then he sailed from the wharf of Yangzhou.
After a few days, they came to the lake of Xuzhou. The water was wild and
the danger great.

When they had come to a place called Xiawan, Master Miao, seeing that
it was late, ordered the boatman to lay up for the night. Now it was that
his life was done, and the fate that he could not escape was upon him. The
boatmen he had engaged, Chen the Third and Weng the Eighth, were both
thieves. But, as the proverb says: 'The Devil cannot get into a house without someone to let him in.' Miao Qing had a burning hatred for his master
and was waiting to get his revenge. He reflected that here was a chance for
him. He might conspire with these two boatmen to push his master into
the river, and so make an end of him, then he and the boatmen would share
the plunder, and he would go home, murder his mistress, and enjoy his
master's concubine and the property.

Miao Qing and the boatmen secretly made a plot. He said to them:
"There are a thousand taels of silver in my master's chests. There is silk
worth two thousand taels and many, many clothes. If you two will kill him,
I am prepared to share with you."

The two men laughed. "We had that same idea before you spoke to us," they said.

That night it was very dark. Master Miao and the boy Antong were asleep in the cabin. Miao Qing was on watch. About the third night watch Miao Qing shouted: "Thief! Thief!" Master Miao woke from his dreams and pushed his head out of the cabin to look around. Chen stabbed him in the throat with a sharp knife. They threw him into the water. The boy Antong tried to escape, but Weng thrust at him with a stick, and he fell into the river.

Then the pair of ruffians went into the cabin, opened the chests and took out all that was valuable—gold and silver, silk and garments. These they counted and made ready to share. "If we keep these things," the two men said to Miao Qing, "we shall be identified. But you were his servant. You can take them and sell them in some market and nobody will suspect you." They shared the gold things among themselves and went home. Miao Qing boarded another boat and went to the wharf at Linqing. When the customs officers had examined him, he took all the things to an inn in the city of Qinghe. There he met some old merchants from Yangzhou. He told them that his master was coming later. Then he sold the property he had stolen.

The proverb says: Men think the world ought to be managed in such and such a way, but Providence thinks otherwise. Master Miao was a plain-living, good man, yet he was unexpectedly murdered by his own servant. Such a death was unnatural. He was to be blamed, because he did not take good advice when it was offered, but really there was no escape from the decision of Fate.

Antong was knocked senseless by the stick, but, though he fell into the water, he was not dead. He floated to a shallow place among the reeds. There came a fishing boat, and, in the boat, an old man. He wore on his head a round reed hat, and, on his body, a short coat of straw. When he heard a scream, he rowed his boat in the direction of the sound and found a boy of seventeen or eighteen years of age. He quickly pulled the boy out of the water and asked what had happened. The boy told him that he was the servant of Master Miao of Yangzhou, and that they had been robbed on the river. The old fisherman took the boy into his boat, gave him clothes and food and drink. Then he said: "Do you wish to go back or will you live here with me?"

Antong said: "My master has been murdered, and I can never see him again. What is the use of my going back? I will stay with you."

"Very well," said the fisherman. "Live with me, and we shall, in time, find out something about the robbers. Then we will make new arrangements."

Antong thanked the old man and went to live with him.

One day—it was the last day of the year—it was fated that something of importance should happen. The fisherman and Antong went down the river to sell fish. They came suddenly upon Chen the Third and Weng the Eighth drinking together on their boat. They were wearing the clothes of Antong's master. When they came on shore to buy fish, the boy recognized them. He secretly told the old man. "Now," he said, "my master's death shall be avenged."

"Write an accusation and bring them before the judge," the old man said.

Antong wrote down his charge and took the paper to the office of the Inspector of the River, Major Zhou. The Major saw that the boy brought no witness or evidence with him, so he would have nothing to do with the case, and the boy went to the magistrate's court. Magistrate Xia saw that the case was one of murder and robbery: he accepted the charge and, on the fourteenth day of the first month, sent the watch with Antong to arrest the murderers at Qinghe. When they were examined and saw Antong there, they did not wait to be tortured but told the truth at once. They said that Miao Qing had been concerned with them in the murder, that he had taken a share of the things and gone his own way. Magistrate Xia ordered them to be put back in prison and ordered Miao Qing's arrest. He decided to give sentence when Miao Qing had been brought before him.

It was about the time of the New Year Festival and all the officers were on holiday. For two days the public offices were closed. In the meantime somebody at the office told Miao Qing what had happened. Miao Qing was terrified. He locked up his room at the inn and hid himself in the house of a certain Yue the Third. This Yue the Third was a broker. He lived in Lion Street next door to Han Daoguo, and his wife was on very friendly terms with Wang Liu'er. She often visited Wang Liu'er, and Wang Liu'er, when she had nothing else to do, often visited her. They were on very close terms indeed.

Yue saw that Miao Qing seemed exceedingly distressed and asked him what the trouble was. Miao Qing told him. "Don't worry," Yue said. "My neighbor Han's wife is the mistress of Master Ximen, an officer of the court. Her husband is a servant of his, and both husband and wife are our very good friends. We agree with each other on all points. If I get you out of this trouble, how much are you prepared to offer? Tell me, and I will go and discuss the matter with him."

Miao Qing knelt down. "All I ask," he said, "is to be saved from this trouble. I will most surely give you a great reward and I shall never dare to forget your kindness."

They wrote out a supplication, parceled up fifty taels of silver, put them with two dresses of embroidered satin, and Yue told his wife to take them to

Wang Liu'er. Wang Liu'er was delighted. She took the clothes, the silver and the paper, and waited for Ximen Qing to come.

For several days there was no sign of him but, on the evening of the seventeenth, Wang Liu'er saw Daian, with a wrapper, riding down the street. She went outside her door and called to him: "Where are you going?"

"I have been a long way with my master," the boy said. "We have just come back from Dongpingfu, where we took some presents."

"Has your father come back too?" Wang Liu'er asked.

"Father and Ben the Fourth have come back already," the boy said. Wang Liu'er took the boy into her house, told him all about the case and showed him the paper.

"Aunt Han," Daian said, "you may try to manage this affair, but you will not find it too easy. The two boatmen are already in prison and now this man is wanted. A few paltry taels are not enough for the servants. I want neither more nor less than twenty taels of silver, and then I will ask Father to come here and you can tell him all about it."

Wang Liu'er laughed. "You little oily mouth!" she said, "you may be hungry, but you must not be too greedy. If this case is settled, of course there will be something for you. Even if I get nothing myself, I will see that you get something."

"Aunt Han," said Daian, "don't misunderstand me. The proverb says: 'Honorable men are never ashamed to speak plainly.' The best thing we can do is to agree upon terms and then talk about the matter."

Wang Liu'er prepared some food and entertained Daian. "If I get a red face from drinking wine," the boy said, "my master will scold me."

"Don't trouble about that," Wang Liu'er said. "Tell him you have been here."

The boy drank one cup of wine and went away. As he went, the woman said to him: "Tell your father I am expecting him."

Daian went home, handed in the wrapper and waited for Ximen Qing to have his sleep out. When Ximen came to the room in the wing, the boy went to him quietly and said: "On my way home, Aunt Han stopped me and told me to ask you to go to see her. She has a very important matter to speak to you about."

"What is it?" Ximen said. "I will go."

Then District Examiner Liu came to borrow some silver. Ximen gave it to him and he went away. Ximen, wearing his eyeshades and a small hat, mounted his horse and went with Daian and Qintong to see Wang Liu'er. He went into the parlor and sat down, and Wang Liu'er came and made reverence to him. It was Han Daoguo's turn to sleep at the shop that night, so he did not return. Wang Liu'er had bought many things and had sent for old woman

Feng to cook them. She hastened to bring tea for Ximen Qing. Ximen told Qintong to take his horse to the house opposite and to shut the gate.

At first the woman said nothing about the case. "You must be tired after so many parties during these last few days," she said. "I have heard about your young son's betrothal and must congratulate you."

"It was my relative Wu who suggested the marriage," Ximen said. "The Qiaos have only one daughter. It really is not the most suitable marriage, but I want to get the matter settled."

"It is not a bad marriage," Wang Liu'er said, "but you have a high position and it will be awkward, perhaps, when you meet them."

"That was what I thought," Ximen said.

They talked for a while and Wang Liu'er said, "It is rather cold here. Won't you come into the inner room?" They went into the inner room. There was a chair on either side and a brazier with burning coals. Hesitatingly, the woman showed him Miao Qing's paper. "This man, Miao Qing, asked Mistress Yue to come and see me about it," she said. "Miao Qing is staying with Yue. The two boatmen have accused him falsely. All he wants is to have his name kept out of this case. He sent me a little present and you must do something for him."

When he had read the paper, Ximen Qing said: "How much did he give you?" Wang Liu'er took the fifty taels from her box and showed them to him.

"If the case is settled, he promised to give me two dresses," she said.

Ximen Qing looked at the silver and laughed. "Why did you accept so small a sum?" he said. "You don't understand. This Miao Qing is the servant of Master Miao of Yangzhou. He and the two boatmen murdered their master and threw the body into the river. It is a case of murder and robbery. The corpse has not yet been found. The boy Antong was with them, and both the boy and the boatmen are anxious to get hold of Miao Qing. If he is arrested he will certainly get the punishment of the thousand slashes and the two boatmen will lose their heads. They say that Miao Qing has stuff worth two thousand taels. Why should he send you a paltry sum like this? Send it back to him at once."

Wang Liu'er went into the kitchen and told her maid to go for Mistress Yue. When Mistress Yue came, Wang Liu'er gave her the silver and told her what Ximen Qing had said. When the news was brought to Miao Qing, it was as though a pail of water had been poured over him from head to feet. He was absolutely terrified. He talked over the matter with Yue and said he would give up all he had if only he could save his life.

"Since Master Ximen says this," Yue said, "it is clear that a little more will be of no avail. It looks to me as though it will mean a thousand taels to the two officers, and another thousand taels for the underlings and the policemen."

"But I haven't sold all my things," Miao Qing said. "Where am I to find the ready money?" They told Mistress Yue to go back to Wang Liu'er and find out whether Ximen would accept the goods. "If so, Miao Qing will offer goods to the value of a thousand taels to him. If he will not have them, ask his Lordship to allow Miao Qing two or three days in which to sell them. Then he will go in person to his Lordship to offer the money."

Wang Liu'er took the list of the goods and showed it to Ximen. He looked at it. "In the circumstances," he said, "I will let him have a few days. Then he must bring the money to me himself."

Mistress Yue went back and told Miao Qing what had happened. He was greatly relieved.

Ximen Qing noticed that there was somebody in the next house, so he did not stay long. He drank a few cups of wine, then ordered his horse and went home.

The next day the office closed early, and he did not mention the matter at all. Miao Qing desperately urged Yue to sell the stolen property for him, and, in three days, everything was disposed of for seventeen hundred taels. He gave Wang Liu'er another fifty taels and four dresses of the finest material. On the nineteenth he put a thousand taels into four wine jars, bought a pig and, when it was dark, carried them to Ximen Qing. All the servants knew about the matter, so he gave Daian, Ping'an, Shutong and Qintong ten taels of silver apiece. Daian went to Wang Liu'er and got another ten taels from her.

Ximen Qing came out and sat under the awning. There was no light but the moon was just rising. The presents were brought to him and Miao Qing, dressed in black clothes, kowtowed. "I am so grateful for your generous kindness," he said, "that though my body were beaten to pieces, I could never repay you."

"Your case has not yet been investigated," Ximen said, "but the two boatmen still insist on the truth of what they have said. If you are arrested, you must inevitably be severely punished. But since you have come to me, I will see that your life is saved. You would not be satisfied if I did not take your present, but a half of it I must give to Magistrate Xia, my colleague. You must stay here no longer, but get away as quickly as you can. Where do you live at Yangzhou?"

"I live within the city itself," Miao Qing said. He kowtowed again.

Ximen Qing called for some tea from the back court and Miao Qing drank it, standing beneath a pine tree. Then he kowtowed and prepared to take his leave. Ximen recalled him and said: "Have you attended to the officers of lower rank?" Miao Qing told him that he had. "Then you should go home at once," Ximen said.

Miao Qing gave fifty taels and the remainder of the silk to Yue and his wife. At the fifth night watch, they saddled a horse and he started for Yangzhou.

The next day Ximen Qing and Magistrate Xia left their office together. They were riding side by side. When they came to the middle of the High Street, Magistrate Xia was about to say good-bye to Ximen, but Ximen raised his whip and said: "Will you be kind enough to come to my house for a moment?" Xia went with him. They went into the hall and exchanged the appropriate greetings. Then Xia was asked to go to the arbor, and there he took off his long cloak. The servants brought tea and Daian and Shutong prepared a table.

"Really," Xia said, "I should not put you to all this trouble." Ximen Qing asked him not to say so. Two boys brought chicken, pigs' trotters, goose, duck, fish and other dishes on a large square tray. They ate some and everything was cleared away. Then they drank wine with dessert and fruits, using small golden cups and silver trays. Ximen pressed his colleague to drink more and more, and, while they were drinking, began to talk about the matter of Miao Qing.

"Yesterday," he said, "the fellow got some scholars to come here, and sent presents. I dared not make any decision myself, so I have asked you to come and talk about it." He showed Magistrate Xia the list of presents.

"I leave the decision to you," said Xia, when he had read the list.

"Well," Ximen said, "I suggest that, tomorrow, we send on those two robbers and leave Miao alone. We will ask someone to take Antong away. The matter can be settled when Master Miao's body is found. The present, of course, is yours."

"Not at all," Magistrate Xia said. "I agree with everything you say about the case, but why should you give me the present? You have done well. Certainly I shall not take it." They disputed politely for a long time, and at last Ximen said: "Perhaps we might share it." He put five hundred taels into a food box. Magistrate Xia stood up and made a reverence to him.

"You are very kind," he said, "and if I don't accept, you will take it unkindly. Thank you very much." He had some more wine and then went away.

Ximen Qing told Daian to take the food box to Magistrate Xia's as if he were taking wine. Xia himself came to receive it. He gave the boy a card in return and two taels of silver for himself. The four bearers each received four *qian* of silver. As the proverb says: Just as a pig's head will be cooked when the fire is hot enough, so a case will be settled when money enough is forthcoming.

So Ximen Qing and Xia arranged the matter. The next day they went to the office. The jailers, policemen, and attendants had all been bribed by Yue. In the hall of audience, the instruments of torture were all set out, and Chen and Weng, the two boatmen, were brought forward. When they were questioned, they still declared that they had murdered Master Miao at the instigation of Miao Qing. Ximen Qing professed to be very angry and ordered them to be beaten. "You two thieves have worked the river for years. You have pretended to carry travelers on your boat, but actually you have robbed and murdered. This boy says you killed Master Miao with a knife and threw his body into the water. You struck the boy himself with a stick. Here are the clothes of the boy's master for witness. Why do you still accuse somebody else?"

Then he called for Antong. "Who killed your master? Who pushed you into the water?"

"About the third night watch I heard Miao Qing shout. My master came out of the cabin, then Chen killed him and threw his body into the water. Weng struck me with a stick and I was thrown in too. He did not kill me. I do not know where Miao Qing is now."

"It is clear from what the boy says," Ximen Qing said, "that there is no way out for you." He had fetters put upon their legs and each of them was given thirty blows with a club. Their bones were broken and they screamed like pigs being killed.

The two robbers gave up half of the property they had stolen. They had already spent the rest. A document was written out to be sent with the men and the property to Dongpingfu. The magistrate at Dongpingfu, Hu Shiwen, was Ximen Qing's friend. He accepted the document without question. He sentenced Chen the Third and Weng the Eighth as thieves and murderers to have their heads cut off. Antong was allowed to go. Afterwards, the boy went to the Eastern Capital. There he accused Miao Qing of his master's murder, and of bribing the officers at Qinghe, and so escaping trial. A letter was written and joined to the lad's accusation; he was given money for his journey and sent to the supreme court of Shandong. Thus, more trouble was brewed for Miao Qing, and Ximen Qing was given considerable cause for anxiety in consequence of his action in the matter.

> Evil and good meet with their due reward
> Good Fortune and ill luck walk side by side
> But he who never walks in the wrong path
> Need have no fear when comes the summons in the night.

# CHAPTER 48

# The Censor's Accusation

Antong took the documents and the letter and set off for Shandong. He found that the Imperial Censor on circuit was at Dongchangfu. This was Ceng Xiaoxu, the son of the Censor, Ceng Bu. He had just taken a high place in the examination for the third literary degree, and was a very prudent and just official.

Antong thought that if he simply said he had come with a letter he would never be allowed to approach the Censor, and that it would be better for him to wait until the tablet was brought out. "Then," he said to himself, "I will kneel down, bring out my papers; the Censor will see them and justice will be done."

The boy put the accusation into his breast and took his stand outside the court. After a long time he heard the sound of the castanets announcing the opening of the court. The great gate was opened, Censor Ceng came to the great hall of audience, and a tablet was brought out upon which was written: "The cases of all princely families, princes and nobles." The second said: "The cases of civil and military officials," and the third: "Marriages, lands, and common cases." Then Antong followed the tablet and went in. He waited for all the cases to be decided, then knelt down in the hall before the dais. Attendants asked him what he wanted. He took the letter from his breast and held it up in both hands. The Censor said: "Bring me that letter." Then an officer quickly took the letter and set it down upon the table. The Censor opened it and read it. It said:

Huang Duan, your humble fellow student of the arts, living at the Capital, with all due respect.

To the exalted Censor Ceng. Greetings to your excellency from your younger brother. It is almost a year since your brightness illuminated me. Good friends seldom meet, and a joyful reunion is quickly ended. But the love of my heart is always with you. Last autumn your precious communication reached me. I opened it and read it, and my spirit seemed to wander till I spoke with you face to face. Some time ago you went to the South to see your honorable parents. Then I was told that you were on circuit in Shandong, and was pleased beyond all measure. I congratulate you upon your magnificent loyalty and filial piety. Uprightness as keen as the wind and the frost keeps your mind forever glorious. Your worthy ambition is known and recognized at Court. Now you are going around the provinces and it is possible for you to discover the misdeeds of officials and correct evil customs that have become established. Since I love you, I feel that I must remind you. You are a man of great capacity and at the prime of life. Our Emperor has the wisdom of a Sage, and your father enjoys splendid health. You have a magnificent opportunity to display your learning to advantage and to establish the supremacy of law. You will not permit dishonorable officials to corrupt the administration of justice. You will not allow cunning and evil men to play their scurvy tricks. At this time, there is in Dongping a certain Miao Qing who has escaped the justice of the law. So wrong has been done to Miao Tianxiu, his master. It is beyond my understanding, how in an age of such splendor, these discreditable things can happen. You will, I am sure, go to that place and make examination into the matter, and so the wrongdoing will be set right. I have directed Antong to bring his accusation to you and beg you to examine it. This the sixteenth day of the second month.

When the Censor had finished reading the letter, he asked for the boy's accusation. The attendants came down and said to Antong: "His Excellency asks if you have brought an accusation." Antong took the paper from his breast and they handed it to the Censor.

When he had read it through, Ceng took a brush and wrote upon it: "The officers at Dongpingfu will examine this case justly. They will search for the corpse and examine it, sending their report to me in detail with all the documents." To the boy he said: "Go to Dongpingfu and wait there."

Antong kowtowed, then rose and went out by a side door. Censor Ceng put the papers together with his own notes into a folder, sealed it with his official seal, and gave it to one of his officers to take to Dongpingfu.

When Hu Shiwen, the magistrate of Dongpingfu, read the document that had come from his superior, he was so frightened that he did not know where to put his hands and feet. He sent at once for the Deputy of Yanggu, a certain Di Sibin. This man was a native of Wuyang in Henan, an honest-dealing official. He was not a lover of money, but somewhat hasty and stupid in his investigations of cases. Hence men called him Stupid Di.

Some time before this, Deputy Di had gone to Qinghe. When he was on the shore of the river west of the city, a whirlwind seemed to arise in front of his horse and, as he went along, the whirlwind went with him. "This is curious," Di said to himself, and, reining in his horse, he told one of his attendants to go after the wind to see where it went. The attendant followed the wind and, when it had nearly reached the wharf, it subsided. He came back and told Di what had happened. Di sent for some of the old men of the place and dug up the bank. They found a corpse with the mark of a knife clearly discernible in the throat. Di gave instructions to the coroner to hold an inquest upon it. "What is this place in front of us?" he asked the bystanders. They told him that it was a temple and not far distant. Di sent for the monks and questioned them. The monks told him that, in the tenth month of the previous winter, they had been setting lanterns on the water's edge when they saw a corpse floating down the river. It came to the shallows and the Abbot generously buried it. But of the cause of death they knew nothing.

"It is quite obvious," said Stupid Di, "that the monks themselves murdered the man and buried him there. He must have had money on him. But you will not tell the truth." Without listening to any of the monks' explanations, he had the screws put on the Abbot and gave him a hundred strokes of the rod. The other monks were each given twenty, and they were all thrown into prison. Then he reported the case to Censor Ceng.

The monks clamored for justice, and, when Ceng thought the case over, it occurred to him that, if they had really murdered the man, they would have thrown his body into the river and not buried it on the bank. Besides, it did not seem probable that so many people would conspire to murder one man.

The monks had now been in prison for almost two months. When Antong came, he was taken to identify the corpse. As soon as he saw it, he cried bitterly and said, "This is indeed my master. The thieves murdered him and the mark in his neck can still be seen." The body was carefully examined and a report sent to the Censor. The monks were set free.

Ceng read all the documents about the case. He examined Chen the Third and Weng the Eighth and they both said that the idea of murdering Master Miao had originated with Miao Qing.

The Censor was very angry. He sent a man with a warrant bidding him travel day and night and arrest Miao Qing at Yangzhou. And he wrote a report censuring all those who had accepted bribes and sold justice.

Wang Liu'er had received a hundred taels and four dresses from Miao Qing. She and her husband did not sleep all night. They talked about the ornaments, pins and rings she would have made; how they would send for the tailor to make some clothes; how she would have a new net for her hair, and spend sixteen taels on a new maid, Chunxiang, whom sooner or later she would give to Han Daoguo.

One day Ximen Qing came to see her, Wang Liu'er welcomed him and gave him tea. After a while he went to the inner court to wash his hands and saw a building being set up on the roof of a neighboring house. When he came back, he asked Wang Liu'er whose house it was. She told him it belonged to their neighbor, Yue. "Why should you allow them to interfere with your fengshui?" Ximen said. "Tell him to stop at once. If he refuses to pull it down, I will send the police to deal with him."

"We cannot talk to him like that," Wang Liu'er said afterwards to her husband. "He is our neighbor."

"The best thing we can do," Han Daoguo said, "is to get some wood, say nothing about it, and build another story ourselves. On the top of it we can dry our bean paste, and we can use the inside either as a stable or as a privy."

"That would be silly," Wang Liu'er said. "If we are going to build a roof, we might as well buy tiles and bricks and make two good rooms."

Han Daoguo agreed. They spent thirty taels, built their two rooms and put a flat roof over them. Ximen Qing told Daian to take wine, meat and cakes to give the workers as a reward. The matter was known to everyone who lived in the street.

Magistrate Xia, now that he had received several hundred taels, sent his son Xia Cheng'en to the military college. Every day the young man studied archery and horsemanship with his teachers and friends. Ximen Qing suggested to the two eunuchs, Liu and Xue, Major Zhou, General Jing and Captain Zhang, that they should send a present to Xia in congratulation. They gave him a large scroll.

At Ximen's burying place, he had recently built a mound, an arbor, and some rooms. He had not been to worship his ancestors since he had received his official appointment. Now he sent for Xu, the Master of the Yin Yang, to examine the site, built a gateway and made a path for the spirits. Around the gateway he planted peach trees, willows and pines. On either side he made a small embankment. At the Festival of the Dead he proposed to visit the grave and change the tablet. He prepared pigs and sheep and food.

The festival was on the sixth day of the third month. He sent out many invitations and arranged for a number of people to take the things out to the tomb—wine, rice, vegetables and so forth. He engaged musicians and actors, and arranged for several singing girls to be present. He invited a great number of guests, both men and women. Chunmei, Yingchun, Yuxiao and Lanxiang were to be there also. Twenty-four or more sedan chairs would be needed. But when there was question of the nurse's taking the baby Guan'ge, Wu Yueniang said to Ximen: "It will be better not to take the baby. He is not a year old yet, and old woman Liu tells me that the bones of his head have not yet grown together. He is very nervous, and, if we take him on such a long trip, I am afraid he will be frightened. We will leave him behind. The nurse and old woman Feng can stay at home and look after him so that his mother can go."

Ximen Qing would not agree. "Why are we going to the tombs of my ancestors at all?" he said. "I want both the baby and his mother to go and kowtow to my ancestors. You always believe everything that silly old woman tells you. If the baby's head is not strong enough, he must be wrapped up more carefully. He will be quite safe with his nurse in the sedan chair. There is nothing for you to worry about."

"Have it your own way," Yueniang said.

In the morning all the ladies came to Ximen Qing's house, and they started off together. They left the city by the southern gate, and, when they had gone about eight *li*, they could see the green pine trees that surrounded the tomb. There was the new gateway and the embankment on both sides. Stone walls encircled the tomb, and, in the middle, were the oratory and the way of the spirits. The perfume burners, candlesticks and utensils for the worship of the ancestral spirits were all of white alabaster. Over the gate was placed a new tablet that bore the inscription: "The Ancestral tombs of the valorous Commander Ximen." They went in and around beneath the interlaced branches of the trees. Ximen Qing, wearing his scarlet robes and girdle, set out the pigs, sheep, and food for the worship of his ancestors. First the gentlemen offered their worship, then the ladies. The musicians played. The baby was frightened and hid his face in his nurse's bosom. He whimpered, lying perfectly still.

"Sister," Yueniang whispered to Li Ping'er, "I should tell the nurse to take him away. Don't you see how terrified he is? I said we ought not to bring him, but his stupid father wouldn't listen to me. Now he is frightened into such a state."

Li Ping'er hurriedly told Daian to stop the beating of the drums and gongs. They covered the baby's ears and took him away.

After a time the service was ended. Master Xu read the oration and burned paper offerings. Then Ximen Qing invited the gentlemen to go to the front, and Yueniang invited the ladies to go to the back. They went through the gardens. There were pine trees and pine hedges, bamboos standing beside the paths, and many flowers and grasses.

Beneath the awning the actors played for the ladies, while four young actors entertained the gentlemen, playing instruments and singing in the great hall. Four singing girls served wine in turn for the gentlemen, and the four maids for the ladies. Then they stood at Ximen Dajie's table and had soup and cakes.

Pan Jinlian, Meng Yulou and Ximen Dajie went with Li Guijie and Wu Yin'er to the garden and played on the swings there. Behind the arbor, Ximen had arranged three rooms with furniture and beds, curtains, and things for the toilet. Here, the ladies might dress when they came to visit the tombs. The rooms were covered with paper so white that they seemed like caves of snow. Pictures and scrolls adorned the walls. To this place the nurse, Ruyi'er, brought the baby, and, on the gilded bed, the child lay upon a tiny blanket. Yingchun was there too, playing with the child. Jinlian, alone, came in from the garden, with peach flowers in her hand. When she saw Yingchun, she said: "So you are not attending to your duties in the hall."

"Chunmei, Lanxiang and Yuxiao are there," Yingchun said, "and my mistress told me to come here and look after the baby. I brought some cakes for the nurse."

The nurse welcomed Jinlian and stood up with the child. "Ah," Jinlian said, laughingly. "Ah, little oily mouth, the drums and the gongs frightened you. You're a brave young man, aren't you?" She opened her silken gown, took the child to her breast and kissed him.

Suddenly Chen Jingji pulled up the lattice and came in. When he saw Jinlian playing with the baby, he joined in the play too.

"Now, my young priest," Jinlian said, "let me see you kiss your brother-in-law."

Strangely enough, the child smiled at the young man. Jingji bent over and kissed him several times. Jinlian scolded him. Jingji smiled. "It is a good thing I didn't kiss the wrong person," he said.

Jinlian was afraid the nurse would hear him. She closed her fan and struck the young man. Jingji jumped like a fish. "I am not going to argue with you," Jinlian said.

"Very well," Jingji said, "but you ought to realize that I have feelings. I have only thin clothes on, and there was no need for you to hit me so hard."

"I have no intention of being kind to you," Jinlian said. "I shall hit you every time you offend me."

Ruyi'er saw them playing together and hastily took the child away from them. Jinlian and the young man laughed and joked together. She made the peach flowers into a garland and set it on his head without his noticing it. Jingji went out wearing it. Yulou, Ximen Dajie and Guijie met him. His wife looked at him. "Who did this?" she said. Jingji did not answer, but he took off the garland.

By this time four acts of the play had been performed, and it was beginning to grow dark. Ximen Qing told Ben the Fourth to give each of the chair men a cup of wine, four cakes, and a plate of cooked meat. When the chair men had eaten it, they took the ladies away. The servants followed on horseback. Laixing came with the cooks, bringing all the food boxes. Daian, Laian, Huatong and Qitong followed behind Yueniang's chair; Qintong, with four soldiers, followed behind Ximen Qing's horse. Ruyi'er had a small chair for herself and the baby, who was closely wrapped in bedclothes. Yueniang was still anxious about him and bade Huatong accompany the nurse's chair. She was afraid that they would find the streets very crowded when they came to the city.

When all the chairs had entered the city, those of the Qiao family went their own way. Yueniang reached home, but it was some time before Ximen Qing and Chen Jingji arrived.

When Ximen Qing dismounted, Ping'an said to him: "His Lordship Xia has been here and gone away. He sent messengers for you twice. I don't know what he wanted."

This made Ximen Qing thoughtful. He went to the great hall, where Shutong took his clothes. "What did his Lordship say when he was here?" Ximen asked the boy.

"He didn't say anything to me," Shutong said. "He only asked where you were. He suggested that I should go and ask you to come back because he had something very important to say to you. I told him that you had gone to the tombs to make offering to the dead and that you would be back this evening. He said he would come again. He has sent messengers twice, but I had to tell them you had not returned."

"What is this?" Ximen Qing said to himself.

He was thinking over the matter when Ping'an came and said Magistrate Xia had called once more. It was very dark. The magistrate was in plain clothes and had only two servants with him. When he entered the great hall, he greeted Ximen. "You have just returned from your glorious estate," he said. "Today I have been to worship at my ancestor's tombs," Ximen Qing said. "I ask your forgiveness for being absent when you called."

"I have come especially to bring you news," said Xia. "Shall we go into another room?"

Ximen Qing told Shutong to open the door, and they went in. He ordered all the servants to leave.

"This morning," Magistrate Xia said, "Li came to me and told me that the Censor has sent a report to the Eastern Capital accusing us both. I have had the document copied and here it is. Please read it."

Ximen Qing was alarmed. He paled. He took the paper to the lamp and read it. It said:

I, the Censor and Circuit Commissioner of Shandong, Ceng Xiaoxu, make accusation against certain rapacious and unworthy officials, and implore the Sacred Majesty to dismiss them that the dignity of the Law may be preserved.

I have been instructed that the duty of the Emperor is to go around the country and investigate the morals of the people. To check evil officials and enforce the law is the duty of the censors. In olden times it was written in the Book of Spring and Autumn that the Supreme Monarch went upon an inspection of the Empire and made the whole state subject to himself. So the morals of the people were improved and the exalted principle of the Ruler made manifest. The four peoples became obedient and all men recognized the rule of wisdom.

About a year ago the duty of going around all the districts of Shandong was entrusted to me. I have questioned the officials and found out the truth about the capacity of them all, whether military or civil. Now my tour of duty is almost at an end: I am continuing my investigations and would make report to Your Majesty. Especially would I, with Your Majesty's gracious permission, make the following accusations... .

Xia Yanling, captain of the Royal Guard and a principal magistrate in Shandong, is a man of no merit. He is rapacious and a man of evil conduct. People talk about his behavior and he is a disgrace to his position. Formerly, when he held office at the Capital, he committed many irregularities and was discovered by his subordinates. Now that he is employed in the courts of Shandong he is more rapacious than ever. He is always associating in evil with other officials. He has entered his son at the Military College by making false statements, and procured some other person to take the examination in his son's place, thus utterly demoralizing the students. He has allowed his servant Xia Shou to take bribes. The soldiers complain bitterly and his administration is extremely disorganized. When this Xia receives officers visiting his district, his face is as that of a slave and his knees as those of a maid. For this reason the people call him "Maid." When he investigates a case, his judgment is always uncertain, and his underlings call him "Wooden Image."

His Deputy, Captain Ximen Qing, was originally a street-corner lounger. He obtained his position by bribery and has thus improperly secured military rank. He cannot even distinguish between the flail and the corn. He cannot read a single character. He allows his wife and his concubines to play in the streets, and there have been scandals in his household. He drinks with singing girls in wineshops, and has disgraced the official class to which he belongs. Recently he has been associating with the wife of a certain Han Daoguo. He gives himself up completely to a dissolute life and cares nothing about his conduct. He took bribes from a certain Miao Qing and has irregularly allowed that fellow to escape the justice of the law. So Miao Qing's crime has never been punished.

These two rapacious and unworthy officers have long been the talk of the common people and they should be immediately dismissed from their posts. I pray Your Majesty to hear me, and instruct the Boards to examine these men closely. If it is found that what I have said is true, I pray Your Majesty to dismiss these two men. The morale of the service depends upon it. May the virtue of Your Majesty be glorious for ever and ever.

When he had finished reading this, Ximen Qing could only look at Magistrate Xia. He could find no words to say. "What shall we do?" said Xia.

"There is a proverb," Ximen Qing said, "that says: When soldiers come against us, we send out a general. When the flood comes, we build a dike. So, when in trouble, we must take steps to meet the situation. We must get ready presents and send them to the Imperial Tutor in the Eastern Capital."

Magistrate Xia hurried home and got ready two hundred taels of silver and two silver vases. Ximen prepared a chest full of gold, jade, and precious things, and three hundred taels of silver. Xia ordered his servant Shou, and Ximen his man Laibao, to take charge of these gifts. He had a letter written to the comptroller Zhai. The two men hired horses and went off, traveling as fast as they were able, to the Eastern Capital.

When the baby Guan'ge returned from the tomb, he cried all night and would not take his food. Everything he swallowed he disgorged again. Li Ping'er was alarmed. She came to Yueniang and told her.

"I said that a baby not a year old should not be taken outside the city," Yueniang said, "but the foolish man would not listen to me. He said the whole purpose of going to the tombs of his ancestors was that you and the child might offer worship there. He glared and shouted at me as if he were a savage. Now, what I anticipated has happened."

Li Ping'er did not know what to do.

Ximen Qing, after talking to Xia about the Censor's report, was getting the presents ready to send off. He felt very depressed about things in general. Now the baby was ill too.

Yueniang sent a boy for old woman Liu and also for a doctor who specialized in children's ailments. The gate was opened, and there was much shouting and running about all night. Old woman Liu said that the baby had been frightened and that he must have met the General of the Road. "It is of no great importance," she told them. " Burn a few paper offerings and we shall get rid of the devil, sure enough." She gave them two red pills, peppermint and lamp wick, and, when the baby had taken them, he quietened and went to sleep. He stopped crying and did not disgorge his milk any more. But the fever did not leave him. Li Ping'er gave old woman Liu a tael of silver for some papers. The old woman returned with her husband and another witch-woman. They burned the papers and danced the spirit dance in the arbor.

At the fifth night watch, Ximen Qing got up to see Laibao and Xia Shou away on their errand. Then he went to Magistrate Xia's, and together they went to Dongpingfu to Hu's place to hear what news there was of Miao Qing.

After Yueniang had been told that the baby had been frightened on the way home, she reproached Ruyi'er for not looking after the child properly. "He was frightened while he was in the sedan chair," she said. "If not, why should he not have got better?"

"I wrapped him up very carefully in the bedclothes," Ruyi'er said, "and he was not frightened. You sent Huatong to follow my chair, and he was all right then. It was only when we came into the city that he suddenly began to shiver. We were quite close to home. It was then he began to refuse his milk and to cry."

Laibao and Xia Shou made all the haste they could and reached the capital in six days. They went at once to the Imperial Tutor's palace, saw Comptroller Zhai, and handed over the presents to him. Zhai read Ximen Qing's letter. "The Censor's report has not yet reached the Capital," he said. "You had better stay here for a few days. The Imperial Tutor has recently sent a memorial to his Majesty that contains seven suggestions. This has not yet been returned. By the time it does return, perhaps the Censor's report will have arrived. I will warn his Eminence, and suggest that he should do no more than send the report to the Board of Military Affairs. Then I will send word to the Minister of War, Yu, and ask him to suppress it. Tell your master there is nothing to worry about. I can promise that nothing serious will come of the matter."

He entertained the two men. Then they went to their inn to rest and wait for further news.

One day, the Memorial of the Imperial Tutor Cai came back from the Court. Laibao asked one of the officers of the Imperial Tutor's household to copy it that he might take back a copy to Ximen Qing. Comptroller Zhai wrote a letter of thanks and gave Laibao five taels of silver. The two men went home again.

When they reached Qinghe, Ximen was living in a state of extreme anxiety. While they were away Magistrate Xia had been calling every day in the hope of hearing some news of their mission. The two men went at once to the inner court and Laibao gave Ximen an account of everything that had happened. "Master Zhai," he said, "read your letter, but he said there would be nothing very serious and certainly no need for you to be anxious. This Censor's tour of duty is nearly at an end and he will be succeeded by somebody else. His report has not yet reached the Capital, and, when it does, Master Zhai will speak to the Imperial Tutor and see that, however serious it may be, his Eminence sends it to the Board of Military Affairs. Zhai himself will go there and persuade the Minister to register it but not to let it go any further. So, no matter how serious the report may be, you will suffer no harm from it."

This was a great relief to Ximen Qing. He asked how it was that the Censor's report had not yet reached the Court. "When we went to the Capital," Laibao said, "we traveled posthaste and got there in five days. On our way back we met the couriers with the report. At least, we saw post-horses with bells and riders with yellow wrappers. The pennants bore pheasants' feathers."

"So long as the document reached the Capital after you did," Ximen said, "all will be well, but if you had been too late . . ."

"There is no need to worry," Laibao said. "I have other good news for you."

"What is that?" Ximen Qing asked.

"Recently, the Imperial Tutor sent a Memorial to the Emperor with seven suggestions that his Majesty will approve. The Imperial Tutor's relative Han, the Vice President of the Board of Domestic Affairs, proposes to open the salt monopoly in Shaanxi, and, in every district, to set up official granaries for the sale of rice. Wealthy people will pay their contribution of rice to these granaries and get their official receipt from them. The government will issue salt certificates. The old grain certificates will rate at seventy percent and the new ones at thirty. Some time ago, we and your relative Qiao put in to the excise office of Gao Yang thirty thousand grain certificates and thirty thousand salt certificates. The Board of Domestic Affairs has now appointed Cai, the President of the Academy, to be Salt Commissioner for the Two Huais. He is to leave the Capital shortly. He will certainly make an excellent inspector."

Ximen asked if this was true.

"If you do not believe me," Laibao said, "here is a copy of the document." He took a paper from a letter case and handed it to Ximen Qing. Ximen looked at it, and, as there were many unusual characters, sent for Chen Jingji to read it for him. Jingji read half of it, and then stopped. So many of the characters were strange to him. Then Shutong was sent for, and he read it with perfect ease from start to finish, for he had come from a wealthy household and had been well taught. The paper said:

The humble memorial of Cai Jing, Great Scholar of the Hall of Supreme Authority, Prime Minister, and Duke of Lu Guo.

These foolish suggestions are put forward that he may expend his futile energies upon the securing of men of capacity; that an efficient administration may be secured; the financial state of the country strengthened, and the welfare of the people fostered.

Thus may the glory of the Imperial Wisdom be made manifest:

**First**: the public examinations should be abolished and men should be given appointments direct from the colleges.

**Second**: the hitherto existing Board of Finance should be abolished.

**Third**: the present trade in salt should be done away with.

**Fourth**: the promulgation of a law upon coining.

**Fifth**: the buying and selling of cereals should be placed upon a sound footing.

When Ximen Qing had heard this and had read Comptroller Zhai's letter again, he knew that his present had been safely delivered, and that President Cai had been appointed Salt Commissioner, and would pass through Qinghe on his way to assume office. He was delighted. He sent Xia Shou home to give the news to Magistrate Xia, and gave Laibao five taels of silver, two jars of wine and a piece of meat. Then Laibao went to his place to rest.

# Chapter 49
# The Monk from India

Xia Shou went home and told his master the news. Then Magistrate Xia came to Ximen Qing and thanked him. "You have saved my life," he said. "Without your influence and your authority, I should have been in a very grave position."

Ximen Qing laughed. "Do not mention it. We did nothing wrong and, though the Censor spoke harshly about us, the Imperial Tutor will arrange everything." He entertained his guest in the great hall. They laughed and talked, and it was evening before Xia went home. The next day they both went to their office and attended to their duties as before.

Censor Ceng saw that, though his report had reached the Court, nothing happened. He understood that bribery had been at work, and was very indignant. He knew, moreover, that the five suggestions of the Imperial Tutor would lead to serious trouble. They would work to the detriment of the common people and the advantage of the officials. So he went himself to the Capital to put his case before the Emperor, and presented a memorial suggesting that it was well for the country that money should circulate instead of being collected and hoarded in the Capital. The new method of dealing in foodstuffs he considered impracticable. The new coinage, in which each coin was worth ten pence, had many disadvantages, and free trade in salt ought not so frequently to be abolished. He pointed out that, when such raids are made upon the people's resources, the safety of the realm is endangered.

The Imperial Tutor was furious. He told the Emperor Huizong that the Censor was rebellious and undisciplined, that he was concerning himself unduly in matters of policy. He summoned Ceng to appear before the Board of Civil Service, which degraded him and made him Magistrate of Qingzhou in Shaanxi.

The Censor and Commissioner of Shaanxi, Song Pan, was the Imperial Tutor's brother-in-law. Cai Yu secretly ordered Song Pan to accuse Ceng. Ceng's servants were arrested and persuaded to bring false accusations against their master. His name was cut out of the roll and he was banished to the Salt Mountain. So did the Imperial Tutor get his revenge.

Ximen Qing told Han Daoguo and Cui Ben to go with Master Qiao's nephew and take the grain certificates to the officer of the Board of Domestic Affairs at Gaoyangguan and register them. Laibao stayed at home to attend to the preparations for a great banquet. He also went to find out whether there was any word of the arrival of the Salt Commissioner's boat.

One day Laibao heard that Cai and Song had started together from the Capital and had now reached Dongchangfu. He brought the news to Ximen Qing, and Ximen invited Magistrate Xia to accompany him. Laibao had already visited the Commissioner on his boat and presented some gifts. Ximen Qing and Xia journeyed for fifty *li* to receive the notables at the new wharf at Bojiacun. They went on board the boat and told Cai that they would like to invite his colleague Song. Cai agreed and said that it was their intention to visit the office of the prefecture together.

Hu, the magistrate of Dongpingfu, and all his officers, military and civil, from all the districts; the scholars, Buddhist and Daoist priests, and the Masters of the Yin Yang were present to welcome the notables. They sent in their cards. Major Zhou, General Jing, and Zhang, the Captain of Militia, with horses and men, attended in full state. People were sent in advance to spread the news, and even the chickens and ducks kept out of the way. There was music to welcome Song when he entered the prefectural office at Dongpingfu. The officers presented their credentials. Song spent the night resting and, the next day, the gatekeeper came to inform him that the Salt Commissioner had come to visit him.

Censor Song immediately came out to receive him. They greeted one another and took the places proper to host and guest.

"How long do you propose to stay here?" said Song.

"I shall probably stay a day or two," Cai said. "I have a friend at Qinghe, a certain Captain Ximen, a man of excellent character, wealthy but modest. He is under the protection of the Imperial Tutor, and that is how I know him. He was good enough to come a very long way to meet me and I am going to stay with him a while."

"What rank does this Ximen hold?" Song asked.

"He is a junior magistrate," Cai said. "One of those who came to pay their respects to you yesterday."

Song ordered a servant to bring him all the visiting cards. Among them he found the names of Ximen and Xia. "Is not this the man who is a friend of Zhai the Comptroller?" he said.

"Yes," Cai said. "As a matter of fact, he is outside now. He asked me to invite you to take dinner with him."

"As the Censor for this place," said Song, "I am afraid it would be hardly becoming for me to accept."

"Why should you be afraid?" said Cai. "Our friend Zhai would like it. What harm is there in it?"

They called for their sedan chairs and made ready to start together. As soon as their order for the sedan chairs came out, word was brought to Ximen Qing. He, Laibao and Ben the Fourth rode home in great haste to make everything ready for the banquet. Awnings had already been set up outside the gate, forming a gaily decorated reception room. Two bands of musicians had been engaged and actors and other performers were in attendance.

Censor Song did not bring all his attendants, only a few men with blue pennants to clear the way, and a few officers. He and Cai seated themselves in two large sedan chairs; attendants carrying huge umbrellas accompanied them, and so they came to Ximen Qing's house.

Everybody in Dongpingfu knew of this visit, and it was especially remarked at Qinghe. Word went from mouth to mouth that the Censor was a friend of Ximen Qing and was coming to visit him at his house. The military officers, Zhou, Jing, and Zhang, were greatly excited, and sent soldiers, both horse and foot, to take post at each end of the street. Ximen Qing dressed in black robes, wearing his ceremonial girdle, went a considerable distance to meet his guests. Then the musicians began to play, the sedan chairs reached the gate. The two officers got down from their chairs. Both wore scarlet embroidered clothes, ceremonial hats and boots, and red girdles like a stork's beak. Attendants followed them, bearing two large fans.

The bamboo lattices were rolled high, and embroidered screens were placed in the great hall where the two guests were to be received. At the upper end two tables were set with delicacies and sweetmeats of the most delectable variety. The two officers bowed one to the other before they entered, and, when they went in, they made a reverence to Ximen Qing. Cai summoned his servant to offer the presents he had brought for Ximen. There were two rolls of silk, a case of collected works of literature, four parcels of tender tea shoots, and an ink slab of Duanxi stone. Song presented a red visiting card on which was written: "The respectful compliments of Song Qiaonian."

"The Lanxiang of your name has long been known to me," Song said. "I have only just come to this place and I am ashamed to appear before you without some offering. My brother Cai urged me to come, however, and, but for him, I should not have had the pleasure of seeing your glorious countenance."

Ximen Qing fell upon his knees. "Your humble servant," he said, "is but a plain soldier, one subject to your commands. It is an honor to receive from you a visit which brings enlightenment to this poor hovel." He rose and bowed with the utmost politeness, and Censor Song returned his greeting.

Then Cai invited his companion to take the place of honor and took the seat beside him. Ximen respectfully seated himself with them. When they had drunk their tea, the musicians played and the drums were beaten. Ximen Qing offered his guests wine, and set places before the table. Servants carried in the food. The banquet surpassed all powers of description. Music, songs, dances and splendor seemed to be crowded within the confines of a tiny space, and there was a marvelous abundance of refreshment. To the servants of the two censors, Ximen gave fifty bottles of wine, five hundred cakes and a hundred measures of cooked meat, and these were taken away. The subordinate officers were entertained in other rooms. That day Ximen Qing expended a thousand taels of silver.

Censor Song was a native of Nanchang in Jiangxi, a volatile fellow. He did not stay long, and listened to but one act of the play. Then he stood up. Ximen Qing pressed him to stay, and Cai also tried to persuade him. "Brother," he said, "unless you have business to attend to, why not stay a little longer? Why go away so soon?"

"Brother," said Song, "you stay. I must go to my office and see about various matters."

Ximen Qing had bidden his servants pack two complete services of gold and silver in food boxes. There were twenty such boxes. For Song there was a whole set for the table, two jars of wine, two sheep, two pairs of golden flowers, two rolls of red silk, a set of gold dishes, two silver wine pots, ten silver wine cups, two small silver jars and a pair of ivory chopsticks. There was an exactly similar set for Cai. Ximen Qing presented his list of gifts.

"I dare not accept such a present," Song said. He looked at Cai.

"Brother," said Cai, "this is your sphere of jurisdiction, and it is right and proper that you should accept. But, for me, the case is different.'"

"They are but trifles," Ximen Qing said, "so that you may drink a cup of wine. Why treat the matter as one of ceremony?"

The two officers still hesitated, but the boxes were taken away and Song could only end by accepting them.

"I have never had the pleasure of meeting you before," he said, "yet you have entertained me nobly and given me this valuable present. I do not know how I can return such kindness, but I will endeavor to do so by degrees," He said to Cai: "Brother, I must go now, but do you stay here." Then he started. Ximen Qing would have taken him well on his way, but Song begged him not to do so, bowed, and got into his chair. Ximen Qing went back to Cai. They removed their robes of ceremony and went to sit under the arbor. The musicians were sent away and only the actors remained. Ximen called for food, and rare dishes and fruits were set before them. They settled down to enjoy their wine.

"Brother Song and I have visited you today," Cai said. "That was pleasure enough for us, but for all this excellent entertainment and the rest I don't know how to thank you."

Ximen Qing smiled. "I only fear that everything has been too poor for you. All I could do was but a slight indication of my feelings." Then he said: "What is his Lordship's honorable title?"

"His name is Songquan," Cai said. "He would not have come today, but I told him you were under the protection of the Prime Minister and he decided to come. He knows that you and Zhai are connected."

"My relative Zhai must have spoken to him," Ximen Qing said. "I must say his manner seems to me a little strange."

"He is from Jiangxi," Cai said, "but I don't think there is anything strange about him. Perhaps the first time he meets you he thinks he must stand on his dignity." He smiled.

"It is getting late," Ximen said, "and you cannot return to your boat tonight."

"The boat sails tomorrow morning," Cai said.

"Stay the night here," Ximen said, "and tomorrow I will take you to your boat."

"You are very kind indeed," Censor Cai said. He dismissed all his servants but two, bidding the others come for him the following morning.

When Ximen saw that they had gone, he whispered to Daian and told him to go to the bawdy house for Dong Jiao'er and Han Yuchuan. "Bring them in by the back door," he said, "and don't let anyone see you." The boy went away. Ximen returned to the table and drank wine with the Censor. The actors sang for them.

"How long did you stay at home?" Ximen asked, "and how is your lady mother?"

"My old mother is very well. I stayed about six months; then I went back to the Court. Unfortunately an accusation was brought against me by Cao He. I and thirteen others were brought before the Academy of History, and we were all reduced to provincial rank. That is how I came to be appointed Salt Commissioner. Song is a favorite of the Imperial Tutor."

"Where is venerable Master An now?" Ximen Qing said.

"An Fengshan has been appointed to the Board of Works," Cai said. "He has gone to Qingzhou as Superintendent of the Imperial Forests. That is quite a good post for him."

Ximen Qing called for the actors. When they had served wine, he asked them to sing "The Fisherman's Pride." While they were singing, Daian came and asked Ximen to go out and speak to him. "Dong Jiao'er and Han Yuchuan are here," he said. "They are in the Great Lady's room."

"Tell the sedan chair men to take the chairs away," said Ximen. Daian told him that he had already done this. Then Ximen went to his wife's room. The two singing girls kowtowed to him.

"Today," Ximen said to them, "I want you to wait upon his Excellency Cai. He is both Censor and Commissioner of Salt. If you are careful what you are about, he will certainly make you a handsome present."

Yuchuan laughed. "You need not be so explicit. We understand."

"He is a Southerner," Ximen Qing said, "and likes things done in the Southern style. You must not be too shy with your hands and feet."

"Mother," Dong Jiao'er said to Wu Yueniang, "do you hear that? Father is like one of those ram's-horn onions that is planted against a southern wall and grows hotter and hotter. We are to kowtow before a royal palace, but we mustn't drink the water in the well."

Ximen Qing laughed and went back to the outer court. When he came to the second door, he met Laibao and Chen Jingji with a visiting card. They gave the card to him and said: "Your relative, Master Qiao, says that if his Excellency the Censor is not engaged now will you please speak about this matter to him. He supposes that his Excellency will be going away tomorrow, and asked us to write this card." Ximen Qing told Laibao to go with him. The man waited outside the window of the arbor.

Ximen drank with Cai. After a while he said: "There is a little business I should like to mention, but I hesitate to trouble you."

"Tell me anything that is in your mind," said Cai. "Your commands shall be obeyed, whatever they may be."

"Last year," Ximen said, "one of my relatives paid the rice tribute and was given some salt certificates. He was appointed Collector at Yangzhou, within your jurisdiction. It would be very kind of you, when you take up your appointment, if you would let them have their salt a little earlier." He handed to Censor Cai the paper that Laibao had brought. It said: 'Laibao and Cui Ben are entitled to 30,000 *yin* of salt. May it be granted them as early as possible.' Censor Cai smiled.

"This is a trifle," he said, "I should like to see Laibao." Ximen Qing summoned Laibao to kowtow to the Censor. "When I get to Yangzhou," Cai said, "come to my office, and I will see that the matter is settled one month earlier for you than for anyone else."

"It is very kind of you," Ximen said, "but ten days would be quite sufficient."

Cai put the paper in his sleeve. Shutong served wine and the actors sang again. When the song was over, it was getting late. "I have burdened you for a whole day," Cai said, "and I must not drink any more." He stood up. The servants were about to light the lamps, but Ximen Qing stopped them.

"I am going to take his Excellency to the inner court to change his clothes," he said. He took Cai to the garden. They looked around it for a while, then Ximen took his guest to the Hall of the Kingfisher. The lattice was rolled down, candles were burning brightly, and wine and refreshments had been set out.

Ximen Qing dismissed the actors. Shutong saw that everything was cleared away in the arbor, and the corner gate was closed. The two singing girls, beautifully dressed, came to the steps and kowtowed four times to the Censor.

> Their faces so charming, their dresses gold embroidered
> They do not trouble the fragrant dust
> As they come down the stairs.
> With water splashes still wet upon their silken skirts
> As though they were just back from Wu Mountain
> Where they had brought the rain.

Cai seemed dumbfounded when he saw them. "You are too kind to me," he said. "This is indeed too much."

Ximen Qing smiled. "It is not very different," he said, "from that entertainment that once there was upon the Eastern Mountains."

"I fear I have not the learning of Wang Anshi," Cai said, "though you, Sir, have the elevated sensibilities of Wang Yuzhun." In the moonlight he took the hands of the two singing girls, feeling as excited as Liu Yuan at the Tiantai. They went into the Hall of the Kingfisher. Writing materials were lying there and, taking paper and brush, Cai prepared to write a poem to give to the girls. Ximen Qing told Shutong to take the ink slab, grind some thick ink, and arrange the flower-patterned paper. His Excellency was possessed of the accomplishments becoming his position. Taking the brush, he wrote without any hesitation, the characters springing like dragons beneath it. Under the lamplight he finished the poem without once stopping.

> Six months have passed since last I visited you
> But brush and paper wait for me in this room.
> The rain is over. Shutong is tending the sweet-smelling herbs
> The wind has changed. An angel walks among the flower beds.
> When I would drink my fill, the bells ring urgently
> When I have written my poem, the night watch will call me away
> But when I go from you, I must expect new sorrow
> I know not when I shall return.

When Cai had finished this poem, he bade Shutong put it on the wall in memory of his visit. Then he asked the names of the two girls. One said: "My name is Dong Jiao'er," and the other: "My name is Han Yuchuan." Then Cai asked them by what familiar names they were called. "We are but humble girls," Dong Jiao'er said, "it would not befit us to have familiar names." But the Censor pressed them, and at last Han Yuchuan said: "Mine is Yuqing [Treasure of Jade]." Dong Jiao'er said: "Mine is Weixian [Fairy of the Purple Flower]." The last one delighted Cai particularly, and he did not forget it. He asked Shutong to bring the chess pieces and played a game with Dong Jiao'er. Ximen Qing looked on while Yuchuan served the wine and Shutong sang. The Censor won, and Dong Jiao'er had to drink a cup of wine, but first she offered one to the victor. At the same time Han Yuchuan offered a cup to Ximen Qing. They played a second game. This time Dong Jiao'er won, and she quickly offered wine to the Censor. Ximen drank again.

Then Cai said: "It is late and I can drink no more." They went out and stood for a while amid the flowers. It was the middle of the fourth month, and the moon had just risen.

"It is still early," Ximen Qing said, "and Han Yuchuan has not offered wine to you yet."

"That is true," the Censor said. "Let her bring a cup here, and I will drink it among the flowers."

Han Yuchuan brought a large gold cup shaped like a peach blossom and offered it with her slender fingers. Dong Jiao'er stood beside her with a dish of fruit. The Censor drank his wine and offered a cup to Dong Jiao'er. Then he said to Ximen Qing: "I have indeed taken too much wine. Will you not ask your servants to clear away?" He took Ximen Qing's hand. "You show me so much kindness," he said, "that my mind is confused. If you had not been by nature a scholar, you could not have been so kind. I have not forgotten the loan you made me a few months ago. I told the Comptroller all about it, and, if it should happen that promotion comes to me, I shall never dare to forget your generosity."

"Please do not mention it," Ximen Qing said. "Think no more of it."

Han Yuchuan saw the Censor holding Dong Jiao'er 's hand. She knew what this meant and went to the inner court. When she came to the Upper Room, Yueniang said to her: "Why did you not stay?" Han Yuchuan smiled.

"He has Dong Jiao'er," she said. "I was not wanted any longer." A little later, Ximen Qing said good night to the Salt Commissioner and came in. He told Laixing to prepare food, wine, cakes and dishes, and, the next morning before dawn, to go with the cooks to the Temple of Eternal Felicity, where they would take leave of his Excellency. He must not forget the two young actors.

"But tomorrow is the Second Lady's birthday," Laixing said, "and there are not enough people to attend to things at home."

"Let Qitong buy the things," Ximen said. "The cooks must use the large oven."

Shutong and Daian cleared everything away and took a pot of excellent tea to Cai in the garden. In the Hall of the Kingfisher, the bed and furniture were arranged to perfection. Cai saw that Dong Jiao'er was carrying a speckled bamboo fan of gilded paper. On it was painted in black ink a picture of orchids growing beside a rivulet. She asked him to write a poem upon it for her. "I can't think what to write," he said. "I had better take your other name, Fairy of the Purple Flower." Taking up a brush, he wrote four columns upon the fan.

> All is still and silent in the courtyard
> The moonbeams cast their light upon the windows.
> They meet, so chance has ordered, and the night is early
> He of the purple shrub and the maid of purple blossom.

Dong Jiao'er made a reverence to the Censor and thanked him. They went to bed. Shutong, Daian and his Excellency's servants slept in a room near by.

The next morning the Censor gave Dong Jiao'er a tael of silver wrapped in red paper. She took it to the inner court and showed it to Ximen Qing. Ximen smiled. "He is a civil officer, and, of course, could not make you a very large present. This is as high a mark as you can expect." He told Yueniang to give each of the girls five *qian* of silver and let them out by the back way. Shutong brought water and aided his master to dress. Then Ximen Qing went to the great hall and ate rice gruel with Censor Cai.

Cai's servants came with horses and a sedan chair. He said good-bye to Ximen Qing and thanked him repeatedly.

"Please do not forget the matter of which I spoke to you yesterday," Ximen said. "I will write to you when you reach your post. And I am greatly obliged to you."

"There is no need to write," Cai said. "Send a servant with a blank sheet of paper and I will do anything you ask."

They mounted their horses and, followed by their attendants, went as far as the Temple of Eternal Felicity. There they lunched in the Abbot's parlor. Laixing and the cooks had made all kinds of preparations and the two young actors, Li Ming and Wu Hui, were waiting. They drank a few cups of wine together and Cai stood up. The horses and sedan chair were waiting outside the gate. Ximen Qing spoke to him about the

Miao Qing affair. "Miao Qing," he said, "is a friend of mine who was falsely accused by the late censor. The papers for his arrest have been sent to Yangzhou. The case has already been settled here, so, if you should see his Excellency Song in Yangzhou, please speak in his favor. I shall be very grateful to you."

"Do not worry," Cai said. "When I see my brother Song, I will ask him to free Miao Qing if he should be arrested." Ximen Qing bowed and thanked him.

> Justice and friendship lie in opposing camps
> Friendship and justice cannot be reconciled.
> He who deals justly, loses all his friends
> He who to friendship yields, abandons justice.

(Some time later, when Censor Song was going to Jinan, he happened to be traveling on the same boat with Cai. The officers arrested Miao Qing, but Cai said to his friend: "This is an affair that goes back to Censor Ceng's administration. Why should you do anything about it?" So Miao Qing was set at liberty and orders were sent to Dongpingfu that the two boatmen were to be executed at once, and the boy Antong allowed to go.)

Ximen Qing would have gone all the way to the boat with Cai, but the Censor asked him not to do so. "Pray do not come any farther," he said. "We will part here."

"Take great care of yourself," Ximen Qing said. "I shall send my servant for news of you."

Cai got into his sedan chair and was carried away. Ximen Qing went back to the Abbot's rooms and the Abbot came to make reverence to him and offer tea. Ximen returned the greeting. He saw that the Abbot's eyebrows were white as snow. "Venerable Sir," he said, "how old are you?"

"The humble monk before you," replied the Abbot, "is seventy-four years of age."

"You seem very strong," Ximen said, and asked his name in religion.

"My name is Daojian," the Abbot said. Ximen asked how many novices the Abbot had.

"No more than two now," the Abbot said, "but there are more than thirty wandering priests in my temple."

"Your temple," Ximen Qing said, "is very large and spacious, but it seems to need repair."

"The truth is," the Abbot said, "that this temple was built by the venerable Zhou Xiu, but we have no fixed endowment, and it is almost utterly ruined now."

"So your temple belongs to Major Zhou? I remember now that his estate is quite close. You ought to ask him to open a subscription. I should be glad to help."

Daojian made a reverence and thanked him. Ximen Qing told Daian to give the Abbot a tael of silver. "I have given you much trouble today," he said. The Abbot apologized for the inadequacy of his preparations. Then Ximen told the priest that he would like to go to the inner court to change his clothes. Daojian told one of his novices to open the door. Behind the Abbot's quarters, Ximen found a large hall, as large as five rooms. A number of wandering monks were chanting from their sacred books and beating their wooden fish. Ximen looked around the hall. There was one monk of very curious appearance. His head was like a leopard's and his eyes were round. His color was that of purple liver, and upon his head he wore a cock's crest. His tattered robe was flesh-colored; his shaggy beard all matted together. By all seeming he might have been a veritable Arhat, a fiery-tempered dragon. He was lying upon the bench of contemplation, his head bowed and his shoulders hunched upon his chest. The stream of matter from his nostrils looked like chopsticks of jade.

Ximen Qing thought that this must certainly be a wonder-working monk, so unusual was his appearance. "I will arouse him," he said to himself, "and question him." Then, in a loud voice, he said to the holy man: "Where do you come from? Where is your monastery?" There was no answer. He repeated his questions, but still there was no reply. He asked a third time, and now the monk came down from the bench of contemplation, stretched himself, put forth a hand and straightened his body, and opened one eye. He made a slight inclination of the head to Ximen Qing and said in a hoarse voice:

"Why do you ask me these questions? I am only a poor monk. My name is everywhere the same. I come from a foreign land, from the deep pine forests of India, from the temple of the Frozen Mansions. I roam about the world, dispensing remedies to give ease to men. What would you say to me?"

"Since you have remedies to give ease to men," Ximen Qing said, "I should be glad to have something that would inspire me with new ardor. Have you any such medicine?"

"I have," the Indian Monk said.

"I should like to ask you to come to my house," Ximen Qing said. "Will you come?"

"I will come. I will come."

"If you are willing," Ximen Qing said, "let us start at once."

The Indian Monk rose, took his iron staff and a long leathern bag in which were two gourds of medicine, and they went out of the great hall. Ximen told Daian to bring two donkeys and bade him ride together with the monk.

"Not so," said the monk. "You go first on your horse. I need no animal on which to ride, but I shall be there before you."

"This must indeed be a wonder-working monk," Ximen said to himself, "or he would not make such rash promises." He was afraid the monk might go somewhere else, and told Daian to accompany him. He took leave of the Abbot and mounted his horse, and all his servants followed him. It was the seventeenth day of the fourth month, Wang Liu'er's birthday. It was also the birthday of Li Jiao'er, and a few ladies had come to congratulate her.

In the afternoon Wang Liu'er sent her brother Wang Jing to ask Ximen Qing to go and see her. She had no one else to send. "Go and look out for Daian," she told him, "and, if you do not see him, wait outside the gate."

Wang Jing waited at the gate. When he had waited two hours or so, Wu Yueniang and Li Jiao'er came out with old woman Li. Yueniang, seeing a small boy about fifteen years old, asked him what he wanted.

"I have come from the Han household to see my brother An," he said.

"Which brother An?" Yueniang asked.

Ping'an was standing near, and, fearing lest Yueniang should discover that the boy came from Wang Liu'er, he went forward and pushed him aside.

"He has come from Han Daoguo," he said. "He wants to see Daian to find out when Han is to come."

Yueniang was deceived. She said no more and went back into the house. Then Daian and the Indian Monk came to the gate. Daian's legs were very weary and his whole body was covered with sweat. He was in a very bad way, but the Indian Monk was perfectly comfortable and did not even puff. Ping'an told Daian about the visit from Wang Jing. "The Great Lady saw him, but, fortunately, I was here, and passed the matter over. Otherwise the cat would have been out of the bag. If Mother asks you any questions tell her the same story that I did."

Daian opened his eyes wide and fanned himself. "My luck is certainly out today," he said. "Father told me to bring this bald rascal home with me and we have walked all the way from the temple without stopping. I can hardly breathe. Father said we were to take two donkeys, but the monk would not hear of it. It is all very well for him to walk that long way, but my poor legs have certainly suffered. The soles are torn off my boots and my feet are torn too. What a dirty business!" "What does Father want with him?" Ping'an said.

"Who knows?" Daian said. "Perhaps he hopes to get some medicine out of him."

As they were talking, they heard the sound of the attendants clearing the way. Ximen Qing arrived. When he found the monk already there, he said: "Master, you are indeed a wonder worker to get here before I did." He asked the monk to go into the great hall. Ximen Qing gave his clothes to Shutong and changed his hat. He sat down with the monk, and they drank tea. The Indian Monk gazed around the great hall and saw how deep and spacious it was; how large and quiet the courtyard. Over the door hung a bamboo lattice made of shrimps' feelers with a tortoiseshell design. The floor was covered with rugs, with a pattern of lions rolling balls. In the middle of the hall was a table colored black, with dragonflies on the legs and the praying mantis upon the edges. There was a marble screen upon the table, with a fretted pattern and a base shaped like a mountain. Around it were several large cedar chairs, substantial and heavy, with eels' heads for decoration. The pictures on the walls were hung on purple rods bound with silk. The ends of the rolls were of cornelian.

When the Indian Monk had looked around him, Ximen Qing said to him: "Master, do you drink wine?"

"I drink wine and eat meat," the monk said.

Ximen sent a boy to the kitchen to tell them not to prepare vegetarian dishes but to bring wine and food. As it was Li Jiao'er's birthday, all kinds of food were already prepared. A table was set and the food brought. There were three or four plates of fruits, four smaller and four larger dishes to accompany the wine. There was one dish of fish head, one of preserved duck, one of chicken and one of sea perch. Then four dishes to be eaten with rice, one of little nuts of meat roasted with ram's-horn onions, one of little pasties of finely minced meat, shaped like a periwinkle, one of plump sausages, and one of bright and slippery eels. Then soup was brought. In the soup were two balls of meat and a garnished sausage between them. This soup was known as "The Dragon playing with two pearls." Then there was a great dish of stuffed buns with little openings at the top.

Ximen Qing asked the monk to eat, and bade Qintong bring a jar of wine with a round handle, a beak-shaped mouth and a neck like that of a chicken. The boy opened a large jar that had come from Yaozhou. From it he poured a tiny stream of wine as white as snow, extremely fortifying. He poured it into a high-stemmed cup shaped like a lotus upside down. He handed the cup to the Indian Monk, who took it and emptied it at one draft. More dishes were brought, one of sausages about an inch long, one of preserved goose neck. There were fruits for the monk to eat with his wine, grapes mottled as though they had the pox and red plums juicy at the center. Finally a great bowl of noodles and eels with vegetables.

The monk gobbled everything up till his eyes almost stood out of his head. Then he said: "I have had enough." Ximen Qing told a boy to clear away the table. Then he asked the monk to give him some medicines to enhance his skill in the arts of love.

"I have one medicine made by Laozi, to whom the Queen Mother of the West gave the secret. None are able to secure this medicine but those of whom I think well. You have been kind to me and I will give you a few pills." He took a gourd from his long bag and emptied about a hundred pills. "Take one on each occasion," he said, "but no more. Take it with a drop of spirits." He opened the other gourd and took from it some red powder about two *qian*'s weight. "Every time you use it," said the monk, "take two grains and no more. Should you feel a burning sensation, take your weapon in your hand and stroke your thighs a hundred times or so. Then all will be well. Be judicious in your use of these remedies and give none to anyone else."

Ximen Qing took the medicines in both hands. "Tell me," he said, "what is the merit of this medicine?"

> Shaped like an egg
> Yellow like a duck
> In three successive processes Laozi prepared it
> At the bidding of the Queen Mother.
> To him who glances at it heedlessly
> It seems like earth or dung
> But, when its merits are known, its worth is more than jewels.
> No gold will buy it
> And jade is valueless compared with it.
> Though you are girt with gold and robed in purple
> Though you are dressed in sable
> And ride upon the plumpest chargers,
> Though you uphold the pillars of the state
> Take but a speck of this, set it upon you, then
> Rush like a whirlwind to the bridal chamber
> There you will find spring always young
> All will be bright and gay.
> There will be no ruins on the jade mountain
> And the moonbeams will shine bright upon your window.
> The first engagement will leave you full of vigor
> The second, even stronger than before.
> Though twelve exquisite beauties, all arrayed in scarlet, wait your onset,
> You may enjoy each one, according to your fancy

And, all night through, erect your spear will stand.
Soon, new strength will be given to limbs and belly
It will refresh the testicles, invigorate the penis.
In a hundred days, hair and beard will be black once more
In a thousand days, your body will know its power.
Your teeth will be strong, your eyes more bright,
Your manhood stiffened. Then at the first planting
The seed will germinate.
I fear that this may seem beyond belief.
Pray try the medicine on the cat.
After three days he'll burn with fire
Four days will see him quite beyond control
And, if a white cat, he will soon be black
Then cease to piss and shit, and so will die.

Though in the summer you may sleep exposed
And in the winter plunge yourself in water
Yet, if you cannot keep your bowels free
Your hair you'll surely lose.

Each time, take but a grain or so.
Your weapon will be merciless.
Ten women in one night will be as one to you
You'll feel no slackening of vital power.
The old woman will knit her brows
The young one's strength will hardly stay the course.

When you are sated, and would give up the fight
Swallow a mouthful of cold water. Then withdraw your weapon
You will not be harmed.
In pleasure and enjoyment you will spend your nights
The joys of spring will fill the orchid chamber.
I make this gift only to those
Who worthily appreciate its qualities.
Take it, I pray, and may your manly vigor flourish evermore.

Ximen Qing listened. When the old monk had done, he asked for the recipe. "When I send for a doctor," he said, "I insist upon having a good one, and, when I have medicine, I like to know what it's made of. When I have finished it, and can't get any more from you, it will be most awkward. I don't mind how much you ask, you shall have it." He said to Daian:

"Go to the back and bring thirty taels of white gold." He offered the gold to the monk and again asked for the recipe. The monk laughed.

"I am a poor monk," he said, "and I roam all over the world. Gold is valueless to me. Keep your money." He rose and prepared to go away.

Ximen Qing saw that he would not get the recipe from the old man. He said: "If you will not take my gold, let me offer you a roll of cloth, fifteen feet long, to make a habit for yourself." He bade a servant bring a roll and presented it to the Indian Monk with both hands. The monk thanked him and made a reverence. Before he went away, he cautioned Ximen Qing, telling him not to take more than the proper dose. Then he picked up his long bag and his staff, went out of the door, and mysteriously disappeared.

# CHAPTER 50
# The Indian Monk's Medicine

Before she drew the perfumed curtains
And settled to the work of love,
Her brows were knit in sadness at the thought
The night would be so short.
She bade her lover hasten to the bed
And warm the silk-embroidered coverlets.
Then was their love as that of butterflies and bees.
They stripped themselves: their passion knew no bounds.
She left the lamp to burn beside the curtains
That he from time to time might gaze
Upon the beauty of her face.

It was the birthday of Li Jiao'er. Nun Wang came from the temple of Guanyin, bringing with her Nun Xue from the Temple of Lotus Blossoms. With them came two young novices, Miaofeng and Miaoqu. Wu Yueniang had been told that Xue was deeply versed in matters of religion and hastened to welcome her. The nun was wearing a religious hat, and a long robe the color of tea leaves. Her hair was tonsured. She was very stout and big. Her mouth was like that of a fish; her cheeks like those of a pig. When she came in, she made reverence to Yueniang and the others; and Yueniang and the others returned her greeting. The nun raised her eyebrows, closed her eyes, put on all sorts of airs, and spoke in an extremely affected voice. The ladies addressed her as "Noble Xue." She, in return, called Wu Yueniang Buddha of the Household or else My Lady. This made Yueniang think highly of her.

That day Aunt Wu and Aunt Yang had come to call and Yueniang entertained them so well that the tables overflowed. It was far beyond the ordinary range of entertainment.

The two novices, Miaofeng and Miaoqu, were no more than fourteen or fifteen years old, and they were very sedate. They were given something to eat and drink. Then everybody went to the upper room, and the ladies listened to a sermon from the nun.

Yueniang saw Shutong carrying things from the outer court and said to him: "Has that monk who eats meat and drinks wine gone yet?"

"Yes," Shutong said, "he has just gone. Father saw him to the door."

Aunt Wu asked: "Where did he meet that monk?"

"My husband went to see Censor Cai on his way," Yueniang said, "and he brought the monk back with him from the temple. He eats meat and drinks wine. My husband has been asking him for some medicine or other. The monk would take no money, and I have no idea how they got on with their business."

"The question of taking meat and wine is one of great delicacy," Nun Xue said. "Nuns generally observe the vow of abstinence, but monks do not seem to trouble much about it. As a matter of fact, the Scriptures say that, if we take but a mouthful of meat, we shall suffer for it in the next life."

"We eat meat every day," Aunt Wu said, "so we must be committing a great many sins."

"Oh, but it is different for you," the nun said. "You are able to enjoy meat as a reward for virtue in your last life. It is right and proper that you should enjoy both wealth and comfort. If plants are set in the ground in the spring, we may expect a harvest in the autumn."

Meanwhile, Ximen Qing had parted from the Indian monk and returned to his room. Daian whispered to him: "Aunt Han has sent her brother to ask you to go to her. It is her birthday today and she would very much like to see you."

Ximen Qing now had the medicine the monk had given him, and he desired nothing better than to try its effects. Wang Liu'er's invitation came at the right moment. He told Daian to prepare his horse and sent Qintong to the woman's house with a jar of wine. Then he went to Pan Jinlian's room for his case of instruments. Wearing plain clothes, with an ordinary hat and eyeshades, he rode to Wang Liu'er's house. When he got there, he told Qintong to stay and sent Daian back with the horse. "If anyone asks where I am," he told the boy, " say that I am going through the accounts at the house in Lion Street." Daian went back on his master's horse.

Wang Liu'er came out and kowtowed to Ximen Qing. Then she sat down beside him. "I only asked you to come that you might have some amusement," she said. "It was good of you to send the wine."

"I had forgotten that it is your birthday today," Ximen said. "I have been to say farewell to someone outside the city and have only this moment come back." He took a present from his sleeve and gave it to her. "I have brought you something," he said. The woman took the gift and examined it. It was a pair of gold pins with the lucky character *shou*.

"It is very pretty," Wang Liu'er said, and made a reverence to thank him. Ximen gave her five *qian* of silver and asked her to give a boy something and send him for a jar of Southern spirits. Wang Liu'er laughed. "Are you tired of ordinary wine," she said, "that you need Southern spirits?" But she hastened to give the boy five *fen* and sent him for the spirits. Then she took Ximen's cloak and asked him to go to the inner room. She made some excellent tea for him and set out a small table. They played dominoes for a while, then she warmed some wine.

Daian went home. He was very weary after walking so far with the monk. He went to sleep and slept till evening. Then he woke up, rubbed his eyes, and saw that it was late. He went to the inner court to get a lantern and make ready to go for Ximen Qing. But he stood there for a while without doing anything. Yueniang spoke to him. "Your father saw the monk to the door, but, instead of coming to change his clothes, he suddenly went out. Where did he go?"

"Father went to Lion Street to inspect the accounts," Daian said.

"He can't be inspecting accounts all day," said Yueniang.

"No," Daian said. "When he had finished the books, he had something to drink all by himself."

"All by himself, indeed!" Yueniang said. "You are lying. A boy came from Han Daoguo after him. What did he want?"

"The boy came to find out when Uncle Han would be here."

"You young rascal!" Yueniang said. "You are up to some trick or other."

Daian dared say no more. Yueniang told Xiaoyu to give him a lantern. "Tell your father," she said, "that the Second Lady is waiting for him to come and celebrate her birthday."

Daian went to the shop. Shutong and Clerk Fu were sitting behind the counter. On it were a bottle of wine, several dishes, and a plate of tripe. Ping'an came in bringing two jars of fish paste. "Excellent!" said Daian, putting down his lantern, "I have come just in time." Then he said jokingly to Shutong: "Ah, you naughty little strumpet. I have been looking everywhere for you, and you have been hiding here all this time, drinking."

"What did you want me for?" Shutong said. "Do you wish me to adopt you as my grandson for a while?"

"Little boy," Daian said, "would you bandy words with me? I was looking for you because I want to do some business with your behind." He pushed him onto the couch and kissed him, but the boy freed himself.

"You queer creature," he said, "I find it hard to scold you as I should like. Now you've hurt my mouth and knocked my hat off."

Clerk Fu saw Shutong's hat on the ground. "Why, that's a new hat," he said, and told Ping'an to pick it up before somebody stepped on it.

Shutong picked up the hat and threw it on a couch. His face was very red.

"Well, you strumpet," Daian said, "I was only playing with you. Why do you get so angry?" He dragged Shutong to the bed and spat in his mouth. They overturned the wine, and it was spilled on the counter. Clerk Fu was afraid it would stain the account books. He hastily found a cloth and dried it up.

"Don't play the fool any more," he said, "or you will get angry with one another."

"I don't know where this strumpet can have been brought up," Daian said, "to make him as stubborn as this." Shutong's hair was in disorder.

"A game is a game," he said, "but this is not a game. You have filled my mouth with your filthy spittle."

"Ah, you slave," said Daian, "this is not the first time you have swallowed such a liquid. You are always doing it, and who can tell how often?"

Ping'an heated some wine and gave it to Daian. "Drink this and go for our master. You can settle with him when you come back."

"Yes," Daian said, "wait for me. When I come back, I will have a word with you. Unless I make you see spirits and ghosts, you will think I am not to be feared. I shall spit on you again. I am the son of no human parents, so I can do whatever I like." He drank his wine, summoned two small boys to accompany him with the lantern, and himself rode on horseback. When he came to Wang Liu'er's house, he knocked at the door and asked Qintong where their master was. "He is asleep," said Qintong. They shut the gate and went to the kitchen.

There, old woman Feng said to him: "Your Aunt Han waited a long time for you, but you did not come. Here is your supper." She took from a cupboard a plate of ass's flesh, a dish of cold roast chicken, two bowls of birthday noodles, and a pot of wine.

Daian drank some wine. Then he said to Qintong: "Come here. I can't drink all this wine. You must drink some for me."

"It is yours," said Qintong. "Drink it yourself." Daian said he had already had some wine. The two boys finished it off together.

Then Daian said to old woman Feng: "If you will excuse me, there is something I should like to tell you. You are really attached to the household of our Sixth Lady and are supposed to work only for her. But I am always finding you here working for Aunt Han. I am afraid I shall have to tell the Sixth Lady."

The old woman cut him short. "Oh, you funny young monkey," she said. "You keep quiet! If you say a word to her, she will never forgive me and I shall not be able to go and see her."

While Daian and old woman Feng were talking, Qintong slyly went to the window of the inner room, listened, and peeped in to see what was going on there.

Ximen Qing took a pill with the spirit, undressed himself and sat down on the side of the bed. Then he opened the case in which he kept his instruments. First he put the silver clasp on the root of his penis, and fixed a sulfur ring on top of it. Then he took a little of the red powder from a silver box, no more than the prescribed dose, and put it into the horse's eye. The medicine worked at once. The penis's erection was amazingly aggressive; its head swelled and the single eye opened wide; the lateral sinews stood out plainly; it was as dark as liver in color, seven inches long, and much thicker than usual. Ximen Qing was highly pleased: he decided that the medicine was a very fine thing. She sat naked on his knee, took his penis in her hands and said: "So this is why you wished to drink spirits. You wished to make him like this." She asked Ximen where he had obtained the medicine, and he told her about the Indian Monk.

She laid herself upon the bed, with two pillows under her. He wanted to put his penis to work, but its head was so swollen that it was a long time before he met with any success, and even then he made very little progress. Eventually the juices of love flowed from her and the path became gradually easier; the prick advanced, but its head was hardly covered. Then the wine that he had drunk came to the rescue; he withdrew a little, then plunged in deep and enjoyed untold rapture. She also had an exquisite orgasm; she lay on the bed as if unable to move, and said tearfully, "Dearest of men, your wonderful prick has killed me." Soon she whispered, "My darling, my dearest, would you like to enjoy the flower of my bottom?" He turned her onto her stomach and his penis returned to action, so violently that it made a loud noise. "Shove, darling, shove," cried Wang Liu'er, "don't be afraid. If you like, bring a candle, and the pleasure will be greater." The candle was moved nearer, and below him she opened her legs wide. Ximen withdrew and plunged in, while she moved her thighs to meet him and titillated the flower in her womb with her trembling hand.

"I am going to send your husband to Yangzhou," Ximen Qing said. "He shall go with Laibao and Cui Ben to get the salt. When that business is done, I will send him to Huzhou to buy some silk."

"Darling," said Wang Liu'er, "send him where you like. Why should you keep him here in idleness? But who will take charge of the shop?"

"I will put Ben the Fourth to look after the shop," Ximen said.

"Yes," said Wang Liu'er, "Ben the Fourth can look after it. That is a good idea."

So these two went about the business of love and Qintong watched them through the window. Daian came along from the kitchen and tapped Qintong on the back. "You must not stand here," he said. "Come away before they get up." Qintong went with Daian, and Daian said to him: "In the lane behind here there is a bawdy house where there are two young girls who have but lately come. One day when I was riding that way, I happened to see them. It was at Long-legged Lu's place. One is called Jin'er and the other Sai'er. Neither of them is more than eighteen. We will make the other boys stay here, and we will go and have some fun with the girls."

They told the boys to watch the door, washed their hands, and said: "If we are wanted, come to the lane behind and call us." Then they went off to the lane. The moon was shining. The lane was known as Butterfly Alley. There were not more than ten houses in it and all were for the accommodation of the public.

Daian was a little drunk. He made a loud rat-tat at the door. Some time passed. The brothel keeper Wang Ba and the procuress Long-legged Lu had been weighing silver with a balance by the light of a candle when in rushed the two boys like a couple of demons. The light was blown out, but the brothel keeper recognized Daian as Ximen Qing's servant and asked them to take a seat.

"Call the two singing girls to sing us a song," said Daian.

"I am afraid you are too late, masters," Wang Ba the brothel keeper said. "They have both got visitors."

Daian wasted no words, but dashed into the inner room. There was no light but that of the moon, but he could see two men with white felt hats on the bed. One was actually lying on the bed and the other was taking off his boots. "Who is this?" one of them cried.

"My dagger to your mother's cunt," Daian said, and let fly his fist.

"Ai ya," cried the man. He ran away without troubling to put on his boots. The other got off the bed and ran away too. Daian demanded that the lamps be lit.

"The thieves, the rogues!" he cried. "How dare they ask who I am? I would have pulled out all their hair. It is lucky for them I let them get away. I ought to have sent them to the police court and let them taste the new thumbscrews there."

Long-legged Lu came and lighted the lamps. "Please do not be angry, young masters," she said. "They were strangers and did not know you. Don't treat it too seriously." She told the two girls to sing for the boys.

The two girls were wearing dresses of red and white, and their hair was done like a bundle of silk. "We did not expect you," they said. "It is late, and we have made no preparations." They brought four dishes of dried fruits, ducks' eggs, dried prawns and salt fish, besides pig's head and sausages. Daian looked closely at the girls. Sai'er had a tiny pink silk satchel for perfume, and he gave her his handkerchief in exchange for it. Then wine was brought. Sai'er took a cup and poured wine for Daian. Jin'er took up her lute, and, after offering wine to Qintong, sang this song:

> In the camp of the flowers of the mist
> Life is not easy.
> I may not choose to sit, or yet to stand
> All day I must be ready to welcome strangers.
> On me the fortune of this house depends
> When evening comes, the procuress
> Makes me give up my earnings.
> What does she care whether I live or die?
> I stand beside the gate till midnight
> When I come in, none asks if I am hungry.
> If I must live for but a few years more
> Among the flowers of the mist
> My life will be a living death.
> The tears drop from my cheeks like falling petals
> I cannot hold them back;
> Only when the iron tree comes into blossom,
> Will I ever get my reward.

Jin'er finished her song, and Sai'er gave Daian a cup of wine. Then she, in turn, took the lute and was about to sing when a boy suddenly came in. Daian rose and said to Sai'er: "I will come and see you another day." Then he went back to Wang Liu'er's house, where Ximen Qing had got up and was drinking with his lover.

The two boys went to the kitchen and asked old woman Feng if their master had called for them. "No," she said, "he asked if his horse had come, and I said it had. That was all."

The boys sat down and asked old woman Feng to give them some tea. While they were drinking it, Daian told the other boys to light the lantern and bring out the horse.

Ximen Qing got up to go. "The wine is good and hot," Wang Liu'er said to him. "Won't you drink another cup, or are you going to have more when you reach home?"

"No, I'm not going to drink any more at home," Ximen Qing said. He drank the cup she offered him.

"When will you come again?" the woman asked.

"I will come when I have sent your husband on this business." The maid brought a cup of tea so that Ximen Qing might rinse his mouth. Wang Liu'er took him to the door; he mounted his horse and rode home.

*          *          *

Pan Jinlian was listening with the others to Nun Xue and the two young novices singing their sacred songs when she suddenly remembered that Yueniang had scolded Daian and said she did not know what tricks he was playing. She went to her room and found that the love instruments had disappeared. She asked Chunmei about them. "Yes, Father came here," the maid said. "He looked in the drawers and in the bed, but I don't know where he found them."

"When did he come?" Jinlian asked.

"You were in the inner court with Nun Xue. I asked him what he was looking for, but he would not tell me."

"He has taken them to the bawdy house," Jinlian said. "I will find out when he comes back." She went back to the inner court.

It was very late when Ximen Qing returned. He did not go to the inner court. Qintong took a lantern to light him, and they went through the garden gate to the rooms of Li Ping'er. Qintong took his master's hat and clothes and gave them to Xiaoyu. When Yueniang saw the boy, she asked if his master had returned. "Yes," the boy said. "He has gone to the Sixth Lady's room."

"The fellow hasn't the slightest regard for decent behavior," Yueniang said. "Here we have all been waiting for him and he doesn't come."

Li Ping'er went quickly to her room and said to Ximen Qing: "The Second Lady is waiting to offer you wine on her birthday. Why have you come here?"

Ximen Qing laughed. "I have had too much wine already," he said. "I will see her tomorrow."

"Even so," said Li Ping'er, "you must come with me and take a cup of wine in the inner court. If you do not, you will offend the Second Lady." She compelled him to go. Li Jiao'er offered him wine.

"Have you been alone all this time?" Yueniang asked him.

"I have been drinking wine with Brother Ying," Ximen Qing told her.

"Of course!" Yueniang said. "I knew you couldn't be drinking by yourself." She said no more.

Ximen Qing did not stay very long. He staggered over to Li Ping'er's rooms. He had not fully eased himself when he was with Wang Liu'er, because of the Indian Monk's pill that he had taken. He had worked long and lustily, yet his weapon was harder than ever, as stiff as an iron rod. He went into the room, gave his clothes to Yingchun, and asked Li Ping'er to let him go to bed. She had not expected him and was already in bed with Guan'ge. Now she said to him: "Please go somewhere else. The baby has just gone to sleep. Besides, I am not very well. Don't be silly. Go to some-body else." But Ximen embraced her and kissed her.

"I particularly want to stay here," he said. He showed her his weapon. It gave her a start.

"However did you make it so big?" she said.

Ximen Qing laughed. He told her about the Indian Monk and said: "If you won't let me sleep here, I shall die."

"But how can I?" Li Ping'er said. "I have been unwell for two days and I am not better yet. When I am better, I will certainly sleep with you, but please go to the Fifth Lady's room tonight. It is all the same to you."

"I don't know why," Ximen said, "but I feel I want you today. I am afraid I must insist. Tell the maid to bring some water, wash yourself, and we will sleep together."

"You make me laugh," Li Ping'er said. "You must be drunk or you wouldn't behave so scandalously. Even if I do wash, it won't be very pleas-ant. If, at a time like this, my juices meet a man, bad luck follows. If this means my death, I will certainly come and haunt you."

She could not get rid of him, and, at last, she told Yingchun to bring some water, and washed herself. They got to bed together. Strangely enough, the baby Guan'ge, who had gone to sleep, woke up the moment she turned her head. This he did three times. Li Ping'er told Yingchun to give him a comforter and take him to the nurse. Afterwards, they were able to enjoy themselves more freely.

Ximen Qing sat down inside the net, and she got onto hands and knees. He plunged in, admiring the ivory white of her legs in the candlelight. He maneuvered himself to enjoy the sight of the moving prick. He reached halfway, but could go no further; she was afraid that blood would flow, and tried to dry herself with a handkerchief. Ximen struggled for an hour, and at last he held her legs apart and achieved so clear a passage that they stroked each other with their pubic hair.

His orgasm was greater than imaginable, but she said, "Come carefully, please, that hurts."

"Now you will have all of me", he replied. On the table there was a cool potion; when he had drunk it the sperm flowed like water. His limbs relaxed comfortably, and he felt as fresh as the spring. He was beginning to appreciate the marvel of the Indian Monk's medicine. It was the third night watch when he went to sleep.

When Jinlian knew that Ximen had gone to Li Ping'er, she was quite sure that he had taken the instruments there. It never occurred to her that he might have been elsewhere too. She bit her lips with her silvery teeth and went to sleep.

That night Yueniang slept with the two nuns, Xue and Wang. Wang secretly gave her the afterbirth of a baby boy, which Nun Xue had made into a charm. Xue told Yueniang to pick out a *renzi* day, take the medicine with a little wine, and then sleep with her husband. "Do not let anyone know about this," she said, "and you will have a baby."

Yueniang took the medicine and thanked the two nuns. "I expected you in the first month," she said to Wang, "but you did not come."

"It is easy to promise," said Wang, "but not so easy to get such things as this. Fortunately Nun Xue was equal to the occasion. She gave an old woman three *qian* of silver and got this from a young lady who had just given birth to her first baby. We got alum water and cleaned it, and cooked it on two new tiles. Everything was done in proper form. We sifted it through a very fine sieve, mingled it with drugs and charms, and here it is."

Again Yueniang thanked them. Then she gave them two taels of silver and said: "If this is successful, Nun Xue shall have some yellow silk."

Nun Xue made a reverence to her. "Your Ladyship is very kind," she said. "Remember the proverb that says: 'Sometimes, though we try for ten days, it is impossible to sell a load of genuine stuff; yet in one day we can dispose of three loads that are not genuine.'

# CHAPTER 51

# Pan Jinlian Makes Mischief

Pan Jinlian was so angry when she thought that Ximen Qing had taken the love instruments to Li Ping'er that she tossed about the whole night through. She hated Li Ping'er. The next morning, when she knew that Ximen had gone to the office, she went to the inner court to see Wu Yueniang.

"The Sixth Lady," she said, "has been saying nasty things about you behind your back. She says you take undue advantage of your position and that you are overbearing. Last night, she says, our husband came in drunk and went to her room. She was in the inner court, and you shamed her before everybody there. She was angry, went to the other court and forced him to come to your room. He didn't wish to come, and went back again to her as soon as he could. They talked all night. He has given himself to her, heart, entrails and all."

This made Yueniang very angry. Aunt Wu and Meng Yulou were present, and she said to them: "You two were here yesterday. I said nothing that anyone could take exception to. When the boy brought the lantern, I asked him why his master had not come, and he said his master had gone to the Sixth Lady's room. Then I said: 'The Second Lady is expecting him and he ought to come.' There was nothing wrong about that. What does she mean by saying that I take undue advantage of my position? I used to think she was a good woman, but, evidently, I was judging by appearances, and did not realize what her mind was like. You never can tell. Now I see that she is like a needle hidden out of sight, a thorn in the flesh. How do I know what stories she may have been telling my husband? No wonder he was so anxious to go and see her yesterday. But never mind, my foolish lady. Even if he goes to you every day, it shall not worry me. You can have him, you people who cannot bear the strain of widowhood. Think of it! But when I first came here, and that rogue treated me without due respect, I managed to survive."

"Lady," Aunt Wu said, "say no more. There is the child, you know. Those in authority always have much to put up with. You are the mistress of the house, and the mistress is like a jar that has to hold all sorts of water. Both good and bad are your portion."

"One of these days," Yueniang said, "I will certainly ask her what she meant by saying I was overbearing."

This alarmed Jinlian. "Sister," she said, "you must forgive her. There is an old saying that tells us that the truly great do not concern themselves with the doings of those who are less worthy. And what person of that baser sort is without faults? We all suffer from the way she talks to our husband, especially I, who am her nearest neighbor. If I were as bad as she, there would be desperate trouble. And things are by no means better for us now that she has had this baby. She says more. She says that when her son grows up, there will be kindness for those who have been kind to her and revenge for those who have been unkind to her. We shall all die of starvation. But, of course, you knew nothing of this."

Aunt Wu said: "Lady, how can you say such things?" Yueniang said nothing.

When people get to discussing matters in this way, there are always some who speak for fire and some who speak for candles. Ximen's daughter, Ximen Dajie, was friendly with Li Ping'er, who had always given her needles, thread and cloth when she wanted them. She had given her fine silk and other things besides, and two or three excellent handkerchiefs. She never expected any return. So, when Ximen Dajie heard this conversation, she naturally went to tell Li Ping'er.

The Sixth Lady was sitting in her room making a charm for the baby to wear at the Dragon Boat Festival. She was also making different kinds of millet dumplings and delicacies to eat. When Ximen Dajie came in, she asked her to sit down, and told Yingchun to bring some tea.

"When we asked you to come and take tea with us, why didn't you come?" Ximen Dajie said.

"When your father went away, I began to make these things for the baby, now that it is cool."

"I want to tell you something," Ximen Dajie said. "Now, please realize, I don't wish to talk scandal, but have you done anything to displease the Fifth Lady? She has been telling the Great Lady that you said she was an interfering busybody. Mother is going to ask you what you meant by it. But when she asks you, don't tell her that I spoke to you about it, or she will be angry with me. You must think out your answer beforehand."

When Li Ping'er heard this, she could hardly hold her needle; she was so paralyzed by astonishment. For a long time she could not answer and tears rolled down her cheeks. "I never said a single word," she said at last. "Last night, I was in the inner court and the boy came to tell me that your father had gone to my room. I came and asked him to go to the inner court, and that was all. The Great Lady has been very kind to me. Do you think I don't know how to distinguish good from evil? How dare Jinlian say such things? I will have this out with her, face to face."

"She did seem to be disturbed when the Great Lady said she would talk to you about it," Ximen Dajie said. "If I were you, I should certainly challenge her."

"No," Li Ping'er said, "she is too clever for me. Her mouth is sharper than mine. Day and night she schemes to kill my child and me. I can only put my trust in Heaven. But one of these days she will be the end of me." She sobbed as she spoke.

Ximen Dajie stayed for a while to comfort her, then Xiaoyu came to ask them both to go to dinner. Li Ping'er put down her sewing and went with Ximen Dajie, but she could eat nothing and went back to her room to lie down.

When Ximen Qing came back from the office and found Li Ping'er lying on the bed, he asked Yingchun what was amiss. The maid told him that she had had nothing to eat. He became excited and asked: "Why couldn't you eat anything? Tell me. I see your eyes are very red. How are you feeling?"

Li Ping'er got up quickly, rubbed her eyes and said: "My eyes have been bothering me, but it is nothing very serious. I just wasn't hungry." She did not say a word about the trouble, but she could not get it out of her mind.

In the inner court, Ximen Dajie said to Yueniang: "I have been speaking to the Sixth Lady about the things the Fifth Lady says. She swears she never said anything, and cried bitterly. She says she could not possibly say anything of the sort after you have been so kind to her."

"I don't believe a word the Fifth Lady says," Aunt Wu said. "The Sixth Lady is much too good a woman to say things like that."

"I fancy there is some trouble between Li Ping'er and Jinlian," Yueniang said. "Perhaps Jinlian could not get her husband to go and visit her, and that is why she comes and tells me such tales. I am the one who has to suffer."

"You must be fair in your judgments, Lady," Aunt Wu said. "It would take a hundred like the Fifth Lady to make one like the Sixth. She has been here three years now, and never has she done anything she should not have done."

As they were talking, Qintong came in with a large parcel wrapped up in blue cloth. Yueniang asked him what was in it. "There are thirty thousand salt certificates here," the boy said. "Clerk Han and Cui Ben have been to have them registered at the Excise office. Father is giving them something to eat, and seeing about the money. The day after tomorrow is a lucky day, and they will start for Yangzhou."

"Master Ximen will be coming now," Aunt Wu said. "I had better go with the two holy teachers to the Second Lady's room." Before she finished speaking Ximen Qing appeared.

"What is that thievish, fat, bald-headed old whore Xue doing here?" he asked his wife.

"Why do you use such unbecoming language?" Yueniang said. "Since you do not offer them charity, there is no call for you to make such rude remarks. She has done you no harm. And how did you know her name?"

"Don't you know her history?" Ximen Qing said. "She got Counselor Chen's young daughter away to her temple where she carried on with some young fellow. For that she received three taels of silver. When the business came out, I had old Xue arrested. She was given twenty strokes and ordered to return to lay life and get married. I should like to know why she hasn't got married yet. Perhaps she would like me to put the thumbscrews on her."

"You must not speak evil of the servants of Buddha," Yueniang said. "She is religious and observes her vows. Why should she return to the secular life? You don't appreciate her holiness."

"Holiness!" said Ximen Qing. "Ask her how many men she welcomes in one night."

"Don't be so vulgar," Yueniang said, "or I shall tell you what I think of you." Then she said: "When are you going to send the men to Yangzhou?"

"I have sent Laibao to see our relative Qiao," Ximen said. "I want five hundred taels from him. I myself am contributing another five hundred taels: I shall send them off the day after tomorrow."

"Who is going to take charge of the shop?" Yueniang said.

Ximen told her that he had arranged for Ben the Fourth to do so. Then Yueniang opened a chest and took out the silver. It was weighed and wrapped up. Ximen gave each man five taels of silver as journey money.

Ying Bojue came while this was being done. "What are you doing, Brother?" he asked. Ximen Qing told him. "I congratulate you, Brother," Bojue said, bowing. "You will certainly do well out of the transaction."

Ximen Qing asked him to sit down and called for tea. Then he asked when Li and Huang were going to get their money. "Within a month, I expect," Ying Bojue said. "They told me yesterday that there is another contract going in Dongpingfu for twenty thousand lots of incense. They are very eager to get your backing to the extent of five hundred taels and, as soon as they get the money, they will bring it to you without even touching it."

"As you see," Ximen said, "I am sending people to Yangzhou and I have had to borrow five hundred taels from Qiao. How can I spare money for them?"

"Well," Ying Bojue said, "they said to me with much insistence that one guest does not trouble two hosts. If you do not do them this favor, they don't know where to get the money."

"Xu the Fourth, in East Street, outside the walls, owes me five hundred taels," Ximen Qing said. "They shall have that."

"Splendid," cried Ying Bojue.

At that moment Ping'an brought a visiting card and said that Xia Shou had come to invite Ximen Qing to go and visit Magistrate Xia next day. Ximen Qing looked at the card. "Good," he said.

"Brother," Ying Bojue said, "I have news for you. Have you heard about Li Guijie? Has she been here recently?"

"She has not been here since the end of the first month. I can't imagine what's been happening to her."

"General Wang's third son," Ying Bojue said, "is a nephew by marriage of Grand Marshal Huang of the Eastern Capital. In the first month, this young man went to the Capital to celebrate the New Year, and the old gentleman gave a thousand taels to the young couple as a New Year's gift. Oh, you have no idea of the beauty of Grand Marshal Huang's niece. No artist could paint more than a half of it. I have never seen so beautiful a woman. Since you have been staying at home with your own ladies, old Sun, Pockmarked Zhu, and Little Zhang have been spending all their time in the bawdy house with this young man. In Second Alley he has taken up with a girl called Qi Xiang'er, and sometimes he goes to Guijie's house. He stole his wife's ornaments and pawned them. This distressed his wife so much that she even tried to hang herself. The other day was the old gentleman's birthday. Wang's wife went to the Eastern Capital and told him all about it. The old gentleman was terribly annoyed. He had the names of all the naughty fellows set down and sent the paper to Marshal Zhu. Marshal Zhu has sent it here with orders to arrest the people named. So, yesterday, old Sun, Pockmarked Zhu and Little Zhang were arrested at Guijie's house. Guijie herself escaped to a neighbor's and spent the night there. They have asked me to come and beg you to help them."

"Only a month or two ago I said they were a pack of cadgers," Ximen Qing said. "Pockmarked Zhu even tried his tricks on me."

"I will be off," Ying Bojue said. "I expect Guijie will be coming to see you, and, whether you listen to her or not, she is sure to blame me for putting a finger in the pie."

"One moment," Ximen Qing said, "if you see Li, don't tell him I am going to let them have the money. Wait till I have got it from Xu, and then I'll talk to you again."

Bojue promised. As he went out of the gate, Guijie's sedan chair arrived. She was getting out of it, but Bojue went straight on.

Ximen Qing was telling Chen Jingji to go to Xu the Fourth's for the money when Qintong came and said: "The Great Lady would like to see

you in the inner court. Guijie is here." Ximen went to the back court. Guijie was wearing a dun-colored dress. There was no powder on her face, and
her head was hidden in a white kerchief. There were no ornaments in her
hair and she seemed extremely miserable. She kowtowed to Ximen Qing.

"Whatever shall I do, Father?" she said, sobbing. "The fates have abandoned me. I was sitting quietly at home, when disaster seemed to drop
suddenly from the skies. There is a certain young master Wang. He was a
stranger to me, but, one day, old Sun and Pockmarked Zhu brought him
to our house to see my sister. My sister was not at home, and I said to my
mother: 'Don't let them in,' but, the older my mother grows, the bigger fool
she becomes. It was the day of my aunt's birthday. I wanted to get into my
sedan chair and come here, but Zhu went down on his knees and implored
me not to come until I had at least given them a cup of tea. He made
it impossible for me to get away. Suddenly, a number of policemen came
to arrest them. Wang slipped away, and I managed to escape to a neighbor's house. When everything was quiet again, our servant came to take me
home again. My mother was frightened out of her wits. She talked about
killing herself.

"Today the runners came with a warrant from the office and spent the
whole morning at our place questioning us. They mentioned my name
and wanted to take me to the Eastern Capital. Father, you must take pity
on me and save me. I don't know what to do. Mother, won't you say a
word for me?"

Ximen Qing laughed. "Get up," he said. "What other names were there
on the document?"

"Qi Xiang'er's name was there," Guijie said. "It was young Master Wang
who made her a woman. But it was right for her name to be there, for she
took his money. But if I ever took a penny from him, may my eyeballs fall
out. And if I ever allowed him to set hands on me, may a beastly sore grow
at every one of my pores."

"You really must do something for her," Yueniang said. "Don't make her
take these terrible oaths."

"Has Qi Xiang'er been arrested?" Ximen Qing asked.

"Not yet," Guijie said. "She went to the Wangs' house."

"The best thing you can do," Ximen Qing said, "is to stay here for a
few days, and I will see what I can do for you at the district office." He told
Shutong to write a letter and go at once to the office to see Magistrate Li.
He was to tell Li that Guijie was at Ximen Qing's house, and ask that she
should not be arrested.

Shutong put on his black clothes and went on this errand. In a short
time he was back again with a card from Li. "His Lordship told me,"

the boy said, "that he will gladly do anything else you wish, but he can't do this. In this case the document has come from the Eastern Capital. His Lordship must see that the people are arrested, and the best he can do for you is to allow her two days' grace. If you wish to do anything for her, you will have to send to the Capital."

When Ximen Qing heard this, he muttered a while. Then he said: "Laibao is about to go somewhere else, and I have no one to send to the Eastern Capital."

"Why not send the other two to Yangzhou, and keep Laibao?" Yueniang said, "Then he can go to the Eastern Capital for Guijie. There will still be the other two to go to Yangzhou. See how terrified the girl is."

Guijie kowtowed to Yueniang and Ximen Qing. Ximen sent for Laibao. "You will not go on the twentieth," he said. "I am going to send the others to Yangzhou, and you must set off tomorrow for the Eastern Capital to get this business of Guijie's settled. You will go and see Uncle Zhai and ask him to get the affair disposed of at the courts."

Guijie hastily made a reverence to Laibao. He made reverence in return and said: "I will start immediately."

Ximen Qing told Shutong to write a letter thanking Zhai for what he had done in the matter of Censor Ceng. He sealed up twenty taels of silver to go with the letter and gave it to Laibao. Guijie was greatly relieved. She offered five taels of silver to Laibao. "When you come back," she said, "my mother will reward you suitably." Ximen Qing took the five taels and returned them to the girl, telling Yueniang to give Laibao another five taels in place of them. "But this is quite wrong," Guijie said. "You are taking all this trouble on my account and I cannot allow you to spend your money as well."

"Do you think I don't have five taels," Ximen said, "so that I must ask you to pay him for me?"

Guijie put away her five taels and made reverence after reverence to Laibao. "Brother," she said, "please start early tomorrow. I am so afraid you may be too late."

"I will start at the fifth night watch, the break of dawn," Laibao said. He took the letter and went to Han Daoguo's house in Lion Street.

Wang Liu'er was making clothes in her room. She saw Laibao through the window and said to him: "What can we do for you? Please come in. My husband is not at home. He has gone to the tailor's for some clothes, but he will be back in a moment." She said to the maid: "Go to Xu's, the tailor's, and tell your father Uncle Bao is here."

"I have come to say that I am not going with him tomorrow. I have to go to the Eastern Capital instead. Guijie pleaded urgently with my master to do something for her, and I have been ordered to start tomorrow morning.

Your husband and Cui will have to go by themselves and I shall join them later on. What are you making, Sister-in-law?"

"Underclothes for my husband," Wang Liu'er said.

"Tell him not to take much in the way of clothes," Laibao said. "The place to which we are going is the very home of silk, so why bother about clothes?"

As they were talking, Han Daoguo came in. The two men greeted one another, and Laibao told Han what he had told Wang Liu'er. "I will join you in Yangzhou," he said.

"Our master has given instructions that we are to stay at Wang Boru's inn," Han said. "Wang's father was a friend of his Lordship's father. He has a very large inn, and there are always many merchants there. Our money and our goods will be safe there. That is where you will find us."

"Sister-in-law," Laibao said to Wang Liu'er, "I am going to the Eastern Capital. Is there anything you would like me to take to your daughter?"

"Her father has had a pair of hairpins made, and I have made two pairs of shoes. Would you be so kind as to take them?" She wrapped them in a kerchief and gave them to Laibao. Then she told her maid to bring something to eat and to warm some wine. She laid down her sewing and set the table.

"Sister-in-law," Laibao said, "do not take any trouble on my account. I must not stay. I must go home and pack my luggage so as to be ready to start first thing in the morning."

Wang Liu'er smiled. "Why do you stand on ceremony with us? We are colleagues in business, and it is only right that we should entertain you and that you should drink a cup of wine with us." She said to Han Daoguo: "Now, old sobersides! Help me to get the table ready and ask Uncle Bao to sit down. Don't look as though you did not wish him to stay."

Dishes were brought, and they offered Laibao wine. Wang Liu'er sat with the two men. When Laibao had drunk a few cups, he said again that he must go. "It is late, and my house is shut up early." Han Daoguo asked what arrangements had been made about the horses, and Laibao told him that they were to be hired early the following morning. "If I were you," he said, "I should hand over the keys and the accounts to Ben the Fourth, and not go to the shop. Take a rest at home in preparation for your journey."

"I am going to give them to him tomorrow," Han Daoguo said.

Again Wang Liu'er urged Laibao to drink. "Just this one cup, Uncle," she said, "I will not ask you to drink any more."

"If I must drink," Laibao said, "may I have a cup of very hot wine?" Wang Liu'er poured the wine into the pot and told the little maid to heat it. Then she poured it out again and offered it with both hands to Laibao. "I am sorry that I have nothing better to offer you to eat," she said.

"I thank you, Sister-in-law," Laibao said. "We do not, of course, stand on ceremony since we are all members of one household." He took the wine and drank with Wang Liu'er. Then he got up. She gave him the shoes to take to her daughter.

"Go to the palace, Uncle," she said, "and see whether my daughter is well." Then she and her husband together took him to the gate. Laibao went home, packed his baggage, and, next day, set off for the Eastern Capital.

Uncle Wu came to talk to Ximen Qing. "A document," he said, "has come from the Capital to Dongpingfu appointing me Keeper of the Seals and Controller of the Granary in this city. I am to be on six months' probation and, if my work is well done, I am to be promoted; and, if not, reported by the Censor. Brother-in-law, if you can spare the money, I should be glad if you would lend me some. I will pay you back when I get paid myself."

"How much do you need?" Ximen Qing asked. "You shall have it."

"It is very kind of you, Brother-in-law. Perhaps twenty taels." They went together to Wu Yueniang's room. Yueniang took out twenty taels and gave them to her brother. Then they had tea, but, as there were lady guests, Uncle Wu could not stay in the inner court, and Yueniang asked her husband to entertain him in the great hall.

While they were drinking, Chen Jingji came in. He made a reverence to Uncle Wu, and said to Ximen Qing: "Xu asks to be allowed a few days in which to make his payment."

"Rubbish," Ximen said, "I need the money now. You will have to speak to him severely."

Uncle Wu asked Jingji to sit down and drink with them.

In the inner court, Aunt Wu and Aunt Yang, Ximen's ladies, and Guijie were drinking wine together. Miss Yu sang to them the first act in *The Western Wing* play cycle. When she had finished and laid down her lute, Meng Yulou gave her some wine. "What a terribly long ditty," she said, "I don't like you at all." Pan Jinlian, with a pair of large chopsticks, took a piece of meat and dangled it before Miss Yu's nose, to tease her.

"Sister," Guijie said to Yuxiao, "give me the lute, and I will sing a song for the ladies."

"But you are in trouble," Yueniang said. "You can't feel like singing."

"Now that you and Father have made things all right, I have nothing to worry about," Guijie said.

"Guijie," Yulou said, "I suppose you are able to change the parts you play so quickly because of where you come from. When you first came, your brows were knit and you would not even take a drop of tea. Now you laugh and talk readily enough."

Guijie stretched her delicate fingers, plucked the strings and sang to them. While she was singing, Qintong came with the things from the outer court. Yueniang asked if Uncle Wu had gone and was told that he had. "It must be time for my brother-in-law to come here," Aunt Wu said. "We had better go elsewhere." Qintong told them that Ximen Qing had gone to the Fifth Lady's room.

When she heard this, Jinlian was on tenterhooks. She lifted first one foot and then the other in her anxiety to get away, but she felt that it would not be polite to go. At last Yueniang said to her: "Get off to your room since he is there. Don't sit there looking like a guest who can get nothing to eat."

Jinlian tried to pretend to be in no great haste, but her feet carried her quickly away. When she came to her room, Ximen Qing had already taken some of the Indian Monk's medicine. Chunmei had taken his clothes and he was sitting on the bed.

"Ah, my son," Jinlian said, "you could not wait for your mother to come, but went to bed first. I have been drinking in the inner court. Guijie was singing there, and I have had several large cups of wine. I had to find my way here alone in the dark, one foot in the air and the other on the ground. Really, I don't know how I got here." She asked Chunmei for some tea. When the maid brought it, Jinlian drank it and made a sign to her. Chunmei understood and went to heat some water for her. The woman washed herself with sandalwood water and alum and took off her headdress so that her hair was held by a single golden pin. She stood before the mirror, reddened her lips and put some fragrant tea into her mouth. Then she came back and Chunmei brought her sleeping shoes. The maid went away and made fast the door behind her.

The woman took the lamp and set it beside the bed. Then she pulled down the curtains, took off her scarlet trousers, and stripped her jade body. Ximen Qing was sitting on the bed, the silver clasp in position upon a fierce-looking weapon. Jinlian was startled when she looked at it. It was too great for one hand to grasp, full-blooded and heavy. She stared at Ximen Qing and said: "I know what you've been doing. You've been taking some of that monk's medicine to make it like that. Then you think you'll come here to show what a mighty fellow you are. Fresh wine and fresh meat for others. I have to content myself with the defeated champion. I can serve the meanest of your purposes. Then you pretend to be fair to me. Why, the other day, when I was not in my room, you came and ran off with the instruments to the Sixth Lady's room and carried on your games there. And she pretends to be one of those pure, pious people. You wretched little creature, you can be twisted around anybody's finger. When I think about it, I swear I won't have anything to do with you for a hundred days."

Ximen Qing laughed. "Come here, you little strumpet," he said, "and see if your mouth can make this smaller; if you can, I'll give you a tael of silver."

"I'm ashamed of you, you rascal," she said. "How can it get smaller when you have drunk that potion?" But she lay on the bed and put his penis between her red lips. "It's so huge," she said, "that it hurts my mouth." Then she sucked and teased the prick's head with her tongue, licking the outer skin and rubbing it up and down with her lips. But, although she stroked the giant with her cheeks and played a thousand love games with it, it merely became longer and thicker. Ximen looked at her. Her beautiful body gleamed among the silk sheets. She took his hairy monster in her delicate fingers, put it between her lips, and took it all in her mouth; when she released it, it was limp.

Beside them lay a long-haired white cat. Watching the movement of this hairy thing, the cat crouched ready to spring. Ximen had a gold speckled fan in his hand and with it he teased the cat. Jinlian seized the fan and struck a hard blow at the cat. It ran quickly away. She looked up at Ximen Qing and said: "You terrible fellow. You are amusing yourself with me, and that isn't enough for you, you must play with the cat. Suppose it claws me. What then? Do you think I shall go on playing this game?"

"You funny little whore," Ximen said, "you would talk anybody to death."

"Why don't you ask Li Ping'er to play these games with you?" Jinlian went on. "You ask me every time you come here. What that medicine you have been taking may be I don't know; I could suck it all day without success."

Ximen took from his sleeve a little silver box and from it picked out with a toothpick some of the reddish ointment. He put it upon the horse's mouth. He lay down and made her ride on top of him. "Let me get into position first," she said. "If I do, perhaps you'll be able to penetrate me." But the head of his penis was so broad that they both struggled hard and long before even a little of it would go in. She rode on top of him, up and down, hither and thither, but could not conceal her pain. "Darling," she said, "that hurts me so much that I can't bear it any longer," and feeling around with her hand she found that less than half the penis was inside her. She collected some of her spittle and moistened the inside of her cunt with it to make the path easier. Then she moved up and down and gradually the penis went the whole way into her vagina.

"Darling," the woman said, "the medicine you always used to take gave me a tremendous feeling of burning inside, but this makes me feel a coldness that reaches even to my heart. My whole body seems numb. I shall certainly die at your hands today."

Ximen Qing laughed. "I will tell you a story," he said. "I heard it from Brother Ying. Once upon a time a man died and went down to the infernal regions. The King of Hades put an ass's skin upon his body and told him that in his next life he must be a donkey. But the record keeper looked in his books and found that the man still had thirty years to live. They sent him back to earth. His wife perceived that, except for his weapon, his body was as it had been before, but he had still the donkey's weapon. 'I will go back to Hell and change it,' he said to his wife. 'No, my dear,' said the wife. 'They might not let you come back again. I will put up with it somehow.' "

Jinlian struck him with the fan. "Beggar Ying's wife is able to put up with a donkey's weapon," she said. "That is obvious. You are a foul-mouthed thing, and I ought to hit you harder."

They went on with their work, but Ximen Qing did not give forth. He closed his eyes and made the woman move. She, wriggled and writhed with terrible moans. Then they changed places. He held her legs, and thrust in his penis with all his might. He worked hard in the face-down position, but he felt very little, and she did not become wet. They changed places again; she embraced his neck and hurled herself at him, put the tongue in the mouth, and pressed the whole penis inside herself. Then she whispered gently, "Darling, finish it off or I'll die." Soon she drooped; her tongue was as ice, and the juices of love flowed from her. Ximen felt that her cunt was warm, his passions were aroused, and he felt an enormous orgasm. Both their juices flowed like rivers. She mopped them up with a handkerchief. Then they embraced and kissed each other—but the penis was still erect. They slept for an hour; after that Jinlian, still unsated, climbed on top of him and played with him again. The juices again flowed, but at last began to exhaust themselves. Ximen Qing was undaunted. He could only marvel at the medicine that the Indian Monk had given him. Then they heard the cock crow. It was just before dawn.

"If it doesn't go down, come back to me tonight and my lips will make it do so."

"You can never do so," Ximen said, "there is only one thing that will."

Jinlian asked what that was, but he said: "This is not a thing to be told to other ears. Wait till tonight and I will tell you then."

In the morning he rose and Chunmei helped him to dress. Han Daoguo and Cui Ben were waiting. Ximen went out and gave them two letters, one to introduce them to Wang Boru, who kept the inn at Yangzhou, and the other to Miao Qing to ask if his affair had been settled satisfactorily. He told them that, if they needed more money, he would send it later by Laibao. "You said you were writing to Censor Cai," Cui Ben said, but Ximen said the letter had not been written and that he would send it by Laibao. Then the two men set out upon their journey.

Ximen Qing put on his hat and robe of ceremony and went to the office. He thanked Magistrate Xia for his invitation. "It will be a great honor if you visit me today," Xia said. "There will be no other guests." They attended to their business, then each went to his own home.

An official on horseback, carrying a parcel, with sweat rolling down his cheeks, came to the gate and asked Ping'an if Ximen Qing lived there. Ping'an asked his business. The man dismounted, bowed to Ping'an, and said: "I come from An, the Warden of the Royal Forests, with presents for your master. My master and Huang, the Controller of the Brick Fields, are now at Dongpingfu, at Master Hu's place, drinking wine. My master wishes to visit his Lordship, and I have come to see if he is at home." Ping'an asked for a card, and the man took one from the wrapper and gave it with the presents to the gatekeeper. The boy took them and showed them to Ximen Qing. On the list of presents he read: "Zhejiang silk, two rolls; four measures of Hu brocade; a scented girdle; and an ancient mirror." Ximen told him to give the messenger five *qian* of silver and a card in return, and to say that Ximen would be happy to receive his master. The man went away and Ximen hastily made the necessary preparations.

The two gentlemen arrived about noon. They came in sedan chairs with a fine array of umbrellas and men to clear the way for them. They sent in visiting cards with their names An Shen and Huang Baoguang. Both were dressed in ceremonial attire, with black hats and black boots. They got down from their sedan chairs and Ximen Qing went to the gate to meet them. They went into the hall and exchanged salutations. Then they sat down, Huang on the left and An on the right.

"Your fragrant renown has long been known to me," Huang said. "I am only sorry that my visit has been so long delayed."

"The kindness is on your side," Ximen said, "it was for me to come and see you first. May I ask your illustrious name?"

An answered for his colleague. "Brother Huang's name is Taiyu. It is expressive of the principle that earth is made peaceful by the glory that comes from Heaven."

"May I ask your name?" Huang said.

"My unworthy name," Ximen said, "is Siquan. I was so called because, on my poor estate, there is a well with four openings."

"The other day," An said, "I met Brother Cai. He told me how he and Song had inflicted themselves upon you."

"Yes," Ximen Qing said, "I had orders from my friend Zhai, and besides, his Excellency Song is my superior officer. It was only fitting that I should entertain them. When my servant was at the Capital, I heard of the exalted rank you had attained and I can only apologize for not having come in person to congratulate you. When did you set out?"

"Last year, after I left you, I went home to marry again. Then, in the first month of the new year I went to the Capital and was appointed to the Board of Works. Now I have been detailed to superintend the transport of the imperial timber from Jingzhou. I had to pass this way, and, of course, felt bound to come and pay my respects to you."

"I am grateful for your precious gifts," Ximen Qing said. He asked them to change their clothes, and summoned the servants to lay a table. But Huang rose, and An said: "Indeed, we have to go to drink wine with the prefect of Dongpingfu. We only called in passing, and we will trouble you some other day."

"It is a long way from here to Dongpingfu," Ximen Qing said, "and if you are not hungry yourselves, there are still your servants to consider. I shall not offer you anything very special, merely common, everyday food, and when your servants have been refreshed by a meal, you will travel more quickly." A table was set with food of all kinds, delicious dishes, soups, and pastries. Ximen took a small golden cup and offered three cups to each of them. The servants were entertained. Then the two officers stood up and An said:

"We are giving a little party tomorrow and should be very honored if you would come. The party will be at Chamberlain Liu's place. He is a friend of my brother Huang. Will you give us the pleasure of your company?"

"Since you are good enough to invite me," said Ximen, "I dare not refuse."

He escorted them to the gate. Just as they went away in their sedan chairs, a man came from Magistrate Xia to remind Ximen Qing. "I will come at once," he said. He ordered his horse to be brought, went to the inner court to change his clothes, then came out again and mounted. Qintong and Daian followed him, and soldiers went before him to clear the way. When he reached his colleague's house, he went to the hall. The two men saluted each other. Ximen said: "Their Lordships An and Huang have just been to see me. They stayed a long time or I should have been here earlier." Two tables were set in the hall. Ximen Qing sat on the left, and, next to him, the graduate Ni. They talked to one another and Ximen asked Ni his second name. "My name is Ni Peng, and my second name Shiyuan. I am also known as Guiyan. I am on the staff of the college of this prefecture, and at present am coaching his Lordship's son for his examination. I am ashamed to say I am too ignorant to have many friends." The two young actors came up and kowtowed.

When Jinlian had said good-bye to her husband, she went to bed again and did not get up before midday. Even then, she was too languid to dress her hair. She was afraid those in the inner court would remark it, so, when Yueniang sent for her to go to dinner, she would not go but said she was unwell. Not until afternoon did she go to the inner court.

Yueniang, taking advantage of Ximen Qing's absence, decided to hear Nun Xue expounding the teachings of Buddha and interpreting the *Diamond Sutra*. An altar was prepared and incense burned. The two nuns, Wang and Xue, sat down facing each other, and the two novices, Miaoqu and Miaofeng, stood beside them. The service began. All Ximen's ladies were present, with Aunt Wu and Aunt Yang. They gathered round and listened to Xue recite.

"It has been said," Xue began, "that lightning and brightness soon pass away but that stone and fire are everlasting. The withered blossom can never return to the tree on which it grew and flowing water can never go back to the spring from which it came. In painted halls and tapestried chambers, life is but emptiness. The noblest and the greatest die, and all is but a dream. Gold and jade are no more than fountains of trouble. Silken garments are wasted labor. Wives and children can never spend a hundred years together and, in the darkness beyond, a thousandfold sufferings await.

"When you have lain upon your dying bed and your spirit has gone to the realms below, only in history will your name be recorded. It will avail you nothing, and the yellow earth will cover your corrupting bones. Your fields and gardens, though they cover ten thousand acres, will be divided and cause strife among those who come after you. Your chests of silks and satins, though they are a thousand, will give you not a moment's pleasure. Before life is half done, white hairs assail us. When we have received the congratulations of one guest, he will be followed by another who comes to condole with our children. It is bitter, bitter, bitter. Our spirit is transformed into vapor and our body goes beneath the ground. On go the transmigrations, ceaselessly, and so our heads and countenances are ever changed.

"Hail to the limitless void of the Dharma Realm, to the Three Treasures of the Buddhas of Past and Future, the Dharma, and the Holy Orders.

"Oh, highest, deepest, most admirable Law! Through a hundred, a thousand, ten thousand ages, it is difficult of attainment. Let us now behold it, hearken to it, receive it, hold fast to it. Let us vow to grasp the Buddha's great Truth."

Then Nun Wang said: "Shakyamuni Buddha was the ancestor of all the Buddhas, the Founder of our religion. Do you know how he left his home? Hear me tell of it." Then Nun Xue sang:

The Buddha Shakyamuni was a prince in India.

He left his kingdom and went forth to the Himalayas

Where he cut off his flesh to feed the eagles, magpies nested on his
    head.

He cultivated his purity until the nine dragons spittle made him a
    body of gold,

And became the Perfect One, the Buddha of the Great Vehicle.

Then Nun Wang said: "Now that you have heard of Shakyamuni, I will
tell you how the Bodhisatva Guanyin strove after perfection, attained hundreds of manifestations, and attained the fullest power of the Path. Would
you like to hear?"

Xue was about to sing again when Ping'an came rushing in and said:
"His Excellency Song has sent two runners and a servant with a number of
presents."

Yueniang was flurried. "Your father has gone to Magistrate Xia's," she
said. "Who is there to accept the presents?"

Daian came in, put down his wrapper and said: "Don't worry, lady. I
will take the card and go and tell my father. Meanwhile I will ask Master
Chen to entertain the servants here." He took the card, mounted a horse,
rode quickly to Xia's place and told his master. On the card was written: "A
freshly slaughtered pig; two jars of Jinhua wine; four quires of writing paper
and a miniature book." It was signed: "With the respects of the junior official Song Qiaonian." Ximen Qing told the boy to go home and ask Shutong
to write a card with his full title, and give the servant three taels of silver and
two handkerchiefs, and five *qian* to each of the runners.

Daian hurried home. He looked everywhere for Shutong but could not
find him. This made him so excited that he ran around like an ox going
around the grindstone. Nor could he find Chen Jingji. Clerk Fu had to
come and entertain the men. Daian went to the inner court to get the silver
and the handkerchiefs. There was nobody to wrap them up, and he had to
go to the shop to have a parcel made of them. He asked Clerk Fu to write
the necessary card. Then he asked Ping'an where Shutong was. "He was
here when Master Chen was here," Ping'an said, "and when Master Chen
went to get some money, he disappeared."

"I suppose the young rascal has gone off after some girl," Daian said.

At that moment, Chen Jingji and Shutong came riding along on the
same mule. Daian scolded the boy and bade him quickly write the card.
They dismissed the men who had brought the presents.

"You rascally young scamp," Daian said to Shutong. "You are too ready
to roam about. When Father is not at home, you think you can go too. You

have been after your girl, beyond a doubt. Father never told you to go out with Master Chen. Wait till he comes back and see what I tell him."

"Tell him what you like," Shutong said. "If you don't, I shall know you are afraid of me, and I shall consider you my boy."

"What, you dog!" Daian cried. "Do you dare me?" He went up to Shutong and kicked him. The pair rolled about on the ground struggling. Daian gained the upper hand and spat upon Shutong's face. "I am going for Father now," he said, "but when I come back I will settle my score with you."

In the inner court, Yueniang gave the two nuns some tea and refreshments, and they continued their hymns and their preachings. Jinlian grew impatient and tugged at Yulou, but Yulou would not move. Then she thought of suggesting to Li Ping'er that they might go, but she was afraid Yueniang would reprove her.

"Sixth Sister," Yueniang said, "she wants you to go with her. I think you had better go. She is so very impatient." Li Ping'er went out with Jinlian. Yueniang looked after them. "Now that the turnips are out of the way," she said, "we shall have more room. We don't want her here, jumping about like a rabbit. She is not the sort of woman to listen to religion."

Jinlian, holding Li Ping'er by the hand, came to the second door. "The Great Lady," she said, "is very fond of that sort of thing. But there isn't anybody dead in the household, and I don't see why we should have the nuns to read stuff of that sort. I have had enough of it; that's why I asked you to come out. Let us go and see what Ximen Dajie is doing." They passed through the great hall. There was a light in one of the side rooms. Ximen Dajie and Chen Jingji were quarreling over the disappearance of some money. Jinlian tapped at the window.

"So, instead of going to the inner court to hear the nuns, you are squabbling here."

Chen Jingji came out. "It is a lucky thing I didn't curse you. Fifth Mother and Sixth Mother, won't you come in?"

They found Ximen Dajie busy making shoes. "It is late and very hot," Jinlian said. "Why are you making shoes now?" She asked what they were quarreling about.

"Father told me to go outside the city walls to get some money," Chen Jingji said, "and my wife gave me three *qian* to buy her a handkerchief. Unfortunately, when I got there, I couldn't find the money. I couldn't buy it for her. When I got back, she said I had spent the money on some woman. She scolded me and made me take oath upon my body. When the maid was cleaning the floor, the money was found. She has taken it, yet still she tells me I must buy a handkerchief for her tomorrow. You two ladies can judge which of us is in the wrong."

"You thievish rascal," his wife said. "You say you don't keep a woman, but what were you doing out with Shutong? You must have heard Daian cursing him. I have no doubt that you and that boy went to some strumpet together. That's why you came back so late. Where is this money you were sent for?"

"Have you found the other money?" Jinlian asked.

"Yes, the maid picked it up when she was sweeping the floor. I have it now."

"Don't worry," Jinlian said to Jingji, "I will give you some money and you can buy two handkerchiefs for me." And Li Ping'er said:

"If there are handkerchiefs to be bought outside the city, please buy some for me."

"Outside the city," Jingji said, "there is a Kerchief Lane where some well-known merchants are having a special sale of kerchiefs of all sorts. Some are woven with gold; others have jade trimmings. They can supply as many as you like. Tell me what color you like and what kind of pattern you want and I will get them for you tomorrow."

"I will have an orange-colored one, with gold and green, and a phoenix among the flowers," Li Ping'er said.

"Mother," Jingji said, "orange and gold don't look at all well together."

"Mind your own business," said Li Ping'er. "I want another of pink wavy silk, with the design of Eight Precious Treasures, and still another of shimmering silk with gold and flowers."

"What design do you want, Fifth Mother?" Jingji asked Jinlian.

"I have only a little money, so two will be enough for me. One the color of jade, with edges of lace and gold."

"You are not an old woman," Jingji said. "What do you want with white?"

"Don't think you know better than I do," Jinlian said. "I shall use it when I have to wear mourning."

"Then you will need a colored one too."

"Yes, I want one of the most delicate purple grape shade, made of Sichuan silk, gold and green, with a pattern of crossed squares, and in every square a pair of love symbols. On the lace I must have tassels and pearls and other bits of jewelry."

"Ai ya! Ai ya!" Chen Jingji cried. "You are like the melon-seed seller, who sneezed when he opened his box, and scattered the seeds all over the place."

"You horrid man," Jinlian said. "Since it is my money, I shall buy what I like. It is a question of taste and nothing to do with you."

Li Ping'er took a piece of silver from her purse and gave it to Jingji. "This will pay for the Fifth Lady's too," she said. Jinlian shook her head.

"No," she said, "I will pay for my own."

"We are asking Brother-in-law to buy them all at the same time. Why should you bother?"

"Even so," said Jingji, "it is more than enough." He took a balance and weighed the silver. It weighed a tael and nine *qian*.

"With the rest," Li Ping'er said, "buy two handkerchiefs for your wife."

Ximen Dajie stood up and made a reverence to Li Ping'er. "Now the Sixth Lady has paid for your handkerchiefs," Jinlian said to her, "you ought to hand over those three *qian* of silver. You and your husband can draw lots to decide which of you shall be our host. If it is not enough, we will ask the Sixth Lady for some more. Your father will be out tomorrow; we will buy roast duck and white wine and enjoy them together."

"Yes," said Jingji, "hand over that silver."

Ximen Dajie gave the silver to Jinlian, and Jinlian passed it to Li Ping'er for safe keeping. They found some cards, and Ximen Dajie and her husband played. Jinlian helped Ximen Dajie, and she won three games. Then they heard a knocking at the gate. Ximen Qing had returned. Jinlian and Li Ping'er went to their rooms and Jingji went to tell Ximen that Xu the Fourth would pay two hundred and fifty taels in a day or two, and the remainder the following month. Ximen Qing cursed, for he was drunk. He did not go to the inner court but straight to Jinlian's room.

# CHAPTER 52

# Ying Bojue Teases Li Guijie

That day, Ximen Qing had been entertained by Xia and presents had come to him from Censor Song. He was utterly delighted, and Xia was impressed. He shut the door and urged Ximen to drink more and more wine, refusing to let him go before midnight, the third night watch.

Pan Jinlian had taken off her headdress, prepared the bed and washed her cunt with perfumed water. She was waiting for Ximen Qing to come. When he came, he was drunk. She quickly undressed him; Chunmei brought him tea, and he went to bed. Jinlian, quite naked, sat on the side of the bed and bent over to tie the ribbons of her shoes to her white ankles. The shoes were low-heeled and scarlet. The sight aroused Ximen's passion, and his handle stood up sharply. He asked her for the love instruments, and she brought them out from beneath the bed and gave them to him. He put on two silver clasps, and then threw his arm around her. "Today," he said, "I want to play with the flower in the back court. Will you let me?"

"You shameless fellow," the woman said, "you have played that game often enough with Shutong. Why need you ask me? If that is what you want, go to the slave."

Ximen Qing laughed. "Little oily mouth," he said, "if you will let me do this, I shall want the boy no more. Don't you understand that I am particularly fond of this kind of play. I will only put it there for a little while."

Thus urged, the woman said: "I don't believe you can do it. Your thing is too big. But take the ring from its head and I will try."

Ximen Qing took off the sulfur ring and left only the clasps at the root. He told her to get onto the bed on hands and knees and raise her buttocks high. He rubbed his penis with spittle and moved in gradually. But its cruel, proud head refused to go farther than a little way. She grimaced and bit a handkerchief. "Darling," she said, "be careful not to go in too quickly; my bottom isn't like a door. I feel you inside me like a burning fire."

"Never mind," Ximen said, "tomorrow you shall have a dress of fine embroidery."

"I have clothes like that already," Jinlian said. "What I want is a dress like that of Li Guijie, a lined skirt of gold and silver with jade-colored ribbons and fur. It is very beautiful, and everybody but me has such a skirt.

I don't know how much it will cost, but please buy me one."

"Don't worry," Ximen said, "I will buy one for you." He plunged violently forward.

The woman turned her head and looked at him. "Darling," she said, "it is painful enough. Why are you so violent? Won't you let yourself go now?"

But Ximen Qing would not. He held her legs while he looked at his penis going in and out, and cried, "Give me my way, you little strumpet, and call me 'darling.' Then you will have all of me."

The woman closed her eyes and said something like the whisper of a bird. She gently shook her willow-like waist and thrust her sweet body forward to meet his, her enticements and tender words beyond description. After a time, Ximen felt that the essence of his manhood was ready. He grasped her buttocks, then launched himself into her, with the sound of constant slapping against her buttocks. The woman under him could only mumble inarticulately. When the time came, he pulled her against himself and pushed it in to the root, into the final recess, enjoying exquisite pleasure. Contented, the semen flowed freely. The woman received it all, and they lay stuck together on the bed. After a long while he withdrew his penis, but it looked bloody, and liquid was oozing slowly from its mouth; she wiped it with a handkerchief, and they both slept.

The next day Ximen Qing went to his office. When he returned, invitations had come from the two dignitaries Huang and An, asking him to go early on the twenty-second to a party at Eunuch Liu's place. Ximen Qing dismissed the man who had brought the invitations, then went to the upper room and had some gruel. When he came to the great hall, he met Zhou the barber. Zhou knelt down and kowtowed. "You have come at the right moment," Ximen Qing said. "My hair needs attention."

They went to the Hall of the Kingfishers. Ximen sat down beneath an awning, took off his hat and hairnet and pulled down his hair. Barber Zhou took out his combs to dress it. He cleaned it and examined the color. When he knelt down to receive payment, he said: "There will be further promotion for you this year, my Lord, for your hair is in excellent condition." Ximen Qing was very pleased. When his hair had been combed, he told the barber to cleanse his ears and massage his body. The barber had his instruments with him and gave Ximen's body a thorough rolling. Then he exercised the muscles so that Ximen began to feel extremely fit everywhere. Ximen gave him five *qian* of silver and some food, and he was told to wait and shave the baby's head. Then Ximen Qing went to his study, lay down on a great marble bed, and fell asleep.

That day Aunt Yang went away and the two nuns Wang and Xue also made ready to go. Wu Yueniang packed their boxes with sweet things and

cakes and gave each of them five *qian* of silver. To each of the novices she
gave a small roll of cloth. As they were leaving, Xue told Yueniang not to fail
to take the medicine on a *renzi* day and she would be sure to have a child.

"Lady Xue," Yueniang said, "my birthday comes in the eighth month.
You must come to see me then. I want you especially." The nun made a
reverence and promised to come. All the ladies went to see them off. Afterwards, Yueniang and Aunt Wu went back to the upper room, and the other
ladies went to the garden with Guijie and the baby.

"Sister Guijie," Li Ping'er said, "won't you give me the baby?"

"No," said Guijie, "I love carrying him."

Yulou said: "Sister Guijie, you have not seen Father's new study yet."

Jinlian saw how beautifully the roses were blooming, and she plucked
two of them for Guijie. They went along the pine-hedged walks till they
came to the Hall of the Kingfishers. Beds, curtains, screens, tables, books,
pictures, musical instruments and chess, were all tastefully set out. A silken
net was held in position over the bed by two silver hooks, and the light
summer pillows and mattress were spread upon it.

Ximen Qing was lying fast asleep. Beside him was a small gold incense
burner in which some Dragon's Spittle incense was burning. The green windows were partly open, and light was reflected through them by the palm
leaves outside. Jinlian took the incense box from the table and examined
it. Li Ping'er and Meng Yulou sat down on chairs. Suddenly Ximen Qing
turned over and saw the ladies. "What are you doing here?" he said.

"Sister Guijie wanted to see your study," Jinlian said. "So we brought
her here." Then Ximen saw his son Guan'ge with them and played with
him for a while.

Unexpectedly, Huatong came and said: "Uncle Ying is here." The ladies
hurried away to the rooms of Li Ping'er. When Ying Bojue came to the
pines, he saw Guijie with Guan'ge in her arms, and said to her maliciously:

"Ah, Guijie! So you are here! When did you come?"

Guijie did not stop. "Beggar Ying," she said, "pray don't meddle in my
affairs."

"Your affairs or not, you little strumpet," Bojue said, "I am going to kiss
you." He went up to her, but she pushed him away.

"You unpleasant fellow," she said, "if I were not afraid of frightening the
baby, I would use my fan on you."

Then Ximen Qing came and said to Ying Bojue: "Don't frighten my
son, you funny dog." He told Shutong to take the child to the Sixth Lady's
room. The boy took him and carried him to his nurse, Ruyi'er, who was
watching them from the corner. Ruyi'er took him away.

"What has happened about you?" Ying Bojue said to Guijie.

"Father was very kind. He has sent Brother Laibao to the Eastern Capital."

"That is good," Bojue said, "I suppose you are satisfied now."

Guijie would have gone to the inner court, but Bojue said: "Come here, you little strumpet, I want to talk to you."

"I shall be back before long," Guijie said. She went to visit Li Ping'er.

Ying Bojue made a reverence to Ximen Qing, and they sat down together. "Yesterday," Ximen said, "I went to Magistrate Xia's place. Censor Song sent me some presents. Among them was a pig. I didn't want to keep it too long so, this morning, I told the cook to cut it up and cook the head with peppers. Don't go away. I will send for Xie Xida and we will play backgammon." He said to Qintong: "Go and ask your Uncle Xie to come. Tell him Uncle Ying is here."

Bojue asked Ximen whether he had yet received Xu's money.

"The dog has only paid two hundred and fifty taels of what he owes me. You must tell your friends to wait a few days. I will get the rest for them somehow."

"That will be all right," Bojue said. "I should not be surprised if they brought you some present today."

"Don't let them spend their money on me," Ximen said. He asked if old Sun and Pockmarked Zhu had started or not.

"After they were arrested at Guijie's place, they spent a night in jail," Bojue said. "The next day they were taken to the Eastern Capital, three of them on one chain. It doesn't seem likely that any of them will come back as comfortable as he went. Trying to earn an honest living is not a simple matter in these days. What a hard time they will have. In this roasting weather, they have to bear that big iron chain, and they haven't a penny in their pockets. I can't think what will become of them."

"You funny dog," Ximen Qing said, laughing, "if they could not bear this punishment, why did they interfere with young Wang? They deserved all they get."

"You are right, Brother," Bojue said. "Flies can never make their way into an egg unless there is a crack in it. Why didn't Wang ask me and Xie Xida to go about with him? But the good go with the good, and the bad with the bad."

While they were talking, Xie Xida came. He sat down and fanned himself busily. "What has made you so hot?" Ximen Qing said to him.

"Ah, Brother, you don't know. Today, an unexpected trouble descended upon me. Early this morning, old woman Sun came to my house and said I had taken her husband away from her. That old whore! Her husband spent all his time at the bawdy house, ate and drank a tremendous lot, and spent all his money there. 'Have you come from Hell?' I said to her. 'Everybody knows you yourself have taken money from the people in the bawdy house.' I gave her a good talking-to and she went away. Then your boy came to invite me."

"I have just been saying to our brother," Bojue said, "that if we put newly vinted wine into two bottles, we shall see which is pure and which is not. Didn't I tell you that anybody who went about with young Wang would certainly get into trouble? Now it has happened, and they have nothing to complain about."

"I can't see how young Wang dared have anything to do with the girls," Ximen Qing said. "He is not properly grown up yet. Conduct like his would be shameful even in a corpse."

"The boy hasn't seen much of the world," Bojue said. "He is not like you. If I mentioned your name to him, he would be frightened to death."

The boys brought tea. Ximen Qing said: "You two play backgammon, and I will tell a boy to buy us some noodles." Qintong set the table, and Huatong brought four small dishes on a square tray, some garlic sauce, and a large bowl of stewed pork with a silver ladle in it. He set everything upon the table with three pairs of ivory chopsticks. The three men sat down and the boys brought three bowls of noodles. Each helped himself to the stew, the garlic sauce, and the vinegar. Ying Bojue and Xie Xida took up their chopsticks. In three helpings and two gulps each finished one bowl, and so on till they had had seven. They finished the seven before Ximen Qing had finished two.

"My sons," Ximen said, "how can you eat so much?"

"Brother," Ying Bojue said, "who has cooked these noodles? They are delicious."

"The stew is perfect," Xie Xida said. "It is most unfortunate that I have just had my dinner. I should have liked to eat another bowl."

The two friends felt hot and took off their coats. Qintong came to clear the table, and they asked him for water to rinse their mouths. "Cold tea will do," Xie Xida said, "but I won't have hot. It would make my breath smell of garlic." Huatong brought three cups of tea. Afterwards, they went to stroll among the flowers.

Huang the Fourth sent four boxes of presents to Ximen Qing, and Ping'an brought them in. There was a box of freshwater chestnuts, another box of a different kind of chestnut, four fine shad in ice, and a box of loquat fruits.

"What splendid delicacies!" Ying Bojue said. "I can't think how he managed to get them. Let me try one." He picked up several and handed two to Xie Xida. "There must be people who have never tasted such things in all their lives."

"You funny dog," Ximen Qing said. "I have not offered them to Buddha, yet you start tasting them."

"Why offer them to Buddha?" Bojue said. "They suit my palate admirably."

Ximen Qing told a boy to go to the inner court and get three *qian* of silver for the man who had brought the presents. "Who brought them?" Bojue said. "Was it Li Zhi or Huang Ning?"

"Huang Ning," said Ping'an.

"Lucky dog," Bojue said. "That's another three *qian* of silver for him." The two friends played backgammon, and Ximen Qing looked on.

After dinner, Yueniang and the others sat under the eaves. Little Zhou the barber peeped in from behind the screen. "Zhou," said Li Ping'er, "you have just come at the right moment. Come and shave my son's head. His hair is very long."

The barber came forward and kowtowed. "That is what Master said," he told them.

Yueniang said: "Sixth Sister, we must look at the calendar first and make sure that it is a lucky day."

Jinlian told Xiaoyu to fetch the calendar. When the maid brought it, Jinlian looked at it and said: "Today is the twenty-first day of the fourth month. It is a *gengxu* day, and under the influence of the Golden Dog. It is a good day for divine worship, for starting on a journey, making clothes, bathing, shaving and building. The afternoon is the most auspicious part of the day."

"In that case," Yueniang said, "the maid shall bring some hot water to wash the baby's head." She told the barber to amuse the baby while he was having his head shaved, and Xiaoyu to stand beside him with a kerchief to catch the hair. After a few strokes of the razor the child howled lustily. The barber was going on in spite of the crying, when, suddenly, the baby screamed and fell in a fit. No sound came from him and his face went purple. This frightened Li Ping'er. She cried: "Stop! Stop!" Zhou put his instruments together and went hastily away.

"The baby is not strong enough," Yueniang said. "We should have cut his hair ourselves instead of having him shaved. See what a state he's got into."

The baby gasped for a long time and at last began to howl again. Li Ping'er was greatly relieved. She began to play with him. "Did Little Zhou dare to come and shave my boy?" she said to him. "Did he shave half his head and treat him roughly? Let us bring him back and punish him." She took the child to Yueniang.

"You naughty little beggar," Yueniang said. "Crying like that when you are shaved. Now the part that has been left unshaven makes you look like a tonsured thief."

They played with him for a while, and Li Ping'er gave him to the nurse. "Don't give him any milk now," Yueniang said. "Let him sleep a while and then feed him." The nurse took him to the front court.

Laian came for the barber's instruments. "Zhou is so frightened that his face is as white as a sheet," he said. Yueniang asked whether the barber had been given anything to eat. "Yes," Laian said, "and my father has given him five *qian* of silver."

"Take him a pot of wine," said Yueniang. "We don't want to terrify him. He has a hard enough life." Xiaoyu heated some wine and gave it to Laian with a dish of preserved meat. The boy took it to the barber.

"Look at the calendar," Yueniang said to Jinlian," and tell me when the next *renzi* day is."

"It is the twenty-third," Jinlian said. "About the time of the day of Corn in the Ear. Why do you wish to know?"

"Oh, no particular reason," Yueniang said. "I was just wondering."

Guijie took the calendar and examined it. "The twenty-fourth is my mother's birthday. What a pity I won't be at home for it."

"The tenth of last month was your sister's birthday," Jinlian said. "Now it is your mother's. You people in the bawdy house suffer from two diseases on the same day and have three birthdays. In the daytime you have the money disease and at night the husband disease. In the morning, it is your mother's birthday; at noon, your sister's; and your own in the evening. It is very funny, all these birthdays coming in a lump. When your husband has any money, you had better make the best of the opportunity and celebrate all your birthdays together." Guijie laughed.

Ximen Qing sent Huatong to summon Guijie. She went to Yueniang's room to powder her face and then to the garden. Under the arbor a square table had been set, and on it were two large plates of roasted pork and many other dishes. The friends were eating, and Guijie served them with wine.

"Let me say this in your father's hearing," Ying Bojue said. "I am not talking for the sake of talking. I want to say that this business of yours is settled. Your father has done what was necessary at the district office, and you will not be arrested. But to whom do you owe this kindness? To me, who urged your father so strongly that he decided to intervene on your behalf. Now you must sing one of your favorite songs as a return to me, while I am drinking my wine."

Guijie laughed. "You ghostly beggar," she said. "You think too much of yourself. I don't believe Father pays the slightest attention to you."

"You little whore," Bojue said. "The sacred texts are not yet read, and already you would strike the priest. But don't go too far. Don't laugh at the priest because he hasn't got a mother-in-law. If I were a priest, I could deal with you myself, you young strumpet. And don't make fun of me. There are still some limbs that I can move."

Guijie struck him as hard as she could with the fan she held. Ximen Qing laughed. "You dog," he said, "your sons will be thieves and your daughters whores. And even that will not be as much as you deserve."

They all laughed. Guijie slowly took her lute and put it across her knees. She opened her scarlet lips and showed the whiteness of her teeth. Then she sang the song of the orioles.

> Who would have dreamed that this so fragrant body
> Could have been wasted and brought low by suffering?
> Her mirror is tarnished and she has no heart
> To polish it.
> She is too languid to adorn her face with powder,
> Too languid to set flowers in her hair.
> Her brows are knit in bitterness.

"You used to like him," Bojue said, "and you should be tender with him now. You ought not to treat him so unkindly."

"I don't know what you're talking about," Guijie said, and went on with her song.

> Most hard to bear is the sound of the horn
> Which the watchman blows on his Tower of vigil.
> It breaks her heart.

"Your heart is not broken yet," Bojue said, "but I warn you not to put too great a strain upon it. The string may break."

Guijie hit him hard. "You rascal," she scolded. "Are you quite mad today, that you fool with me like this?" She sang about the meeting of the virtuous guests.

> The windows are calm and silent
> The moon shines brightly.
> Alone, she leans upon the screen.
> She hears the sudden cry of a wild goose that has lost her mate,
> Calling outside the hall.
> It wakes her to the memory of ten thousand griefs.
> The night watch passes like an age
> The water clock moves slowly.
> She does not see the dimness of the lamps

The burned-out ashes of the incense.
She tries to sleep, but how can sleep
Come peacefully to her?

"Oh, you foolish little whore," Bojue said, "why can't you sleep in peace? Nobody's arrested you yet. Why don't you sleep at home? You managed to escape into somebody's house, and still you are worried all day long. You won't be happy till the man comes back from the Eastern Capital."

This made Guijie angry. "Father," she said, "listen to Beggar Ying amusing himself at my expense. I don't know why he does it."

"Yes," Bojue said. "Now you realize that he is your father."

Guijie did not answer him. She took up her lute and went on with her song.

When I think of him, when I think of him
How can my heart not be troubled?
When I am alone, when I am alone
Tears fall from my cheeks like pearls.

"There was once a man," Bojue said, "who was always piddling. One day his mother died, and, in due observance of the rites, he slept before the coffin. He piddled again. Someone came and saw that the bedclothes were wet, and asked what had happened. The man didn't know what to say. 'Can't you see?' he said. 'It was the tears falling from my stomach.' It is just the same with your song. The girl could not think what to say, so she had to howl in secret."

"You shameless little boy," Guijie said. "Were you there to see? You're crazy." She continued her song.

I hate him. I hate him.
I can never tell the things he did.
To this place I have fled, hating myself
Because I dealt with him so faithfully.

"Oh, you foolish little whore," Bojue said. "In these days it is impossible to deceive even a three-year-old child. How could anyone expect you to be honest with the clients of your house of joy? Now I'll sing you one of the songs of the South."

In these days we cannot say
Who is straight and who is crooked.

The world is full of cunning spooks
And all pretend to love us dearly.
They plot to bury us alive
And put a jar upon our heads.
The old whores think of nothing but cash
And the poor little whores stretch out their necks
To make the business flourish.
Their bitterness is as great
As that of drowning in the river.
The grief we get of them
Drives us to seek a well.
When will their cup of bitterness be full?
Far better would it be to live as horse or donkey.
Than make a living by such dirty business.

Guijie began to cry. Ximen Qing slapped Ying Bojue and said, laughingly: "You will kill somebody with those silly jokes of yours." To Guijie he said: "Don't cry. Go on with your songs and don't mind him."

"Brother Ying," Xie Xida said, "why are you so rude to my daughter, treating her so unkindly? If you say another word, may you grow a big sore on your mouth."

After a while Guijie took up her lute again and sang:

Men all say that he is noble and true . . .

Bojue began to say something, but Xie Xida clapped a hand to his mouth. He bade Guijie continue and pay no attention to Bojue.

But the rogue is a deceiver.
His eyes are open wide, but lips and heart
Speak different stories.

Xie Xida took his hand away from Bojue's mouth. "If they did speak the same language, there would be no harm done," Bojue said. "But of course they never do. Why, the mouth might not agree even if your 'tiger's mouth' does—at least after two or three cones of moxa are burned there."

"Have you seen that done, you white-browed, red-eyed fellow?" said Guijie.

"Of course I've seen it. I saw it in the Hall of the Joy Star."

Ximen Qing and the others laughed. Guijie continued.

He swore by mountain and by ocean.
He lied as though he spoke the truth.
Nearly did I suffer from love sickness for him,
That deceiver.
Now I know his deceit, but what can I do?

"What does life hold in store for you indeed?" Bojue said. "Why, he will certainly become a general one of these days."

Guijie sang again.

Every day we are farther and farther apart.
When shall we meet again?
You have wronged me, who have waited for you
With such longing and such patience.
Even in my dreams I know
The clouds and rain upon Wu Mountain
Can never meet again.
All my life long I must be
The widowed phoenix, you my widower.

She brought the song to an end.

Your love has waned, you leave me lonely.
All that life meant is now but emptiness.

"Excellent! Excellent!" Xie Xida cried. "You take the lute," he said to Shutong," and I will offer her a cup of wine to put her in a better humor."

"Yes," said Bojue, "and I will offer her something to eat. I seem to be no use to anybody, so I'll make this offering as amends for my evil deeds."

"Go away, you beggar," Guijie said. "Who wants your attentions? First you strike a man with your fist and then pat him on the back."

Xie Xida offered Guijie three cups of wine one after the other. Then he said to Bojue: "We have still a couple of games to play." They began to play again. Ximen Qing made a sign to Guijie and went out.

"Brother," Bojue said, as Ximen was going, "if you are going to the inner court, bring me some fragrant tea leaves. The garlic I had is making my breath smell."

"Where am I to get any fragrant tea?" Ximen said.

"Now, Brother, don't try to hoodwink me. I happen to know that Liu, the educational officer at Hangzhou, sent you a lot. Surely you don't want to keep it all for yourself." Ximen Qing laughed and went away. Guijie went out too.

She plucked a few flowers and then disappeared. Bojue and Xie Xida played three games. Then, as Ximen Qing did not return, they said to Huatong: "What is your father doing in the inner court?"

"He will be back soon," the boy replied.

"Will he?" said Bojue. "There is something funny about this." He said to Xie Xida: "You wait here, and I'll go and look for him." Xie Xida and Huatong played chess together.

Ximen Qing had gone to Li Ping'er's room to get some of his medicine. Then he came to the Arbor of Wild Roses and there met Guijie. He took her to the Snow Cavern. He shut the door, sat down on a small bed, and took Guijie on his knee. He showed his weapon to her and she was startled by it. "How did you make it so huge?" she said. Ximen told her about the Indian Monk. Then he asked her to bend her white neck, open her red lips and toy with it for a while. He gently lifted her two tiny feet, raised her in his arms, set her upon a chair and got to work. Meanwhile, Ying Bojue was looking everywhere for him without success. At last, he went through a small grotto under the mound of greenery, and so came to the Arbor of Wild Roses. Then he passed the Arbor of Grapes and so came to the Snow Cavern. It was deeply hidden in the thicknesses of the bamboos and pine trees.

He could hear someone laughing softly, but could not make out where the sound was coming from. He went on tiptoe to the cavern and pulled up the lattice. But the door was fast. He could hear Guijie's trembling voice calling Ximen Qing her darling. "Oh, please be quick," he heard her say, "I am afraid of someone coming." Then Ying Bojue gave a shout and pushed open the door. Ximen Qing, with Guijie's legs around him, was doing splendid work.

"Quick," cried Bojue, "fetch some water. There is a fight going on here."

"You frightened me, you silly thing, rushing in like that," Guijie said.

"You said you wished to make an end quickly," said Bojue, "but it is not so easy as all that. Things have to reach a certain pitch first. You were afraid someone would come and catch you, and here I am. I shall have to come to an understanding with you."

"You funny dog," said Ximen, "be off at once. Don't play tricks and let all the servants know."

"You must talk to me nicely, you little whore," Bojue said, "or I shall shout at the top of my voice, and all the ladies will know. They have accepted you as a daughter, and have been good enough to let you stay here. Now, here you are stealing their man, and, if it comes out, I don't know what will happen to you."

"Go away, you beggar," Guijie said.

"I will go when you have given me a kiss," said Bojue. He kissed her and went out.

"Come back, you dog. Why don't you shut the door?"

Ying Bojue came back and shut the door. "Strike hard, my son," he said to Ximen Qing, "and if you demolish her bottom, it will not worry me."

He went as far as the pine trees and came back again. "Where are the fragrant tea leaves you promised me?"

"I will give them to you later," Ximen said. "Why do you need to come back again now?"

Bojue went off laughing. "Really," said Guijie, "the man does not know how to behave." For a full hour she sported with Ximen, and then they ate a red date that allowed them to reach a climax. They set their clothes in order and came out of the Cavern of Snow. Guijie took some fragrant tea leaves from his sleeve and put them in her own. Ximen Qing was bathed in sweat. He was puffing and blowing. He went to a blooming lantana and piddled. Guijie took a small mirror from her girdle, dressed her hair by the window and went to the inner court. Ximen Qing went to the rooms of Li Ping'er, washed his hands, and rejoined his friends. Ying Bojue again asked for the tea leaves.

"You beggar," Ximen Qing said, "you might be going to die if you didn't get it. What makes you such a nuisance?" He gave a pinch to each of them.

"Is this all?" Bojue said. "Well, never mind, I'll ask the little whore for some."

Li Ming came and kowtowed to them. "Where have you come from?" Bojue said, "and how is that business of yours going?"

"Thanks to Father's kindness," Li Ming said, "the officers have not interfered with us for the last day or two. We are waiting to hear from the Eastern Capital."

"Has that little wench Qi Xiang'er come out yet?" Bojue asked.

"No," said Li Ming, "she is still at Wang's place. Guijie is safe here. No one would dare to come to this house for her."

"It would have been very awkward," Bojue said, "but fortunately, I and Uncle Xie won over your father. We told him that if he did nothing to help your sister, no one would."

"Oh," Li Ming said, "without Father's help, it would have been hopeless. The old lady is not very bright, and, besides, what could she do?"

"If I am right, it is the old lady's birthday some time now," Bojue said. "I must persuade your father to go with me to congratulate her."

"Pray do not put yourself about," Li Ming said. "When this matter is settled, she and Guijie will invite you, of course."

"Then we will congratulate her afterwards," Bojue said. "Come and drink this cup of wine for me. I have been drinking all day and I can't drink any more." The boy took the silver cup and knelt down to drink it. Xie Xida told Qintong to give him another cup.

"I feel sure you have not had anything to eat," Bojue said to Li Ming. "Here is a plate of cakes." Xie Xida took two plates of roast pork and duck and handed them to Li Ming. With his chopsticks, Ying Bojue helped the boy to half a shad fish. "I can see you haven't tasted any of this fish this year," he said. "Here is something seasonable for you."

"You funny dog," Ximen Qing cried. "Why don't you give him all the fish and be done with it?"

"I will eat the rest myself when I feel hungry again, after I have had some more wine. Don't you realize that fish of this sort is only to be had once a year? Why! When you pick your teeth, it still tastes sweet. This is no ordinary fish. I very much doubt whether you could even find it at Court. Certainly I could not get any anywhere else but here."

Huatong brought more dishes, water chestnuts, lotus roots and loquat fruits. Before Ximen Qing had time to eat any of them, Ying Bojue had emptied the plate into his sleeve. "You must leave some for me," said Xie Xida, taking another dish and leaving only the loquats on the table. Ximen Qing took one and put it into his mouth, then gave the rest to Li Ming. He told Huatong to go to the kitchen and bring two loquat fruits for Li Ming, who, when he had eaten them, sang a song for which Ying Bojue specially asked. The three men drank until evening. Then rice gruel with dried peas was brought for them. When they had eaten it, Bojue and Xie Xida made ready to go.

"Brother," Bojue said, "I understand that you are taking wine with his Excellency An tomorrow. I will tell Li and Huang to come about their business the day after tomorrow." Ximen Qing nodded. They did not wait for him to take them to the door, but went away by themselves. Ximen Qing told Shutong to clear the table and went to Yulou's room.

The next morning he did not go to the office, but dressed immediately after breakfast and, with Shutong and Daian, rode to Eunuch Liu's place. It was distant from the city about forty *li*.

Jinlian took advantage of Ximen Qing's absence to ask Li Ping'er to spend the three *qian* of silver that Chen Jingji had lost, adding another seven *qian* to them. They asked Laixing to buy a roast duck, two chickens, a jar of Jinhua wine, a bottle of white wine, fruit pastries and other things, and arranged for his wife to prepare them. Then Jinlian said to Yueniang: "The other day, Ximen Dajie was playing cards with her husband, and won three *qian* of silver from him. The Sixth Lady has added some more to it, and we have arranged to have a little feast. We should be glad if you would come and enjoy it with us in the garden." So Wu Yueniang, Meng Yulou, Li Jiao'er, Sun Xue'e, Ximen Dajie and Li Guijie all went to the arbor and joined in the feast. They took some of the food to the artificial mound. There, some of them played chess and some played darts.

"Why has our host not come?" Yueniang said.

"Father sent him to Xu's for some money," Ximen Dajie said, "but I don't think he will be long."

Chen Jingji soon came. He made a reverence to the ladies and sat down beside his wife. He told Yueniang that he had brought two hundred and fifty taels from Xu and given them to Yuxiao. The wine was passed around, and they all enjoyed themselves immensely. Yueniang, Li Jiao'er, and Guijie played chess, Yulou and the others strolled about the garden admiring the flowers. Jinlian, alone, fanning herself with a white silk fan, went in search of coolness to the deepest part of the banana palm glade behind the artificial mound. She saw on the grass a wild purple flower that was very delightful and went to gather it. She did not imagine that when he saw her go, Chen Jingji would quietly follow her by impulse. Suddenly he spoke from behind her. "What are you looking for, my lady? The grass is slippery, and I shouldn't like you to fall. It would hurt me if you did."

Jinlian glanced at him over her shoulder. Half smiling, half reproving, she said: "Why should it hurt you if I fell, you young scamp? I don't need you to look after me. What are you doing here? Aren't you afraid somebody will see us? What about those handkerchiefs you were to buy for me?"

"Here are the handkerchiefs," Jingji said, smiling. He took them from his sleeve. "What will you give me for them?" He drew nearer, but she pushed him away. Just then, Li Ping'er with Guan'ge in her arms came through the pine alleys with the nurse. They could see the movement of the white fan in Jinlian's hand, but not that she was pushing Jingji aside with it. They thought she was catching butterflies.

"Fifth Mother," Li Ping'er said, "catch a butterfly for my baby."

Jingji hurriedly slipped behind the artificial mound. Jinlian wondered whether Li Ping'er had seen him. She said: "Has our brother given you any handkerchiefs?"

"No, no yet," Li Ping'er said.

"He has brought them," Jinlian said, "but he did not like to give them to us in front of his wife, so he gave them to me secretly." They sat down in the shade of the plantains, opened the packet, and divided them.

After a while Li Ping'er said to Ruyi'er: "It is very cool and pleasant here. Go and tell Yingchun to bring the baby's pillow and bed, and also a set of dominoes. I will have a game with the Fifth Lady. You stay in my room."

The nurse went away, and Yingchun came with the things. Li Ping'er spread out the bed and put the baby upon it. While the baby was playing, she had a game of dominoes with Jinlian. Then she told Yingchun to bring a pot of tea. Yulou, who was in the smaller arbor, caught sight of them. She beckoned to Li Ping'er. "Come here," she said, "I have something to tell you."

Li Ping'er left the baby in Jinlian's care and went to speak to Yulou. But Jinlian was thinking about Chen Jingji who was still hiding in the grotto, and she forgot about the baby. She hurried into the cave and said to Jingji: "There is nobody about now. Come out at once." Jingji asked her to go and look at a huge mushroom that he said was there. She went in. Then Jingji knelt down and begged Jinlian to grant him her favors. They kissed.

When Li Ping'er came to the arbor, Yueniang said to her: "Yulou has been playing darts with Guijie. She was beaten. We want you to play for her."

"But there is nobody to look after my baby," Li Ping'er said.

"Jinlian is there," Yulou said. "There is no reason why you should worry." Yueniang asked Yulou to go and look after the child.

"Bring him here," Li Ping'er said. She told Xiaoyu to bring the baby's bed. Yulou and the maid went to the grove of plantains. The baby was screaming upon his bed, and there was no sign of Jinlian. A big black cat stood beside the child. It ran away when they came near.

"Where is the Fifth Lady?" Yulou said. "She has left the baby here, and the cat has terrified him."

Jinlian hurried out of the grotto. "I have just been to wash my hands, that's all. Where is this cat that is supposed to have frightened the baby? What are you so excited about?"

Yulou did not look into the grotto. She picked up the baby and went back to the arbor, trying to pacify him. Xiaoyu brought the bed, and Jinlian, afraid that they would tell the true story, went with them.

"Why is the baby crying?" Yueniang said.

"When we got there," Yulou said, "there was a big black cat standing near his head."

"He must have been frightened," Yueniang said.

"But the Fifth Lady was looking after him," said Li Ping'er.

"She had gone into the grotto to wash her hands," Yulou said.

"How can you say such a thing!" Jinlian said. "And where is this cat of yours? The baby is hungry and wants some milk. That's all."

Yingchun brought tea, and Li Ping'er told the nurse to feed the child.

Chen Jingji, now that there was nobody about, came out of the grotto and slipped away between the pine hedges. Yueniang, seeing that the baby refused to feed and would do nothing but cry, told Li Ping'er to take him to her room and put him to sleep. The party broke up. Chen Jingji, who had been disappointed in his hopes of enjoying Jinlian, went sadly to his own room.

# CHAPTER 53

# Pan Jinlian Is Unfaithful

In the little courtyard the jade steps are deserted
At the corner of the wall a few orchids put forth new shoots.
Lilies and pomegranates blossom there
The flowers beloved by those who long for children.
Let not the wind and rain beat down those flowers
May Heaven foster them.
May they not turn into the cuckoo flowers
Whose colors quickly change
And whose fragrance fades away.

Ximen Qing went to take wine with the two dignitaries An and Huang. With the serving boys, he came to Eunuch Liu's place. The two gentlemen came out to welcome him. Eunuch Liu was acting as host, and he, too, came out to meet Ximen, taking him by the hand as soon as he dismounted. "We have been waiting for you for a long time," he said. "You are late."

"You are very kind," Ximen said, "but I had some trifling business to attend to at home and this caused me to keep you waiting. I am very, very sorry." They all bowed profoundly and went into the hall. Ximen Qing again made reverence to them. They asked him to take the seat of honor and Eunuch Liu to take the second place. Eunuch Liu declined.

"This is my house," he said, "and you are my guests."

An insisted: "It is your proper place," he said. Ximen Qing supported him.

"On the score of age alone," he said, "you should take it, most noble sir." Liu could protest no more.

"Then," he said, "I must be presumptuous enough to take the second place." Huang and An sat in the hosts' seats. Some young actors came and kowtowed. Tea was served and then wine.

When the tables had been laid, the young actors took their instruments, string and wind, tuned them and sang the song "In Springtime, the Gentle Rain Falls Softly." When the song was done, Liu raised his cup and asked the company to drink.

"What an exquisitely beautiful song that was. Quite incomparable!"

An said. "It must have been written by a true scholar. And the singers' voices are so sweet. One can imagine them holding back the floating clouds. You will agree with me, I am sure, when I say that, in both respects, we have here an example of absolute beauty."

"With regard to that," Ximen Qing said, "I can express no opinion. But I certainly would call this a marvelous party, with you two gentlemen as hosts and noble Liu here as the master of the house."

"That is not quite a true statement of the case," Huang said. "This party is remarkable because of the presence at it of noble Liu, who has gone daily in and out of the purple forbidden city, and witnessed the appearance of the Dragon. Is he not an illustrious chamberlain? And here, too, is noble Ximen, whose gold is as a mountain and whose jade is beyond price. We may well compare him with Tao Zhu, a wealthy man indeed. We have here two men, one of unusually exalted rank, the other extremely rich. This is indeed cause for admiration."

They laughed heartily and drank together. One of the actors took a long flute and played a melodious tune. The others sang a new song, "Where the Peach Flowers and Willows Blossom beside the Stream." This song too, met with approval.

Chen Jingji was driven to desperation by the foiling of his desire to possess Pan Jinlian. Ximen Qing did not return, and Jingji went quietly backwards and forwards, continually peeping in at the inner court. Jinlian herself, after the advances the young man had made to her, was ill at ease. There was nobody about, and she pondered the matter, resting her cheeks upon her hands. Suddenly, in the darkness, Chen Jingji came in. It seemed as though he would have devoured her. Desperately, he came up behind her and took her in his arms. "Woman mine," he said, "it nearly killed me when Meng Yulou came and disturbed us."

Jinlian was startled, for she had not noticed his coming. When she turned her head and saw who it was, she was half frightened, half pleased. "You young thief," she said, "let me go. Someone will see us." But Jingji would not let her go. He fumbled at her trousers, trying to unloose them. Jinlian half yielded, half resisted, but he had already torn the ribbon that held them. She pretended to be alarmed. "You thief," she said. "Are you so ignorant of the laws of propriety that you dare thus to approach your mother?"

"Mother," Jingji said earnestly, "should you ask for my heart and liver that you might make them into soup, I would gladly cut them out of my body for you. You must be kind to me."

As he spoke, he brought forward that which was below his waist. It was firm, and he pushed it forward against the single garment Jinlian was wearing. The touch of it made her cheeks as rosy as the peach blossom. She still made a show of refusal, but, as he persisted in his entreaties, she could not keep her hand from touching him. Jiṅgji pulled up her skirt and shoved with all his might. At the first thrust he gained access, for she had long been aroused and was already wet, so there was nothing in their way. They stood up against the railing and sported furiously. Jingji was not satisfied. "Lie on the ground," he said, "and I will give you all you want."

Jinlian feared that her hair would be disordered or that someone might come. "Not this time," she said. "Let us be content for now. We shall meet again." They called each other many tender names and played together for a long time. Then they heard voices on the other side of the wall and were compelled to separate. They were still unsatisfied. The noise they heard was that of Shutong and Daian coming in with Ximen's hat, girdle, and boxes. The two boys were tipsy and made a great deal of noise.

Yueniang heard them and thought that Ximen had come. She sent Xiaoyu to make sure. The boys told her he was on his way, that they had come before him. When Ximen came, he was drunk. He went to Yueniang's room and carried her to her bed. But it was the next day, which happened to be a *renzi* day, on which she wished him to come to her. So she said: "I am not very well. Go somewhere else tonight."

Ximen laughed. "Oh, I know," he said, "you don't want me because I am drunk. Very well. I won't upset you. I'll go away and come tomorrow."

Yueniang smiled. "Really I am not very well," she said. "It isn't that I do not want you. Do please come tomorrow."

Ximen Qing went to Jinlian. She was resting on the bed after her bout with Chen Jingji. She rose hastily and said: "I suppose you have just come back from the party?"

Ximen did not answer. He took her in his arms and kissed her. Then he touched her cunt. "You wicked little strumpet. Of whom have you been thinking that you are as wet as this?"

Jinlian said nothing. She pushed him aside and went to wash herself. The happiness they enjoyed that night is beyond description.

The next day was the twenty-third and a *renzi* day. Yueniang got up and dressed herself. She told Xiaoyu to set out a table, and on it she placed an incense burner and burned some precious incense. Then she placed on the table a volume of the Scripture of the White-robed Guanyin. Yueniang knelt towards the west, added more incense, and opened the book. She read it once and knelt down once, and so twenty-four times, reading and kneeling time and time again. She took the medicine from a small box, put it on the table and knelt down four times. Then she made this prayer: "The woman Wu prays to Heaven most high that, by the help of this medicine, prepared by the nuns Xue and Wang she may be blessed with a male child." She took the wine that Xiaoyu had warmed and knelt towards the west again. Then she swallowed the pills and the powders. When the medicine passed her throat, it tasted very fishy, and she had to gulp it down. She made reverence four times more, then went back to her own room and remained there.

The next day, when Ximen Qing had got up in Jinlian's room, he sent Shutong with a card to thank Huang and An for the banquet they had given him. Ying Bojue came. He made a reverence to Ximen and said: "Brother, what time was it when you came back from Liu's place yesterday?"

"They were very kind and pressed me to drink a great deal of wine," Ximen said. "I had a long way to come home, and it was after the first night watch when I got here. I was drunk. That is why I am so late getting up."

Daian brought breakfast, and the two friends ate it together. A servant came and announced their Excellencies An and Huang. Ximen Qing dressed, and told the servants to make haste and clear the table. Ying Bojue disappeared into another room. An and Huang got out of their chairs and greeted Ximen Qing. They came in, and the servants brought tea.

"We were lacking in politeness last night," the two gentlemen said.

"You were most kind," Ximen said, "and I was just thinking of coming to see you when you arrived."

"You cannot possibly have been satisfied with your entertainment or you would not have left so early," said An.

"I fear I was very drunk last night," Ximen said. "When it was time for me to leave, noble Liu gave me more than ten cups of grape wine. I was almost sick as I rode home, but I managed somehow to control myself. I have only just waked up and even now I am not quite sober."

They laughed, drank three cups of wine, then talked for a while and took their leave. Ying Bojue said he had business to attend to and went home.

Ximen Qing went to the inner court and had lunch. Afterwards, he got into a sedan chair and went to pay a return call upon An and Huang. He had two red present cards written and told Daian to buy two sets of presents. These he took with him.

That evening, when he came home, Yueniang had made every preparation for him. As soon as he arrived she told Xiaoyu to bring food and heat wine. Husband and wife sat together. "Last night," he said, "I was drunk and you wouldn't let me stay. You tried to pretend you were not well, but you were only fooling me."

"No," Yueniang said, "I really was not well. Why should husband and wife not be free and open with one another?"

Ximen Qing drank ten cups of wine, ate some fish and some duck, then would not eat any more. Yueniang told her maids to clear away.

Xiaoyu perfumed the bedclothes. They bathed and went to bed. That night they enjoyed delight beyond all measure. Yueniang's monthly sickness was just over, and she had every reason to hope that the joy she sought would be granted her. She was as lively as a fish in the water. So a child was conceived.

The next day, when Ximen Qing got up, Yueniang prepared for him lamb, wine, eggs and kidneys, and he went to his office. When he returned, he went to Li Ping'er's room to see Guan'ge. He found her nursing the baby.

"Some time ago," she said to him, "I vowed to make a sacrifice, but I have not done so. These last few days, every time I go for a certain purpose, I lose a little blood. I ought to carry out my vow, but, so far, I have been too busy."

"If you like," Ximen Qing said, "I will send Daian for Nun Wang and you can talk to her about it." He gave the necessary instructions to Daian, and the boy went away at once.

Shutong came and said: "Uncle Ying and Uncle Chang are here." Ximen Qing went out to see them.

"The other day, when Xie Xida and I had wine with you," Bojue said, "I told you about that matter of Huang and Li, and you promised they should have the money."

"But where am I to find the money?" Ximen said.

"The other day you promised. Why have you changed your mind? Brother, don't try to pretend. You are such a rich man that it is no use your professing not to have any money. You must give them some."

Ximen Qing did not answer. He looked at Chang Zhijie.

"It is a long time since I last saw you," Chang Zhijie said. "How is your young son?"

"Thank you," Ximen said. "My wife has just been telling me that she is anxious to have a service for him. I have sent for a nun called Wang to see about it."

"When people have money," Ying Bojue said, "children make a great difference. When a child comes into the world, he needs the utmost care. It is like planting seeds. They must be watered when they are young if they are ever to come to anything. My little brother is more valuable than ten thousand pieces of gold. He is a pearl upon your palm. You can't help taking more care of him than common people do. There is always trouble with children in their second year, the sixth, and again in the ninth. There is always danger of smallpox and scarlet fever. Forgive my plain speaking, but I feel that you should indeed offer sacrifice for your child, and so secure the happiness that you have already. If my sister-in-law wishes it, it must be done. Then your troubles will end and the rearing of the baby will be a simple matter."

Daian came and said: "Nun Wang was not at the temple. She had gone to Wang's palace. I went there to look for her. After I had waited a long time, she came out and I gave her the message. She promised to come at once."

Ximen continued his conversation with Ying Bojue and Chang Zhijie. Shutong brought them tea.

"Brother," Ying Bojue said, "you have been very kind to me, but I have never ventured to ask you to come and see me, because my house is so unsuited for your entertainment. But if you are free tomorrow or the day after, I hope you and Brother Chang will come and spend a day with me in the country, and so give me an opportunity to show my friendship."

"I am sure you cannot fail to appreciate the motives of my friend Ying, and I hope you will accept his invitation," said Chang.

"I am not busy tomorrow," Ximen Qing said, "but I do not like to bother you."

"I cannot remember the number of times I have bothered you," Bojue said. "Besides, I am making no very great preparations. Just a poor cup of wine."

"I will keep tomorrow free for you," Ximen said.

"I have engaged the young actors," Bojue said, "but perhaps it would be more satisfactory to have two singing girls."

"Don't let that trouble you," Ximen said, "I will arrange for Wu Yin'er and Han Jinchuan to come." He told Qintong to go at once to the two singing girls and tell them that, the next day, they must go to the park outside the city.

Before long, Nun Wang came. She made a reverence to Ximen Qing. "You sent for me," she said. "May I hear your commands? I was at his Lordship Wang's place and could not get away before."

"This is the situation," Ximen Qing said. "When Guan'ge was born, we promised to have a service of thanksgiving, but we have been so busy that we have omitted to do so. We wish to give thanks to Heaven for protecting him so far and letting him grow so big. In the first place, I wish to thank Buddha for his favor, and, secondly, to forestall any calamities and troubles that might be in store for him, and ensure his long life. So I sent for you."

"The young master's body is worth ten thousand pieces of gold," Nun Wang said, "and we must trust in Buddha's protection for him. Your Lordship may not know it, but in the Sacred Scriptures of Buddha it is written that in the world of men there prowl demons and devils whose business it is to inflict injuries upon people and destroy their children. When a child dies before its birth, or in its infancy, some demon is always responsible. The best thing we can do for your son will be to read the sacred texts and implore the assistance of Buddha. Anything else would be inappropriate."

"What is the most suitable form for our devotions to take?" Ximen Qing asked.

"First," Nun Wang said, "we will go through the scripture of the Master of Medicine. Then, I suggest that we prepare two Tuoluo charms. They cannot fail to be efficacious."

"And when will you begin reading the scriptures?"

"Tomorrow is an excellent day; I will have the service at my temple."

Ximen Qing agreed. Nun Wang went to the inner court to see Yueniang and the others. They were with Li Ping'er. She made a reverence to them all. Yueniang said: "We are anxious for you to do something for the baby. When will you do it?" Nun Wang said that she would begin at her temple the following day. Xiaoyu brought tea for her.

"Teacher," Li Ping'er said to her, "I have something to say to you." The nun begged her to speak. "Since I have had this baby," Li Ping'er said, "I have never been quite well. When you read the sacred scriptures, pray for me too. I will see that you are well paid for it."

"That will be no trouble," Nun Wang said. "When I write out the prayers, I will put down your name. That is all."


End of Volume One